Crafting Prose

Crafting Prose

Don Richard Cox
University of Tennessee

•

Elizabeth Giddens
Auburn University

HBJ

HARCOURT BRACE JOVANOVICH, PUBLISHERS
San Diego   New York   Chicago   Austin
London   Sydney   Tokyo   Toronto

Preface

Crafting Prose assumes that the aims of discourse are far more important than the modes of discourse. It obviously owes much to the work of James Kinneavy, whose book, *A Theory of Discourse* (1971), revised the way many people think about discourse in general and writing in particular. We have generally adopted Kinneavy's premises about the *writer-reader-reality* triangle (which he labels the *encoder-decoder-reality* triangle), and about the kinds of writing that an emphasis on each component of that triangle generates. We have modified the titles of these aims of discourse slightly from Expressive, Persuasive, and Referential to Expressive, Persuasive, and Informative. We have also omitted entirely the category of literary discourse (which emphasizes, according to Kinneavy, the *signal*), on the admittedly somewhat arbitrary grounds that most college English departments shunt "literary" or "creative" writing off to other courses. In going along with this convention of viewing creative writing as a discipline unto itself, we are not necessarily disagreeing with Kinneavy's assumptions, but instead are simply conforming to the practice most commonly found in classrooms.

Using these aims of discourse as an organizing principle, we have divided the book into four major sections — an Introduction, devoted to the principle elements of composition, and three remaining sections — Crafting Expressive Prose, Crafting Informative Prose, and Crafting Persuasive Prose. We allow for some degree of overlap within these divisions and understand that these aims are seldom, if ever, found in completely pure forms. In our Introduction we assume that most instructors will wish to instill a sense of composition's basic elements — invention, composing, and revision — right away. That is, instructors will not want to spend several weeks on invention alone and leave revision for the distant future, because students usually need to be writing complete compositions in the first weeks of a term. We include several workable heuristics in the Introduction, but touch on other invention strategies and heuristics later. We focus here on the *process* of writing. Although the debate between emphasizing process or product in a writing class would seem to have been declared a victory for the process approach years ago, simply subscribing to a "process approach" does not completely explain all the strategies that one may employ in the classroom.

The remaining three divisions of the text move beyond the basic elements of teaching writing as process to present the three fundamental aims of discourse — expressive, informative, and persuasive writing. Within each section we provide a general introduction discussing the basic principles of that specific aim, followed by readings that demonstrate these principles. Persuasive prose is probably the most familiar of these aims to many teachers, for the argumentative essay is generally the staple of most college composition classes. Traditionally, expressive and informative prose have played lesser roles, with expressive prose sometimes being encouraged with the assignment of journals or freewriting exercises and informative prose occasionally touched on in the context of research writing. We contend that these two major aims — expressive and informative prose — also have their place in textbooks and in the classroom, and within these sections (as within the section on persuasive prose) we have purposely chosen a wide variety of readings and have avoided selecting only those pieces that might fit into the traditional "essay" format. These readings, which represent a broad spectrum of writing tasks drawn from all three realms of discourse, provide students not so much with "models," at least as the term is most narrowly construed, but with representative samples of the many possibilities that exist in the universe of discourse.

We hope that students will use these readings to guide and shape their own compositions and, more inportant, allow these authors to expand their perception of what constitutes good writing. By including these representative samples and by asking students to write similar pieces, we hope to broaden a sense of discourse and make their freshman English writing more relevant to their writing in their other college classes and to their lives after college. In that world they may be called on to draft expressive or informative prose as frequently as, if not more frequently than, they will create purely persuasive prose. Although we do not necessarily intend this book to be a writing-across-the-curriculum text, it accepts some of the premises of that movement, because it attempts to expand the boundaries of what students traditionally write and read in college English classes and reflect a larger view of the universe of discourse than one usually finds in more traditional texts.

We structured *Crafting Prose* to present the aims of discourse in an order that gradually becomes more difficult for students. The movement from expressive prose to informative prose to persuasive prose, however, follows what we believe is also an appropriately "natural" progression. Students seem to write most easily about themselves, find it slightly more difficult to report on the world around them, and have the most difficulty persuading others of the validity of their opinions. The problems students encounter as they work their way through this progression may suggest to teachers that they should not devote equal amounts of class time to each of the three aims of discourse. Although that may be the case, we caution against omitting any section entirely. Certainly, because crafting clear and coherent persuasive prose is difficult for most students, it makes sense to allot a substantial portion of the academic term to dealing with this aim and devote less of the term to other aims. In the not-too-distant past, as Janet Emig's landmark study *The Composing Process of Twelfth Graders* (1971) attests, students felt far less comfortable with personal, subjective, or "reflexive" writing than they did with more distanced, objective or "extensive" prose. That situation has changed somewhat (partly, no doubt, as a result of Emig's book), but because the pendulum of pedagogical theory constantly swings back and forth, we cannot assume that any group of sudents will enter the college classroom already skilled in, and comfortable with, any form, genre, or aim of discourse.

Finally, a comment on *modes* of discourse. In differentiating between *modes* and *aims* of discourse, we make what we believe is an absolutely crucial distinction. Traditionally, a mode of discourse is a *format* or *form*. Comparison/Contrast, for example, is a format in which material can be presented. It is not, however, an aim or goal of discourse. To teach writing by emphasizing the modes of discourse over the goals or aims of discourse severely distorts the nature of the task at hand. Such an approach produces assignments in which students are asked to present the format first and ignore the purpose or use of the material they are creating. Frequently students create "correct" prose that satisfies the assignment, but prose that, beyond that assignment, has no real reason for existing. Focusing primarily on modes suggests that formats are an end in themselves, rather than a means to an end. It is the end — the goal, the aim — of a piece of prose that deserves the emphasis and focus. For this reason we wish to place the *function* or purpose of the prose first, the format or mode of the discourse second. For this reason, for example, descriptive prose is a form found within the section on Crafting Expressive Prose. Descriptive prose is not an end in itself, because, except in some college English classes, writers do not sit down with the intention of simply writing a narrative or a description; they begin with the goal of expressing themselves, or informing a reader, or persuading an audience. Similarly, it is also misleading simply to ask students to do an "interview" assignment, as though the point of the exercise is again its overall form or structure. Before a writer decides to do an interview, something in the relationship of writer, reader, and subject, something within the context of the communicative situation, should suggest that an interview would be the most appropriate format to choose. Form (or format) should follow function. Sometimes, of course, a piece of prose may have more than one function, more than one purpose, so we therefore include a number of questions within each section, questions students should use to guide them towards defining their aims, their goals, and, at times, their formats. Overall, we contend, this system of focusing on function first, rather than form, produces far better and more significant prose, and ultimately creates far better crafters of that prose.

We agree with Donald Murray, who, in *A Writer Teaches Writing*, argues for open assignments rather than closed ones, asserting that with open assignments students "will make their own discoveries — they will think — and they will discover a voice that is appropriate to them, to the subject, and to their own audience." Stressing format over function will not allow this creative process to take place.

All books owe much to others. Clearly we owe a debt to many theorists and practitioners. James Kinneavy we have mentioned; Donald Murray also needs to be singled out as a major influence. Other theorists we attempt to acknowledge in the course of the book; like Tennyson's Ulysses we have become "a part of all [we] have met." Beyond these theorists who have taught us, we are grateful to our many students, who, though unnamed, through their queries and insights have forced us to make decisions and judgments about what we in turn advocate and believe. Five of these students — Mary Rhea, Greg Maine, Sybil Adams, Bill Estep, and Dwayne Ferrell — do need to be singled out for their specific contributions to this book. We would like to thank Joseph Trahern and Edward Bratton for their support and encouragement over the past several years, as well as colleagues such as Donald Ploch, Richard Kelly, B. J. Leggett, Tom Wheeler, Sandra Ballard, Karen Sprague, and Bonnie Winsbro, who have provided us with insights, information, criticisms, and speculations. Thanks also to Donita Owings, Donna Giddens, Michael, Vickie, Steve, Patsy, Dawn, Andrea, and Woody for their particular contributions during the writing process. We are also indebted to Judith G. Gardner, University of Texas at San Antonio; Peter Goodrich, University of Northern Michigan; Mary Sue MacNealy, Memphis State University; and Richard J. Zbaracki, Iowa State University, for reviewing our manuscript.

Finally we would like to thank the book team at Harcourt Brace Jovanovich: Eleanor Garner, permissions editor; Cheryl Hauser, manuscript editor; Niamh Foley-Homan and Kristina Sanfilippo, production editors; Ann Smith and Kay Faust, designers; Paulette Russo, art editor; and Sarah Randall and Mary Kay Yearin, production managers. Most of all we thank Bill McLane, executive editor, who was willing to take a chance on us, and whose own patience and good humor allowed us to produce the book we wanted to create. There are not many in the textbook publishing business like him.

Don Richard Cox
Elizabeth J. Giddens

Contents

SECTION I

SECTION III ▸ Crafting Informative Prose   156

Concerns in Informative Prose   157

8 ▸ Basic Features of Informative Prose 158

A Thesis or Not?   158

Objectivity and Subjectivity   161

Factors Affecting the Fairness of Informative Prose   162

9 ▸ Informative Prose: The Writer's View   166

Stance of the Writer   166

Specialized Knowledge and Methods from a Field of Expertise   169

Logical Thinking   169

10 ▸ Avenues of Inquiry   175

• • • •
•
• **SECTION IV** ▶ Crafting
Persuasive Prose   312

13 ▶ **Logical Appeals**   **315**

14 ▶ **Emotional Appeals**   **333**

15 ▶ **Ethical Appeals**   **344**

16 ▶ **The Goals of Persuasion**   **350**

READINGS • PERSUASIVE PROSE   364

UNDERSTANDING THE TASK

Writing is complex. This announcement may not be news, but sometimes an obvious statement deserves contemplation, unpacking. First we have to decide what we actually mean by that overwhelming, ominous noun — "writing." Do we mean handwriting or typing? Or are we referring to the words that a somewhat nervous and tentative author, businessperson, or student scrawls across a page, onto a grocery list, or into a love letter? Could we also mean the complicated and occasionally inexplicably odd system of grammar and good use that makes up what English teachers call Standard English? What about the whole routine of gathering up the right pen and the right kind of paper, finding a quiet corner in a library, and then settling in to think about something — a topic, a point of concern, or doubt — and trying, just trying, to put those thoughts down in sentences so that you don't forget them and maybe even so someone else can read them? Is that writing?

What if, just to be generous, we allow that writing is all of these things — and more. We've said nothing so far about making outlines, fulfilling assignments, conducting interviews, reading expert sources, analyzing others' arguments. These activities could be writing too, because they could be, and often are, included in the act of writing. Perhaps, then, it's best for us to think about writing as both a thing you do — a process — and a thing you create — a product like a finished letter, a newspaper story, a book review, or a personal essay.

Also, if the goal of writing is to communicate something to someone, whether it be in an exam, a letter of complaint, a proposal for a new traffic light, or a diary written only for your older self to read years from now, then writing encompasses much more than just the process and the eventual product; it includes a concern for surrounding events, situations, and human relationships. The people involved, the places they live and work, their opinions of the writer and the cause she represents, the time of day and season of the year, all influence a writer and what she writes.

No wonder we find writing hard! No wonder we squirm a little when we know we're going to have to write several essays, term papers, or lab reports in a class.

Writing is complex, and for most of us writing takes time, energy, and concentration. It's harder than thinking and much less natural than speaking. It's governed by legions of rules, some of which are unspoken, unwritten, and even unknown.

What to do? Panic, of course, is an option. But you have other options as well, and they are healthier; sometimes these options can even be fun. Mostly, we have to breathe deeply and take a logical tack: practice, get advice, rework drafts, polish, and send writing out to be read. In short, we learn a writing process that helps us produce sentences that make sense to ourselves and to our readers. The central tenets of this textbook are that (1) writing comprises both a product and a process, and (2) all writing involves a series of choices. In this book we will try to make you aware of many of the choices you will face when you write, and we will attempt to give you the skills and confidence to make those choices well.

The first step is to think for a minute about the factors relevant to any writing task: a writer, a reader, the world or environment influencing the writer and reader, and finally the text, the written piece itself that mediates between the other three factors. Many people find it helpful to visualize these factors and their relationships by thinking of the writing triangle. It looks like this:

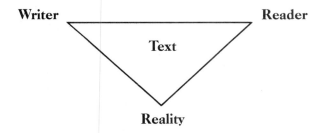

This diagram clearly shows that writer, reader, and reality all influence the text; in other words, a writer produces a text, the reader reads it, and reality gives it a meaningful context. Further, without any one of these factors, we would not really have a writing situation; the factors are interdependent. (Some of you might suggest that a reader is not always required, say, for instance, if you write in a diary. But we would argue that a reader is required, even if the writer becomes her own reader.)

Nevertheless, we should not take this interdependence of factors too far; although all of them are present to some degree in every writing situation, quite often one of these factors is more important than the other two. In many writing situations one factor is the star, the focus; it is under the spotlight and the others, still present, are waiting in the wings, never quite offstage. For example, if the writer puts herself under the spotlight in order to tell a story about a personal experience, the goal of the written text is her self-expression and revelation. She finds her material for writing in her own past or in her thoughts. Her writing process is largely guided by an effort to recreate an experience or explain something about herself. Sure, she's somewhat concerned about her readers' reactions and expectations; she has to produce a written artifact that accurately gets her meaning across, and the experiences she describes and the thoughts she explains must have some connection to reality to have meaning. But all the same, the focus is on herself. So she approaches writing with an effort to reveal herself and thus de-emphasizes her concern for the other factors (reader, reality, and text).

In short, this writer decides on a basic goal for her project by emphasizing her own desire to express herself. And that goal determines at least some, if not most, of the choices she makes as she writes. Starting off with one goal in mind is a useful, manageable concept. A goal gives some rough, embryonic shape to a writing project, and it can help you see which options are relevant to a particular project. We encourage you to use a goal as a point of departure in your writing, but not to cling to this goal too tightly. A goal will give you a rough sense of direction, a general sense of purpose; it's meant to fit loosely and comfortably, like an old sweatshirt (which is also a good thing to wear when you write).

It's possible to emphasize each of the four factors of the writing triangle, thus creating four basic goals that encompass all writing. This illustration demonstrates these relationships:

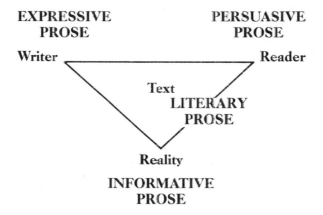

An emphasis on the writer, then, produces *expressive prose*; emphasis on reality makes for *informative prose*; focus on the reader creates *persuasive prose*; and stress on the text results in *literary prose* (which is not covered in this book, but is covered in other courses, usually under the label of *creative writing*). For example, a letter from a friend describing his first calamitous attempt at windsurfing would be *expressive*; a magazine article explaining how to buy the best windsurfing board for the money would be *informative*; an advertisement or brochure selling a particular brand of windsurfing board would be *persuasive*; and a story that vividly re-creates the experience of windsurfing, transforming that experience into a symbol of freedom, would be *literary*. Although the subjects in these four texts are related, the writers' purposes are quite distinct. Furthermore, it's easy to see that the letter writer, the reporter, the advertiser, and the artist would make vastly different decisions about how to research their projects and how to write their texts. Consequently, you can see how a goal can affect the way you go about writing a specific piece.

The first section of the book introduces the basic process common in all writing, so that you can find some useful suggestions to help you design your own process. The three subsequent sections contain advice for expressive, informative, and persuasive writing. They will help you adapt your process to specific goals. At the end of each of these sections, you will find readings illustrating the three goals; they have been chosen to illustrate the range of writing purposes available to you as well as the options all writers have. You may get some ideas from them; you may just enjoy reading them. We hope they will help you see that good writing takes many diverse forms. One last point: Despite this notion of different goals in writing, it's important to recognize that your writing purposes may overlap. Remember that even though one factor is spotlighted, the others remain onstage. This notion of overlap, of degree, should help you remain aware of the complexity and interrelatedness of all writing goals. The readings, as you will see, further attest to this overlap. Enjoy them, and yourself, as you progress through the book.

Crafting Prose

CHAPTER 1

▶ Advice for Writers

The purpose of this section is to provide you with general advice about how to approach a writing project and how to sustain your interest and self-confidence as you write. Attitudes and expectations are the keys to this puzzle. Writing is an intensely personal, mental, and psychological activity. No doubt, part of the difficulty of writing rests in its cerebral nature. Writers often feel that when they commit thoughts to words on paper they are putting themselves on the line. They believe they are taking a risk, pinning themselves down, and exposing themselves to attack. It's only natural for this feeling to make them reluctant to write, and so they adopt the most common defense strategies: avoidance and procrastination. Unfortunately, these strategies do not help anyone write; they make it harder, and the risk of disappointment, disapproval, or even embarrassment grows once writers become edgy and defensive about their work. Writers must overcome these attitudes to continue writing and to improve their work.

The sense of risking your self-esteem when you write may haunt you to some extent, but you can learn techniques to help you skirt the difficulties. Most of these techniques involve adopting practical methods and attitudes; to some degree they are mental games — ways to think creatively and constructively about writing and ways to view yourself as a writer. They can lessen the stress of writing. Here are some basic pointers:

- ▶ View yourself as a writer.
- ▶ Make writing interesting for yourself.
- ▶ Set up a comfortable writing environment.
- ▶ Adopt a process approach.
- ▶ Identify and control writing problems.
- ▶ Build your self-confidence as a writer.

View yourself as a writer.   Most of us equate the title writer with high status, intelligence, and talent. Yet the word simply means "one who writes": you are a writer if you write a history exam, a letter to an editor, a cover letter for a job, or a memo to your boss. You do not have to be comparable to Shakespeare to earn the title; it is better to recognize that while you are writing you are a writer. Think of the word as a job description. If you are doing the job of a writer, you qualify.

This attitude opens the door to writing well because it helps you begin to have faith in your own thoughts, insights, and ability to express these ideas in words. Instead of doubting your instincts when you write, follow them, develop them, and refine them. Begin to consider how your ideas and experiences are interesting and would be intriguing for a reader too. Simply put, you must learn to believe that you do have something to say; then you may work on learning how to get those thoughts down into sentences and across to a reader.

Another helpful technique is to recognize that, since you are a writer, it's worthwhile to develop your own writing persona. Developing a persona does not mean that you should predetermine your stance in your writing — that you should set out always to be funny or sophisticated, but that you should pay attention to the tone of your voice and to your personality. Do you want your voice and personality to be heard through your writing? Could these personal characteristics help you develop a writing process that complements your temperament? For instance, consider whether you are patient or impatient, serious or lighthearted, cavalier or committed, or anything between these extremes. How might these traits help you write? If you are impatient, perhaps you should try to write drafts quickly to get your ideas down fast. If you're lighthearted, entertain fanciful, amusing approaches to writing such as brainstorming about a topic while you dance or throw a Frisbee with a friend. Then jot down your notes on the back of an envelope. A more orderly person might, however, write best by taking meticulous notes and arranging them carefully in an elaborate outline. In brief, consider your own personality and adopt a stance toward writing that accesses the path of least resistance to getting words on paper. Once you get these words down, no matter how hurriedly or injudiciously they have been scrawled, you can go back over them, alter them, and ultimately produce a piece sensible enough for a reader. Find ways for your temperament to help you write, rather than working against what comes naturally.

> Advice to young writers? Always the same advice: learn to trust your own judgement, learn inner independence, learn to trust that time will sort the good from the bad — including your own bad.
>
> — DORIS LESSING

> A man who writes well writes not as others write, but as he himself writes; it is often in speaking badly that he speaks well.
>
> — MONTIESQUIEU

> This is what I find encouraging about the writing trades: they allow mediocre people who are patient and industrious to revise their stupidity, to edit themselves into something like intelligence. They also allow lunatics to seem saner than sane.
>
> — KURT VONNEGUT, JR.

> There is no one right way. Each of us finds a way that works for him. But there is a wrong way. The wrong way is to finish your writing day with no more words on paper than when you began. Writers write.
>
> — ROBERT B. PARKER

Finally, think back over past writing experiences — stories you wrote for your younger brother, postcards dashed off on a trip, and term papers written in school. Make a list of what made some of these good experiences and what made others unpleasant. Identify the factors that helped you write something, like a desire to share an experience, to learn about an intriguing event or issue, to convince someone of the correctness of your opinions. You should attempt to include these factors in all writing projects; they motivated you once; they might motivate you again. Also, try to avoid the kind of situations that made you uncomfortable as a writer: resolve not to wait until the last minute, or not to try to write an essay without learning the facts of your topic first. Find a pattern to your successes and cultivate it into a personalized writing process. Grant your process respect and nurture it attentively; it will offer you an identity as a writer.

Make writing interesting for yourself. This recommendation is perhaps the key to all success in writing. Let's face it, to write you have to have something to say. Paragraphs, even sentences, written down without some incentive behind them will result in empty passages, filling a page, boring your reader, and probably boring yourself. It is physically difficult to write when you're bored, just as it is hard to sing if you are asleep. Writing requires some tension and excitement because the real effort needed to make a thought clear has to be supported by interest and desire. You must have a granule of intrigue, a kink in your thoughts, that makes you want to say something or parse it out into comprehensible words. You may want to write to learn about yourself, to find out what you actually think about an issue, to see if you can inform someone, to discover if you can move or persuade a reader. Look into your thoughts and emotions for the question you want to answer when you write, the pin prick of curiosity that causes you to think and formulate words; then strings of sentences, paragraphs, and longer passages will come accordingly.

It is easy enough to find the intriguing part of writing when you can select your own topic. Then you pursue ideas, hobbies, concerns that are innately interesting to you. But this need for motivation is especially critical when you are assigned a project or topic. To find a purpose for your writing, go for the part that puzzles you a little, that makes you ask questions, that you have yet to figure out on your own. Then the writing process will become a discovery, not a recitation of previously understood information holding no surprises for you, and none for the reader either. Stray off of the worn path and find the new, unexhausted, unusual avenue to tour and write about. Since writing is so complex, so demanding an act, you should feel that your topic is worth the effort. Without this respect, you will probably write dully. Ironically, our uncertainties and worries often lead us to the best ideas because they coax our minds to work, to search for solutions and words to explain these solutions.

I think that in order to write really well and convincingly, one must be somewhat poisoned by emotion. Dislike, displeasure, resentment, fault-finding, imagination, passionate remonstrance, a sense of injustice — they all make fine fuel.

— EDNA FERBER

If we had to say what writing is, we would define it essentially as an act of courage.

— CYNTHIA OZICK

Curiosity urges you on — the driving force.

— JOHN DOS PASSOS

If there's no mystery, for the artist, to solve inside of his art, then there's no point in it. . . . for me, every act of art is the act of solving a mystery.

— TRUMAN CAPOTE

Set up a comfortable writing environment.   Part of your identity as a writer is formed by how and where you write. If you find that a certain time of day, lighting, noise, clothing, food, or drink will help you settle in and begin writing, you should indulge yourself. Let yourself develop some writing rituals, however eccentric they may seem to friends or family. If they help you get in the right mood or frame of mind for writing, they will be worth any teasing you might have to endure. Shape all of your writing eccentricities into a writing environment and routine that helps you make progress. The rationale behind the need for a writing ritual is that, after a while, simply putting yourself into your own personally designed writing space will help you write when you are least enthusiastic about it. Also, many writers feel that having all of the surrounding factors constant enables them to concentrate on their writing; a place you know well may help you focus on the task at hand rather than on the graffiti scratched on a library desk or the pattern of some unusual wallpaper. Further, when you put yourself in your designated writing environment, you will know that the only thing you're supposed to do there is to write; no talking or dreaming allowed there, just writing. This paring down of options helps you settle in to your work. Consider your preferences for some of the following factors and arrange an environment that includes your choices.

- ▸ Find the best time of day to write.
- ▸ What place makes you most comfortable for writing? Home? Office? Library? Kitchen? Den? Desk?
- ▸ Which writing materials suit you best? Buy stocks of your favorite paper, pens, pencils, or arrange to work on a computer, using a word processing program that you know well.
- ▸ What clothes are the most comfortable? Do you have a writing outfit, a special shirt or pair of shoes that are comfortable?
- ▸ Do you like listening to a certain kind of background music, or is silence essential?
- ▸ What do you like to munch on while you compose? Does caffeine get you going or make you too jumpy to sit still?

One useful trick is to re-create the environment in which you wrote your best piece of writing. Wear your lucky sneakers, insist on the same writing materials, play the same music, and put yourself into the identical state of mind you had then. You may even want to read over that letter, essay, or poem before you start on your new task. These rituals bolster your self-confidence: you wrote well in this environment, and it is likely that you can write well here again.

> When I am working on a book or a story, I write every morning as soon after the first light as possible. There is no one to disturb you and it is cool or cold and you come to your work and warm as you write.
>
> — ERNEST HEMINGWAY

> What the writer needs is an empty day ahead. A big round quiet space of empty house to, as it were, tumble about in.
>
> — CATHERINE DRINKER BOWEN

> Every morning between 9 and 12 I go to my room and sit before a piece of paper. Many times I just sit for three hours with no ideas coming to be. But I know one thing: If an idea does come between 9 and 12, I am there ready for it.
>
> — FLANNERY O'CONNOR

Adopt a process approach.   Perhaps the most useful psychological advantage you can give yourself when you write is to view writing as a process, rather than as a one-shot event. According to researchers in composition practices, the biggest difference between student and professional writers is that professionals see the writing process as happening over a period of time, whereas student writers view writing much more as a single-step activity, involving little or no prewriting or revising. This finding suggests that people who write for a living develop a writing process that reduces the stress of getting their words down perfectly the first time. Rather than spending the majority of their time laboring over a first draft, they spend large chunks of time planning, drafting, and revising. In other words, they do not try to sit down and write a finished piece in one intense session. It is a truism to say that making a draft better is easier than making the first draft; time you spend improving your writing, once you have even the roughest of drafts, will be less stressful than the time spent producing that first draft. Consequently, many professional writers draft quickly, producing something they know is disorganized, incomplete, even off the mark entirely, and then they revise thoroughly and repeatedly until they get the content, organization, tone, sentences, and grammar right.

Another pointer from professional writers is that they often do not view the writing process as rigidly progressive, moving from prewriting to drafting, revising, and editing without any backward glances to the earlier stages. Instead, they often return to planning and drafting in the middle of revision, or they begin drafting before they have finished all of their research and organizing (usually part of planning). The best word to describe this kind of process is *recursive*, meaning that professionals go through various writing stages again and again, spending time researching a little more if necessary or adding a passage that their evaluation of a draft reveals as critical. To some extent, then, they allow their *progress* on an article to determine their *process*.

Quite literally, a process approach to writing is a kind, forgiving, and humane approach; it gives you more than one attempt to produce good writing, and since writing is so complex, involving so many concerns (about content, form, voice, grammar, spelling, etc.), most of us improve our writing tremendously when we view writing as a process. The trick is to let a draft be terrible at first and to continue writing it, knowing you can go back and change it once you have something in hand. Regard writing as a process activity, something worked on and built up over time, like an oil painting. Try not to see writing as a single performance; for most professionals writing is not like an Olympic diver's last dive off the platform, a dive that will determine whether he wins the gold or fails entirely. Better to take writing easily, work on a project over time, and give yourself as many chances and revisions as you need to get the words down right.

> I write a lot — every day, seven days a week — and I throw a lot away. Sometimes I think I write to throw away; it's a process of distillation.
>
> —DONALD BARTHELME

> I have often written — often several times — every word I have ever published. My pencils outlast their erasers.
>
> —VLADIMIR NABOKOV

> There are days when the result is so bad that no fewer than five revisions are required. In contrast, when I'm greatly inspired, only four revisions are needed.
>
> —JOHN KENNETH GALBRAITH

> I start off but I don't know where I'm going; I try this avenue and that avenue, that turns out to be a dead end, this is a dead end, and so on. The search takes a long time and I have to back-track often.
>
> —GALWAY KINNELL

Identify and control writing problems. A high hurdle to writing well confronts each of us when we recognize that we are not perfect writers, that we have problems with diction, comma use, verb form, or paragraph organization. Often we know what our weaknesses are — we have been told hundreds of times that we can't spell or that we have a problem with run-on sentences. This knowledge that we're not perfect, that, in fact, we're inferior as writers and as users of our native tongue, paralyzes us. We feel defeated before we start since we know that no matter how hard our labor, how earnest our attempt, how inspired our thoughts, the letter or essay will end up flawed, marked by our interminable, obvious deficiencies as writers.

While it's healthy to know about your weaknesses as a writer, it's certainly not encouraging to think about them while you plan and draft. First, dwelling on writing problems does not encourage creative thought or energy. Second, during the planning and drafting stages it does no good for you to worry over the details of writing anyway. For instance, you may spend fifteen minutes with a thesaurus searching for the best word with all the right connotations only to strike out the paragraph or even the section while revising. Why sweat the details before you're sure of the larger plan and direction of the whole piece? Don't waste time this way; it only inspires frustration.

Generally it's better to push all anxiety about your writing problems out of your mind until you begin evaluating and revising a draft. You write knowing errors, misstatements, and confusing sentences lurk in your draft. You know you can find them later. Fret over correctness once you've got the bigger factors in hand such as your main point, your basic organization, your paragraph structure, your use of examples, illustrations, and quotations. Then — after you like the thrust of your draft — you can usefully pay attention to the fine points (and we will give you some pointers on how to work on your problem areas). Of course, this attitude toward weaknesses will work only if you develop your writing process; a one-step process won't give you the additional chances you'll need to find and correct problems, so you will have to adopt the recursive strategy mentioned above.

Two other common writing problems, besides the concern for correctness and quality, include writer's block and the pressure of working under a deadline. In some cases, you can't do much to get out of the binds of time limits; you simply have to plan your work as well as possible and hack away at your task, trying to make progress steadily, trying to avoid pitfalls that will waste time. One of the biggest pitfalls is the paralysis that comes from too much concern for perfection: writer's block. Again, a process approach will help you keep writing and it should help you defuse the anxiety of writing so that you can learn to meet deadlines. The most common remedies for writer's block — the inability to write anything — are (1) to lower your standards and (2) to let your ideas brew for a designated (and not too lengthy) period of time. If you lower your standards for your writing by telling yourself that you're going to set off to write something, anything, even if it's inferior or off the mark, you can usually get your project underway. Later you can go back and revise or throw out the passages that are truly terrible and irrelevant to your goal. Letting your thoughts about a project brew a while can help you a lot if the brooding period leads you back to writing. Sometimes it's best to take a break from writing when it gets too hard, when you're tired or frustrated, or when you can't keep your mind on track. Then when you're fresher — an hour later or the next day — come back to the draft and get back into it. The point is not to let a writing problem unnerve you. Remember that writing is a mental game; sometimes you have to write poorly to write well later on, and sometimes you have to admit temporary defeat, only to return a little later to write with self-confidence and determination.

> One should lower his standards until there is no felt threshold to go over in writing. It's easy to write. You just shouldn't have standards that inhibit you from writing.
> — WILLIAM STAFFORD

It's a matter of letting go. You have to work hard, you have to punch a clock, you have to put in your time. But somehow there's a trick of letting go to let the best writing take place.
— WALKER PERCY

Build your self-confidence as a writer. Writing involves balancing optimism about your abilities, interest in your topic, and realistic appraisal of your work. Most of us have very little trouble criticizing our writing, and once you get going, maintaining your own interest comes easily. Yet keeping up your self-confidence about a work in progress is usually much more difficult. This game requires that we honestly recognize any strides we do make on a project, and sometimes it demands that we reward ourselves for well-intentioned efforts at writing, regardless of the result. One way to build your self-confidence as a writer is to set up a routine that makes you write — or attempt writing — for a fixed period of time each day. You simply put in your time, writing steadily; when the period has elapsed, you stop. Putting your time in makes you feel that you have lived up to an agreement you made with yourself. You will not have to feel guilty about not trying hard enough or not being disciplined enough. Some days you may write very little, but they will be balanced by the days that are productive.

Another way you can avoid guilt and procrastination is to determine that you will write a prescribed amount each day, one or two pages, a small section at a time. If you break the project into small enough tasks — your introduction or your first example — completing one or even several of them will seem easy, but you will be making real progress just the same. In addition to these methods for gently disciplining yourself as a writer, you need to learn how to recognize (and sometimes reward) your own good behavior and accomplishments. If you keep a bargain with yourself, stick to your schedule, write a little more than you had planned, or meet a deadline, admit that you're working the way professionals do and congratulate yourself for your hard work and perseverance. Don't belittle the small triumphs; think positively about them and let them bolster you further in your routine and writing efforts. If, despite hard work and discipline, you are disappointed by your writing, remember that you can always revise. Also, recognize that becoming a good writer takes practice and time. Realize that you are still developing as a writer, so if you solve one of your writing problems, you have killed a big dragon. The remaining dragons can be challenged and conquered another day, in another project. Be patient and industrious; your writing will improve, perhaps slowly, but it will improve.

The first discipline is the realization that there is a discipline — that all art begins and ends with discipline — that any art is first and foremost a craft.
— ARCHIBALD MacLEISH

Talent is cheap. What matters is discipline.
— ANDRE DUBUS

I love being a writer. What I can't stand is the paperwork.
— PETER DE VRIES

FOCUS · · · · · · · · · · · · ·
SUGGESTIONS FOR WRITING

These suggestions are meant to give you ideas to pursue in writing. They may be the focus of freewriting, a journal entry, a paragraph to be discussed with classmates, or the point of departure for a more formal essay. These suggestions are intended to prompt you to think critically about your own writing attitudes, habits, and process so you can evaluate their effectiveness. You or your instructor should decide the specific requirements for writing successfully on one of these topics.

1. Think of an analogy for your writing process; in other words, describe what writing is like for you. Try to get at your psychological state when you write. Is writing like cooking? Could it be compared to spelunking? Is it similar to trying to remember the words of a song that you never really memorized? Once you find a suitable analogy, discuss why it accurately explains your attitude toward writing.

2. Reread the quotations about writing included in this chapter. Which is your favorite? Write out this quotation and explain why you like it, or create your own writing maxim and explain it.

3. Think of a time when your writing seemed to come particularly easy for you. Why was this so? Make a list of the reasons that seem to account for this success.

4. Think of a time when writing was particularly difficult for you. How do you explain this difficulty? What could you do to avoid the factors that seemed to make writing difficult? Write down some guidelines, things you in particular are to avoid, if you are to be a successful writer. Compare your list with those other students in your class have made. What similarities do you find? What differences?

5. Ask your friends or members of your family what strategies they employ when they attempt to write. Make a list of these strategies and try them yourself. Do certain strategies — writing early in the morning or using a particular kind of pen — work better than others in particular writing situations, or do you find yourself returning to a familiar formula?

CHAPTER

2 ▸ Options for Invention

As you might expect, the word *invention* refers to the writer's process of coming up with ideas. Invention is a big part of the prewriting and planning stage. Although occasionally a topic will simply — and fortuitously — leap to mind, many writers have to coax these ideas out, and often they do it by practicing one or several invention techniques — ways of thinking while writing that lead to concrete topics and notions of how to treat these topics in an essay or article. Further, once you have the topic in mind, invention techniques can enable you to explore all of its relevant facets; in this way invention techniques lead you gradually into drafting or more formal planning.

With that said, the only preparation you need for using these techniques is to realize that your attitude is all-important. Be open to all the thoughts you have, no matter how silly or tangential they seem. You should try to capture your thoughts first, and then edit out the ones that you don't like or that you think would be hard to write about. The process is somewhat like that of the sculptor who sculpts a statue of a horse by beginning with a large block of granite and then removing all the parts of it that don't resemble a horse. Think of invention as the act of pulling topics, ideas, details, and memories out of your mind. The ideas are already inside you (like the horse inside the granite); all you need to do during invention, then, is to be open to them and write them down as they come to you. As you write these thoughts down, new ones will appear. New questions, theories about relationships between ideas, and details that may be enlightening will occur to you because you are actively thinking and recording those thoughts. Often a consideration of obvious matters will lead you to new insights that can become the focus of your writing. In general, invention techniques provide you with some raw material, "stuff," roughly expressed ideas, to help you start writing. But for invention techniques to work — for them to help you plan and prepare for writing — you have to believe that they will help. Peter Elbow, a composition theorist, calls this attitude "the believing game," because you have to try these techniques with faith that they will help you; otherwise they will seem like — and probably will be — a waste of time.

This chapter describes several common invention techniques. Try out the ones that appeal to you, and if one doesn't work, try another. Eventually you'll find the right technique; thoughts and words will come to you, and you will have begun writing with a minimum of anxiety.

FREEWRITING, FOCUSED FREEWRITING, AND LOOPING

Freewriting is a technique that invites you to write down whatever is on your mind without stopping to reflect on your thoughts too deeply. You can write about what's around you, what has happened to you during the day, or how you feel about a writing assignment. You can write about anything at all. The point is to get started right away putting words and rough sentences down on paper. It's a stream-of-consciousness exercise, so don't worry over what you're saying or how you say it. Don't stop to think of the best words or look up the correct spelling of a word; just keep writing, as steadily as possible, without pauses and creeping self-doubt. The only goal is to get words on paper. If you use a word processor (and in many ways a computer is an ideal tool for freewriting), you can let your sentences ramble on; you can restart them in the middle of a thought, or combine several different sentences or approaches to sentences together into one long, ungainly, extremely ungrammatical "sentence." Then you can go back later and (like the sculptor finding the horse in the granite block) remove the extraneous material and find your real sentences.

Many writers choose this technique when they have a lot of resistance to getting started on a project, when procrastination is taking hold of them. They select this strategy because it does not require any forethought and because it enables them to produce sentences, paragraphs, even pages of writing painlessly. Beyond this, sometimes it's just fun to let yourself go — unrestrained — and see where you end up. Often it's a good idea to do a timed freewriting exercise, where you set out to write nonstop for a short period of time, say five minutes. The sustained effort of writing will usually lead you to ideas and topics. For example, read over the freewriting exercise below. It was written in about five minutes, and is a response to a teacher's request for students to begin a personal essay by first writing steadily for a short time on whatever came to mind. This example is an *unfocused* freewriting assignment. In it the writer moves from a state in which she has really nothing to say — a perfectly "cold" beginning — to a point where a story has come to mind. She still doesn't know what to make of her story, but she's got a start on a personal essay.

An idea. That's what I need. Something to get my mind going. It's rainy, gray February. Boring. Pen, white paper, blue lines. Words and sentences. Let's see yesterday I thought of a couple of intriguing sentences, like something that could begin a story or that described relationships. What were they? One was "She looked at them as if they were speaking a foreign language." I can't remember the other one now and this one's not so good, although it intrigued me yesterday as I walked from the bank to the Humanities Building. Who was I thinking about then? I think I was thinking about my mother for some reason. Don't remember the details, the little curls of thought that called this sentence to mind, although my mother often gets a look on her face that makes me feel that I'm saying strange things, making sounds that she can't comprehend as words or sentences. Of course, some of the things she says to me turn out the same way. One of the most mysterious things that I remember her saying when I was a teenager, had my first car — a brownish/blackish/greenish Falcon — was that, whenever I left the house, particularly if I were going somewhere I had not been before, she would call to me "Whatever you do, don't go across the river." Usually she said this when I was going nowhere near the river, and I came to think about the river as a mysterious symbol of danger and adventure. If you crossed it, you might not come back. What was over there? Was the bridge across a one-way street? Would I get lost? Were there no telephones on the other side? For years I just answered her "ok" and then forgot her warning, never coming close enough to the river to be in danger of crossing it. Funny thing, though, years later I learned that other mothers, my friends' mothers, had the same habit. A particular incident was when Laura's fiancee was going out to look around the city — he was in town for their wedding the next week and decided to strike off on his own. As he got out to his car — so Laura says — her mother jumped from the breakfast table and ran to the door, waving and shouting him down, just to say to this grown man "Whatever you do, don't go across the river!" Laura said she thought that was the only time Chip had serious doubts about marrying into her family.

Well what is across the river? I've been there a couple of times now; just another side of town. When I picture it I picture warehouses, nothing really sinister or unusual. Maybe both of these mothers knew of some crime that happened there, maybe a crime involving a child, and they will forever associate that river with that memory. And they will forever warn their own precious children not to go across. No matter how old they are. I don't really know.

Once the writer got this material to work from, she read it over, thinking about why it interested her and what she could make of it. She continued with freewriting for several more minutes, this time closing in on an idea she had about family stories. At this stage she was engaged in a *focused* freewriting exercise, an attempt to elaborate on some of the thoughts and emotions behind the first exercise.

Well, I've read over this stuff. What can I do with it? It's just an old story, a piece of my family's folklore. I have a theory that every family has a mythology of its own — a series of stories that somehow illustrates their beliefs, values, sense of itself, and sense of humor. What does this story say about that? Not sure, but maybe I can write about my ideas about family lore, use this story as one of the examples. What others? When Tom said "Bee flies weeelll be back" as a 2-year-old? What about when Joy spent hours "facing" the belt of that yellow dress she was going to make all alone? Or Hal's generally lucky nature. I'm not sure what I can make of all of this, but I've always liked hearing & telling these stories. What's their purpose? Do they give me an identity? Do they give me a sense of what my family means to me? Hmmm. Perhaps. I think I need to think up some more examples, maybe talk to some friends about their family mythology, maybe read some psychology on the topic.

The process of freewriting, reading, and freewriting again is called looping because it allows the writer to go back over a passage, pick up the thread of an attractive thought, and then write a little more about it. This process allows a writer to zero in on a particularly interesting idea over a series of steps, without continually straining for the point. Also, freewriting is an easy way to fill up a page or two with writing; it bolsters the writer's confidence by giving her some tangible evidence of her day's efforts.

LISTING AND GROUPING

This technique involves little more than the obvious. Simply start writing down words and phrases that come to mind. Put them down without concern for order or meaning. The only thing that counts is quantity. Write down as much as you can to help you get going; later you can rewrite your list to exclude unrelated ideas or to group related ones together.

In the following example the writer began with the idea that he wanted to write about his definition of sophistication, so that's the first word on his list. From that point he just let his mind wander, writing down whatever occurred to him.

sophistication

what is in

ability to see & accept other cultures

knowledge of other cultures

savoir faire, tact, poise, refinement — dullness, ennui, hollowness, shallowness/naivete, freshness, enthusiasm

big city, cultural center/regionalism, provincialism

Washington — diversity, variety of cultures
   Ethiopian food, sushi — fondness for, celebration of variety, but not an acceptance of it

accents — lack of distinct regional accent is good!?
   approved, but recognition of accents acceptable, local color, expressions declasse

knowledge of variety of regional, international cultures, but no participation in them, knowledge w/out acceptance or enthusiasm for culture

status-conscious, labeling, prestige (awareness in academe)

produces people who know, but don't feel, people aware of culture but too timid, shallow? to embrace one

Herb/Linda — Oscar Wilde/Grandma Moses

recognition of what is flavorful, unique, rich about a particular culture; no condemnation of a culture for what it doesn't have

true sophistication: positive rather than negative, characterized by interest, not boredom or haughtiness

celebration of diversity: for a rich, informed life, tolerance, understanding,
    w/out stereotypical judgment

who is the most truly sophisticated person I know?
    someone who has traveled
        is open to other cultures
        with a culture of his/her own
        with curiosity & enthusiasm about people

Prof. S?   Steve & Vickie?

what about examples?   Tennessee
    sushi bar
    Uncle Bud's Catfish Cabin
    music, dancing, customs, holidays, celebrations, religions

Portrait of a Lady — characters

homogeneity xxx

awareness of the existence of good and bad in every culture

my trips to Juarez & Ireland
    dog racing

It's interesting to note that some of the items on this list have meaning only for the writer himself because he included bits of personal history, words, and stories. At this point, he was not trying to communicate with anyone, so his ideas didn't need explanation; he was just trying to come up with raw material. Later, when he drafts his essay, he will have to decide whether or not he wants to include the personal examples or if he wants to develop and explain these anecdotes to a reader.

After writing this list, the writer reread it, paying attention to the opinions he saw developing in his list. Then a basic idea dawned on him: what was usually labeled "sophisticated" he viewed as shallow and trendy. So he rewrote his list, grouping together words and phrases that were related to his developing concept of the differences in the way sophistication is usually defined and what he thinks it actually means or should mean.

Common Definition of Sophistication

outward appearance of savoir faire, tact, poise, refinement

knows about other cultures: sees and accepts

aware of diversity and variety in cultures

is not provincial or regional — no accent
    cosmopolitan, urbane
    w/out clear affiliation to any group or set of beliefs

Becomes a False Sophistication (ironic)

status-conscious

produces people who know but don't feel, aware of many cultures but too
    timid/shallow to embrace one

concern for appearances and fashionable beliefs

someone w/out an identity, or w/ an identity that is so repressed that it's hidden, denied.

emptiness/life as game/social climbing

True Sophistication

positive rather than negative, characterized by interest, not boredom or haughtiness

recognition of what is flavorful, unique, rich about a culture, no condemnation of a culture for what it doesn't have

tolerance, understanding, no stereotypical judgment

does not enjoy propriety as much as uniqueness

awareness of good & bad in every culture

someone traveled
   who has a cultural identity of his own
   with curiosity and enthusiasm about people
   kind, capable of empathy, no narrow definitions of acceptability
   not jaded or bored with people
   recognizes the hollowness of fashion and trends

This grouped list is still only a rough guide for the writer. Now he needs to think more about what he means by key terms such as *culture*. He will also want to think about the kinds of examples and illustrations that he will need in a draft. He can review his first list for suggestions about people, places, and practices that would illustrate his ideas. From this point, however, he can move into more structured planning such as outlining, or into drafting, if he thinks he's ready. Note that the writer has actually begun to organize his essay, since the grouped list suggests a movement or line of development for an essay. Whether that suggested organization will be maintained and elaborated, or changed altogether, will depend on the drafting and revising stages to come.

BRANCHING

Branching is very similar to listing and grouping, except that it lets you put your ideas down spatially rather than sequentially. Usually a writer begins a branching exercise with a focus and a desire to push herself to discover the relevant parts of the idea as well as how these facets relate to the focus and to each other. So branching begins with the writer putting a word in the center of a sheet of paper. Next, she thinks of all the related topics and writes them in, spreading them wheel-fashion around the central word. Connecting lines and arrows can be drawn to show relationships between ideas and to suggest ways of grouping them. The branching exercise on page 21 gives you an idea of how this technique can help you generate material for writing.

old family photos

↑

gambling uncles

↑

stories about
her mother - "headaches"
her father - Christmas
                    drinking
she denied these
          stories

her own life
cleaned
fixed meals

↑

her "woman"

2nd husband
"Pop"

↑

1st husband

↑

her personality
gentility
social graces
somewhat snobbish

her illness - oxygen tank
emphysema   thin

Spring Hill, TN
small town
one stop light

now sold   front parlor
              staircase
              circular drive
                      columns
Hampstead Manor
other old houses in
                        town
Roderick House
((across street)
someone's house

the will
(the piano)
$100.
the houses + stipulation
about Martha's marriage

Aunt Kirk
Hazel Marton

- plantation
- 3rd floor slaves

1st cousins
Dad - Joe Torrence
        Marthea Torrence ← lived with for
                                        years

Jan & JoAnn

Old South

↓

the cannonball
from the civil war

↓

the old cemetary
- overgrown
- clean up days

periodic
visits
gifts
Sherry
veggies
      candy

my brother's fantasy
          to buy the Hampstead
          & Roderick

↓

her sisters
aunt Tenn.
aunt Iby
Aunt Gold

↓

what she meant
      to him   →

↓

her funeral shortly
      after Dad's

love of family history
- several written
      family histories
- one she wrote (left out all
      scandalous stories)

- efforts made to hold on to this family history
- genteel version of Old South
- how I feel removed from all this

Branching works well in helping writers to see the richness of their topics; it enables them to become aware of the variety of angles from which a single topic may be approached. For instance, in the exercise on page 21 the writer could choose to focus on her aunt's life and personality, the places she lived, her family history, or she could center on her own family's relationship to the aunt and to the past that the aunt represents for them.

The key to branching is to let the exercise show you a range of approaches from which you choose the best. Do not hesitate to shift the focus of your project from your starting point (that first word) to another idea that comes out of the exercise. Final note: Branching is just one of the more visually oriented invention techniques. Your teacher may encourage you to use others such as *mapping, diagramming, drawing,* and *flowcharting*. These options work well for writers who think pictorially or spatially. Also, some topics lend themselves naturally to the drawing of caricatures, maps, diagrams, and flowcharts. Often a rough sketch, a time line, or a floor plan can help you organize information. Be aware of these possibilities and use them anytime they will help you start writing more quickly than word-oriented strategies.

PAIRING QUESTIONS

Another useful technique, particularly good for encouraging you to analyze situations and contexts of events, is to ask yourself paired questions. First answer the reporter's questions of *Who, What, Where, When, How,* and *Why*. Then pair these questions to see how the various aspects of the topic are interdependent. That is, ask yourself about the relationships between the facets of the event in order to analyze the motivations of the people involved, and judge how the context of the situation affected those people. For example, pair the who and where questions to ask yourself "What is significant about the participants being in this place?" Or a pairing of what and when questions would prompt you to wonder about how the event was influenced by the time in which it took place. Ultimately, you would ask yourself about the connections suggested by all the possible pairs of questions, gaining insights into your topic along the way. The basic questions and their pairs are listed below.

Reporter's Questions	*Question Pairs*	*Question Pairs*
Who?	Who?/What?	What?/Why?
What?	Who?/Where?	Where?/How?
Where?	Who?/How?	Where?/When?
When?	Who?/When?	Where?/Why?
How?	Who?/Why?	How?/When?
Why?	What?/Where?	How?/Why?
	What?/How?	When?/Why?
	What?/When?	

JOURNALS

Keeping a journal is one of the best ways to help yourself become a writer. A journal allows you to write down your thoughts and ideas as they occur to you, so when you're faced with a writing assignment or project you can read through your journal, an informal record of your thoughts and experiences, to locate ideas. Also, the writing practice a journal provides will help you write more freely later. You will simply become more comfortable as a writer if you write regularly, a habit that keeping a journal fosters.

Please refer to the excerpts from Scott Turow's "One L" (p. 96) and Bob Greene's "Good Morning Merry Sunshine" (p. 91) for some examples of journal entries. Also, note their personal, informal nature and how they treat a range of topics briefly. Below is a list of guidelines for keeping a journal.

- ▸ Select a special notebook in which to write. Keep all of your entries together so you can see how your thoughts change and develop.

- ▸ Write in your journal regularly. Try writing an entry once a day at a scheduled time. It might be easiest to write an entry first thing in the morning or before going to bed; these times allow you a few minutes to reflect about the day.

- ▸ Try carrying your journal around with you to write down words, thoughts, bits of conversations, pithy remarks, and questions. Use your journal as a commonplace book, like Elizabethans did, to record anything you might want to recall later. In this way your journal can become a kind of personal reference work, containing notes about your experiences and reflections.

- ▸ Use your journal as a problem-solving mechanism to help you sort out conflicting thoughts and emotions. Writing about problems — personal or otherwise — can help you see situations clearly and make wise decisions.

- ▸ Write out your impressions about your classwork, lectures you attend, and articles, books, or stories you read. It's a good idea to write a brief response to textbook chapters or other material as soon as you finish reading. This exercise will help you remember the details of what you have read, and it encourages critical and creative thought, both sources of writing topics.

- ▸ Keep track of your daily progress on all kinds of projects or interests. Many athletes keep journals of their workouts; travelers take notes about what places they visit and how they like them; businesspeople keep records of meetings and appointments; artists often record their dreams to help them tap into ideas for future development; scientists carefully record their experiments and results to help them develop their understanding of phenomena and to use as a basis for speculation. Keep a log of one of your own ongoing activities and observe your progress over time. Or plan future activities for the months and weeks to come, listing and considering places you want to go, books you want to read, activities you want to do.

- ▸ Try to make your journal more than a diary. Don't simply create a list or catalog of each day's activities. Reflect on or analyze your experiences. Make your journal a place where you think about many of the topics that interest you — your hobbies, schoolwork, job, long-range goals, friendships, and family. A multidimensional journal will give you a more accurate sense of the richness and complexity of your own life and thoughts than a single-topic journal and will be a better source for writing topics.

▶ Don't worry if your journal entries seem to offer little in the way of concrete writing suggestions. After reading over several entries you can do another invention exercise that will help you develop one of the ideas in your journal.

RESEARCHING

Research involves looking outside of yourself for writing topics and information. There are many different research techniques such as observing, interviewing, reading, and surveying. Specific advice for these methods is provided in Section III: Crafting Informative Prose. Before you start on one kind of research activity, you can adopt the attitude of a researcher by practicing the suggestions discussed below. For the most part they are logical, even prosaic, methods for finding topics, and they can work especially well if you're having trouble pulling ideas from your own personal memories, thoughts, and interests.

Adopting a questioning intellect is a basic way of finding a topic. Think of subjects you would like to know more about. Think of issues that interest you and might interest your audience. Much writing usually takes as its subject the external world of events, discoveries, timely issues, people, and places, so while you are generating topic ideas make a concerted effort to look around yourself at your community, state, nation, and world. While surveying the possibilities, ask yourself questions; be curious, questioning, even doubtful of facts you hear reported and their usual explanations. Try some of the following activities for finding an interesting topic.

1. Skim through a local, state, or national newspaper or newsmagazine and make notes about events that concern or puzzle you.

2. From any news source, find a local event or issue that needs more study.

3. From any news source, find a national event or issue that can be researched from a local angle.

4. Think about your job or occupation. What unanswered questions do you have about your business, institution, or school?

5. What things would you like to learn about for your personal interest or enjoyment? Think of activities you would like to learn to do, places you would like to visit, skills you would like to acquire, health or financial questions you would like answered.

6. Consider the community you live in. What are its characteristics? What is unique about the area? What industries, businesses, restaurants, recreation spots, community activities, or conditions are of note? Could you find out more about one of them?

7. What kind of people interest you? People who have interesting jobs, who have had unique experiences, who have lived through periods or events that are noteworthy, who are celebrities of local or national renown? Could you meet and interview someone?

8. Look through your journal for questions about your surroundings that you want answered.

Remember that if you find a topic that interests you, an essay, article, or report about that topic will probably interest an audience too.

Once you have a topic in mind, no matter how sketchy it seems, you can continue to generate ideas by *surveying standard works* on that topic. Even personal reflections on topics you believe you are familiar with — your hometown, for example — can benefit from acquiring additional information about the general subject you are exploring. You might look up your topic in an encyclopedia or specialized dictionary. You might find a brief history of the person, place, event, or thing in a biographical dictionary, encyclopedia, newspaper or magazine, textbook, or other reference work. For instance, if you were fascinated by the history of the electoral college in U.S. national elections and its function and impact on recent elections, you might look up the topic in a reputable encyclopedia or political science textbook to get some basic background information. From that source you could move to other standard works by looking at the list of works cited. If you were writing a profile of a person who is close to you — your father, for instance — you probably could not expect to find him written up in an encyclopedia or other reference work. But you could turn to unpublished "reference works" — a family scrapbook or photograph album — to seek out information that you had forgotten or never known.

Your goal at this stage should be to gain a familiarity with the subject. The amount of background reading you should do depends on (a) your previous knowledge of the topic, (b) the complexity of the topic, (c) the amount of historical background necessary to understand the parameters of the topic, and (d) the amount of time you have. Even though reading widely and generally about a subject is hardly ever a mistake, realize that if you read too long and too widely you can waste time and become confused about your own approach to the topic. Learn when to call it quits on background reading and move on to more directed research and planning.

Another beginning research strategy is to *inventory sources* that may be useful to you. This technique requires that you make a list of who, what, where, and how you can gain information on your topic. Can you visit a place or observe an event significant to your topic? Who could you interview about the topic that would be an expert or eye witness? What kinds of written sources are suitable for your project — almanacs, scholarly works, popular newspapers, or magazines? Could you write to a business or government office for information? Is there a public information service that could supply some facts — the Better Business Bureau, the county clerk, or the Office of Consumer Affairs? Could you devise a survey or other experiment to gain information? Consider all the options available for researching your topic by asking yourself who would know about a certain aspect of your project. If you draw a blank, meet with a reference librarian for some pointers on written information and talk to friends and family for their ideas. The point of this exercise is to force yourself to start thinking as tangibly and specifically as possible about what you can learn and how you can learn it. You may not need to pursue all of your sources, but developing a clear sense of the research options available will help you define your topic, discover the facets of your topic you want to pursue, and locate a variety of sources.

AUDIENCE ANALYSIS

Up to this point, we have discussed invention techniques that encourage you to find your topic and your approach to it either by locating ideas within yourself or within the world around you. If you think back to our discussion of the writing triangle, you will see that we have suggested exercises that focus on the writer and on reality. Another approach to invention focuses on the intended audience, or reader of a piece of writing. This approach requires that you have a topic in mind, so if you already have a sense of topic this technique will help you refine it further.

An important consideration in all writing is what your reader needs in order to be able to read easily, follow, and remember an article. Therefore, it is sometimes useful to consider your reader even during the earliest stages of invention. You may find that thinking about the questions your reader may ask, the confused preconceptions he may have, and his interest in the topic will help you decide what to pursue during planning and what to include in your finished piece. For invention purposes, you should simply put yourself in a reader's shoes or talk over your project with someone who qualifies as a reader of your article. Ask yourself or your prospective reader the following questions:

1. Who is your reader? What do you think he will like, and what does he already know about the topic?
2. How interested will your reader be in the topic? Will he want to read your article or will he be required to read it?
3. How can you engage a reader who may not initially view the topic as relevant or interesting to him?
4. What anecdotes could you tell to gain your reader's attention, interest, understanding?
5. What background information does your reader need, and what should you tell him about the purpose of your essay or article?
6. For what terms and processes will your reader need definitions, explanations, examples, and instructions?
7. What broad organization for your article would make the topic accessible to your reader? Try thinking about what a reader will need to know first, second, third, and so forth.
8. What sources would be particularly convincing to your reader?

9. Will your reader recognize an expert or will you need to explain why a source has the authority of an expert?

10. What style will be appropriate for your reader? Should you be formal or informal to reach this reader?

11. What will your reader's expectations be when he reads the title of your piece or learns of the topic? Will you want to meet these expectations directly, or will you want to surprise a reader by taking an approach to the topic that is different from the one he expects?

These questions should be helpful to you in pinpointing problems that you will need to solve when you research and draft. One warning: If you are unfamiliar with your topic, it may be very difficult to decide what your reader needs. In this case, do some research and drafting before answering these questions. Go ahead and learn about your topic and then return to thinking about how you can present it to someone else. In short, don't feel that you have to have your reader analyzed before you have a good understanding of your topic; too much early concern for a reader may make you overly anxious about him and hinder your grasping the topic fully during invention and research.

LIMITING YOUR TOPIC

Once you've identified an area of interest and have done some background reading on your subject, it's time to face honestly the constraints of your writing project. Weigh the complexity of your subject and the amount of research it will require against the constraints of (1) article length, (2) closeness of your deadline or due date, (3) the depth of investigation your assignment calls for, and (4) the likely interests, patience, and sophistication of your audience (if you know who your readers will be). It's a good idea to make up a timetable to use to organize your project. Make up a calendar and set aside blocks of time for inventing, researching, drafting, revising, editing, and preparing your project in "publishable" form. Be painfully honest with yourself here so that you don't begin a project that's going to demand more time than you can ever give it. Also, be sure that your subject will be large enough to meet minimum requirements; don't stay with a topic that's too simple or shallow to meet a length requirement effectively or an audience's expectations.

If you feel your topic doesn't fit your assignment or writing situation, think of ways to limit or expand it. Here are some suggestions:

To Limit:

1. Treat a national issue from a local point of view.

2. Limit your topic to a study of one perspective or angle — how a change in federal funding will affect a single local school, for example, or an individual

class within that school, or a single student within that class — and be sure to make this limitation clear to a reader when you write the piece.

3. Determine if you can de-emphasize certain aspects of your project without skewing the issue. If you can, select which points demand the most attention; plan to summarize the ones that are subordinate.

4. Reduce the number of sources you plan to use, but be careful that you don't cut out significant ones.

5. Restrict the amount of original research you do and use secondary (usually written) sources more than you first planned. Again, be careful not to bias your research when you limit it in this way.

6. See if you can write a series of articles on this topic, rather than just one long one.

To Expand:

1. Consider how a local issue may have a national application.

2. Compare two or more instances of the phenomenon that you have chosen.

3. Determine if you can include more detailed descriptions, anecdotes, or meaty quotations in your article than you may have originally planned. Be sure that you don't just include "filler," but add more useful detail about your topic.

4. Try to think of additional relevant sources and perspectives on your topic.

5. See if you can look more thoroughly at the complexities of your topic and find ways to elucidate them in your article.

6. Connect your current topic to a related one and discuss both of them.

7. Try to establish relationships between the individual examples you have chosen and larger issues or trends.

By suggesting these methods of tailoring your topic to fit the needs of your situation, we are not implying that you either overlook important issues or that you add useless, meaningless filler to your article. Limiting a topic is not objectionable as long as those limitations are presented straightforwardly to your reader. That is, you don't want to imply in your writing that you have discussed more or less than you actually have. Your goal in limiting your topic should be to find a comfortable and realistic compromise between the time and space constraints you face and a satisfying treatment of your subject.

FOCUS . . . .
SUGGESTIONS FOR WRITING

1. Write an autobiography of yourself as a writer. Think back over the most memorable and formative experiences that shaped your attitudes toward writing, considering how each one influenced you. What generalizations can you make about yourself as a writer?

2. Recalling one particularly successful or disappointing writing project, write about how you went about working on that project. What was your process? Do you think that your methods helped or hindered you? What mental games did you play as you wrote this piece? Did they work?

3. Returning to the lists you were asked to make on page 18, describe in detail the writing process and environment that you envision as perfect, for both inspiration and productive writing. How can you adapt your vision of the perfect method and place to your actual writing circumstances?

4. Practice "looping" by choosing one of the following words (*courage, friendship, hate, brotherhood, achievement, disaster*) and engaging first in an unfocused freewriting exercise for five minutes. Then focus your freewriting on certain elements of what you have written for further examination.

5. Choose one of the following subjects (*childhood shoes, space exploration, illness, machinery*) and use a branching exercise to develop a number of topics related to the central subject. Let your mind range freely over the possibilities for at least ten minutes.

6. Make a list of the invention techniques you usually use. Write about why you think they work for you and what kinds of writing they help you produce. Try to cite examples of particular assignments or projects that you have begun by freewriting, brainstorming, or research. Do you feel that these techniques were adequate in helping you generate good ideas? Now that you have the benefit of hindsight, which other techniques might you have employed for better or different results?

► Drafting

GUIDE TO DRAFTING AND REVISION

This chapter and the one that follows sketch the process of drafting and revising writing. Mostly, they are meant to provide you with practical, everyday techniques for producing that first draft and the eventual finished essay or article. You, of course, will have to stretch, alter, and re-design this one-size-fits-all process to meet your own writing needs and habits. You may discover that you like to write one or two working drafts before you find your focus, or that you do best to outline meticulously before writing a draft at all, or that you are most comfortable writing many drafts quickly, revising each time with special attention to one factor or concern. All of these drafting behaviors — and many other variations — can produce good writing. You simply need to experiment until you find the drafting and revising strategies that work for you. Feel free to mix and match techniques. Be flexible about your process, making an extra revision if you think your essay needs it, or asking for a reader's reaction during the drafting stages if that will give you a sense of where you are. In short, learn to follow whatever leads or hunches you have when you draft and revise. If you're stuck, try one or two techniques that might get you started again.

In general, we encourage you to think of drafting and revising as gradual and recursive activities. The first goal is to create a draft that is meaningful to you, one that says what you want to say. Then you can evaluate, revise, and edit to help tailor your writing for a reader. The final goal is to produce a finished piece of writing that serves both as an accurate expression of your own thoughts and an effective presentation or communication of them to your reader. To use current terminology, coined by composition theorist Linda Flower, first you produce *writer-based prose* that gets your ideas on paper; then you alter that draft until it becomes *reader-based*, or a clear and effective communication of your own ideas, polished and ready for a reader. (This concept is touched on again in Section II: Crafting Expressive Prose.) It's important for you to recognize the need to make the shift from writing for yourself to writing for a reader. Remember that your writing will almost always make sense to you. After all, you put the words down, you came up with the ideas. But communicating to a reader, who may be distant from you and who may be a very different person from you, is a much more difficult undertaking, demanding that you express your thoughts clearly, arrange them in an accessible order, support them with illustrations, facts, and quotations, and follow all the conventions of good use and correct grammar. Ultimately it does not matter how many drafts you write or how you go about revising; your goal is to develop a process enabling you to produce work that is clear and accessible to a reader.

In this chapter, we examine how to find your purpose for writing and explore methods for discovering a suitable organization and creating a first draft. The following chapter discusses the evaluation and revision of that draft. As you read the sections that describe this generic drafting, evaluating, and revising process, do not mistake the order in which the parts themselves are presented as a prescription for when you should decide on a focus, for example, or on an organizational structure. Professional writers make these decisions at different times depending on their personalities and their current projects. For instance, you don't have to have either a focus or a firm organization before you begin to draft, or even before you finish a first draft. Many writers draft and then make choices about focus and structure. In other words, they use the drafting stage to help them discover their ideas rather than just to copy them down. Keep these options in mind, and, whatever you do, don't put off beginning to draft just because you're not quite sure about how you want your finished project to appear. Take a stab at drafting and then shape your writing afterwards.

FINDING A PURPOSE

Writers have to say something when they write. They must write about something, and they must say something meaningful, insightful, interesting, or new about their topics. In short, you have to have a purpose for writing, a point to make, a reason to compose sentences and ask others to read them. Sometimes your purpose will be clear: you will want to complain about the lack of parking spaces on campus, or you will write to your best friend about your decision to major in city planning and architecture. In these cases, you not only know what you want to write about, you also know why, and that sense of purpose will help you make many decisions as you compose. For instance, it will be easy for you to determine the limits of your topic, the structure of your piece, and the significant point you want to make. Lucky you! In such situations some of the hardest work is already done.

On the other hand, many times you will have to discover your purpose as you invent, research, and draft. Often you will have a topic in mind, but just what you're going to do with it will be undecided. At these times you will need to draw on some of the techniques described below. They can help you find your purpose for writing, and they can lead you to your focus and thesis.

Before we get to these specific suggestions, however, let's discuss the nature of a writer's focus and thesis. These terms and concepts are actually refinements of a writer's purpose since they provide a controlling idea that helps a writer decide what to include in her essay or article and how to shape her drafts. *A focus designates the area of study, the limits of the essay, the angle of approach to the topic. A thesis serves a more specific role since it states the major idea that the essay will discuss, support, and advocate.* A thesis is the heart of the essay, the bull's eye of the target that you want to hit when you write, the central point that your reader will need to recognize and understand. Here are two lists of questions that will help you test your focus and thesis.

Test for a Reasonable Focus

1. Does my focus allow me to limit my topic and make decisions about what is relevant, what deserves inclusion, and what is extraneous?

2. Does my focus inform me of the perspective or approach I'm going to take in developing my ideas and writing about them? For instance, do I know if I want to treat my topic from a personal, impersonal, local, or national angle? Do I want to focus on causes or on effects, general principles or specific manifestations of these principles?

3. Does my focus give me a direction for formulating a thesis, drafting the work, and researching my topic?

4. Is my focus large or small enough to treat adequately in an essay of the necessary length?

5. Can my focus be pursued, researched, and successfully examined within my limitations of time and access to reliable information?

Test for a Workable Thesis

1. Is my thesis clearly stated?

2. Is my thesis stated specifically enough to be understandable to a reader? Have I avoided using abstract terms whose meanings may be different for my reader than they are for me?

3. Does my thesis state only one idea? Is it unified so that I will attempt to support only one major idea or opinion in my essay?

4. Does my thesis say something of interest? Is it an opinion or interpretation of facts or information that will intrigue a reader? If my thesis is a statement of fact, is this fact already well known or obvious? If so, how can I develop it into something more meaningful?

5. Can my thesis be supported? A workable thesis needs the support of facts, explanations, examples, descriptions, or quotations from experts, eyewitnesses, or interested parties.

By way of example, we will examine the process through which Greg Maine, a composition student, found his focus and thesis for an essay about one of the central crossroads on his campus, a courtyard. Greg had already decided to write about the courtyard that lay outside his own dormitory because he thought it a unique spot on campus. He also enjoyed sitting in the courtyard and visiting with his friends when the weather was pleasant. But what was he going to say about it? What fascinated him about it? He didn't know. So he decided to go out to the courtyard with his notebook and take notes, closely recording what he saw and what he thought. Next he wrote a draft that got down some of his ideas into sentences and encouraged him to think seriously about the nature of the courtyard. Here is his draft:

I step outside into the crisp morning air and shiver when that first cool blast of wind hits me. Surveying the scene before me, I see an empty space, barren except for those few, like myself, who are forced out of their warm beds so early. The cold, hard concrete that surrounds the islands of grass and trees seems to stare at me as I quickly walk across it. Hours later, when I return, the same hateful space has changed personality. People now walk across it freely, not afraid of what lies beneath their feet. Even the birds, who had hidden in the trees before, now come to life to take advantage of this daily friendliness to forage for food.

As the day draws on, I return again to see the calm and hospitable turn wild, drawing parties out of thin air. Finally, I retire to the safety of the dormitory while the schizophrenic courtyard slowly evolves into the beast again

In reality the surface is not alive. It is nothing but common sand mixed with cement, gravel, and water. It is not even strong enough to hold itself together. It must be held together with steel. At no time is it actually a living, breathing organism. Even when it is poured out to form the courtyard it is not alive. This surface, made of common materials, can only be alive in the context of the role it plays in drawing life. It will never live. It is forever dead.

In the midst of death there is life in the courtyard. Randomly scattered about the yard are islands of grass and trees. Each is about the same size as the dormitory rooms which line the perimeter of the courtyard. Like the rooms, they are havens for life. Birds sit in the trees and sing their songs to the people who walk below. The people pass to and fro constantly. Their voices carry to all parts of the yard setting a cheerful mood.

The living and the dead combine to make the courtyard atmosphere. The green of the grass and trees livens up the nearby area. People sit in the islands and talk. Footballs and Frisbees constantly sail through the air overhead. Friends and lovers stroll across the yard casually.

The question is which is more significant — the surface or the life? Without the surface the people would disappear because of the lack of a clean place to congregate. The concrete is necessary for the people to be there. On the other hand, what good is a surface without people to use it? The concrete would just crack after years of disuse, unjustified. So both the life and the structure which draws the life are necessary to form the courtyard.

We can look at this draft to see how Greg's thoughts developed. He begins with the most accessible details and describes the courtyard as it appears to him throughout the day, recording the changes in atmosphere. In this way, he treats the courtyard as something alive, even calling it a "beast." Then in his third, fourth, and fifth paragraphs he begins to question this idea and finds that the place is not really alive; it is the people who pass through the courtyard who make it seem alive. He seems unable to make up his mind: Is the courtyard alive or dead? What can he say to make sense of it? In the last paragraph he resolves this point of confusion by deciding that the courtyard is actually a place composed of two entities — the dead surface of concrete and the living people, plants, and animals who frequent it. The courtyard, like all places, is a composite of dead and living entities.

After Greg finished this draft he read over it. He liked some of the details he had included and felt pretty good about the idea developed in the last paragraph. Returning to a planning stage, he decided that he would focus on the split personality of the courtyard and that his thesis would be the point he makes at the end, that people and surface are interdependent and together account for the reality of the courtyard. He had discovered what he wanted to say.

He was then ready to evaluate his draft and consider how he might revise it to give his readers a more vivid sense of the atmosphere of the courtyard by describing people and their activities in more detail. Also, he wanted to change the tone of the essay to make it less mysterious and more humorous. He felt he had a good opportunity for a humorous treatment of himself and his fellow students. Other questions cropped up during evaluation too. He wondered whether he should identify the place more specifically by name and include a factual description of it as background information for readers who would not know the place he was discussing. Yes, he decided, was his answer to both questions. One feature of the draft that he did decide to leave intact was his general organization of the essay, which allowed him to build up to the thesis throughout the body of the paper. He thought this order worked more naturally than stating his thesis early on. At this time he moved into a period of organizing and revision.

Activities for Finding a Purpose

1. *Write a narrative account of your invention and research process.* Often this exercise will lead you to consider why you settled on your topic and what is most interesting about the ideas or information you have found.

2. *Write a letter to yourself* detailing what you know or have learned about your topic. Ask yourself what you want to say or accomplish in your essay or article. What do you need to do next to move forward in your project? What options do you see for selecting a focus or thesis? Which one seems most promising?

3. *Draft several versions of a thesis sentence* (which you may or may not include in the text of your essay). Evaluate each version for its clarity, unity, specificity, and interest. Select the version that most intrigues you and that holds up best to scrutiny. Do the same with a "lead" or first sentence.

4. *Talk over your topic, focus, or thesis ideas with a friend or classmate.* Try to explain your ideas to your friend and encourage her to ask questions about what she doesn't understand. Often it's a good idea to discuss your topic in a relaxed environment and when you do not have notes, preprinting, or drafts handy. Without these props you will need to synthesize your thoughts, and you won't be tempted just to have your friend read these and do your thinking for you.

5. *Zero in on your focus by brainstorming for key words and phrases* relevant to your topic. Make a list of these and then review it, looking for your reason for writing or for your salient opinion about the topic.

6. *List potential titles for your essay or article.* Given that a good title suggests the thesis, this exercise will enable you to identify a variety of foci and thesis statements quickly. Try to write out fifteen to twenty different titles in ten to fifteen minutes. Afterwards you can select the one that seems to fit your ideas and opinions best and use it as a point of departure for drafting.

THINKING ABOUT ORGANIZATION

Organizing your ideas — either before or after drafting — is not a mysterious concept. It's simply the process by which you determine when to say what. Perhaps the most important guideline is to let the content, the raw material, of your work in progress suggest an organization. In other words, it's usually a bad idea to set out to write with a rigidly fixed notion of the number of paragraphs you need or the number of sentences that are required for each paragraph. Very few sophisticated ideas are adequately presented and discussed in an essay with five predetermined paragraphs. Although patterns can sometimes be useful and essential to writers of news stories, scientific reports, and letters, they should never become so important as to inhibit a writer's ability to develop his topic. A useful distinction to make when you organize your writing is the difference between formula and order. A formula is predictable and does not respond to the particular demands of the topic or reader, while an order is logical and accessible; it is also flexible enough to allow a writer the freedom to follow the demands of his situation. This ordering approach to organization enables the structure of the essay to be determined by its content.

A good rule of thumb for organizing is the adage "form follows function." This maxim summarizes the philosophy of a famous American architect, Louis Sullivan, and writers can adopt it because it encourages them to think of the structure of a work as emerging from the ideas they want to communicate. In other words, the organization of an article or essay should be prompted by its content and should complement, rather than fix or control, what you want to say.

Sybil Adams, a student in a composition class, took this ordering approach when she worked on organizing her material for an article about feline leukemia virus. She had already read about the disease, interviewed a local expert, and observed cats who had the disease. Also, she had decided to focus on explaining the danger and progress of the disease with the purpose of encouraging all cat owners to have their pets vaccinated. With these thoughts in mind, she sat down to organize her information and begin drafting. First she simply made a list of points to include in her article:

> no cure
>
> how the disease is spread
>
> description of cats with virus — one sick, one just a carrier, how disease manifests itself
>
> introduce vet. & describe hospital
>
> definition of FLV
>
> need for vaccination by owners, must educate public

Once Sybil had collected her list of main points, she thought about how she should begin her article. Initially she considered beginning with a definition of the disease and the introduction of her expert source, the veterinarian. After a moment, however, she decided that would make her paper too textbooklike. She wanted to fascinate her readers, even alarm them since she felt most pet owners were too unconcerned about this issue. So she decided to place the most emotional and moving information she had in the first paragraph: an anecdote about a sick kitten she had seen and a description of its symptoms. Next, she arranged her ideas in an order she thought would keep the interest of her readers and still let her present all the information she needed to make her point about the seriousness of FLV. She wrote the following "flowchart" for her article:

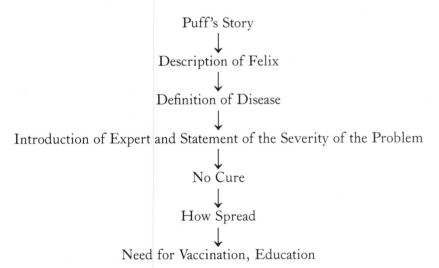

Puff's Story
↓
Description of Felix
↓
Definition of Disease
↓
Introduction of Expert and Statement of the Severity of the Problem
↓
No Cure
↓
How Spread
↓
Need for Vaccination, Education

After she constructed this loose order for her ideas, she felt ready to select specific details and quotations from her notes, match them up with the most appropriate sections, and begin to draft. After several drafting sessions she produced the following article. Notice the smooth progression of ideas and information. Here is her third draft:

Feline Leukemia Virus

Puff was a birthday present for Lucy Thompson's sixth birthday. The adorable, little ball of white fluff has grown in the past year into a sleek, elegant feline. But the future is grim for Lucy's kitty and the entire household is upset. Puff is constantly fighting off infections of one sort or another with very few good days in between. First she had a nasty bladder infection, the painful ulcers in her mouth that kept her from eating, and now she is in the hospital with a respiratory infection that will probably kill her.

Felix is the neighborhood tomcat. His large scarred jowls, tattered ears, and snubbed tail are the only remnants of the fierce, screaming battles fought defending his territory. While Felix remains outwardly quite healthy, he is actively spreading a horrible disease to many other cats.

Both Puff and Felix are infected with feline leukemia virus. There is information available about this disease, but there still remained some unanswered questions in my mind. Being an avid cat fancier, I felt I needed the most current information on this "plague" that could pose a potential health problem to my own precious cats. This quest for knowledge took me to the University of Tennessee Veterinary Hospital, a major center for research and learning, and a meeting with Dr. Bill Adams, a first year resident.

"No," said Dr. Adams sadly shaking his head. "We don't have all of the answers. We know the disease is caused by a virus that, among other things, affects the immune system making the cat defenseless against infections. We call it 'kitty AIDS' because it works very much like the human form of that disease." Much to my relief the doctor quickly assured me that the feline leukemia virus affects cats only.

As we walked down the long, sterile halls toward the intensive care unit, I began to realize the seriousness of this disease.

"How does a cat get feline leukemia?" I asked him. I was trying very hard to mask my growing concern as I thought about my own dear kitties.

"Well," said Dr. Adams as we rounded the corner into ICU, "this disease has reached epidemic proportions among the cat population, and any cat that is outside or ever exposed to other cats is at risk. The virus is shed in the saliva, urine, and feces of infected cats but is most frequently transmitted when cats eat out of common bowls or lick or bite each other. A major problem in controlling this disease," he said with a look of frustration, "is that there are many cats out there who are carriers but never get sick themselves. They will spend a lifetime spreading feline leukemia virus to other cats."

At this point we were standing in ICU with all of its medicinal smells and elaborate life-saving equipment. Directly in front of us was one of many cages, inside of which was a very flat, skinny cat. The only evidence of life was the strained movement of its chest as the cat struggled for air.

"Many cats with feline leukemia virus present like this case," he said in his doctor's dialect. "Puff has had multiple infections over the past six months, and it looks like this respiratory infection may be her last. Lymphosarcoma and cancers of the blood cells do occur, but most cases are like this one where an overwhelming infection causes the death of the cat."

"Isn't there anything you can do for her?" I asked, my heart going out to the pathetic creature.

"There is no cure," he said with finality. "All we can do is try to prevent other cats from getting feline leukemia by encouraging owners to have their cats vaccinated. We can save a lot of suffering, both of cats and of their grieving owners, if we can just educate the public about the seriousness of this disease and about the fact that there is a vaccine available which can prevent it."

I thanked Dr. Adams for his time, and not wanting to waste a moment, made a beeline for my car. Now that I was equipped with accurate information, I could take action. I would have my cats vaccinated as soon as possible and keep my fingers crossed that I wasn't already too late.

Notice how the article builds on itself logically and continually presents the reader with interesting facts and details. Furthermore, Sybil's article is not formulaic because she never set out to follow a pattern; she let her purpose, focus, and ordering decisions guide her paragraphing and organization. In addition, she has been sensitive to the needs of the reader, always providing him with the information he needs to understand her points, such as her introduction to the vet and her descriptions of the hospital. Sybil has successfully organized her article so that it is controlled by her focus and purpose. Notice also that this third draft does not exactly follow her flowchart; during the drafting and revising stages she altered and refined her plans. Here are some suggestions for your drafts:

Pointers for Organizing Your Ideas

1. *Don't organize; jump into drafting* to see how you will naturally select and organize your ideas. Then revise the structure of your draft by considering the needs of your reader as well as the effect your current organization will have on him. Once you have a draft, consider if it begins in an interesting way, clearly presents information in a reasonable order, maintains your reader's interest, and satisfies his need for a conclusion.

2. *Group and shuffle note cards*, trying out a variety of sequences of information and ideas. This method works particularly well for arranging material gained from research since it allows you to group together related information from a variety of sources. Even if your piece is largely based on your own thoughts, you may want to write key thoughts on note cards to facilitate your arranging them into an order for a reader. Cluster related cards and match them up with examples, quotations, and statistics. Then play with the sequence until you find an order that you like.

3. *Fit your material to conventional ordering patterns*. These are familiar patterns which may work well for your topic.

   ▶ Move from specific examples to general conclusions.
   ▶ Move from general conclusions to specific examples.
   ▶ Arrange events and their related ideas chronologically. What happened first, second, third, and so forth?
   ▶ Order the major points of your article according to their importance. You may want to begin with the least important point and build toward the most

significant, or you may want to order your article so that the critical information is presented early in the piece. Don't forget that readers remember first and last points more vividly than those in the middle.

> ▸ Use a spatial plan. For instance, you might want to discuss local events and issues before national ones, so that the movement of your piece would be to broaden toward points of universal significance. Or if you are describing a person or place you might organize details according to a movement from inside to outside, top to bottom, etc.

4. *Find a movement for your writing.* Consider where you want to begin and end in discussing your topic. Find a sequence of steps that clearly presents the important points you want to make. For example, you might want to begin an essay with descriptions or definitions that will provide your reader with a context for the more specialized or abstract information to come later. Or you might discover that it's most appropriate to reveal how several events lead to a conclusion; in that case you might want to organize your article by naming and discussing a series of causes and effects. Make a flowchart of the progress of ideas and examples that your reader will need.

5. *Scratch out notes and rough outlines* that will allow you to visualize potential organizational schemes for your work. Write down your plans so that you can get a perspective on the whole of your essay before drafting.

6. *Refine organizational plans by constructing a formal or detailed outline.* Many writers gain confidence and a sense of control by writing an outline, which may be composed of sentences or phrases. Outlines usually conform to the pattern illustrated below.

    I. Major topic.
      A. Subtopic of I.
      B. Subtopic of I.
        1. Subtopic of B.
        2. Subtopic of B.
          a) Subtopic of 2.
          b) Subtopic of 2.
            (1) Subtopic of b)
            (2) Subtopic of b)
              (a) Subtopic of (2)
              (b) Subtopic of (2)
                (i) Subtopic of (b)
                (ii) Subtopic of (b)
    II. Major topic.

    Notice that anytime you subdivide a section you need to have two items in the section beneath it.

    You may want to begin outlining by first delineating the major divisions of your topic. After you decide on these sections you can determine what you need to subdivide. You may also want to predetermine which examples, facts, and quotations to include in each major section and write them in your outline. This activity can streamline drafting since it decreases the number of decisions you need to make while writing. Of course, some writers find this approach too rigid and confining; they like to make these choices in the heat of composition.

DRAFTING

To many writers drafting is the big event. This activity indicates whether or not their ideas, their research, and their planning are going to pay off. At this time they must concentrate most fully on their writing and must work hardest to give their work a shape and a meaning. For these reasons, drafting sessions can be periods of intense, exhausting, and emotional work. While you draft you may see all of your thoughts synthesizing into a coherent essay, or you may suddenly discover big obstacles in the way of the logic of your argument. Drafting can be exhilarating or frustrating. As with the writing process, the best advice for drafting is to follow any tactics, techniques, or eccentricities that will help you begin and continue drafting. Whatever you can do to make a drafting session more productive and less difficult, you should do. Follow your hunches and whims while you write. If they don't pay off directly with an inspired draft, they will help you see what needs to be changed in the next one. Adopt the attitude that you expect to evaluate and revise whatever you write in a draft. Believe that the quality of a draft is never so important as its existence. Once you have sentences on paper, you can always improve on them. Remember that drafting is still part of the discovery process.

CASE STUDY, PART ONE

The following paragraphs begin a case study of one student's experience in drafting, evaluating, and revising an essay. As you read, consider your own process. This case study will illustrate how a writer's thoughts grow and develop throughout the writing process. In addition, it will show the ups and downs of writing.

Mary Rhea had decided she wanted to write about her uncle. Since her childhood, she had known about his bravery as a marine during World War II. She had sat for hours around his kitchen table listening to his stories about Guadalcanal and Peleliu. But it wasn't the events that fascinated her: she had always been amazed that such a sweet, jovial man had once been a determined soldier involved in hand-to-hand combat. How did these two sides of him fit together? What were the details of his experiences? Up to now she had only paid enough attention to his stories to remember her own imaginings and vague impressions of his adventures.

She decided she needed more information. During the upcoming weekend at home she would visit him and get him to talk once more about his life as a marine. She knew he would be pleased that she asked him about it. So she dropped by to see him and talked to him while he worked in his garage, changing the spark plugs on one of his daughters' cars. This time she paid more attention to the details and to his tone of voice; she jotted down names and dates to keep them straight.

When she got back to her dorm room, she had lots of ideas and pages of notes, mostly transcriptions of his remarks. After arranging, rearranging, and selecting her material, she decided that she wanted to focus on her uncle's faith in the Marine Corps, in God, and in his own abilities. This faith, she had learned, was what he thought had brought him through the war alive. With these ideas in mind, she drafted her essay. It took her two sessions of about three hours each (with breaks) to complete her draft. She wrote first in longhand and then typed up each session's work, restraining herself from editing and polishing sentences and paragraphs since she didn't believe that she would keep all of them. As she wrote, she followed a rough outline and often referred to the notes she had taken. Here is her draft:

Having Faith (First Complete Draft)

Blaine E. Rhea is a war veteran, a proud Marine, and a perfect example of a man guarded by an angel. After surviving many battles, wounds, and diseases, Blaine firmly believes he has an appointed protector watching over him.

Blaine entered the Marines when he was just seventeen. For those of us who know him, it is difficult to imagine him as a ruthless commander of one hundred to two hundred soldiers. Many people picture him as an affectionate father of two daughters and the owner of a sheet metal business which started in 1876. Blaine takes pride in the Marines' history and will be the first to tell you how lucky he is to be here today.

Unless you knew him well, you would probably never know that he fought for Chesty Puller, the Marine Corps' most famous and most decorated general. Blaine lives by the motto "once a Marine, always a Marine." He says that he would go back today if the occasion arose. "Just tell me what time the bus leaves," he says. "I'd go in a minute's notice. It would take me forever to get back into shape, and I know I couldn't run and fight hand to hand like I did when I was seventeen, but there are a lot of things I could do and I'd do them until every bit of me was gone."

When Blaine was still at the young age of seventeen, he and the Marines hit Guadalcanal. He had barely enough food to last him three days. After fighting twenty-three days under constant artillery fire, he began eating rice and bugs in order to stay alive. Shortly after Guadalcanal, Blaine was treated for shrapnel wounds, malaria, and yellow jaundice. While resting in a sick bay tent, live enemy shells landed beside him. Instead of exploding, the shells stuck dormantly in the mud. Blaine shook his head when he looked back and said, "Things like that don't just happen by themselves. You'd better believe that we knew how to pray. If we hadn't, none of us would have survived. Without some help from up there, I'd have been blown to pieces many times."

The following autumn in Peleliu, Blaine remained the only member of his old company of one hundred and ninety men still on foot. The rest were either dead, missing, or permanently disabled. Blaine's eyes filled with tears when he remembered his war-time buddies and his brow wrinkled showing years of hardship.

He quivered when he stated that it was in fall, forty-four years ago, that he was buried under the lifeless bodies of his fellow soldiers waiting for help on Peleliu. Blaine said he has many sleepless nights in the fall when he remembers the trauma he experienced the same time years ago.

Blaine left the Marines to go into the sheet metal business with his uncle. His civilian career did not last long because on Thanksgiving Day in 1950, he joined the military again. Physically he was not able to be in the infantry and spent those next sixteen years as a metal worker on fighter aircraft. When he rejoined, he signed away a permanent disability allocation (compensation for the damage caused by his shrapnel injuries and diseases from the old days in the Pacific).

In 1966, Blaine reluctantly retired. He knew that civilian life would test him just as the Marine Corps had tested him. He said it was hard to leave such a disciplined life and walk into the foot-loose ways of civilian life. He feels the best thing the old Marine could do is to stay in the Corps but knows that would not be possible nor reasonable.

Blaine paused and rested his hand on his chair before he said, "the big battles of the Pacific are over, and I hope they stay over, but all the old Marines, the good ones, want the memory of those who didn't come back from the Pacific to remain alive after names like Peleliu have been forgotten. It is best to try to forget some things like the horror and the blood in the sand, but there are those men we'd better never forget."

In order to keep his love alive for the Corps, Blaine has attended a number of reunions and celebrations. At these gatherings, the remaining soldiers remember the old days and express their shock at what the years have done to thin their hair and to thicken their waistlines.

Blaine stood back and grinned when asked what he thought about the modern day Marine Corps. He then winked mischievously and said, "We know there are a few old Marines out there, but as you know, there's always been just a few of us." This is a Marine. They are few and they are proud, but as long as the old leathernecks like Blaine Rhea are around, the story of the proud few will continue to be told.

Once she had finished this first complete draft, she was both pleased and dissatisfied. It had been exciting to write about someone she cared about, and she wanted to present him accurately. But she felt her draft fell short of this goal and that she wasn't really getting at the true nature of her uncle and his faith. She also had had some surprises while she was drafting: it was fun to interweave her uncle's words, via quotations, into her narrative of his life. That part she liked; the quotations added drama. Nonetheless, she was sick of working on the essay and wanted to get away from it. If she didn't look at it for a couple of days, she knew she would like it more, and she would then be objective enough in her reading of it to think about revising, which she could already see was a necessity.

Mary's essay is discussed further on pages 46–47 where her evaluation of this draft is described. To conclude this chapter, here are some guidelines to help you with your drafting.

Activities for Drafting Quickly and Steadily

1. *Write the easiest or hardest part first*. Writers often gain momentum once they get going, so whatever you can write to get started, even if it's the last section of an article or a description of someone, will help you get the project underway. Some people like to start with getting the easiest parts of their piece written, quickly and painlessly producing a part that is not difficult but that will help them get going. Others prefer to complete the trickiest parts early on, such as an introduction or detailed discussion, so that they can feel that the rest of the drafting will be downhill. Select the way that works best for you, but remember that you don't have to draft from start to finish.

2. *Pace yourself and settle into the project* by setting reasonable daily goals for drafting. Also, you may want to make up a schedule for drafting during which you assign yourself deadlines for small parts of your project, say drafting two pages a day for a week to complete an eight-to-ten-page article. That way you can limit the amount of time you write each day so that you don't feel overwhelmed but still make steady progress.

3. *Expect for your draft to be a mess*, full of weaknesses, inconsistencies, and digressions. Try not to become disgruntled when you draft just because it's not perfect the first time. Tell yourself that you can and will revise to clear up problems.

4. *Keep your judgment at bay*. When you are drafting don't become too critical about your ideas, word choice, or phrasing. Even if you know some parts are "all wrong," don't stop generating ideas and sentences to correct them. Such a shift to critical evaluation may cause you to lose your train of thought and forget to write down good ideas.

5. *Refer often to notes, brainstorming exercises, and outlines* to remind yourself of key words and phrases as well as the direction you want your draft to go in. Many times this reference to the ideas gained from invention and planning stages can keep you on track while drafting.

6. *End a drafting session when you know where and how you want to begin drafting the next day*. Consider stopping in the middle of a sentence or paragraph so that it will be easy for you to continue. Another option is to write a note to yourself detailing what you want to write next so that some decisions are made at the end of a successful drafting session rather than at the unsteady beginning of one.

7. *Keep going* until you complete your draft, however flawed. Remind yourself that once you have a finished draft you can revise it, a much less stressful undertaking than producing the first draft.

8. *Read your partial draft aloud or recopy it* to get back into the rhythm of your work at the beginning of a drafting session. This technique can also help you get unstuck by revealing to you what you need to say next or what you forgot to include earlier.

FOCUS · · · · · · · · · · · · ·
SUGGESTIONS FOR WRITING

1. Make a list of your writing problems and explain how you think you acquired them. What prescription for changing your attitudes or methods would help you overcome or control these problems? Assuming that these problems are what makes writing difficult, what beliefs, experiences, or attitudes make writing rewarding?

2. Who has most influenced you as a writer? Describe how this person affected you and consider whether you need to break free of this influence or if you need to cherish it.

3. A draft is somewhat analogous to a sketch. You should always think of it as something that can be revised, substantially altered, or even tossed aside and started again. Practice drafting by writing a number of introductory paragraphs to an essay entitled "My Worst Argument." Begin your first draft with the classic opening "Once upon a time . . . ." Make your second draft of your introductory paragraph begin with a question. Begin a third draft of this paragraph with a statement that might shock or surprise your reader. Write a fourth draft of this paragraph and begin it with an excerpt of dialogue. Review your introductory paragraphs, select the one you prefer, and finish your essay using this beginning.

4. Brainstorm on how you go about drafting a piece of writing. Write an account of the drafting stage of your process for one essay, article, letter, term paper, or lab report that you have written in the past year. What generalizations can you make about your mood, thoughts, and habits during drafting? How might an improved awareness of these intangible elements help you write more comfortably in the future?

4 ▶ Evaluating and Revising

EVALUATING

When you begin to evaluate your work, you start shifting your perspective from your own efforts in generating and expressing your thoughts to your concern for how well the reader of your work will be able to understand what you have said. Now you begin to step back from your draft, study it, find its strengths and weaknesses, and look at it from a more objective, critical stance. If we recall Linda Flower's terminology, this stage begins the shift from writer-based prose to reader-based prose.

It is important for your growth as a writer and for the success of your essay that you recognize and attend to this shift. Remember that since you are the writer of your own work, it will make sense to you. You know how you want a reader to interpret your vocabulary, ideas, and emphases because you have already told yourself, to some degree at least, what you want your essay to say and how you want it to be said. Consequently, your natural tendency will be to read your own writing with the predetermined belief that it says what you mean. For example, it's often very difficult for a writer to see when a sentence is too long, complex, or convoluted to strike a reader in the intended way. The writer, after all, understands it; what's the reader's problem? But that's just the point. A reader has to be introduced to the writer's tone and style; he needs to learn the topic and terminology. He may even need basic concepts and background information to be provided and explained. To some extent he needs to be walked through your ideas and draft; he may even need to be pampered a little. You are *not* automatically assuming that your reader is stupid, or ignorant of your topic. But it is necessary for you to entertain the possibility that he *might* be one or both of these. Also, you need to consider how he might miss an important point if you don't emphasize it or state it clearly.

To prevent possible misreading on your reader's part and to assess your current draft for what it actually does say (rather than for what you think it says) you need to evaluate your draft. Your goal during this stage will be to find what needs to be changed during revision.

CASE STUDY, PART TWO

When Mary returned to her essay, she read through it once. She was heartened to find that she still liked her use of quotations and that through them she had captured some of her uncle's spirit. Yet she also recognized that some changes would have to be made: even she lost track of her thesis when reading the draft, but she wasn't sure where she went astray or how she could alter her draft to make it clearer. She needed to evaluate her draft thoroughly to decide which paragraphs needed changing and which ones could be kept the same.

Mary decided to write a descriptive outline—a description of each paragraph in terms of (1) what is said in it, and (2) what is accomplished, or done, in it to support her thesis. This exercise enables a writer to see the progression of ideas throughout an essay; it is perfect for discovering a thesis and for determining whether you have deserted it along the way.

Descriptive Outline of "Having Faith"

Para-
graph
#

1. *says:* Blaine is a veteran Marine & believes he has a protector.
   does: Introduces my uncle & the idea of his faith; maybe sounds too spiritual too soon.

2. *says:* Explains when he entered the Marines, how we see him now, and that he takes pride in being a Marine.
   does: Furthers introduction, starts telling story of his life, mentions luck.

3. *says:* Served under Puller, still dedicated to Marines.
   does: Begins to discuss his loyalty to the Marines & his faith in them.

4. *says:* Story of his experience at Guadalcanal, narrow escapes in the face of death.
   does: Detail about experience in the Marines and discussion of how his faith in God helped him through.

5. *says:* Mention of Peleliu, his survival, & his buddies' deaths, mention of undefined "years of hardship."
   does: Shows Blaine as blessed or protected once again at Peleliu.

6. *says:* Horror of Peleliu & his strong memory of it.
   does: Detail of his experiences & how they still affect him.

7. *says:* Brief civilian career and reenlistment in the Marines.
   does: Continues story of his life.

8. *says:* Blaine retires & returns to civilian life.
   does: Continues story; fate of all Marines?

9. *says:* Blaine's memories, loyalty to dead Marines.
   does: Discusses the need for remembering those who died.

10. *says:* Blaine attends reunions, how he and others like him have grown old.
    does: Discusses how Blaine still remains loyal to the Corps.

11. *says:* That the Marines who survive are still proud of their past.
    does: Establishes that they will always be remembered. Heightens the tone and mood of the piece, establishes Blaine's integrity.

Mary learned a lot from writing this outline. It showed her that after paragraph six she did not talk directly about her uncle's faith; in fact, she discovered that her first idea, although still relevant, began to take a backseat to the notion that Blaine's experiences in the marines during World War II had greatly influenced the rest of his life, and that, moreover, they had transformed his life, causing him to become a devoted patriot and Marine Corps loyalist. So Mary realized that she really had two controlling ideas at work; ultimately she would have to choose one and shape the whole essay to support it, leaving out or recasting paragraphs that were not directly relevant.

As her next evaluative technique, she asked a classmate to read her draft and point out places that were unclear. After he finished reading, her classmate Dwayne immediately praised her use of quotations; he thought Blaine's remarks about Peleliu were particularly forceful and memorable. However, at the end of his reading, he could not really tell Mary what he thought her thesis was; he just liked the story of the marine's life and dedication. Dwayne's fuzziness on this point served as a further clue of her need to work on the thesis during revision. Dwayne also liked the title, but wished that at some point Mary would spell out who had faith and what that faith was in. On the local level, Dwayne raised questions about what Blaine looked like, where the battle of Peleliu took place, what its importance was in the war, and why Blaine decided to reenlist in 1950. He also said that he had heard of Guadalcanal, perhaps even seen a movie about it, but that more background information about it would be very helpful.

Mary took notes of all Dwayne's remarks; she wasn't yet sure if she would answer all his questions, but she decided to think about how she could sastisfy his curiosity without confusing herself and her reader more. Mary had not been surprised by what she learned from Dwayne in light of her own evaluation, but his opinions did help to confirm her belief that the most important thing was for her to revise her essay so that it supported one idea clearly and fully.

Next, Mary set out to plan her revision strategy. This strategy is described in the next section of this chapter, following this list of techniques for evaluating a draft.

Options for Evaluating a Draft

1. *Take a break; then read over your draft.* Allow a day or at least a few hours to elapse between drafting and revising sessions. In this way you should become the first reader of your work in progress.

GUIDELINES FOR READING A DRAFT CRITICALLY

Read the draft through. Next number the paragraphs in the margin and review the draft to answer the questions below for the writer. Remember that your job as a reader is to help the writer find weaknesses in the draft. You do not want to be either too nice or too cruel in your critique; be honest and diplomatic. The worst thing to do is to say that a troublesome draft is "okay" or "pretty good." You may want to balance negative and positive remarks, but don't just give your writer a whitewashed, polite comment when you see big trouble.

1. Identify and evaluate the thesis of the draft. Is it stated clearly and specifically? If not, is it clearly implied? Do you sense that the draft says something?
2. Does the thesis appear at a point in the essay that seems natural? Explain how you as a reader respond to the thesis, its placement, and its clarity.
3. Review the draft, paying particular attention to topic sentences. Identify the topic sentence of each paragraph and mark them on the draft. On a separate sheet of paper write the paragraph numbers of the topic sentences that seem directly related to the thesis. Explain how they meet your expectations as a reader and how they further your understanding of the thesis.
4. Write down the paragraph numbers of the topic sentences that do *not* seem to support the thesis. Explain why they seem unrelated.

2. *Make lists of the draft's strengths and weaknesses.* Question yourself specifically about (1) whether or not the draft sticks to its focus or thesis, (2) the interest of your draft to a reader, (3) the clarity of your writing, (4) the amount of support included in your work, and (5) the draft's logical and smooth progression from point to point.

3. *Write a descriptive outline of your draft.* Read through your draft a paragraph at a time. For each paragraph write two sentences. One should summarize what the paragraph says, and the other should explain what the paragraph accomplishes, or rather how it furthers your thesis or supports your opinions. When you complete the descriptive outline, study it to see if what you say helps you accomplish your writing purpose and supports your thesis, and if the paragraphs are ordered logically for a reader to follow the development and growth of your ideas.

4. *Have a friend, classmate, or teacher read your draft.* Interview the reader for his responses to the draft. Ask him what he thinks your purpose is and where he got confused or bored while he read. Listen carefully to his responses and

5. Now concentrate on the support each paragraph provides. Write down the numbers of paragraphs whose support is (1) hard to understand, (2) not introduced properly, (3) not explained thoroughly for a reader, (4) not clearly related to the thesis or topic sentence. Explain the problem in writing.

6. Now evaluate the order of paragraphs and the organization of the essay as a whole. Do any sections or paragraphs seem out of place? How might they be rearranged?

7. Does your writer fail to make any important points? What are they?

8. Are any important points not adequately supported? What are they?

9. Critique the introduction. Is it interesting? Does it clearly set forth the topic of the essay? How might it be improved with anecdotes, examples, explanations, quotations?

10. Does the introduction give you a sense of the direction the essay is to take? Does the thesis appear at a point where you can comprehend it, or is it unceremoniously announced?

11. Next look at the conclusion carefully. Is it satisfying? Does it make the essay seem complete? Does it do more than summarize the essay by giving you a sense of the ultimate significance of the topic of the essay?

12. Suggest some ways to improve the conclusion by adding a memorable final example, anecdote, quotation, or statement.

13. What should the writer focus on first to improve the draft? Make a list of priorities for the writer.

then go through your draft again, marking the places that your reader feels need work.

5. *Read your draft aloud slowly*. Listen to your writing. Do your sentences and ideas seem connected? Can you think of questions a reader might have about your article? Write such comments and questions in the margins of your paper so that you can work on these spots later.

6. *Have a friend or fellow writer critique your draft* by filling out a peer review sheet, a list of specific questions about your draft. An example of a peer review sheet that you might request a reader to complete is given in the box above.

REVISING

The word *revision* is a word that is a combination of two terms: *re* meaning *again* and *vision* meaning *seeing*. Literally, then, revision means "seeing again." When this word is applied to a discussion of the writing process, its meaning is extended to refer to a combination of activities that a writer can perform in order to alter and improve her writing. Revision can prompt a thorough reworking of an existing draft or a total replacement of the earlier draft. It can help the writer find a thesis that is more complex, sophisticated, interesting, or subtle than her original one. The range of revision activities is suggested in the following list:

1. Discovering a new purpose, focus, or thesis for your project.
2. Altering your draft so that it is more accessible to a reader.
3. Reorganizing your draft so that the development is logical and natural.
4. Adding to your draft sentences or sections that will further support or clarify a thesis.
5. Cutting out irrelevant passages or recasting them so that they no longer seem unrelated to your purpose.
6. Refining the paragraphing, organization, sentence structure, diction, and grammar of a draft to put it in final form.

Although writers have much to accomplish during revision, most find revising a draft to be less difficult than creating the first one. In this sense, revision signals a turning point in the writing process. Revision may take you just as long as drafting or even longer, but usually you feel that you're nearing the home stretch in completing a project. No doubt, part of this notion stems from the fact that revision involves your critical and creative abilities in equal parts, whereas drafting is largely creative.

A useful method for revising your writing is to divide the task into two stages. First, during *global revision* make all the decisions and changes that are necessary on a large scale. In brief, your goal during global revision is to get the thrust of your essay right. Make final decisions about your writing purpose, the information that you are going to include, and the order in which you will present it.

After these big decisions are made, revise once again on the paragraph and sentence level. This second stage is called *local revision*, and its purpose is for you to clarify, polish, and refine the smaller elements of your draft. For instance, during local revision you would want to question the organization of individual paragraphs, the phrasing of individual sentences, the sharpness of your descriptions, the accuracy of your word choice, and the correctness of your punctuation and grammar. You focus on the small elements that affect the clarity and smoothness of your writing. It is now worthwhile for you to tinker with syntax, play with connotations of individual words, deliberate over comma placement, and consider the need for extra sensory detail. You can be particular and picky about how you say something since you have already decided what to say.

One final word: even though we have suggested a two-step revision method, you should not feel confined to this approach. You may want and need to revise your writing several times, on one or both levels; again the best rule of thumb is to revise as much as you honestly think is useful. Don't let revision become a never-ending task, but let it help you improve your writing as much as possible. There is no preferred number of versions, drafts, or revisions; *you* must make the decision about how much is enough.

CASE STUDY, PART THREE

Mary revised her essay by using the two-part method of global and local revision suggested by her teacher. Therefore her first task was to decide once and for all about her focus and thesis. Because she liked her title so much and felt that it best represented her uncle's personality, she decided to stick with her idea about how important her uncle's faith in his own abilities, his God, and the Marine Corps had been to him. Also, she thought that in the conclusion she might be able to imply her secondary idea that this faith had deeply affected his whole life. With that settled, she went through her draft and crossed out sections that were unrelated to her thesis. This step was difficult; she didn't like deleting whole paragraphs, but she knew it was essential. Mostly, she marked off paragraphs that discussed Blaine's life outside the marines; those parts did not seem relevant to her purpose.

Next she determined that to answer Dwayne's questions she would have to read about the battles her uncle discussed. She wanted to place them in a historical and geographical perspective. So an afternoon of library research and reading became necessary. She found most of what she needed in an *Encyclopedia Britannica* article on World War II and in a book about the marines' role in the war — Fletcher Pratt's *The Marines' War* (New York: William Sloane Associates, 1948). This reading paid off because it made her recognize the great difference between her general attitude toward war and her uncle's attitude. This notion she planned to include in her introduction, and it underscored why she was so impressed by her uncle's faith in the military; his attitudes were not really tinged with the cynicism and distrust of the post-Vietnam era, as hers were.

Then she drafted a new version of her essay. She began with material that put her uncle's experiences and views into a historical perspective and rewrote the majority of the narrative, adding more facts and details along the way as answers to Dwayne's questions. Also, she included more quotations from her original interview. (She had saved all her notes just in case she found a need for them later.) Drafting this second version took her two sessions, one lasting two hours, and the other taking nearly an hour.

Pleased with her progress, Mary took a day off and returned to her draft when she was fresh and ready for local revision. Now it was time to edit and polish, so she read her draft aloud and marked awkward sentences and words that didn't suit her meaning. She also learned that her conclusion needed more work, but for the moment she focused on the smoothness of the essay's movement and development. She recast sentences and varied her diction by using a dictionary and thesaurus. Then she revised her conclusion, echoing the earlier ideas about differences in perspective. This part took about two hours of concentrated work, but she knew it was important for her to get the connotations of her words and statements right. For example, in the conclusion she had to be careful not to imply that her uncle's attitude was naive or that baby boomers were totally wrongheaded in their views on war and the military. Her goal was to give her reader a sense of the differences in attitudes; she did not want to judge anyone.

After this period of local revision, she worked another thirty minutes on checking spelling, punctuation, and grammar. Mary knew she had a tendency to shift tenses and overlook misspellings, so she double-checked for these errors. Finally, she typed and proofread her final draft. Her completed essay is reprinted below. Once she had completed it, she felt it accurately conveyed her thoughts about her uncle's experiences. She was pleased with her essay's focus on the essence of faith; that was always the notion that had fascinated her.

Having Faith (Final Version)

World War II ended over forty years ago, and for many of us who were born after it, the details, dates, names of heroes and battlefields are just terms vaguely recalled from history textbooks. But for many of our parents and older relatives, the memories are much more vivid and powerful. These memories have shaped their lives and continue to shape their beliefs. World War II is not ancient history for them; it has afforded them faith in the most basic concerns of their lives: their country, their God, and their own abilities.

This is the striking realization that a conversation with a World War II veteran provides. Blaine E. Rhea is such a man. As a World War II veteran with a record of twenty years' service in the Marine Corps, he exemplifies the traditional values that sometimes seem to exist only as part of the legend of American greatness, a legend that reminds post–World War II Americans of the idealistic bravery and patriotism of John Wayne's war movies.

Blaine is not a movie idol though. Now he is a man in his mid sixties with a slight paunch and a friendly face accented by deep green eyes. As the owner of a sheet metal business and an affectionate father of two daughters, it's a little hard to imagine him as a commander engaging in hand-to-hand combat and supervising nearly two hundred soldiers, but his fire and determination are not far below the surface once he starts reminiscing about his days in the Pacific.

Blaine entered the marines when he was seventeen, became a member of the U.S. 1st Marine Division, and fought under L. B. "Chesty" Puller, the Marine Corps' most famous and most decorated general. These details are a source of great pride to Blaine even now, a fact emphasized by the motto "Once a Marine, always a Marine" that he lives by. But beyond this pride in his military service lies a deep faith in and respect for the Marine Corps and for God. He credits both of these with his life, saying that "if it weren't for the leadership and discipline of one and the protection of the other" he would never have survived his many close calls with the enemy, tropical diseases, and shrapnel. This faith is well illustrated by Blaine's account of his experiences at Guadalcanal and Peleliu, the sites of two important and hard-won battles.

On August 7, 1942, the 1st Marine Division landed on Guadalcanal, an island toward the south of the Solomon Islands. Their purpose was to initiate a drive that would secure a clear sea and communications link from Midway Island to Australia. Although the marines were able to occupy the island without large numbers of casualties, most of their supplies were soon destroyed by a Japanese air attack. Blaine narrates these textbook facts calmly, but becomes more emotional when he talks about his personal situation. After the enemy air attack, he had barely enough food to last him three days. Over a period of twenty-three days, Blaine fought under constant artillery fire and lived on a diet of rice and bugs, and he felt lucky to have that.

During the battle of Guadalcanal, Blaine was wounded and received treatment for shrapnel wounds, malaria, and jaundice. While resting in a sick bay tent, live enemy shells landed beside him. Instead of exploding, the shells stuck dormant in the mud. Blaine shook his head as he finished this story and said, "Things like that don't just happen by themselves. You'd better believe that we knew how to pray. If we hadn't, none of us would have survived. Without some help from up there, I'd have been blown to pieces many times."

Another one of Blaine's narrow escapes occurred during the battle of Peleliu, an island located in the Palau group roughly 500 miles east of the Philippines. This battle became part of the Allies' effort to force the Japanese retreat from the Philippines. Blaine's division went ashore on September 15, 1944, and faced an extended period of heavy casualties and fierce fighting. By that time Blaine remained the only member of his old company of 190 men still on foot. The rest were either dead, missing, or permanently disabled. This remarkable fact still moves and startles Blaine; his eyes fill with tears when he remembers wartime buddies, wondering how and why he survived when they didn't. In fact, he quivers when he recalls that it was in the fall, forty-four years ago, that he was buried under the lifeless bodies of his fellow soldiers waiting for help from reinforcements. He says he still has many sleepless fall nights when he remembers the trauma he experienced years ago. The only way that he can reconcile his conflicting feelings of regret for the loss of his friends and wonder at his own survival is to defer to his belief in God and in the discipline and training that the Marine Corps gave him: "I just kept doing my job as best I could. It wasn't easy, and maybe I was just lucky or blessed by a guardian angel or something. Sometimes the way things turn out doesn't make sense; you just got to have faith that everything will be okay."

Blaine's devotion to the marines outlasted the war. After a brief sally into civilian life, on Thanksgiving Day 1950 he reenlisted in the Corps and spent the next sixteen years as a metal worker on fighter aircraft. Even though he had to sign away a permanent disability allocation (compensation for the damage caused by shrapnel injuries and diseases from the old days in the Pacific), Blaine felt that he had made the best decision for himself and his family. By that time he was a dedicated, dyed-in-the-wool marine: "I was used to the disciplined life of the Corps. I liked being a marine, too. Always made me feel that I was serving my country and living up to the best of my abilities. I was too old to fight or be in the infantry, but I could sure be a part of it. It was a choice I have never regretted." Even after his reluctant retirement in 1966, Blaine felt that the best thing an old marine could do, if possible, was to stay in the Corps: "It's a good life, and you don't get tired of it like you do a civilian job. It never loses its meaning, always rewarding, you know."

Since his retirement, Blaine has remained faithful to the beliefs that his marine experiences fostered in him. He firmly believes in God's protection of him and of our country during World War II. He is devoted to the Corps and keeps his love for it alive by attending reunions and celebrations with the other survivors from his old division. At these gatherings, the old soldiers remember their experiences in the Pacific and express their shock at what the years have done to thin their hair and thicken their waistlines. Beyond these light-hearted admissions of the changes brought by time, the larger purpose of these reunions is for Blaine and his brothers-in-arms to keep the faith for the friends they fought with and lost. This keeping of the faith is a part of Blaine's worldview, his sense of patriotism, honor, and devotion to the Corps: "The big battles of the Pacific are over, and I hope they stay over, but all the old marines, the good ones, want the memory of those who didn't come back from the Pacific to remain alive after names like Peleliu have been forgotten. It's best to try to forget some things like the horror and the blood in the sand, but there are those men we'd better never forget."

Perhaps Blaine gives all of us a good reason for learning about how the war affected our elders: it shaped their lives and to a degree it has shaped ours. We have inherited their legacy. We, too, must keep the faith and honor the rightfully proud leathernecks who have done so much for our country. This is certainly a different perspective from our post-Vietnam cynicism and distrust of war and of the integrity of the military, but to some extent we must recognize and appreciate the validity of Blaine's patriotism. Isn't that, after all, part of having faith?

Here are some tips Mary used that will also help you with your revision:

Hints for Global Revision

1. *Think big*. Consider the large, pervasive aspects of your draft and how to improve them. Don't spend time perfecting the phrasing of a minor point or checking the punctuation of your sentences. Work on revising the ideas, order, and support in your essay.

2. *Consider the reader*. What information will he need that you haven't provided? Will he be able to follow your explanations? Will he respond favorably to your writing? You might find it helpful to think in terms of courtesy to your reader. As a writer, assume the role of a willing host; invite your reader into the topic and show him around it in a considerate and intelligible manner. Revise terminology or passages that might confuse your reader.

3. *Rethink your focus and thesis*. Is it clearly stated or clearly implied for a reader? Does it control and pervade the whole piece? Is the controlling idea of interest or importance to your reader, or will he ask "So what?" as he finishes reading? If you discover that you don't have a clear purpose, recast your thesis or reorganize your paragraphs so that they will support your main point.

4. *Don't be dull*. Maintain interest by varying your method of presenting information from your sources; use quotations, paraphrases, descriptions, and definitions. Revise the beginning of your draft so that it is both interesting and clear. Recast the end of your essay so it is memorable and meaningful.

5. *Adapt the tone of your draft to your readers' needs and expectations*. Determine what your choices are for an appropriate tone. Can you be funny, informal, personal? Or does your topic and situation require a serious, formal, or businesslike approach? Try to strike the right tone; you want one that will both satisfy your goals for the piece and that will enable you to reach and appeal to your readers. Be sure to avoid all sexist and racist language and overtones.

6. *Add more support for your ideas*, especially when it's needed for clarity, authority, or richness. Consider whether you could improve your draft's effectiveness by adding one or more of the following:

   quotations, dialogue

   definitions

   facts, statistics

   illustrations, examples, case studies

   descriptions

   explanations, interpretations

   references to your thesis

7. *Trim out dead ends and digressions*. Locate and strike out passages and paragraphs that are not related to your purpose. Remember that you have to have a clear sense of your article's focus to identify extraneous, distracting sentences and passages.

8. *Discover new questions arising from your draft*. As you read and revise your draft,

you may find "holes" in your argument or unanswered questions. You may need to do more research or invention exercises to find answers to these questions.

Guidelines for Local Revision

1. *Think small*. Now it's time to look carefully at the smaller factors affecting the clarity of your draft. Work on revising the phrasing of sentences, word choice, and connections between sentences.

2. *Mark fuzzy spots*. Read through your draft, marking sentences that are hard to follow and comprehend as well as words that don't seem to fit your ideas. Recast these sentences and try to select words that are more appropriate and have the right connotations. You may want to use a thesaurus for help with diction, but resist the temptation to use words that sound good if you don't really understand them. It's a good idea for you to double-check the meanings of words you find in a thesaurus in a dictionary.

3. *Look for clichés and unsupported abstractions*. Often we phrase our ideas in the easiest way possible when we draft; consequently clichés and vague terms, whose meanings are clear to us, can lead a reader astray. Remember that a reader might not understand your use of a cliché or your meaning for a loaded abstraction such as *honor, loyalty*, or *friendship*. You have the choice of either defining your terminology or of substituting words that are not as likely to be misinterpreted.

4. *Make connections between sentences and paragraphs*. Pay special attention to the flow of your sentences, or the way in which one prepares a reader for the next. You may find choppy sentences that need combining, long sentences that need shortening, and neighboring sentences that need to be connected in idea and diction. One corrective device for this last difficulty is to link sentences by the use of repeated key words and their synonyms. Also, you may resort to using transitional phrases such as *for example, in conclusion, despite the fact that, consequently*, and others. Sometimes you may need to add transitional sentences and paragraphs to bridge gaps between ideas.

5. *Check the unity of your draft and select a title that suggests the overall force of the piece*. Remember that a title should accurately summarize the purpose of your writing. Often you will find that your draft is coherent if you can select a title that faithfully implies the focus.

6. *Identify points that need verification and check them*. Attention to accuracy becomes more necessary as a draft becomes more complete and stable. Double-check dates, the spelling of names and places, and the accuracy of titles (of people, events, associations). You may need to make a brief follow-up telephone interview or check facts in a reference book.

7. *Edit and polish your draft*. Once you've worked out the problems in your draft that have to do with purpose, organization, unity, and clarity on both the local and global levels, it's time to work on punctuation, grammar, and spelling mistakes. Try the following techniques:

    ▶ Listen to your writing as you read it aloud to see if you can hear grammar mistakes.

▶ Read your draft backwards, sentence by sentence, and look for errors. This technique interrupts the flow of ideas and allows you to concentrate on the correctness of your writing.

▶ Look for common errors. If you know that you tend to make particular mistakes, proofread your draft several times, each time looking for only one of your typical errors. Focus on verb agreement, tense shifts, or punctuation as you read by checking each sentence.

▶ Check for misspellings. You may want to run a computer spell check on your draft, but if you don't have access to this software, simply look up every questionable word in a dictionary.

8. *Prepare the final copy of your work.* Either recopy, type, or print the final copy of your piece. Make this draft as neat as possible so that your writing is legible and inviting to a reader.

RECOGNIZING YOUR ACHIEVEMENT

What is success? In writing, as in everything else, success may be many things. Perhaps success is simply finishing the project or controlling a long-lived and much hated writing problem such as digressions, confusing sentences, or even comma placement. It may be that success is gaining a reader's interest, laughter, agreement, or favorable assessment. It may be getting a good grade on a writing assignment. Success also may be having your writing published or gaining a wide readership. Success has many levels and flavors. A writer may ultimately strive to experience all of these successes, but the one that is the most important for her development must be her own recognition of the achievement in each writing project.

That achievement could be located in a single moving description, a text without tense shifts, a comfortable writing process, a discovery of a new research or drafting technique. Whatever it is, you should learn to look for it as you complete a project. That one improvement or accomplishment will build your confidence and abilities as a writer. Writing is hard, so when you finish a project look for the successes and congratulate yourself on them. Remember that writing is a hands-on learning experience; it can't be done without thought, effort, and concentration. Consequently, each writing experience will teach you about your own interests, talents, tendencies, and opinions. The finished product serves as physical evidence of your work. In turn you should allow that completed essay to give you something back, and that something should be a sense of what you did well, what was achieved. That lesson will inform all your future writing efforts, eventually helping you grow as a writer and thinker. Consider the writing process to be larger than what happens when you work on one project; it further designates the process that you go through over time to become a competent writer and to keep improving as a writer.

As you complete a project, mull over the following questions as a way to begin thinking about your achievement.

1. What did I learn about myself and my topic while I worked on this project?

2. What was enjoyable about planning, researching, drafting, or revising this piece?

3. What was difficult about working on this project? How well did I manage the difficulties? In my next writing project will I manage them differently or in the same way?

4. What is my favorite part of the finished piece? Why do I like it?

5. What was my writing process for this project? How was it different from what I usually do? Did I use any new techniques?

6. How well did my process work? Did it help me write or did it hinder me?

7. What surprised me about my work on this project?

8. What am I most pleased about now that I have finished this project? What are my successes in this piece?

9. When I begin my next project, how will my experience with this piece affect my approach to the new one?

FOCUS • • • • • • • • • • • • • •
SUGGESTIONS FOR WRITING

1. Consider the percentages of time you spend prewriting, drafting, revising, and editing. Do you think these percentages are right for you, or do you need to spend more time on some stages and less on others? How would shifting these percentages affect the writing that you produce? Draft a proposal for improving your allotment of time.

2. Return to a writing assignment that you have successfully completed. Answer the following questions in a short essay. What made this assignment successful for you? What aspects of it can you repeat in a future assignment? Were there any aspects that seemed to work against the project's success? How might you eliminate these from any future writing assignments?

3. Once you have written a draft of one of these suggestions, swap yours with a classmate. Read and respond to the draft, make recommendations to the writer, and pick up some more anecdotes, ideas, and advice about writing. Consider how your classmate's ideas and experiences are different from yours. Make a list of pointers that you have learned.

4. Frequently, revision is an easier process when it is not our own deathless prose we are changing. As an exercise in revision, exchange drafts with a classmate. Now, revise for submission the essay you have been given. Later, when you have completed your revision of your classmate's paper, exchange the finished product with her again. What changes has she made in your original draft? Are these changes you yourself might have made? Would you have revised as freely as she did?

5. Create a descriptive outline (p. 46) of a recent writing assignment, analyzing what each paragraph in your essay both *says* and *does*. What discrepancies do you find between what you wanted to say, and in fact did say? Revise your draft accordingly.

▼

Crafting Expressive Prose

CONCERNS IN EXPRESSIVE PROSE

Expressive prose is writer-oriented prose. It is not necessarily prose we write only for ourselves and we may not be the sole audience (although that sometimes is the case). Expressive prose is writer-oriented because it primarily seeks to express the writer's feelings, thoughts, and emotions. Unlike persuasive prose, it does not attempt to influence or persuade an audience to think or act differently; unlike informative prose, it does not attempt to focus on a subject and inform a reader. We may use expressive prose as a means of recording our thoughts and feelings, our impressions. Or we may use it as a way of examining our remembrances and reminiscences, a way of exploring our past and coming to understand it better. Expressive prose may be private writing, as in a diary, journal, or lab notes, or it may be writing that we intend for others to read, as in a memoir or autobiographical piece. Expressive prose can be quiet, passive, and reflective, as in a letter describing an idyllic fall afternoon, or assertive and declarative, as in a political manifesto or religious credo. In any case, expressive writing begins with the writer and flows from her thoughts, her reactions, her interactions with others and her world. It creates a reflection of the writer, a reflection others can use to understand her better, a reflection she too can use to understand herself. Here, in general, are the features of expressive prose:

1. Reference to the writer, rather than the reader or objective reality.
2. An emphasis on expressing beliefs or emotions rather than presenting objective information or changing a reader's mind.
3. A style that focuses on the writer's feelings and emphasizes subjective emotions.
4. A degree of probability that depends on the writer's ability to articulate emotions and feelings. The reality presented in expressive prose is not necessarily a false reality, but it may be a personal or private reality.

CHAPTER 5 ► Language and Storytelling

WRITER–BASED PROSE

Because expressive prose tends to be more spontaneous than persuasive and informative writing, it is in some instances less structured and ordered. For many writers, in fact, expressive prose comes more easily than does persuasive or informative prose, generally because it seems more natural to them and therefore flows more smoothly. The natural or unrestrained quality of certain expressive prose is genuine. The writer can write more freely since she knows only she will be asked to make sense out of her writing. Expressive writing meant for the writer alone does not need to be intelligible to anyone else. For example, if you are writing a note to yourself, a reminder that no one but you will ever see, you do not need to write in complete sentences (or in sentences at all). You can use a private code to identify people and places, and you can draw arrows or boxes to indicate relationships you do not want to express in words. If you wish, you can even create a kind of private language that only you will ever understand.

Writing that is not really intended for others to read has been labeled *writer-based prose* (a term we touched on in Chapter 3), but the title also applies to prose that is simply difficult for readers to understand because the text is organized in a way that is more clear to the writer than it is to the reader. *Writer-based prose* is different from *reader-based prose*, which is organized and presented so that a reader can easily comprehend it, and created with the reader's needs consciously in the writer's mind. Reader-based prose is not necessarily structured in the manner that comes naturally to the writer as she sits down and begins to write. The classic example of writer-based prose is the "apartment tour" description, a study that has been frequently replicated. When asked to describe their apartment (or home), writers almost invariably create a "tour" that begins at the front door. They "guide" their readers much the way they might guide guests, taking them through the rooms in sequence just as they would walk through them, "backing" out of bedrooms and bathrooms that are dead ends, and looping back around to "finish" the tour at the entrance or starting place.

When asked to visualize the floor plan of an apartment, or, more difficult yet, sketch the floor plan, readers who take one of these "apartment tours" usually struggle. The viewpoint of the writer as "tour guide" is something like the viewpoint of a camera that comes in the door and moves from room to room. To create a floor plan one needs an overhead view. That perspective, the overhead view or overall plan, is generally neglected by writers; these writers are familiar with their homes, of course, and overlook their readers' ignorance of a general floor plan.

The tour-guide perspective of the apartment description we can call writer-based prose. The overhead-view perspective we can call reader-based prose; that is, it provides a reader with a description of the apartment that is easier for him to visualize, a perspective he can more easily understand than the tour-guide view. On some occasions the tour-guide viewpoint is preferable. This method, a sequential set of instructions, is the one we frequently use when we give people directions: "Go down two blocks; turn right at the first stop sign you come to; it's the third house on the left; you can't miss it." For some simple sets of directions this sequential or linear set of instructions works just fine. If the directions are more complicated, however, we usually resort to drawing a map. Maps, of course, provide an overview, an overhead perspective, and in most instances provide us with clear guidance. Of course we cannot "speak" a map; we have to draw it. Maps represent nonverbal communication; they provide a kind of picture of the terrain, not a verbal statement. To understand the differences between maps and sets of instructions, between nonverbal and verbal communication, we need to examine language, thought, and the relationship between the two.

LANGUAGE AND LINEAR THINKING

Language is linear. When language is written down and printed as it is on this page, one letter follows the next on the page in an orderly row; each word follows the one before it; and the sentences arrange themselves from top to bottom on the page in rows of military precision. When we read written language our eyes scan the page, reading each word in sequence, finishing each sentence before we move on to the next. When we look at a picture (or a map), we do not have to begin in the upper left-hand corner and move our eyes across it. We can look at the whole picture, or study a detail in any portion of it. When we read we may be able to *see* the whole page at one time, or cast our eyes at the bottom of the page and then gradually move our gaze to the top but we cannot *read* the page this way. In order to read we are required to respond in a linear fashion. Spoken language has a linear nature too. We cannot say several words at once, for example. We must speak one word at a time if we are to be understood, and our language is arranged in thin air much as it is on the page: each word follows the word that preceded it; sentences line up one after the other.

It has been suggested that our thinking in Western culture has been affected by the linear nature of our language. The philosopher Bertrand Russell, in fact, has gone as far as stating that "almost all thinking that purports to be philosophical or logical consists in attributing to the world the properties of language." Since the invention of the printing press and the resulting popularity of books and other printed matter, the reasoning goes, we have been trained by our language to arrange our thoughts in a linear fashion. A book, after all, is just one long line of printed words that has been arranged, for convenience, into lines of print that snake back and forth across pages. We could, if we did not wish to bend and fold our lines of words, simply publish them in one long narrow string of print several thousand feet long. Then we could stretch this line of print down a fence, perhaps, and stroll along the fence reading our "book." Slow readers might possibly need extra clothes or a picnic lunch on their hike through a long novel; fast readers would get plenty of exercise as they jogged their way through a collection of short stories. Fortunately, books are not published this way. But more to the point, they are conceptualized in a linear sequence, written in a linear sequence, and, in a manner of speaking, published in a (conveniently folded) linear sequence. Expressive prose (like all prose) is linear.

This linear influence of print and language shapes our attempts to present information. We give directions or describe an apartment in a sequence, because that comes easiest; our language suggests this idea and influences us to express ourselves sequentially. The language does not suggest a global overview, so the overview does not seem as natural to us. What seems natural here is somewhat misleading, because nature, that is, the world, is not linear. We simply force it into linear patterns. We create a concept of time, for example, and then arrange it into a linear pattern of days, weeks, years — the past, present, and future. We look "back" into this past, or "ahead" into the future, as though history were a kind of road or line we were moving along. When we do think in nonlinear ways it is difficult to articulate our thoughts, because in order to communicate them we must first translate them into linear language.

Imagine, for example, that you are walking down the street on a sunny May morning. Out of the corner of your eye you notice a red car passing through a nearby intersection. You once had a car the same color — not the same make, but the same color. You recall buying the car, and a friend who went with you to pick it out. You recall that this friend, whom you have not seen for years, is now living in northern Nevada, a place you have never been. You do, however, remember visiting Hoover Dam, which is in southern Nevada, on the Nevada-Arizona border; you went there once with your uncle, who is now dead. You begin to remember other times you spent with this uncle, Christmases when he visited you, summers when you visited him. Stop. If this were a freewriting exercise you would have filled several pages by now. Through this cluster of associations you have moved from a red car to a summer you spent visiting your uncle in California. Thoughts and memories have tumbled into your head, to be replaced by other thoughts and memories, associations that are sometimes clear and sharp, other times vague and hazy. Is there a linear pattern here? You have to examine your own thought processes, but most thinkers say No, there is not a linear pattern to these associative "thought clusters."

STORYTELLING—SHAPING IMPRESSIONS ... **63**

Of course, describing these patterns as we have, in linear language, allows us to trace a linear movement. The language itself — "you have *moved from* a red car *to* . . ." — nearly forces us to see linear thought. *From* and *to* clearly imply direction; *movement* suggests linearity, because objects move in specific directions. In this case it would seem we are virtually forced, as Russell says, to "attribute to the world the powers of language." Clearly the world as we experience it differs from the world as we describe it in language. Our goal, in writing expressive prose, is to make these two worlds — the world we live in and the world we write about — coincide as closely as possible.

STORYTELLING—SHAPING IMPRESSIONS

Ralph Waldo Emerson once wrote, "if only a man knew how to choose among what he calls his experiences that which is really his experience, and how to record truth fully." Recounting our experiences, to ourselves or to others, is an activity that occupies much of our time. We call our friends to tell them what happened when we went shopping yesterday, to report on what took place in class, to relate how we are feeling, what we think, how we are coping with life. At the center of these conversations are stories, stories about what took place, what we were told, how we reacted, what we expect will happen next. We are all storytellers, continually telling each other the stories that make up our lives, the stories that are our lives.

We all follow certain rules for storytelling, rules that we do not violate. "But," you may say, "I am not a storyteller following rules; I am simply explaining to my friend what happened to me on my shopping trip to the mall yesterday. I am simply relating life." But life, as we have seen, is different from language, and stories are created from language. To understand this point let us look at a very short story:

> Once upon a time there was a little boy named George. One day George got up very early. He quietly brushed his teeth and dressed. Then he went downstairs.
> THE END

What if your friend had telephoned you early this morning, awakened you out of sound sleep, told you that you just had to hear what had happened to a friend of his, then told you a story similar to this one? What would your reaction be? Anger? Disappointment? Bewilderment? Why? What are the problems with this story? Although the story begins in a fashion that appears normal enough, it ends too quickly; it does not seem to have a real conclusion. Also, and this is particularly disconcerting if we have been awakened to hear this tale, the story does not seem to have a point; it just ends. Our reaction is to ask what comes next, or simply say "So what?"

This short (and not very good) story violates at least two rules of storytelling: it does not have a proper ending, and it does not seem to make any point or have any apparent reason for being told. Stories are not life, they are only pieces of life, segments that we believe have significance and meaning.

When we tell a story we must first of all determine that we have had an "experience"; that is, we must ascertain that "something" has taken place. Of course, "things" are taking place around us all the time; the world is filled with activity. But we do not always see that activity as significant, as constituting meaningful "events." You may, for example, sit in the library and read quietly for an hour. If a friend wanders by and chats with you, you may see that conversation as an event. If the fire alarm suddenly goes off, or if you drift off to sleep, you may see those happenings as "events." But the rest of the hour you spend reading, if nothing noteworthy "happens," is literally *uneventful*. That is a time, you might conclude, when "nothing happened." But of course many things happened. You turned pages, and (perhaps) learned something. Your heart kept beating; your breathing continued (if these body functions had stopped, an "event" would surely have happened). You yawned, scratched your ear when it began to itch, and paused to wonder whether you should go eat when you finished. But these are not activities that you would want to tell your friends about; these are not the material for stories, unless you want to tell stories like the story about George.

To be good storytellers, we need to understand the fluid nature of our experiences. Before we can tell a story, it is imperative that we conceptualize the existence of an event — an incident, a happening — so that we understand there was a "something" that actually "took place." When we do this we are generally inferring that we have seen a meaning or relevance in the afternoon's activities, that we have a point to make, a conclusion we wish to draw about what took place. Once we have concluded that we have had an experience we wish to recount, that is, as Emerson says, decided what our experience *is*, we must shape this experience into a story.

Stories have definite beginnings and endings, so we must begin our story in an appropriate place. If you are relating how you dozed off in the library and were then startled into consciousness by the fire alarm, you must decide where the appropriate point for beginning your story is. You probably do not want to begin with breakfast that morning and tell your listener everything that happened to you for the six-hour period between breakfast and the alarm jarring you awake. Your listener may herself fall asleep at such a string of irrelevant details, or simply urge you to "get to the point." You must also decide where your experience ended, and thereby give your story an appropriate ending (that is one place the story of George leaves us unsatisfied). Does the story end when the alarm went off, or does it include an account of what you witnessed then — people leaving the building or fire engines arriving?

Where our stories end usually depends on the point we are trying to make with them. That is, we have come to learn that stories, unlike life, have a definite shape. Stories look like this:

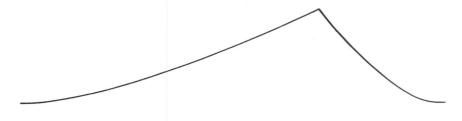

They have a beginning, and some complications which create a rising action; they then generally build toward a climax of some type, and finish with an appropriate conclusion. Now this shape has no doubt been sketched for you before in some literature class, where it was presented as a basic plot outline for a short story, play, or novel. But this shape also reflects the form our own stories take. If we are any good as storytellers our stories will begin at the right point, move to a climax, and round off with an appropriate conclusion. Sometimes we even add a moral or message for our listeners in the event they might misunderstand our point. Life, of course, does not come to us in this neat shape, and it certainly does not come with built in messages or lessons. Life does not have a shape at all. It consists of a nebulous continuum of experience, and it is up to us to transform this continuum into packets of meaning we label events or experiences. Notice, for example, how Gloria Steinem, in "Ruth's Song (Because She Could Not Sing It)," records a number of moments or events that stand out in her memory. These packets of experience are not Steinem's only memories of her mother, but the ones she lists seem to be especially significant and the basis for many of her final judgments; the message or conclusion she draws flows from them. Like Steinem, we must sort through our experiences, determine which of these events are major and which are minor, decide what are climaxes and anticlimaxes, and resolve what should be dismissed and relegated to the category of irrelevant details. Then we must use these judgments to create a meaningful set of stories, the stories that we weave into the larger story of our lives. If we do this well, if we know, as Emerson says, how to choose among our experiences that which *really is* our experience, and then come to express that experience accurately and truthfully, we will come to understand our lives more fully. Allowing us to arrive at such understanding is among the most significant functions — and rewards — of expressive prose.

6 ▶ Options for Expressive Prose

FREE ASSOCIATION—LISTING, CLUSTERING, MAPPING

Because our experience comes to us in a nonlinear form, one technique that is particularly helpful in recording our impressions is free association, a technique psychologists sometimes use to understand intricate psychological relationships. When we use free association to assist us in expressive writing, however, we do not use it as an analytical technique; instead we attempt to focus on a subject and then record as fully as we can the cluster of impressions we associate with that person, place, or event. We might begin a simple reminiscence by thinking about elementary school, for example, and then jotting down the thoughts and impressions that immediately come to mind. Although we may begin this free association or brainstorming by simply making a list of our impressions (see Listing and Grouping, Chapter 2), we usually soon find that a list is in itself too much of a linear arrangement, that we need to connect ideas and impressions with lines, arrows, brackets, and circles. These steps are quite similar to the branching exercise to develop a topic discussed earlier. The finished product, the "picture" of our impressions may cover a page or more; although it may start out looking something like a list or an outline, it generally finishes as a tangled snarl of lines, a web of relationships like the illustration on page 21. And that is normal.

TRANSFORMING TECHNIQUES

Translating this web of relationships into expressive prose is our next task. The problem of transforming experience into prose involves, like all problem-solving situations, certain thought processes that may be intuitive, unconscious, or even inexpressible. They can, however, be generally described. Usually we begin with a sense of incongruence; we are aware of a sticking point, a difficulty, an interference, a clash between what we want and what we have. In simplest terms, this incongruence might be translated into the realization that our web of associations cannot be easily communicated to another person. After we have sensed that there is a difficulty, the second stage in the process consists of defining the problem. In the illustration on page 21 that means ascertaining the specific aspects of the "cluster map" that make it difficult to communicate this experience.

Then comes the most difficult and at times the murkiest part of the procedure, the incubation stage, the point at which we wrestle with the problem we have defined, striving to solve it. We consume gallons of coffee or diet soda, sharpen our pencils endlessly (or even more pointlessly time-consuming, look up esoteric formatting commands in our word-processing manuals), and figuratively, if not literally, beat our heads against the wall in the attempt. But if we work at it hard and long enough, we will usually arrive at a resolution, a path that takes us from our web of experience, that tangle of yet to be fully articulated sensings, gropings, and half-formed thoughts, and delivers us to our destination, a finished piece of articulate, expressive prose.

We may adopt several strategies to guide us through the most treacherous part of this journey, the incubation stage, but because our experiences vary greatly it is difficult to generalize about which strategy works best as a transforming technique. One successful strategy may need to be discarded on another occasion and replaced with a different paradigm. Think of these strategies as being like lenses we can use to view the cluster of free associations and sort them out into expressible patterns. In one situation one lens may allow us to see more clearly; in another situation another lens may give us the needed insight.

Stream of Consciousness

One way to transform the web of association to prose is to attempt to replicate the interior monologue, the stream of impressions that produced this web. The word *stream* of course suggests a linear movement, a linear progression that may not precisely reflect the thought processes we went through in our free association. But we can attempt to reproduce this stream of conscious thought, this stream of consciousness, by recording all the twists and turns of our thinking process, all the apparent digressions as they occurred. Compelling fiction is sometimes created in this manner; for example, large portions of James Joyce's novel *Ulysses* and William Faulkner's novel *The Sound and the Fury* are written in just this way. If you have read either of these books you know that a stream-of-consciousness narrative can at first be confusing, even, at times, seem bewildering or unintelligible. But after spending a few minutes exploring the pasts of these characters whose minds you are invited into, you can come to follow the twists and turns of their psyches — even the simple world of Faulkner's retarded Benjy, or the insanely twisted world of Benjy's brother Quentin.

A stream-of-consciousness narrative, however, does present obstacles to a reader, who may not have the time or inclination to trace out all the relationships it contains. A true interior monologue is frequently recursive and even repetitive, or it can loop off into tangents that may require several additional pages of explanation. For these reasons a stream-of-consciousness narrative should usually be seen as an intermediate draft, writer-based prose that falls somewhere between free association and true reader-based prose. Other methods of translating these freely associated clusters of experiences into prose may be used in addition to, or in place of, a stream-of-consciousness interior monologue.

The Reporter's Questions

To shape an interior monologue further, one may want to ask the familiar reporter's questions (*who, what, where, when, how,* and *why*), presented in Chapter 2, and then extract from the monologue the appropriate answers. The answers to these questions will suggest which parts of your experience, which parts of your monologue, are central to the experience. Pairing the questions as suggested in Chapter 2 will shed further insight on the nature of your experience. The answers to the reporter's questions do provide a list of primary features you may want your finished document to contain. Once you have decided on the primary features, you can sort through your remaining material to see which parts affect or influence the primary features of your monologue, and then determine which aspects merit inclusion. Identifying your primary features does not mean that all other details are irrelevant; to the contrary, it is from just these details that the meaning of an experience frequently flows.

Identity — Particle, Wave, Field

Seeing something as having a discrete identity, that is, seeing something as a "thing" and correspondingly naming it, translates that object from the hazy realm of boundless experience into the sharp and more precisely circumscribed world of language, a world where words sharply and artificially delineate the boundaries between objects. As we have seen, establishing that an event has taken place requires that you create certain beginnings and endings, that you remove this situation from the web of experience.

Three language theorists, Richard Young, Alton Becker, and Kenneth Pike, have proposed that any topic can be viewed from three perspectives and seen as a *particle*, a *wave*, or a *field*. To understand these concepts, you need to ask yourself questions about this event, this circumstance you have partly created, and view it from the perspective Young, Becker, and Pike suggest. Viewing it as a particle, for instance, simply means you see your event as a complete unit, separate and distinct from other units of experience that might be roughly similar in their nature. When you view your experience as a particle, you should ask yourself these questions:

1. How is this experience like other experiences you have had? How is it different from them?
2. Are there any elements this experience shares with other experiences you have had? What are these shared elements?

3. Are there reasons that these experiences have these elements in common? What are these reasons?

Viewing an event as a wave, rather than as a particle, simply involves viewing it as a dynamic, rather than as a static, entity. Waves crashing on a shore are changing, fluid, and dynamic; it is difficult to see where one wave begins and another ends, for the waves blur into each other. Particles, on the other hand, are like rocks or pebbles lying on the beach. They are distinct, separate, static, and unchanging. To see your event as a wave you should ask yourself these questions:

1. What are the limits of the experience? Are these limits clearly defined or are they shifting?
2. Does the event change? Has it changed? What causes it to change? Time? Circumstances? Other experiences? Your attitude about it?
3. How much can the experience change and still remain the same? If it changes into something else, what changes? Does anything remain the same? If so, what?
4. How do these changes take place?

Seeing an experience as a field necessitates that we look at it two ways. First we should see it as something composed of smaller parts, as a network of smaller components; it is a system created from a relationship of lesser subsystems. Second, viewing a topic as a field also involves looking at it from the other end of the microscope, as it were, and seeing the event as itself a component in a still larger network of experience. To examine your experience from the field perspective, you should ask yourself these questions:

1. What components comprise this experience?
2. Can these components themselves be broken down into even smaller subsystems? How are these parts, these subsystems, related to each other? How are they related to the event as a whole?
3. What larger system of relationships does this event fit into? What are some of the other components within this larger overall system? What is the relationship of this event to these other components?

To illustrate how the particle-wave-field approach works, let us examine a hypothetical situation. If you have ever visited France in July, you know the entire country essentially stops for the running of the Tour de France, the longest and most prestigious bicycle race in the world. Unless you are actually a participant in the race (and even then your viewpoint would be limited) it is nearly impossible to "see" even one full day's ride in this event that stretches over three weeks and approximately 2,300 miles. In order to watch the race, most observers simply select what they believe is a good vantage point, then stand or sit by the road, frequently with a picnic lunch and several bottles of wine, and await the whir of riders. When the riders get close they are first preceded by a caravan of promotional vehicles advertising various commercial products; a great deal of commotion and hoopla ensues as samples of sponsors' products are thrown into the crowd. This caravan tends to run some distance ahead of the actual racers, so hours can pass before the race officials' motorcycles actually appear in the distance, accompanied by cars and trucks filled with newspaper and television camera crews, and even several press helicopters.

At this point chaos really begins to break loose. The first riders appear, then the pack, or peloton, rides into view, and finally, after some time, the race stragglers come limping along. Interspersed between the riders are more press crews and team vehicles passing out drinks and food to the weary cyclists. The crowd cheers on its favorites and even gives a tired rider a push when necessary. Because each day's stage is very long, frequently over a hundred miles, it can easily take over an hour for the several hundred riders to pass any given point on the race course. After all the riders come even more support vehicles and commercial vans. When the last "sag wagon" finally appears the race is "over" at any specific vantage point. Of course, many miles down the road some race fans are at their favorite viewing spots, just watching the first riders pull into sight. Twenty million people watch the Tour de France just this way each year, lining the French roadsides and waiting for a glimpse of the Tour as it races by.

To see a day at the Tour de France as a *particle*, you would want to view it as a sporting event and compare it with other single sporting events you have witnessed, basketball or football games perhaps, or even automobile races. These events also have contestants and teams, and the competition is roughly similar to the Tour. The Tour is a big national event, something like our own Super Bowl, and the winner receives as much attention and acclaim as the star players in one of those games. These are obvious similarities and the differences are obvious also. The Tour de France is different from most sporting events we are familiar with in that it occurs over a number of days, of course, instead of a single afternoon, and there is no formal procedure — such as buying tickets — necessary for viewing it. The crowd's common practice of pushing exhausted riders is also somewhat unusual to us, and clearly different from our customary notions of athletic events, where the athletes must perform entirely on their own, without the benefit of any crowd participation.

To see a day at the Tour de France as a *wave* involves contemplating the nature of the experience itself. No one at any observation point could argue she really "saw" the Tour, because the race ebbs and flows over the course of a day, and ebbs and flows even more over the course of the three weeks necessary to complete it. Even a single day's experience is quite fluid, consisting of number of emotional crescendos as various parts of the Tour pass by. The leading cyclists are not "the Tour," nor is the pack "the Tour." One could even argue that the cyclists as a whole are not "the Tour," because the commercial and journalistic extravaganza sur-rounding the race is an integral part also. The Tour itself changes over the years as the course is modified; these course changes in turn affect the chances of individual racers and teams from year to year, for those who are best in the mountains are not always the fastest in the flat sprints and time trials. Because the course always changes, and because there are so many unplanned variables — rain or cold weather — it is very difficult for a single rider or team to repeat as champion. The fact that the Tour de France is always changing, that it is not just a static race, not just a single sporting event or particle, is part of what creates its appeal to the millions who eagerly await it each year.

To see a day at the Tour de France as *field*, we can first break it down into subsystems: the commercial aspects and the sponsors; the riders and their bicycles; the support crews, mechanics, trainers, race officials; the hundreds of journalists who cover the race; and the millions of fans who stand, watch, and cheer. Within the teams are individuals of course, who are competing both for their teams and for their own personal glory. All of these components comprise the race. But we can also see the race as part of a larger field. A day's competition is only part of the overall race. The Tour itself is only part of a professional cycling season; winning the Tour once, or several times, constitutes only part of a professional cyclist's career. The Tour de France is a very complicated field indeed.

FOCUS . . . .
SUGGESTIONS FOR WRITING

1. Review your journal for ideas you can return to. Are there emotions or ideas contained in it that suggest they might be described further? Do you have several entries describing the same experience or event? What is there about this event that caused you to return to it in your journal more than once? Can you express your feelings about this event to others?

2. Reflect on the last year of your life. If you were to make a list of the most significant things that happened to you in the last year, what items would you include on this list? Has the passing of time altered your perspective any on what might be described as a significant event? That is, is there anything you have decided not to include on this list that six months ago you might have included? Why?

3. Expand the list of significant events to include the most significant events of the last five years, or of your entire life. Which events seem to have shaped you the most? Which of these significant events has shaped you the least? Why?

4. Write an essay on an extreme condition you once experienced, for example, "The Coldest I Have Ever Been," "The Hottest I Have Ever Been," "The Wettest . . . ," "The Most Isolated . . . ." In this essay try to convey to your reader the intensity of your experience so that he can experience it also.

5. Use the particle-wave-field method to analyze the experience you described in the exercise above. How does your view of the experience alter as you view it from each of these perspectives? Rewrite your essay, using the new perspective you find most accurately describes your experience as you remember it.

6. Attempt to write a stream-of-consciousness narrative describing an apparently simple recent event — walking to class, eating breakfast, reading a newspaper.

What difficulties do you encounter in writing this narrative? What difficulties might a reader encounter? What changes might you make to clarify your narrative for a reader?

7. Using the branching technique, create a "map" of your impressions on one of these topics: classical music, Fourth of July, exercise, cafeteria lunches. Explain your cluster map to a classmate. All of these topics are fairly broad and could not be covered adequately in a short piece of writing. Select one aspect of your cluster map and write a short essay focusing on these impressions. Let your classmates read your essay and reexamine your map. What changes should you make for your classmate to clarify your impression?

CHAPTER 7 ▸ Structures for Expressive Writing

REFLEXIVE PROSE, NARRATIVE PROSE, DESCRIPTIVE PROSE

Reflexive Prose

Reflexive prose conveys our emotions, what we feel. We find reflexive prose in diaries, and personal letters, as well as in some more official expressions of our beliefs, such as religious and political documents. We should tentatively distinguish between our *emotions*, what we feel or believe, and our *opinions*, those conclusions we arrive at after careful thought and study. Our emotional judgments are not necessarily different from our logical conclusions, but many times they are. We do not fall in love, for example, on the basis of logic and reason; we cannot add up a rational or logical scorecard to make a decision about our emotional state if we suspect we are bordering on this condition. Or, to cite another example, we do not necessarily dislike our enemies for logical reasons. Behavior we blithely ignore in our friends, we can find intolerable in people we have already made emotional judgments against. We do not necessarily have logical or rational grounds for our feelings about our country, our loyalties to a school, city, state, or region, or the intense feelings we may have about nature, religion, or certain political and ideological principles. It is not always our heads that guide us in such situations; sometimes it is our hearts that have taken control.

Yelena Bonner, for example, the wife of the late Soviet dissident Andrei Sakharov, writes wistfully in "A Farewell to America" about the simple wants and desires she feels as she prepares to leave New York and return to the Soviet Union. She wants a house of her own; she wants to be able to telephone her children frequently; she wants her husband and her mother to be near her. With no real rational evidence beyond her own intuition, Yelena Bonner asserts that all the citizens of the United States, from the President on down, share her desires — "I maintain that Americans do not want war. What Americans want is a house." Yelena Bonner's longing for fairly simple symbols of peace and security are somewhat surprising, when we consider the international political roles she and her husband have played. A person who might be expected to make a strong political statement at the point of her departure instead turns her attention to new shoots of grass and the coming of spring. Clearly she is speaking from the heart here, and most of us have found ourselves in similar circumstances. We certainly have all known occasions when our logic told us to act or speak a certain way, yet our emotions would not let us do so. Sometimes speaking our heart was the right thing to do in these situations; sometimes it was not. But if our feelings are not always rational, we should not automatically assume they are always irrational either. Our emotions can be shaped by what we read, what we have studied, what we have had presented to us in rational discourse. The whole premise of a liberal arts education, in fact, is that one's judgments and attitudes can be shaped, presumably for the better, by exposure to a broad variety of doctrines and ideas. So when F. Scott Fitzgerald writes his daughter (in "Letters to Frances Scott Fitzgerald") about "duty" and "happiness" and "misery," his judgments are both the result of his own experiences and the many books he frequently suggests that his daughter should read. The immediacy and spontaneity of his letters suggest their emotional, rather than their purely logical, origins. Reflexive writing captures our emotional states rather than our rational arguments; it presents our moods, our attitudes, our aspirations and desires. It focuses on these inner truths rather than external realities, and gives us a chance to speak what is in our hearts.

At its most fundamental and common level, reflexive prose is simply the expletive you utter when you accidentally bang your shin on an open drawer. You are speaking to no one in particular, even though a deity or deities may be addressed directly or indirectly. The point of your profanity is simply the release of your feelings, an verbal effusion that reflects your own anger, pain, and frustration. Reflexive prose is usually much more than a simple emotional outburst, but this example suggests the extremely close connections between such prose and our inner sensations. Language, to be sure, can at times have a kind of therapeutic function for us. The link between what we feel and the immediate expression of our feelings can shape our understanding of those emotions. We are not trying to "understand" our feelings when we shout after banging our shin, but saying something can, and usually does, make us feel better about our mistake.

Our more complicated feelings and emotions are also affected by our verbalizations of them. For example, we have all known the relief it sometimes brings when we talk over our problems with someone else. Sometimes our discussions help us solve our problems, and sometimes they do not. But even when we are unable to solve our problems by discussing them, we usually feel better simply because we have talked about them. Frequently, talking about situations allows us to come to understand our problems better, for by verbalizing them we are able to give them shape and structure. We often know what we wish to say before we say it, but many times we do not know what we believe until we try to give that belief form in language. Reflexive prose can provide us with an inner window that allows us to grasp the form of our private beliefs, a means of understanding our feelings and articulating them so that others too can come to understand how we feel.

A common way of producing reflexive prose is the practice of freewriting described in Chapter 2. In freewriting you simply pick up your pencil or pen and begin writing, without stopping, without pausing to worry over spelling or punctuation, without letting yourself hesitate over the direction your prose will take. Some writers advocate that you never even lift your pen from the page, because even such tiny pauses may diminish the flow of language you are attempting to encourage. The principle behind freewriting is a simple one. Presumably, your thoughts have a natural direction and coherence, and it is this natural coherence you are striving to generate. Ideally, you are hoping to create a direct channel between your emotions and the tip of your pen on the page, a kind of "automatic writing." For some people, of course, a typewriter or a word processor provides a smoother channel for these thoughts than a pen or pencil and if this is true of you also you should practice your freewriting at a keyboard. The important thing is that you learn how to transfer your thoughts into written language in the manner that is most efficient for you. The precise mechanics of the process are not as important as the results the medium you choose produces.

Freewriting might be either focused or unfocused; that is, you might begin your freewriting with a general topic in mind, or you might start freewriting with no specific direction whatsoever (see Focused and Unfocused Freewriting in Chapter 2). Naturally, in either case, the prose your freewriting produces is almost pure writer-based prose. Because you have written without stopping to reflect or correct, it may not be written in complete sentences; it may not even be written in sentences at all in places, but simply presents the thought clusters or stream of consciousness discussed in Chapter 6. Moving from this writer-based reflexive prose to reader-based prose will require that you find the center or focus of your freewriting exercise. You begin your search for the center by looking for key words, or ideas that are repeated or touched on frequently. Do these repetitions or key words suggest a relationship among your ideas? If your freewriting has been a purely unfocused exercise, you are looking for a topic that has drawn your interest. If you have been focusing on a single topic or subject, you are looking for a particular position or opinion you are expressing on this subject. Once you have identified a belief or opinion, you should ask yourself the following questions:

1. What am I trying to say here? Am I expressing a belief, articulating a perspective, or simply evoking a mood?

2. Are my views here consistent with each other? Are they consistent with opinions I have previously expressed on similar topics? How might they differ? Why do they differ?

3. What experiences have I had that may have shaped these beliefs? Have I had other experiences that also might be relevant to these beliefs? What are they? Why are they relevant? Would a branching exercise or a cluster map be helpful at this point?

4. Finally, what do these beliefs lead to, if anything? What do they suggest about me and my interaction with the world? What am I trying to say, if anything, about that world?

Narrative Prose

Narration is probably the most common form of expressive writing we encounter. Narration tells a story; it relates a series of incidents; it explains what happened. We find it most frequently in autobiographies, journals, diaries, and even lab reports. It attempts to portray a sequence of events as it happens, to record the flow of life through time.

Narratives are fundamentally linear, taking us from point A to point B to point C. The story we told of George follows this form, establishing a beginning — "Once upon a time" — and then follows a traditional narrative sequence: first this happened, then this happened, then this happened. Michael Arlen's "Thirty Seconds," a record of how an AT&T television commercial was conceived, filmed, and broadcast, follows this fairly simple framework also. Such narratives are generally easy to construct because they simply reflect the natural progression of events; we record the sequence of circumstances as it transpired, and there is our narrative, in just the right order. Arlen's narrative, for example, moves along smoothly with the flow of a calendar, providing readers with exact dates and occasionally the precise time of day — "At 11:48:00 . . . At 11:48:30 . . . At 11:49:00" — and this chronological flow becomes the dominant structure of his book; within this larger chronological structure he frequently reports the conversation as it occurs — "Tanner says . . . Carson says . . . Tanner says . . ." — as though he were a court reporter providing a transcript or a sportscaster giving a blow-by-blow account. By carefully presenting these events in the precise sequence in which they occur, Arlen is able to emphasize exactly what he wants to emphasize, the elaborate preparations that underlie what seems to be a simple thirty-second television commercial.

The story about George also presents events in the sequence in which they occur, but it ends too quickly, of course, and thus reflects one of the ways we can construct a faulty narrative. As we have already noted, we must know where to begin a story, and we also must know where it should end. In Arlen's case ending the narrative would appear to be fairly simple, because this story ends with the first broadcast of the AT&T commercial. Even so, he adds a "Coda" (a musical term identifying a passage that marks the formal close of a composition) to his essay in which he gives a final reaction to the broadcast. Simply closing with a traditional signal — "The End" — is not always satisfactory; in the case of the story of George, for example, it is very unsettling, because we perceive that this signal contradicts the sense of the narrative.

Not every narrative needs to begin with "once upon a time," or even begin precisely at the beginning. We have all read books or seen movies that begin somewhere in the middle of a narrative, sometimes at the very climax of a story. Then, through flashbacks, these narratives return to the real beginning and relate the events that lead up to the point where they seemed to begin. This movement, which begins with point B, and then returns to point A before coming back to points B and C is at times even more effective than the traditional A, B, C pattern, because it allows us to grasp our reader's interest immediately with an anecdote or incident we know will make an instant impression.

Endings and beginnings are not the only places you need to be sensitive to when you are creating narratives. We have all heard and read stories that jumped ahead too quickly, that omitted necessary details, or became sidetracked with needless digressions. Very often even what we might call "simple" narratives involve the weaving together of two or more separate sets of circumstances, the confluence of several chains of apparently unrelated incidents. Your reaction to a remark a friend made today is influenced by other situations from the past. Explaining your reaction, then, sometimes involves the reconstruction of several separate stories. These chains of circumstances must be intertwined in the proper sequence in order for readers and listeners to follow the narrative successfully.

When creating a narrative, then, there are several questions to keep in mind:

1. Does each incident you include significantly contribute to the overall sequence of events you are recording? Is each incident essential to your overall narrative?
2. Have you overlooked any important incidents or not explained them fully? Are you presenting your events in the proper sequence? Would they be more clear if they were reordered?
3. Do any supporting details appear in an order that might prove confusing to your reader? How might they be rearranged to be more effective?
4. If your narrative involves the intertwining of separate sets of incidents (as does the Gloria Steinem essay "Ruth's Song," for example), are the relationships between these subnarratives clear?
5. Do any of these subnarratives digress substantially from the central story you are trying to tell? How might they be revised?
6. If you employ flashbacks (or flash forwards), is their relationship to the overall narrative clear?
7. Finally, remember the story about George. Does your narrative have a point to make? Is that point made clear by your presentation?

Descriptive Prose

Description is the third form of expressive writing we most frequently encounter. Descriptive writing falls into two categories: that which is scientifically or realistically descriptive, and that which is figuratively or metaphorically descriptive. Realistic description attempts to depict a person or object as fully and accurately as possible; it is the kind of description we might find in an encyclopedia entry, a description that captures a scientific or literal reality. Realistic description commonly employs a spatial ordering. That is, when we describe a person's appearance, we might start at his head and work down to his shoes. Or we might describe a room by starting with one wall and then moving around it, much as we might pan a camera. Spatial ordering is very similar to the sequential ordering we use in narratives; it represents the somewhat natural movement of our eyes as we sweep our gaze over an object.

But just as we have options for the order of narratives, we may choose to vary our descriptions. Sometimes our gaze moves slowly across a scene, but often it does not. Frequently our eyes move to a single arresting detail first, and it is only later that we become aware of other features. If we walk into a room that is dominated by a grand piano, then the piano would probably also become the focal point of our observation and of any description we might create. It would be possible to begin our description of the room with the carpet, or the first piece of furniture on our right, but this would also be somewhat misleading, and perhaps would create a description that was not as effective as it might be. In this situation we might wish to begin with the central feature of the room — a single dominant impression — and then fill in details around this.

Description, of course, does not need to be limited to visual information; our sense of touch, taste, scent, and hearing also contribute to our experiences, and we sometimes need to include these sensations in our descriptive prose, particularly when these perceptions overpower the visual impressions and create a dominant impression. For example, the single strongest impression you receive when entering an old house might be the odor of musty books, the smell of old furniture, the scent of fresh flowers on the mantle, the ticking of an antique clock, or the creaks and squeaks of the floor. Almost every building has distinct aromas and sounds like these that contribute to its atmosphere. Filling in details around one of these dominant impressions would present a faithful reflection of the realistic appearance of the room, as well as provide an accurate psychological record of the impression the room made.

In the excerpt from Eudora Welty's autobiography, *One Writer's Beginnings*, she uses this technique of seizing on a dominant sensation repeatedly. She begins an overall description of her youth with a single dominant impression — a striking clock. When she begins her description of her father, she does not commence with his physical appearance, but begins by describing his library table and the contents of one of its drawers. Her description of her living room, or "library," begins with the central feature — the bookcase — and then moves to the details of what the bookcase contains. Welty, who of course is a consummate fiction writer also, is well aware of how to achieve an accurate psychological impression with a minimum of prose.

A psychological impression is also what we are attempting to record when we use a figurative or metaphorical description. If we look up the word "skylark," in Merriam Webster's *Third International Dictionary*, for example, we find the following: "a common Old World lark (*Alauda arvensis*) with dark brown upper parts, a buff throat and breast streaked with brown, and creamy white abdomen that inhabits chiefly open country and is noted for its song esp. as uttered in vertical flight." Although it might not be possible to sketch the bird on the basis of this very brief notation, we possibly could use this description to pick a skylark out of a group of birds. The English poet Shelley wrote a poem entitled "To a Skylark," in which he also describes the bird. But Shelley does not use any of the language we find in the Webster's definition. Instead he likens the bird to, among other things, a "cloud of fire," a "star of Heaven," a "rose," a "glow-worm golden," and a "high-born maiden." Shelley's descriptions are clearly not to be taken literally. They do not represent a scientific description, but instead provide us with a series of metaphorical descriptions. "What thou art we know not," says Shelley, so he asks "What is most like thee?"

The many comparisons he draws in his poem reflect his attempt to describe the bird's essence (not simply its physical appearance), and to define what is "most like" it. The dictionary definition, on the other hand, does not devote any space to the "essence" of the skylark or how it might affect us emotionally; it restricts itself to the literal appearance of the bird — what it is, as opposed to what it is like. When we create metaphorical descriptions we try to draw comparisons between two different objects, emphasizing the similarities we find. Sometimes, like Shelley, we are making a comparison between what we *see* (or taste, smell, or hear) and what we *feel*. When we do this we are reaching for a psychological or emotional truth, a description of an inner reality rather than an external reality.

When you are creating a realistic description, you should ask yourself the following questions:

1. Is the scene, person, or object I am describing something that lends itself to a spatial ordering, a viewpoint that moves across it from side to side or up and down? If so, have I chosen the most effective spatial ordering?

2. If a spatially ordered description resembles the view of a camera panning across a scene, have I "placed my camera" in the best possible position? Would another position produce a more accurate, or more interesting, perspective?

3. Is my spatial ordering consistent? Have I skipped over details or placed them out of their proper sequence? Are there good reasons for these variations or omissions?

4. If I have chosen to begin with a central feature, a dominant impression, rather than employ spatial ordering, what are my reasons? Have I chosen the proper feature — or features — to build my description around?

5. Is it clear why I am choosing to emphasize this central feature or aspect, and, correspondingly, de-emphasize other aspects? Would my description be more effective if I began with another feature as my central focus?

6. Is a visual description effective in this situation? Would it be better to emphasize taste, touch, scent, or sound? What is the dominant impression here?

7. Can I use analogy to draw a comparison between my subject and something else that may be familiar to my audience?

If you are creating a figurative description, you may want to begin by asking yourself these questions:

1. What impressions are generated by the subject?

2. What is your subject's most distinctive feature? What does this feature resemble? One can create a metaphorical comparison, as Shelley does, by attempting to define the "essence" of an object. Such connections are probably arrived at intuitively rather than analytically, but you can still ask yourself, as Shelley does, what similarities might exist, what is "most like" this thing?

3. If your subject is an abstract concept, what might it look like if it could take on a shape? What might it feel like if it could be touched? What might it taste like? Smell like? Sound like?

4. If your subject were another object entirely, what would it be? If it were living, or (vice-versa) if it were inanimate, what would it be?

5. Finally, apply the particle-wave-field heuristic to your subject and ask yourself what it might resemble if it could be seen as a particle, or a process, or a network of relationships. What is the essence of this subject's identity?

6. How much would it have to change before it lost that identity and became something else? How much can it change and still remain the same?

FOCUS . . . .
SUGGESTIONS FOR WRITING

1. Reflect on your happiest occasions. What tends to make you happy? Is there any discernible pattern to your happiness? What is that pattern and why do you think it exists? Use the questions above to create a figurative description of your happiness.

2. Reflect on the occasions in your life in which you have been the most angry or upset. Is there any discernible pattern you can find running throughout these moments of distress? What is that pattern and why do you think it exists? Attempt to differentiate between stages or levels of anger. How does your extreme anger differ from your anger in less serious situations?

3. What are your most firmly held beliefs? If you were asked to risk your life for a cause, a principle, or a person, would you do so? What cause or causes might you be willing to take such a risk for? Are there any causes or principles that others might be willing to risk their lives for that you would reject outright? What are these causes or principles? Why would you differ from others on these issues?

4. Think of a time when you felt special, completely different from other people around you. Write a letter to your best friend in which you describe this special time and explain as best you can why you felt different. Was there a reason for this feeling that you can put your finger on?

5. We have all been frightened at times. Think of the time when you were the most frightened. What was threatening you? Have there been other times when you were nearly as frightened? Are there any similarities these experiences have in common? What are they? Is there any common pattern you can find running through the situations in which you have been frightened? What is it? Is there a reason for this you can identify? How do these experiences differ? What is the difference in terms of your sensations between being really frightened (as you might be in a life-threatening situation) and just a little bit frightened (as you might be at a horror movie)?

READINGS

• • • • • • • • • • •

EXPRESSIVE PROSE

Expressive prose emphasizes the writer and his emotions. It focuses on presenting beliefs or emotions rather than objective information. Expressive prose is most frequently found in journals, diaries, letters, declarations of independence, manifestos, utopia plans, contracts, constitutions, myths, and religious credos. The following readings represent various forms of expressive prose.

LETTERS TO FRANCES SCOTT FITZGERALD

F. Scott Fitzgerald

Scott Fitzgerald, the author of The Great Gatsby *and* Tender Is the Night, *was one of the premier novelists of the 1920s. After Fitzgerald's flamboyant wife, Zelda, became hospitalized with mental problems, the rearing of their only child became his sole responsibility. These are only a small sample of the many letters Fitzgerald wrote to his daughter Frances (nicknamed Scottie) while she was away at school.*

August 8, 1933
La Paix, Rodgers' Forge,
Towson, Maryland

Dear Pie:

I feel very strongly about you doing duty. Would you give me a little more documentation about your reading in French? I am glad you are happy — but I never believe much in happiness. I never believe in misery either. Those are things you see on the stage or the screen or the printed page, they never really happen to you in life.

All I believe in in life is the rewards for virtue (according to your talents) and the *punishment* for not fulfilling your duties, which are doubly costly. If there is such a volume in the camp library, will you ask Mrs. Tyson to let you look up a sonnet of Shakespeare's in which the line occurs *Lilies that fester smell far worse than weeds.*

Have had no thoughts today, life seems composed of getting up a *Saturday Evening Post* story. I think of you, and always pleasantly; but if you call me "Pappy" again I am going to take the White Cat out and beat his bottom *hard, six times for every time you are impertinent*. Do you react to that?

I will arrange the camp bill.

Half-wit, I will conclude. Things to worry about:

    Worry about courage
    Worry about cleanliness
    Worry about efficiency
    Worry about horsemanship . . .

Things not to worry about:

    Don't worry about popular opinion
    Don't worry about dolls
    Don't worry about the past
    Don't worry about the future
    Don't worry about growing up
    Don't worry about anybody getting ahead of you
    Don't worry about triumph

Don't worry about failure unless it comes through your own fault

    Don't worry about mosquitoes
    Don't worry about flies
    Don't worry about insects in general
    Don't worry about parents
    Don't worry about boys
    Don't worry about disappointments
    Don't worry about pleasures
    Don't worry about satisfactions

Things to think about:

    What am I really aiming at?
    How good am I really in comparison to my contemporaries in regard to:
      (a) Scholarship
      (b) Do I really understand about people and am I able to get along with them?
      (c) Am I trying to make my body a useful instrument or am I neglecting it?
              With dearest love,

Spring, 1940

Spring was always an awful time for me about work. I always felt that in the long boredom of winter there was nothing else to do but study. But I lost the feeling in the long, dreamy spring days and managed to be in scholastic hot water by June. I can't tell you what to do about it — all my suggestions seem to be very remote and academic. But if I were with you and we could talk again like we used to, I might lift you out of your trouble about concentration. It really isn't so hard, even with dreamy people like you and me — it's just that we feel so damned secure at times as long as there's enough in the bank to buy the next meal, and enough moral stuff in reserve to take us through the next ordeal. Our danger is imagining we have resources — material and moral —

which we haven't got. One of the reasons I find myself so consistently in valleys of depression is that every few years I seem to be climbing uphill to recover from some bankruptcy. Do you know what bankruptcy exactly means? It means drawing on resources which one does not possess. I thought I was so strong that I never would be ill and suddenly I was ill for three years, and faced with a long, slow uphill climb. Wiser people seem to manage to pile up a reserve — so that if on a night you had set aside to study for a philosophy test, you learned that your best friend was in trouble and needed your help, you could skip that night and find you had a reserve of one or two days preparation to draw on. But I think that, like me, you will be something of a fool in that regard all your life, so I am wasting my words.

April 27, 1940

Musical comedy is fun — I suppose more "fun" than anything else a literary person can put their talents to and it always has an air of glamour around it. . . .

I was particularly interested in your line about "feeling that you had lost your favorite child." God, haven't I felt that so many times. Often I think writing is a sheer paring away of oneself, leaving always something thinner, barer, more meagre. However, that's not anything to worry about in your case for another twenty years. I am glad you are going to Princeton with whom you are going. I feel you have now somehow jumped a class. Boys like **** and **** are on a guess more "full of direction" than most of the happy-go-luckies in Cap and Gown. I don't mean more ambition, which is a sort of general attribute at youth and is five parts hope to five parts good will, but I mean some calculated path, stemming from a talent or money or a careful directive or all of these things, to find your way through the bourgeois maze — if you feel it is worth finding. Remember this, though, among those on both sides of the fence there are a lot of slow developers, people of quality and distinction whom you should not overlook.

You are always welcome in California, though. We are even opening our arms to Chamberlain in case the British oust him. We need him for Governor, because we are afraid the Asiatics are going to land from Chinese parasols. Never mind — Santa Barbara will be our Narvik and we'll defend it to our last producer. And remember, even England still has Noel Coward.

I actually have a formulating plan for part of your summer — if it pleases you — and I think I'll have the money to make it good. I'm working hard, guiding by the fever which now hovers quietly around the 99.2 level, which is fairly harmless. Tell Frances Kilpatrick that, though I never met her father, he is still one of my heroes, in spite of the fact that he robbed Princeton of a football championship singlehanded — he was probably the greatest end who ever played football. In the future please send me clippings even though you do crack at me in the course of your interviews. I'd rather get them than have you send me accounts of what literary sourbellies write about me in their books. I've been criticized by experts including myself.

I think I've about finished a swell flicker piece. Did you read me in the current *Esquire* about Orson Welles? Is it funny? Tell me. You haven't answered a question for six letters. Better do so or I'll dock five dollars next week to show you I'm the same old meany.

June 20, 1940

I wish I were with you this afternoon. At the moment I am sitting rather dismally contemplating the loss of a three year old Ford and a thirty-three year old tooth. The Ford (heavily mortgaged) I shall probably get back, according to the police, because it is just a childish prank of the California boys to steal them and then abandon them. But the tooth I had grown to love. . . .

In recompense I found in *Collier's* a story by myself. I started it just before I broke my shoulder in 1936 and wrote it in intervals over the next couple of years. It seemed terrible to me. That I will ever be able to recover the art of the popular short story is doubtful. At present I'm doing a masterpiece for *Esquire* and waiting to see if my producer can sell the *Babylon Revisited* screen play to Shirley Temple. If this happens, everything will look very much brighter. . . .

The police have just called up telling me they've recovered my car. The thief ran out of gas and abandoned it in the middle of Hollywood Boulevard. The poor lad was evidently afraid to call anybody to help him push it to the curb. I hope next time he gets a nice big producer's car with plenty of gas in it and a loaded revolver in each side pocket and he can embark on a career of crime in earnest. I don't like to see any education left hanging in the air.

July 12, 1940

Haven't you got a carbon of the *New Yorker* article? I've heard that John Mason Brown is a great favorite as a lecturer and I think it's very modern to be taking dramatic criticism, though it reminds me vaguely of the school for Roxy Ushers. It seems a trifle detached from drama itself. I suppose the thing's to get *really* removed from the subject, and the final removal would be a school for teaching critics of teachers of dramatic criticism. . . .

Isn't the world a lousy place — I've just finished a copy of *Life* and I'm dashing around to a Boris Karloff movie to cheer up. It is an inspirational thing called "The Corpse in the Breakfast Food." . . .

Once I thought that Lake Forest was the most glamorous place in the world. Maybe it was.

QUESTIONS

1. Fitzgerald's daughter was only eleven when he wrote the August 8, 1933, letter. What elements of this letter suggest that he is writing to a child? What image of himself does he project in this letter? Why do you think he presents himself this way?

2. How do Fitzgerald's letters change when he writes in 1940? What suggests that he is now writing a young woman rather than a child?

3. As time passed Fitzgerald's own life became bleaker. His work progressed unsuccessfully, and the cost of his wife's continued hospitalization, along with his own failing health, sapped his resources considerably. What elements of this personal tragedy do you find in these letters? What evidence do you find that these letters were written for Fitzgerald himself, rather than for his daughter?

A FAREWELL TO AMERICA

Yelena Bonner

Yelena Bonner is an author and the widow of the late Soviet physicist Andrei Sakharov, a well-known dissident and activist for peace. Bonner came to the United States in late 1985 for medical treatments, leaving her husband behind her in Moscow. In June of 1986, her surgery and recuperation complete, Bonner returned to the Soviet Union to rejoin her husband. Before she left New York, however, she left this essay that was published in Newsweek, *and reprinted later in her book* Alone Together *(1986).*

I AM convinced that Americans want peace. I don't know about America — I'm not a specialist, like the schoolchildren who travel around the world on peace missions and can explain everything about rockets and so on. But while I am not as competent to judge, I maintain that Americans do not want war. What Americans want is a house.

This desire expresses a national trait, the desire for privacy. The house is a symbol of independence, spiritual and physical. The First Lady says that when the president retires, they will sell the house in which they lived before the presidency. The children are grown and the place is too big for them, so they will buy a smaller house. A wonderful plan! And it's wonderful that the whole country knows it. The president doesn't want war, he wants a new house.

I also want a house in addition to my usual wants that everyone be together and healthy and that there be no war. With enough land around it, and no more, for me to plant flowers. For the sake of nostalgia I could grow an ordinary Russian daisy and a single birch tree. I don't need a lot of bedrooms, just one for us and one for Mother, a guest room and one more so that I'm always ready for our grandchildren. And I'd like a room where I could at last spread out my books and where Andrei could make a mess. What nonsense I'm writing! I want a house! This is me, who should be counting the days, no, the hours of my freedom to do what I want, ever to type this freely, to type all my unattainable nonsense, such as "I want a house."

But you know, I'm 63, and I've never had a house; not only that, I've never had a corner I could call my own. I started out like everyone else: a normal childhood, but then came a strange orphanhood — father and mother were arrested and no one knowing whether they were alive or not. Later, after the war, we had a room in a communal apartment — there were 48 people in one apartment and one toilet. I think the first time I was mistress of my own place was — it's hard to believe — in Gorky, in exile.

I do not want that. I want a house. My dream, my own house, is unattainable for my husband and myself, as unattainable as heaven on earth. But I want a house. If not for me, then for my son and his family in America. My son and I plan to buy one. And I am learning many new things. The house should be near good schools; my granddaughter is three and schooling is not far off in the future. It should be in the suburbs — vacations are short and a child should not have to grow up in a polluted city. It should be close to their work — both parents have jobs and there is only one car. It should have a full foundation and basement (I had never known such considerations to exist). It should have three bedrooms so that my mother can be with them, or at least visit. It should have a studio—my son Alyosha needs a work room for his mathematics. But the cost is . . . oh! I want, I want, I want. More than the children, I want. But it's time for me to pack my bags. The children live here, I live over there.

I wish Andrei were here. I wish my mother could sit in a rocker in the shade near those sweet, sleep-inducing oleanders I saw when I visited the Virgin Islands, and I wish I could pick up the phone once a week and hear the calm voices of my children. Paradise, it turns out, is so simple and so unattainable.

My husband told me just six months ago (God, I haven't seen him in six months and want to be with him so much!), "The world is further away from war than it has been in a long time." I believe him, and on that score, I live calmly, especially since I have more than enough worries, cares and misfortunes of my own.

What difference does it make if Gorbachev and Reagan meet in June or some other month? What difference does it make which of them is being cranky? First Gorbachev plays hard to get, like a girl invited for a date, pouting, considering: "I don't know, I have to think about it, probably not." Then Reagan sounds like a jealous girl: "It's her or me. Now or never." I must be one of the world's least interested people in the problems that Reagan and Gorbachev are threatening to discuss or not discuss, when and if they meet or don't meet. I want a house. I don't want a war. Americans want a house, too. Americans don't want war.

So now with my surgically repaired organ of feelings and circulation, I am writing in a hotel in New York, which is simultaneously a city and a country and a world. I am on the eighth floor in a corner room. One window opens on 61st Street, the other on Central Park. In two directions, unfolding from an angle, stretches a panorama that needs nothing added to it. Against the blue of the sky are the gray silhouettes of buildings that pierce it (light gray in the sun, darker in shadow), lines, lines, lines. How can anyone say that New York is not beautiful? For me it is the city of cities, ready for the future.

Today I saw something amazing from the windows of this room. I got up early, a bit after 6. The haze of burgeoning buds barely showed over the trees, and the grass had not yet taken on a greenish hue. It was still yellow, the color of grass shoots. And now it's noon, and there is a delicate green smoke over the trees and the grass has turned green, a tender, tender green. So quickly, spring came in six hours. Lord, I want the whole world to feel this good. They say New York is at its best in the springtime. And now I'm going downstairs into the city.

QUESTIONS

1. *Newsweek* labeled Bonner's statement a "quirky" farewell when it was first published. Do you agree? What about it seems quirky to you? What does not seem quirky about Bonner's reflections?

2. Bonner begins her essay with the flat statement that Americans want peace, and then goes on to assert that what Americans really want is "a house." What is Bonner's evidence for these remarks? Has she accurately depicted the wishes of most Americans? Is she justified in making the statements she makes? Why or why not?

3. It has been suggested that American culture has a seductive effect on those from other countries who are exposed to it for the first time. What evidence of that effect do you find in Bonner's reflections? Has she become "Americanized" at all in her six-month visit?

4. Write your own "A Farewell to . . ." essay, inserting your topic. You might say farewell to an apartment, a friend, a car, or an old pair of shoes.

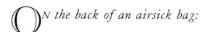

JAPANESE CRASH VICTIMS: GOOD–BYE LETTERS

Japanese Crash Victims

When a Japanese airliner crashed into a mountain and burned on August 13, 1985, only four of the 524 passengers on board survived. Because the passengers knew their plane was in trouble before the crash, some of them took a few minutes to write hurried notes to loved ones, notes that were later found in the wreckage. The Associated Press reprinted several of these tragic letters that literally present some of the passengers' final thoughts.

O*N the back of an airsick bag:*

Osaka
Mino

Machiko, please take care of my children.

Masakazu Taniguchi
6:30

On the back of an architectural firm document:

I want you to be strong.

Kazuo Yoshimura

On the pages of an appointment calendar:

Be good to each other and work hard.
Help your mother.
I'm very sad, but I'm sure I won't make it.
I don't know the reason.
I don't want to take any more planes.
Please, Lord, help me.
To think that our dinner last night was the last time.

There was smoke that seemed to come
from an explosion in the cabin,
and we began making a descent.
What will happen from here?

Tsuyoshi, I'm counting on you.

Mother, to think something like this would happen.
It's too bad. Good-bye.
Please take care of the children.

It's 6:30 now.
The plane is rolling and descending rapidly.

I am grateful for the truly happy life I have enjoyed until now.

Hirotsugu Kawaguchi

QUESTIONS

1. The three letters reproduced here do not seem to be the hasty remarks of panic-stricken victims. What accounts for this? What might we expect these letters to say?

2. What similarities do you see in these messages? What do these similarities tell you about the reactions of people who are facing a crisis?

3. The Japanese names do not indicate to most of us the sex of the passengers who wrote these letters. What are your speculations about the sex, age, or profession of these letter writers?

RESPONSE TO OLIVER NORTH

George J. Mitchell

In the summer of 1987, Congress began open hearings into what had become known as the "Iran-Contra affair." During an embargo on arms shipments to Iran, members of the Reagan administration were accused of secretly attempting to sell weapons and weapons parts to the Iranians in exchange for the release of U.S. citizens held in Libya. An added twist to this already complex deal was the divergence of funds received from these arm sales to the antigovernment (contra) forces in Nicaragua. At the public hearings many government officials testified on their roles in this convoluted scheme, but none caught the public's imagination as much as Lieutenant Colonel Oliver North, a member of the National Security Council staff. North, whom President Reagan called "a national hero," became the darling of some viewers, who saw him as a sterling example of patriotism, and was soundly condemned by others, who saw him as the epitome of power gone wrong. One who was not impressed by North's brand of patriotism was Senator George Mitchell of Maine, a member of the Congressional committee investigating the scandal. Here is the response he made at the hearings to North's impassioned testimony.

B UT I want to—my time is nearly up and I want to make some closing observations because you have, as I indicated, expressed several points of view with respect to which there are other points of view, and I think they ought to be expressed. And I'd like to do that now. You've talked here often and eloquently about the need for a democratic outcome in Nicaragua. There's no disagreement on that. There is disagreement over how best to achieve that objective. Many Americans agreed with the President's policy. Many do not. Many patriotic Americans, strongly anti-Communist, believe there's a better way to contain the Sandinistas, to bring about a democratic outcome in Nicaragua and to bring peace to Central America. And many patriotic Americans are concerned that in the pursuit of democracy abroad we not compromise it in any way here at home. You and others have urged consistency in our policies. You've said repeatedly that if we are not consistent our allies and other nations will question our reliability. That's a real concern. But if it's bad to change policies, it's worse to have two different policies at the same time; one public policy and an opposite policy in private. It's difficult to conceive of a greater inconsistency than that. It's hard to imagine anything that would give our allies more cause to consider us unreliable, than that we say one thing in public and secretly do the opposite. And that's exactly what was done when arms were sold to Iran, and arms were swapped for hostages.

Now, you've talked a lot about patriotism and the love of our country. Most nations derive from a single tribe, a single race. They practice a single religion. Common racial, ethnic, religious heritages are the glue of nationhood for many.

The United States is different. We have all races, all religions. We have a limited common heritage. The glue of nationhood for us is the American ideal of individual liberty and equal justice. The rule of law is critical in our society. It's the great equalizer, because in America everybody is equal before the law.

We must never allow the end to justify the means, where the law is concerned, however important and noble an objective. And surely, democracy abroad is important, and is noble. It cannot be achieved at the expense of the rule of law in our country.

And our diversity is very broad. You talked about your background, and it was really very compelling; and is obviously one of the reasons why the American people are attracted to you. Let me tell you a story from my background.

Before I entered the Senate, I had the great honor of serving as a federal judge. In that position I had great power. The one I most enjoyed exercising was the power to make people American citizens. From time to time I presided at what we call "naturalization" ceremonies. They're citizenship ceremonies.

These are people who came from all over the world, risked their lives, sometimes left their families and their fortunes behind, to come here. They'd gone through the required procedures, and I, in the final act, administered to them the oath of allegiance to the United States, and I made them American citizens. To this moment, to this moment, it was the most exciting thing I've ever done in my life. Ceremonies were always moving for me because my mother was an immigrant, my father, the orphan son of immigrants. Neither of them had any education, and they worked at very menial tasks in our society. But, because of the openness of America, because of "Equal Justice Under Law" in America, I sit here today, a United States Senator. And, after every one of these ceremonies, I made it a point to speak to these new Americans. I asked them why they came, how they came, and their stories, each of them, were inspiring.

I think you would be interested and moved by them, given the views you've expressed on this country. And, when I asked them why they came, they said several things, mostly two: The first is, they said, "We came because, here in America, everybody has a chance, opportunity." And, they also said, over and over again, particularly people from totalitarian societies who came here because here in America, you can criticize the government without looking over your shoulder. "Freedom to disagree with the government."

Now, you've addressed several pleas to this Committee, very eloquently, none more eloquent than last Friday, when in response to a question by Representative Cheney, you asked that Congress not cut off aid to the contras "For the love of God and for the love of country." I now address a plea to you. Of all the qualities which the American people find compelling about you, none is more impressing than your obvious deep devotion to this country. Please remember that others share that devotion, and recognize that it is possible for an American to disagree with you on aid to the contras and still love God and still love this country just as much as you do.

Although he's regularly asked to do so, God does not take sides in American politics, and in America disagreement with the policies of the government is not evidence of lack of patriotism. I want to repeat that. IN AMERICA, DISAGREEMENT WITH THE POLICIES OF THE GOVERNMENT IS NOT EVIDENCE OF LACK OF PATRIOTISM. Indeed, it's the very fact that Americans can criticize their government openly and without fear of reprisal that is the essence of our freedom and that will keep us free.

Now, I have one final plea. Debate this issue forcefully and vigorously, as you have and as you surely will, but please do it in a way that respects the patriotism and the motives of those who disagree with you, as you would have them respect yours.

Thank you very much, Colonel. Mr. Chairman, I have no further questions.

QUESTIONS

1. Mitchell's heartfelt remarks were partly generated by the sympathy some of North's comments had received from the public, a sympathy Mitchell obviously felt was misplaced. What stories does he tell, what examples does he cite, that might win some sympathy from the public for his point of view?

2. North's polite and respectful military manner during his questioning was one element of his testimony that won him much support. Mitchell's rebuttal to North could not seem unreasonable or disrespectful then, or he and the committee would appear to be political demagogues grinding away on a patriotic marine who was only following orders. Can you find evidence within the text of his speech that suggests Mitchell is trying to appear to be calm, fair, and reasonable?

3. In his closing Mitchell invokes a kind of political "golden rule" on patriotism and dissent. What effect does he hope this "golden rule" will have?

4. Mitchell's statement is not intended to persuade North as much as it is simply to express an alternative viewpoint. Do you find his remarks convincing or persuasive? Why or why not? Write a brief essay explaining your position.

• • • • •

GOOD MORNING, MERRY SUNSHINE

Bob Greene

Bob Greene is the author of a widely syndicated Chicago Tribune *newspaper column. This piece, "Good Morning, Merry Sunshine," is an excerpt from Greene's book of the same name, a book fully explained by its subtitle:* A Father's Journal of His Child's First Year.

June 11

AMANDA Sue was in trouble. I had yet to meet her; my wife was in her tenth hour of labor, and the fetal monitor attached to her stomach indicated that our baby's heart rate was dipping alarmingly low. We had decided months before that the child would be named Amanda Sue; now, as I stared at the computerized machine that measured the beating of her tiny heart, my insides tightened as I wondered what might happen next, and tried not to think about the possible answers.

There were three doctors and four nurses in the room. We were in the basement of Chicago's Michael Reese Hospital, in Labor Room No. 9. We had left our home at 2:30 a.m.

The cab ride to the hospital was eerie. The city was asleep, and we were almost alone on Lake Shore Drive. We both knew it was unlike any other late-night ride we had ever taken, or would ever take again. The first few hours in the labor room were so easy, they could have been a Lamaze teacher's dream. Every time a contraction would come, Susan would do her breathing, and the pain would pass; it was a breeze. But in the last hours leading up to this moment, the pain had become agonizing. I thought of all the lessons in Lamaze class, from a teacher promising the women that getting through labor would be eminently manageable without drugs; I felt angry, resentful, and helpless as I looked at Susan in the worst pain she had ever experienced. Maybe the breathing exercises were tool enough for some women; but I wished that all of the other expectant mothers in our class could have seen films of something like this, rather than the propaganda of some young mother whizzing her way through labor on a breath and a smile.

An anesthesiologist had given Susan an epidural block with a long needle, after an intravenous injection of Demerol had failed to provide any relief; the insertion of the needle in her back was the only time the doctors had suggested that I leave the room. When I returned she was still crying out; an orangish antiseptic solution dripped down her back, and the table was soaked with blood.

Dr. Allan Charles, Dr. William Alpern, Dr. Martin Motew, and four nurses stood together looking at the printout from the fetal monitor. On the right side of the paper a moving needle charted the intensity of the labor contractions. On the left side another needle recorded the baby's heart. This was accompanied by a steady beeping, keeping time with the heartbeat. I did not have to talk to the doctors to know they were concerned; the very fact that all three of them were huddled here was testimony enough.

Earlier in the day they had joked with me about my nervousness. Every time Dr. Charles would leave the labor room to go into the physicians' lounge, I would follow him in there several minutes later and just sort of hang around. He got the point: I thought he should be in the labor room all the time. "You have to give me a few minutes with my pacifier," he said once, holding up a big cigar. We had laughed. Now that was over.

The doctors conferred quietly. For some reason — they weren't sure why — the baby's heart would beat normally for a few minutes, then slow dramatically. They theorized that something inside Susan was applying pressure on the baby, putting the child in distress and endangering her. They were encouraged that every time this happened, it seemed to correct itself. Still, the graph paper from the monitor was telling a story they really would rather not have been seeing.

And Susan kept crying out. I knew I would rather be here than in the waiting room of my father's generation; the way she kept looking over at me as the pains drove her flat against the table, and as the doctors talked about the baby's heart, I realized that my presence was the only thing keeping her from complete panic. But this wasn't how it was supposed to be. This wasn't some pleasant trip we were taking together; this was trouble of the worst kind, and I could tell that the doctors would have been just as happy without the father in the room.

Just before two-thirty Dr. Charles said he wanted to try to deliver the baby. Outside it was a warm, sunny June afternoon in Chicago; I had not yet seen the day. The doctors, nurses, and I were in scrub suits; now we put on caps and masks, and Susan was wheeled into the delivery room.

I stood at the head of the operating table. The medical personnel surrounded the other sides; Dr. Charles moved swiftly. "You have to help me now," he said to Susan. "You can't tell me how much it hurts. This is it. This is what it's all been about. You have to help get your baby out."

Susan pushed. "That's it," Dr. Charles said. "That's it. Do it again." A nurse took me by the arm and led me to the foot of the table, beside the doctor. "Look at that," she said to me. "Here comes the top of your baby's head."

"Okay, push again," Dr. Charles said. I went back to the other end of the table. I was watching it in a mirror placed behind the doctor.

"It's going to be a tight squeeze," he said. He asked for forceps. They looked like giant, ugly shoehorns. He inserted them and said, "Here comes your baby." In an instant Amanda Sue was there — not crying right away, but waving her arms and legs. She looked fine. A nurse carried her over to a warming table, and a few seconds later she began to cry — and a few seconds after that a pediatrician examined her and said she was in good health. The heartbeat was normal.

The nurse carried her back to Susan and said, "Here's your baby." Susan held Amanda against her chest. Dr. Charles came around and shook my hand. "The problem with the heart came from a low-lying placenta," he said. "It was pressing against the baby, and that's why the heart slowed down. I almost decided to do a caesarean three times. Ten years ago I would have had to, but these new fetal monitors are so sophisticated — the monitor told me that the baby was bouncing back okay every time, so I knew it would be all right to go ahead."

I didn't say anything. I could feel myself shaking.

"You think this was bad," Dr. Charles said. "Wait until she goes on her first date. Now that's bad. My own daughter . . . I tell her to be in at ten o'clock, and she says, 'Dad, what can I do at two in the morning that I couldn't do at ten at night if I wanted to?'"

This was bizarre. We were standing there laughing at the doctor's story, and two feet away Amanda Sue lay moving against my wife's chest. Susan looked up at me and let out a long breath. And then, for the first time, I reached down and touched my daughter.

The nurses let us stay with the baby for fifteen minutes or so before she was taken up to the nursery. Then one of the nurses wheeled Susan into the recovery room, where she would stay for ninety minutes before being taken to her room.

I saw Amanda Sue lying in a heated transport unit in the corridor. Susan must have seen her, too, because in the recovery room she said to me, "I feel funny with her lying there all alone." So I went out and looked at the baby and pretended that I had something to do out there until the nurse came back to take Amanda Sue to the elevator. "That blanket's not going to cut off her breathing, is it?" I said, and the nurse assured me that it would not.

In the recovery room Susan and I sat together behind a curtain. We just kept looking at each other. The moment was full of a new kind of feeling for me — the feeling of family — and then I heard something from the other side of the curtain.

A black woman from Chicago's South Side had given birth perhaps two hours before; she had no husband, and no man had accompanied her to the hospital. She had had her baby alone, and she had lain in the recovery room alone, and now she was leaving alone. I thought of the joy I was seeing on my own wife's face in the moments after the birth of a child, the beginning of a family. And then I looked out to see this other woman being wheeled away, alone.

Her eyes locked with the nurse who sat by the door. The nurse said to her, "You take care of yourself, now." The woman nodded, and then she was gone.

People talk about the emotions that come when a baby is born: exuberance, relief, giddiness, pure ecstasy. The thought that you have seen a miracle in front of your eyes.

I knew I was supposed to be feeling all of those things, and of course I did. But the dominant emotion inside me was a more basic one. I was scared; scared of what I knew was sure to come, and more scared about what I didn't know. I am of a generation that has made self-indulgence a kind of secular religion. I looked down at that baby, and suddenly, I felt that a whole part of my life had just ended, been cut off, and I was beginning something for which I had no preparation.

That's what went through me as I watched my baby enter the world; a sense of fear unlike any I have felt in my life. Fear that sprang from the place where the greatest fears have always lurked: fear of the totally unknown.

June 12

I slept fitfully. Alone in the apartment, I kept waking up with a nagging feeling that there was something I should remember. I was groggy from the long day before; it took me several seconds to recall what it was. Amanda had been born. I lay awake and stared at the ceiling, trying to comprehend it.

I had called my parents and Susan's parents within half an hour of the birth. Now, the morning after, I took time to phone other people I wanted to tell. Most of my friends don't have children; their words of congratulations were mixed with a genuine sense of confusion and wonder. Their questions about what it had been like were elementary, not cosmic; this was virgin territory for them as well as for me, and suddenly they were addressing me as if I were the expert.

It was as if, in the last twenty-four hours, I had become a different person. They were asking me things about being a father that they wouldn't have thought to ask just one day before. I told them that I was too new at it to know anything; for all that had changed overnight, the fact remained that Amanda was still less than one day old.

She had microscopic fingernails and a scrawny, funny ducktail hairdo and tiny replicas of a wizened old man's hands. I stared down at Amanda Sue; she lay in a see-through hospital bassinet in room 808 of Michael Reese.

Susan was in bed next to the bassinet. A document had arrived with Amanda's vital statistics. A piece of paper said that she had weighed six pounds, fifteen ounces at birth, and had been twenty-and-one-half inches long.

"She can't be that long," I said.

"Of course she is," Susan said.

"My column's only sixteen inches long, and she isn't as long as the column," I said.

It was true. I write my newspaper column on a computer-generated video display terminal every day, and there is a measuring function in the upper right-hand corner of the screen that tells me how long the story is. When it reaches sixteen inches, the column is finished.

There was a *Chicago Tribune* lying on a chair in the hospital room. I picked it up and carried it over to Amanda's bassinet. I unfolded the paper and opened it to my column. I reached in and placed it next to Amanda. She was, indeed, a little longer than that day's effort.

"Well, she looks shorter," I said.

Susan held her as if she had been doing it all her life. When she handed Amanda to me, I felt like I was trying to balance twenty crystal goblets on my forearms. Every time the baby moved I thought I was going to drop her. I don't see how anyone ever gets used to this.

Amanda started crying. I leaned over the bassinet and said, "Shhh, Helen." Helen is my cat.

The men and women who work in maternity units behave as if they are specially blessed, and in a way they are. My previous experiences with hospitals, both personal and professional, have been unhappy ones — I suspect most people's are — and until you are in a ward devoted to new life, you neglect the fact that this one part of a hospital complex is devoted to happiness.

You could feel it: the doctors and nurses on the floor were used to dealing with people who were glad to be seeing them. I don't know what makes a nurse decide to specialize in newborns instead of, say, cardiac cases; but the people I kept running into were clearly up about their work. They seemed to relish coming here each day.

It made me wish that Amanda and Susan could stay in the hospital a little longer than the standard three days. I felt comfortable and confident with these people around. Once we got home, I didn't know what I'd do if something started to go wrong with that fragile, tenuous baby. Here all we had to do was push a button and help was seconds away. I imagine that kind of fear will be the hardest to kick.

I went outside for a walk and ran into Dr. Charles. He was in a sport coat and tie, and was getting into his car. Our hours with him had been so awesome to me; for the rest of my life I will see him lifting Amanda into the world for her first breath. I had lost sight of the fact that he does this virtually every day. It must be remarkable — to be that important to so many lives.

We shook hands. I asked him if he had been working all day.

"I just came in for a quickie," he said. Another day, another new life. He got into his car and drove off.

A moment for the memory:

Susan had her own room; there were two beds, but the other one wasn't occupied. Amanda had drifted off to sleep, and Susan, exhausted from the past twenty-four hours, was fading, too.

I took my shoes off and climbed up onto the other bed. And in the middle of the afternoon, for the first time, the three of us fell asleep together.

I imagine I'm going to realize all of this through the little things that happen. Late in the afternoon, after my visiting hours were over, I was back downtown. I was walking up the street, and a woman next to me was pushing a little boy in a stroller.

"How old is that baby?" I said.

"Fifteen months," she said.

I have never asked that question before in my life.

QUESTIONS

1. Greene's fears and nervousness reflect the reactions many new parents experience. What is special about his situation that would make him different from the average parent?
2. Greene's journal, like many journals, consists of both *narration*, the recounting of events, and *reflection*, the analysis of those events. Which parts of the journal do you, as an outsider observer, find to be the most interesting? Why? Which parts do you think Greene, as the one who lived through these events, will find to be most interesting as he looks back over these entries in the years to come? Which parts might his daughter, Amanda Sue, find the most interesting?
3. Greene is a journalist, and he may have had thoughts of publishing his journal while he was writing it. Do you find anything in these excerpts that suggests he always intended — or anything that suggests he did not intend — to publish this journal?
4. Turn to your own personal journal and rewrite for a classmate a series of entries dealing with a single topic.

• • • • •

ONE L

Scott Turow

One L is a book-length journal that records the triumphs and traumas encountered in Scott Turow's first year at Harvard Law School. Although a popular novel, movie, and television series were based on a similar experience — John Jay Osborn's The Paper Chase — *Turow's journal projects a realism and immediacy that the fictionalized dramatization lacked.*

11/17/75

It is Monday morning, and when I walk into the central building I can feel my stomach clench. For the next five days I will assume that I am somewhat less intelligent than anyone around me. At most moments I'll suspect that the privilege I enjoy was conferred as some kind of peculiar hoax. I will be certain that no matter what I do, I will not do it well enough; and when I fail, I know that I will burn with shame. By Friday my nerves will be so brittle from sleeplessness and pressure and intellectual fatigue that I will not be certain I can make it through the day. After years off, I have begun to smoke cigarettes again; lately, I seem to be drinking a little every night. I do not have the time to read a novel or a magazine, and I am so far removed from the news of world events that I often feel as if I've fallen off the dark side of the planet. I am distracted at most times and have difficulty keeping up a conversation, even with my wife. At random instants, I am likely to be stricken with acute feelings of panic, depression, indefinite need, and the pep talks and irony I practice on myself only seem to make it worse.

I am a law student in my first year at the law, and there are many moments when I am simply a mess. . . .

9/25/75 (Saturday)

The student life is still a treadmill, class and books all day, closed up in my study briefing cases every evening. And never enough sleep. The only time I get to see Annette, during the week, is over dinner. On the weekends, thus far, I've managed to take off Friday and Saturday nights for movies, music, restaurants; but even then I'm sure I'm not the best of company. Right now, law's my greatest enthusiasm, yet after losing me to the legal world all week, it's the last thing Annette wants to hear about. Even when she's willing to listen, the strange language and the intricacy of all of it makes it difficult for me to convey just what's so exciting. To A., I'm sure it all seems a jumble and a bore. I continually make resolutions to talk about other subjects, which I somehow never keep.

In those first few weeks, I gradually became aware that second-year and third-year students were moving through a world much different than that of a 1L. Upperclassmen have no required courses and their work load is lighter. Many participate in the numerous law-related extracurricular activities from which 1Ls are usually excluded. Much of the energy of 2Ls and 3Ls does not go into school at all. They are busy looking for work for the forthcoming summer or after graduation, a process with which most 1Ls are not involved.

Yet what made the 2Ls and 3Ls seem most distinct was simply that they had survived their first years. They were initiates, part-way attorneys, people no longer fazed by the things which confused us. All of my classmates seemed to have some second-year or third-year student on whom they relied for advice, and I was no exception.

I often solicited wisdom from Mike Wald. Even more frequently, I would go with questions to our BSA advisor Peter Geocaris. Peter was a generous guide in acquainting me and my cohorts in our Methods group with the customs of the law school. I was intrigued from the start by the earnestness with which Peter regarded HLS's institutions. Other upperclassmen came on jaded about the school and about studying law. But Peter took Harvard Law School quite seriously.

One day in mid-September I was talking to him about the amazing pace at which the first-year students seemed to be driving themselves, the amount of work we were doing, and the relentless stress we all seemed to place on doing that work well.

"That's what I love most about the law school," he told me. "People want to come here because they think it's the best and they demand the best from themselves. There's a real standard of excellence here, a standard of achievement."

The phrase "standard of excellence" reminded me of a Cadillac commercial and I tended at first to dismiss what Peter had said. But thinking it over, I understood. I had already noted in my classmates, and sometimes in myself, a demand for achievement which went beyond a mere orientation toward success or competition. As Peter suggested, there was something about Harvard Law School which inspired people to use their capacities fully, to do things in a way that would make them proud of what they'd done and of themselves. I regarded that as something affirmative, and in time it was Peter himself whom I began to see as the embodiment of all of that. In Methods class he always spoke of law and lawyer's work as something sober and exalted. He regularly talked of "achievement" and "excellence," and when he did, mention of the *Harvard Law Review* was seldom far behind.

To Peter, the Review seemed the symbol of those things around HLS he most admired, and at times he appeared almost fixated with the subject. In his first meeting with the Methods group during registration week, Peter had explained that he was not a member of the Law Review. I had been struck by his tone of apology, and also that that was nearly the first thing he'd told us about himself. Peter's talk about the Review always sounded that way, half awe, half sadness. . . .

10/21/75 (Tuesday)

A difficult day. A disturbing incident at lunch.

For a while, I've felt that there's a cohesion lacking in my studying and it has seemed to me that the study group could help provide some focusing. In talking it over, I found that everyone else felt the same way. It seemed time for a meeting, to see if we could hash over the problems with the study group and consolidate purposes, and so, with the exception of Stephen, who had a date for lunch, we all got together at noon.

The complaints about the group came out at once: too disorganized, too uncommitted, rudderless, overaggressive in discussion (Aubrey's point, aimed at me, I think), and too many people.

The last was Kyle's complaint, and he kept hammering at it.

"We've got too many people. We can't have effective discussions. We can't concentrate on anything. We're going to keep BS'ing." Finally, Kyle said, "We've got to narrow the group to four people, five at the most."

The suggestion pretty plainly was that we throw somebody out, and it offended me. I was telling Kyle exactly that when Sandy Stern, guileless or guilty, suddenly spoke up.

"You're not going to throw me out, are you?" Sandy asked. "Not just because I'm in two groups?"

Two? we all asked. Sandy quickly admitted that he was part of another group which had been busy all term outlining courses and preparing review notes. He had joined our group too, he said, because we seemed more interested in high-minded, speculative talk about the law, which he felt was missing in the other.

"Hey," Terry told him, "we don't wanna do that kind of jiving around anymore. We wanna start putting it all together now."

Sandy refused to take the hint. He sat there pulling at his big scraggly moustache and proposing compromises: One day, with him present, we could speculate. On the second, without him, we could review. As a last hope, he even offered to make copies for us of the outline he was preparing for the other group.

It did no good. Kyle, pointedly, kept repeating, "Somebody's gotta go, someone *has* to."

I told Sandy that it should be his decision. I said that I was against his sudden exclusion and that if he wanted to stay it would be okay with me, but I also told him that I felt it had been deceptive to conceal his membership in the other group, and that so far as I knew everyone always assumed study groups were exclusive.

Sandy debated my points but finally said that he would do whatever we preferred. Aubrey seemed to hold the crucial weight and he shook his head no. He had wanted a smaller group from the start.

With apologies issued all around, Sandy gathered his books and departed. We stayed to plan further activities for the group. But the whole event stayed with me all day. I felt a frustrated pity, angered by Sandy's obtuseness but ashamed that we had been so hard-nosed as to boot him. What difference is it to us really if he thinks he can handle being in two groups? I was disturbed by what had emerged in each of us. Kyle had been ruthless and Aubrey a little matter-of-fact. Terry all along was bothered by Sandy's mincing way and was visibly anxious to have him gone. I had hardly been stalwart in defending Sandy's right to stay.

When I told the story to Stephen tonight on the phone, he was dismayed.

"That goddamn Kyle," he said.

I admitted that none of us had been shown to much advantage this afternoon. I'm beginning to get some idea of what might be involved in meeting my enemy.

QUESTIONS

1. Turow's book begins with the November entry that begins this selection and then drops back to September when school actually began for him. What effect does this reordering have on the narrative? Is it justifiable?

2. Turow's account retains much of the slang terminology he encountered — 2Ls, BS'ing. Does this slang add or detract? Why?

3. Compare the Turow journal to Bob Greene's account in "Good Morning, Merry Sunshine." Which seems more natural and spontaneous? Why? Which can you identify more easily with? Why? Which do you prefer? Why?

4. Do you find any evidence that this journal has been altered or touched up for publication?

INVASIVE PROCEDURES

Mark Kramer

Mark Kramer's book, Invasive Procedures, *is subtitled,* A Year in the World of Two Surgeons. *Before he begins his journalistic exploration into the lives of two different doctors, he begins with a Prologue (from which this excerpt is taken) in which he approaches a medical problem from the viewpoint of the person who is most concerned — the patient.*

WHEN I was twenty-three, a bump crawled onto my hip. One day it wasn't there, I'm sure. The next it was. I looked down and it had come — the surfaced knuckle of some buried fist, mimicking the tip of the pelvic bone an inch away. It signaled corruption, through and through, of the body I'd inhabited without suspicion until the moment before. I went to a doctor just off Fifth Avenue, whose office door opened only after negotiation by intercom.

"Who did you say?"

I shouted my name a second time.

"Delivery or appointment?"

"What?"

The door buzzed. Eventually, the doctor saw me.

He said, "This bump troubles me." I signed into the hospital the next day. It was a Friday. One should begin hospital stays on Monday mornings. I'd been declared officially sick, but for days they didn't do anything to me; things slow up for weekends. I felt as well as I had the week before, except more worried. I had been working as a journalist. I carried on from my cranked-up bed, with a portable typewriter propped on my knees, and it felt a little bit heroic.

You're supposed to eagerly conform to all doctors' orders because you want to do whatever you can to get better and get back to the office. I wanted to deny that I was sick, that I needed the hospital and the doctors. So I bridled at regulations. I wouldn't stay put. Sunday afternoon I wandered off in my bathrobe on an excursion to the farthest wings of the hospital while, it turned out, nurses were hunting for me so they could send me to X-ray. "Where have *you* been?" one said when I finally showed up in my room, where my supper tray was already cooling on the bed table. The nurse said, "We're responsible for you." I'm sure my answer was vague, and I later was to wonder if it had cost me, in slowed postsurgical bedpan service.

All weekend and Monday, too, when normal people were off at work, I took long languid baths, two a day, in milky disinfectant, cleansing myself in preparation for the surgeon. Monday afternoon, an orderly with a green wheelchair strode in and said he was to transport me to X-ray — the trip I'd missed the day before. I got in. Then I stepped back out. I folded my arms across my chest and refused to move. I told the man I'd just been all over on foot, and they hadn't done anything yet to slow me down except feed me hospital food. The man stood behind the green wheelchair and reasoned, with surprising patience and understanding, about insurance, his orders, usual procedure, this had never happened to him before, he only worked here. Then he called the head nurse, and she came and went away and came back again with a handsome doctor, young but white-haired, whose blue eyes read me and transmitted his contempt. He just shook his head, but I felt my cheeks redden. I was awed by his detachment, by his authority as a doctor. Suddenly, I knew how very scared I was of the bump, and I thought he must know it too. I needed him and his colleagues. I buckled. I felt sick. I rode down to X-ray, cowed. Once back in my room, I felt fury — not about hospital routine now, but about being ill. My surgeon visited for a moment that evening. He turned out to be short and swarthy, and he had a little neat pompadour combed into his hair. He'd heard about me and the wheelchair. He had a cheerful manner. He kidded me about the folly of resisting the will of nurses, then left.

That night I experimented with holding the absolute knowledge that I was fatally ill: "Cancer had invaded my bones and life has been short and has served little purpose." Then I'd haul myself out of self-pity and experiment with the absolute knowledge that I was well, that this was a mistake, just me being too worried, or that it wasn't me at all, or that the odds I'd been quoted by the surgeon: "Eighty percent chance it's nothing," were so strong that a little scary experience would do me good, purify the spirit. On the strength of that certainty I'd go back to the typewriter for half an hour and then grow afraid again.

At ten or eleven at night, a nurse's aide, a Haitian with reddened eyes, a loping island accent, and a gleeful laugh, befriended me. My college French was not up to her explanations about her family and children back home. A nurse sent her away and gave me a sleeping pill. I found myself fighting it for hours until it wore off. The Haitian aide came back in the middle of the night, closed the door to my room, and shared vodka and orange juice with me. Home in the midst of despair, I finally slept.

The surgeon stopped by again, shortly after dawn. He was paunchy, jolly in the day as well as the night, and so recently shaved that his chin shone slate-blue. He told me numbers — boring details of incredible interest to me. Two hours or so in surgery. Four hours in the recovery room. Ten more days in the hospital, gathering strength. Verdict as soon as I woke up. By the way, did I play basketball? I remember feeling a moment's love for him then. I was very interested in him. He was about to get to know me intimately.

A few minutes later, an olive-drab anesthesiologist with an Indian accent came by, guessed my weight to within five pounds, and asked about allergies. I slept again, awakened, scared, and was sucking on a Marlboro, my last, desperate, cigarette of a lifetime, when a huge black male nurse, as bald and muscular as Mr. Clean, stuck me with a sedative. I lost what little will I had left.

I recall, I think, lying on the cart, inside what must have been the surgical corridor, surprised that everyone ran around in pastel-blue scrubsuits. I was free of choices, adrift in their hands. In a moment of inane surprise, I noticed another young man parked next to me, staring back, then asleep.

I'm quite sure I remember the coolness of the draping sheets as they hauled me from the cart onto the table. And I awakened, for just one minute, in the recovery room, with the surgeon jiggling a tube that ran into my nose, and shouting, "Not cancer."

Moments or hours before or after that, someone adjusted the tube in the nose again. I can recreate the gritty intracranial tugging. And still later, the surgeon leaned over and quietly said he's taken away a small block of hip, then had flared the edge of the remaining bone, "so your pants will hang on you, and not fall down." A joke. He told me he'd done a beautiful job. I took heart from the evidence that he was thinking of my future. I slept all day and knew even when I slept that I hurt.

The next day, my family, and a few nurses, told me things had gone well. I didn't believe them. The pain was far stronger than any I'd ever experienced. Now I can't remember what it felt like at all, but I have known during my few other moments of pain that nothing compared to the power of the hurting hip the day after surgery.

Under morphine, I dreamed obsessively of a broad living room, where each piece of furniture stood far from each other, and whose cantilevered beams were laminated of cement and pain. Every beam had a name and the names were secret. A girl in Russian peasant clothes, a tiny figure at the far end of the room, danced a kazatsky. She was bald, alabaster-headed; features had been drawn on her face in India ink. It doesn't make sense now, but at the time it was my world — far more reasonable and consuming than the momentary chats with hospital visitors.

On the third evening after surgery, a friend showed up, on his way to work, carrying a banjo case. I paid attention. He made me laugh so much I cried in pain and had to ask him not to say anything. Then we got the agonizing giggles, like schoolboys under discipline. That night, the pain dulled and I came fully to my senses. For the first time I looked around the bland room and took note of gray pebble-grained wallpaper and a nice view of the city. I knew that in my infidel way, I was born again. General anesthesia sends the soul off. It had inserted what I then took to be an experienceless time, a blank space, into my life. It had rendered my being, which had been continuous since childhood, discontinuous — on, then off, then turned back on again, this one time at least.

The Haitian nurse's aide showed up again on the late shift. She sat on my bed, smelling of musky rose, sweeping wax, and alcohol, and beamed at me in the dim night-light. I eased myself up in bed, a few inches. She stroked my cheek.

"Well, *petit monsieur*, you are not feeling all so good tonight?"

"Better than yesterday, thank you."

"And what is the result?"

"They say it was a benign thing — nothing — that grew there and now they've taken it away."

"*Est-ce-que tu peux les croire?*" she asked, smiling still — can you believe them?

"I think I do."

"Surgeons never tell the truth. They tell what makes it easy for themselves." She spoke dramatically, in a breathy whisper.

It took me a day to understand how devastating she'd been, and during that day I homed in on bitter lines from John Donne's "Noctourne upon St. Lucie's Day":

Study me then, you who shall lovers be
At the next world, that is, at the next spring:
    For I am every dead thing . . .
He ruined me, and I am re-begot
Of absence, darkness, death; things which are not.

Bandaged and invaded, robbed of my bone, I felt a kinship with Donne, who had written those lines dressed up in his shroud. I sided with the dead against the living.

We dead are an ignored minority. We have our plight too. It seemed like a reasonable position.

Later, as I recovered strength, I came up with a mundane axiom: The body leads the mind. My trust, my spirit, curiosity, and affection slowly grew as I healed. After I had been home for a few months, I invited one of the nurses out to supper and watched her carefully over the antipasto to see if she acted as if she were visiting with a dead man. I felt reassured.

Still, life had become odd. I went back to work, but I was like a child who, having thought about how he walks, now stumbled at every step. I let things fall apart. After a few more months I was gone from New York, and was writing newspaper columns from a farm in the New England hills. The surgeon who had operated on me was vacationing in the area and he came by to visit. After lunch, I told him how disorienting my hospitalization had been, but he said that what went on in the hospital didn't have much to do with him. I couldn't understand his feelings, so detached from the effects of his work. We changed the subject and talked farming, and some about basketball.

QUESTIONS

1. Most of us have gone to the doctor with a puzzling ailment at one time or another. Which parts of Kramer's speculations seem familiar to you? Why? Which seem unfamiliar? Why?

2. Do any aspects of Kramer's account make him seem to be "a typical patient"? Do any aspects make him seem atypical?

3. A certain mystique surrounds physicians and the world of medicine, and it is partly because of that mystique that Kramer is writing his book. What does he include in this account that might add to or detract from that mystique?

4. Kramer's reaction to his surgery is perhaps unusual. Months after it occurs he goes to dinner with one of his nurses and appraises her reaction to him. Still later he visits with the surgeon and attempts to discuss the hospitalization with him. Kramer shrugs off his fascination in the last sentence of this selection, but still he seems inordinately interested in what was a routine procedure for the hospital staff. What evidence do you find in the excerpt that Kramer might be making too much out of his experience? What is the nature of his reaction? What reaction would you expect?

5. Write your own record of a recent trip to a doctor or dentist.

ONE WRITER'S BEGINNINGS

Eudora Welty

Mississippi novelist Eudora Welty is acknowledged to be one of the finest American fiction writers of the twentieth century. Her short stories "The Petrified Man," "Why I Live at the P. O.," and "A Worn Path" are familiar to many college students. This selection is taken from her autobiography, One Writer's Beginnings.

IN our house on North Congress Street in Jackson, Mississippi, where I was born, the oldest of three children, in 1909, we grew up to the striking of clocks. There was a mission-style oak grandfather clock standing in the hall, which sent its gong-like strokes through the livingroom, diningroom, kitchen, and pantry, and up the sounding board of the stairwell. Through the night, it could find its way into our ears; sometimes, even on the sleeping porch, midnight could wake us up. My parents' bedroom had a smaller striking clock that answered it. Though the kitchen clock did nothing but show the time, the diningroom clock was a cuckoo clock with weights on long chains, on one of which my baby brother, after climbing on a chair to the top of the china closet, once succeeded in suspending the cat for a moment. I don't know whether or not my father's Ohio family, in having been Swiss back in the 1700s before the first three Welty brothers came to America, had anything to do with this; but we all of us have been time-minded all our lives. This was good at least for a future fiction writer, being able to learn so penetratingly, and almost first of all, about chronology. It was one of a good many things I learned almost without knowing it; it would be there when I needed it.

My father loved all instruments that would instruct and fascinate. His place to keep things was the drawer in the "library table" where lying on top of his folded maps was a telescope with brass extensions, to find the moon and the Big Dipper after supper in our front yard, and to keep appointments with eclipses. There was a folding Kodak that was brought out for Christmas, birthdays, and trips. In the back of the drawer you could find a magnifying glass, a kaleidoscope, and a gyroscope kept in a black buckram box, which he would set dancing for us on a string pulled tight. He had also supplied himself with an assortment of puzzles composed of metal rings and intersecting links and keys chained together, impossible for the rest of us, however patiently shown, to take apart; he had an almost childlike love of the ingenious.

In time, a barometer was added to our diningroom wall; but we didn't really need it. My father had the country boy's accurate knowledge of the weather and its skies. He went out and stood on our front steps first thing in the morning and took a look at it and a sniff. He was a pretty good weather prophet.

"Well, I'm *not*," my mother would say with enormous self-satisfaction.

He told us children what to do if we were lost in a strange country. "Look for where the sky is brightest along the horizon," he said. "That reflects the nearest river. Strike out for a river and you will find habitation." Eventualities were much on his mind. In his care for us children he cautioned us to take measures against such things as being struck by lightning. He drew us all away from the windows during the severe electrical storms that are common where we live. My mother stood apart, scoffing at caution as a character failing. "Why, I always loved a storm! High winds never bothered me in West Virginia! Just listen at that! I wasn't a bit afraid of a little lightning and thunder! I'd go out on the mountain and spread my arms wide and *run* in a good big storm!"

So I developed a strong meterological sensibility. In years ahead when I wrote stories, atmosphere took its influential role from the start. Commotion in the weather and the inner feelings aroused by such a hovering disturbance emerged connected in dramatic form. (I tried a tornado first, in a story called "The Winds.")

From our earliest Christmas times, Santa Claus brought us toys that instruct boys and girls (separately) how to build things — stone blocks cut to the castle-building style, Tinker Toys, and Erector sets. Daddy made for us himself elaborate kites that needed to be taken miles out of town to a pasture long enough (and my father was not afraid of horses and cows watching) for him to run with and get up on a long cord to which my mother held the spindle, and then we children were given it to hold, tugging like something alive at our hands. They were beautiful, sound, shapely box kites, smelling delicately of office glue for their entire short lives. And of course, as soon as the boys attained anywhere near the right age, there was an electric train, the engine with its pea-sized working headlight, its line of cars, tracks equipped with switches, semaphores, its station, its bridges, and its tunnel, which blocked off all other traffic in the upstairs hall. Even from downstairs, and through the cries of excited children, the elegant rush and click of the train could be heard through the ceiling, running around and around its figure eight.

All of this, but especially the train, represents my father's fondest beliefs — in progress, in the future. With these gifts, he was preparing his children.

And so was my mother with her different gifts.

I learned from the age of two or three that any room in our house, at any time of day, was there to read in, or to be read to. My mother read to me. She'd read to me in the big bedroom in the mornings, when we were in her rocker together, which ticked in rhythm as we rocked, as though we had a cricket accompanying the story. She'd read to me in the diningroom on winter afternoons in front of the coal fire, with our cuckoo clock ending the story with "Cuckoo," and at night when I'd got in my own bed. I must have given her no peace. Sometimes she read to me in the kitchen while she sat churning, and the churning sobbed along with *any* story. It was my ambition to have her read to me while *I* churned; once she granted my wish, but she read off my story before I brought her butter. She was an expressive reader. When she was reading "Puss in Boots," for instance, it was impossible not to know that she distrusted *all* cats.

It had been startling and disappointing to me to find out that story books had been written by *people*, that books were not natural wonders, coming up of themselves like grass. Yet regardless of where they came from, I cannot remember a time when I was not in love with them — with the books themselves, cover and binding and the paper they were printed on, with their smell and their weight and with their possession in my arms, captured and carried off to myself. Still illiterate, I was ready for them, committed to all the reading I could give them.

Neither of my parents had come from homes that could afford to buy many books, but though it must have been something of a strain on his salary, as the youngest officer in a young insurance company, my father was all the while carefully selecting and ordering away for what he and Mother thought we children should grow up with. They bought first for the future.

Besides the bookcase in the livingroom, which was always called "the library," there were the encyclopedia tables and dictionary stand under windows in our diningroom. Here to help us grow up arguing around the diningroom table were the Unabridged Webster, the Columbia Encyclopedia, Compton's Pictured Encyclopedia, the Lincoln Library of Information, and later the Book of Knowledge. And the year we moved into our new house, there was room to celebrate it with the new 1925 edition of the Britannica, which my father, his face always deliberately turned toward the future, was of course disposed to think better than any previous edition.

In "the library," inside the mission-style bookcase with its three diamond-latticed glass doors, with my father's Morris chair and the glass-shaded lamp on its table beside it, were books I could soon begin on — and I did, reading them all alike and as they came, straight down their rows, top shelf to bottom. There was the set of Stoddard's Lectures, in all its late nineteenth-century vocabulary and vignettes of peasant life and quaint beliefs and customs, with matching halftone illustrations: Vesuvius erupting, Venice by moonlight, gypsies glimpsed by their campfires. I didn't know then the clue they were to my father's longing to see the rest of the world. I read straight through his other love-from-afar: the Victrola Book of the Opera, with opera after opera in synopsis, with portraits in costume of Melba, Caruso, Galli-Curci, and Geraldine Farrar, some of whose voices we could listen to on our Red Seal records.

My mother read secondarily for information; she sank as a hedonist into novels. She read Dickens in the spirit in which she would have eloped with him. The novels of her girlhood that had stayed on in her imagination, besides those of Dickens and Scott and Robert Louis Stevenson, were *Jane Eyre*, *Trilby*, *The Woman in White*, *Green Mansions*, *King Solomon's Mines*. Marie Corelli's name would crop up but I understood she had gone out of favor with my mother, who had only kept *Ardath* out of loyalty. In time she absorbed herself in Galsworthy, Edith Wharton, above all in Thomas Mann of the *Joseph* volumes.

St. Elmo was not in our house; I saw it often in other houses. This wildly popular Southern novel is where all the Edna Earles in our population started coming from. They're all named for the heroine, who succeeded in bringing a dissolute, sinning roué and atheist of a lover (St. Elmo) to his knees. My mother was able to forgo it. But she remembered the classic advice given to rose growers on how to water their bushes long enough: "Take a chair and *St. Elmo*."

To both my parents I owe my early acquaintance with a beloved Mark Twain. There was a full set of Mark Twain and a short set of Ring Lardner in our bookcase, and those were the volumes that in time united us all, parents and children.

Reading everything that stood before me was how I came upon a worn old book without a back that had belonged to my father as a child. It was called *Sanford and Merton*. Is there anyone left who recognizes it, I wonder? It is the famous moral tale written by Thomas Day in the 1780s, but of him no mention is made on the title page of *this* book; here it is *Sanford and Merton in Words of One Syllable* by Mary Godolphin. Here are the rich boy and the poor boy and Mr. Barlow, their teacher and interlocutor, in long discourses alternating with dramatic scenes — danger and rescue allotted to the rich and the poor respectively. It may have only words of one syllable, but one of them is "quoth." It ends with not one but two morals, both engraved on rings: "Do what you ought, come what may," and "If we would be great, we must first learn to be good."

This book was lacking its front cover, the back held on by strips of pasted paper, now turned golden, in several layers, and the pages stained, flecked, and tattered around the edges; its garish illustrations had come unattached but were preserved, laid in. I had the feeling even in my heedless childhood that this was the only book my father as a little boy had had of his own. He had held onto it, and might have gone to sleep on its coverless face: he had lost his mother when he was seven. My father had never made any mention to his own children of the book, but he had brought it along with him from Ohio to our house and shelved it in our bookcase.

My mother had brought from West Virginia that set of Dickens; those books looked sad, too — they had been through fire and water before I was born, she told me, and there they were, lined up — as I later realized, waiting for *me*.

I was presented, from as early as I can remember, with books of my own, which appeared on my birthday and Christmas morning. Indeed, my parents could not give me books enough. They must have sacrified to give me on my sixth or seventh birthday — it was after I became a reader for myself — the ten-volume set of Our Wonder World. These were beautifully made, heavy books I would lie down with on the floor in front of the diningroom hearth, and more often than the rest volume 5, *Every Child's Story Book*, was under my eyes. There were the fairy tales — Grimm, Andersen, the English, the French, "Ali Baba and the Forty Thieves"; and there were Aesop and Reynard the Fox; there were the myths and legends, Robin Hood, King Arthur, and St. George and the Dragon, even the history of Joan of Arc; a whack of *Pilgrim's Progress* and a long piece of *Gulliver*. They all carried their classic illustrations. I located myself in these pages and could go straight to the stories and pictures I loved; very often "The Yellow Dwarf" was first choice, with Walter Crane's Yellow Dwarf in full color making his terrifying appearance flanked by turkeys. Now that volume is as worn and backless and hanging apart as my father's poor *Sanford and Merton*. The precious page with Edward Lear's "Jumblies" on it has been in danger of slipping out for all these years. One measure of my love for Our Wonder World was that for a long time I wondered if I would go through fire and water for it as my mother had done for Charles Dickens; and the only comfort was to think I could ask my mother to do it for me.

I believe I'm the only child I know of who grew up with this treasure in the house. I used to ask others, "Did you have Our Wonder World?" I'd have to tell them The Book of Knowledge could not hold a candle to it.

I live in gratitude to my parents for initiating me — and as early as I begged for it, without keeping me waiting — into knowledge of the word, into reading and spelling, by way of the alphabet. They taught it to me at home in time for me to begin to read before starting to school. I believe the alphabet is no longer considered an essential piece of equipment for traveling through life. In my day it was the keystone to knowledge. You learned the alphabet as you learned to count to ten, as you learned "Now I lay me" and the Lord's Prayer and your father's and mother's name and address and telephone number, all in case you were lost.

My love for the alphabet, which endures, grew out of reciting it but, before that, out of seeing the letters on the page. In my own story books, before I could read them for myself, I fell in love with various winding, enchanted-looking initials drawn by

Walter Crane at the heads of fairy tales. In "Once upon a time," an "O" had a rabbit running it as a treadmill, his feet upon flowers. When the day came, years later, for me to see the Book of Kells, all the wizardry of letter, initial, and word swept over me a thousand times over, and the illumination, the gold, seemed a part of the world's beauty and holiness that had been there from the start.

QUESTIONS

1. Welty describes her father by first describing some of her father's possessions. What do these things tell us about the man who owns them? If you were to describe yourself by first describing some of your possession, what would you choose to describe? Why?

2. Welty obviously believes it is important to describe in some detail the books her family owned (and in one case did not own). Why? What do these books say about her and her family? What about the books your family owns? What do they say about you?

3. Welty's description depends on her memory of her childhood, on what she can now recall that seems to have been important to her. How would her description have been different if she had written this memoir as a child instead of as an elderly woman? What comments might she not have included if this had been written sixty years ago?

4. If you were to catalog the gifts your parents have given to you, what would you place at the top of the list? Why?

5. Write a description of your childhood home, using Welty's essay as a model or starting point.

• • • • •

MY FATHER

Joan Baez

Joan Baez first became famous as a folk singer and songwriter in the 1960s. Always devoted to humanitarian causes, she has frequently taken controversial and uncompromising stands on social issues in which she believes. In this excerpt from her autobiography Daybreak *(dedicated, significantly, "to the men who find themselves facing imprisonment for resisting the draft") we see that some of her tough-minded idealism is inherited from her father.*

MY father is short, honest, dark, and very handsome. He's good, he's a good man. He was born in Mexico, and brought up in Brooklyn. His father was a Mexican who left the Catholic church to become a Methodist minister. My father worked hard in school. He loved God and the church and his parents. At one time in his life he was going to be a minister, but the hypocrisy of the church bothered him and he became a scientist instead. He has a vision of how science can play the major role in saving the world. This vision puts a light into his eyes. He is a compulsive worker, and I know that he will never stop his work long enough to have a look at some of the things in his life which are blind and tragic. But it's not my business to print. About me and my father I don't know. I keep thinking of how hard it was for him to say anything nice about me to my face. Maybe he favored me and felt guilty about it, but he couldn't say anything nice. A lot of times I thought he would break my heart. Once he complimented me for something I was wearing. "You ought to wear that kind of thing more often," he said, and I looked into the mirror and I was wearing a black dress which I hated. I was fourteen then and I remember thinking, "Hah. I remind him of his mother in this thing."

My father is the saint of the family. You work at something until you exhaust yourself, so that you can be good at it, and with it you try to improve the lot of the sad ones, the hungry ones, the sick ones. You raise your children trying to teach them decency and respect for human life. Once when I was about thirteen he asked me if I would accept a large sum of money for the death of a man who was going to die anyway. I didn't quite understand. If I was off the hook, and just standing by, and then the man was killed by someone else, why shouldn't I take a couple of million? I told him sure, I'd take the money, and he laughed his head off. "That's immoral," he said. I didn't know what immoral meant, but I knew something was definitely wrong taking money for a man's life.

Once in my life I spent a month alone with my father. In 1950, when he was assigned to a project in Baghdad, Iraq, for UNESCO, my sisters got jaundice, and couldn't leave the States. My father left on schedule, for a month of briefing in Paris before going to Baghdad. I had jaundice too, but I didn't tell anyone. I wanted very badly to go to Paris. So despite bad pains in my stomach and black urine which I flushed in a hurry so he wouldn't see, and a general yellow hue which was creeping over my skin, and sometimes seemed to tint everything I looked at, I took full advantage of that time with my old man in Gay Paree. We bicycled everywhere, and bought long fresh bread and cheese and milk. We sat in outdoor cafés and had tea, and while he was busy at UNESCO house, I would run the elevators and visit secretaries and draw pictures of everyone and go off to feed pigeons in the park. Neither of us spoke French, but we faked it. One night in a restaurant, we couldn't understand anything on the dessert menu, so my father took a gamble and said, "*Ça, s'il vous plaît,*" pointing to the word "*Confiture,*" and they bought him a dish of strawberry jam, which he ate.

Once the family was together in Baghdad, I developed a terrible fear that my father was going to die. The fact is he almost killed himself tampering with the stupid brick oven which had to be lit in order to get hot bath water. He was "experimenting" with it — trying to determine how fast he could get the fire going by increasing the flow of kerosene into the oven. It exploded in his face, setting his clothes on fire and giving him third degree burns on his hands and face. He covered his eyes instinctively, or he would probably have been blinded, but his eyelashes and eyebrows were burned off anyway. Pauline passed out after telling Mother that "Popsy is on fire," and Mother wrapped him up in a sheet and called the English hospital for an ambulance. While we waited for the ambulance, my father tapped his feet in rhythm on the kitchen tiles, and cleared his throat every four or five seconds. He smelled terrible, and except for Mother, we just stood there. I was probably praying. Mother took me to the hospital to see him once, and I felt bad because I got dizzy when I saw his hands. They had big pussy blisters on them, and his face looked like a Rice Krispie, and I wanted to make him feel better, but I also wanted to go stick my head out the window and get some fresh air. When he came home from the hospital he was bandaged so that all you could see were his eyes and his ears. He held classes for his students at home. He is a brilliant teacher, and they loved him. I know they loved him, because the room smelled so awful from burnt flesh and Middle East medication that I felt sick every time I passed his door. And they came every day to learn and to see him.

My father teaches physics. He is a Ph.D. in physics, and we all wish he'd had just one boy who wasn't so opposed to school, to degrees, to formal education of any kind. One child to show some interest when he does physics experiments at the dinner table. But then it must be partly because we felt obligated to be student-types that we have all rebelled so completely. I can barely read. That is to say, I would rather do a thousand things before sitting down to read.

He used to tell us we should read the dictionary. He said it was fun and very educational. I've never gotten into it.

When we lived in Clarence Center, New York (it was a town of eight hundred people, and as far as they knew, we were niggers; Mother says that someone yelled out the window to me, "Hey, nigger!" and I said, "You ought to see me in the summertime!"), my father had a job working in Buffalo. It was some kind of armaments work. I just knew that it was secret, or part of it was secret, and that we began to get new things like a vacuum cleaner, a refrigerator, a fancy coffee pot, and one day my father came home with a little Crosley car. We were so excited about it that we drove it all over the front lawn, around the trees and through the piles of leaves. He was driving, Mother was in the front seat, and we three kids were in the back. The neighbors knew we were odd to begin with, but this confirmed it. Mother was embarrassed and she kept clutching my father's arm and saying, "Oh, Abo!" but he would take a quick corner around a tree and we'd all scream with laughter and Mother gave up and had hysterics.

Then something started my father going to Quaker meetings. We all had to go. It meant we had to sit and squelch giggles for about twenty minutes, and then go off with some kind old lady who planted each of us a bean in a tin can, and told us it was a miracle that it would push its little head up above the damp earth and grow into a plant. We knew it was a miracle, and we knew she was kind, but we made terrible fun of her the entire time and felt guilty about it afterwards.

While we were in the side room with the kind old lady, watching our beans perform miracles, my father was in the grown-up room, the room where they observe silence for a whole hour, and he was having a fight with his conscience. It took him less than a year of those confrontations with himself in that once a week silence to realize that he would have to give up either the silences or his job. Next thing I knew we were packing up and moving across the country. My father had taken a job as a professor of physics at the University of Redlands for about one-half the pay, and one-tenth the prestige — against the advice of everyone he knew except my mother. Since leaving Buffalo in 1947, he's never accepted a job that had anything to do with armaments, offense, defense, or whatever they prefer to call it. Last night I had a dream about him. I dreamed he was sitting next to himself in a theater. One of him was as he is now, and the other was the man of thirty years ago. I kept trying to get him to look at himself and say hello. Both faces smiled very understandingly, but neither would turn to greet the other.

I don't think he's ever understood me very well. He's never understood my compulsiveness, my brashness, my neuroses, my fears, my antinationalism (though he's changing on that), my sex habits, my loose way of handling money. I think often I startle him, and many times I please him. Sometimes I have put him through hell, like when I decided to live with Michael when I was twenty. "You mean you're going to . . . *live* with him?" "Yes," I said, and my father took a sleeping bag and went to the beach for two days, because Michael was staying in the house. Years later he sent me an article by Bertrand Russell, whom he respects very much, underlining the part which said that if young people could have a chance at "experimental marriages" while they were in college, they might know more about what it's all about before they actually got married. My father wrote that it always amazed him how I came to conclusions intuitively which took him years to realize.

At one time, my father couldn't stand to have a bottle of wine in the house. Whenever my aunt on my mother's side came to visit us in Cambridge, Mother would buy a bottle of wine, and she and my aunt would have a glass of wine before dinner. Sometimes my sisters and I took a glass, too, though I think Pauline was the only one who ever actually drank it down. One time, after my aunt had left, Father called a powwow, and we all gathered in the kitchen. Father's forehead was crumpled and overcast. He cleared his throat about a hundred times and made some vague opening statements about this generation and how we were still kids, and how he didn't really know how to deal with the problem at hand. Mother finally asked him what he was talking about, and he said, "Well, if any of my kids turns out to be an alcoholic, I'll know where it started. Right here in my own home." We looked at Mother to feel out the appropriate reaction, and she tried to be serious but couldn't be so we got into a half-humorous argument with Father. I told him he was lucky because none of us was at all interested in booze, and most of our friends got crocked every weekend, if not more often, and he said where were our standards, that his father would have had to leave home if he'd ever so much as tasted alcohol. It was all so entirely ridiculous that we ladies had to check ourselves to keep from making too much fun, or his feelings would be hurt, and he would get really angry. A few years later, my mother and father moved to Paris, and he learned to drink, and I think even to enjoy wine with dinner. Knowing the way I am, it's amazing that my father's puritanism about liquor did not set me up nicely for dipsomania, but for some reason, I have a total dislike for alcohol. And for cigarettes. And for the more recent fads: I don't smoke marijuana, or, needless to say, use any other drugs. I get high as a cloud on one sleeping pill, if that's what it means to get high, and it's not a whole lot different from what I feel like on a fall day in New England, or listening to the Faure Requiem, or dancing to soul music or singing in a Mississippi church. . . .

Lately my father has told me, off and on, that he is 100 percent behind me in the things I do. I think that's hard for him to say, for lots of reasons, one being the reason I mentioned earlier — that he has trouble telling me nice things about myself or what I do. Another is that he hasn't always gone along with my radical ideas of nonviolence and antinationalism, or my feelings that formal education is meaningless at best, and that universities are baby-sitting operations. Even though he was peace-marching long before I was, when I swung, I swung all the way, and left my father looking and acting, in my opinion, fairly moderate. But he has changed very much in the last five years, and I know that when my mother and Mimi and I went to jail for doing Civil Disobedience at the Army induction center, he had no doubts that we were doing the right thing, and he took over the Institute for Non-Violence for the weekend seminars. I think that all the while he was working with UNESCO in Paris, traveling around the world, trying to help find ways of teaching science in underdeveloped countries, he was more concerned than he admitted to himself about two problems: One was how he could teach people the wonders of science and at the same time keep them from simply trying to ape the powerful nations of the world and race to discover new scientific ways to destroy themselves and each other. The temptation for power is so great, and unfortunately, what power has always meant is one's ability and efficiency to murder one's neighbor. The other problem that haunted my father had to do with UNESCO itself: It was filled with power-hungry and money-hungry individuals, and he never wanted to admit it. My mother told me of a time when they were at a dinner party of UNESCO science division men and their wives. Some of the men were loosening up on wine and my father was talking about his difficulties in South America. His colleagues were not really interested in his successes or failures in teaching science to Brazilians, and that fact became more and more apparent. Finally, one of them said something to the effect of, "Aw c'mon, Baez, you don't really give a damn about science teaching methods, do you?" My mother was completely floored by this, and she said, "That's what we're here for," and asked the man why *he* was with UNESCO. He had a publishing job, the man said, and it hadn't really paid much: UNESCO paid a hell of a lot more, plus you got to travel, so he had gone to work for UNESCO and ended up in Paris. Not a bad deal all the way around. He went on kidding my father, who was struck dumb; and Mother did something she doesn't do unless she's in a state of shock or fury — she gave something resembling a speech, "My husband was an idealist when he came to work for UNESCO. He's a pacifist. He's concerned about the fact that people are starving to death and he thought the best way he could help out would be through UNESCO, to spread the uses of science to people who need it. Maybe we're just crazy, but I never imagined anyone came to work here for any other reason."

While he was with UNESCO, he seemed to lose his sense of humor. When I would visit them in Paris, sometimes it seemed that all I ever heard him say was, "I have this deadline . . . You know I just have to keep to this schedule . . ." He was trying to finish a book, which took him eight years to write. A basic text in physics. I seriously thought he would not ever complete that book, that it was like an eternally incomplete project he had to have to keep himself worn out. And I thought he was afraid to get it printed. But it was published while he was still in Paris. It's beautiful. The introduction is preceded by a picture of a huge rock suspended over the ocean. The picture makes you want to sit down heavily on the floor, or throw a paperweight out the window and watch it hit the sidewalk. There are little bits of human philosophy preceding each chapter, over eight hundred pictures, and the book is dedicated to "my wife, Joan, and my three daughters, Pauline, Joanie, and Mimi." And on page 274 there is a drawing which illustrates how an image is projected onto a television screen, and the image being projected is of a familiar-looking girl with long black hair, who stands holding a guitar.

In my estimation, my old man got his sense of humor back when he left Paris, and returned to the States. Toward the end of a course he was teaching at Harvard, a crash summer course, based on his book, he gave what he later described to me as the "demonstration of the century." He told the class that he was going to give an example of jet propulsion. He had a little red wagon brought in, and then he took the fire extinguisher off the wall and sat down in the wagon and jet propelled himself in circles around the front of the room, explaining, at the top of his voice, exactly what was happening technically. The students stood on their chairs and gave him an ovation, and it was all so overwhelming that he repeated the experiment. He shouted halfway through it for someone to open the door, and shot himself out into the hall, and disappeared. When he came back the bell had rung and the class was still there, cheering.

Right now, in 1967, my mother has planted my father and herself in a beautiful place in Carmel Valley, about one mile from my house, and not far from Pauline. A while after they began to be settled, I asked him if he could give himself permission to enjoy the luxury of his new home, his swimming pool, the endless beauty of the hills around. He tried to avoid my question by making a joke, but I said I was serious. We were sitting on the floor on a nice carpet, and he smoothed his hands over it as he leaned back against the wall. He looked very brown and Mexican in that moment, and I watched his profile against the valley hills as he struggled with himself. He said something about other people in the world, and about hunger. Then he looked up and gave me a smile of such a combination of things. "Yes, honey," he said, "I think I can enjoy it . . . if I keep myself busy enough . . ."

QUESTIONS

1. Baez recounts her relationship with her father in a very economical fashion. She uses simple sentences and few descriptive modifiers. How does this style affect the portrait she is creating? How would a more colorful and flamboyant style affect her message?

2. What character traits does Baez attribute to her father? How does she go about demonstrating that he possesses these traits? Which incidents contribute the most to her portrait? Why? Are there any details you wish she had included? What are they?

3. Although this section of Baez's autobiography is entitled "My Father," her mother and sisters also figure prominently in several of the incidents. Based on this simple selection, how would you characterize the part that the other members of Joan Baez's family played in her development?

4. Which member of your own family has had the most influence on you, your values, and your ideals? How would you characterize the contributions this individual has made to your development? Write an essay about this person.

RUTH'S SONG (BECAUSE SHE COULD NOT SING IT)

Gloria Steinem

As the editor of Ms. *magazine, and as a writer, speaker, and social critic, Gloria Steinem has consistently been one of the most prominent leaders of the contemporary feminist movement. In this essay, taken from her collection* Outrageous Acts *and* Everyday Rebellions, *she explores her association with her mother, a woman whose mental illness and ensuing chemical dependency placed a severe strain on their relationship.*

HAPPY or unhappy, families are all mysterious. We have only to imagine how differently we would be described — and will be, after our deaths — by each of the family members who believe they know us. The only question is, Why are some mysteries more important than others?

The fate of my Uncle Ed was a mystery of importance in our family. We lavished years of speculation on his transformation from a brilliant young electrical engineer to the town handyman. What could have changed this elegant, Lincolnesque student voted "Best Dressed" by his classmates to the gaunt, unshaven man I remember? Why did he leave a young son and a first wife of the "proper" class and religion, marry a much less educated woman of the "wrong" religion, and raise a second family in a house near an abandoned airstrip; a house whose walls were patched with metal signs to stop the wind? Why did he never talk about his transformation?

For years, I assumed that some secret and dramatic events of a year he spent in Alaska had made the differene. Then I discovered that the trip had come after his change and probably been made because of it. Strangers he worked for as a much-loved handyman talked about him as one more tragedy of the Depression, and it was true that Uncle Ed's father, my paternal grandfather, had lost his money in the stockmarket Crash and died of (depending on who was telling the story) pneumonia or a broken heart. But the Crash of 1929 also had come long after Uncle Ed's transformation. Another theory was that he was afflicted with a mental problem that lasted most of his life, and asked for help from no one.

Perhaps he had fallen under the spell of a radical professor in the early days of the century, the height of this country's romance with socialism and anarchism. That was the theory of another uncle on my mother's side. I do remember that no matter how much Uncle Ed needed money, he would charge no more for his work than materials plus 10 percent, and I never saw him in anything other than ancient boots and overalls held up with strategic safety pins. Was he really trying to replace socialism-in-one-country with socialism-in-one-man? If so, why did my grandmother, a woman who herself had run for the school board in coalition with anarchists and socialists, mistrust his judgment so much that she left his share of her estate in trust, even though he was over fifty when she died? And why did Uncle Ed seem uninterested in all other political words and acts? Was it true instead that, as another relative insisted, Uncle Ed had chosen poverty to disprove the myths of Jews and money?

Years after my uncle's death, I asked a son in his second family if he had the key to this family mystery. No, he said. He had never known his father any other way. For that cousin, there had been no question. For the rest of us, there was to be no answer.

For many years I also never imagined my mother any way other than the person she had become before I was born. She was just a fact of life when I was growing up; someone to be worried about and cared for; an invalid who lay in bed with eyes closed and lips moving in occasional response to voices only she could hear; a woman to whom I brought an endless stream of toast and coffee, bologna sandwiches and dime pies, in a child's version of what meals should be. She was a loving, intelligent, terrorized woman who tried hard to clean our littered house whenever she emerged from her private world, but who could rarely be counted on to finish one task. In many ways, our roles were reversed: I was the mother and she was the child. Yet that didn't help her, for she still worried about me with all the intensity of a frightened mother, plus the special fears of her own world full of threats and hostile voices.

Even then I suppose I must have known that, years before she was thirty-five and I was born, she had been a spirited, adventurous young woman who struggled out of a working-class family and into college, who found work she loved and continued to do, even after she was married and my older sister was there to be cared for. Certainly, our immediate family and nearby relatives, of whom I was by far the youngest, must have remembered her life as a whole and functioning person. She was thirty before she gave up her own career to help my father run the Michigan summer resort that was the most practical of his many dreams, and she worked hard there as everything from book-keeper to bar manager. The family must have watched this energetic, fun-loving, book-loving woman turn into someone who was afraid to be alone, who could not hang on to reality long enough to hold a job, and who could rarely concentrate enough to read a book.

Yet I don't remember any family speculation about the mystery of my mother's transformation. To the kind ones and those who liked her, this new Ruth was simply a sad event, perhaps a mental case, a family problem to be accepted and cared for until some natural process made her better. To the less kind or those who had resented her earlier independence, she was a willful failure, someone who lived in a filthy house, a woman who simply would not pull herself together.

Unlike the case of my Uncle Ed, exterior events were never suggested as reason enough for her problems. Giving up her own career was never cited as her personal parallel of the Depression. (Nor was there discussion of the Depression itself, though my mother, like millions of others, had made potato soup and cut up blankets to make my sister's winter clothes.) Her fears of dependence and poverty were no match for my uncle's possible political beliefs. The real influence of newspaper editors who had praised her reporting was not taken as seriously as the possible influence of one radical professor.

Even the explanation of mental illness seemed to contain more personal fault when applied to my mother. She had suffered her first "nervous breakdown," as she and everyone else called it, before I was born and when my sister was about five. It followed years of trying to take care of a baby, be the wife of a kind but financially irresponsible man with show-business dreams, and still keep her much-loved job as reporter and newspaper editor. After many months in a sanatorium, she was pronounced recovered. That is, she was able to take care of my sister again, to move away from the city and the job she loved, and to work with my father at the isolated rural lake in Michigan he was trying to transform into a resort worthy of the big dance bands of the 1930s.

But she was never again completely without the spells of depression, anxiety, and visions into some other world that eventually were to turn her into the nonperson I remember. And she was never again without a bottle of dark, acrid-smelling liquid she called "Doc Howard's medicine": a solution of chloral hydrate that I later learned was the main ingredient of "Mickey Finns" or "knockout drops," and that probably made my mother and her doctor the pioneers of modern tranquilizers. Though friends and relatives saw this medicine as one more evidence of weakness and indulgence, to me it always seemed an embarrassing but necessary evil. It slurred her speech and slowed her coordination, making our neighbors and my school friends believe she was a drunk. But without it, she would not sleep for days, even a week at a time, and her feverish eyes began to see only that private world in which wars and hostile voices threatened the people she loved.

Because my parents had divorced and my sister was working in a faraway city, my mother and I were alone together then, living off the meager fixed income that my mother got from leasing her share of the remaining land in Michigan. I remember a long Thanksgiving weekend spent hanging on to her with one hand and holding my eighth-grade assignment of *Tale of Two Cities* in the other, because the war outside our house was so real to my mother that she had plunged her hand through a window, badly cutting her arm in an effort to help us escape. Only when she finally agreed to swallow the medicine could she sleep, and only then could I end the terrible calm that comes with crisis and admit to myself how afraid I had been.

No wonder that no relative in my memory challenged the doctor who prescribed this medicine, asked if some of her suffering and hallucinating might be due to overdose or withdrawal, or even consulted another doctor about its use. It was our relief as well as hers.

But why was she never returned even to that first sanatorium? Or to help that might come from other doctors? It's hard to say. Partly, it was her own fear of returning. Partly, it was too little money, and a family's not-unusual assumption that mental illness is an inevitable part of someone's personality. Or perhaps other family members had feared something like my experience when, one hot and desperate summer between the sixth and seventh grade, I finally persuaded her to let me take her to the only doctor from those sanatorium days whom she remembered without fear.

Yes, this brusque old man told me after talking to my abstracted, timid mother for twenty minutes: She definitely belongs in a state hospital. I should put her there right away. But even at that age, *Life* magazine and newspaper exposés had told me what horrors went on inside those hospitals. Assuming there to be no other alternative, I took her home and never tried again.

In retrospect, perhaps the biggest reason my mother was cared for but not helped for twenty years was the simplest: her functioning was not that necessary to the world. Like women alcoholics who drink in their kitchens while costly programs are constructed for executives who drink, or like the homemakers subdued with tranquilizers while male patients get therapy and personal attention instead, my mother was not an important worker. She was not even the caretaker of a very young child, as she had been when she was hospitalized the first time. My father had patiently brought home the groceries and kept our odd household going until I was eight or so and my sister went away to college. Two years later when wartime gas rationing closed his summer resort and he had to travel to buy and sell in summer as well as winter, he said: How can I travel and take care of your mother? How can I make a living? He was right. It was impossible to do both. I did not blame him for leaving once I was old enough to be the bringer of meals and answerer of my mother's questions. ("Has your sister been killed in a car crash?" "Are there German soldiers outside?") I replaced my father, my mother was left with one more way of maintaining a sad status quo, and the world went on undisturbed.

That's why our lives, my mother's from forty-six to fifty-three, and my own from ten to seventeen, were spent alone together. There was one sane winter in a house we rented to be near my sister's college in Massachusetts, then one bad summer spent house-sitting in suburbia while my mother hallucinated and my sister struggled to hold down a summer job in New York. But the rest of those years were lived in Toledo where both my mother and father had been born, and on whose city newspapers an earlier Ruth had worked.

First we moved into a basement apartment in a good neighborhood. In those rooms behind a furnace, I made one last stab at being a child. By pretending to be much sicker with a cold than I really was, I hoped my mother would suddenly turn into a sane and cheerful woman bringing me chicken soup à la Hollywood. Of course, she could not. It only made her feel worse that she could not. I stopped pretending.

But for most of those years, we lived in the upstairs of the house my mother had grown up in and that her parents left her — a deteriorating farm house engulfed by the city, with poor but newer houses stacked against it and a major highway a few feet from its sagging front porch. For a while, we could rent the two downstairs apartments to a newlywed factory worker and a local butcher's family. Then the health department condemned our ancient furnace for the final time, sealing it so tight that even my resourceful Uncle Ed couldn't produce illegal heat.

In that house, I remember:

lying in the bed my mother and I shared for warmth, listening on the early morning radio to the royal wedding of Princess Elizabeth and Prince Philip being broadcast live, while we tried to ignore and thus protect each other from the unmistakable sounds of the factory worker downstairs beating up and locking out his pregnant wife.

. . . hanging paper drapes I had bought in the dime store; stacking books and papers in the shape of two armchairs and covering them with blankets; evolving my own dishwashing system (I waited until all the dishes were dirty, then put them in the bathtub); and listening to my mother's high praise for these housekeeping efforts to bring order from chaos, though in retrospect I think they probably depressed her further.

. . . coming back from one of the Eagles' Club shows where I and other veterans of a local tap-dancing school made ten dollars a night for two shows, and finding my mother waiting with a flashlight and no coat in the dark cold of the bus stop, worried about my safety walking home

. . . . in a good period, when my mother's native adventurousness came through, answering a classified ad together for an amateur acting troupe that performed Biblical dramas in churches, and doing several very corny performances of *Noah's Ark* while my proud mother shook metal sheets backstage to make thunder.

. . . on a hot summer night, being bitten by one of the rats that shared our house and its back alley. It was a terrifying night that turned into a touching one when my mother, summoning courage from some unknown reservoir of love, became a calm, comforting parent who took me to a hospital emergency room despite her terror at leaving home.

. . . coming home from a local library with the three books a week into which I regularly escaped, and discovering that for once there was no need to escape. My mother was calmly planting hollyhocks in the vacant lot next door.

But there were also times when she woke in the early winter dark, too frightened and disoriented to remember that I was at my usual afterschool job, and so called the police to find me. Humiliated in front of my friends by sirens and policemen, I would yell at her — and she would bow her head in fear and say "I'm sorry, I'm sorry, I'm sorry," just as she had done so often when my otherwise-kindhearted father had yelled at her in frustration. Perhaps the worst thing about suffering is that it finally hardens the hearts of those around it.

And there were many, many times when I badgered her until her shaking hands had written a small check to cash at the corner grocery and I could leave her alone while I escaped to the comfort of well-heated dime stores that smelled of fresh doughnuts, or to air-conditioned Saturday-afternoon movies that were windows on a very different world.

But my ultimate protection was this: I was just passing through, a guest in the house; perhaps this wasn't my mother at all. Though I knew very well that I was her daughter, I sometimes imagined that I had been adopted and that my real parents would find me, a fantasy I've since discovered is common. (If children wrote more and grown-ups less, being adopted might be seen not only as a fear but also as a hope.) Certainly, I didn't mourn the wasted life of this woman who was scarcely older than I am now. I worried only about the times when she got worse.

Pity takes distance and a certainty of surviving. It was only after our house was bought for demolition by the church next door, and after my sister had performed the miracle of persuading my father to give me a carefree time before college by taking my mother with him to California for a year, that I could afford to think about the sadness of her life. Suddenly, I was far away in Washington, living with my sister and sharing a house with several of her friends. While I finished high school and discovered to my surprise that my classmates felt sorry for me because my mother *wasn't* there, I also realized that my sister, at least in her early childhood, had known a very different person who lived inside our mother, an earlier Ruth.

She was a woman I met for the first time in a mental hospital near Baltimore, a humane place with gardens and trees where I visited her each weekend of the summer after my first year away in college. Fortunately, my sister hadn't been able to work and be our mother's caretaker, too. After my father's year was up, my sister had carefully researched hospitals and found the courage to break the family chain.

At first, this Ruth was the same abstracted, frightened woman I had lived with all those years; though now all the sadder for being approached through long hospital corridors and many locked doors. But gradually she began to talk about her past life, memories that doctors there must have been awakening. I began to meet a Ruth I had never known.

QUESTIONS

1. Steinem sees her mother as being to some extent the victim of her culture. What were the contributing social factors in her mother's decline?

2. Steinem characterizes her family as one in which the traditional roles were reversed; she became the parent to her mother, who had become childlike. Does she seem resentful of this role her mother has thrust upon her? What does her attitude about her mother seem to be while she is growing up? When does it change? Why does it change?

3. Steinem recounts a series of incidents (pp. 117–18) that have stuck in her memory. What is the effect of relating these scenes without comment? What do these scenes contribute to the overall effect Steinem is trying to create? How do they do this?

4. Steinem points out that her fantasy of being adopted is a common one; many children have it. Although most of us have not lived through the kind of tragedy that Steinem did, many adolescents and teenagers go through a period of rejection, a time when they become frustrated with, or ashamed of, their parents. Was Steinem's frustration and shame substantially different from that of your own at that period in your life? In what ways did her experience differ from yours?

5. What can you learn from Gloria Steinem's struggle? What did she learn?

* * * * *

TEN TON OF STUN

Noel Perrin

Noel Perrin's books on nature and Vermont country life have been compared to the writings of Thoreau. This essay comes from Second Person Rural, *the second volume in a series (along with* First Person Rural *and* Third Person Rural*) that characterizes him as "a sometime farmer."*

ANYONE who owns land in Vermont has rocks to deal with. Anyone who both owns land and farms it becomes a specialist in rocks. He has to. Rocks are natural enemies of farm equipment. A boulder sticking up as little as two inches can catch your cutter bar when you're mowing hay — and few thuds are more sickening. Hitting, say, five rocks in the course of an afternoon's mowing can reduce a man to quivering jelly. I have known a sober middle-aged farmer to leap off his tractor and peer through the tall grass like Tarzan tracking elephants, because he thought he caught a glimpse of a gray hump in the next swath.

Stones in plowland are even worse. No worry about the ones above ground; here you can easily see them, and, at some cost to the straightness of your furrows, detour around. But the ones just under the surface are another matter. You fear that at any second the plowshare will smash into one. A Vermonter plowing a strange field consequently wears the cautious expression of a pilot guiding a ship into a harbor that he knows to be full of shoals and reefs and quite possibly minefields.

For these reasons, a good farmer will go to quite a lot of trouble to get the stones out of his fields. I myself am not a good farmer. Oh, I've pulled a few boulders out with my tractor, loaded them onto a borrowed stoneboat, and dragged them to the nearest swamp. I've even incorporated a few into stone walls. But I only attack the little ones — say, up to a thousand pounds. The big ones I learn to avoid when I mow. As for plowing, I don't do any. I'm too chicken.

I have a young neighbor, though, who shows signs of becoming one of the best farmers around. For the last several years Ellis has been growing corn on a four-acre piece of plowland that his father and grandfather worked before him. It's good land, too: level and well watered.

Long ago — probably in the eighteenth century — some farmer took out all the stones that could be moved with a team of oxen. More recently, Ellis's father got some still bigger ones with his tractor. What that left was a beautiful clear field with about eight giant boulders dotted across it, ranging in size from half a Honda to a whole Chevy II. Some were half out of the ground, some nearly flush. A couple more lurked five or six inches under the surface, with soil carefully built up over them by Ellis's father and grandfather, the way a balding man combs his hair over the bald spot. From my point of view, those rocks were as enduring a part of our local landscape as Potato Hill, or the Pompanoosuc River.

One Sunday last August, though, I was walking past Ellis's cornfield on my side of the boundary and I noticed a scene of unusual activity. There were a tractor, a backhoe, and a little bulldozer gathered around one of the boulders. They weren't messing up the corn, because last year Ellis planted corn only on the upper side of the field, where there are no rocks. Naturally, I stopped to watch.

The backhoe had already dug a deep trench around the rock, which was one of the half-buried ones. And someone had already fixed slender logging chains around the rock, and the rock had visibly shifted forward in its bed.

At the moment I arrived, Ellis was sitting on his old Allis-Chalmers tractor, which was chained to the front of the rock. Ed Paige, his father, was beside him on the little bulldozer, similarly chained. A neighbor named Alford Stone, who's a professional equipment operator, had his backhoe to one side. By extending the boom as far as it would reach, Alford was just able to get the hoe teeth under the back of the rock. The tractor whined, the bulldozer growled and spun its worn treads, the backhoe made a throaty roar — and the rock moved forward in its hole maybe an inch.

Undismayed, Alford dismounted from his backhoe and jumped lightly onto the rock. "We'll get this stun," he said. He rearranged the chains so that the angle of pull would be slightly different. Then the tractor whined, the bulldozer growled, the backhoe roared. The rock crept forward and up out of the hole almost a foot.

Twenty minutes later, the rock was half out of the hole, and apparently coming no farther. The last two pulls hadn't moved it at all. Alford only smiled. He got Ed to take his place on the backhoe, and hopped on the bulldozer (which he owns). Ellis unchained it, and Alford calmly backed it down what looked to me like a sixty-degree slope into the bottom of the now quite large pit behind the rock. There was just room for it. He set the blade against the back of the rock, and once again every machine strained to the limit. The rock moved about half an inch.

"Maybe you could use another tractor," I said to Ellis, and he agreed that another one could do no harm. It took me less than ten minutes to come snorting back on my International Harvester 504. Alford chained me to the front, next to Ellis. Then all four of us, mounted on our machines, pulled and pushed, and the great rock came lurching out of its hole.

No one broke out any champagne. Instead, Ed, Ellis, and Alford set about making a train. It had two engines, one car, and a caboose. First came Ellis's tractor, tightly chained to the bulldozer blade. Then the bulldozer, tightly chained to the rock. Then the boulder itself, looking enormous now that it was all above ground. Finally the backhoe, which Alford had turned around, so that now his bucket loader was pressed against the back of the rock.

Instead of someone blowing a whistle, Ed shouted, "Let's go," and the train moved off on a hundred-yard journey to a piece of wet ground at the bottom of the field. There the boulder was pushed up against four others they had already taken out. The crew, not knowing anything about railroad rules on what constitutes a day's work, immediately set out on the next run.

Two days later, on my way out to my woodlot, I took a steel tape and measured the stone I had helped to pull out. It is nine feet long by eight feet wide, and at the center nearly four feet thick. Solid granite. Granite weighs 165 pounds per cubic foot. Making full allowance for irregularities and thin places near the edges, I calculate that boulder at well over ten tons.

Talk about weight lifters! Vermont farmers may well be the national champions.

QUESTIONS

1. Does this ten ton boulder really need to be moved? Why? Is it possible that they move it "for the fun of it"?

2. New Englanders are legendary for being terse, closemouthed, and fairly uncommunicative. Is there any indication of this stereotype in this narrative?

3. Why does Perrin feel this story needs to be told? What point is he trying to make?

4. Have you ever accomplished something similar to this feat? What? How did you feel when you had finished your task? Describe your struggle in a reflective essay.

WEST WITH THE NIGHT

Beryl Markham

Although she was born in England in 1902, Beryl Markham grew up on her father's farm in Kenya, where she played and hunted with the native Murani children, learned to breed and train race horses, and survived a serious attack and mauling from a neighbor's "pet" lion. In 1931 she learned to fly and began work as a bush pilot, venturing to remote places through East Africa carrying passengers, mail, and supplies. On a bet from a friend, she became the first solo pilot to cross the Atlantic traveling east to west from England to North America. The following excerpt from her memoir West with the Night *describes her twenty-one-hour flight in September 1936.*

I HAVE seldom dreamed a dream worth dreaming again, or at least none worth recording. Mine are not enigmatic dreams; they are peopled with characters who are plausible and who do plausible things, and I am the most plausible amongst them. All the characters in my dreams have quiet voices like the voice of the man who telephoned me at Elstree one morning in September of nineteen-thirty-six and told me that there was rain and strong head winds over the west of England and over the Irish Sea, and that there were variable winds and clear skies in mid-Atlantic and fog off the coast of Newfoundland.

"If you are still determined to fly the Atlantic this late in the year," the voice said, "the Air Ministry suggests that the weather it is able to forecast for tonight, and for tomorrow morning, will be about the best you can expect."

The voice had a few other things to say, but not many, and then it was gone, and I lay in bed half-suspecting that the telephone call and the man who made it were only parts of the mediocre dream I had been dreaming. I felt that if I closed my eyes the unreal quality of the message would be re-established, and that, when I opened them again, this would be another ordinary day with its usual beginning and its usual routine.

But of course I could not close my eyes, nor my mind, nor my memory. I could lie there for a few moments — remembering how it had begun, and telling myself, with senseless repetition, that by tomorrow morning I should either have flown the Atlantic to America — or I should not have flown it. In either case this was the day I would try.

I could stare up at the ceiling of my bedroom in Aldenham House, which was a ceiling undistinguished as ceilings go, and feel less resolute than anxious, much less brave than foolhardy. I could say to myself, "You needn't do it, of course," knowing at the same time that nothing is so inexorable as a promise to your pride.

I could ask, "Why risk it?" as I have been asked since, and I could answer, "Each to his element." By his nature a sailor must sail, by his nature a flyer must fly. I could compute that I had flown a quarter of a million miles; and I could foresee that, so long as I had a plane and the sky was there, I should go on flying more miles.

There was nothing extraordinary in this. I had learned a craft and had worked hard learning it. My hands had been taught to seek the controls of a plane. Usage had taught them. They were at ease clinging to a stick, as a cobbler's fingers are in repose grasping an awl. No human pursuit achieves dignity until it can be called work, and when you can experience a physical loneliness for the tools of your trade, you see that the other things — the experiments, the irrelevant vocations, the vanities you used to hold — were false to you.

Record flights had actually never interested me very much for myself. There were people who thought that such flights were done for admiration and publicity, and worse. But of all the records — from Louis Blériot's first crossing of the English Channel in nineteen hundred and nine, through and beyond Kingsford Smith's flight from San Francisco to Sydney, Australia — none had been made by amateurs, nor by novices, nor by men or women less than hardened to failure, or less than masters of their trade. None of these was false. They were a company that simple respect and simple ambition made it worth more than an effort to follow.

The Carberrys (of Seramai) were in London and I could remember everything about their dinner party — even the menu. I could remember June Carberry and all her guests, and the man named McCarthy, who lived in Zanzibar, leaning across the table and saying, "J. C., why don't you finance Beryl for a record flight?"

I could lie there staring lazily at the ceiling and recall J. C.'s dry answer: "A number of pilots have flown the North Atlantic, west to east. Only Jim Mollison has done it alone the other way — from Ireland. Nobody has done it alone from England — man or woman. I'd be interested in that, but nothing else. If you want to try it, Burl, I'll back you. I think Edgar Percival could build a plane that would do it, provided you can fly it. Want to chance it?"

"Yes."

I could remember saying that better than I could remember anything — except J. C.'s almost ghoulish grin, and his remark that sealed the agreement: "It's a deal, Burl. I'll furnish the plane and you fly the Atlantic — but, gee, I wouldn't tackle it for a million. Think of all that black water! Think how cold it is!"

And I had thought of both.

I had thought of both for a while, and then there had been other things to think about. I had moved to Elstree, half-hour's flight from the Percival Aircraft Works at Gravesend, and almost daily for three months now I had flown down to the factory in a hired plane and watched the Vega Gull they were making for me. I had watched her birth and watched her growth. I had watched her wings take shape, and seen wood and fabric moulded to her ribs to form her long, sleek belly, and I had seen her engine cradled into her frame, and made fast.

The Gull had a turquoise-blue body and silver wings. Egar Percival had made her with care, with skill, and with worry — the care of a veteran flyer, the skill of a master designer, and the worry of a friend. Actually the plane was a standard sport model with a range of only six hundred and sixty miles. But she had a special undercarriage built to carry the weight of her extra oil and petrol tanks. The tanks were fixed into the wings, into the centre section, and into the cabin itself. In the cabin they formed a wall around my seat, and each tank had a petcock of its own. The petcocks were important.

"If you open one," said Percival, "without shutting the other first, you may get an airlock. You know the tanks in the cabin have no gauges, so it may be best to let one run completely dry before opening the next. Your motor might go dead in the interval — but she'll start again. She's a De Havilland Gipsy — and Gipsys never stop."

I had talked to Tom. We had spent hours going over the Atlantic chart, and I had realized that the tinker of Molo, now one of England's great pilots, had traded his dreams and had got in return a better thing. Tom had grown older too; he had jet-tisoned a deadweight of irrelevant hopes and wonders, and had left himself a realistic code that had no room for temporizing or easy sentiment.

"I'm glad you're going to do it, Beryl. It won't be simple. If you can get off the ground in the first place, with such an immense load of fuel, you'll be alone in that plane about a night and a day — mostly night. Doing it east to west, the wind's against you. In September, so is the weather. You won't have a radio. If you misjudge your course only a few degrees, you'll end up in Labrador or in the sea — so don't misjudge anything."

Tom could still grin. He had grinned; he had said: "Anyway, it ought to amuse you to think that your financial backer lives on a farm called 'Place of Death' and your plane is being built at 'Gravesend.' If you were consistent, you'd christen the Gull 'The Flying Tombstone.'"

I hadn't been that consistent. I had watched the building of the plane and I had trained for the flight like an athlete. And now, as I lay in bed, fully awake, I could still hear the quiet voice of the man from the Air Ministry intoning, like the voice of a dispassionate court clerk: " . . . the weather for tonight and tomorrow . . . will be about the best you can expect." I should have liked to discuss the flight once more with Tom before I took off, but he was on a special job up north. I got out of bed and bathed and put on my flying clothes and took some cold chicken packed in a cardboard box and flew over to the military field at Abingdon, where the Vega Gull waited for me under the care of the R.A.F. I remember that the weather was clear and still.

You can live a lifetime and, at the end of it, know more about other people than you know about yourself. You learn to watch other people, but you never watch yourself because you strive against loneliness. If you read a book, or shuffle a deck of cards, or care for a dog, you are avoiding yourself. The abhorrence of loneliness is as natural as wanting to live at all. If it were otherwise, men would never have bothered to make an alphabet, nor to have fashioned words out of what were only animal sounds, nor to have crossed continents — each man to see what the other looked like.

Being alone in an aeroplane for even so short a time as a night and a day, irrevocably alone, with nothing to observe but your instruments and your own hands in semi-darkness, nothing to contemplate but the size of your small courage, nothing to wonder about but the beliefs, the faces, and the hopes rooted in your mind — such an experience can be as startling as the first awareness of a stranger walking by your side at night. You are the stranger.

It is dark already and I am over the south of Ireland. There are the lights of Cork and the lights are wet; they are drenched in Irish rain, and I am above them and dry. I am above them and the plane roars in a sobbing world, but it imparts no sadness to me. I feel the security of solitude, the exhilaration of escape. So long as I can see the lights and imagine the people walking under them, I feel selfishly triumphant, as if I have eluded care and left even the small sorrow of rain in other hands.

It is a little over an hour now since I left Abingdon. England, Wales, and the Irish Sea are behind me like so much time used up. On a long flight distance and time are the same. But there had been a moment when Time stopped — and Distance too. It was the moment I lifted the blue-and-silver Gull from the aerodrome, the moment the photographers aimed their cameras, the moment I felt the craft refuse its burden and strain toward the earth in sullen rebellion, only to listen at last to the persuasion of stick and elevators, the dogmatic argument of blueprints that said she *had* to fly because the figures proved it.

So she had flown, and once airborne, once she had yielded to the sophistry of a draughtsman's board, she had said, "There: I have lifted the weight. Now, where are we bound?" — and the question had frightened me.

"We are bound for a place thirty-six hundred miles from here — two thousand miles of it unbroken ocean. Most of the way it will be night. We are flying west with the night."

So there behind me is Cork; and ahead of me is Berehaven Lighthouse. It is the last light, standing on the last land. I watch it, courting the frequency of its flashes — so many to the minute. Then I pass it and fly out to sea.

The fear is gone now — not overcome nor reasoned away. It is gone because something else has taken its place; the confidence and the trust, the inherent belief in the security of land underfoot — now this faith is transferred to my plane, because the land has vanished and there is no other tangible thing to fix faith upon. Flight is but momentary escape from the eternal custody of earth.

Rain continues to fall, and outside the cabin it is totally dark. My altimeter says that the Atlantic is two thousand feet below me, my Sperry Artificial Horizon says that I am flying level. I judge my drift at three degrees more than my weather chart suggests, and fly accordingly. I am flying blind. A beam to follow would help. So would a radio — but then, so would clear weather. The voice of the man at the Air Ministry had not promised storm.

I feel the wind rising and the rain falls hard. The smell of petrol in the cabin is so strong and the roar of the plane so loud that my senses are almost deadened. Gradually it becomes unthinkable that existence was ever otherwise.

At ten o'clock P.M. I am flying along the Great Circle Course for Harbour Grace, Newfoundland, into a forty-mile headwind at a speed of one hundred and thirty miles an hour. Because of the weather, I cannot be sure of how many more hours I have to fly, but I think it must be between sixteen and eighteen.

At ten-thirty I am still flying on the large cabin tank of petrol, hoping to use it up and put an end to the liquid swirl that has rocked the plane since my take-off. The tank has no gauge, but written on its side is the assurance: "This tank is good for four hours."

There is nothing ambiguous about such a guaranty. I believe it, but at twenty-five minutes to eleven, my motor coughs and dies, and the Gull is powerless above the sea.

I realize that the heavy drone of the plane has been, until this moment, complete and comforting silence. It is the actual silence following the last splutter of the engine that stuns me. I can't feel any fear; I can't feel anything. I can only observe with a kind of stupid disinterest that my hands are violently active and know that, while they move, I am being hypnotized by the needle of my altimeter.

I suppose that the denial of natural impulse is what is meant by "keeping calm," but impulse has reason in it. If it is night and you are sitting in an aeroplane with a stalled motor, and there are two thousand feet between you and the sea, nothing can be more reasonable than the impulse to pull back your stick in the hope of adding to that two thousand, if only by a little. The thought, the knowledge, the law that tells you that your hope lies not in this, but in a contrary act — the act of directing your impotent craft toward the water—seems a terrifying abandonment, not only of reason, but of sanity. Your mind and your heart reject it. It is your hands—your stranger's hands—that follow with unfeeling precision the letter of the law.

I sit there and watch my hands push forward on the stick and feel the Gull respond and begin its dive to the sea. Of course it is a simple thing; surely the cabin tank has run dry too soon. I need only to turn another petcock . . .

But it is dark in the cabin. It is easy to see the luminous dial of the altimeter and to note that my height is now eleven hundred feet, but it is not easy to see a petcock that is somewhere near the floor of the plane. A hand gropes and reappears with an electric torch, and fingers, moving with agonizing composure, find the petcock and turn it; and I wait.

At three hundred feet the motor is still dead, and I am conscious that the needle of my altimeter seems to whirl like the spoke of a spindle winding up the remaining distance between the plane and the water. There is some lightning, but the quick flash only serves to emphasize the darkness. How high can waves reach—twenty feet, perhaps? Thirty?

It is impossible to avoid the thought that this is the end of my flight, but my reactions are not orthodox; the various incidents of my entire life do not run through my mind like a motion-picture film gone mad. I only feel that all this has happened before—and it has. It has all happened a hundred times in my mind, in my sleep, so that now I am not really caught in terror; I recognize a familiar scene, a familiar story with its climax dulled by too much telling.

I do not know how close to the waves I am when the motor explodes to life again. But the sound is almost meaningless. I see my hand easing back on the stick, and I feel the Gull climb up into the storm, and I see the altimeter whirl like a spindle again, paying out the distance between myself and the sea.

The storm is strong. It is comforting. It is like a friend shaking me and saying, "Wake up! You were only dreaming."

But soon I am thinking. By simple calculation I find that my motor had been silent for perhaps an instant more than thirty seconds.

I ought to thank God—and I do, though indirectly. I thank Geoffrey De Havilland who designed the indomitable Gipsy, and who, after all, must have been designed by God in the first place.

A lighted ship—the daybreak—some steep cliffs standing in the sea. The meaning of these will never change for pilots. If one day an ocean can be flown within an hour, if men can build a plane that so masters time, the sight of land will be no less welcome to the steersman of that fantastic craft. He will have cheated laws that the cunning of science has taught him how to cheat, and he will feel his guilt and be eager for the sanctuary of the soil.

I saw the ship and the daybreak, and then I saw the cliffs of Newfoundland wound in ribbons of fog. I felt the elation I had so long imagined, and I felt the happy guilt of having circumvented the stern authority of the weather and the sea. But mine was a minor triumph; my swift Gull was not so swift as to have escaped unnoticed. The night and the storm had caught her and we had flown blind for nineteen hours.

I was tired now, and cold. Ice began to film the glass of the cabin windows and the fog played a magician's game with the land. But the land was there. I could not see it, but I had seen it. I could not afford to believe that it was any land but the land I wanted.

I could not afford to believe that my navigation was at fault, because there was no time for doubt.

South to Cape Race, west to Sydney on Cape Breton Island. With my protractor, my map, and my compass, I set my new course, humming the ditty that Tom had taught me: 'Variation West — magnetic best. Variation East — magnetic least.' A silly rhyme, but it served to placate, for the moment, two warring poles — the magnetic and the true. I flew south and found the lighthouse of Cape Race protruding from the fog like a warning finger. I circled twice and went on over the Gulf of Saint Lawrence.

After a while there would be New Brunswick, and then Maine — and then New York. I could anticipate. I could almost say, "Well, if you stay awake, you'll find it's only a matter of time now" — but there was no question of staying awake. I was tired and I had not moved an inch since that uncertain moment at Abingdon when the Gull had elected to rise with her load and fly, but I could not have closed my eyes. I could sit there in the cabin, walled in glass and petrol tanks, and be grateful for the sun and the light, and the fact that I could see the water under me. They were almost the last waves I had to pass. Four hundred miles of water, but then the land again — Cape Breton. I would stop at Sydney to refuel and go on. It was easy now. It would be like stopping at Kisumu and going on.

Success breeds confidence. But who has a right to confidence except the Gods? I had a following wind, my last tank of petrol was more than three-quarters full, and the world was as bright to me as if it were a new world, never touched. If I had been wiser, I might have known that such moments are, like innocence, short-lived. My engine began to shudder before I saw the land. It died, it spluttered, it started again and limped along. It coughed and spat black exhaust toward the sea.

There are words for everything. There was a word for this — airlock, I thought. This had to be an airlock because there was petrol enough. I thought I might clear it by turning on and turning off all the empty tanks, and so I did that. The handles of the petcocks were sharp little pins of metal, and when I had opened and closed them a dozen times, I saw that my hands were bleeding and that the blood was dropping on my maps and on my clothes, but the effort wasn't any good. I coasted along on a sick and halting engine. The oil pressure and the oil temperature gauges were normal, the magnetos working, and yet I lost altitude slowly while the realization of failure seeped into my heart. If I made the land, I should have been the first to fly the North Atlantic from England, but from my point of view, from a pilot's point of view, a forced landing was failure because New York was my goal. If only I could land and then take off, I would make it still . . . if only, if only . . .

The engine cuts again, and then catches, and each time it spurts to life I climb as high as I can get, and then it splutters and stops and I glide once more toward the water, to rise again and descend again, like a hunting sea bird.

I find the land. Visibility is perfect now and I see land forty or fifty miles ahead. If I am on my course, that will be Cape Breton. Minute after minute goes by. The minutes almost materialize; they pass before my eyes like links in a long slow-moving chain, and each time the engine cuts, I see a broken link in the chain and catch my breath until it passes.

The land is under me. I snatch my map and stare at it to confirm my whereabouts. I am, even at my present crippled speed, only twelve minutes from Sydney Airport, where I can land for repairs and then go on.

The engine cuts once more and I begin to glide, but now I am not worried; she will start again, as she has done, and I will gain altitude and fly into Sydney.

But she doesn't start. This time she's dead as death; the Gull settles earthward and it isn't any earth I know. It is black earth stuck with boulders and I hang above it, on hope and on a motionless propeller. Only I cannot hang above it long. The earth hurries to meet me, I bank, turn, and sideslip to dodge the boulders, my wheels touch, and I feel them submerge. The nose of the plane is engulfed in mud, and I go forward striking my head on the glass of the cabin front, hearing it shatter, feeling blood pour over my face.

I stumble out of the plane and sink to my knees in muck and stand there foolishly staring, not at the lifeless land, but at my watch.

Twenty-one hours and twenty-five minutes.

Atlantic flight. Abingdon, England, to a nameless swamp — nonstop.

A Cape Breton Islander found me — a fisherman trudging over the bog saw the Gull with her tail in the air and her nose buried, and then he saw me floundering in the embracing soil of his native land. I had been wandering for an hour and the black mud had got up to my waist and the blood from the cut in my head had met the mud halfway.

From a distance, the fisherman directed me with his arms and with shouts toward the firm places in the bog, and for another hour I walked on them and came toward him like a citizen of Hades blinded by the sun, but it wasn't the sun; I hadn't slept for forty hours.

He took me to his hut on the edge of the coast and I found that built upon the rocks there was a little cubicle that housed an ancient telephone — put there in case of shipwrecks.

I telephoned to Sydney Airport to say that I was safe and to prevent a needless search being made. On the following morning I did step out of a plane at Floyd Bennett Field and there was a crowd of people still waiting there to greet me, but the plane I stepped from was not the Gull, and for days while I was in New York I kept thinking about that and wishing over and over again that it had been the Gull, until the wish lost its significance, and time moved on, overcoming many things it met on the way.

QUESTIONS

1. In Markham's flight she must contend with fatigue and boredom as much as anything else. What strategies does she employ to fight boredom?

2. Markham says she was never very interested in record flights. Why, then, does she decide to make this flight?

3. Throughout her narrative Markham seems detached and distant from herself, her friends, and her adventure. Does this detachment make her story seem more — or less — interesting? Why?

4. Unlike Lindbergh, who landed at a crowded Paris airfield, Markham unceremoniously crashed her plane into a swamp. What overall effect does this crash have on her estimate of her flight's success? Does she exaggerate the importance of this particular conclusion to her flight?

5. Beryl Markham was the first pilot, male or female, to cross the Atlantic flying west from England. Successfully completing such an aviation first should make her a hero, but in her account she doesn't seem very heroic. Why is this? Is she too modest? What does her narrative suggest about heroism?

6. Have you ever done anything that might be considered "heroic" or especially virtuous (feel free to stretch the definition of these terms so that they might apply to day-to-day situations). Describe this event in a brief essay.

• • • • •

THIRTY SECONDS

Michael J. Arlen

Although Michael Arlen won the National Book Award in 1975 for Passage to Ararat, *he is perhaps better known for the dozens of articles about television he has written for* The New Yorker. *In his 1980 book,* Thirty Seconds, *from which this excerpt is taken, he traces the history of a thirty-second AT&T commercial. The commercial, which took six months and nearly a million dollars to make, is followed by Arlen from its initial conception to its first national broadcast. This selection records the final stages in this lengthy process.*

Client Approval

FINALLY, on Tuesday, June 19, the two senior N. W. Ayer vice-presidents on the project, George Eversman and Jerry Pfiffner, take cassettes of "Tap Dancing," and also of several other AT&T commercials that are virtually completed, out to AT&T Long Lines headquarters in Bedminster, New Jersey, for client approval.

The Long Lines headquarters is in itself a wonder of modern corporate techno-aesthetics. To begin with, it is not so much set down, or "located," in one of those few remaining tranquil countryside areas an hour and a half from New York as it is more or less hidden there. On either side of the road south from Morristown one sees only green rolling hills and green leafy woods. No vast buildings on the horizon; not even a sign on the highway. At last, there is a modest roadside sign announcing "Bedminster," and then a turnoff into more greenery, and then a really tiny sign announcing "AT&T Long Lines" (the kind of sign one imagines that Howard Hughes would have liked to have, for it tells the world you're there, but not so loudly that the world, driving by at 55 m.p.h., would ever know it), and then a long, carefully tended driveway or feeder road, with *nothing* on either side — only well-mowed grass and suitably arranged shrubs. No guards, no people, and, that morning, no visible vehicles: the entrance, perhaps, to Paradise or else to the King of Switzerland's convention center. And then, not at all looming, despite its obvious size — not yet even truly visible — but, rather, stretched out almost somnolently beside the leafy woods, somewhat like a sleeping dragon, the Long Line headquarters: not so much a complex as a single building that looks like a complex — the equivalent, in fact, of a thirty-five-story skyscraper laid on its side, so that its upper stories barely rise above the treetops.

Inside the building, there is a feeling of great size and of great hush, and also of considerable sums of money having been expended to obtain one with the other. Acres of tactfully carpeted floor stretch in all directions. Huge plants bloom in skylit atriums. Occasional men and women walk hither and yon. A group of Swedish tourists passes by, led by a guide, on the way to the Network Operations Center: a huge cavern of a room, perhaps a hundred feet long, on one of whose walls is an enormous map of the United States and its surrounding oceans, with all the major long-distance trunk routes traced in lights; the map also shows the daily position of cable-laying vessels, and next to it is a huge electronic bulletin board displaying information about sections of the system which are experiencing malfunctions or overload.

Now Phil Shyposh, solid and genial as ever, arrives to lead the Ayer vice-presidents through a security checkpoint and then to his office, which they reach by walking down what should most certainly not be called a maze of corridors, since a great deal of design effort clearly went into its not appearing mazelike; and which, considering the corporate position of the incumbent, is surprisingly small (and is not at all unlike the N. W. Ayer offices of Pfiffner and Eversman). It appears, however, that Phil Shyposh is not really the *top*; Walt Cannon is the *top*. Phil Shyposh makes the day-to-day tactical decisions, but Walt Cannon makes strategy. And Walt Cannon gives client approval.

Somewhere upstairs, Walt Cannon awaits the deputation, but temporarily he is busy. Coffee is brought into Phil Shyposh's office. Fred McClafferty arrives. The Ayer people show Phil Shyposh the commercial: Shyposh sits behind his desk; George and Jerry sit on chairs in front of him; Fred works the TV-cassette machine at the side of the room.

Jerry says: "We reversed the yoga scene of the white girl and the baby. We wanted the baby going down while the girl was upside down. We might have to work on that some more. Also, we want to go still tighter on the hockey player at the end."

The commercial plays through in its allotted thirty seconds.

"Bryan Trottier looked good," says Phil Shyposh.

"I think he worked out very well," says Jerry. "But we have to go tighter before we go into the mortise."

George Eversman says: "I just love that music. You know, back home I sometimes sit watching those Coke commercials with my tongue hanging out, but I think we're doing every bit as well right here."

Jerry says: "Thanks, George. What hurts us is we have to throw out so much good stuff."

Now the phone rings on Shyposh's desk. Phil picks it up. "Shyposh here," he says. Then: "Yes, Walt." Then: "Ready when you are, Walt."

In the senior-executive area, the spaces are larger and the hush is more pronounced. Beige carpet everywhere. Dark wood furniture. Prints and drawings hanging on all the walls—there are over twelve hundred of them, in fact, in the entire building. Phil Shyposh walks ahead of the three Ayer men down a corridor so wide that it can scarcely be called a corridor; here and there in its broad expanse are large dark wood desks, and at them are women—not more than four or five in a space about eighty feet long—working as secretaries. An electronic beep-beep-beep can be heard approaching from another corridor, and shortly a robot mail cart, carrying piles of pre-sorted mail, stops at one of the desks, whereupon the secretary takes up a pile of letters, puts some others in a basket on the cart, and taps the rear of the machine, and off it beeps down the corridor.

J. Walton Cannon, vice-president in charge of public relations for AT&T Long Lines, is an affable, dark-haired man in his late forties, wearing a dark suit, a white shirt, and a striped necktie, who has the air of someone about to break into a laugh without actually ever getting around to it. His office is very large and very tasteful: a brown carpet; a large desk; a variety of comfortably upholstered chairs; a leather couch off to one side of the room, near a marble-topped table covered with magazines; the usual prints and plants. But perhaps more noticeable than the interior of the room (which has clearly been designed not to be much noticed) is the exterior: the view from the large picture window, which is as if from a tree house — an expanse of treetops and soft green New Jersey countryside.

Cannon greets the Ayer men, and they arrange themselves in chairs in front of his desk. Cannon sits behind his desk but swiveled sidewise toward a TV set.

This time Phil Shyposh does the honors with the cassette machine.

"Do you know how to work it, Phil?" says Walt.

"I think I do, Walt," says Phil.

A picture appears on the screen of the TV set: Paul Reed in top hat and tails. *Your audience is ready, so put on your dancin' shoes* . . . Now Tiffany Blake beaming and tapping. *Reach out, reach out and touch someone* . . . Back to Reed. His feet are tap-tap-tapping . . . *Reach out* . . . Now the white yoga girl. *And turn 'em upside down* . . . Now the black yoga girl. *When you have a great day, reach for the phone* . . . Now the cowboy, now the pretty equestrienne. *And share the occasion* . . . Now the Marine in the phone booth. *With people back home* . . . Now the barber, and Billy Longo in the barber chair. *Reach out* . . . Now the toothless little boy, now Bryan Trottier in the locker room, now the toothless boy again. *And touch a winning smile!* Trottier's arm upraised, Trottier's smile!

Cannon is silent.

Jerry says: "Walt, there are still several things we want to do here. We want to tighten up at the end. When it goes into the mortise, we want to have it tight. Then, with the Marine and the barber, we're going to put a move on them, we're going to drift in."

Walt says: "How's the color?"

Jerry says: "The color adjustment still needs to be done."

Walt says: "It seems a bit heavy on the red."

George says: "The red will be taken care of. Isn't that right, Jerry?"

Jerry says: "Yes, we're already planning to do something about the red."

Walt says: "I thought it was too red."

Fred McClafferty says: "It was very red."

Jerry says: "I agree. We're planning on fixing the red."

George says: "Walt, mind you, this is without the opticals. They still have to do some things — go tighter on the hockey player . . ."

Jerry says: "Drift in on the barber . . ."

Walt says: "Well, it's fine."

Phil Shyposh says: "It has some very exciting moments."

Walt says: "It's fine. When do we air?"

Fred says: "I think we have some slots for it around the third week in July."

Walt says: "Well, O.K. Just try to lighten up on the red."

On their way out of the Long Lines building, as the Ayer men head for their separate cars, George Eversman says to Jerry: "That was some really beautiful stuff. It really gave me a tingle."

Jerry says: "Well, it's been a long haul."

George says: "And let me till you this: Coca-Cola never did anything better. *Never.*"

The Première

On the night of July 27, Johnny Carson is chatting on *The Tonight Show* with Roscoe Tanner, the tennis player from Lookout Mountain, Tennessee, who has just lost a close five-set Wimbledon final to Björn Borg.

Tanner says: "I didn't feel all that bad about losing."

Carson says: "You mean, just getting there was something."

Tanner says: "Look, I felt I played some of the best tennis I ever played in my life."

Carson says: "You had your whole ground game working."

Tanner says: "I had my ground game most of the time. The main thing, I think, was I had my concentration."

Carson says: "I can't ever concentrate enough. That's probably why I never reached the finals."

Tanner says: "You have to concentrate. Dennis Ralston taught me that."

Carson says: "He's been a good coach?"

Tanner says: "He's been a wonderful coach. He shows you the positive side of things. He's a very positive guy."

Carson says: "Somehow it seemed as if you were a lot looser on the court this year."

Tanner says: "This year, Wimbledon really lifted me up. I had a good feeling out there. Last year, I was real nervous. You know, the Queen and everyone being there."

Carson says: "My impression is that the Queen is not such a big tennis fan. My impression is that they sort of had to hustle the Queen over to the courts. I think we have some commercials coming up here. I mean, did you notice that when the Queen applauded, which wasn't often, she did it like this, with one hand—definitely restrained. All right, we have some commercials and then we'll be back."

At 11:48:00, there is a commercial for Clairol Herbal Essence shampoo, showing a pretty girl walking across a lawn, with long closeups on the pretty girl's face and hair as she turns her head this way and that, and then looks at the camera and says: "You're gonna swear, you got more hair!"

At 11:48:30, there is a commercial for the Volkswagen Rabbit, showing a man driving down the road while an offscreen voice asks: "Why are you driving a Rabbit?" and then the man in the car says: "Because it has more head room than my Rolls-Royce," and the car pulls up to a hotel and the voice asks: "Is that such a big deal?" and the man in the car gets out—a giant of a man—and says: "It is if you're Wilt Chamberlain."

At 11:49:00, Paul Reed appears, telephone in hand, tapping his shoes to the music, while a voice sings, "Your audience is ready, so put on your dancin' shoes . . ." Then the little girl in the red-white-and-blue dress appears, then the white yoga girl upside down, with the baby, then the black yoga girl, then the cowboy, then the pretty equestrienne, then the young Marine in the phone booth, then the barber and his customer, then the little kid, then the hockey player, then his little kid again, grinning without teeth, then the hockey player again, arm waving, grinning, also without teeth, big smile, while the music concludes and a voice announces, "Reach out and touch someone far away. Give 'em a call." And the logo of the Telephone Company's bell appears just below the hockey player.

At 11:49:30, there is a commercial for a car company, showing three men standing in a showroom full of cars. One of the men talks about the spectacular values that the cars in the showroom represent. Then the three men walk to different corners of the showroom and wave to the camera.

At 11:50:00, Johnny Carson reappears, still talking to Roscoe Tanner.

Tanner says: "Well, if you're talking about satisfaction, every time you take Borg to five sets you feel satisfied."

Carson says: "No regrets?"

Tanner says: "I don't know about regrets, but I feel satisfied."

Coda

Jerry Pfiffner, dressed in bluejeans and sports shirt but now barefoot, stands in the middle of his living room watching the TV set, where Johnny Carson and Roscoe Tanner are about to demonstrate serving tennis balls into an electrical timing device.

"I thought it was very good," his wife says.

"Yes, it was nice," Jerry says.

"It was more than nice," she says. "It has a lot of style. And terrific music."

"I agree," says Jerry. "I think it came out just about right."

The phone on the desk rings, and he picks it up. "Hello, Gaston," he says. "Yes, we were just watching it." Then: "I think it looks pretty good. Everything but the color. . . . No, the red is fine, but we lost a lot of the color in the rodeo scene . . . No, the equestrienne was good. We picked up color in that one. Just the rodeo, really. . . . Yes, O.K. Well, see you Monday. . . . No, I guess I'm going to take the week off."

After Jerry hangs up the phone, his wife says: "The color seemed fine. Besides, if it was a bit off, nobody will notice."

Jerry says: "They'll notice."

His wife says: "Not in thirty seconds."

Jerry says: "In thirty seconds, everybody notices *everything*."

QUESTIONS

1. What does this excerpt tell you about television and advertising that you did not know? Is there anything here that surprises you?

2. How would you characterize Arlen's point of view in this selection? Does he have an opinion about this process or is he simply recording the objective facts as they occur?

3. In the section titled The Première, Arlen presents us with the seemingly unrelated conversation of Johnny Carson and the tennis player Roscoe Tanner. Why does he do this? What does this dialogue contribute to his overall narrative?

4. Arlen's book is structured as a series of extremely short chapters, three of which are given here. Why do you think he chose to construct his book in this fashion? What does this structure contribute to the story he is trying to tell? How does this structure affect his message?

5. In a piece similar to Arlen's, describe a project in which you have participated.

• • • • •

LIVING LIKE WEASELS

Annie Dillard

Annie Dillard's first book, Pilgrim at Tinker Creek *(1984), established her as one of the foremost contemporary nature writers and won her a Pulitzer Prize. Like Thoreau, she is a special kind of nature writer, finding nature informative and uplifting, a source of meditation and insight. This essay on weasels is taken from her 1982 book* Teaching a Stone to Talk: Expeditions and Encounters.

A WEASEL is wild. Who knows what he thinks? He sleeps in his underground den, his tail draped over his nose. Sometimes he lives in his den for two days without leaving. Outside, he stalks rabbits, mice, muskrats, and birds, killing more bodies than he can eat warm, and often dragging the carcasses home. Obedient to instinct, he bites his prey at the neck, either splitting the jugular vein at the throat or crunching the brain at the base of the skull, and he does not let go. One naturalist refused to kill a weasel who was socketed into his hand deeply as a rattlesnake. The man could in no way pry the tiny weasel off, and he had to walk half a mile to water, the weasel dangling from his palm, and soak him off like a stubborn label.

And once, says Ernest Thompson Seton — once, a man shot an eagle out of the sky. He examined the eagle and found the dry skull of a weasel fixed by the jaws to his throat. The supposition is that the eagle had pounced on the weasel and the weasel swiveled and bit as instinct taught him, tooth to neck, and nearly won. I would like to have seen that eagle from the air a few weeks or months before he was shot: was the whole weasel still attached to his feathered throat, a fur pendant? Or did the eagle eat what he could reach, gutting the living weasel with his talons before his breast, bending his beak, cleaning the beautiful airborne bones?

I have been reading about weasels because I saw one last week. I startled a weasel who startled me, and we exchanged a long glance.

Twenty minutes from my house, through the woods by the quarry and across the highway, is Hollins Pond, a remarkable piece of shallowness, where I like to go at sunset and sit on a tree trunk. Hollins Pond is also called Murray's Pond; it covers two acres of bottomland near Tinker Creek with six inches of water and six thousand lily pads. In winter, brown-and-white steers stand in the middle of it, merely dampening their hooves; from the distant shore they look like miracle itself, complete with miracle's nonchalance. Now, in summer, the steers are gone. The water lilies have blossomed and spread to a green horizontal plane that is terra firma to plodding blackbirds, and tremulous ceiling to black leeches, crayfish, and carp.

This is, mind you, suburbia. It is a five-minute walk in three directions to rows of houses, though none is visible here. There's a 55 mph highway at one end of the pond, and a nesting pair of wood ducks at the other. Under every bush is a muskrat hole or a beer can. The far end is an alternating series of fields and woods, fields and woods, threaded everywhere with motorcycle tracks — in whose bare clay wild turtles lay eggs.

So. I had crossed the highway, stepped over two low barbed-wire fences, and traced the motorcycle path in all gratitude through the wild rose and poison ivy of the pond's shoreline up into high grassy fields. Then I cut down through the woods to the mossy fallen tree where I sit. This tree is excellent. It makes a dry, upholstered bench at the upper, marshy end of the pond, a plush jetty raised from the thorny shore between a shallow blue body of water and a deep blue body of sky.

The sun had just set. I was relaxed on the tree trunk, ensconced in the lap of lichen, watching the lily pads at my feet tremble and part dreamily over the thrusting path of a carp. A yellow bird appeared to my right and flew behind me. It caught my eye; I swiveled around — and the next instant, inexplicably, I was looking down at a weasel, who was looking up at me.

Weasel! I'd never seen one wild before. He was ten inches long, thin as a curve, a muscled ribbon, brown as fruitwood, soft-furred, alert. His face was fierce, small and pointed as a lizard's; he would have made a good arrowhead. There was just a dot of chin, maybe two brown hairs' worth, and then the pure white fur began that spread down his underside. He had two black eyes I didn't see, any more than you see a window.

The weasel was stunned into stillness as he was emerging from beneath an enormous shaggy wild rose bush four feet away. I was stunned into stillness twisted backward on the tree trunk. Our eyes locked, and someone threw away the key.

Our look was as if two lovers, or deadly enemies, met unexpectedly on an overgrown path when each had been thinking of something else: a clearing blow to the gut. It was also a bright blow to the brain, or a sudden beating of brains, with all the charge and intimate grate of rubbed balloons. It emptied our lungs. It felled the forest, moved the fields, and drained the pond; the world dismantled and tumbled into that black hole of eyes. If you and I looked at each other that way, our skulls would split and drop to our shoulders. But we don't. We keep our skulls. So.

He disappeared. This was only last week, and already, I don't remember what shattered the enchantment. I think I blinked, I think I retrieved my brain from the weasel's brain, and tried to memorize what I was seeing, and the weasel felt the yank of separation, the careening splashdown into real life and the urgent current of instinct. He vanished under the wild rose. I waited motionless, my mind suddenly full of data and my spirit with pleadings, but he didn't return.

Please do not tell me about "approach-avoidance conflicts." I tell you I've been in that weasel's brain for sixty seconds, and he was in mine. Brains are private places, muttering through unique and secret tapes — but the weasel and I both plugged into another tape simultaneously, for a sweet and shocking time. Can I help it if it was a blank?

What goes on in his brain the rest of the time? What does a weasel think about? He won't say. His journal is tracks in clay, a spray of feathers, mouse blood and bone: uncollected, unconnected, loose-leaf, and blown.

I would like to learn, or remember, how to live. I come to Hollins Pond not so much to learn how to live as, frankly, to forget about it. That is, I don't think I can learn from a wild animal how to live in particular — shall I suck warm blood, hold my tail high, walk with my footprints precisely over the prints of my hands? — but I might learn something of mindlessness, something of the purity of living in the physical senses and the dignity of living without bias or motive. The weasel lives in necessity and we live in choice, hating necessity and dying at the last ignobly in its talons. I would like to live as I should, as the weasel lives as he should. And I suspect that for me the way is like the weasel's: open to time and death painlessly, noticing everything, remembering nothing, choosing the given with a fierce and pointed will.

I missed my chance. I should have gone for the throat. I should have lunged for that streak of white under the weasel's chin and held on, held on through mud and into the wild rose, held on for a dearer life. We could live under the wild rose wild as weasels, mute and uncomprehending. I could very calmly go wild. I could live two days in the den, curled, leaning on mouse fur, sniffing bird bones, blinking, licking, breathing musk, my hair tangled in the roots of grasses. Down is a good place to go, where the mind is single. Down is out, out of your ever-loving mind and back to your careless senses. I remember muteness as a prolonged and giddy fast, where every moment is a feast of utterance received. Time and events are merely poured, unremarked, and ingested directly, like blood pulsed into my gut through a jugular vein. Could two live that way? Could two live under the wild rose, and explore by the pond, so that the smooth mind of each is as everywhere present to the other, and as received and as unchallenged, as falling snow?

We could, you know. We can live any way we want. People take vows of poverty, chastity, and obedience — even of silence — by choice. The thing is to stalk your calling in a certain skilled and supple way, to locate the most tender and live spot and plug into that pulse. This is yielding, not fighting. A weasel doesn't "attack" anything; a weasel lives as he's meant to, yielding at every moment to the perfect freedom of single necessity.

I think it would be well, and proper, and obedient, and pure, to grasp your one necessity and not let it go, to dangle from it limp wherever it takes you. Then even death, where you're going no matter how you live, cannot you part. Seize it and let it seize you up aloft even, till your eyes burn out and drop; let your musky flesh fall off in shreds, and let your very bones unhinge and scatter, loosened over fields, over fields and woods, lightly, thoughtless, from any height at all, from as high as eagles.

QUESTIONS

1. Dillard begins with two anecdotes about weasels. What point is she trying to make with these stories? How do these stories relate to the overall thrust of her thoughts?

2. When Annie Dillard sees her weasel she describes the encounter as though it were some metaphysical event. Can you understand the significance of this confrontation? Is the exact nature of this encounter inexpressible?

3. Seeing the weasel becomes a catalyst for Dillard, a stimulus that allows her to meditate on other things. What is her essay really about? When she says that we can all "live like weasels," what is she suggesting?

4. Weasels do not have a very positive reputation among most people. Calling someone a weasel is usually considered to be an insult. Is there a reason that Dillard specifically chose a weasel for the subject of her thoughts? Would another animal have done just as well? What animal might she have used?

5. Choose another animal, one you feel is particularly appropriate, for your own essay "Living Like . . . ."

•   •   •   •   •

THE CRIME OF THE TOOTH: DENTISTRY IN THE CHAIR

Peter Freundlich

Going to the dentist seems to be a universally dreaded necessity; no matter how many advances or painless techniques modern dentistry develops, sitting helplessly with one's mouth open while someone else probes this cavity with sharp instruments is not a happy way to spend a morning. Peter Freundlich, a former writer for CBS News, records his experience in this article that originally appeared in Harper's.

IF you are anything like me (and you must pray, of course, that you are not, and behave yourself besides, or your prayers will be denied), you will have experienced this. Just before eye-crack on a sunny day, warm light on the eyelids only, and already a trickle of pleasure, a soft worm in the ear, an electric tingle to which — still asleep — your muscles react, tightening in preparation for the flinging back of the covers and the springing up from the bed.

And then, awesome quick change of weather, there is a blackness across the sun and a dampness in the soul. You recollect, at the very moment of the leap from bed, with feet high and arms wide, that this is the day you go to the dentist.

How well, as Auden wrote, the Old Masters understood suffering. How the calamity happens on a mild golden day, and goes unseen by the happy and the hard at work. Auden was talking about the fall of Icarus, and so am I, for what else is the sudden recollection of an appointment with the dentist than a terrible chuteless fall from hopeful, sleepy midair, a melting — no, a vaporizing — of the wax wings of dream and a blind drop to the killing ground.

The truth on such a morning is that in half an hour you will be laid out on a morgue slab rigged to look like a reclining chair, with Dr. Kaliper's masked face filling your entire sky, and all eight of his hands at play in your mouth.

The knowledge that you are going to the dentist changes everything. Where a minute ago the sunlight seemed marmalade, richly spread across your window, now it is a mockery. It does not beckon, it jeers.

You would have jumped into your clothes before, all eager cinchings and zippings and knottings. Now you drag your leggings on, shrug mournfully into your shirt, fuss thick-fingered with every button. Your face in the mirror is smudged with worry.

It is not the local pain that causes dread, but the *greater* pain: the loss of speech, the pinioning, the drool tides coming in and washing out, the marooning of the brain. For two hours, the brain is Robinson Crusoe alone in the bone cup of the skull, peering out at faraway chrome implements and rubber-sheathed fingers and cotton cylinders red with blood, peering out but forbidden to signal for help.

Pushing open the lobby door, you descend three marble steps into the anteroom of the underworld. In place of Charon, there is only a buzzer to conduct you across this Styx; you are vacuumed into the starched white smile of the receptionist and, behind her, the starched white smile of the hygienist and, behind her, the green-tunic smile of Kaliper himself.

There is perfunctory talk. How are you today? You are fine. (Or would be, if not here.) And how is the practitioner this morning? He too is fine.

Meanwhile you have been settling yourself into Kaliper's astronaut's couch, in preparation for the launching.

Of course, he would not have you go uninformed into that good night. He explains at length his objectives and methods while showing you what looks to be the seating plan of a Greek amphitheater, two opposed semicircles with many Xs along the perimeters. These do not mark reserved seats but the sites of work to be done.

Kaliper continues to hold forth on such matters as roots and canals and crowns and tiaras and diadems. You pretend to follow it all, but in fact have already turned your attention inward, into your mouth, which is independently alive: All the little under-skin creatures — the stalks and cones and antlered antennae — are nervously atwit, snuffling, shuffling, pawing, like forest animals before a storm.

You have had the X-rays already. The lead blanket was laid on your chest and you were told to be still while that timid funnel-beaked behemoth with its triple-jointed metal neck poked its snout against your face. Though eyeless, the creature still managed an audible wink wherever it stopped tenderly to nuzzle. All that by which you are everywhere known to be you and not someone else — your entire exterior, your features, hair color, eye color, skin color, marks commemorating your birth and child-hood diseases — the funnel-beaked thing sees not at all. It is blind except to your insides.

Now Dr. Kaliper stands by the X-ray lightbox and points to the snapshots: a valley to be filled, a ridge to be rounded off, a cave in which something rotten lurks. Kaliper will turn spelunker, go into the cave and yank out the rot. You continue to nod sagely; the underskin animals are braying wildly now.

He asks, rhetorically, if you are ready. Then, pressing a button that makes the machinery of the chair moan, he causes your head to be lowered. You turn pink as blood sloshes down from your feet and legs.

They must be taught in school not to let their patients see the needles and the instruments coming. Kaliper manages the sleight of hand nicely. His forearm grazing your nose, he takes the novocaine-filled syringe from the hygienist. Then he brings the thing down along your jawline, too low for your radar to pick up. Finally, he has it under your chin, then up, aimed, and ready. It is now too close for you to focus on; you have only an impression — an orange cylinder and a glint.

Hold on just a bit, he says, *you're going to feel this.*

There is a small intrusion into your gum, a cold, sharp pinch, as if a steel no-see-um had landed there. Then the midge grows suddenly much heavier, sinking in. It is Kaliper, of course, his arm behind the work now.

Okay, we'll give that a minute or two to numb you up.

It seems that your upper lip is growing not numb but far and thick, as if swollen with liquid. It is now out beyond the tip of your nose, billowing in a spinnaker curve until finally it is so big and heavy that it hangs down even over your lower lip.

Starting to work?

You mutter as much of a *yeah* as you can with your lower lip alone, the upper answering to no authority now.

Kaliper is ready to begin.

And your brain, crazy Crusoe, settles in a hunker on a bone ridge.

This, unless you ask for fumes, is one of the few things in life from which you cannot turn away. It is an event that happens *on* you, *in* you: a subcutaneous circus, a riot under your nose.

And only your brain, that ball bearing in its bone cup, only your brain is free. Under any other circumstances, you would flee before these chrome threats. All your greater muscles would clench and work — legs wildly pumping, arms wildly swinging — and you'd be gone in a flash from a masked mugger like Kaliper. But now all your retreats must be microscopic, tics and twitches and tremors only. All you can do, on a large scale, is think.

And you do. What *don't* you think?

This is what a road would feel, if it were sentient, when the yellow trucks of early spring bring burly armed men and pots of tar to repair frost heaves. Just so, you are being worked on: jackhammered, steam-chiseled, bulldozed.

You yourself, having become a structure, are sentient in a different way now. You feel a pounding in your joists, as if the dentist were a carpenter working in your attic. The thudding he causes with his little mallets and mauls is conducted down through your studs, raising a pulse to rival the heart's.

Why was Shakespeare silent on this subject? Hath not a Jew teeth? Does he not cry out to high heaven when, molar-pierced, he feels the iron worm in the velvet hand, and hears the keening of his own resisting bone?

There are no dentists in nature. Animals doctor themselves and each other, probing and licking and tamping on wounds mud- and spittle-bound grass. But no animal puts on rubber gloves and . . .

Wider. Open wider.

Wider? The corners of your mouth have already met at the back of your head, and Dr. Kaliper blandly asks for easier access. To what?

How fine to feel your bronchioles warmed by his lamp, and the fresh breeze from his nostrils rippling your intestines.

Turn toward me.

Only lovemaking happens at this range: Arm's length is otherwise the closest we come, but this is finger's length, and finger's width, and less.

What confidence these men must have to work so very close to hostile observers, offering themselves for microscopic inspection, aware as they must be that their every pore looks like a dreadful hole from this vantage point. Look: the tapioca surface of the skin, the thick upstanding face-hair bristles grown out from that cheesy plain like cacti, like the legs of half-buried scorpions struggling to right themselves.

But then this is the scale at which they work (and tit for tat): they, nose up against your breath, digging with microshovels in the topsoil of your tooth-rot, and you, threatened by their follicles.

Our mouths should be full of horn, sharp wedges of antler, or tortoise shell, grinders that grow like fingernails trimmed weekly to a new, fresh edge.

There is music playing, yes. *Music*: old tunes made toothless by accordions and violas and clarinets. Soothing music, Kaliper must think it is. But it is not music enough to catch the ear, or really to engage the brain. It is just a mask for the drill sounds, and ineffective even at that. The drill plays an octave higher than any instrument on the radio.

The body rejects foreign objects and Kaliper is most foreign. You gag and guff and hack, your throat-flap lashed by drill-storm, a minuscule typhoon of spray.

You have down your gullet already air-jets and water-jets and a teeny goddamn bilge pump on a metal hook. Now comes a vacuum cleaner on a stick put in your mouth to slurp up more of your juices.

Hold on now. Be still a moment.

You would laugh sardonically, if you could. Snake-fingered Gorgon Kaliper, who has long since turned you to stone, now commands stillness.

Through your mouth he is drilling holes in your wallet.

Last night, you remember now, you had a dream. You were eating money. Your own money, green and fibrous, vegetal. Next to you was an insurance-looking man. He threw coins into your mouth, a nickel for every dollar of your own. Looking up beyond him, you saw a vast herd of big-eyed dentists, all of them placidly grazing in a field of rippling sawbucks.

What is the prayer for surcease from dentistry?

You remember your daughter's first tooth, and the joy: she in that scootling thing she had, a sling seat hung in a wheeled metal frame with a fore-mounted tray, and one day in the wide smile, a glint of white in the upper pink ridge. A toof! A toof! Lookit, lookit, clap clap clap. The sight made you break into ecstatic Eddie Cantorish dumbshow, palms pushed repeatedly flat together, fingers straight up, just below the chin. A toof, a toof, welcome to toddler's estate.

And welcome to all this.

Dentists are our alchemists, transmuting rot into gold.

There was an Ancient Dentist, and he drilleth one of three. Then he drilleth the other two. Then he billeth.

There is no fetish involving teeth. Men secretly adore feet and buttocks and thighs and axillae. But Krafft-Ebing never lapsed into Latin over teeth. Some aborigines wear teeth around their necks: they ought to wear dentists — little shriveled sun-dried dentists.

It is high tide in your mouth now. Your nose is Cape Horn, and, God help you, Kaliper means to round it, to point his chrome prow toward the rocky promontories of your teeth, to find safe passage between them. He means to land somewhere under your uvula.

Peace, peace. You are here for a reason and you must hug close the promise, which is that you will have a smile of tourist-attraction quality, a smile of such perfection and brilliance that omnibuses bursting with camera-strewn pilgrims will pull up at your door, Japanese, Germans, Italians, all with their heads cocked attentively toward their bull-horned tour-guides who, in their respective languages, will tell the tale of your teeth, will put your teeth in their proper dento-historical contexts, who will make plain to the milling bell-shaped women and the big-nosed men that, in your mouth, they will be seeing the dental Sistine ceiling, the periodontal Pietà, the bridgework Winged Victory of Samothrace.

You will feel the long lenses and the moist eyes trained upon you, and you will favor the pilgrims with a glimpse of the fabled teeth. But slowly, gradually, so as not literally to knock them arse over teakettle with the splendor of the sight. You will be impoverished, yes, but with God's own smile.

The Brits will not come, of course, they of the gnarled yellow choppers, over-lapped, jagged. A people of deplorable dental cavalierness, the Brits would rather invest their money in Savile Row tailoring and Harley Street doctoring and Bentley motor cars and manor houses. A fine thing. The thirtieth Duke approaches, tall, fair-skinned, as richly veined about the nose and cheeks as Stilton cheese, in balmoral and balmacaan, walking stick at the ready; says hello and, beneath the grenadier's mus-tache, shows chiaroscuro smile, some teeth long and tending toward the spiral, some squat and striated, as rune-covered as river rocks. Of course he has money, having forsworn dentistry.

Why exactly does Kaliper wear a mask? Is it to hide his own teeth? Do they become, when he's working, black and pointed or blood-red and outward-curled, like the tips of Turkish slippers?

Kaliper is hot with enthusiasm now. His hands fly about the tray held by his mechanical butler, selecting picks and spears. Inside your mouth, your pulse must be visible again, a growing and shrinking of the veins. Kaliper construes this, you sup-pose, as a readiness to reach a dental climax, in tandem with him.

Nearly there, he says, *nearly there*.

How do they endure this, the famous? They must endure it with great regularity, for, as is well known, the teeth of the famous are not teeth at all. They are wonderful facsimiles, made by master technicians and implanted by master dentists. If Michel-angelo were alive today, he'd be carving teeth in Hollywood.

The drill sounds like a winch now, makes the sound the winch makes when, the mourners having turned to go, the coffin begins to be lowered. You feel pain, not in your teeth, but everywhere else — the small of your back, your legs, your neck, your shoulders, and especially your face because you've been holding your mouth scream-wide for so long.

Or you *were* holding your mouth open. Now it is stuffed, overstuffed, filled to cracking, with egg-beaters and chrome tricycles and socket wrenches and antique wristwatches, small prams, suits of armor, coffee-makers.

You think you feel the lower end of a ramp being placed on your tongue, and you think you hear, from a distance, the sound of a motor being cranked. Kaliper must be mounting an expedition into your interior, with fresh supplies loaded aboard a Land-Rover.

You gurgle.

You alright? Kaliper asks.

You gurgle again.

Good, he says.

Kaliper is maneuvering into position, for a trial fitting, the crown he has had made. It is a bit of porcelain-covered metal, very like a tooth. But it is not a tooth, and your flesh knows it.

You are given a mirror to see what Kaliper has wrought. And of course your eyes, stupid gelatinous organs, are fooled.

Looks good, you mumble.

And you mean it: the simulacrum *does* look good. But your tongue worries the thing, frets and pushes at it as would an animal at something dead. Your gum, the flesh most directly intruded upon, pulses, is offended. And there is an undulation in your cheek, a threadwide, millimeters-long surf—your cheek is offended on behalf of your gum.

Kaliper has emptied your mouth of his gear. His work now, a tightly controlled scratching, has an air of finality. You think he may be etching his name on the permanently installed crown. You will have *Kaliper fecit* inscribed on the dark side of the not-tooth, a joke to be appreciated someday by the coroner.

All done, he says.

And his assistant swings away an arm of the chair on which you have been marooned, so that you may stand.

Which you do, crowned now, and dizzy.

QUESTIONS

1. Freundlich begins with a reference to W. H. Auden's poem "Musée des Beaux Arts." If you are not familiar with this poem, look it up. How does this poem relate to the trip to the dentist that Freundlich describes?

2. Freundlich, in an obviously playful mood, compares the dentist chair to a "morgue slab," and suggests the dentist will have eight hands "at play in your mouth." What other descriptions and comparisons does he use to characterize his plight? What effect do these descriptions have on the overall tone of his essay?

3. Freundlich suggests that it is not specifically the pain that is upsetting for him, but the isolation one encounters in the chair, the fact that one sits immobile simply wondering about what is going on and reacting to the unexpected probings. Would you agree? Is this the essence of what makes a trip to the dentist uncomfortable for most of us?

4. Freundlich's essay is essentially humorous. Why? Can you imagine another point of view he might have taken? What would that essay have been like?

5. Have you ever had any of the thoughts Freundlich has while you were sitting in a dentist's chair? Is his experience in any sense "universal"? What other experiences can you think of that would be comparable to the one Freundlich describes?

UNCIVIL LIBERTIES

Calvin Trillin

This piece appeared as a column in The Nation, *a weekly political magazine with a decidedly liberal perspective. The author, Calvin Trillin, is a regular contributor, who has also written for* Time *and* The New Yorker. *Trillin's column was published shortly after the Iran-Contra hearings began to be televised regularly in 1987.*

AFTER only a week or so of having the soap operas pre-empted by Congressional hearings on the Iran arms sale scandal, thousands of soap opera fans called the networks to demand their regular programs back. I wasn't surprised. On *General Hospital* nobody takes the Fifth. Declining to answer a question may be perfectly supportable on constitutional grounds, but it sure doesn't do much for dramatic tension.

Occasionally, someone on a soap opera may respond to a question by saying something like, "I can't answer that question now, Mark, but someday I will, and I hope that when I do, you and Brenda will realize that what I did, I did for you, whatever your father and the public health authorities say." Usually, though, somebody on a soap opera who is asked a question answers it, often at great length ("Yes, Rob, I did realize that Bruce would someday learn of my combined face lift and sex change operation, but I thought I could buy time — time to heal the wounds Bruce had suffered after Brenda's cat was eaten, time to pull my own life together so that what happened on the bridge that night between Hilary and Bruce's father and that perfectly dreadful Airedale . . .").

In fact, television programming of all sorts is based on the assumption that anyone who is asked a question will answer it. If a tight end is asked by the sportscaster how it felt to grab that ball in the end zone with only thirty seconds left on the clock, he can be counted on to say, "It felt great, Tony." Even if he said, "The next sportscaster to ask me how it felt to do something is going to find out how it feels to eat a football," that would be an answer of sorts.

If a contestant on a game show is asked if he wants to stop now that he has won $1,400 or try for the super deluxe toaster oven that is valued at $3,200, he may hesitate for a moment to think it over ("Boy, a toaster oven with power steering and factory air is just what I've always wanted . . . on the other hand, with $1,400 I could pay off the dog-track debt and get that mob enforcer off my back . . . on the other hand, if I quit now that knockout blonde in the third row might think I'm a wimp . . ."), but he would never simply refuse to say.

If everybody got the idea that it was O.K. not to answer questions — if the dippy starlet on the talk show responded to a question about her love life by saying "none of your beeswax" — television could be crippled. Think of the letdown on a soap opera if Bruce Sutherland, the dashing but cash-short lawyer with the fatal auto accident and incestuous affair and severe acne in his past, asked Melissa Brent, the rich and extraordinarily attractive but left-handed young widow, if she was indeed the one with guilty knowledge of who ate Brenda's cat so that Todd and Kimberly's divorce case had to go into extra innings, or if she'll marry him instead, and she said, "I reluctantly inform you that, on the advice of my counsel, I must decline to answer your question, based on the rights afforded to me by the Fifth Amendment of the Constitution." If that happened, the voice heard over the theme music at the end of the show would have to say something like, "Will Melissa marry Bruce? Is it possible that Kimberly ate Brenda's cat? Tune in tomorrow, when we will not find out the answer to any of those questions."

All of this must be why Republican senators and even the White House people started calling for the witnesses to quit taking the Fifth. Those Republicans don't want a dog with a low rating on their hands. Oddly enough, I think the hearings will do pretty well against the soaps as soon as the witnesses start talking. The lives of some of those arms dealers the White House dealt with sound pretty much like what happened on the bridge that night between Hilary and Bruce's father and that perfectly dreadful Airedale. A lot of the White House people, who say they didn't know about anything ever, could be taught to testify with the dramatic touch of one of those soap opera characters who acknowledges having been overwhelmed by the complications in his past — the character who says, "Oh, sure, if I had noticed that my wife had just left me, and Joey had burned the house down, and my business had failed, sure, I might have acted differently toward you, Kimberly, but I was so preoccupied with the question of who ate Brenda's cat . . ."

If the rest of the White House people decide not to answer questions, it would help, of course, if they did it more in the soap opera manner — something like, "I can't answer that question, but someday I will, and when I do I hope you'll realize that what I did, I did for you."

QUESTIONS

1. What is the specific situation Trillin is reacting to? How would you characterize his attitude and tone?
2. Trillin makes several points about the nature of contemporary television. Are his observations accurate? What do his remarks, if they are accurate, suggest about our culture?
3. *The Nation* is a political magazine, and Trillin is responding to public reaction to a political hearing. What political and social statement is Trillin making? Are his comments valid?
4. Trillin is writing for an audience that probably shares his political perspective. Would he have to change his remarks, his tone, his argument, if he were writing for a more middle of the road magazine such as *Newsweek*? How might he change his presentation to make it appeal to a more general audience?

RESPONSE TO THE GOVERNMENT

Nelson Mandela

The racial strife that has continued for decades in South Africa has made a legendary figure out of Nelson Mandela, the anti-Apartheid leader and organizer of the African National Congress. Mandela has been in trouble with the government since 1956, when he first was put on trial for treason. He was acquitted of these charges, but was later arrested and sentenced to five years in prison. Before completing this sentence Mandela was again charged with sabotage and sentenced to life in prison, where he stayed from 1962 until his release in 1990. In January 1985, the President of South Africa, P. W. Botha, offered to release Mandela from prison if Mandela in turn "unconditionally rejected violence as a political weapon." Mandela's response, delivered from Pollsmoor Prison, was the following statement.

I AM a member of the African National Congress. I have always been a member of the African National Congress and I will remain a member of the African National Congress until the day I die. Oliver Tambo is much more than a brother to me. He is my greatest friend and comrade for nearly fifty years. If there is any one amongst you who cherishes my freedom, Oliver Tambo cherishes it more, and I know that he would give his life to see me free. There is no difference between his views and mine.

I am surprised at the conditions that the government wants to impose on me. I am not a violent man. My colleagues and I wrote in 1952 to Malan asking for a round table conference to find a solution to the problems of our country, but that was ignored. When Strijdom was in power, we made the same offer. Again it was ignored. When Verwoerd was in power we asked for a national convention for all the people in South Africa to decide on their future. This, too, was in vain.

It was only then, when all other forms of resistance were no longer open to us, that we turned to armed struggle. Let Botha show that he is different to Malan, Strijdom and Verwoerd. Let him renounce violence. Let him say that he will dismantle apartheid. Let him unban the people's organisation, the African National Congress. Let him free all who have been imprisoned, banished or exiled for their opposition to apartheid. Let him guarantee free political activity so that people may decide who will govern them.

I cherish my own freedom dearly, but I care even more for your freedom. Too many have died since I went to prison. Too many have suffered for the love of freedom. I owe it to their widows, to their orphans, to their mothers and to their fathers who have grieved and wept for them. Not only I have suffered during these long, lonely, wasted years. I am not less life-loving than you are. But I cannot sell my birthright, nor am I prepared to sell the birthright of the people to be free. I am in prison as the representative of the people and of your organisation, the African National Congress, which was banned.

What freedom am I being offered while the organisation of the people remains banned? What freedom am I being offered when I may be arrested on a pass offence? What freedom am I being offered to live my life as a family with my dear wife who remains in banishment in Brandfort? What freedom am I being offered when I must ask for permission to live in an urban area? What freedom am I being offered when I need a stamp in my pass to seek work? What freedom am I being offered when my very South African citizenship is not respected?

Only free men can negotiate. Prisoners cannot enter into contracts. Herman Toivo ja Toivo, when freed, never gave any undertaking, nor was he called upon to do so.

I cannot and will not give any undertaking at a time when I and you, the people, are not free.

Your freedom and mine cannot be separated. I will return.

QUESTIONS

1. Mandela's response rejects Botha's offer of "freedom" on what grounds? Does his argument make sense?
2. How would you characterize Mandela's style? Is this style effective? How might you change it?
3. If you were the President of South Africa, and you wished to respond sincerely to Mandela's statement, what would you say? What argument could you make that would respect the sincerity of Mandela's position? Write your response to Mandela.

• • • • •

FREEDOM CHARTER

National Action Council of the Congress of the People, Johannesburg, South Africa

As the statements of Nelson Mandela indicate (p. 145), he is a member of the African National Congress, an anti-Apartheid organization that was banned in South Africa in 1960. Although the racial problems in South Africa have only recently been garnering headlines around the world, racial unrest has simmered there for decades. In 1955, for example, thousands of leaflets were distributed throughout South Africa calling the people together to a Congress of the People, a meeting at which a Freedom Charter, a statement not unlike our own Declaration of Independence, would be drafted. The following political document, which the ANC accepts as its position statement, is the result of that June 1955 Congress of the People.

Preamble

We, the people of South Africa, declare for all our country and the world to know:

That South Africa belongs to all who live in it, black and white, and that no government can justly claim authority unless it is based on the will of the people;

That our people have been robbed of their birthright to land, liberty and peace by a form of government founded on injustice and inequality;

That our country will never be prosperous or free until all our people live in brotherhood, enjoying equal rights and opportunities;

That only a democratic state, based on the will of all the people, can secure to all their birthright without distinction of colour, race, sex or belief;

And therefore, we, the people of South Africa, black and white, together — equals, countrymen and brothers — adopt this FREEDOM CHARTER. And we pledge ourselves to strive together, sparing nothing of our strength and courage, until the democratic changes here set out have been won.

The People Shall Govern!

Every man and woman shall have the right to vote for and stand as a candidate for all bodies which make laws.

All the people shall be entitled to take part in the administration of the country.

The rights of the people shall be the same regardless of race, colour or sex.

All bodies of minority rule, advisory boards, councils and authorities shall be replaced by democratic organs of self-government.

All National Groups Shall Have Equal Rights!

There shall be equal status in the bodies of state, in the courts, and in the schools for all national groups and races;

All people shall have equal rights to use their own languages and to develop their own folk culture and customs;

All national groups shall be protected by law against insults to their race and national pride;

The preaching and practice of national, race or colour discrimination and contempt shall be a punishable crime;

All apartheid laws and practices shall be set aside.

The People Shall Share in the Country's Wealth!

The national wealth of our country, the heritage of all South Africans, shall be restored to the people;

The mineral wealth beneath the soil, the banks and monopoly industry shall be transferred to the ownership of the people as a whole;

All other industries and trade shall be controlled to assist the well-being of the people;

All people shall have equal rights to trade where they choose, to manufacture and to enter all trades, crafts and professions.

The Land Shall Be Shared among Those Who Work It!

Restriction of land ownership on a racial basis shall be ended, and all the land re-divided amongst those who work it, to banish famine and land hunger;

The state shall help the peasants with implements, seed, tractors and dams to save the soil and assist the tillers;

Freedom of movement shall be guaranteed to all who work on the land;

All shall have the right to occupy land wherever they choose;

People shall not be robbed of their cattle, and forced labour and farm prisons shall be abolished.

All Shall Be Equal before The Law!

No one shall be imprisoned, deported or restricted without a fair trial;

No one shall be condemned by the order of any Government official;

The courts shall be representative of all the people;

Imprisonment shall be only for serious crimes against the people, and shall aim at re-education, not vengeance;

The police force and army shall be open to all on an equal basis and shall be the helpers and protectors of the people;

All laws which discriminate on grounds of race, colour or belief shall be repealed.

All Shall Enjoy Equal Human Rights!

The law shall guarantee to all their right to speak, to organise, to meet together, to publish, to preach, to worship and to educate their children;

The privacy of the house from police raids shall be protected by law;

All shall be free to travel without restriction from countryside to town, from province to province, and from South Africa abroad;

Pass laws, permits and all other laws restricting these freedoms shall be abolished.

There Shall Be Work and Security!

All who work shall be free to form trade unions, to elect their officers and to make wage agreements with their employers;

The state shall recognise the right and duty of all to work; and to draw full unemployment benefits;

Men and women of all races shall receive equal pay for equal work;

There shall be a forty-hour working week, a national minimum wage, paid annual leave, and sick leave for all workers, and maternity leave on full pay for all working mothers;

Miners, domestic workers, farm workers and civil servants shall have the same rights as all others who work;

Child labour, compound labour, the tot system and contract labour shall be abolished.

The Doors of Learning and of Culture Shall Be Opened!

The government shall discover, develop and encourage national talent for the enhancement of our cultural life;

All the cultural treasures of mankind shall be open to all, by free exchange of books, ideas and contact with other lands;

The aim of education shall be to teach the youth to love their people and their culture, to honour human brotherhood, liberty and peace;

Education shall be free, compulsory, universal and equal for all children;

Higher education and technical training shall be opened to all by means of state allowances and scholarships awarded on the basis of merit;

Adult illiteracy shall be ended by a mass state education plan;

Teachers shall have all the rights of other citizens;

The colour bar in cultural life, in sport and in education shall be abolished.

There Shall Be Houses, Security and Comfort!

All people shall have the right to live where they choose, to be decently housed, and to bring up their families in comfort and security;

Unused housing space to be made available to the people;

Rent and prices shall be lowered, food plentiful and no one shall go hungry;

A preventive health scheme shall be run by the state;

Free medical care and hospitalisation shall be provided for all, with special care for mothers and young children;

Slums shall be demolished, and new suburbs built where all have transport, roads, lighting, playing fields, crèches and social centres;

The aged, the ophans, the disabled and the sick shall be cared for by the state;

Rest, leisure and recreation shall be the right of all;

Fenced locations and ghettos shall be abolished, and laws which break up families shall be repealed.

There Shall Be Peace and Friendship!

South Africa shall be a fully independent state, which respects the rights and sovereignty of all nations;

South Africa shall strive to maintain world peace and the settlement of all international disputes by negotiation — not war;

Peace and friendship amongst all our people shall be secured by upholding the equal rights, opportunities and status of all;

The people of the protectorates — Basutoland, Bechuanaland and Swaziland* — shall be free to decide for themselves their own future;

The right of all the peoples of Africa to independence and self-government shall be recognised, and shall be the basis of close co-operation.

Let all who love their people and their country now say, as we say here:
'THESE FREEDOMS WE WILL FIGHT FOR, SIDE BY SIDE, THROUGH-OUT OUR LIVES, UNTIL WE HAVE WON OUR LIBERTY.'

QUESTIONS

1. As a political statement, do the demands of the Freedom Charter seem reasonable and just? Are there any parts of this document that you personally find unacceptable? Why do you think this charter has been rejected by the government of South Africa?

2. How is this charter organized? What points are made first? Why? Are there ways it might be rearranged? How would you go about doing this?

3. Compare this document with our own political documents such as the Constitution or the Bill of Rights. What differences do you find? How do you account for these differences?

---

*Now the independent States of Lesotho, Botswana, and Swaziland.

4. There is a sense in which the Charter apparently attempts to mandate conditions no government could maintain — that food shall be plentiful, for example, and that no one shall go hungry. Is this charter too idealistic in some respects, too impractical? Why or why not?

• • • • •

THE GREENPEACE PHILOSOPHY

Greenpeace USA

Greenpeace is an ecological organization that does not believe in only talking about ecology. With their ship, the Rainbow Warrior, *for instance, members of Greenpeace have staged the nautical equivalent of protest marches and sitdown strikes by sailing into whaling grounds and placing themselves between the whaling boats and their endangered quarry. Greenpeace's efforts to save seals, whales, dolphins, and other threatened species by directly confronting those who are hunting and killing these animals has angered some and inspired others. The recent destruction of Greenpeace's* Rainbow Warrior *while it sat in a New Zealand harbor demonstrates just how strongly some foes of Greenpeace object to the organization's spirited passive resistance.*

THE
GREENPEACE PHILOSOPHY

*ℰcology teaches us that humankind
is not the center of life on the planet.
Ecology has taught us that the whole earth is part
of our "body" and that we must learn to respect it as
we respect ourselves. As we feel for ourselves,
we must feel for all forms of life —
the whales, the seals, the forests, the seas.
The tremendous beauty of ecological thought is
that it shows us a pathway back to an
understanding and an appreciation of life itself —
an understanding and appreciation that is
imperative to that very way of life.*

As with the whales and the seals,
life must be saved by non-violent confrontations
and by what the Quakers call "bearing witness."
A person bearing witness must accept
responsibility for being aware of an injustice.
That person may then choose to do something or stand
by, but he may not turn away in ignorance.
The Greenpeace ethic is not only to personally
bear witness to atrocities against life; it is to take
direct action to prevent them. While action must
be direct, it must also be non-violent.
We must obstruct a wrong without
offering personal violence to its perpetrators.
Our greatest strength must be life itself,
and the commitment to direct our own
lives to protect others.

GREENPEACE USA
1611 Connecticut Ave. N.W.
P.O. Box 3720, Washington, D.C. 20007

QUESTIONS

1. What parts of the Greenpeace philosphy suggest that the organization is not going to tolerate quietly what it perceives as injustice?

2. What is the difference between "direct action" and "violence"? Can direct action always be distinguished from violence? Does one lead to the other?

3. Some have argued that Greenpeace's philosophy is too militant, that it almost contradicts the ecological spirit the organization hopes to preserve. Do you agree? Why or why not?

4. If you were to draft your own ecological philosophy or charter, what would it be? Write up your principles in a format similar to those of Greenpeace.

REFLECTIONS OF POPE JOHN XXIII

Pope John XXIII

John XXIII, who was pope in the years 1958–63, has been both praised and blamed for the sweeping changes the Roman Catholic church underwent in the 1960s. Although it is true that Pope John XXIII initiated Vatican II, a pastoral council that reviewed and subsequently revised many longstanding Church policies, he himself did not live to oversee all of the changes Vatican II brought about; he died several years before this revolutionary council completed its work. Still, fairly or unfairly, Pope John XXIII is usually credited with "opening the windows" of the modern Catholic church to the breezes of change. In the following reflections, taken from a collection called Prayers and Devotions of Pope John XXIII, *he attempts to explain the role of the Church, and the role of Catholics, as he saw it.*

What Is a Saint?

What does the world know of that mysterious force which stirs in the depths of so many souls who seem unsatisfied in this world because they follow another light, an ideal which never fails to attract them?

In recent times, because of a fashion that seems to me a legitimate reaction from certain traditional methods of recounting the lives of holy men (methods according to which the saints were plucked by the hair and dragged out of the society in which they lived, and even out of themselves, to be turned into demi-Gods), we have, perhaps a little too eagerly, turned to the opposite excess and concentrated too much on the study of the human element in the saint, and by so doing have to some extent failed to give enough consideration to the work of grace.

What is a saint? Recent distortions have tended to spoil our conception of the saints; they have been tricked out and coloured with certain garish tints, which might perhaps be tolerated in a novel but which are out of place in the real world and in practical life.

To deny oneself at all times, to suppress, within oneself and in external show all that the world would deem worthy of praise, to guard in one's own heart the flame of a most pure love for God, far surpassing the frail affections of this world, to give all and sacrifice all for the good of others, and with humility and trust, in the love of God and of one's fellow men, to obey the laws laid down by Providence, and follow the way which leads chosen souls to the fulfillment of their mission — and everyone has his own mission — this is holiness, and all holiness is but this.

We Are All Called to Be Saints

The daily anxious thought of the great importance, or rather the necessity, that the souls entrusted to our care should be directed to the purest sources of human and Christian perfection is always near to our heart. They should turn back to the most solid foundations of the spiritual life, for safe guidance in the ways of righteousness, evangelical charity and holiness. Yes, of holiness too, for we are all called to be saints.

Every one of us has heard, and still hears, ringing in his conscience, the command: "Climb higher"; higher, ever higher, until while we are still on this earth we can reach up to grasp the heavens, until we can join our saints, whether they be the venerable saints of old or the wonderful saints of modern times, who were our own contemporaries, and in whom our Mother the Church already rejoices.

The Divine Origin of Marriage

In jealously guarding the indissolubility of the bond of marriage and the sanctity of the "Great Sacrament," the Church is defending a law which is not only ecclesiastical and civil but above all natural and divine.

These two great and necessary principles, which the veil of passion and prejudice at times obscures so much that they are easily forgotten, are established, the one by natural law engraved indelibly on the human conscience, and the other by the divine law of our Lord Jesus Christ. So it is not a question of decrees and regulations which circumstances require and which succeeding generations may modify; it is a question of the divine will, of the inviolable order established by God himself to safeguard the first fundamental nucleus of civilized society. It is the primordial divine law, which in the fullness of time Christ himself restored to its original integrity, "but from the beginning it was not so" (Matt. 19. 8).

The Church does not defend class interests or obsolete customs. Her glorious hymn, her title of honour, is heard in the Lord's Prayer, Our Father: thy will be done, on earth as it is in heaven.

What she preaches and defends in this world is the will of God, in which will be founded the peace, serenity, and even the material welfare, of all his children.

Women's Work

There has been and still is much debate about this or that aspect of the advisability of women applying themselves to a given work or profession. It is necessary to consider the actual facts, which show that women are becoming more and more frequently employed, and more and more generally conscious of the need to undertake some activity which can make them financially independent and free from anxiety.

The problem interests us all, and especially parents, from the time when girls leave their childhood behind, and when the problems of existence and the urgent necessities of the family induce their parents to think of a source of profitable employment for them, or to prepare them by education for future professions and occupations.

But although the economic independence of the woman brings certain advantages, it also gives rise to many problems regarding her own fundamental mission in life, which is that of forming new creatures! Therefore new situations arise which urgently require solution and need preparation and a spirit of adaptability and self-denial.

Woman's Mission

A woman's professional occupation must take into account those particular characteristics with which her Creator has endowed her. It is true that the conditions of our life tend in practice to establish almost absolute equality between man and woman. Nevertheless, although the rightly proclaimed equality of rights must be acknowledged in all that pertains to her human person and dignity, in no way does it imply similarity of function. The Creator has given woman talents, inclinations and natural dispositions which are proper to her, and differ from those he has given to man; this means that he has also assigned to her a particular function. If we did not clearly recognize the diversity of the respective functions of man and woman and the ways in which they inevitably complement each other, we should be working against nature, and we should end by humiliating the woman and depriving her of the true foundation of her dignity.

. . . The special purpose to which the Creator has directed a woman's whole being is motherhood. This maternal vocation is so proper and natural to her that it is present and active even when she does not actually give birth to children.

We must therefore give the woman all necessary assistance in the choice of her occupation, and in the training and perfection of her own gifts, and to do this it is necessary that she should find in the exercise of her profession the means of constantly developing and expressing her maternal affections.

Finally, we must always bear in mind the special needs of the family, the principal centre of a woman's activities, in which her presence is indispensable.

The Church's Mission

The Church, continuing to bear witness to Jesus Christ, does not wish to divest man of any of his rights: she does not dispute his claim to his achievements or the merit of the efforts he has made. She wants to help him to rediscover himself and to recognize himself for what he is, to reach that fullness of knowledge and conviction which has at all times been desired by wise men, even by those who have not received divine revelation.

In this immense field of activity which opens before her the Church embraces all men with her motherly affection, and wishes to persuade them to accept the divine Christian message, which gives a sure direction to individual and social life.

This is the mission of the Church, catholic and apostolic, to re-unite men whom selfishness and disillusionment might keep apart, to show them how to pray, to bring them to contrition for their sins and to forgiveness, to feed them with the Eucharistic Bread, and to bind them together with the bonds of charity.

The Church does not claim to effect every day the miraculous transformation worked in the apostles and disciples at the first Pentecost. She does not claim this — but she works for it, and never ceases to pray to God for the repetition of this miracle.

She is not surprised to find that men do not immediately understand her language, that they are tempted to reduce to the small scale of their own lives and personal interests the perfect law of individual salvation and of social progress, and that some-times they slacken their pace. She continues to exhort, to implore and to encourage.

The Church teaches that there can be no discontinuity or break between the religious practice of the individual and the laws that govern human society.

As she has inherited the truth she wishes to enter every field; she prays God to grant her the grace of sanctifying all things in the domestic, civic and international order.

The Church in the Modern World

Nearly all contemporary writers are full of pessimism, and the rulers of this earth now confess their powerlessness to raise man to greater heights, or to create for him that realm of happiness and prosperity which he always so ardently desires.

The Catholic Church has never said she wishes to dispense men from the hard law of suffering and death. She has not tried to deceive them, or to drug them with the compassionate opium of illusion. Instead, she has always insisted that our life here is a pilgrimage, but she has taught her children to join in that song of hope which, in spite of all, is still heard in this world.

Man is now, as it were, bewildered by the scientific progress he has made and is at last aware that none of these conquests can bring him happiness. He sees the continual appearances and disappearances of all those who promised eternal youth and easy prosperity. It is therefore right and natural that the Church should raise her authoritative and persuasive voice, to offer all men the comfort of her doctrine, and of truly Christian brotherhood which prepares the splendour of the eternal day for which man was made.

Undaunted by the difficulties which her children are encountering, and which impede the service she wishes to render to truth, justice and love, still faithful to the orders of her divine Founder, she wishes to speak to men about him, about Christ Jesus as Master, Christ Jesus as Shepherd, and about Christ Jesus as victim and expiatory sacrifice for our redemption.

QUESTIONS

1. Even though Pope John XXIII has been seen as one who initiated great changes, many of his statements may seem old-fashioned, even repressive. Which of his points do you find objectionable? Why?

2. Needless to say, the pope often finds himself in a tough position, between doctrine he believes is correct and a world that seems ever to be in conflict with that doctrine. Which points does Pope John XXIII make well? What points do you find particularly convincing? How does he make these points convincing to you?

3. Pope John XXIII was frequently praised for his good nature and his benevolence. In his reflection on the Church's mission, he says that the Church "is not surprised to find that men do not immediately understand her language," an apparent acknowledgment of the fact that people may find Church doctrine hard to follow. What does this admission contribute to Pope John XXIII's message?

4. How would you characterize the persona who is speaking in these reflections? What role or image does he seem to be projecting?

5. Select one of Pope John's topics and write an essay that agrees or disagrees with his philosophy.

▼

Crafting Informative Prose

CONCERNS IN INFORMATIVE PROSE

Much more than expressive or persuasive writing, informative writing accepts as its goal making readers aware of people, places, issues, ideas, discoveries. This goal is simple, but also requires careful attention to details, shades of meaning in phrasing, and interpretation of facts. Although an expressive and emotional letter may chronicle a vacation and a persuasive proposal for a new shopping mall may present the physical characteristics of the construction site, their primary purposes are to accomplish something more than simply providing interesting and useful information. But the overriding duty of informative writing is to report facts, opinions, and ideas. Jefferson Morgan's "Traveling with Taste: Nashville," for example, discusses the range of restaurants from French cuisine to home-style cooking available to a visitor to Music City USA. And Bob Greene's article about a condom factory describes both the appearance and location of the place where Trojans are made. These authors do not expect their readers to attach great emotional or sentimental value to these subjects nor do they want to challenge overtly those readers' opinions about any issues related to the topics. In fact, both articles are particularly light in tone. Informative writing can certainly treat weighty issues, but the nature of informative writing is that a reader learns something, maybe something amusing, intriguing, helpful, or alarming; most important she picks up some information that was previously unknown. The specific shape of the informative writing you will do will be determined by your context and the relationship between reader, writer, and subject matter. Whatever you write — interview, history, definition, news release — what remains constant is your aim, the need to report information to a reader. The basic features of informative writing follow:

1. Reference to the world, to objective reality.
2. An emphasis on providing information, rather than on expressing the writer's beliefs or emotions or on changing a reader's mind.
3. A style that is levelheaded and rational, containing many references to verifiable facts.
4. A high degree of probability in all interpretations and analyses of data.

► Basic
Features of
Informative
Prose

As implied in the introduction of this section, the simple goal of informative writing is not always easy to achieve. As we have seen in Section II on expressive prose, language itself is interpretive, so words and sentences do not often behave as fair, unemotional transmitters of knowledge. Facts as well are usually very difficult to separate entirely from interpetations without losing some of their meaning and significance. Also, the basic notion of a controlling device for an article or essay such as a thesis or focus implies that the writer does some orchestrating and manipulating of the information. This sort of arranging is necessary to present the topic effectively to a reader who needs background information, linking of important facts and ideas, and a context to make the piece understandable.

So how it is possible to make writing, which is naturally emotive and persuasive, serve the purpose of an informative aim? It must be granted that although language can never be completely objective, it can be objective to a degree, and a writer can honestly attempt objectivity if she is sensitive to shades of meaning in words and the impact of tone and organization on the message. In this chapter we discuss issues in informative writing that, when ignored, can undermine a writer's attempt to inform, and when recognized and controlled can go a long way to establish the writer's fairness and authority in her writing.

A THESIS OR NOT?

Should there be a thesis controlling an informative essay, article, or news story? Usually we think of a *thesis* as a statement of the writer's opinion on the topic at hand. Because of this definition, the informative writer may see the thesis as subversive to her goal and creed of providing new information. However, a thesis can also be the general point she wants to make in the whole work, and the presence of a thesis does not automatically disqualify an article from having a primarily informative aim. Other options in informative writing are that the thesis can modulate into a *focus*, which is a statement of the general area of inquiry, or a *lead* sentence (mostly used in news writing), which is a summary statement of the most important facts in the story. The sort of controlling device a writer chooses should depend on at least two factors: (1) the degree to which the writer wants or needs to interpret the information for her reader, and (2) the kind of piece the writer is producing (for example, a news story will probably need a lead, while an encyclopedia article may only need a focusing statement). Comparing some thesis statements, focus sentences, and lead sentences will help us understand fully how each can be used in informative writing. Look at a thesis statement from Colin Turnbull's chapter about the tropical rain forests of the Belgian Congo, which begins his book *The Forest People*, an anthropological study of pygmies. Here is Turnbull's thesis for this chapter:

> The world of the forest is a closed, possessive world, hostile to all those who do not understand it.

This thesis is fully supported by evidence explaining the different attitudes of the villagers, who fear and avoid the forest, and the pygmies, who view it as a safe, enchanted home. How then does this thesis differ in substance from a persuasive or expressive thesis statement? Like any thesis, it states an opinion and is backed by arguments that lend it credence. The difference is in the basic aim of the entire chapter — Turnbull's desire to inform you about a topic he has carefully studied and about which he feels he can voice accurate generalizations. Turnbull is not merely expressing an opinion; his opinion is an expert's synthesis of research and unbiased thought. Furthermore, the thesis and chapter do not overtly attempt to change the reader's mind, but they sincerely set about to inform that reader. The distinction between a persuasive or expressive thesis and an informative one is often slight indeed. It is more useful, we believe, to consider your basic goals as a writer when phrasing a thesis. Ask yourself what your main purpose is. Remember, persuasion and self-expression are not usually absent in informative writing; they are simply de-emphasized.

It's much easier to see the distinctive flavor of informative writing when an article is controlled by a *focusing statement* or *heading*. A focus will supply a reader with a direction for the piece and with the limitations of the topic. For instance consider the focusing statement of Robin Marantz Henig's article "The Big Sneeze: New Advances in Treating Allergies" (p. 250):

> But now some recent medical advances may be changing the outlook for allergy sufferers.

There is hardly a forceful opinion or interpretation in this remark. Mostly the writer has signalled to the reader that a discussion of new drugs and treatments for allergy sufferers will follow. She has set a direction and limited her article to a specific topic, and that's all she needs to do. Like Turnbull, Henig's focusing statements are clear and frank, without emotional coloring. Another example of a focusing statement can be found in the introduction to Cokie Roberts' news article that was broadcast on a National Public Radio (NPR) program (p. 266). Here, the program's host, Bob Edwards, succinctly introduces the topic and the reporter:

> In the first of a three-part series on Congress and the Constitution, NPR's Cokie Roberts examines the questions surrounding a second Constitutional Congress.

Roberts presents a variety of opinions on this subject, all of which are expressed by quotations from experts. Roberts compiles these viewpoints and arranges them in a coherent order for a listener. The focusing statement, however, has already provided the listener with a meaningful context for the piece.

Of course, the most obvious focus is a heading in an encyclopedia or dictionary. In *The Oxford Companion to Twentieth-Century Art*, the heading "Calder, Alexander (1898–1976)" (p. 204) prepares a reader for a brief factual biography of a significant American sculptor. Similarly, the chapter heading "Yacht Racing," in *The Rule Book: The Authoritative, Up-to-Date, Illustrated Guide to the Regulations, History, and Object of All Major Sports*, unceremoniously prepares a reader for a description of the sport that will include all of the elements mentioned in the book's subtitle. Note that the most important features of focusing statements and headings are that they limit the topic and give the reader a clear sense of the substance of the article, definition, or entry to come.

The third distinctive controlling device for informative writing is the *lead*. A lead is the sentence or first few sentences beginning a news story. Leads summarize the most important facts contained in the entire article and quite often leads quickly answer the five journalistic questions (of who, what, where, how, and when) for a reader who wants to get the gist of a story without reading the entire article. Take a look at Jon Nordheimer's two-sentence, two-paragraph lead to the *New York Times* article "To Neighbors of Shunned Family, AIDS Fear Outweighs Sympathy" (p. 224). Note also that the dateline "ARCADIA, Fla., Aug. 30" instantly answers two of the five questions.

> ARCADIA, Fla., Aug. 30 — The day after Clifford and Louise Ray decided to quit this town, citing the suspicious fire that gutted their house Friday night, those who fought to keep the couple's children out of school are saying the battle was not really against the Ray family. To them the enemy was AIDS, a dark and sinister force that threatened their own children, no matter how many authorities assured them there was no risk in casual contact among school children.

As news story leads go, this one is long. The length is necessary, however, to answer all five questions and to announce to the reader that the article is an interpretive one. It contains Nordheimer's evaluation of the mood and rationale of the Arcadia townspeople, trying to explain their reaction to the AIDS-infected Ray children. Some purists might contend that the reporter exceeds his mission of reporting just the facts of the matter, but the purpose here is to treat the story from a new, revealing angle. Most previous articles on this topic concentrate on the family and what happened to them; this article centers on the townspeople. Some interpretation, therefore, is essential to making the article meaningful. Nordheimer's lead answers all five journalistic questions by presenting the reporter's generalization about the townspeople. It also proposes an answer to the question of why — which goes beyond what is knowable by pure factual reporting. Because the article continues by supporting Nordheimer's generalization with many quotations from prominent townspeople and with details about the recent AIDS-related incidents, Nordheimer's lead is both acceptable and helpful for a reader. Thus, a lead provides a reader with an accurate summary of the major facts of a news story at the beginning of the article.

As you can see, the decision of whether to choose a *thesis*, *focus*, or *lead* to control a piece of writing should usually be determined by your choice of genre (essay, article, news story, definition). Unfortunately, this choice does not always tell you how objective or interpretive that controlling device needs to be. Informative writing may contain opinions, evaluations, and interpretations, but the subjective elements should be subservient to the writer's desire to inform and they should be supported by solid inferences from, or syntheses of, evidence.

OBJECTIVITY AND SUBJECTIVITY

The concepts of objectivity and subjectivity comprise the next important issue in informative writing. We have already seen how elusive pure objectivity in writing can be in our discussion of thesis statements. The problem rests ultimately in the richness of language and in its virtual inability to present a topic neutrally. Also, we must admit that many subjects suitable for informative treatment cannot be discussed in purely objective terms. The best examples of this type of subject in the readings are Colin Turnbull's explanation of attitudes that different groups of people have toward the tropical rain forest, and on Nordheimer's account of the mood and beliefs of the townspeople of Arcadia, Florida.

In writing that attempts to enumerate, explain, and clarify a person or group's moods, feelings, beliefs, and world views, strict objectivity becomes impossible, even undesirable. For sufficiently meaningful treatment of these intangible topics, a writer — even one with the most objective purpose — will have to draw on her own human compassion and empathy to be able to interpret the attitudes of others. Usually such a reference to the emotional and psychological sides of human behavior calls for the use of subjectively descriptive diction, organization, and emphasis. Before we look at specific factors affecting the objectivity and subjectivity of a piece of writing, let's clarify the meaning of these two polar terms by comparing synonyms of each adjective:

objective	*subjective*
neutral	partisan
unbiased	biased
impersonal	humane

continued

continued from page 161

objective	*subjective*
disinterested (not uninterested)	interested
dispassionate	compassionate
detached	sympathetic/empathetic
fair-minded	warm-hearted
rational/logical	moral/emotional/psychological
nonethical (not unethical)	ethical
factual	interpretive

The point of this comparison is not for you as an informative writer to adopt a rigorously objective stance toward your topic and writing, but for you to recognize that many topics for informative writing will compel you to make at least some use of the subjective side of your personality. The degree to which you do should depend on the amount of interpretation necessary to reveal the subjective facets of the topic at hand. For example, in his essay on the liver, Richard Selzer subjectively describes the damage that cirrhosis of the liver represents to the human body in order to impress the reader with the dangers of this disease. Please note that Selzer has already established a metaphor of the liver as a house:

> But there are limits [to what the liver can take]. Along comes that thousandth literary lunch and — Pow! the dreaded wrecking ball of cirrhosis is unslung. The roofs and walls of the hallways, complaining under their burden of excess fat, groan and buckle. Inflammation sets in, and whole roomfuls of liver cells implode and die, and in their place comes the scarring that twists and distorts the channels, pulling them into impossible angulation. Avalanches block the flow of bile and heavy tangles of fiber impede the absorption and secretion. . . . The obstructed bile, no longer able to flow down to the gut, backs up into the bloodstream to light up the skin and eye with the sickly lamp of jaundice. . . . The carnage spreads. The entire body is discommoded.

The subjective, emotive images of this description are essential to Selzer's point about the seriousness of cirrhosis. Yes, he exaggerates some, but we readers know he's doing it for a reason — to educate us about the disease in a memorable, scary, and even entertaining fashion. Therefore a *fair-minded* (probably an easier term to live with than *objective*) approach is desirable, but you should not view fair-mindedness as a demanding god that requires the sacrifice of all human feeling and personality in informative writing. Writing is an activity done by people for other people; we don't have to become machines to inform.

FACTORS AFFECTING THE FAIRNESS OF INFORMATIVE PROSE

The *denotation* and *connotation* of a word unite to form that word's complete meaning. The denotative meaning of a word is its factual reference to a thing, person, or idea, and the connotative meaning is the suggestive meaning, or flavor. A word may have either a positive or negative connotative meaning, and when a writer chooses a word that has a strong connotation, she may *slant*, or influence, the denotative meaning of a sentence or an article. A good example of the effect of connotation on meaning can be seen in Barbara Tuchman's discussion of the French colonization of Vietnam (then called Indochina) before World War II. Tuchman describes how the French administration was exploitative and demeaning to the Vietnamese people. Then she points out that the French named their system "la mission civilisatrice," a term which portrays their occupation as a kindly protectorship fostering modernization in the third world, which it certainly wasn't. Such historical examples remind us of the power of a name and of shades of meaning. As a writer, you should develop a sensitivity to shades of meaning and consider the difference in impact particular words may have. Remember that synonyms such as *bureaucrat*, *public servant*, and *government official* may all describe the same person, but only the last of these terms is neutral. Check the meaning of a word in usage notes in standard dictionaries or in a usage dictionary before you select an unfamiliar synonym.

The *selection* of which facts, examples, opinions, and quotations are included in an article also determines the fairness of the piece. As an informative writer, you should try to include all significant elements without giving preference to those that mirror your personal taste, and without purposefully "forgetting" those that offend you or ones with which you disagree. Selection becomes especially important when you write about a controversial or political topic; you have a responsibility to present all notable views on the topic. For instance, in her discussion of the problems surrounding the call for a second Constitutional Convention, Cokie Roberts carefully summarizes the views of all the interested parties: President Reagan; leading proponents and opponents, including those considered liberal and conservative; and scholars of American history and political science. It would not be enough for her to interview only those who brought the issue up; to give an unbiased account she seeks out and reports all relevant opinions and facts.

Placement of information within an article influences a reader's perception of the topic as well. The key to this element is to recognize that readers of essays are most likely to remember paragraphs they read first and last. When reading news stories, readers usually remember the lead and the next few paragraphs; often readers don't even finish news stories. So a biased writer can bury information in the middle paragraphs of an essay and at the ends of news articles, knowing that these sections are less likely to get attention. These spots are the equivalent of fine print in contracts. In his news story about the attitudes of Arcadia, Florida, citizens toward AIDS-infected Ray children, Jon Nordheimer had to be particularly careful to point out both the sympathetic and hostile attitudes early on in the article to avoid portraying Arcadia in a misleading light. He manages (and thus weights) the quotations he includes to show a range of attitudes. Rather than beginning with the most hostile, he first quotes a minister who preaches tolerance and charity; then he inserts the sentiments of a sympathetic but genuinely alarmed mother. After these two opinions a summary of past events and scientists' views follows. The most hostile view comes last; it's the opinion of two anonymous senior citizens. This arrangement, revealing the honest concerns and fears of prominent citizens first and ending with the more hostile, callous views, portrays a range of attitudes without enabling the reader immediately to adopt the misleading stereotypical view of all Arcadians as being uneducated hicks. Nordheimer delicately manipulates his information to prevent a reader either from seeing his report as biased or from thinking the worst of the townspeople.

Proportion of information within an article may have the same effect as placement by causing a reader to interpret certain facts, statements, or paragraphs as more or less important than others because of organization and the amount of coverage. Often the informative writer's role is to balance her discussion of a topic by allowing opposing sides equal time to present their arguments. A good illustration of careful balancing in organization can be found in Jefferson Morgan's discussion of Nashville cuisine. Even his thesis is phrased to reveal his fairness. It states very simply that "Nashville is a classic example of a city with a split personality." From this point in the article, Morgan gives equal time to the two sides which he delineates as one part Music City USA and one part the genteel yet contemporary South. With matching enthusiasm and epicurean delight he narrates his visits to dinettes and cafes featuring country cooking, to a legendary honky tonk that doesn't serve imported beer, and to a lavish, restored hotel whose menu is "extensive and innovative." Morgan's balanced approach lends his article credibility because he has tried to look objectively at the range of restaurants available and has sampled the most significant of each type.

Like proportion, *emphasis* in phrasing may influence meaning on the sentence level. Sometimes the meaning of a statement can be greatly altered by a change from a coordinating structure to a subordinating one and by a switch in the ordering of words. These variations on one of Morgan's sentences about the variety of Nashville show how a change in phrasing can change meaning too. The altered words are underlined.

Original sentence: Nashville is a city of museums and graceful public buildings set cheek by jowl with places such as the renovated Second Avenue districts of once-decaying warehouses along the Cumberland River.

Coordinating Constructions:

(a) Nashville can be a city of museums and graceful public buildings, or it can be one of places such as the renovated Second Avenue districts of once-decaying warehouses along the Cumberland River.

(b) Nashville is a city of such places as the renovated Second Avenue districts of once-decaying warehouses along the Cumberland River and also one of museums and graceful public buildings.

(c) Nashville is a city of museums and graceful public buildings, yet there are places like the renovated Second Avenue districts of once-decaying warehouses along the Cumberland River.

Subordinating Constructions:

(d) Although Nashville is a city of museums and graceful public buildings, they are set cheek by jowl with places such as the renovated Second Avenue districts of once-decaying warehouses along the Cumberland River.

(e) <u>Even though</u> Nashville is a city of places such as the renovated Second Avenue districts of once-decaying warehouses along the Cumberland River, <u>it is also one of</u> museums and graceful public buildings.

If you read these variations aloud while thinking about the subtle differences in emphasis, you can see how slight changes in phrasing alone can alter the meaning and tone of the entire sentence. Try a few additional alterations by substituting other connnecting words like *as well as*, *besides*, and *along with* into the coordinating sentences. Change the subordinating constructions around by substituting *despite the fact that* and *if*.

Clearly, Morgan's original sentence is structured to illustrate the variety of the city without making an additional comment on whether or not one of its areas dominates or influences the character of the other. As a writer sensitive to the effect of the implications of phrasing, he chooses the phrasing that provides his reader with the balance contained in his thesis. The point is not that an informative writer should avoid constructions that emphasize particular words and ideas, but that he should be aware of how easy it is to imply that one is more significant than another — without overtly stating that emphasis.

CHAPTER 9 ▶ Informative Prose: The Writer's View

STANCE OF THE WRITER

Should an informative writer use first or third person in an article? Can he present some topics humorously and others seriously? How much of his personality should the reader be able to pick up from an article, dictionary definition, news story, or historical narrative? All of these questions concern the stance of the writer in informative writing — the attitude a writer has toward his topic and audience. It includes his decision of how formal and self-effacing he should be and how much he feels he can develop a rapport with his readers.

Usually, we think of informative writing as being as dull and dry, like an accounting textbook. We assume that the writer must rope in and repress all hints of his own personality. Sometimes this approach is necessary, particularly in reference works like encyclopedias, handbooks, textbooks, and dictionaries. News writing often requires the reporter to eradicate all vestiges of personal opinion and preference from his writing. Nevertheless, many genres of very useful and important informative writing permit the writer to be a recognizable presence behind his words, if not a personality. These more interpretive, essay-type genres include magazine articles, eyewitness accounts, how-to books, and interpretive studies.

While he is drafting, an informative writer must decide whether he will write exclusively in third person, or if some first-person observations and statements of opinion will be acceptable and effective. *Third person* writing uses objects, ideas, people, and the third-person pronouns that refer to them (he, she, it, them) as the subjects of its sentences. Therefore a writer using third-person phrases all ideas as though they are expressed by an unself-conscious, self-effacing speaker; no first person pronouns (I, we) are used to imply that the writer is in any way personally involved in his subject matter. To understand the nature of third-person writing, look at the following sentences from some of the readings:

1. The three main types of engraving may be classified as (1) Relief or cameo, (2) Intaglio, and (3) Surface or planar.

2. Using sail power only, competitors aim to complete a prescribed course in the shortest time.

3. For all of its impressive armor, a hard disk isn't terribly different from the lowly floppy disk. Data is recorded as magnetic patterns written in circles around the hub of the disk.

4. In the past few months, Dr. Rebecca H. Buckley, chief of pediatric allergy and immunology at Duke University, and her colleagues have identified the compound responsible for IgE production as Interlukin IV.

5. In 1919 at the Versailles Peace Conference, Ho Chi Minh tried to present an appeal for Vietnamese independence but was turned away without being heard.

Please notice, however, that the use of third person does not rule out judgment and evaluation in writing; look closely at the effect of the adjectives "impressive" and "lowly" in sentence 3, and consider the effect of the final phrase of sentence 5, "but was turned away without being heard." Perhaps it is more accurate to say that third person creates an illusion of an impersonal approach for a reader. Third person allows the writer to shine a spotlight on the topic and keep out of the limelight himself, but clearly the connotative power of language allows that same writer to control the effect of his prose.

On the other hand, writing that uses *first-person* pronouns naturally allows a degree of personal involvement on the writer's part. Often this touch of personality is accompanied by the writer's expert opinion and advice about the topic, which may be about the best information to which a reader can gain access. First person also has the appeal of a personal narrative while it presents factual information in an interesting way.

A good example of the expert's use of first person as a vehicle for giving advice can be found in Bob Cerullo's article about how to fix electrical problems in automobiles. The first section of his article is an anecdote about how he usually solves short circuits and current drains. In that section he explains to his customer, and to his reader, that "The key to success in electrical repairs is never to assume anything," a valuable tip to those of us who might otherwise presume we need to replace the battery no matter what goes wrong. Furthermore, the anecdote vicariously places the reader in the customer's situation and teaches him how to best approach a similar problem, possibly before it happens.

Fred H. Harrington's account of his research on wolf cries in "The Man Who Cries Wolf" demonstrates the role that a first-person point of view can play in attracting a reader to an article about research in a specialized field. Harrington wisely begins his article with an fascinating description of his nightly research ritual:

The winter night was perfect for howling. The air was cold and motionless. Light, fluffy snow blanketed the ground, cushioning my steps as I edged closer to the wolf pack. Best of all, a full moon hung in the clear, black sky, illuminating my way and perhaps stirring a few primordial howls within the wolves. Soon I came across wolf tracks that crossed the road and headed toward a spruce bog. I tried to follow, but at every third step I broke through the crust and was left floundering midthigh in powdery snow. I stopped trying to walk, set my microphone on its tripod, and switched on my tape recorder. Then I howled.

This first paragraph sets the scene. It provides a visual, eerie picture of the Superior National Forest in Michigan where Harrington researched wolves. It shows us the ethologist's difficulty in gaining data and draws us into the substance of the article. Yet much of the suspense and humor of the paragraph is created by the first-person observation and narrative; we become immediately fascinated by Harrington's singular and slightly silly experience imitating wolves. Used in this way, a first-person point of view lends informative writing some of the emotion and allure of expressive writing, but it also functions to establish the author as an expert who has individually researched his topic.

A writer's decision of whether he should adopt first- or third-person point of view should be determined by (a) the kind of piece he wants to produce (e.g. encyclopedia article, essay, advice column), (b) the extent of the writer's personal experience and first-hand knowledge about the topic, and (c) the response he wants from his reader. Again we find that informative prose is a balancing of the primary aim to present information with the need to include and exclude the expressive and persuasive aspects of all writing in accordance with the demands of fair-mindedness and appeal to a reader.

A significant distinguishing feature of informative writing is the author's need to either become an expert or present the views of experts. Informative prose gains credibility from the knowledge of its writer. Often, informative articles are written by people who have conducted research and are well qualified to report their findings to an audience. Peter Norton and Robert Jourdain, the authors of *The Hard Disk Companion*, are good examples. They are computer experts who can clearly explain the workings of hard disks and offer valuable opinions about what kind of hard disk to buy and how to maintain and organize information on one.

If you are not already an expert on your topic, you have two options: (1) become as well versed as possible about your topic so you can present information accurately, or (2) find and interview experts in the field for their judgments and opinions. If the experts in a field disagree, then the writer's obligation is to present all views equally. Also, a controversial issue may prompt you to make yourself into an expert on your topic so that your generalizations will be as helpful and reliable as possible. Obviously, becoming an expert often requires much study, reading, and research, so if your time is limited, you will probably need to refer to a range of experts, as Cokie Roberts does in her article about the issues surrounding a second Constitutional Convention.

Please refer to Chapters 11 and 12 for pointers on how to research a topic for informative writing. Remember that since your purpose is to present information, the quality of your facts, inferences, and opinions must be of the highest caliber.

SPECIALIZED KNOWLEDGE AND METHODS FROM A FIELD OF EXPERTISE

Writers and readers of informative prose must realize that when experts discuss a topic, they draw on the literature, assumptions, and methods particular to their fields of expertise. In other words, experts look at a topic from a certain angle and will characteristically suggest solutions to problems or opinions on controversies that are consonant with the premises of their field. Experts are wise to admit the limitations of their knowledge and make others aware that they are supplying only one specialized outlook on a subject rather than the final and whole truth. David Baltimore, for instance, is a virologist and AIDS expert. In his interview for *U.S. News & World Report* titled "Quarantining Will Help No One," he carefully delineates his area of expertise, which is understanding the life cycle of the virus and making basic predictions about the epidemiology of the disease. When asked how to educate people, he explicitly defers to advertisers for a specific answer since they are trained to broadcast messages to the general public. Baltimore's deference to advertisers does not weaken the substance of what he does know, however. In fact, it gains him the reader's trust; most people respect those who recognize and admit their limitations. Readers can be reassured of Baltimore's expertise in his field when he recognizes its limits.

Writers and readers of informative prose also find it useful to think about the bias of articles by experts. Fred H. Harrington is an ethologist, a specialist in the study of animal behavior. This field causes him to conduct research in a certain way and make observations that are useful to it. A photographer or park ranger would have spent his evenings in the forest in a very different way and probably would have written a very different article from Harrington's "The Man Who Cries Wolf." Similarly, Barbara Tuchman's account of the beginnings of U.S. involvement in Vietnam would differ greatly if she were, say, looking at this time period from the perspective of a French journalist. The article would also be different if she had been a political advisor to or biographer of Presidents Roosevelt or Truman, instead of a historian. Expert opinions and advice are central to informative prose, but very rarely can one expert or one specialized approach tell us all the relevant information. As writers we should recognize our own limitations and try to suggest the value of other fields and sources in understanding one topic. As readers we should grant experts authority only in the areas they can claim it in and be open to a variety of perspectives on one topic.

LOGICAL THINKING

When you plan an informative writing assignment, reason, rather than emotions or preconceptions, should guide you. To present accurate, reliable information, it is imperative that you think logically about what facts need to be learned and included, what perspectives on your topic need to be covered, and what conclusions can be reasonably reached. Since we are all human and have emotional and ethical responses to many issues, we must guard against viewing topics too narrowly.

One way to be a logical thinker and a good informative writer is to develop a cogent, or logically sound, *world view*. Your world view is the set of inherited and acquired personal values and background beliefs, religious, philosophical, and ethical in nature, that influences your outlook on the world and on the human condition. This term refers to everything that makes up your general approach to life — whether you think people are generally good or bad, whether you are prejudiced toward others, whether you have a defined moral code, and whether you make decisions based on wishful thinking, past experiences, superstitions, logical inferences, or realistic assessments of situations and probable outcomes. A sound world view — which involves an attitude more than it does the acquisition of a body of knowledge — is one that is reasonable, fair, and scientifically informed. It should meet the following criteria:

1. Consistency
2. A base of accurate information from reliable sources
3. Reasonable theories of human motivation
4. Resistance to self-deception and wishful thinking
5. Resistance to belief in unverified stereotypes
6. A scientific view of the universe that does not fall prey to pseudoscience
7. Lessons learned from the past (both the personal and historical past)
8. Realistic appraisal of one's own chances and abilities

A writer's world view is important because it often, either consciously or unconsciously, causes a writer to slant the facts or twist the presentation of information to fit his own set of beliefs. Biasing your writing in this way subverts the basic goal of informative writing by forcing the reader to view and interpret a topic according to your beliefs, not according to a fair-minded presentation of all relevant information. For all practical purposes it is probably impossible for any writer to disregard his world view; consequently, the soundness of a writer's world view becomes vital to good informative writing.

A logical approach to a topic is further enabled by an understanding of the basics of formal logical reasoning. When a writer studies an issue he must become aware of the arguments, or reasoned conclusions from evidence, that concern his topic. He should be able to determine whether those arguments are accurate (valid) or fallacious (invalid). This determination is made by recognizing the parts of an argument and judging their individual and combined validity.

All arguments are made up of *premises* and *conclusions*. Premises are the initial statements of fact, opinion, or presupposition from which one derives a conclusion; they comprise the reasons why the conclusion, also called the inference, can be posited. For example, consider an argument from the David Baltimore interview published in *U.S. News & World Report*:

Q Surveys show that a majority of the public believes AIDS victims should be quarantined. What do you think?

Quarantining will help no one. Most AIDS patients are too sick to be transmitting the virus. The virus is being spread largely by people who do not have AIDS but are infected with the virus, and they may or may not even know it. Quarantining would be totally futile.

If we break Baltimore's argument down into premises and conclusions, it looks something like this:

Premise: AIDS patients are too sick to transmit the virus.

Premise: The virus is spread by people who do not have AIDS but are infected with the virus, and they may or may not even know it.

Premise (unstated): It would be a waste of effort and money to quarantine a group of people who are not spreading the virus.

Conclusion: Therefore, quarantining AIDS patients will help no one.

There are two things to notice about Baltimore's argument as it is originally stated in comparison to its transformation into a formal argument.

Notice that in his statement the conclusion of the argument comes first and is followed by the premises. Position alone does not indicate whether a point is a premise or a conclusion. A reader or listener must determine whether the point is a *reason* for a conclusion or if it is the final point itself before labeling the premises and conclusion. Some key words usually signal a premise or reason: *because*, *since*, *the facts are*, and *the evidence consists of*. Phrases and words signalling a conclusion are *therefore*, *consequently*, *to sum up*, *in conclusion*, *the facts suggest that*, and *the point is*. Although these clues are not always present in arguments, you can usually identify premises if you look for the supporting statements of the main idea; the conclusion is the main idea.

The second point to notice is that Baltimore's argument contains at least one unstated premise, which he merely implies. This is often the case with arguments contained in conversations and writing. Therefore it may be helpful for you to consider the possibility of implied premises and try to fill them in before you analyze the argument for validity.

Also, some arguments imply a conclusion without explicitly stating it. So you may want to ask yourself if a group of sentences that seems only like an anecdote or description implies a course of action, result, or opinion that should be understood as a conclusion. In that case the anecdote can be labeled as the premise(s) and the implied result as the conclusion.

Determining the validity of an argument is the next step in analyzing an argument. Basically when you test an argument for validity you must consider three things:

1. The reasonableness of the premises,
2. Whether the premises include all the relevant information,
3. Whether the premises clearly and reasonably support the stated conclusion.

This last test for validity involves the form of the argument and the way the premises combine to support the conclusion. Structural validity, as well as a more detailed treatment of argument form, is discussed is Chapter 13. But for now, the important thing to recognize is that to test the validity of David Baltimore's argument, or any other argument, you can question one or more of the premises, decide whether any relevant information has been omitted and see if the premises "add up to" the conclusion.

How can analyzing arguments help you in the invention stage of the writing process? It helps you to evaluate your own ideas and preconceptions about a topic as well as those of others you find during research. In other words, while you plan and research an informative article, you will constantly construct your own arguments about a topic, and you will continually come across the arguments of experts and other people concerned with your topic. Before you accept any of these arguments as valid, you will need to test them against your cogent world view and against the criteria for a valid argument. This testing process may reveal to you errors in your own thinking, new questions that need to be answered in research, and the incomplete or biased nature of others' perspectives and opinions. This logical thought should gain you valuable insights into the complexities of your topic, making a truly fair-minded and informative article possible.

For example, suppose you are writing an informative article on how acid rain has affected the flora and fauna of the Great Smoky Mountains National Park located in Tennessee and North Carolina. You begin planning your essay by remembering your last hike up Mt. Le Conte, one of the highest peaks of the park, where you noticed the diseased pine trees and mountain laurel bushes on the summit. A park ranger later suggested that the trees were dying because of acid rain. And you vaguely remember newspaper articles to the same effect. Although these memories impress you with the harmfulness of acid rain, you realize you have very little verifiable information for an article. During your planning you sketch out your argument about acid rain:

> **Premise:** I saw the damaged trees and bushes on Mt. Le Conte.
>
> **Premise:** The ranger attributed this damage to acid rain.
>
> **Premise:** I also remember reading about how acid rain was damaging the park.
>
> **Premise:** These memories are alarming and convincing to me.
>
> **Conclusion:** So acid rain must be doing a lot of damage to the flora and fauna of the park.

Next you analyze your line of thought by using the tests of validity and immediately see that you need more information.

Test #1: Are the premises reasonable?

Despite your personal conviction that acid rain has damaged the park, when you look objectively at the second and third premises you see how vague they are. One is only the casual remark of a ranger, whose authority is unknown to you, and the other is only a fuzzy memory. Both of these premises need to be substantiated with more factual information and more qualified expertise on the issue.

Test #2: Do the premises include all the relevant information?

Clearly, your argument has numerous shortcomings here. You need to know:

1. Exactly what kind of visible damage does acid rain cause?
2. What is acid rain exactly?
3. What are the most probable sources of acid rain that would reach the park?
4. How probable is it that acid rain from neighboring industries would reach the park and cause damage of a measurable and destructive level?
5. What could be other causes for the damage witnessed?
6. What do park, environmental, industry, and government spokespersons have to say about this topic?

This test gives you some specific routes to follow in your research.

Test #3: Do the premises clearly and reasonably support your conclusion?

In one glance you realize that none of your premises say anything about how acid rain affects the animal life of the park, one of your main concerns. Also, the sketchiness of your premises doesn't really allow you to conclude convincingly that acid rain has done any damage at all. This test further inspires you to dive into research.

Test #4 (The Cogent World View Test): Is your thinking about this topic reasonable, fair, and scientifically informed?

Your answer has to be no, not really. You admit that you are inspired to write the article because you have always been concerned about the environment. Maybe your approach up to this point has been based more on personal convictions rather than on much knowledge of the details of this particular topic. Also, have you been fair to industry at all? You don't even know what the point of view of the surrounding industrial plants and supposed polluters might be. Recognizing these limitations, you see that it's now necessary for you to cool down emotionally and find out the facts before you raise the cry of alarm and disgust about acid rain.

These tests might initially depress you because after you think about your topic in this way, you realize how little you actually know. But on the positive side, they have helped you get the parameters of your topic in mind and have prepared you for the research stage. Furthermore, they have pushed you beyond the vague, uneasy, wondering stage of planning your article; you now know what you need to do. Your next step in working on this article will probably be to determine specifically from whom you can learn the answers to your list of questions.

FOCUS . . . .
SUGGESTIONS FOR WRITING

1. Review your journal for ideas that you could develop through research. You may want to be especially on the lookout for topics that you don't know much about. Set out to learn about some issue or answer a question through your research and writing.

2. Browse through some current newspapers and magazines. Make a list of intriguing topics and then consider whether one could be pursued from a local angle.

3. Select a news story from a local paper. The story is probably written in the third person, so for practice rewrite it using the first person. Then write an analysis of the differences between the two stories. Did the story become more, or less, subjective? Did the changes slant the story in a particular way? Is it possible to rewrite the story without slanting it?

4. Select a topic from the following list and draft a series of premises about the topic. What conclusion do your premises lead to? Apply the four tests of validity to your premises as they are applied in the example above about acid rain. What work needs to be done in order for you write a informative essay on this topic?

    television evangelists
    fast food restaurants
    "shuttle" diplomacy
    compact discs
    World War I
    tulips

10 ▶ Avenues of Inquiry

While you plan and research your writing project, you will want to ask yourself detailed questions about exactly what kind of information to present in your article, how you might both conduct research to find the facts you need, and how you might organize these pieces of information into paragraphs, sections, and a finished article. One useful method is to question yourself in a brainstorming exercise that forces you to answer modal questions, or rather questions derived from traditional modes of inquiry and development. In the past you may have set out to write essays according to one mode, but whatever your past experience, you will now want to use modes as avenues of inquiry, not as patterns by which you shape an entire project. Below we list several questions that each mode prompts a writer to ask herself. Once you have selected a topic, work through this list. Ask yourself each question. Decide if you want or need to pursue your topic in the manner suggested by the question. Take notes about what you know already and about what you need to learn.

Explanation

- ▶ What is the context surrounding my topic?
- ▶ How is my subject connected to other issues, events, or people?
- ▶ What are the interrelationships between my subject and these other relevant elements?

Analysis

- ▶ How can I break my subject down into parts?
- ▶ What can I learn about each of these parts that will make the whole subject more understandable?

▸ How does this division of my subject into parts help me understand the whole better?

Definition, Classification

▸ How can I define my subject?
▸ What are its distinguishing characteristics?
▸ How can I classify my subject? What type is it?

Description, Illustration

▸ What does my subject look like?
▸ What other sensory details can I use to help a reader understand it?
▸ What specific examples of my subject can I present in detail?

Comparison

▸ How is my subject like or unlike something else?
▸ Are these two subjects more different than similar or vice versa?
▸ Are these differences or similarities obvious? Subtle? Surprising? Important?
▸ What can I learn about my topic by comparing it with something else?

Narration

▸ Can I tell a meaningful or relevant story about my subject?
▸ What is its history?
▸ What are the beginning, middle, and end of this story or history?
▸ How will telling this story help my reader understand the subject?

Causal Analysis

▸ Is my subject a cause or effect of something else?
▸ What has caused it?
▸ What have been the effects of my subject?
▸ How should I evaluate these causes and effects? Are they major or minor, obvious or hidden, primary or remote?
▸ What are the contributing causes of my subject?
▸ Is there one or more sufficient cause(s) that could alone result in the occurrence?

Process Analysis

▸ How does my subject happen? Do I need to explain this process?
▸ How does my subject work? Do I need to explain this process?

▸ What are the steps in the process?

▸ Do I need to supply instructions for my reader to make or operate my subject?

Once you have worked through this list of questions, you will be better able to decide on the kind of research you need to do. Also, you may now be able to develop a preliminary scheme for organizing your article. For instance, the questions may help you recognize a need for particular definitions, examples, explanations, and descriptions in your finished article. Perhaps you will want to make a rough outline of your article at this point, including sections that you now see as necessary. Of course, all of these plans are tentative and will probably change during research and drafting, but right now they can gain you a focus on your project.

FOCUS · · · · · · · · · · · · ·
SUGGESTIONS FOR WRITING

1. Make a list of activities, people, hobbies, or issues that you know about. Putting yourself in the role of expert or local authority, write an article detailing some of the fine points or demystifying some of the complexities surrounding one of the items on your list. As an invention technique, ask yourself the modal questions.

2. Exchange your article with a classmate and have her critique it by making a list of things she would like to have explained further. What kinds of details did you overlook? What may have caused you to overlook them? What steps could you take in the future to avoid such oversights?

Approaches to Research — Observation, Interviewing

11

The word *research* often conjures up pictures of lonely students poring over huge tomes in a dingy library basement. Or it may bring forth visions of a laboratory scientist carefully conducting complex and delicate experiments. To most of us the word suggests difficult, solitary endeavor. Although research can be this kind of work, it can also be public, interactive, and engrossing. Observing a city council meeting, interviewing a local celebrity, writing a senator, or polling your dorm's residents for their opinions about cafeteria food are all forms of research. The point is that research means "finding out," finding out needed information about your topic through one or more of the methods mentioned above and described in this section. Research is what informative writers from all professions — academe, journalism, business, government, and public service — do to master their fields and prepare for writing. And it can be usefully conducted in many ways. This chapter and the next one provide guidelines for basic research techniques for informative writing.

OBSERVING

Perhaps the most basic research technique is observing, simply spending time watching your subject, whether it be a person, place, activity, or event related to your topic. This method can provide you with useful and interesting descriptive detail as well as insights into the values, motivations, and personalities of individuals and organizations. Descriptive detail can be a great way to involve a reader by directly showing him the issue or problem you want to discuss. The resulting insights may eventually lead you to important connections and realizations about your topic. Never underestimate the power of description; one filled with sensory detail can quickly and memorably gain your reader's attention. The following pointers should help you discover the options for observation that your topic provides.

1. *Selecting an observation subject.*
   ▸ Make a list of the people, places, events, and activities that can provide meaningful information about your topic through observation.
   ▸ Determine which of these possibilities would be most valuable.
   ▸ Determine which of these possibilities you have or can gain access to. Some offices, meetings, and events may require letters of introduction, formal written requests, or official approval.
   ▸ Which of your options can be accomplished during your time frame?
   ▸ Be resourceful in coming up with options. Can you
     a. watch someone at work? at play?
     b. observe a meeting, rally, demonstration, performance, or press conference?
     c. tour a building, campus, complex, city, farm, park, or geographical region?
   ▸ Consider the sensory qualities (sight, sound, taste, smell, texture, and weight) of your observation subject. Unless you have a special purpose in mind, it's probably a good idea to pursue the most dramatic and visual subject available.

2. *Determining observation goals.*
   ▸ Think ahead about what you hope to see, learn, or find from your observation.
   ▸ Do you want to develop your observation into a *case study* of a particular kind of person or place? For instance, you could do a case study of an Alzheimer's patient, of a typical school for the deaf, of a stock broker, family doctor, or state senator during a session of your state's legislature. Case studies can also be conducted on various kinds of industry such as car manufacturers, wineries, and department stores. Observation such as this, with a specific goal in mind, is the basis of the scientific method. The purpose of such a case study is to learn about the typical features, problems, and challenges of your topic by studying one example very closely. In general, you use your information about one person or organization to help your reader understand the basic character of all such individuals and groups. Unique features of your subject may be recognized and noted, but in a case study they are not as important as the qualities your subject shares with those that are comparable.
   ▸ Is the purpose of your observation to uncover the distinguishing features of your topic, those that make it unique or especially important? This sort of purpose forces the researcher to pursue the individualizing qualities of the subject. You may find that your purpose is to answer questions such as the following:
     a. Why is this physician so loved and respected by his community?
     b. What makes this person such an exceptional lawyer?

    c. How does this business clear so much profit each year and remain a leader in research?

    d. Why is this year's drought so much worse than last year's?

▶ Is the purpose of your observation to acquire an *eyewitness account* of some event or activity? Perhaps you want to observe a rescue team training drill, a hang-gliding competition, a town parade or festival, a press conference with a local politician or public official, or an anti-nuclear demonstration. The point of observing an event or activity is to develop an understanding of a relevant issue, learn and report how an activity is performed and discover its purpose, or catalogue some examples and details about an individual or group activity. You will want to gather enough information to enable a reader to visualize what it is like to attend the function or take part in the activity.

3. *Observation pointers.*

▶ Take notes if at all possible. Jot down key words, names, remarks, and details. Don't write sentences, organize material, or search for the best words, just quickly take down information. Use quotation marks for dialogue and direct quotations.

▶ Determine all important features and note sensory information. Answer these kinds of questions:

    a. Is the setting important? What is it?

    b. Is the size of the crowd important?

    c. What is the weather, date, time of day?

    d. What is the atmosphere or mood?

    e. What is the sequence of events?

    f. Who are the important participants?

    g. What do they look like? How do they react to the event?

    h. What can you hear?

    i. What can you smell?

    j. Are the senses of taste or touch important? How?

    k. What is unusual, surprising, or unexpected?

    l. What ideas or questions do you have about what you see?

▶ Draw a diagram or sketch if it is helpful.

▶ Decide whether you need to participate in the event to understand it or gain information. At a press conference, you may want to ask a question, while you may want to try wind surfing at an exhibition.

▶ Keep asking yourself about the point of what you see. What does your observation tell you?

▶ After you finish taking notes, read over them. Add details that you left out. Ponder over what you witnessed and try to decide on what most impressed you. Write down ideas and interpretations of what you saw.

▶ If necessary, organize or recopy your notes. You may now want to group details and remarks into categories.

▸ Determine which questions arise from your notes and how you can answer them.

4. *Using observation notes in writing.*

   ▸ You may want to develop your notes into an anecdote, example, or report.

   ▸ Descriptions of people and places can be included in your article to give it life and gain a reader's attention and trust.

   ▸ Think about what your reader needs to "see" to follow your article or believe your interpretations.

   ▸ Consider whether you need to observe anything else or if you need to visit your original observation site once more.

INTERVIEWING

Interviewing is a common and often rewarding research method. It can gain you access to compact explanations and statements of opinions from experts, replacing hours of reading about a topic. And, as Mary Rhea discovered when she interviewed her uncle for her paper "Having Faith," interviewing can provide insights into the personality, values, and life-styles of interesting individuals, whether they are celebrities, officials, highly skilled people with interesting jobs, or those with important stories to tell. Furthermore, you will often find that people are happy to tell you about themselves or their areas of expertise. Usually they are flattered to learn that someone believes they have an interesting story to tell, an important job, or an expert's status. This research technique, however, does require you to be aware of and sensitive to the subject's ego, schedule, motivations, and situation. Usually preliminary attention to your subject's willingness to talk and his expectations about the interview will enable you to conduct a productive and even enjoyable interview.

Deciding on the Right Kind of Interview

Do you want to interview a specialist who can provide you with an expert's opinions about your topic? If so, consider that your subject may have a biased view of the controversial aspects of your topic. Perhaps you will want to interview two or more experts to get all sides of an issue. Some examples of *expert interviews* follow:

1. The local chief of police about crime in your area.
2. Your university's anthropologist who is currently excavating a Cherokee burial ground.
3. An ophthalmologist about new surgical techniques for correcting vision problems.

4. An ecologist about the effects of acid rain or the hole in the ozone layer.

5. An automobile mechanic about the effects of the computer on car service.

To conduct an expert interview, you may need to do some phone calling and leg-work to find a subject who is truly an expert on your topic. However, a university community is often chock full of experts willing to talk, publicize their expertise, and promote their fields of study.

Do you want to interview a celebrity or someone with an interesting past or job? This kind of interview might develop into a profile article, the purpose of which is to present your subject's history, skill, or personality to your readers. Often when you conduct this sort of interview you're not so much interested in what your subject knows as in what he is like. (For example, see Jonathan Cott's interview of Oriana Fallaci in this section's readings.) Remember that wonderful profiles may be written about ordinary people who have unique skills or have had an unusual experience. For example, you might want to interview someone who

1. has built a schooner by hand and sailed around the world in it with his family,

2. lives on the streets because he lost his job,

3. is the conductor of your city's symphony,

4. heads a local civic organization like a "Meals on Wheels" program for the elderly,

5. has a particularly interesting job or occupation.

Is it possible for you to conduct **a face-to-face interview,** *or will you need to settle for a* **phone interview or letter***?* Depending on the time and money you have available for research, you may not be able to interview someone who is out of town. In this case telephone interviews can be conducted, but usually they must be more limited in scope than a personal interview. If you have no success arranging a telephone interview, another alternative is to write your subject and ask for answers to specific questions. Of course, this option is the least desirable since many people are unwilling or slow to take the time to write you back.

PREPARING FOR AN INTERVIEW

Here are some pointers to follow as you plan to conduct an interview:

▸ Set an appointment time that is convenient for your subject and timely for you. It's best not to expect more than an hour (even less for some people) of your subject's time. Try to discover when your subject will have time to relax and become interested in you and your questions; you may want to ask for his slowest time of day rather than attempt to conduct an interview when you have to compete with numerous interruptions.

► When you ask for an appointment, be sure you explain why you want to interview the subject so that he will understand your purpose. For subjects who are reluctant to grant you an interview, you may want to offer a list of questions beforehand.

► Do some background reading about your topic, and, if possible, about your subject. If your subject is a celebrity or expert, you need to be sure you know enough beforehand so that you don't appear uninformed on general knowledge about the individual or on basic facts about the topic. Never spend precious interview time asking your subject questions you could readily find answers to in a biographical dictionary or an encyclopedia. Remember that you want to get information during your interview that cannot be acquired easily elsewhere.

► Determine what your expectations are for the interview. What do you most need to learn from your subject? Decide whether your subject's personal life is important to your research; if you're using the subject as an expert, personality and personal history may or may not be necessary.

► Compose a list of questions you want to ask your subject. Phrase these so that your subject will be encouraged to give you substantial answers.

1. Avoid questions that require only a "yes" or "no" since they will not provide you with useable quotations.

2. Be careful not to ask your subject forced-choice questions that push a subject to choose between one of two alternatives. For example, a forced-choice question is phrased like the following: "Is the proposed bill on gun control good or bad for the country?" In most instances it's better to ask for the same information in a manner that permits more than two acceptable answers, such as "How do you think the proposed bill will affect the nation?"

3. Balance open and closed questions. Open questions encourage a subject to extemporize, answer at length, tell stories, and reveal his personality. Closed questions limit a subject more and enable an interviewer to get answers to specific questions.

INTERVIEW QUESTIONS

The most important feature of interview questions is that they allow the subject to say what he thinks without being led too forcefully.

Order your questions so that you begin with questions that will relax your subject, move into more difficult or controversial areas gracefully in the middle of your interview, and end on a satisfying note. The point of this ordering is that you need to give your subject time to "settle into" the interview before you ask challenging, sensitive, or difficult questions. Let your subject get to know you a little before you hit him with the tough ones.

CONDUCTING AN INTERVIEW

When you actually get to the day of your scheduled interview, remember the following advice:

▸ Arrive promptly and be aware of the time so that you don't inconvenience your subject.

▸ Dress in a manner that will gain your subject's approval, and, if possible, trust. Sometimes this means "dressing up"; sometimes it means "dressing down."

▸ Record the interview or take notes. If you use a tape recorder, be sure it works and that your subject doesn't mind it. You may need to explain that the recorder will simply help you "get things right" and "prevent misquoting." If you take notes, write down only key words and quotations that will enable you to re-create the interview after it's over.

▸ Be tactful and polite especially when you ask about sensitive issues. If a subject resists a question, don't force him to answer. Move on to the next question and only bring the sensitive question back up if you can avoid seeming insolent.

▸ Listen carefully to your subject. Do not become too involved in taking notes to hear what your subject says. If he brings up an issue you had not thought of, don't ignore the signal and miss an opportunity. Try not to follow your prepared questions so closely that you fail to pick up on conversation cues.

▸ Note your subject's appearance, gestures, tone of voice, and expressions. They may help you understand his attitudes and motivations. They may also give you clues to times when he is speaking ironically or deceptively.

▸ Consider telling your subject something about yourself if it will help him relax or trust you. Often people are more willing to discuss sensitive issues if they believe that the interviewer can empathize with their own feelings and situations.

▸ Take observation notes about the setting of your interview, especially if the place reveals something about the subject or his work.

▸ Thank the subject for his time when you end the interview. You may want to ask whether you may call back for a follow-up if new questions occur to you. It is also good policy to offer to send your subject a copy of the completed article that you will write.

Follow-up Pointers

▸ Immediately after the interview ends, check your recording and fill in your notes. If your tape recorder fails you, you can still recall most of the important remarks. If you didn't have time to note gestures and expressions, jot them down now before you forget them. If you did not use a recorder, try to re-create the interview as accurately as possible.

▸ Read over your notes, making an effort to determine what you learned and what information you will want to include in your article. Mark or transcribe important passages. Cluster related remarks and information together to help you plan your essay. It is not essential for you to present interview material in chronological order.

▸ If you are writing a profile article about your interview subject, review your notes and find your focus for the article. When you have difficulty deciding on your focus, try writing a narrative of the interview and then reviewing it for the key moments and statements.

▸ Select the information and quotations you think you want to include in your article. It's important to realize that you probably will not be able to use everything your subject said. Determine what's significant, what should be quoted, what can be summarized, and what you want to leave out.

▸ Determine the extent to which you will use the interview material in your article. Will the interview dominate the article or will it only be used to verify or emphasize important points?

▸ Decide if you need to make a follow-up call or visit. Be aware that you can probably only make one (and it should be brief), without exasperating your subject.

FOCUS • • • • • • • • • • • • •

SUGGESTIONS FOR WRITING

1. Brainstorm about current fads, trends, or issues. Consider writing an article that discusses the origins and characteristics of one.

2. Attend a public meeting, speech, or event and write a news account of it. You may also want to do some background reading to help you understand the people and issues involved.

3. Conduct an interview of one of your classmates on a subject in which he is an expert — his major, a hobby, or his job. Follow the guidelines listed above, treating your subject as though he is "really important" by making an appointment, showing up on time, and so on. After you have interviewed your subject, write your article. What aspects of the interview went more smoothly than you had expected? What aspects were more difficult than you had anticipated? How would you go about this differently next time?

4. Observe a friend, relative, acquaintance, or even a total stranger or group of strangers going about their normal activities in a specific situation. You will want to shape this observation into a short article entitled something like "A

Day in the Life of an X-Ray Technician," "The Saturday Morning of a Four-Year-Old," or "Sunday Afternoon at the Laundromat." If you choose to follow a friend around his job, you will of course need to get his permission (and perhaps the permission of supervisors as well). If you are going to watch what transpires at the laundromat, cafeteria, or basketball game, you will only need to sit quietly in the corner, watch, and record your observations. Aim your article at an audience who has little experience with the activity you are observing; you may, therefore, have to explain even the most elementary details.

12

► Approaches to Research — Reading and Surveying

READING

The amount of reading you do for any one article usually depends on your purpose for reading. Before you begin research reading, it's best to list quickly what you want to find out from written sources. Then use a search strategy that will help you find the best sources in the least amount of time. These steps will keep you from becoming overwhelmed by the sheer number of sources — the hundreds of pages available on most topics. The secret to research reading is facing the fact that you will seldom have the time, need, or endurance to read everything written on your topic, so you learn to tailor your reading to finding answers to questions that are clearly relevant to your topic. In short, select the best and most appropriate sources from what's available; pragmatism about time limitations and the level of expertise you need to reach before drafting should determine the depth of your reading. For a thumbnail guide to reading consider the chart below that roughly matches purpose with amount of reading.

Purpose of Reading	*Amount of Reading*
1. To gain background information about a person, place, event, issue.	One or two good encyclopedia articles, a substantial entry in a biographical dictionary, or a couple of recent and carefully written magazine or newspaper articles.

continued

continued from page 187

Purpose of Reading	*Amount of Reading*
2. To gain a basic familiarity with your topic, an understanding of the most important facts and features of the topic.	Several good sources such as three to five books or periodical articles that place your topic in a larger context and present information in a nontechnical, accessible style.
3. To find one or several expert opinions about your topic.	Background sources should lead you to names of important works and leading experts. Look at a few of these principal works and identify which are most useful. Don't waste time reading books or articles by writers who clearly don't qualify as experts; go for the sure recognizable leaders in the field. If the expert sources are too technical in approach, look for reliable summaries and other books or articles that interpret the experts for a general audience.
4. To do a comprehensive or exhaustive study of a topic.	Identify and read all significant and all recent information about your topic. Pursue the technical, advanced sources in order to become an expert yourself.

Clearly, this chart gives you only a rough guide to reading. It is also important for you to notice when exhaustive research reading is necessary and when it's not. Most writing projects do not require exhaustive reading, so resist the temptation to read everything available. Often this approach robs you of time that would be better spent planning and drafting your own article. Here are some other useful tips:

Beginning a Library Search

Getting Started

- ▸ Determine what you need to learn from reading.
- ▸ Gauge the depth of your research reading.
- ▸ Consider the time you can allot to reading.
- ▸ Identify key terms for your topic that will help you research your topic in card catalogs, computer data bases, and reference books. If you are conducting your search in a library that uses the Library of Congress system, look your topic up in *The Library of Congress Subject Headings List* to learn how it is listed in the card catalog. This step is necessary because Library of Congress headings are based on outdated terms that may not occur to you.

▶ Find background and overview information about your topic in reference books. These are general and specialized encyclopedias, dictionaries, yearbooks, and handbooks. They can provide some general information and lead you to other sources since most contain bibliographies. Here is a sampling of some useful specialized reference books:

Advertising Age Yearbook
Encyclopedia Britannica
The International Dictionary of Sports and Games
The Encyclopedia of Banking and Finance
AMA Management Handbook
Encyclopedia of American Foreign Policy
The Guide to American Law
McGraw-Hill Encyclopedia of Science and Technology
Who's Who in the World
Medical and Health Encyclopedia

▶ Go to the reference room of your city or school library to find this kind of source. Reference librarians can usually direct you to the works that will be most relevant to your topic.

▶ From reference books make a bibliography of other books and articles you want to find. Update it continually by adding titles you find in all the sources you read.

Finding Useful Books

▶ Look up key terms in the card catalog or on-line computer catalog of your library and add relevant book titles to your bibliography. Be on the lookout for published bibliographies on your topic; these are great time-savers.

▶ Find books in the stacks (the shelves) of the library and browse through them before you read them or check them out. Book titles can be misleading, so check out the preface, introduction, table of contents, and index before you take the book home to read.

▶ Read books selectively unless you have a lot of time. Often you may only need to read one or two chapters from a book because they will be the only parts that treat your topic.

Finding Relevant Periodical (Magazine, Newspaper, and Journal) Articles

▶ Look up key terms in periodical indexes. Most library reference rooms have a wide range of subject indexes for both general and specialized magazine and newspaper articles. Usually the title of the index will tell you the sort of magazines and newspapers you can expect to find indexed in it. Ask your librarian to recommend several that might cover your topic. Here's a sampling of some commonly used indexes:

Reader's Guide to Periodical Literature

Magazine Index

National Newspaper Index

American Statistics Index

Business Periodicals Index

Education Index

Social Sciences Index

Public Affairs Information Service

Humanities Index

Applied Science and Technology Index

Index Medicus

Physical Education Index

▶ If necessary, run a computer search on your topic for periodical listings. Most university libraries now offer these for a small fee.

▶ When you find relevant article titles, copy down the citation, being sure you note the article title, periodical title, author, date of publication, and page and volume numbers.

▶ Determine if your library subscribes to the periodicals you want by looking up periodical titles in a *serial holdings list*, which is an alphabetical list of the magazines and newspapers available in the library. When you find a listing you want, copy down its call number and location (stacks, current periodicals, microfilm) in the library.

▶ If your library doesn't carry a periodical you want, consider going to a larger library or requesting a copy from *inter-library loan* (a borrowing system between libraries). This latter option usually takes some time, so decide if you can wait a couple of weeks for the article.

▶ Locate articles in the library and determine if they are useful before you check them out.

Collecting Other Written Sources

Government publications can provide access to a number of studies, census reports, consumer information, and transcripts of congressional sessions and hearings. Large university and city libraries often have separate departments for government indexes and collections; ask a reference librarian for help finding government publications.

Many written sources are available through private organizations, associations, and clubs as well as through the public relations departments of businesses and corporations. Usually the best approach is to write a letter to the association or business you think can help you, explain your research project, and ask if they can mail you copies of relevant pamphlets, brochures, studies, and transcripts. Some organizations will charge for this service, but often businesses supply information free. Find the proper addresses in reference books like the ones listed below. These books are often kept in the reference sections of libraries.

Corporation Addresses

1. *Million Dollar Directory: America's Leading Public and Private Companies*, published by Dun's Marketing Services, Inc., 1990. Lists addresses, phone numbers, and names of corporate officers.
2. *Principal International Businesses (1990): The World Marketing Directory*, published by Dun and Bradstreet Corp. Includes addresses, phone and telex numbers, and usually the managing director's name.
3. *Word's Business Directory: U.S. Private Companies: Largest Private Plus Selected Public Companies*. Lists address, phone number, the name of the Chief Executive Officer.

Association Addresses

1. *Worldwide Chamber of Commerce Directory*, published by the Association of Chambers of Commerce, 1990. Includes address, phone number, and name of the president, secretary, director, and/or ambassador of U.S. chambers of commerce, state boards of tourism, convention and visitors bureaus, foreign chambers of commerce, foreign embassies in the U.S., and U.S. embassies abroad.
2. *The Encyclopedia of Associations*, edited by Koek et al., published by Gale Research Inc., 1990. This is a name and key word index that cites more than 25,000 national and international organizations. Each entry contains the address, phone number, director's name, plus a brief description of the organization, meeting and convention information, the number of members, names of committees and publications, and the group's budget.

Reading Carefully and Critically

Good writers know that there is reading, and there is *reading*. Although you have no doubt been reading since you were very small, you can employ methods to make your reading more efficient:

- ► For books read the preface or introduction; this kind of introductory material can often provide a valuable summary of a book's content or purpose.
- ► Determine which parts of the book or article you will need to read.
- ► Begin reading actively, taking notes, sketching outlines of the information or argument, and asking questions that might occur to you.
- ► If you are using your own copy of a book or article, don't hesitate to mark or underline important sentences or passages. Also jot your questions in the book's margins as they occur to you. These annotations will help you follow

the source carefully, without becoming lulled by the words and simply glossing over pages without really reading them.

▶ If you are using a borrowed book or journal, take notes of your observations. Be sure that you don't deface the pages of a borrowed source.

▶ Consider whether you agree, disagree, or are surprised with the source you are reading. It may be helpful for you to test the arguments contained in a source by sketching out the premises and conclusions and testing them according to the basics of logical thinking as discussed in Chapter 13.

▶ Once you finish reading a source, or a section of one, do a freewriting response to what you have learned from the source, pondering how this new information affects your own thoughts on your topic.

▶ Think about which statements, facts, and opinions from the source you might want to include in your article, either for support for your own facts and observations or as a counterargument that you will want to refute. Be sure you have accurate notes on these points. See page 196 for a discussion of note taking.

SURVEYING

Writers occasionally administer surveys to learn about a specific group's particular opinions or attitudes on an issue. This research technique can provide you with a useful overview of a topic and of the range of opinions on a topic. The technique has the advantage of anonymity for the subjects (unlike interviewing), and it can also be an efficient way for a writer to gather information about a whole group. However, it is important for any writer to recognize that surveying large groups of people, like the entire student population of a university, is a complex matter, involving careful planning and sampling. This sort of formal, large survey requires special training in statistics and in polling methods. So we do not advise you to undertake a large survey unless you have the time and resources to do so.

Small, informal questionnaires of select groups can often be workable and valuable. For example, it is perfectly manageable and reasonable for a writer to poll all the students living on the floor of her dormitory, or all the professors of a particular department, especially if the writer believes she can get a high level of response from the group. It is a much shakier proposition for that writer to poll all of her dorm's residents or the entire university faculty, since it is improbable that she can be sure of a representative sample or of a high response level without using a scientific approach. Here are some guidelines to observe when you are contemplating a survey:

Planning a Survey

▶ First decide on your purpose for conducting a survey. It should be fairly limited in scope, planned to answer no more than several specific questions about your topic.

▶ Determine whom you should poll and whether or not you can reasonably select a representative sample or a large enough percentage of respondents to provide you with accurate, reliable information.

▶ Draft your questionnaire, paying attention to its clarity, its brevity, and the phrasing of your questions. In general, you want your questionnaire to be easy for your respondents to answer. Do not make it too long or complex. Phrase your questions so that they do not lead someone to answer in a particular way. Review the advice about constructing questions for interviews; the same considerations apply here.

▶ As in an interview, you may want to balance open and closed questions. Remember, it's much easier to tally the results of closed, multiple-choice questions, but open questions can provide unforeseen insights and pithy statements to quote in your own article.

▶ Consider how to administer the questionnaire. Do you want to question your respondents orally or over the telephone, marking the answers yourself as you go? Or you may believe you would get more thoughtful responses if you requested that your respondents wrote out their own answers on a prepared form. In this case, you may want to consider mailing the questionnaires to your sample group or, even better, administering them to the whole group at one time when all the members are assembled together and will be motivated to respond.

Administering the Questionnaire

▶ Whatever method of distribution you select, be sure to be polite and considerate of your respondents' time and feelings. Be honest with them, tell them the purpose of the survey, make the form easy to read and respond to, and thank them for their trouble.

▶ Be sure that you do not lead your respondents to believe that you want or expect particular answers to your questions. Your stance should be as neutral as possible so as to encourage them to respond honestly and accurately.

Analyzing Your Findings

▶ Tally the results to the closed questions; you may want to express the results as percentages of certain responses to questions or as a table illustrating all the responses to individual questions.

▶ For the open questions, read all the answers from all questionnaires through once. Create some rough categories with which to group the answers. Reread each answer and determine into which category each should be placed.

▶ Take notes of particularly telling answers to the open questions and select several to use as quotations in your own article. Be sure, however, that these quotations do not skew your reader's perception of the whole survey; they should be striking, but not unrepresentative.

▶ Review your findings and consider what you learned from the survey. Did you get the information you wanted? Are you surprised by your findings?

How can you use this information in your writing project? Remember that you are obligated to be honest about your findings in your project, and guard against the temptation to see only what you wanted or expected to see in your survey results.

RESEARCH SKILLS

Anytime you go beyond your own personal knowledge and experience in writing, you need to consider more factors in selecting and using information. These additional concerns have to do with determining the credibility of your sources and with using the sources you find in an ethical and accurate manner. For the most part, you must act on these concerns while you are researching and drafting so that late in the game of revising and editing you do not have to backtrack. Checking the accuracy of a quotation or verifying a statistic is simple enough when you have the book in hand or are working in a library, but these precautions are time consuming and frustrating when you are trying to finish an article or meet a deadline. This introduction to research skills encourages a writer/researcher to be methodical in checking the reliability of sources, taking notes, and including source material in a draft. Consistency in these areas will simplify drafting and revising of your writing and keep you from spending time doubting the accuracy of your information. Read the following section for pointers in developing your own method of quality control for researching.

Evaluating Sources

Every researcher knows that some sources are better than others. Some books are carefully written and include the latest, most credible information, while others don't. Some experts have a talent for explaining their opinions to a lay audience without confusing or distorting the facts or issues, while others become lost in technicalities. Some eyewitnesses have a good eye for detail and an accurate memory, while others easily forget faces and names or confuse the sequence of events. As a writer/researcher you must make value judgments about the credibility and accuracy of your sources. Evaluating sources can involve background checks, personality judgments, and corroboration from a second source, but the best advice is to use your own sense of what and who is trustworthy in combination with some initial attention to the factors listed below. While only a specialist in a field can judge a source with finality, most of the time a sensitive and skeptical writer can make a reasonably accurate evaluation.

Author, Expert, or Eyewitness An author or expert's professional qualifications can usually be found in a biographical reference book. Also, while you read about an issue you will run across the names of well-respected experts in the field. Pursuing these sources should give you a good chance at locating reliable information. The trustworthiness of an eyewitness, however, is harder to judge. Ask yourself if your source has any reason to give you a slanted account or perspective on your topic. Remember that people who have a vested interest in an issue are less likely to be objective than those who have nothing to gain or lose.

Book Title, Preface, or Introduction   Attention to the title of a book or article plus a careful reading of its preface or introduction will often provide you with useful information about the scope, content, and purpose of the source. Sometimes you can also discover the preferences, attitudes, and world view of an author in the prefatory material.

Publisher   It's a good idea to note the publisher of a source. Have you heard of this publisher before, or have any experts you know heard of it? As you learn more about a field of study you will also learn about the general reputation of the most common publishers in the field, and this information may imply something about the credibility of a book or article it prints. Furthermore, be aware that some publishers have biases and predilections. Two books published by different presses, for example, can possibly have wildly different perspectives on the same topic. Periodicals — scholarly and popular — also have such leanings. For example, *The National Review* and *The Conservative Digest* will usually take a conservative approach to issues, whereas you can expect *The Nation*, *The Village Voice*, and *Mother Jones* to view topics much more liberally.

Timeliness and Date   Determine whether your topic or issue is one which demands the most recent sources available. Remember that some topics develop and change more quickly than others and that when writing about them you will need to guard against obsolete sources. For example, an article on the 1980 presidential election may no longer be relevant for someone writing about yesterday's political battles, whereas a history of election trends may retain its relevance much longer. Or, to take another example, a good deal of information was published on the space program in the early 1970s, shortly after the first moon landing; most of these books are sadly out-of-date today. Furthermore, many older books have been reissued in new covers that make them seem to be new publications; a careful scholar should therefore always check the copyright date of a source on the reverse of the title page.

Documentation   Note how thoroughly a source's information is documented. Footnotes, bibliographies, or references in the text itself should help you discover where an author found his information, either as a check of his credibility or for your own research. Evaluate the sources an author cites; do they seem credible? Do you think they have been carefully researched and documented?

Language and Logic   As you begin to read a source, be sensitive to the author's language and the soundness of his arguments. If his expressions contain highly inflammatory language or if his arguments just don't add up, you may want to double-check the information you gain from this source.

Reviews   If you're new to a field of study, you may want to consult one or more professional reviews of a book. The best reviews, of course, are by other experts in the field who can fairly evaluate the author's work. Ask a reference librarian to help you locate reviews in either *Book Review Index* or *Book Review Digest*. The reviews may also lead you to other useful sources.

Expert Opinions   If you know or can contact a local expert in the field, ask her about the sources you have found, or encourage her to suggest sources that are authoritative. This kind of guidance can save you time in discovering the best sources.

Fact Check and Corroboration   While reading a variety of sources, try to determine which facts and opinions seem to be widely recognized and accepted. These are usually reliable. Don't discount the unconventional notions or maverick data, but acknowledge that these need more support to be credible. If you can't verify information in a second source, make a judgment call about the information; don't just accept it wholesale.

Note Taking

Once you have found good sources for your article or essay, begin taking notes that will help you use the source information in your own writing. While note taking differs from observing, interviewing, and reading, the basic goal does not change: you are trying to collect accurate information methodically that you can later use to write your own essay. The key to all note taking is selection — deciding what to write down and what to omit (and perhaps forget). Generally, observation and interviewing do not allow us the time or perspective to make these selection choices, so it's best to do the selecting of important facts and comments afterwards when you're back at your desk. Still, you will need to be methodical.

Pointers for Observation and Interview Note Taking

- Write on index cards or in a small notebook. Later you will be able to shuffle and organize these notes more easily than notes taken on long sheets.
- Be sure to note names, dates, numbers, other details you might easily forget.
- Jot down key words and phrases.
- Be sure to use quotation marks around exact quotations. If you don't, you may later confuse quotations with the rest of the text.

Pointers for Note Taking from Written Sources

- Begin reading the article or book carefully but not too slowly.
- Make a bibliography card for the source.
- Restrain from recopying all interesting facts on note cards. Only make cards for information that is relevant to your topic, and sometimes more narrowly relevant to a preliminary outline or draft.
- Be selective; note key facts, important opinions, statements that directly apply to your topic.
- On the note card include
  1. The author's name and the page number(s) on which the material appears.
  2. A shortened form of the book's title if you're using two books by the same author.

3. A short heading if you know already how you want to use the noted information. This addition will help you remember later how you originally thought of using the material.

4. Quotation marks for direct quotations to avoid unintentionally plagiarizing your source. Consider quoting most of the time and paraphrasing only to condense long passages. After all, you can always paraphrase a quotation, but you can't reconstruct a quotation from a paraphrase.

5. Ellipsis marks (. . .) if you leave out unnecessary words, phrases or sentences in a quotation.

6. Brackets [ ] if you add words to make a quotation understandable.

▸ Develop a system for organizing groups of cards or notes to facilitate drafting and careful documentation. Arrange notes according to an outline or the sections of a draft.

▸ If you have found a truly significant source consider buying or copying it; then you can write fewer note cards and ensure the accuracy of your research.

Quoting

Quoting is a useful technique for establishing your credibility, plus quotations add variety and interest to writing. The secret of effective quoting is to choose meaningful, striking material to quote. Just as you need to be selective in note taking, you need to be equally selective in quoting. Never include a quotation just because you don't want or know how to make a point yourself; use quotations to back up your own statements and to have an impact on a reader. Also, don't overuse quotations. When you string quotations together without adequate explanation and interpretation, a reader doubts that you know your topic or that you have anything new to say about it. Try to create a satisfying balance of quotations and your own prose. Here are some guidelines for using quotations. The examples are drawn from Cokie Roberts' broadcast article "Congress and the Constitution" and from Barbara Tuchman's essay "America Betrays Herself in Vietnam." The WRONG examples are edited versions, and the RIGHT ones are taken from the authors' texts.

1. Introduce all quotations by identifying the context of the quotation and the identity of the speaker.

WRONG: "They were instructed by their state, by the then Confederation Congress, to devise a few amendments to the Articles of Confederation. . . ."

RIGHT: Fred Barbash's book *The Founding* explains what those conventioneers did two hundred years ago: "They were instructed by their state, by the then Confederation Congress, to devise a few amendments to the Articles of Confederation. . . ."

Quotations gain meaning from the context that surrounds them, and without an explanation of that context, the quotation may only confuse your reader.

2. Introduce quotations with the correct punctuation. Use a comma for brief, grammatically incomplete introductions unless the word *that* precedes the quotation.

> WRONG: Churchill informed Anthony Eden "The President has been more outspoken on that subject than on any other colonial matter, and I imagine that it is one of his principal war aims to liberate Indochina from France."

> RIGHT: The President "has been more outspoken to me on that subject," Churchill informed Anthony Eden, "than on any other colonial matter, and I imagine that it is one of his principal war aims to liberate Indochina from France."

> OR: "The President has been more outspoken to me on that subject," Churchill informed Anthony Eden, "than on any other colonial matter, and I imagine that it is one of his principal war aims to liberate Indochina from France."

> RIGHT: President Roosevelt was more outspoken on that subject, Churchill informed Anthony Eden, "than on any other colonial matter, and I image that it is one of his principal war aims to liberate Indochina from France."

3. Use a colon to separate your own grammatically complete introductions or statements (main clauses) from the quotation.

> WRONG: Professor Burns doubts that a second constitutional convention would end so happily because the cast of characters would not be the same, "That was an extraordinary group of men. . . ."

> RIGHT: Professor Burns doubts that a second constitutional convention would end so happily because the cast of characters would not be the same: "That was an extraordinary group of men. . . ."

4. Integrate quotations into your own sentences. That is, be sure that the quotation functions as a part (usually a direct object) of your own sentences. See RIGHT examples above.

5. Clarify pronouns that have no clear antecedents.

> WRONG: Political Affairs director John Davis claims the convention call serves more as a threat than a reality: "It's our goal to put enough heat on Congress through the state legislatures to force them to act and give the people what they've been wanting for years, a balanced budget amendment to the Constitution."

> RIGHT: Political Affairs director John Davis claims the convention call serves more as a threat than a reality: "It's [*the National Tax Limitation Committee's*] goal to put enough heat on Congress through the state legislatures to force them to act and give the people what they've been wanting for years, a balanced budget amendment to the Constitution."

Brackets [ ] indicate editorial changes that you, not the author, have made to clarify the quotation or to make it fit the grammatical structure of your sentence. Do not use parentheses ( ) to indicate such changes.

6. Block indent and single space any quotation longer than two lines of prose or poetry, still using the standard methods of introduction. Do not use quotation marks around an block indented quotation; the indention itself signals a quotation.

Paraphrasing

Although a paraphrase is usually viewed as a variation of a quotation, these two techniques of including researched information arise from different needs on the part of the writer and create different effects on the reader. Unlike a quotation, a paraphrase condenses and summarizes information, sometimes pages worth. It allows a writer to use source material without directing the focus of the passage away from the writer's argument and style. A paraphrase is a particularly useful technique if you want to repeat the substance of information from a source but do not need or want to reproduce the exact phrasing of the original. However, you must not forget *to introduce and document* paraphrased material in the same way you manage quotations. In fact, it is very important for a reader to recognize when a paraphrase begins and ends so that a reader does not confuse what the writer says with the source's information.

Here are two examples of paraphrased information that is carefully introduced and integrated into the writer's own paragraphs. The following two paragraphs are cited from Robin Marantz Henig's article "The Big Sneeze."

> Hay fever is the most common form of the environmental allergy. According to the National Institute of Allergic and Infectious Diseases, some 17 million Americans, nearly half of all allergy patients, have hay fever, or more properly, allergic rhinitis, from the Latin for inflammation of the nose.
>
> Hay fever is one of the so-called atopic allergies, meaning it seems to run in families. Dr. Michael Sly, chief of allergy and immunology at Children's Hospital National Medical Center in Washington, says a child with one allergic parent runs a 30 percent risk of developing allergies and a child with two allergic parents runs a 60 to 70 percent risk.

These paragraphs are good examples of how to paraphrase researched information because the sources are clearly stated and a reader can easily distinguish between the writer's ideas and the information actually derived from sources. When you paraphrase, follow the pointers listed below.

1. Introduce all paraphrased material by naming the source. Sometimes you may also need to define the source, especially if he is an author or expert who holds a position of authority in the field of interest.

2. Do not use the exact wording of the source in your paraphrase. A good rule of thumb is that no more than three consecutive words should appear in your article that appear in the source. If you have trouble restating source material accurately and fairly, opt to quote the information in question.

3. Consider paraphrasing long passages from your source; a paraphrase is a very useful means of summarizing the basic results of a study and the prominent opinions and ideas of an article or book chapter. Be sure, however, that you are

careful not to misrepresent the thrust of the passage in your paraphrase by over-emphasizing or over-simplifying the source's points.

4. Signal to your reader where your paraphrase ends either by (1) starting a new paragraph, as Henig does, in a format usually used in news articles, or by (2) including a transitional statement that clearly shows that the paraphrase has ended and now you are going to interpret the source material or apply it to your own ideas in the remainder of the paragraph. This is the trickiest part of paraphrasing information. The passage below from James Fallows' article "Japan: Playing By Different Rules" illustrates how to paraphrase accurately. Pay special attention to how Fallows introduces, summarizes, and then applies information from van Wolferen's article, his source.

Fallows' introduction *paraphrase of van Wolferen*	In an article called "The Japan Problem" published in Foreign Affairs late last year, the Dutch journalist Karel van Wolferen, who has lived in Japan for twenty-five years, argued that power in Japan was dispersed among a number of semi-autonomous baronies, each of which promoted its own interests and laughed off any attempt to change course. Prime Minister
Fallows' information *paraphrase of van Wolferen*	Nakasone, viewing the nation's predicament as a whole, might understand that Japan needed to start spending on itself. But, van Wolferen said, all the component parts of the system — the huge industrial companies, the labor unions, MITI, the farmers — were programmed to build market share, cut profit when necessary, resist foreign penetration, and export, export, ex-
Fallows' interpretation	port. Early last year the Japanese government rolled the drums for the Maekawa report, an ambitious proposal to increase imports, improve living standards, shorten the work week to five days, and generally make Japan a nation of economic men. By the end of the year, according to a survey conducted by the Ministry of Labor, the number of firms with a five-day week appeared to have gone down.

Documenting

An article's documentation consists of its system of referring to the sources. The reasons that documentation is necessary are mainly cultural; that is, the Western tradition of scholarship and invention holds as central to its ethics the accurate and fair attribution of ideas, opinions, and information to the individual or group of individuals who first expressed them. In short, an author or speaker is responsible for what he says and should also be given credit for his statements. Our society's notion of individual credit and responsibility also manifests itself in the taboo against plagiarism (the representation of another's work as your own) and in copyright and patent laws and practices.

As you research and draft an article, you need to be aware of what is fair and common practice in regard to documentation for the kind of piece you are writing. Documentation for a news story, for example, may be informal, completely contained within the text of the article, and consisting mostly of clear attribution of quotations and paraphrases. Sometimes a reporter will mention the title of a book or document that is a source, and sometimes he will withhold a source's name to protect her identify. The latter situation usually appears in an attribution to "a Pentagon insider," "a source close to the candidate," or "a highly place state official." This kind of attribution is acceptable in news sources where access to political and sensitive information may be difficult to obtain; however, it also renders the information much less credible and more speculative. Any critical reader will be suspicious of the truth of the information presented in an article that refers only to mysterious "inside sources."

In contrast to the relatively informal documentation of most news stories and popular magazine articles, pieces written for scholarly purposes, either for class-work or publication, are usually documented more exhaustively and according to a prescribed documentation system. Documentation systems vary from field to field, but in general all references in scholarly work contain the following basic information:

1. Author's name.
2. Title of the source, and if the source is an article, title of the magazine or journal in which the source was published.
3. Publication information; usually the publisher's name, city and date of publication.
4. Volume and page numbers in which the cited information appears.

The purpose of scholarly documentation is also more complex; it gives credit to the sources for their contributions, it establishes the reliability and scholarly care of the author, and it provides a reader with all the information she needs to locate source material, either for her own use or in order to double-check the article at hand.

If you are writing an article that calls for scholarly documentation, you must learn which documentation system is appropriate for your field. It's best to familiarize yourself with this system before you research so you can note all the necessary information along the way. Also, look over the style's method of including references in the text of your piece. Differences in this area will affect the phrasing of your introductions to source material. The following list is a sampling of some widely used style manuals for different disciplines.

Biology

Council of Biology Editors. Style Manual Committee. *CBE Style Manual: A Guide for Authors, Editors, and Publishers in the Biological Sciences.* 5th ed. Bethesda: Council of Biology Editors, 1983.

Humanities

Gibaldi, Joseph and Walter S. Achtert. *MLA Handbook for Writers of Research Papers.* 3rd ed. New York: Modern Language Association of America, 1988.

Journalism

Chicago Manual of Style. 13th ed. Chicago: University of Chicago Press, 1982.

Medicine

International Steering Committee of Medical Editors. "Uniform Requirements for Manuscripts Submitted to Biomedical Journals." *Annals of Internal Medicine* 90 (January 1979): 95–99.

Psychology

American Psychological Association. *Publication Manual of the American Psychological Association.* 3rd ed. Washington: American Psychological Assn., 1983.

For style manuals for other disciplines, check with an expert in the field or consult John Bruce Howell's *Style Manuals of the English-Speaking World* (Phoenix: Oryx, 1983).

The other important issue in documentation is determining what should and should not be documented. The rule of thumb for this question is for the writer to decide whether or not a piece of information is common knowledge. The facts that Ronald Reagan was the fortieth president of the United States, that the country of Belize is located on the Caribbean Sea south of Mexico and northeast of Guatemala, and that Greg Louganis won two gold medals in diving in the 1988 Summer Olympics in Seoul, Korea, are all common knowledge since they could readily be checked in a variety of reference books. But any facts that can't be checked easily and may be the result of one person's research should not be considered common knowledge. This information should therefore be documented. Furthermore, an expert's opinion or interpretation of even commonly known facts should be documented too. For instance, it is a statement of fact to say that Oriana Fallaci is a well-respected political interviewer, but it is a statement of opinion for Jonathan Cott to label her, as he does in his article about her, "the greatest political interviewer of modern times." If you cannot decide whether you should document a point because it may be considered common knowledge, play safe and document. That approach will assure your readers that you are a conscientious writer who uses sources honestly and carefully. The pointers listed below will help you make the best choices about documentation.

1. Take down bibliographic information for all sources when you research your topic. Attention to detail at this point will save you time and headaches later.

2. Determine the level of formality in documentation and the style of documentation that your article or essay deserves before you draft.

3. Familiarize yourself with the appropriate style before drafting so that you can make allowances for the special demands of the format during your drafting and revising stages.

4. As you draft and revise, determine which statements could be considered common knowledge and which will need to be documented.

5. Check all the details of documentation when you edit your work. Carelessness at this point can make careful research seem suspicious. Remember that your goal

is to present your documentation as straightforwardly as possible in order to gain credibility as a writer and to inform your readers faithfully.

FOCUS . . . .
SUGGESTIONS FOR WRITING

1. Make a list of your interests, including social causes, hobbies, and pastimes. How might one of these prompt you to write a news story, feature article, or encyclopedia article?

2. Once you find a topic, decide how you might develop it by analyzing the research options available to you. Think about how different research methods might lead you to write different articles or essays. In other words, how could you pursue a topic differently through observation, interviewing, reading, and surveying? Ultimately, of course, you may want to combine research methods, but one might guide you in determining the nature, tone, content, and development of the piece.

3. Review your journal for ideas that you could develop through research. You may want to be especially on the lookout for topics that you don't know much about. Set out to learn about some issue or answer a question through your research and writing.

4. Browse through some current newspapers and magazines. Make a list of intriguing topics and then consider whether one could be pursued from a local angle.

READINGS
• • • • • • • • • •

INFORMATIVE PROSE

Informative prose emphasizes the world, objective reality. It focuses on providing information, rather than on expressing the writer's belief or emotions, or on changing a reader's mind. Informative prose is most frequently found in news releases, reports, definitions, summaries, textbooks, histories, explanations, and encyclopedia articles. The following readings represent various forms of informative prose.

ALEXANDER CALDER

Harold Osborne

We have all used encyclopedias and dictionaries to find basic facts and information quickly. Here is an entry on an important modern artist, Alexander Calder, from The Oxford Companion to Twentieth-Century Art *(1981).*

CALDER, Alexander (1898–1976). American sculptor and painter, born in Lawnton, a suburb of Philadelphia. His grandfather, Alexander Milne Calder, and his father, Alexander Stirling Calder, were sculptors and his mother was a painter. His father had charge of the sculptural work for the Los Angeles World Exhibition in 1912. Alexander Calder, however, studied mechanical engineering from 1915 to 1919 and began to take an interest in landscape painting only in 1922 after having tried his hand at a variety of jobs. In 1923 he enrolled at the School of the Art Students' League, New York, where George LUKS and John SLOAN were among the teachers. Calder and his fellow students made a game of rapidly sketching people in the streets and the underground and Calder was noted for his skills in conveying a sense of movement by a single unbroken line. He also took an interest in sport and circus events and contributed drawings to the satirical *National Police Gazette*. From these activities it was but a step to his wire sculptures, the first of which—a sun-dial in the form of a cock—was done in 1925. In 1927 he made moving toys for the Gould Manufacturing Company and small figures of animals and clowns with which he gave circus performances in his studio. His first exhibition of paintings was in the Artists' Gal., New York, in 1926; his first Paris one-man show was in the Gal. Billiet in 1929 and the Foreword to the catalogue was written by PASCIN, whom he had met the previous year. His wire figures were exhibited by Carl Zigrosser at the Weyhe Gal. and Bookshop, New York, in 1928 and at the Neumann and Nierendorf Gal., Berlin, in 1929, when they were made the subject of a short film by Dr. Hans Cürlis.

During the 1930s Calder became known both in Paris and in America for his wire sculpture and portraits, his abstract constructions and his drawings. In 1931 he joined the ABSTRACTION-CRÉATION association and in the same year produced his first non-figurative moving construction. The constructions which were moved by hand or by motor-power were baptized 'mobiles' in 1932 by Marcel DUCHAMP, and ARP suggested 'stabiles' for the non-moving constructions in the same year. It was in 1934 that Calder began to make the unpowered mobiles for which he is most widely known. Constructed usually from pieces of shaped and painted tin suspended on thin wires or cords, these responded by their own weight to the faintest air currents and were designed to take advantage of effects of changing light created by the movements. They were described by Calder as 'four-dimensional drawings,' and in a letter to Duchamp written in 1932 he spoke of his desire to make 'moving Mondrians.' Calder was in fact greatly impressed by a visit to MONDRIAN in 1930, and no doubt envisaged himself as bringing movement to Mondrian-type geometrical abstracts. Yet the personality and outlook of the two men were very different. Calder's pawky delight in the comic and fantastic, which obtrudes even in his large works, was at the opposite pole from the Messianic seriousness of Mondrian.

Calder continued to do both mobiles and stabiles until the 1970s, sometimes combining the two into one structure. Some of these works were of very large dimensions: *Teodelapia* (1962), a stabile for the city of Spoleto, was 18 m high and 14 m long; *Man*, done for the Montreal World Exhibition in 1967, was 23 m high; *Red Sun* (1967) for the Olympic Stadium, Mexico, was 24 m high and the motorized hanging mobile *Red, Black and Blue* (1967) at Dallas airport was 14 m wide. His interest in animal figures and the circus also continued into the 1970s and in 1971 he was making 'Animobiles' reminiscent of animals. Although he had done gouaches since the late 1920s, he began to take a more serious interest in them and to exhibit them from 1952.

Calder's mobiles were among the forerunners of KINETIC ART and his great reputation depended in part on the fact that he was among the first to incorporate real movement into sculptural art. He concentrated chiefly, however, on free and uncontrolled movement rather than the carefully planned and controlled movements — planned even when they incorporated an element of chance — with which later kinetic artists have been mainly concerned. Among his more important exhibitions were: Gal. Louis Carré, Paris, 1946, for which J.-P. Sartre wrote a now famous essay; exhibition with LÉGER at Stedelijk Mus., Amsterdam, and Kunsthalle, Berne, 1947; retrospectives at The Mus. of Modern Art, New York (1943); Basle (1955); Amsterdam (1959); Solomon R. Guggenheim Mus., New York (1964); Paris (1965); St. Paul-de-Vence (1969); Gal. Maeght, Zürich (1973); Haus der Kunst, Munich, and Kunsthaus, Zürich (1975). A Calder Festival was staged in Chicago in 1974.

QUESTIONS

1. How is this entry arranged? Outline it quickly. Are there other plausible arrangements the author might have used?

2. Glance over some other entries from other encyclopedias. Is there an archetypal format employed in these entries? What variations do you find? ·

3. Like most encyclopedias, *The Oxford Companion* capitalizes words and terms that are also headings in themselves. These terms can then be looked up if more information is needed. What capitalized terms do you find in this article that you do not understand? Are there uncapitalized terms you do not understand? Is is clear to you just what the "Messianic seriousness of Mondrian" really is? Where would you go to find an explanation for this?

4. How would you characterize the audience for this *Companion*? Is this a book for someone who knows nothing about art? What aspects of this entry need to be made more clear to you?

5. Select a topic from the world of art, music, or literature and write an entry on this topic for an imaginary encyclopedia aimed at college freshmen.

• • • • •

ENGRAVING

Peter and Linda Murray

Here is the definition of engraving from The Penguin Dictionary of Art and Artists *(1983). Compare it with the entry on Alexander Calder on page 204.*

ENGRAVING. A generic title often used to cover all the methods of multiplying prints, although strictly the word should apply only to the second of the processes described below. The first distinction to be drawn is between Reproductive and Original Engravings, a reproductive engraving being a means of divulgating an idea expressed in a painting, drawing, statue, or other medium, invented by an artist other than the engraver. An original engraving is an independent work of art invented by the engraver himself.

The three main types of engraving may be classified as (1) Relief or cameo, (2) Intaglio, and (3) Surface or planar. Each of these types corresponds to one or more of the main techniques, and each type has a special method of printing. (1) Relief. The main techniques are Woodcut and Wood-engraving, Linocut and its simpler forms, such as Potato cuts. A plain block of wood, if covered with printing ink and pressed on a sheet of paper, would print as a black rectangle: but if channels were cut into the surface with a gouge these would not catch the ink, and, therefore, would print as white patches. The principle of a woodcut is therefore to leave the black lines or patches as untouched wood and to cut away the parts intended to print as white. A single black line has to have the wood on each side of it cut away, and this is done with special knives and gouges. Woodcuts are done on blocks of soft wood, cut plank-fashion, and will give hundreds, or even thousands, of impressions before wearing out. Lino is often used nowaday, as it is easier to work, but its life is shorter. Colour prints are produced by cutting a special block for each colour as well as a key-block, usually printed black, which carries the linear structure (*see* CHIAROSCURO *woodcut*), and these have to be printed 'in register,' so that the forms do not overlap. The earliest woodcuts date from the end of the 14th century, but wood-engraving hardly occurs before the mid-18th century, and found one of its greatest exponents in Thomas BEWICK, who revived white-line engraving. Wood-engraving is very similar to engraving on copper, using the same kind of tool, called a graver or burin. The main difference between wood-engraving and woodcuts is in the block itself, which is of boxwood, cut across the grain, for wood-engraving. On this smooth, grainless surface the sharply pointed graving tools can plough very fine furrows each of which will print as a fine white line. Obviously, it is far easier to think in terms of white lines on a predominantly black ground, and the great modern revival (since about 1920) of wood-engraving has been of the white-line or Xylographic type, which offers a means of stylized design.

(2) Intaglio (Ital. cut in). The intaglio techniques are all forms of engraving on metal, usually copper, and they are distinguished from the other techniques by the method of printing. When the plate has been engraved by one or more of the processes to be described — and several processes are often used in combination — the plate is dabbed all over with a thin kind of printing ink, which is then rubbed off again with muslin or the palm of the hand, leaving the ink in the engraved furrows. A piece of paper is then damped and laid on the plate and both are rolled through a heavy press not unlike a mangle. The damp paper is forced into the engraved lines and so picks up the ink in them: when dry the engraved lines stand up in relief. This explains the great difference between a copper-engraving, or any other intaglio print, and a wood-engraving which has been cut in a very similar way — the ink lies on the surface of a wood-engraved block instead of being forced into the lines cut (*intagliate*) into the metal plate. A wood-engraving cannot be printed in the intaglio manner as it would break under the great pressure. The main intaglio processes are: (*a*) Line (or copper) engraving, (*b*) Dry-point, (*c*) Etching, including Soft-ground etching, (*d*) Stipple and crayon engraving, (*e*) Mezzotint, and (*f*) Aquatint and the related processes.

(*a*) *Line-engraving*. The sharp graver is pushed into the copper, exactly like a plough into the earth, throwing up small shavings and leaving a line which has a V-section. This is the earliest of the intaglio techniques, as the earliest dated print is of 1446, but it is also the one demanding the greatest discipline and precision of hand since the sharp tool has to be pushed ahead of the hand — and polished copper is very slippery. DÜRER is incomparably the greatest artist in this medium, which was later used mainly for reproducing pictures and other works of art. Seventeenth-century engravers (especially French) brought the art to the pitch of perfection as a didactic medium.

(*b*) *Dry-point*. This is the simplest technique, since it consists of drawing on the metal plate with a 'pencil' made of hard steel, or steel tipped with diamond, ruby, or carborundum (*see* CRAYON ÉLECTRIQUE). The great quality of dry-point lies in the burr, which is the shaving of metal turned up at the side of the furrow. When burr occurs in line-engraving it is scraped off, but it is left in a dry-point because it catches the ink and prints with a richness which adds to the directness of the artist's work. Unfortunately, it is soon crushed by the pressure of printing, so that less than fifty good impressions can be taken. Dry-point is often used to reinforce etching or even engraving; Rembrandt, in particular, often combined it with etching.

(*c*) *Etching.* Here the metal plate is covered with a resinous ground, impervious to acid, and then the etcher draws on the ground with a needle, exposing the copper wherever he wants a line to print. The plate is put in an acid bath, which eats away the exposed parts, but subtlety is given by taking the plate out of the acid as soon as the faintest lines are bitten. These faint lines are then 'stopped-out' with varnish and the plate re-bitten until the medium-dark lines are stopped-out in their turn, and so on. The first dated etching is of 1513 (by URS GRAF), but the great period came with the 17th century, culminating in Rembrandt, and the process has been popular ever since. *Soft-ground Etching* looks like a pencil or chalk drawing, because the ground is mixed tallow, and has a sheet of thin paper laid on it, on to which the etcher draws directly with a pencil; part of the ground sticks to the paper giving a grainy effect when the plate is bitten. CASTIGLIONE may have invented the process. A *Photographic Etching* or *Cliché-Verre* is made by drawing with a stylus on a grounded glass plate which is then treated like a photographic negative and printed on photographic paper. More than sixty such "etchings" were made by Corot from *c.* 1853, but the technique never became popular, even though it permits of limitless prints.

(*d*) *Stipple*, *crayon engraving*, and *colour printing* were popular 18th-century techniques. Stipple and crayon engraving were used particularly for the reproduction of portrait drawings, giving an effect remarkably similar to that of a chalk drawing. It is obtained by a combination of etching and engraving techniques, stippling dots over a grounded plate with the point of an etching needle or, more usually, by the use of special tools; a *Roulette* is a spur-like wheel which gives an effect similar to the grainy quality of chalk, and it can be combined with a *Mattoir*, which is an instrument like a tiny club with sharp points projecting from the head. These points produce a grained effect on the bare copper which prints as black, chalk-like dots. Occasionally the effect of two-colour chalks is obtained by printing from two plates, usually black and red.

Colour engravings of the 18th century fall into two main categories, English and French. The finest English colour prints are usually based on the aquatint process (see (*f*) below) and are made by a single printing from a plate coloured in the appropriate areas. Some English colour prints are, in fact, monochrome aquatints hand-coloured in watercolour, and both GIRTIN and TURNER earned a living colouring engravings at the beginning of their careers.

The French technique, sometimes called *manière de lavis*, is an imitation of a wash drawing or a watercolour obtained by the use of a great number of *roulettes*, *mattoirs* and gravers. The use of these tools gave the tones, but the actual colours were printed from four separate plates — yellow, red, blue, and black, printed in that order, the black being the most important since it defined the contours. The most difficult part of this technique is to ensure that one plate is printed exactly on top of another — 'in register.'

(*e*) *Mezzotint.* This was the great reproductive process of the 18th century (though invented in the 17th century), especially famous and successful in England, where the portraits of Reynolds and Gainsborough were normally reproduced by it. The plate is first covered with a mesh of small burred dots, made by a toothed chisel-like 'rocker.' In this state the plate would print as a solid, rich black. The half-tones and lights are obtained by scraping off the burr with a scraper, or polishing the plate smooth again with a burnisher so that the ink may be wiped off the highest lights. The technique is rarely practised now, as photographic methods have superseded it for reproduction.

(f) *Aquatint.* Like mezzotint, aquatint is a tone process rather than a line method, but it is admirably adapted to the rendering of transparent effects, such as watercolour gives. It is basically a form of etching, but using a porous ground which the acid can penetrate to form a network of fine lines. Any pure whites are stopped out in the usual way before biting begins, then the palest tints are bitten and stopped out, and so on as in etching. Variations of texture can be obtained by pressing a piece of sand-paper on the grounded plate, mixing sugar with the ground, or attacking the plate with sulphur ('sulphur-tint'). Paul SANDBY was the first imaginative artist to use the process, followed by the greatest of all aquatinters, GOYA, but it has been revived by John Piper, and Picasso used the sugar process for his illustrations to Buffon.

(3) Surface Printing. The one major process which involves no cutting into the block or plate, and therefore no 'engraving' in the proper sense, is Lithography, usually executed on a thick slab of stone, although zinc is now more common as it is both lighter and less fragile. The whole technique, invented in 1798 by Alois Senefelder, is based on the fact that water runs off a greasy surface. The design is drawn or painted on the stone with a greasy chalk and then the stone is wetted. When the greasy ink is rolled on the stone it will not 'take' on the wet parts, but it sticks on the parts which are already greasy, off which the water ran. The new process was taken up by several 19th-century artists, including Delacroix, Goya, Géricault, Daumier, Manet, and others, and it is still a popular medium. It is used very widely for posters and other forms of commercial art, since it produces many thousands of prints. Chromolithography, to give it its full name, can be used for colour-printing, with one stone for each colour, printed in register. The first major work produced by this method was BOYS's 'Picturesque Architecture,' 1839. Its great advantage is that there is almost no limit to the number of prints it is possible to take.

QUESTIONS

1. *The Penguin Dictionary* calls itself a dictionary rather than an encyclopedia. Is there a difference in the nature of its entry? Is there a difference in the arrangement or format of its entry? What seem to be the chief differences between an encyclopedia and a specialized dictionary such as this one?

2. Do you find this entry easier to understand than the one on Alexander Calder, or more difficult? Why? What terms would you like to see clarified?

3. It is said that a picture is worth a thousand words. Would illustrations be helpful in allowing readers to understand this entry better? Would illustrations be helpful with the Calder entry? Why or why not?

4. Characterize the audience for which this entry seems to be written.

YACHT RACING

The Diagram Group

Satellites and cable television have exposed us to more sporting events, and more different kinds of sporting events, than ever before. Because a touch of a button can now bring Australian football, Wimbledon, billiard championships, and tractor pulls into our living rooms, we may find that we do not always understand the fine points of all these forms of competition. If you were a bit confused by the recent America's Cup races, here is an explanation of yacht racing that may clarify things somewhat. It is taken from The Rule Book, *a compendium of rules for various sports.*

History

The first recorded yacht race took place in England in 1661, between King Charles II and his brother, the Duke of York. The yachts were attended by the royal barge and kitchen-boat, and the King won the wager of £100.

Organized regattas and small boat sailing races are first recorded in the late nineteenth century; earlier yacht races had been private matches, arranged between the owners of large sea-going yachts. Inshore yacht racing has been included in the Olympic program since the first games of the modern series. The international governing body, the International Yacht Racing Union (IYRU) was founded in 1907.

Synopsis

Using sail power only, competitors aim to complete a prescribed course in the shortest time. Rules described here are for inshore races sailed in daylight over a triangular course.

Competitors and Officials

Competitors   The crew carried by a yacht is specified in her class rules. Crews for classes raced in Olympic Games are as listed.

Officials   Races are controlled by a race committee, who are responsible for setting the course, and for supervising the starting and finishing lines. The control point may be a good vantage point ashore, or a committee boat anchored near the starting line.

Because no referee or umpires accompany the racing yachts, competitors are expected to acknowledge their own rule infringements and enter protests about those of other yachts. Protests are heard by a jury after the conclusion of the race, and may affect the result.

Yachts and Equipment

Yacht classes   All yachts are either keel boats, dinghies, or catamarans. Keel boats and dinghies are further divided into classes. Class rules govern the measurements, shape, weight, buoyancy, and equipment of member yachts, and every yacht

Yacht Racing 1

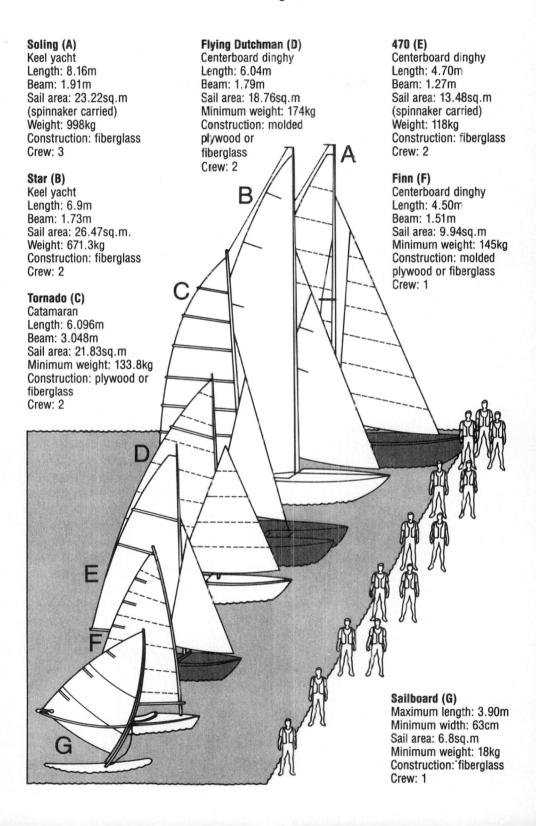

Soling (A)
Keel yacht
Length: 8.16m
Beam: 1.91m
Sail area: 23.22sq.m
(spinnaker carried)
Weight: 998kg
Construction: fiberglass
Crew: 3

Star (B)
Keel yacht
Length: 6.9m
Beam: 1.73m
Sail area: 26.47sq.m.
Weight: 671.3kg
Construction: fiberglass
Crew: 2

Tornado (C)
Catamaran
Length: 6.096m
Beam: 3.048m
Sail area: 21.83sq.m
Minimum weight: 133.8kg
Construction: plywood or
fiberglass
Crew: 2

Flying Dutchman (D)
Centerboard dinghy
Length: 6.04m
Beam: 1.79m
Sail area: 18.76sq.m
Minimum weight: 174kg
Construction: molded
plywood or
fiberglass
Crew: 2

470 (E)
Centerboard dinghy
Length: 4.70m
Beam: 1.27m
Sail area: 13.48sq.m
(spinnaker carried)
Weight: 118kg
Construction: fiberglass
Crew: 2

Finn (F)
Centerboard dinghy
Length: 4.50m
Beam: 1.51m
Sail area: 9.94sq.m
Minimum weight: 145kg
Construction: molded
plywood or fiberglass
Crew: 1

Sailboard (G)
Maximum length: 3.90m
Minimum width: 63cm
Sail area: 6.8sq.m
Minimum weight: 18kg
Construction: fiberglass
Crew: 1

must have official certificates of conformity to class rules. There are many internationally recognized classes, but all are one of three kinds:

(a) one design classes, in which all boats must be identical;

(b) development class, which allows stated variations on the design;

(c) formula class (for keel boats only), in which a number of measurements, such as length, draft, and sail area, are inserted into a complex formula to give a result that does not exceed a given limit.

A yacht must be maintained in accordance with her class rules, and alterations that would invalidate her certificate are prohibited.

A yacht may not eject or release from a container any substance (such as polymer) that might reduce the frictional resistance of her hull to the water.

Olympic classes   The seven international classes currently eligible for the Olympic Games are as illustrated.

Equipment   Required equipment for yachts is prescribed in class rules and in sailing instructions for a specific event. Usual equipment may include an anchor, racing and protest flags, sails with specified identifying inscriptions, and lifesaving equipment.

Ballast carried must conform with class rules, and must be in place the day before the race.

Unless prescribed in the class rules, a yacht may not use any device, such as a trapeze or plank, to project a crewman's weight outboard.

Only manual power may be used unless class rules permit a power winch or windlass for weighing anchor after running aground or fouling an obstruction, or a power pump in an auxiliary yacht.

Dress   The total weight of clothing or equipment worn by a competitor should not exceed 15kg when soaked with water, unless class rules specify a lesser or greater weight which may not exceed 20kg.

Course Layout

Course   There are no restrictions on the size or layout of the course. The course length and direction are determined by the race committee, who take into account local tide and weather conditions, the prevailing wind direction, and the class and numbers of the yachts taking part.

Most courses are triangular: a standard Olympic triangular course is illustrated. Turning points on a course are defined by marks (usually buoys) which must be rounded or passed in the correct order and on the required side.

If necessary, because of foul weather or insufficient wind, the race committee may use flag signals to indicate that the course is shortened or reversed, or that the race is canceled, postponed, or abandoned.

The starting line   may be between two marks, a mark and a sighting post, or an extension from two starting posts. Race instructions may also define a starting area, which should be indicated by buoys.

Yacht Racing 2

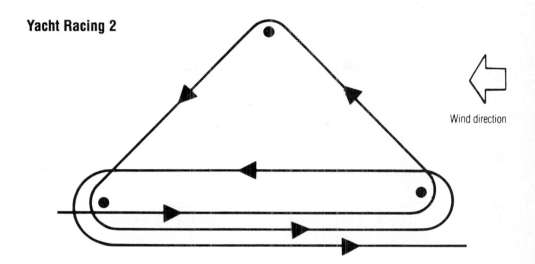

Wind direction

The finishing line   should be marked in the same way as the starting line.

Definitions

Leeward   The leeward side of a yacht is that on which she is or, when head to wind, was carrying her mainsail.

Windward   The windward side is the opposite side to the leeward side.

Luffing   is altering course toward the wind until head to wind (**a**).

Gybing   A yacht begins to gybe when, with the wind behind her, her mainsail crosses her center line. The gybe ends when the mainsail has filled on the other tack.

Bearing away   is altering course away from the wind until the yacht begins to gybe (**b**).

Tacking   is altering course from port (left) (**c**) to starboard (right) (**d**) tack, or vice versa, with the wind ahead. A yacht is tacking from the moment she is beyond head to wind until she has borne away to her course on the new tack.

On a tack   A yacht is on a tack except when she is tacking or gybing. She is on the tack (port or standard) corresponding to her windward side.

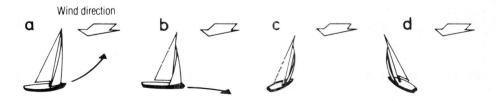

Wind direction

Race Procedure

Sailing the yacht   A yacht may be propelled only by the natural action of wind on the sails and spars, and of water on the hull and underwater surfaces.

When suitable weather conditions exist, a competitor is permitted to surf or plane a yacht by means of a sudden movement of his body backward or forward ("ooching") or by not more than three rapidly repeated trims and releases of any sail ("pumping").

Sailing actions that are prohibited are:
(a) repeated forceful movements of the helm ("sculling");
(b) repeated pumping;
(c) repeated ooching;
(d) persistently rolling the yacht from side to side ("rocking");
(e) persistent or rapidly repeated vertical or side-to-side body movements.
(f) repeated gybing or roll-tacking in calm or near calm conditions.

Starting procedure   Yachts maneuver in the starting area to be in a position to cross the line at the starting signal.

The starting signal is given by three flag signals, usually at five-minute intervals. The flag signals are:
(a) the warning signal, when the flag indicating the class to race is hoisted;
(b) the preparatory signal, when the code flag "P" (the "Blue Peter") is hoisted, or another distinctive signal is displayed;
(c) the starting signal, when both flags are lowered.

Sound signals drawing attention to the flag signals are given with a gun or hooter, but the flag signals are always used for timing purposes.

Starting prematurely   Any yacht over the starting line at the starting signal must recross the line.

Where yachts have been allotted recall numbers, an individual premature start is signaled by displaying the offending yacht's recall number. Where no recall number has been allotted, the offending yacht may be recalled by lowering the class flag to half-mast, or by hailing her sail number. A general recall, if several unidentified yachts are over the line, is signaled by a special flag. All flag recall signals are accompanied by sound signals. Failure of a yacht to see or hear her recall signal does not relieve her of the obligation to cross the starting line correctly.

Rounding a mark   A yacht must sail the course so that she rounds or passes each mark on the required side and in the correct sequence.

If a yacht passes a mark on the wrong side, she must return by that side and then round or pass the mark on the correct side (**1**).

If a yacht touches a mark, or causes a mark to move to avoid touching it, she must:
(a) retire from the race at once; or
(b) protest against another yacht for causing her offense; or

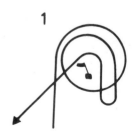

1

(c) when the mark is surrounded by navigable water, absolve herself by completing her rounding of the mark and then re-rounding the same mark without touching it (**2**); or

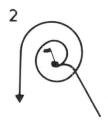

(d) when the mark is not surrounded by navigable water, absolve herself by completing her rounding, and then making a 360° turn at the first reasonable opportunity (**3**).

A yacht that touches a starting mark before she has officially started in the race must comply with one of the above alternatives after she has started racing.

If a yacht touches a finishing mark, she is not considered to have completed the race until she has completed the rounding of the mark and crossed the finishing line again.

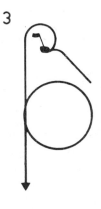

Giving room at a mark Providing that an overlap exists between the yachts when they are at least two boat lengths from a mark or obstruction, the yacht on the outside course must give room where possible to:

(a) overlapping yachts on the same tack;

(b) overlapping yachts on the same or opposite tacks going downwind.

This includes giving room for the inside yacht to tack or gybe if this is an integral part of the maneuver; the inside yacht must tack or gybe at the first opportunity.

Modified rules apply to yachts approaching the starting line before the starting signal has been given.

YACHT RACING 4

Penalties and Scoring

Infringements and protests When a yacht infringes rules or instructions, or causes another yacht to do so, she should retire immediately or observe such other penalty as may be imposed in the sailing instructions. If she fails to do either, then other yachts must still observe racing rules toward her.

The crew member in charge of any yacht finishing must sign a declaration that all rules have been observed and, within a time limit, enter any protests against other yachts. Before making a protest he must usually have flown a "protest flag" during the race and hailed the offending yacht that a protest would be made.

In national events, protests are heard by the race committee or a subcommittee; appeal is to the national authority. In international events, protests are heard by an IYRU jury; there is no appeal. Committees and juries may also instigate hearings where no protest has been made. The outcome of a hearing may penalize a different yacht, or invoke a different rule, from those in the original protest.

If the finishing position of a yacht is materially prejudiced by rendering assistance, being disabled when having the right of way, or by act or omission of the race committee, the race may be canceled or abandoned, or other arrangements made. In the Olympics, a yacht so prejudiced receives points equal to her average points (to the nearest one-tenth) for the other five races.

Penalties for acknowledged infringements   During the race the penalty may be two full turns through 360°, clear of other yachts, and on the same leg of the course as the infringement.

Causing a collision always requires retirement.

After the race the penalty may be to score for finishing in a place worse than the actual finishing place by 20% of the number of starters (minimum of three places lower; maximum of one place less than the number of starters).

Penalties after a hearing   for unacknowledged infringements include:
(a) for an infringement of the sailing instructions, to score for finishing in a place worse than the actual finishing place by 30% of the number of starters;
(b) disqualification from the race;
(c) exclusion from the series;
(d) for a gross infringement, the owner or helmsman or crewman in change may be disqualified from racing for a period of time.

Scoring   In the Olympic Games and most major competitions, points are awarded as follows:
first place, 0 points;
second place, 3 points;
third place, 5.7 points;
fourth place, 8 points;
fifth place, 10 points;
sixth place, 11.7 points;
seventh place and below, place plus 6 points.

Yachts that do not finish, that sail the course incorrectly, or that retire after infringing the rules score the points for a last place finish.

Yachts disqualified, or infringing the rules and not retiring, score as for a last place finish plus points equal to 10% of the number of yachts starting.

Races are usually held in series. In the Olympic Games, there are seven races for each class, and each yacht counts her best six results for her total score. The yacht with the lowest points score is the winner.

Boardsailing

Triangle racing   Sailboard races over a triangular course will be included in the 1984 Olympic Games. Sailboards raced must comply with the [specific] measurements given. Triangle races are sailed under IYRU rules, with some minor amendments. Races may be sailed in heats if so stipulated in the sailing instructions.

Competitors may be divided into groups depending on their bodyweight. Competitors weighing under 72kg in their first event of a racing season compete in the lightweight group; competitors weighing over 72kg compete in the heavyweight group. If, in subsequent events, the weight of a competitor in the lightweight group is found to exceed 75kg, he is transferred to the heavyweight group. If the weight of a competitor in the heavyweight group falls below 70kg, he is transferred to the lightweight group.

Other events are not, as yet, governed by an international body, but by individual class rules or by sailing instructions issued by a particular competition. Examples of different events are described below.

Slalom races are run on a knock-out basis over three laps of a course marked by six buoys. Two sailboats compete in each heat, with the winner going forward to the next round.

Ins and outs combine elements of slalom and triangle racing courses, and are laid out close to the shore, so that competitors must sail "in and out" through surf. Races are run as a series, with points awarded for positions.

Marathon races are long distance massed start races sailed in varying wind and water conditions.

Freestyle events are contested over two rounds. Competitors in the elimination round must perform a set series of tricks on their sailboards. The highest scoring competitors go forward to the second round, and perform a series of tricks of their own choice.

Competitors are judged on the technical difficulty of their tricks, and the artistic merit of their performance.

QUESTIONS

1. How is this entry arranged? Does this seem to be a good format, or could it be improved?

2. One of the primary features of *The Rule Book* is its extensive use of illustrations and diagrams. Do you find these helpful? Is there a need for even more illustrations than we have here? What would you like to see illustrated?

3. What aspects of yacht racing are still unclear to you? How might these points be clarified? Should this description be made longer? Or is it too detailed now?

4. Select an aspect of one of your favorite sports or games (e.g., scoring a run in baseball, the forward pass in football, opening moves in chess) and draft an explanation of it. Limit your topic carefully; you will not easily be able to explain all the rules of any single sport. Feel free to use illustrations if you find them necessary.

SHORT CIRCUITS

Bob Cerullo

Popular Science *is a magazine that attempts to make science and technology clear to the lay person. As part of that mission the magazine publishes a number of articles for readers who are struggling to understand plumbing, home repair, and simple automotive problems. This article, typical of* Popular Science, *advises you on what to do when you find your car's battery dead.*

"Fɪʀsᴛ I replaced the battery, then I replaced the alternator. But the battery still goes dead every few days. I give up." Obviously frustrated at his failure to solve the problem after several hours of effort — and quite a few dollars of expense — this car owner had put his pride in his pocket and brought his car to my service garage in Brooklyn, N.Y.

Raising the car's hood, I asked the driver to describe the symptoms of the problem. "The car starts fine with a boost, or immediately after a battery charge. Then it runs well," he replied. "But if I don't drive it for a few days, the battery goes dead again."

I wish I had a dime for every perfectly good part that is replaced simply because the owner suspects it might be defective, I thought to myself. "The key to success in electrical-circuit repairs is never to assume anything," I explained. "The discharged battery could be caused by a slipping alternator belt, a bad regulator, a loose wire, dirty battery connections, current drains from a defective switch, or any one of a dozen other faults.

"We'll find the problem by methodically running down the list of possibilities," I said. "Without even touching a voltmeter, we already know a few things about the situation. Because the alternator and battery are new, it's safe to assume they are all right.

"My guess is that you may have an unwanted ground, or current drain," I ventured, pulling the cable loose from the positive battery terminal. I clipped the lead of a 12-volt test lamp to the unattached battery cable and touched the probe to the terminal. The light bulb glowed.

"It is a drain," I announced. "Now all we have to do is find the bad circuit." I opened the fuse box and started at one end of the row, removing a fuse labeled "taillight." The light still glowed, so I replaced the fuse. Then I removed the second fuse from a receptacle marked "dome/trunk."

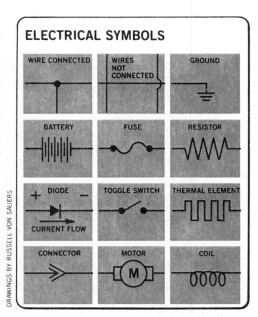

ELECTRICAL SYMBOLS

WIRE CONNECTED	WIRES NOT CONNECTED	GROUND
BATTERY	FUSE	RESISTOR
+ DIODE – CURRENT FLOW	TOGGLE SWITCH	THERMAL ELEMENT
CONNECTOR	MOTOR	COIL

These symbols describe the components found on wiring diagrams. Drawings by Russell Von Sauers.

The test light went out. Not bad. On the second try, after less than five minutes of work, we had found the circuit that was causing the current drain.

The next step took a few minutes longer to complete. Searching through my shelf of service manuals, I found an electrical schematic that matched the customer's make and model of car.

"Do your dome light and cigarette lighter work all right?" I inquired. "They've never caused any trouble," the customer answered.

"Then let's have a look in the trunk." I reconnected the battery, then folded the sedan's rear seat forward and peered behind it. The trunk light was glowing brightly, permanently connected to the battery by a switch stuck in the "on" position. "We found the drain," I proclaimed. The customer seemed overjoyed that a new trunk-light switch would cure the dead-battery problem.

Beginners Welcome

Problems like the one above can be difficult — and expensive — to diagnose if you don't have a grasp of the basics of electrical trouble-shooting. But armed with a modest kit of diagnostic tools, a shop manual, a few basic techniques, and a measure of patience, the weekend mechanic can do as good a job of automotive electrical repair as many professionals.

What's Draining the Battery?

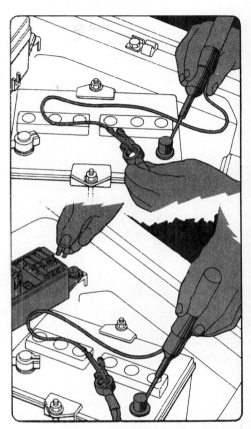

The test light connecting the battery terminal with the disconnected cable clamp glows, indicating a current drain. When the fuse for the offending circuit is pulled, the test light will go out. Check them all, one at a time.

And this is a category of repairs where learning how to do the work yourself can save a sizable service bill; not all troubleshooting goes as quickly as the previous example, so a simple but elusive electrical problem can run up a hefty tab. Besides the money-saving aspect, the low voltage involved probably makes tracing electrical problems one of the safest repair jobs you can perform.

Just be careful with the secondary wiring — the heavy high-voltage cable that connects the coil and spark plugs. And when working on late-model cars with electronic engine controls, make sure you follow the procedures in the factory service manual when you perform any tests on the control module or its sensors and wiring. Mistakes here can damage or destroy expensive components.

Whether confronted with instrument-panel lights that flicker or fuses that blow, you won't have much chance of finding the problem if you don't understand the circuit you're working on. So the place to start isn't under the hood, it's in the schematic wiring diagram for the car. The best schematic is one drawn specifically for your make and model car. These are available from the car maker or in auto-repair manuals sold in book stores.

The schematic diagram is your road map through a maze of thousands of wires. As with any road map, you have to know where you are and how to read the symbols. (The legend identifies most of the commonly used symbols.)

Is There Current in the Circuit?

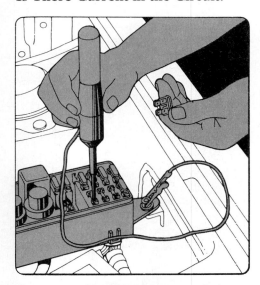

Current reaching the fuse receptacle from the car's battery illuminates the grounded test light. So far so good.

The schematic also tells you what powers the component you are checking, and which other components share the same circuit. Your starting point on the schematic should be the battery. Next locate the questionable component. Then trace the route the current takes from the battery to the failed part. Sometimes it can be helpful to highlight the circuit you are working on with a colored felt-tip pen.

You will often find the component shares its wiring and fuse with some other seemingly unrelated part. A good example of this is an instrument-lamp circuit that shares a fuse with the license-plate lamp. In this case, when the wire to the license-plate lamp is shorted, the fuse blows, causing the instrument-panel lamps to go out as well. Without the schematic to explain it, a connection like this would probably remain a mystery.

Trouble-Shooting Tools

The most basic of these tools is the test lamp. When it glows, you know there is power present in a circuit. You can make a test lamp from a 12-volt taillight bulb and socket with leads and gator clips attached. But you may also want to buy a ready-made light from an auto-parts store. This type usually puts the bulb inside the plastic handle for protection, and its sharp metal tip allows you to probe for current by gently piercing the insulation of a wire.

A battery-powered test lamp is another tool that makes testing isolated circuits for continuity quick and easy. You'll also need an assortment of jumper wires with alligator clips at each end. Use these to bypass dead circuits and to directly connect motors, etc. to the battery for testing. You can save yourself a great deal of grief if you buy a few five-ampere in-line fuse assemblies (available at radio-supply stores) and splice them into your jumper wires. This way the jumper-wire fuse will blow before you can cause damage to most circuits, should you happen to hit the wrong wire.

Cutting pliers, wire strippers, screwdrivers, and electrical tape should also be a part of your basic toolbox. Another important item is a supply of adhesive labels to identify anonymous-looking wires before you forget where they belong. 3M Co. makes handy numbered labels for this purpose. Finally, a volt-ohmmeter, or multimeter, is useful for several tests.

Checking for Current

When a component—the heater blower, for example—doesn't work, the first thing to do is check the fuse for that circuit. If the fuse is OK, the next step is to check for power at the switch that controls the component. Attach one lead of a test light to the heater-blower side of the switch, and ground the other lead. If the light doesn't illuminate, it's time to work backward toward the battery, looking for the place the break occurs.

Make a step-by-step check for voltage between the battery and the switch. Start by removing the fuse and connecting one lead of a test light to the battery side of the fuse socket. When you ground the other lead to the car body, the light will glow if power is reaching the fuse block. If there is no power at the fuse, you know the problem lies somewhere between the battery and the fuse block.

If you find you have power at the fuse, start tracing the circuit in the other direction, using the schematic as a guide. At every connector along the way, check for voltage with the test light. If you find a point where the light doesn't illuminate, you know there's an open or shorted circuit somewhere in the section of wire leading to that point.

What if there is power at the blower switch? The test light should glow intermittently when you work the switch back and forth. Now you know the problem is occurring still farther along the circuit.

When the test lamp indicates current at the connection closest to the motor, the

Does Voltage Drop across Connectors?

The voltmeter leads tap the wires on either side of the connector. A drop of more than 1 V indicates trouble.

motor itself becomes suspect. The first thing to check is the condition of the motor's ground. Often the motor grounds to the car body through its mounting bolts. (This is also common with horns, wiper motors, and so on.) If there isn't a clean connection here, the circuit remains open. By connecting a jumper wire from the motor to a known good ground point, you can answer this question. If the motor runs, the bad ground is the culprit.

Where's the Short Circuit?

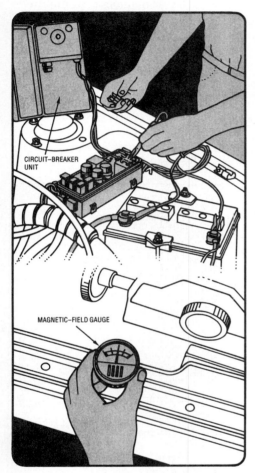

CIRCUIT–BREAKER UNIT

MAGNETIC–FIELD GAUGE

Short-circuit finder's circuit-breaker unit connects to the car battery. It sends a pulsing charge through the circuit from the fuse block. The gauge's needle stops oscillating when it locates a short circuit inside the rocker panel.

Finally, before you start to remove the motor, give it one last chance. Use a jumper wire to connect it directly to the battery. If it's still silent, replace it. If it runs, you missed something along the way.

Detecting a Current Drain

If a car's battery goes dead when the vehicle isn't driven for a few days, it is possible that the battery is simply worn out and won't hold a charge. But if the battery is in good condition, it's likely there is a current drain somewhere. There's a quick and easy test for current drain that requires only a test light.

Remove the positive cable from the battery. Then touch one lead of the test lamp to the battery terminal and the other lead to the disconnected cable clamp. If the lamp illuminates when all the accessories in the car are shut off, this indicates a current drain. A pointer: When performing this test, beware of electric clocks. If the car has one, temporarily remove its fuse to get a reliable reading with the test lamp. (Note: Some cars have computer control circuits that remain continuously energized. In most cases, these chips draw too little current to affect a test-light reading.)

By removing and replacing the fuses one by one as I did for my customer, and repeating this test until the test light goes out, you can isolate the circuit where the drain is occurring. Just think of all the fruitless wire-chasing this eliminates.

Checking for Voltage Drop

Using a voltmeter, you can perform a voltage-drop test that will tell you whether a loose or dirty connection is raising the resistance of a circuit. This is also an alternative method of diagnosing a malfunctioning switch.

Connect the voltmeter's positive lead to the side of the connector or switch that leads to the battery. The negative lead is attached to the other side of the component. If voltage drop across the component reads more than one volt, resistance is probably too high. The most common cause is a connection that is dirty or oxidized.

Short-Circuit Detector

Finding a short circuit in a wire that runs through a plastic conduit, behind a trim panel, or under a carpet can be a time-consuming nightmare. A clever short-circuit finder called Shortell is available from Kent-Moore Tool Group (Sealed Power Corp., 29784 Little Mack, Roseville, Mich. 48066-2298; catalog No. BT 8034-A; $70). This tool makes the job a lot easier.

Shortell uses a circuit breaker powered by the car's battery that sends pulses of current through a lead connected to an individual fuse socket. If there is a short in that particular circuit, the pulsing current sets up an intermittent magnetic field that can be detected with a small hand-held meter.

As you move the meter along the area containing the wire, its needle deflects with the pulses. When you arrive at the point of the short circuit where the pulses of current escape to ground, the needle stops moving. Then you know exactly where to begin excavating. This device can save hours of needlessly tearing up the body and interior, as well as reducing the posibility of creating new electrical problems while trying to fix the original fault.

A last word: Don't replace an electrical component unless you are sure it is defective. If, for example, you believe you have removed a defective motor, take the time to attach it to the battery with two jumper wires to make sure the motor is really dead.

QUESTIONS

1. This how-to article begins with an anecdote (in fact it begins in the middle of an anecdote). Is this a successful strategy? What does it contribute to the article?
2. How much information does this article assume you have about automobiles in general, and electrical problems in particular? Do you think you could perform the tests Cerullo describes?
3. Do you find the tone of this author reassuring? Intimidating? Friendly? Authoritative? What effect is created by including the address where one can purchase the short circuit detector, or by closing with "A last word"?
4. Is there any fundamental information about short circuits you wish this article included? Where should that information be placed?
5. Write a similar essay entitled "What to do when . . ." filling in your own subject (e.g., the lights don't go on, your computer won't respond, your telephone doesn't work). Carefully aim your instructions at an audience of your peers.

TO NEIGHBORS OF SHUNNED FAMILY, AIDS FEAR OUTWEIGHS SYMPATHY

Jon Nordheimer

One of the great current public health problems is AIDS, Acquired Immune Deficiency Syndrome. Millions of dollars have been spent in an attempt to develop a cure for the illness, and health officials have spent countless hours trying to educate the public about the exact nature of the disease and how they might assist in preventing its spread. An incident that took place in Arcadia, Florida, in 1987, reflects the complexity of the many problems AIDS has brought to our culture. Here's the story as it was reported in The New York Times.

ARCADIA, Fla., Aug. 30 — The day after Clifford and Louise Ray decided to quit this town, citing the suspicious fire that gutted their house Friday night, those who fought to keep the couple's children out of school are saying the battle was really not against the Ray family.

To them the enemy was AIDS, a dark and sinister force that threatened their own children, no matter how many authorities assured them there was no risk in casual contact among schoolchildren.

While the Rays — whose three sons have been infected by the AIDS virus — were in seclusion at an undisclosed location, the priest at St. Paul's Catholic Church here urged 300 parishoners at mass this morning to search their hearts.

"It reminds me of the time of leprosy when they rang bells and told people to stay away," the Rev. Michael Hickey said. "There is fear in people."

"The ultimate tragedy is to make them feel outlawed and unwanted. People need to stand by them. They need to look into their own hearts."

Today, the committee formed to close the schoolhouse doors to the three Ray boys, who are hemophiliacs, offered donations of food and clothing to the family.

"There isn't anyone who doesn't feel sympathy for the Ray children," said Sue Ellen Smith, the wife of the Mayor of this ranching and citrus community of 6,000. "But there are too many unanswered questions about this disease, and if you are intelligent and listen and read about AIDS you get scared when it involves your own children, because you realize all the assurances are not based on solid evidence."

Scientists say it would be almost impossible for an infected child to transmit AIDS; all documented cases involve direct contact of blood to infected blood or semen, usually through sexual intercourse or the sharing of hypodermic needles and syringes by drug users.

But such science was not enough for the worried parents here, many of whom kept their own children out of school after the Ray boys — who show no-symptoms of AIDS itself — started classes last week.

"We're All Level-Headed"

Today, fire inspectors had still not determined what caused the fire that razed the Ray house Friday night and convinced the family that Arcadia was no longer their home.

Mr. Ray, who said the family had been getting telephoned threats, believes it was arson, aimed at his three sons: Richard, 10 years, Robert, 9, and Randy, 8.

But others cannot believe things could have gone that far. "We're all level-headed, everyday normal people," said Janet Tew, whose husband is president of Citizens Against AIDS in School. "We don't do something like this when we don't get what we want. We don't want the Rays to leave Arcadia."

At the Trinity Methodist Church, while calling for prayers and understanding on all sides, the Rev. Neil M. Gunsalus objected to the way Arcadia is being portrayed as a town without pity.

"Those boycotting the schools have been very peaceful," he said, "but the media seems to want to paint us as illiterate and belligerent rednecks."

"The outside world," he said after the sermon, "is taking this too seriously," he commented afterwards.

The town has been swept by many rumors in the past week, and the fire at the Ray house kept neighbors buzzing over whether it was arson or not.

"If someone set that fire on purpose," said Martha Clement, owner of a restaurant here, "I sure wouldn't want my children going to school with the children of someone like that."

Rays Won Court Fight

Mr. Ray's brother, Andy, who was the only person at home when the house burned Friday and was treated for smoke inhalation, said today that the family had not decided where they would eventually move. Offers of assistance and schooling for the three Ray boys have poured in since their plight attracted national attention.

But Clifford Ray, who is 29, was a target of scorn for many here in Arcadia because of his yearlong fight to get the local schools to admit his children.

When it was found that the boys had been exposed to AIDS, presumably through the transfusion of blood products they need to ease the effects of their hemophilia, the School Board barred them from classes. Officials first offered to educate the children at home, then proposed that the three be taught in special classrooms that no one else would use.

The Rays persisted, however, and assisted by lawyers in Sarasota they won a ruling two weeks ago from a Federal district judge in Tampa ordering the schools to admit the boys to regular classes.

A boycott was widely backed on the first day of school last Monday, but it sagged as the week progressed and it was called off by Friday.

Mayor George K. Smith and his wife took their 10-year-old son out of the public schools when he was assigned to a class with one of the Rays; they enrolled him in a private school in Port Charlotte, 25 miles southwest of here.

Mrs. Smith is a public school teacher, currently working on her master's degree, and her husband is a graduate of the University of Miami. They both dread the assumptions outsiders may make, but they are steadfast in the belief that blood-to-blood transmission of AIDS is a credible risk between grade-school children.

While sipping from a coffee cup this morning, in the Methodist church basement, the Mayor said a lot of local people, including himself, believed that powerful interests, principally the national gay leaders, had pressured the Government into refraining from taking "legitimate" steps to help contain the spread of AIDS.

"I know I must sound like a country jerk saying this," he said, "but this disease isn't being controlled like any other communicable disease that has threatened a community."

Some Quick to Place Blame

Others were more pointed in their remarks. Two men in their late 60's spent part of a sleepy Sunday afternoon talking in the shade of a moss-draped oak tree that local people call "the tree of knowledge" — beneath its crooked limbs, on wooden benches, men gather to play checkers and swap gossip or common wisdoms.

Jack and Herschel — they would not give their full names — were brutally frank in their opinions of the Ray case.

"This damn Federal judge telling people you can't catch AIDS in school," said Jack, whittling a small piece of red cedar in his strong freckled hands.

Herschel, who retired to Arcadia eight years ago from Tennessee, nodded as he talked about the "plague" that he said homosexuals have brought about, adding, "They pass it on to the decent people."

"They should quarantine every one of 'em, isolate them just like they would do with measles or chickenpox," said Jack, his sharp blade cutting deep, curling slices from the wood.

"Yeah," said his partner, anger setting his jaw. They "want everyone to have some of it."

"And these children in school, they can pass it on by kissing or playing together."

"Yeah," responded Herschel, nodding again. "What's the point of an education for them, huh? They don't need to get an education because according to statistics I've seen, they only have but five years to live."

QUESTIONS

1. Newspaper articles usually adopt a "pyramid" format, with the most important information presented first. Less important details are placed later in the article so that if the story is shortened to fit a limited space important facts will not be cut. Examine the structure of this story. Does it follow the pyramid structure? Are there any details you think should be rearranged?

2. There is, of course, no such thing as truly objective reporting. Evaluate the objectivity of this news story. Where do you find subjective touches? What do you think the author's position is in this situation? Do you think he is trying to keep his attitude from his readers?

3. The title is an important part of every news story. What expectations does the article's present title create? Experiment by creating some alternative titles. How do your titles shape or possibly change a reader's expectations?

4. Select some news stories from your newspaper and retitle them. Share your titles with your classmates and analyze how their expectations are shaped by your alternate titles.

AIDS: SORTING OUT TRUTHS FROM MYTHS

U.S. News and World Report

Newsmagazines try to get as much information to their readers as they can without wasting unnecessary space. Although these magazines usually convey their information through conventional articles, they also rely heavily on graphs, charts, pictures, and other visual devices to convey their messages quickly and efficiently. For this presentation on AIDS, U.S. News and World Report combined a series of questions and answers in a graphic format. It has been reproduced here in paragraph form.

QWHAT is AIDS?

A fatal disease that cripples the immune system, leaving the victim susceptible to illnesses the body can usually fight off, such as pneumonia, meningitis and a cancer called Kaposi's sarcoma.

Q What causes AIDS? What are the symptoms?

AIDS is caused by a virus usually known as human immunodeficiency virus, or HIV. Symptoms of full-blown AIDS include a persistent cough, fever and difficulty in breathing. Multiple purplish blotches and bumps on the skin may indicate Kaposi's sarcoma, a cancer associated with AIDS. The virus can also cause brain damage.

Q How is AIDS diagnosed?

By the appearance of pneumonia and other persistent infections, by tests that show damage to the immune system and by a positive test for antibodies to the AIDS virus.

Q How can you get AIDS?

Mostly by having sex with an infected person or by sharing needles and syringes used to inject drugs. The virus, present in blood, semen and vaginal secretions, can be transmitted from one homosexual partner to another and during sexual intercourse both from a man to a woman and from a woman to a man.

Q Who runs the greatest risk?

Of the more than 29,000 U.S. cases, 65 percent have been homosexual or bisexual men, 25 percent intravenous drug users, 4 percent heterosexuals and 3 percent persons who received blood or blood products, a third of whom have been people with hemophilia or other blood disorders. How 3 percent more caught the disease hasn't been determined. There have been about 400 cases in children.

Q What is the risk for heterosexuals?

The greater the number of sexual partners, the greater the risk. The chances of infection from one encounter are between 1 in 1,000 and 1 in 10.

Q Can AIDS be transmitted from an infected woman to her unborn child?

Yes — about a third of the babies born to mothers with AIDS are infected. Most will develop the disease and die.

Q Can you get AIDS by shaking hands, hugging, social kissing, crying, coughing or sneezing? By French kissing? By eating food prepared by someone with AIDS? By an insect bite?

No known cases have been transmitted in any of these ways.

Q Can you get AIDS by piercing your ears?

Possibly, though as yet no one has. If you plan to get your ears pierced, to have acupuncture treatments or to be tattooed, insist on a sterile needle.

Q Is it dangerous to sit next to someone who has AIDS or who is infected with the virus?

No.

Q Can AIDS be transmitted by someone who is infected but doesn't show symptoms?

Yes. This is mainly how the AIDS virus is transmitted.

Q What's the difference between being infected with the AIDS virus and having AIDS?

People infected with the virus can have a wide range of symptoms — from none to mild to severe. At least a fourth to a half of those infected will develop AIDS within four to 10 years. Many experts think the percentage will be much higher.

Q How can anyone be absolutely certain his or her sex partner is safe?

You can't. But experts believe that couples who have had a totally monogamous relationship for the past decade are safe. A negative blood test, of course, would be near-certain evidence of safety.

Q How can I avoid catching AIDS?

If you test positive for the AIDS antibody, shoot drugs or engage in other activities that increase the chances of catching AIDS, inform your sex partner, and use a condom if you have sex. If your partner tests positive, or if you think he or she has been exposed to AIDS because of past sexual practices or through the use of intravenous drugs, a condom should be used. If you or your partner is in a high-risk group, avoid oral contact with the genitals or rectum, as well as sexual activities that might cut or tear the skin or the tissues of the penis, vagina or rectum. Avoid sex with prostitutes. Many are addicted to drugs and often get AIDS by sharing contaminated needles with other addicts.

Q What are some of the diseases that affect AIDS victims?

Almost all AIDS victims get a parasitic infection of the lungs called *Pneumocystis carinii* pneumonia, a cancer called Kaposi's sarcoma or both. Other ailments include unusually severe yeast infections, herpes and parasites.

Q Who should be tested for AIDS?

Gay men and intravenous drug users. Their sex partners. Anyone who has had several sex partners, if their sexual history is unknown, during any one of the last five years.

Q How accurate is the blood test?

It is very accurate, but not infallible. A more sophisticated and expensive test called the Western Blot is used to confirm borderline cases.

Q What should I do if I test positive?

See a physician immediately for a medical evaluation. Use a condom during sex. Do not donate blood, body organs, other tissue or sperm. Do not share toothbrushes, razors or other implements that could become contaminated with blood.

Q Is banked blood safe?

Yes. It is tested and discarded if contaminated. In addition, people in high-risk groups have been asked not to donate blood.

QUESTIONS

1. The task at hand here was to ask the most necessary questions about AIDS, the questions most readers would want answered. *U.S. News* decided there were nineteen questions readers wanted answered. Did they omit any? Is there anything you would have asked if you had been given the chance? Could any of these questions have been omitted?

2. Some answers require several sentences; other questions are answered in a word, or in a single sentence. Why? What effect does a short answer have?

3. Presumably these questions were prepared for a general audience. Are they clear? Are there any terms or expressions you do not understand?

4. This information was originally printed in a chart format. What are some other ways the same issues might have been explored or presented?

QUARANTINING WILL HELP NO ONE

U.S. News and World Report

There are many ways to tell a story, many ways to present information. Along with the question and answer series on the preceding pages, U.S. News *also presented this interview with Nobel Prize winning microbiologist David Baltimore.*

Q **MR. Baltimore, how serious is the AIDS epidemic?**

In terms of impact on our society, this disease will certainly be the most important public-health problem of the next decade and going into the next century. On an international scale, it threatens to undermine countries, particularly in Africa.

Q What do you mean by "undermine countries"?

It will cause such a significant amount of disease in the middle ages of the population that it will largely reduce the number of people available to carry out the functions of the society. In parts of Africa, it's happening already.

Q Do you think people's basic behavior can be altered in time to stem the AIDS epidemic?

In time to have a significant impact, yes. I don't think we'll be perfect. People will respond differently. But for the homosexual population in San Francisco, the rate of rectal gonorrhea fell 83 percent when a serious educational program was put in place. People were obviously willing to change their behavior when they were made to realize how severe a risk they were taking.

Q What about groups not yet hard hit? Can the message get to them before massive deaths occur?

It is certainly harder to reach people when they don't see the consequences of what they're doing right around them or when the consequences are extremely delayed. I'd guess that's been one of the problems with smokers.

Q How do you reach people?

The advertising industry knows how to do that. They can get people to switch detergents. They are able to get people to buy things they may not particularly need. They ought to be able to get people to look a little more carefully at the consequences of some very basic biological activities. I know that unless we make every effort to reach every type of population on its own terms, we're not going to have any effect. A massive educational campaign is the only thing conceivable at the moment that can help. To not do it would be criminal. To argue that it's difficult and expensive and therefore we shouldn't do it would be self-defeating.

Q What will happen if we don't mount a major campaign?

The consequences will be a spread of the virus that could have been controlled and won't be.

Q With catastrophic results?

The consequences already look catastrophic. A quarter of a million people with a lethal disease is catastrophic — and that's the United States only. And that's the rock-bottom projection for 1991.

Q Who will be the hardest to reach?

Intravenous-drug users, who often exist at the fringe of society. And I'm afraid that the adolescent population just moving into sexual activity may also be difficult. They don't read newspapers and magazines a whole lot, and they have a sense of immortality. It's very hard to take seriously the risk of disease when you're just beginning to feel yourself as an adult human being, and we have to reach these people. I think they're at serious risk.

Q President Reagan has remained virtually silent on the subject of AIDS. What is your feeling about that?

That this a matter of the greatest urgency and requires presidential leadership.

Q Why do you think he hasn't been more outspoken?

You can imagine lots of reasons. Clearly, the communities that were first hit by this disease are not communities that the President feels terribly close to. He may well have made a political calculation that he was better off to be quiet. I think that the political setting is changing as the number of cases increases, and I would hope that he sees now that his greatest gain will come from speaking out on the issue.

Q Surveys show that a majority of the public believes AIDS victims should be quarantined. What do you think?

Quarantining will help no one. Most AIDS patients are too sick to be transmitting the virus. The virus is being spread largely by people who do not have AIDS but are infected with the virus, and they may or may not even know it. Quarantining would be totally futile.

Q Would manadatory testing help?

I believe it would drive the very people you want to test underground. Voluntary, confidential testing is much more appropriate.

Q How can you encourage people to go in for such a traumatic test?

The only thing you can do is convince people that they're better off knowing than not knowing. First, because then they can take action to protect their friends and loved ones and, second, because they can begin to interpret their own symptoms and take whatever action is available.

AIDS is a very serious disease, but it usually reveals its presence through a variety of infections, and many of those infections can be controlled with appropriate drugs.

QUESTIONS

1. Analyze the title of this piece, which is taken from Baltimore's remarks. Does this comment summarize the thrust of his interview? What if another sentence — "The consequences already look catastrophic" — were used as a title? What effect would this have on a reader's expectations? Experiment with alternative titles by using other remarks taken from the interview.

2. This article, obviously, does not address the same questions that were presented in "AIDS: Sorting Out Truths From Myths." How do the questions that are asked of Baltimore differ from the questions that were placed in the question and answer series? Why are they different? How are his answers different from the answers found in the series?

3. Although these two presentations are slightly different, they are both intended to present readers with some basic information in an economical fashion. Which presentation do you find more effective? Why?

•   •   •   •   •

THE GOODS

Bob Greene

Bob Greene is a syndicated columnist for the Chicago Tribune, *a job that also allows him to travel about the country visiting unusual places and meeting interesting people. In this essay he describes his visit to a manufacturing plant that is a bit out of the ordinary, a factory where condoms are made.*

OUT past the railroad tracks in a crumbling industrial section of Trenton, New Jersey, is a long, low-slung, mustard-yellow building. This is the building where they manufacture Trojans.

They manufacture Trojans twenty-four hours a day. More than 1.1 million Trojans on a good day, 170 million Trojans a year. There are other brands of condoms for sale, but in the United States the word "Trojans" has become almost generic. The Trojans brand — which was launched more than fifty years ago — accounts for 57 percent of the condoms sold in drugstores in the U.S.; all of the other manufacturers split the rest of the market.

Nowhere on the outside of the building is the word "Trojans" apparent. Just the name of the parent company: Youngs Rubber Corporation.

The manager of operations and planning at the Trojans plant is Daryl Kress, thirty-seven, a former lieutenant commander in the navy. A trim, serious man in a dark-blue suit and crisp white shirt, he sits behind a tidy desk; in front of him is a coffee cup painted with the legend LIEUTENANT COMMANDER.

At no time does Kress use the term "condom," or "prophylactic," or "rubber" when mentioning the product that is manufactured in this building. Instead he refers to what is made here as "the goods."

"The goods come in seven different varieties," Kress says. "Regular, nipple-end, nipple-end lubricated, ribbed . . ." Or he says, "When the goods are shipped from our plant . . ."

When he is explaining the tensile strength of the product, he reaches into a top desk drawer and comes out with a foil-wrapped Trojan. He opens the package and — still unsmiling — lifts the condom to his mouth. He blows into it and inflates it, then hands it to me for inspection.

Kress says he is married, with two sons, ages fourteen and twelve. He says the world in which his boys are growing up is far more relaxed about Trojans than the world in which previous generations of American males grew up.

"With us, we always hoped we'd get the druggist instead of that gal who worked behind the counter," he says. "Now most of the time they aren't sold behind the counter. They're hung up right next to the cash register. Heck, you just pull as many packages as you need off the rack and go right to the check-out counter."

Kress leads me into the manufacturing area of the Trojans plant. The heat is overwhelming; in some parts of the building the temperatures approach 180 degrees. And the smell — the intense, hot, oppressive smell of liquefied latex — is enough to knock you to your knees.

When it first hits us, I stop in my tracks. I have never smelled anything like it before.

"What is that smell?" I say to Kress.

"I don't smell anything," he says.

The interior of the Trojans plant looks like some woodcut used to illustrate the Iron Age in an old encyclopedia. There is absolutely nothing high-tech about what is done here; the four main manufacturing machines, each as long as a city block, creak and groan and rumble as they do their ceaseless task.

Inside the machine we are standing in front of, 3,412 glass forms in the shape of penises move, pointing downward, along a conveyor belt. The forms are dipped into liquefied latex. They are pulled out of the latex, with a thin rubber coating now formed on the glass. They are heat-dried. They are dipped a second time. A ring is mechanically formed around the top of each new condom. Talc is applied to prevent the condoms from sticking to themselves. The condoms are mechanically rolled off the glass forms in preparation for the next step of the process.

Kress raises his voice to be heard above the sound of the machines. "The goods are tumbled dry to remove the excess talc," he says. "Follow me."

"I guess this puts to rest the joke we all used to tell each other," I say to Kress.

"What joke is that?" he says.

"Well, you know," I say. "When a kid buys a rubber, his friends ask him what size he got. But it's obvious from looking at these things being made that they're all the same size."

"Actually, that's not true," Kress says. "There are two standard sizes in the world for these goods. An American size and a Japanese size."

"What's the difference?" I say.

"The Japanese size is smaller," Kress says. "When you lay one of these goods flat and measure its width, it is fifty-two millimeters wide. It is 7.1 inches long. The Japanese standard is forty-nine millimeters wide and 6.3 inches long."

As we walk through the factory, we pass some of the more than two hundred laborers who divide the three daily shifts at the Trojans plant. They are members of the United Rubber, Cork, Linoleum and Plastic Workers of America.

I ask Kress if the workers are allowed to take samples of the project home.

"There's no official policy on it," he says. "But we wouldn't say anything if they did. We make so many each day, it wouldn't make any real difference."

He says that, despite the recent rugged economy, there have been no layoffs in the Trojans plant.

"In a recession, our business actually goes up a little bit," he says. "People tend to stay home instead of going out."

Each of the million-plus Trojans that are manufactured daily is individually tested for holes or other flaws.

Each Trojan that comes off the line goes to the testing rooms. Here women sitting at long tables slip the Trojans over more forms—called mandrels—that move by on another conveyor belt. These mandrels, also long and erect, are made of metal; they point upward. After the women place Trojans over them, the mandrels are dipped into an electrolytic solution; if any of the charged solution gets through a condom and makes contact with a steel mandrel, a mechanical alarm is tripped and that Trojan is rejected.

The steel mandrels move past the women in rapid, unrelenting succession. In front of each woman is a bin full of new Trojans; all day long she reaches into the bin, comes out with a Trojan, slips it over the top of a mandrel, then reaches back into the bin for another Trojan before the next mandrel moves past her.

Some of the women use their right hands to apply the Trojans to the mandrels. Some use their left hands. Some use both hands. There is no music in the room; there is no visual diversion. Just the mandrels moving by. When you first catch sight of the testers doing their job, you are struck by two immediate impressions: first, this has to be one of the most deadening, monotonous, dreary forms of human endeavor; and second, these women would really make great dates.

As the mandrels pass by the women and the Trojans are slipped over the tops, I approach several of the testers and talk to them. The conveyor belt does not stop; the women continue to work with the Trojans and the mandrels while we speak.

A fifty-three-year-old grandmother named Wilber Holloway tells me she has been doing this for seventeen years. "It took me about six weeks to learn," she says. "The trick is in how you pick them up."

I ask her what she thinks about all day while she is doing this.

"Money and men," Mrs. Holloway says. "I dream of winning the lottery, and I dream of young men."

Cindy Gerner, thirty-three and married, says, "It takes patience at first. You get nervous that you're going to break them when you put them on, and because you're nervous you do break them. You get your system down before long, though."

She says she thinks about different things to get her through the day. "I'm a Baptist," she says. "While I'm doing this I either go over Bible verses in my head, or I think of songs I heard in church."

Terry Scott, twenty-four, says that sometimes at night she dreams of the mandrels moving past her. I ask her what she tells strangers when she meets them and they ask her what she does for a living.

"I tell them, 'Flip rubbers,'" she says.

Daryl Kress leads me through the room where the Trojans are sealed inside foil packets, and then he takes me back to his office.

"The mail is very interesting," he says. "We think we have the best quality-control operation in the business, but when you sell as many goods as we do, you're bound to get some complaints."

He searches through his desk, and finds some correspondence. He flips through the letters and begins to sort them out.

"We had one man write us to complain that his Trojan was all dried out—he said that the lubricant had dried up. He sent us the package, so we took a look at the date on it. The guy had been carrying the thing around for eleven years."

I ask him what the most common complaint is.

"People write us to say that their Trojan won't unroll. Nine out of ten times, they're doing it backwards. They're doing it in the dark, and instead of unrolling it, they're trying to roll it up tighter."

I ask him if people really take the time to write letters about something like that.

"Oh, yes," he says. "They can get pretty eloquent. One man wrote us to accuse a Trojan of 'complete prophylactic recalcitrance.'"

Kress is busy; he is due in another part of the plant, used to test the strength and resilience of the Trojans. Here the condoms are placed on a machine that inflates them automatically.

"You'd be amazed at how big these things can get," Kress says.

And indeed the machine does blow the Trojans up until they are approximately the size of shopping bags.

We walk through the shipping area. Charles Reed, forty-four, who has been working in the Trojans plant for twenty-two years, is packing the individual cartons of Trojans into big brown boxes; the boxes will be loaded onto trucks and distributed around the nation. Reed hardly looks up as he scoops the small packages from the end of the conveyor belt and arranges them in the larger crates.

"When you first come to work here, I guess you think it's going to be a pretty sexy job," Reed says. "I mean, this is an awfully famous product. But before long you quit telling people where you work.

"The reason is that they're going to react one of two ways. Either they're going to think it's tremendously interesting, and they're going to ask you questions all night about it. Or they're going to think it's funny, and make a lot of jokes.

"Now I just say that I'm a machine operator, or a shipping clerk. It makes things easier."

Like the Trojans factory itself, the large brown crates in which the individual packages of condoms are packed for shipping do not have the word "Trojans" printed anywhere on their exteriors.

"That was a conscious decision," Kress says. "These things sit around a lot of docks on their way to their destinations. We feel that if we were to print the name of the product on the outside of the shipping box, it would become a fairly pilferable item in transit."

As I leave the Trojan factory, I pass through the reception area. A secretary is on the telephone; a security camera is sending a black-and-white picture of the parking lot onto a TV monitor; a copy of *Reader's Digest* is placed on a coffee table.

Behind me, behind a series of doors, are the machines and mandrels and pallets and workers. Ahead of me, the real world waits again. On a table, someone has left a package of Trojans. On its front, the design is soft pastel; a young couple is shown in profile, strolling on a deserted beach. The printed slogan is brief and to the point: FOR FEELING IN LOVE.

QUESTIONS

1. Green's title comes from the expression used by the plant manager instead of the word *condom*. What is Greene's attitude about this euphemism? Why does Greene repeatedly point out the anonymity and obscurity that surrounds the manufacturing of this product?

2. Bob Greene uses a fairly matter-of-fact presentation style in this article, yet clearly the article seems humorous. Where does that humor come from? Is it the subject matter or Greene's treatment of the subject? What parts of the article seems funny to you? Why are they funny?

3. Why does Greene include the final vignette, the description of the package he finds lying on a table? What point is he trying to make with this?

4. Visit a local business or factory and write up your visit in an essay similar to Greene's.

A NEW TAPE TO RECORD YOUR FAVORITE NUMBERS

Tom Dworetzky

Not everyone wants to understand the technology that underlies the many electronic marvels that surround us, but some of us do. Explaining a sophisticated process or piece of equipment to a lay person is not easy, but Tom Dworetzky attempts it in this article that appeared recently in Discover *magazine.*

IT has been just four years since the playback-only compact disc (CD) introduced the music lovers of America to digitally recorded sound, but already a new kind of magnetic tape is rivaling the audio quality of CDs—and it can record as well as play back. This system, called DAT, for digital audio tape, blends the latest advances in CD, VCR, and computer technology. Like a CD, it provides sound of master-tape quality. Like a VCR, it employs a rotating drum, containing twin recording/playback heads, that spins rapidly to permit an extraordinary amount of information to be packed onto a tiny tape 4 mm wide. This keeps speed down to a mere 8.15 mm per second, thus reducing wear on the tape.

In conventional video and audio tape recorders, the heads place an electromagnetic representation of light and sound waves directly onto the tape. In DAT machines, a processing chip designed specifically for the task converts sound into binary digits (bits). This is done by slicing the sound into tiny periods of time. Each of these periods, or samples, is translated into binary digits that represent volume, or amplitude, and pitch, or frequency. The samples are then encoded onto the tape. When it's time to play them back, the system translates each sample into sound, and strings the samples together to recreate the music. You don't hear the seams between them for much the same reason you can't see the gaps between movie frames: both forms of recreation occur so fast that the senses can't perceive the interruptions. The DAT does its sampling 48,000 times a second—and each sample is represented by 32 bits (16 per channel).

One reason DATs need so many bits is that they don't record sounds *qua* sounds, as standard audio cassettes do. Thus extraneous noise is a different and bigger issue for DATs. Tape damage that would be heard as just an annoying hiss or pop on a standard analog machine would be interpreted as a number on a DAT system, which could translate that number into, say, unwanted forte in the middle of a delicate pianissimo.

For this reason extra information amounting to almost 40 per cent of the original signal is devoted to error correction. The information is used by elaborate microchip-based Reed-Solomon algorithms, devised in the 1960s by Irving Reed and Gustave Solomon, both then at MIT, that check bit patterns for accuracy and interpolate between true ones to recreate those bits obliterated by dust, tape-stretching, and other noise-producing phenomena. If all else fails, the system can mute the sound for a fleeting moment.

Despite its nearly flawless reproduction, DAT isn't music to record companies' ears. The $4 billion-a-year recording industry has grudgingly come to accept home copying with magnetic tape recorders—which it estimates costs $1.5 billion annually

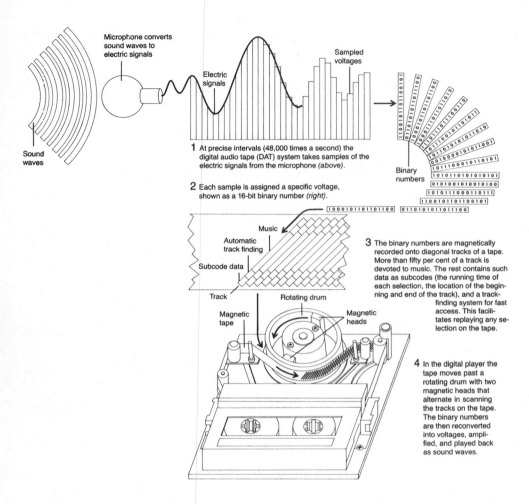

Microphone converts sound waves to electric signals

Sound waves

Electric signals

Sampled voltages

1 At precise intervals (48,000 times a second) the digital audio tape (DAT) system takes samples of the electric signals from the microphone (*above*).

2 Each sample is assigned a specific voltage, shown as a 16-bit binary number (*right*).

Binary numbers

Music

Automatic track finding

Subcode data

Track

Magnetic tape

Rotating drum

Magnetic heads

3 The binary numbers are magnetically recorded onto diagonal tracks of a tape. More than fifty per cent of a track is devoted to music. The rest contains such data as subcodes (the running time of each selection, the location of the beginning and end of the track), and a track-finding system for fast access. This facilitates replaying any selection on the tape.

4 In the digital player the tape moves past a rotating drum with two magnetic heads that alternate in scanning the tracks on the tape. The binary numbers are then reconverted into voltages, amplified, and played back as sound waves.

in lost sales. DATs would permit duplications of unparalleled quality, but audio equipment companies claim to have made digital-to-digital duping impossible: the sampling rate at which DATs record isn't the same as those of CDs and pre-recorded DAT tapes. Nonetheless, the music industry says that audiophiles will be quick to get around this.

The duping issue has touched off a major lobbying war in Washington between the mostly U.S. music biz and the mainly Japanese hardware manufacturers. Says Stanley Gortikov, president of the Recording Industry Association of America, "The creators of music shouldn't be victims of a new technology, especially when that technology's future is dependent on their music."

Last August more than 80 electronics manufacturers met in Tokyo to nail down common DAT technical standards. In early October Japanese manufacturers unveiled prototypes of DAT player-recorders and minicassettes (each approximately two-thirds the size of a standard audio cassette) at the Tokyo Audio Fair. The American unveiling of these prototypes at the Consumer Electronics Show in Las Vegas in January outraged music industry representatives, who argue that some sort of anti-copying device should be installed in the machines before they're sold. Congress has heard the cries of alarm — and is now considering legislation forbidding DATs without such duping spoilers.

The music companies' stand may not prove all that wise, if history is any guide. Hollywood succeeded in stalling the pay TV boom from the late 1940s until the 1970s (it was aided mightily in this effort by the technological shortcomings of early pay-TV systems). And the VCR was hardly welcomed by film makers. Yet these technologies created enormous new home markets for movies — for example, ones too stinko to make a buck in theaters. Sales of pre-recorded DAT tapes, which could be cheaper to make than CDs, could also prove profitable enough to offset piracy losses. In any case, says Marc Finer, an electronics industry consultant, "the format is so good it's bound to succeed."

QUESTIONS

1. This article bristles with initials — DAT, VCR, CD, MIT. Is this distracting? Is it necessary? Would it be easier for readers to understand if these abbreviations were not used?

2. Dworetzky assumes his readers have some familiarity with other technical products — VCRs and CD players. What other assumptions about his readers' knowledge does he also make?

3. Where is Dworetzky's prose most technical? Where is it the most informal? Why does it shift?

4. Does the illustration clarify this process for you at all? Could you understand the principles involved without the illustration?

INSIDE HARD DISK TECHNOLOGY

Peter Norton and Robert Jourdain

To those who work with them on a daily basis, computers and their wonders have become commonplace. When they malfunction, however, or break down, their complexities become marvelous indeed. Peter Norton is the creator of the famous program Norton Utilities, *used, among other things, to recover lost and missing data. The following is an excerpt from the handbook he wrote with Robert Jourdain,* The Hard Disk Companion *(1988).*

AN OVERVIEW

Few people have ever seen a hard disk. Unlike floppies, delicate hard disks must be permanently enclosed in a protective aluminum shell. All that's visible is a *hard disk drive* — a metal box with some circuitry on it. There's no easy way to get inside the box to view the rotating disk; to open the drive is to fatally contaminate it. Drives may be opened only in **clean rooms**, where workers wear surgical garb and all dust is filtered from the air. Some disks are enclosed in removable cartridges that are inserted into the drive, but most are non-removable. IBM invented small non-removable drives and informally dubbed them **Winchester drives** (apparently because the drive's code number matched the model number of a popular Winchester rifle).

Tracks, Sectors, and Heads

For all its impressive armor, a hard disk isn't terribly different from the lowly floppy disk. Data is recorded as magnetic patterns written in circles around the hub of the disk. Each of the concentric circles makes up a **track**, and each track is divided into a number of equal segments called **sectors**. A **read/write head** moves from the outer edge of the disk toward the hub, stopping over the track containing the information the computer needs. Once in position, the head waits for the correct sector of the track to revolve to it, and then it reads or writes data as the sector passes beneath.

Hard disks are distinguished from floppies by the high densities at which data is recorded on the disk surface and by the high speed at which they operate. While a standard 360K floppy disk holds 40 tracks, hard disks of the same diameter may have over 1,000. And they may pack up to four times as much data onto each track. Such high data densities require a very small read/write head positioned very close to the disk surface. Any flexibility in the disk would make it bounce up and strike the read/write head. And so the disks are made *hard* using rigid aluminum plates coated with a magnetic material.

Hard disks are also famed for their speed. While a floppy disk drive turns at 300 or 360 revolutions per minute, most hard disks spin at 3,600 rpm. Also, hard disk drives move their read/write heads from track to track several times faster than floppy drives. Such high performance requires extremely precise machining and assembly.

Platters

To increase the drive's capacity, most hard disk drives actually contain two or more disks. The disks, referred to as **platters**, are mounted around an axle called the **spin-**

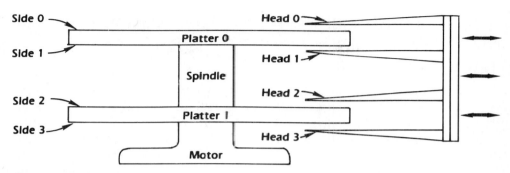

Heads and platters

dle. All platters turn together. The motor that turns the platters may be built into the spindle, or it may reside below the spindle as a **pancake motor**.

Both sides of a platter hold data. Because it would be impractical for a single read/write head to serve all platter sides, each platter side has its own head. The heads are ganged together on a comb-like armature that moves all of the heads in tandem, as shown in Figure 2.2. The accuracy of this mechanism is astounding. The platters and heads must interleave precisely at every track position, with each head positioned only 1/100,000 of an inch from the platter surface. This precise geometry is maintained as the lightweight heads rapidly shunt back and forth over the heavy gyrating platters. High-tech indeed!

The heads are able to stay so close to the platters without touching because they actually *fly* over the surface on a cushion of air created by the disk's rotation. The heads slowly lift off when the drive starts up, and they gently land when power is shut off and the platters grind to a halt. The heads rest against the disk surface when power is off.

Disk Controllers

Most disk drives are accompanied by a **controller card** that plugs into one of the computer's card slots. When data is read from the disk surface, it passes from the heads through the disk-drive circuitry onto the controller card electronics. As we'll see later, not all hard disks require a separate controller card to intermediate between drive and computer. But all drives operating in IBM PCs, ATs, and some PS/2s require some kind of adapter that takes up a slot on the computer's motherboard.

Data sent from the disk surface to the controller card arrives at a buffer — a small patch of memory acting as a temporary holding area for data. Once the data transfers to the buffer, the controller card sends a signal to the computer's **central processing unit** (CPU) — the 8088, 80286, or 80386 chip at the heart of any IBM personal computer. The signal tells the CPU to begin moving the data into the computer's own memory chips.

DMA

The data is moved by one of two techniques. In the IBM AT and PS/2 machines, the CPU does the job itself. But IBM PCs and XTs use **direct memory access (DMA)**. DMA relies on a special chip that shifts the data directly from the controller to memory in a single step, rather than through the two-step process of moving it first to the CPU and then to system memory. PCs and XTs use DMA because their 8088 CPUs cannot keep up with a hard disk's data transfer rate.

DOS Buffers

The data goes into system memory (RAM) in areas set aside as **DOS buffers**. The number of buffers may be set by the user as we'll see later. Each buffer holds one disk sector, which in DOS contains a 512-byte swatch of a file. Typically, computers equipped with a hard disk run with twenty buffers. As a file is read, its sectors fill the buffers; once all buffers are occupied, a sector transfers to the buffer least recently accessed by a program, overwriting that buffer's contents. In the last step on the journey, DOS extracts data from the buffers and lays it down at particular memory locations requested by application software. The figure below shows the path taken by data.

Writing Data

When the computer *writes* data on a disk, the entire process is reversed. An application program tells DOS where to find data in memory. DOS moves it to its buffers and then transfers it to the holding buffer on the hard disk controller. Then the disk controller begins writing, specifying the sector on the track on the platter side to receive the data, sending commands to the disk drive that move the read/write head into position. Then the drive electronics take over, carefully monitoring the disk surface for exactly the right moment to begin. At that moment, the head emits a stream of magnetic pulses that encode the data in a line along the disk surface.

The Disk Surface

A disk is uniformly covered with a **medium** that holds the data. DOS lays out the data in 512-byte sequences called **sectors**, but, in fact, an operating system may impose any organization upon the disk it chooses. We look only at DOS in this section; the general principles we discuss apply to any common microcomputer operating system.

Flux Changes

The surface of a hard disk contains magnetized particles of metal. Each particle has a north and south pole, just like larger magnets. A read/write head can apply a magnetic field to a tiny group of these particles, reversing their polarity, so that what

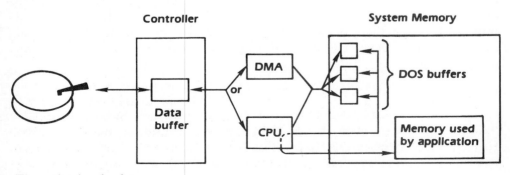

The path taken by data

was north becomes south, or vice-versa. The smallest area of disk surface that can hold one of these **flux changes** constitutes a **magnetic domain**. Thousands of domains taken together make up a track. As the disk spins beneath the head, the head constantly changes the polarity of its magnetic field, creating a sequence of polarity changes on the disk.

Data Encoding

All information in computers is stored as patterns of "1s" and "0s," "Yeses" and "Nos," "Ons" and "Offs." For example, when you type the letter "A" in a document, the character is subsequently stored on disk in the pattern **On**-Off-Off-Off-Off-Off-**On**-Off. These are the eight **bits** that make up a byte of data. (The pattern, incidentally, is arbitrary; it is part of the **ASCII standard**, making it an **ASCII character**.) When the character is written to the disk, the read/write head rhythmically changes its polarity to transfer the pattern to a sequence of eight magnetic domains along a track. A change in polarity indicates an "On" (a binary 1), and a lack of a change indicates an "Off" (a binary 0).

When a drive reads back the data, it essentially reverses the process. The head passively hovers over the disk surface, and, as the tiny magnets that make up the magnetic domains pass beneath, they ever so slightly influence the head's magnetic field. Circuitry on the disk drive greatly amplifies these slight perturbations into patterns of "Ons" and "Offs" that are fed into the computer's memory chips.

Even a floppy disk can pack a staggering number of these magnetic domains ("Ons" and "Offs") onto one track — well over 30,000 domains — enough to hold two screens of text (25 rows of 80 characters, with eight domains per character). Hard disks write at least 10,000 domains *per inch* of track. If you consider that hard drives rotate at 3,600 revolutions per minute, you'll realize that the read/write head is working very quickly indeed. At least 5 million domains pass under a read/write head in a second.

MAGNETIC MEDIA

If you were curious (and unwise) enough to open your disk drive with a screwdriver, inside you'd find either platters covered with the familiar reddish-brown iron oxide coating of floppy disks or bright shiny platters reminiscent of chrome auto bumpers. The first would typify **coated media**, and the second, **plated media**. In either case, not far below the surface is a finely machined aluminum **blank** upon which the medium is applied. The surface is what matters, though.

Until recently, most IBM microcomputer drives were made with coated oxide, including the drives IBM built into the IBM XT and AT. Some forty years old, the technology is well understood. The oxide coating is little more than rust particles held in place by a binding agent. The coating is relatively easy to apply at the precise and regular thickness required. Plated media, on the other hand, are made by applying pure metal to the aluminum blank, either by vapor deposition or by a technique called **sputtering**. Because working with vaporized metal is difficult, the industry took many years to arrive at techniques that produce near-perfect disk surfaces at a reasonable cost. Today, plated media are reserved mostly for drives of high capacity, high speed, and high price.

Coated vs. Plated Media

An oxide coating is roughly ten times thicker than a plated surface (which is but a few millionths of an inch), and it holds much larger magnetic particles. So much binding agent is required in oxide coatings that the magnetic particles are held relatively far apart. In plated media, on the other hand, the particles are packed against one another. The absence of a binding agent makes the coating much thinner, and often plated media are called **thin-film media**. Even though the oxide coating for hard disks is denser than that for standard floppy disks, it still cannot pack as many magnetic domains on the disk surface as plated media can.

While coated media can hold up to 20,000 magnetic domains on an inch of track, plated media have exceeded 50,000 domains in laboratory prototypes. Even higher densities may be achieved by **perpendicular recording**, in which the magnetic domains extend from the disk surface inward rather than end-to-end along the track. As disks move toward higher and higher data densities, there is an inexorable trend toward plated media.

HEAD CRASHES

Plated media have another advantage: They are extremely hard, making them resistant to **head crashes**. Most users have heard of a head crash or at least know that a disk can "crash," but few understand what a crash is. The origin of the term is unclear. The first experimental hard disk drives were giant contraptions with mammoth platters rotated by powerful motors. A mishap in the laboratory would cause the drive literally to tear itself to pieces. These calamitous events may have given rise to the term "crash."

These days a disk crash is a much more genteel affair. Severe vibrations or a mechanical failure cause a read/write head to strike the surface of an oxide-coated platter and cut a tiny furrow in the medium. The momentum of the spinning platters adds considerable energy to the collision. Where a head cuts, data can no longer be held, and if it is a place where data has been recorded, the data is lost. Worse, particles of magnetic material are loosened, freeing them to roam inside the drive. These particles may be much larger than the gap that separates the heads and platter surfaces; when a head hits one, it may fly up, crash back down, and damage more data. Sometimes the particles adhere to the head and interfere with the head's magnetic field.

Sometimes DOS can write upon a lightly damaged point on the disk and the new data is successfully preserved. But when the damage is more severe, with a deep gouge made in the coating, data won't hold at all. The disk has developed a **bad sector**. DOS issues the message "Error reading drive X:" or "Sector not found reading drive X:" when it encounters these gaps in the data. To repair the damage, the sectors must be placed off bounds from DOS's use. Some software utilities perform this service (as we'll see in Chapter 9). Or you can back up all your files, reformat the disk, and then restore the files, including the backups you (presumably) made of the files that were damaged. The damaged area will be marked offbounds during reformatting. We'll discuss these techniques in detail in Chapter 9, Surviving Head Disk Disasters.

When a head crash occurs over the outermost tracks, the damage can be much more serious. These tracks contain special DOS files, the disk's main directory, and information about disk space allocation. If the heads dive into this data, DOS will not be able to read from the disk at all, and all data will effectively be "lost," even though every byte remains intact elsewhere on the platters. This is the most feared of all types of head crash. There *are* ways to get some kinds of data back from the disk but only through great effort and expense (we'll discuss these techniques in Chapter 9 also). Because the read/write heads spend a good deal of time hovering over these outer tracks, head crashes of this kind are relatively common.

For all but the saintly, a hard disk crash is cause for fury and vituperation. "The maker is incompetent: the dealer is a cheat: the consultant is a quack." Remember that when the first IBM PC was released, small Winchester hard disk drives were barely a viable mass-market technology. The rate of technical progress has been remarkable, and quality rises year after year, even as prices fall. Besides, if the disk crashes and data is lost, the real cause for anger is clear: The owner has neglected to make backups.

Crash-Resistant Designs

Engineers are working on other kinds of disk media more resistant to head-crash damage. A particularly promising technology, developed by 3M Company, is called **SRR**, for **stretch-surface recording**, in which a special magnetic-coated film is applied to an aluminum blank with raised rims at the outer edge and center hole. The film is *stretched* between the rims so that the magnetic surface hangs slightly above the surface of the disk. As the head flies above the medium, the air cushion pushes a "dimple" into the surface. When the head crashes onto the surface, the medium can much better absorb the force, and it imparts much less energy to the head. Laboratory prototypes show recording densities almost as high as those for plated media.

Failures That Aren't Crashes

Although many people call any hard disk failure a "crash," much can go wrong that has nothing to do with damage to the medium. Electronic components can fail, the motor that drives the platters can burn out, or the actuator that moves the read/write heads can shift out of alignment. And an actual crash can lead to a different kind of problem: The head itself may become contaminated or damaged. Contamination usually occurs in drives with iron oxide coatings: the soft coating material adheres to the read/write heads, causing errors. Plated media, on the other hand, are so hard that they can smash the delicate heads. In either case, the drive must go in for repairs, and this often means total loss of data.

Soft and Hard Errors

Often **soft errors** occur. In these errors, the hardware is intact, but data is unsuccessfully read or written. **Hard errors**, on the other hand, are those in which the data has been physically mangled or the equipment is malfunctioning. Soft errors sometimes occur when a power surge passes through the circuitry, or when the bearings that support the platters begin to wear, causing a platter to wobble slightly so that it pulls away from the head's magnetic field. The controller can usually recover from a soft error simply by trying to read or write the data again. IBM controllers automatically try ten times before reporting an error to DOS. DOS in turn tries reading or writing data three times before it gives up and displays an error massage. So a total of thirty tries may be made. In Chapter 9 we'll see how software can keep an eye on soft error rates and warn you about impending disk failure.

SECTORS

Although it's possible to lay out data in one long sequence along the entire circumference of a track, generally it's not done this way. Instead, the disk is divided into **sectors** like so many pie slices, and accordingly the tracks are divided into pieces. These pieces of track are themselves commonly called "sectors," so that an expression like "a bad sector" means that only a part of one track has gone bad, not a whole slice of the disk.

Formatting Levels

The sectors are created when the disk is formatted. Actually, formatting proceeds in two stages: low-level and high-level formatting. Low-level formatting defines the sectors, laying down a sequence of special codes that tell the controller where a sector begins. Then it writes special identification numbers so that each sector has its own label (the controller knows the track number by virtue of having moved the heads to that position).

Standard 360K floppy disks are usually formatted in nine sectors; the AT's 1.2-megabyte floppy drives have fifteen; and the 720K and 1.44-megabyte 3½-inch floppies in the PS/2 line have nine and eighteen sectors, respectively. Most hard disks have seventeen sectors per track. The number of sectors is set by the operating system for its own purposes. The physically uniform disk surface can be magnetically cut up in any pattern.

There is something about the word "sector" that encourages people to think of disk sectors as little wedges of data written at regular intervals along the disk surface. This conception is wrong, though. The read/write head projects only one magnetic field onto the disk, and so it can read and write only one magnetic domain at each position along a track. Accordingly, the data is written as a single thin line.

Sector Size

DOS, which fits 512 bytes of data into each sector, applies this sector size to hard disks as well as floppies. Of course, tracks along the outer edge of a disk are much longer than inner tracks, and they could hold a lot more data — but they don't. Operating systems are complicated creatures, and one further complication DOS avoids is having different numbers of sectors on different tracks. The result is a good deal of wasted disk space. (Actually, some drives do vary the number of sectors per track. For example, on some 40-megabyte hardcards, Plus Development Corporation puts 28 sectors on inner tracks and 34 sectors on outer tracks. But the extra sectors are electronically represented as belonging to separate tracks so that DOS "sees" a disk in which all tracks have the same number of sectors.)

We'll see later that some high-capacity hard disks use 1,024- or 2,048-byte sectors. But larger sectors don't in themselves lead to high data densities. Fewer large sectors fit on a track. The amount of data that can be written is limited by the speed at which the heads can make flux changes and by the minimum amount of magnetic medium required to store a flux change.

CYLINDERS

When no more data can be crammed onto the side of a disk, the main approach to higher disk drive capacity is by adding more platters. Drives in the 10- to 40-megabyte range tend to have two platters; high-capacity drives may have six or more. The sides of the platters are numbered starting from 0, with the first platter holding sides 0 and 1, the second platter holding sides 2 and 3, and so on.

Because the read/write heads move in tandem across the platter surfaces, all heads are positioned at a given track at any one time. Because individual files tend to become scattered around the disk surfaces, it would be preferable for the heads to move independently. As one head reads from one track, another head could shift over to the track at which a file continues. But the mechanics would be prohibitively expensive.

How DOS Fills the Disk

To make the best of this situation, DOS tries to fit as much of a file as possible into all tracks at a given head position. For example, were DOS to record a new file starting from track 15, it would first fill all of track 15 on sides 0 and 1, then would continue at track 15 on the next platter with sides 2 and 3. Only when all tracks numbered 15 are filled would DOS initiate the time-consuming task of moving the read-write heads to track 16, where it would go on writing the file from side 0.

Taking all platter sides together, all tracks numbered 15 are called "cylinder 15." The concept is easy to grasp, because a cylinder would be formed if you joined the tracks from side to side. You will often see the term "cylinder" instead of "track" in hard disk documentation, and logically they are often interchangeable. The 10-megabyte hard disk in an IBM XT has 306 cylinders; an AT's 20-megabyte disk has 615. This is precisely the same as saying that a side of a platter in an XT has 306 tracks and an AT, 615.

Cylinder Density

An important concept is **cylinder density**. Unlike **track density**, which tells how many concentric tracks fit along an inch of a disk's radius, the cylinder density gives the *number of sectors* held in a cylinder. It is the number of sectors per track multiplied by the number of platter sides. Disks with a high cylinder density are desirable because they can fit a large file into fewer cylinders. Thus, fewer head seeks are needed to read the file, and the drive performs more quickly. Manufacturers increase cylinder density either by creating drives with more platters or by using media and electronics that can achieve greater data densities, allowing more sectors on a track.

INTERLEAVE

The rate at which data passes beneath a read/write head doesn't necessarily equal the rate at which the computer can read or write data. There are limits to how fast various circuits can move data. The disk controller transfers data between the disk surface and an internal holding buffer, and then either the CPU or DMA (direct memory access) chips move the data between the controller's buffer and system RAM. The platters are spinning at 60 rotations per second (3,600 rpm), moving seventeen sectors under the read/write heads with each revolution. At 512 bytes of data per sector, 522,240 bytes pass beneath the heads in a second. Actually, on a typical disk, about

625,000 bytes can be packed on a track when the track isn't divided into sectors. Because each byte is made of eight bits ("Ons" or "Offs"), roughly five million bits pass beneath a head during a second.

This calculation is the origin of the 5-megabit data-transfer rate attributed to most drives. Many people wrongly believe that the electronics set the transfer rate. Indeed, the electronics must be fast enough to read and write data at the rate it passes by the heads. But faster electronics couldn't transfer data more quickly, because the data couldn't be physically presented to the heads more rapidly without speeding up the drive motor. (Note that "megabits" is abbreviated as **Mb**, "megabytes" as **MB**.)

The 5-megabit data-transfer rate doesn't indicate the actual rate at which data is transferred to system memory. When data is read, the disk controller's buffer fills at this rate, but then the read operation must stop until the data is transferred (by CPU or DMA) to DOS buffers. The delay may be prolonged if the CPU then shifts the data elsewhere in memory, perhaps processing it along the way.

Think about what this means from the point of view of the spinning disk. A sector moves under the read/write heads and its data is transferred to the controller buffer. The next sector is coming up in a minuscule fraction of a second, and if the read/write head is to make use of it, the data from the prior sector must be moved out of the buffer and into memory in a big hurry. But most 8088 and 80286 machines cannot make this transfer quickly enough. So the next disk sector flies by without being read. In fact, in an IBM XT, five sectors pass under the head before the controller is ready to read data again. Because ATs run faster, they're ready to read again after only one or two sectors pass by.

Sector Contiguity

If the second sector of a file's data is laid down on the disk surface right next to the first, the sectors are said to be "physically contiguous." Often, this isn't the ideal condition. Because the controller isn't ready to read the second sector when it physically follows the first, the disk must complete an entire revolution before the data passes under the head again. On an XT, the controller is ready to receive data in only a third as much time, wasting precious milliseconds. With the disk turning 60 times per second, waiting two-thirds of a revolution to read the next sector wastes 11 milliseconds. Reading 17 sectors in a row this way squanders 187 milliseconds — nearly a fifth of a second. Disks with four tracks to the cylinder (the most common case) magnify this loss to three-quarters of a second per cylinder. When a file spans many cylinders, you'd be strumming your fingertips waiting for the disk access to end.

Fortunately, there is no intrinsic need for disk drives to operate so inefficiently. On an XT, the file's next sector of data is simply placed six sectors from the first. The read/write head reaches this sector just as the controller becomes ready to receive more data. The figure [on page 249] diagrams the sector pattern in a 3:1 interleave. The sectors are no longer *physically* contiguous, but they are *logically* contiguous.

The Interleave Factor

This logical patterning of sectors is called the disk's **interleave**. Every disk has an interleave factor. On a standard IBM XT, the factor is 6:1, or simply "6." This means that a file continues at every sixth sector. Expressed differently, an "interleave of 6"

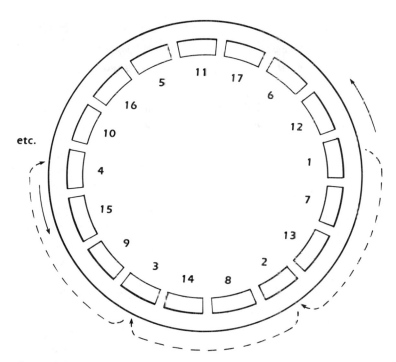

A 3:1 interleave

means that it takes six rotations of the disk to read all data completely from a track. The faster AT uses a 3:1 interleave. A disk in which the data follows the sequence of physical sectors has an interleave of 1:1; all data is read from a track in one turn of the disk. This is the ideal interleave, but it takes a fast 80386 computer to handle it.

A disk's interleave is set when it undergoes **low-level formatting**. (We'll discuss types of formatting in Chapter 4; for now, note that this process breaks up tracks into sectors.) During low-level formatting, each sector is tagged with an identifying number. The numbers may be written in any order, setting the interleave. The interleave can be changed simply by redoing the format with a different interleave factor so that the sectors are numbered differently.

QUESTIONS

1. Presumably those who consult a semi-technical book like *The Hard Disk Companion* know what they are getting into before they begin. What clues do you find in this excerpt that might suggest this guide is not for someone who is a complete novice when it comes to computer technology? What clues do you find that suggest it is not necessarily a book for experts? How would you define the audience of this book?

2. What function do the running subheadings serve? What are the pros and cons of using subheadings in this way?

3. Do computers seem more, or less, mysterious after you have read this clarification? What other kinds of information would you like this explanation to contain?

THE BIG SNEEZE: NEW ADVANCES IN TREATING ALLERGIES

Robin Marantz Henig

*Allergies are no laughing matter to those who suffer from them, and, according to this article, at least 35 million Americans suffer from some type of allergy. Robin Marantz Henig is a free-lance author who has published books on other medical concerns (*How a Woman Ages *and* The Myth of Senility*); this particular article appeared in the* Washington Post. *The article is followed by a sidebar that appeared with it in the newspaper.*

THERE were times I itched so bad I couldn't do anything but sit in the house, keep cool, wear light clothes and drink ice water," says Shirley Meachum, 38, of Washington, recalling her childhood allergies. "I had red eyes, scratchy throat, runny nose and all that itching — especially in the early spring and summer. It was miserable for me, miserable for all of us."

Meachum, her mother and her older sister all had asthma and hay fever. They all still do. And so does Meachum's son, 14-year-old Michael. In fact, she says, "Michael's allergic to everything — mold, dust, smoke, cologne, cats, dogs, people."

For the nation's 35 million allergy sufferers, getting relief has been hard. Over-the-counter allergy medicines that relieve symptoms often lead to intolerable drowsiness; nose sprays can become habit-forming; "desensitization" shots, designed to help build up a tolerance for certain allergens with regular injections, can be costly, time-consuming and ineffective — and, in rare cases, create the very reactions they were designed to prevent.

At the same time, promises of quick fixes for allergies, such as under-the-tongue "neutralizing" drops and urine auto-injections, have led to dashed hopes, emptied wallets and, occasionally, hazardous side effects.

But now some recent medical advances may be changing the outlook for allergy sufferers. As Washington's hay fever season shifts from the tree pollens of May to the grass pollens of June, allergists have some new agents to offer such as steroid nose sprays and inhalers that can be used for a long period of time, a prescription antihistamine that doesn't cause drowsiness, and another prescription drug — cromolyn sodium — that seems to prevent allergy attacks.

What's more, researchers are designing ways of beefing up allergy shots to allow for much higher doses, which is expected to lead to remissions, and maybe even actual cures, in a matter of months rather than years.

The Science of Allergies

An allergy is an over-zealous reaction to a particular irritant. Known as an allergen, the irritating substance triggers the body to produce antibodies to protect itself against the invader. In non-allergic individuals, most common allergens lead to no immune response at all — and hence, no antibodies. But for some reason, allergic people react to an otherwise harmless substance by producing a particular antibody known as immunoglobulin E, or IgE, the so-called allergy antibody.

IgE is present in small amounts in non-allergic people. It is thought to play a role in protecting people from parasites. But some people with allergies may have levels of IgE many times higher than normal.

Exactly how the body mass produces these allergy antibodies is not clear. Researchers are just beginning to learn what regulates this immune reaction. In the past few months, Dr. Rebecca H. Buckley, chief of pediatric allergy and immunology at Duke University, and her colleagues have identified the compound responsible for IgE production as Interleukin IV.

Both types of immune system lymphocytes, the T cells and the B cells, are involved in the process, she says. T cells produce Interleukin IV, and B cells react to its presence by producing IgE.

"Now we are asking what it is about people who are born to become allergic that causes their B cells to mount this response," Buckley says. "Do their T cells produce more Interleukin IV in the first place, or are their B cells less responsive to things that would down-regulate IgE synthesis?"

Once a high level of allergy antibodies have been produced, it is in a certain type of cell — the mast cell — where the action takes place. Mast cells are found along the linings of the respiratory tract, the gastrointestinal tract and the skin — and cells much like them, basophils, are found in the bloodstream. On the surface, a mast cell can carry up to 500,000 IgE antibodies. Inside, it harbors a kind of stink bomb of allergic reactions: tiny packets of chemicals, among them the notorious histamine, that can wreak havoc throughout the body.

The interaction of an antigen with the IgE molecule specifically directed against it is what forces the mast cell to release its store of chemicals — and the allergy attack begins.

Ordinarily, histamine is produced only in response to an actual pathogen — a virus, for example — as it enters the nose. "In a healthy defense mechanism, histamine probably increases the ability of white blood cells to get into the system," says Dr. Glenn Silber, an allergist at the Columbia Medical Plan in Columbia, Md. In addition, he says, the sneezing, dripping and coughing stimulated by histamine release help expel the virus from the nose altogether.

But in an allergy, "that same defense mechanism is triggered by what should be an inert substance," Silber says.

Sneezy, Drippy and Dopey

The site of mast cells involved in an allergic response determines the allergy's symptoms. When histamine is released in the lungs, the person develops the symptoms of asthma — coughing, wheezing, shortness of breath.

In the skin, histamine leads to hives or eczema; in the digestive tract, to abdominal pain, constipation, diarrhea, nausea and vomiting. And in the linings of the nose, sinuses, eyelids and throat, histamine leads to sneezing, sniffing, runny nose, itchy eyes, scratchy throat and conjunctivitis — the telltale signs of hay fever.

Hay fever is the most common form of environmental allergy. According to the National Institute of Allergic and Infectious Diseases, some 17 million Americans, nearly half of all allergy patients, have hay fever, or more properly, allergic rhinitis, from the Latin for inflammation of the nose.

Hay fever is one of the so-called atopic allergies, meaning it seems to run in families. Dr. Michael Sly, chief of allergy and immunology at Children's Hospital National Medical Center in Washington, says a child with one allergic parent runs a 30 percent risk of developing allergies and a child with two allergic parents runs a 60 to 70 percent risk.

"If the parents have asthma," Sly says, "the children run an especially high risk, not necessarily of developing asthma but of developing some allergies."

Different forms of hay fever react to different types of allergens, and this determines which season is "hay fever season"; usually either spring (if the allergen is tree pollen), early summer (if the allergen is grass pollen), or fall (if the allergen is ragweed).

Other allergies — such as allergies to animal dander (skin flakes shed from the hair), house dust mites, mold spores, cockroach excrement or feathers — also can cause hay fever-like symptoms. For people with these allergies, hay fever season lasts all year.

Hay Fever Remedies

The first line of defense against allergies is to stay away from the allergen. This is possible when the allergen is a drug, a food or a house pet, but not it's not so easy if the offending culprit is in the air.

Pollen allergies can be alleviated by staying indoors during hay fever season and by using air conditioners and air filters. But for people with allergies to more than one type of pollen, this can prove all but impossible. In the Washington area, allergenic pollen is in the air, almost without a break, from March through the end of September. And holing up in the house may end up increasing a person's exposure to other substances, such as mold and dust, that usually irritate the allergy-prone.

Dust allergies can be curtailed by giving dust mites fewer places to live — especially in the bedroom, where the allergy sufferer spends eight or ten hours every day. This means no rugs or drapes, plastic linings for the mattresses and pillows, frequent vacuuming and wet mopping, and no pets in the bedroom — except maybe a goldfish.

"When you allergy-proof the bedroom you can see some impressive results," says Silber. "But it doesn't always work. Often, we see someone who is universally sensitive — making it more difficult to avoid all allergens in the environment."

The next best thing in hay fever control is treating the symptoms. The drugs available for this are better today than they were even five years ago — and new drugs are being developed. In the not-too-distant future, people may be able to get over-the-counter nose sprays or eye drops that they can take before an allergy attack, to head off the body's over-reaction even before it gets started.

For now, over-the-counter antihistamines like Chlor-Trimeton and Benedril are "easy, cheap and readily available," says Silber. And in people with a clearly defined hay fever season — like the eight weeks or so when grass pollen is in the air — they are enough.

Yet the more effective the antihistamines, the more likely they are to produce disquieting side effects, such as drowsiness, agitation, dry mouth and blurred vision. These occur because antihistamines pass directly into the central nervous system, easily slipping by the blood-brain barrier.

Allergists say that some side effects can be reduced by lowering the dosage, switching brands or taking the medicine only at bedtime.

A new, non-sedating antihistamine, which does not pass through the blood-brain barrier, is currently available by prescription. When the drug, known by the brand name Seldane, was introduced in 1985, it became the No. 1-selling prescription drug before the year was out—even though it cost twice as much as its over-the-counter competitors.

Seldane's success was testimony not only to the large numbers of allergy sufferers but also to a smart marketing strategy aimed at patients. It was one of the first prescription drugs to target advertisements not just to physicians, who write the prescriptions, but directly to the consumers.

Seldane has already increased the number of hay fever sufferers who can be helped by antihistamines, says Sly. "With newer non-sedating antihistamines, some of which are not yet on the market, we're no longer limited to modest doses," he says. As the doses can be increased, the histamines released during an allergy attack can be better inhibited.

Two other non-sedating antihistamines expected to receive FDA approval within the next few years are Histmanal and Claritin, both of which are longer-acting than Seldane. This means they can be taken less frequently.

When such non-sedating antihistamines become available over the counter, allergy specialists predict these drugs will have a major impact on self-medication for hay fever symptoms.

Another new medication that seems to prevent allergy attack is cromolyn sodium sold as prescription drugs under the brand names Nasalcrom (a nose spray) and Opticrom (eyedrops).

Research suggests that cromolyn prevents the release of chemicals stored in the mast cell that trigger an allergic response. "It actually stabilizes the cell so the chemicals cannot be released," says Silber.

Nasalcrom is sprayed into the nose, and Opticrom dropped into the eyes, two or three times a day whether or not symptoms are present. The only significant side effect seems to be an occasional nosebleed.

In addition, steroid nose sprays also are becoming a popular way of easing hay fever symptoms. Their primary action is anti-inflammatory, but they also ease muscle spasm and reduce mucus production. The steroid sprays, sold under the brand names Vancenase, Beconase and Nasalide, are available by prescription only.

Unlike steroids given by mouth, which can lead to suppression of the adrenal glands, steroid nose sprays don't get into the system for long enough to create problems. With virtually no side effects, some allergists recommend use of steroid sprays for long periods, even in young children.

"Intranasal steroid sprays are effective more often than cromolyn is," says Sly. "There's some absorption of the steroid from the nose, but it's such a small dose involved—a spray or two in each nostril two or three times a day—that you get no measurable adrenal suppression."

Steroid nose sprays are quite different from the over-the-counter nasal decongestants, like Neo-Synephrine, that act by constricting the blood vessels. "These nose sprays can be habit-forming, leading to something called a rebound phenomenon,"

Silber said. The body responds to the drug in the nose spray by producing more mucus, meaning the decongestant is needed even more.

"We tell our patients not to use them at all, except for a severe cold," says Silber, "and never to use them for more than three to five days."

Lastly, Allergy Shots

And then there are shots. Desensitization shots have been called annuities for allergists, and there's no doubt that they guarantee a string of patients, coming in once or twice a week, who pay $10 to $20 a shot.

Immunotherapy appears to be effective in treating allergies to pollen — from grass, from trees or from ragweed — and to dust mites, mold spores, animal dander, even cockroach droppings.

Effectiveness, in this case, is not necessarily cure. Even after allergy shots a person will still have allergies, but symptoms may be eased to the point that they are not bothersome or can be easily controlled with drugs.

One problem is that because of the way immunotherapy works, it's a long, slow process. A person must be sensitized to the offending allergens in concentrations dilute enough not to set off an allergy attack. As a result, a typical course of injections can take three to five years. A year may go by before most patients see any improvement in symptoms, and three to five years before they can expect a long-term remission — by which time many of them might have outgrown their allergies anyway.

What's more, the effectiveness of allergy shots has never been scientifically demonstrated. "A lot of the practice has been based on case reports: 'I used it once, it seemed to work, let's see if it works if I use it again,'" Silber says. Now he is involved in a four-year study at John Hopkins University, sponsored by the National Institute of Allergic and Infectious Diseases, to see if allergy shots actually lead to allergy cures.

"The current data suggest that a significant portion of patients — about 30 to 40 percent — will be cured or will have prolonged clinical improvement," Silber says, "and that another 30 to 40 percent will still have some symptoms, but they won't be as bad as before." The Hopkins research is designed to refine those numbers and results of the study are expected in the early 1990s.

Meanwhile, changes in how shots are given — and what they contain — suggest that immunotherapy might be even more effective in the near future. These changes include:

▸ More-refined mixtures. At one time, patients were tested for allergies to tree mix or dander mix and were treated with combination extracts that "wasted space in the shot," Silber says. Now skin testing is more refined. If a person tests positive for tree mix, for instance, he or she is retested for the 40 individual pollens in that mix, and only treated with extracts from those trees to which the allergic response is most vigorous. "We're using fewer allergens and giving them in higher concentrations," Silber says.

▸ New extracts. Only recently have dust mite and cat allergen extracts come on the market. While many allergists welcome the chance to give shots for dust allergy — one of the hardest to control environmentally — certain dust extracts have been criticized for poor quality control, according to Consumer Reports.

"The raw material for several such extracts comes from the contents of vacuum cleaner bags," the magazine notes. "Analyses show that the extracts contain anything from dog and cat dander to allergens associated with dust mites, rodent hairs, molds and other substances."

As for the cat dander extract, most allergists will not give allergy shots just so someone can keep a cat. Currently, cat allergy shots are given as part of a mixture to someone already getting shots anyway for allergens that are more difficult to avoid. No good extracts exist to sensitize those allergic to dogs.

▶ New polymers. The National Institute of Allergy and Infectious Diseases is sponsoring studies of polymerized extracts, which allow higher concentrations of allergens to be used — for a faster resolution of symptoms — with fewer allergic side effects. A polymer, says Dr. Roy Patterson, chairman of medicine at Northwestern University, is a more efficient way to deliver the allergen because it puts the extracts into one package that is more easily tolerated by the person undergoing immunotherapy. "If you eat 1,000 grains of salt, you taste a lot of saltiness," he says. "But if those same 1,000 grains are all tied into one lump, it would hit fewer receptors on your tongue, and it would taste less salty."

The polymers, now awaiting approval by the Food and Drug Administration, have been shown in some published studies to reduce the course of allergy shot treatment to as little as three months.

All this is leading to a new mood of optimism about the future role of allergy immunotherapy.

"Allergy injections will work in almost every case when the diagnosis is correct," says Patterson.

Still, for the moment, no doctor or patient enters into immunotherapy lightly. "Shots are a long-term commitment," says Silber, "and we reserve them for people with severe disease."

In general, allergy sufferers are looking not so much for a cure as for a way to manage. Sometimes that means hibernating during certain seasons. Michael Meachum, for example, suffers through the spring and summer in his stripped-down, air-conditioned room. Then the teen-ager emerges each winter. "When it's frigid outside," his mother says, "he can run around like crazy."

As the pollen count continues to stay high, most Washingtonians with hay fever will sniffle and cope through the rest of the summer with the help of over-the-counter medicines and air-conditioning.

Yet for those with severe allergies, it is a victory just to keep to a schedule that looks normal. As Michael's mother says: "It's like a job, the daily routine of making sure Michael gets the right medication at the right time."

"But we know that as long as he does what he's supposed to, and as long as he stays calm, he'll be okay."

• • •

WHO GETS ALLERGIES?

The great majority of people with allergies have symptoms they can live with. For a few months every year, they have itchy eyes, scratchy throats and runny noses. Usually, their symptoms can be all but eliminated by avoiding the offending allergen —

which may mean shutting themselves indoors during pollen season — and taking an over-the-counter antihistamine or decongestant.

But for a significant minority of allergy sufferers, possibly one in four, their "bad" season lasts all year. For them, symptoms may be severe enough at times to keep them home from school or work in the refuge of an air-conditioned bedroom.

According to the National Institute of Allergy and Infectious Diseases, asthma and allergies account for more than 16 million days lost from work and school, 46 million visits to the doctor and $614 million in drug expenditures every year.

About half of the nation's 35 million allergy sufferers have hay fever, or allergic rhinitis. Roughly 9 million, including some who also have hay fever, suffer from asthma. Many also are allergic to more than one thing at a time.

In addition to pollens, grasses, house dust and molds, certain foods, medicines, plants and animals also trigger allergic reactions in susceptible people. Common offenders are milk, nuts, shellfish, penicillin, poison ivy, bee stings and cats.

Folklore has it that most people outgrow their allergies — and for many sufferers, this appears to be true. Allergies typically start between the ages of 6 and 12, and a significant number of highly allergic children seem to have fewer and fewer problems after puberty.

"Symptoms often decline in the teen years," says Dr. Roy Patterson, chairman of medicine at Northwestern University. "We're not sure why this occurs. It may be a spontaneous decrease in the production of IgE, or what is called the allergy antibody, or it may be a change in the body's physiology."

Dr. Glenn Silber of the Columbia (Maryland) Medical Plan says estimates of the proportion of childhood allergy suffers who will get better on their own range from 30 to 70 percent. "But a significant [number] don't have problems at all until adulthood," Silber adds, and no one knows why. "That's where the research interest is going now."

Some doctors think individuals who become allergic in middle age are carrying allergic genes that weren't destined to express themselves until later in life. But the mechanism of this timing is poorly understood. "I've had adult patients say to me, 'I've taken penicillin at various times my entire life with no problem at all; why do I suddenly have a pencillin allergy?'" Patterson says. "I can't answer that. The tendency to react to environmental allergens by producing IgE declines with age, but still it can occur at any time in any person."

There's no question that allergies, or at least tendencies toward allergies, run in families. Research has shown that the child of one allergic parent runs one chance in three of developing an allergy — and if both parents are allergic, the chances of the child having allergies are more than two in three. Children don't inherit the particular allergies of their parents; they inherit the tendency.

Steps can be taken to minimize the chance that an allergy-prone child will have allergies, but these steps usually don't prevent allergies altogether. The best they can do, allergists say, is forestall the inevitable. The allergy preventive tricks begin even before the baby is born. In a highly allergic family, some pediatricians recommend that during pregnancy women should stay away from foods most likely to touch off allergies in their unborn children: eggs, milk products, nuts, peanut butter.

These same foods should be avoided while a mother nurses, the experts say, since they can be passed on to the allergy-prone baby in the mother's milk. If a woman watches her diet, she is actually doing her allergy-prone baby much good by breast-feeding. Several studies indicate that nursing a baby who is going to develop allergies at least delays the onset of allergic symptoms.

"If I had a child who was going to develop allergies," says Dr. Michael Sly, chief of allergy and immunology at Children's Hospital National Medical Center, "I'd much rather he developed them at nine months rather than three months. The older the child, the better able we are to manage the allergies."

QUESTIONS

1. Because it appeared in a newspaper, this article is obviously intended for a fairly general audience. Are there any aspects of it you feel a general reader might have problems with? Why or why not?

2. What effect is created by beginning this story with a quotation? The story returns to this speaker at its conclusion for another quotation. Why? Would it be appropriate to include more of these statements within the article?

3. Because it was originally published in a newspaper and published in narrow columns, this article has many short paragraphs (that of course seem longer when it is published in columns). Does the publication format affect the style and readability of this article? What would happen if you simply tried to combine some of these short paragraphs into longer paragraphs that would be more appropriate for book publication?

4. What information would you represent graphically, in charts, graphs, or pictures?

• • • • •

RALEIGH TRI-LITE

John Derven

With the increasing interest in physical fitness in recent years came a corresponding rise in endurance sports such as marathon running and triathlons. Equipment for these sports, as well as for less serious recreational activities, is regularly analyzed and reviewed in articles such as this one, from Bicycle Guide *magazine.*

THERE'S no question that triathlon participants are a major force in the entry-level racing bike market. The Bud Lite USTS, the nation's largest triathlon series, attracted over 20,000 participants in 1986. Compared to approximately 20,000 USCF licensees, it's obvious that many more new racing bikes will wind up at triathlon transition areas than in Category IV pelotons.

"Tri-Lite," as Raleigh has christened its new racing bike, is a double entendre that acknowledges the triathlete market and, at the same time, emphasizes that the three main tubes of its frame are made from aluminum. The Tri-Lites are part of Raleigh's Technium line, a series of bikes constructed by brazing the chrome-moly seat and chainstays into the steel seat lug and bottom bracket, and then gluing these to the aluminum main tubes and steel head tube. This approach allows Raleigh to exploit the merit of aluminum for shock dampening, light weight and rigidity (in a large diameter format) and of steel for resistance to abrasion and ample rigidity with conventional diameters at the stays.

Our Tri-Lite test bike, which will sell for about $450, is the first of two racing models in the Technium line (the other is the Tinley Tri-Lite, which will sell for around $600 retail). As such, it shares certain features with Raleigh's Technium sport-touring bikes. Nearly identical lugs are used, giving the Tri-Lite the same 73-degree parallel geometry and 22½-inch top tube combination as Raleigh's 480 sport-tourer (tested in August, 1986), but the Tri-Lite's chainstays are one inch shorter. This not only stiffens the frame, but also hikes up the rear of the bike a little; the resulting frame angles are 73½ degrees relative to the ground.

The chrome-moly fork on the Tri-Lite is likewise shorter to accommodate short-reach brakes and 700C wheels, and the fork rake is increased to give the bike a bit less trail. Raleigh's Product Manager, Hugh Walton, calls the geometry, ". . . relaxed, easy to steer and comfortable." Indeed, the bike's handling is predictable: the 2⅛ inches of trail gives good straightline stability, and keeps the steering light. Although the 39⅜-inch wheelbase and 23¼-inch front center are on the long side for a racing bike of this size, the stretched dimensions enhance the Tri-Lite's ability to absorb road shock, making it well suited for long road rides.

On the road, the combination of slightly oversize aluminum main tubes (1¼ and 1⅛ inches) and chrome-moly chainstays (with beefy 1-mm wall thickness) keeps the frame adequately rigid when sprinting out of the saddle or climbing hills, but the bike remains comfortable on rough pavement. Although shock absorption is mostly a function of the tires, the aluminum tubes provide additional dampening and are probably partially responsible for the Tri-Lite's smooth ride.

To complement the Tri-Lite frame, Raleigh has picked through 1987's new product bins. The derailleurs and shift levers are Sun Tour's new Alpha 5000 series, with AccuShift indexing. The 5000 series includes some of the refinements described in last month's report on the new Superbe Pro group: shift levers are switchable between standard and indexed modes without giving up the friction adjustment on the D-ring, all Allen fittings have been standardized to five mm, and tolerances have been tightened to allow precise chain alignment during indexed shifts. The 5000 levers do not have the Superbe's Ultra-7 speed capability or the ratcheting feature in the standard mode, but the indexing mechanism in the 5000 levers is more compact. The levers were comfortable to grip and worked — well, like indexed levers, which is to say, perfectly. Except for our test bike's unusual demand for the occasional front detailleur trim adjustment (more on that later), one could fall asleep behind the bars.

Dia-Compe's Alpha 5000 brakes and Alpha aero levers are also new. The levers are composites, with a resin body and aluminum lever arm, and are spring-loaded to work as a "balanced response system" with the Alpha 5000 brakes. Forged aluminum arms and an aggressive pad compound beef up the technical specs, and the stopping power of the Dia-Compe binders was well above the standard I've come to expect on bikes in this price range. I was impressed by their smooth, easily modulated feel.

Although Rigida 1320s were among the first narrow clincher rims on the market, they are still one of the lightest available (around 400 grams) and are here combined with Malliard hubs and stainless steel spokes to create smooth-running, practical wheels.

Our prototype Tri-Lite wasn't completely trouble free. The supplied Hatta bottom bracket axle skewed the chainline out to 48 mm, making front derailleur adjustment more difficult, and a too-short brake cable housing caused an annoying rattle inside the top tube. Both problems were attributed to our bike's pilot-production status, and Walton claims that they won't be seen on production bikes.

UPS AND DOWNS

UPS

Frame: Polyurethane paint; bonded composite frame construction; full braze-ons
Components: Alpha 5000 derailleurs with index shifting; spring-loaded aero levers; rigid calipers; proportionally sized components

DOWNS

Wheels: 36 spokes instead of 32
Seatpost: 200mm length could be longer
Bottom bracket: Incorrect axle supplied

RALEIGH TRI-LITE

$400–$450 (price may vary)
Sizes available: 50, 54, 58, 63 centimeters
Size tested: 58 cm center to center

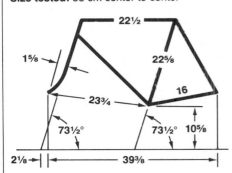

Total weight: 23 lbs. 11 oz
Frame without fork: 5 lbs
Fork only: 1 lb. 10 oz
Front wheel only: 2 lbs. 15 oz
Rear wheel only: 4 lbs. 4 oz
Frame: 6061-T8 aluminum thermally bonded to chrome-moly lugs; chrome-moly stays and fork; forged dropouts. Internal top tube cable guide; riveted bosses for two water bottles and shift levers, bosses for pump and chain hanger, rack eyelets, nylon derailleur cable guides. YST 8002 cone and cup headset
Rims: Rigida 1320 aluminum, heat treated and anodized, 700C
Spokes: 36 stainless Ohio rod spokes, 14 gauge, laced three cross

Hubs: Maillard Atom Sport 400 small flange with quick-release
Tires: IRC Road Lite II, 700 × 25C, 115 psi
Crank: SR SX, 170 mm arms, Hatta cup and cone bottom bracket
Derailleurs: SunTour Alpha 5000 front and rear, Alpha 5000 down tube-mounted indexed levers
Freewheel: SunTour Alpha 6S, 6-speed
Chain: D.I.D.
GEARING in inches

**	40	52
13	83	108
15	72	94
17	64	83
19	57	74
22	49	64
26	42	54

Saddle: Selle Royal Futura, nylon base with foam padding and vinyl cover
Seatpost: Elite micro-adjust, 200 mm long, 26.8 mm diameter
Brakes: Dia-Compe Alpha 5000 with Alpha levers
Pedals: SR SP 250 platform with SR nylon straps and large toeclips
Handlebars: SR CT maes bend, 41 cm wide with SR Custom stem, 10.5 cm reach
Manufactured by: Raleigh Cycle Company of America, 22710 72nd Avenue South, Kent, WA 98032

The Tri-Lite is an excellent value, a good performer and fun to ride. If Raleigh's production models are up to snuff, its triathlete audience is in for a taste of what real racing bikes can do.

QUESTIONS

1. *Bicycle Guide* is read by cycling enthusiasts, a group that usually distinguishes itself from triathletes. (Triathletes must divide their attention among three sports, while cyclists can devote themselves to only one.) What signals do you get in this article that might suggest a certain "snobbishness" about cycling? Would you have noticed this distinction if it had not been pointed out to you?

2. Are the features that attract the attention of the reviewer the same features that might attract your attention? What might you want to know about this bicycle? What aspects of the bicycle really do not interest you as a potential purchaser?

3. As a college student you belong to a demographic group that has been targeted by many industries. The manufacturers of bicycles, sporting goods, cameras, and stereo equipment, to name only a few, would like to attract your attention — and your business. How do you familiarize yourself with the many products in the marketplace that are vying for your cash? Where do you look for guidance in making purchases? How do you know you can trust the advice you receive?

4. Select a piece of equipment from a hobby or sport in which you participate, and write up a product review of it that is similar to this one.

●　　●　　●　　●　　●

ORIANA FALLACI: THE ART OF UNCLOTHING AN EMPEROR

Jonathan Cott

Oriana Fallaci's interviews are as famous in Europe as those of Barbara Walters in the United States. Fallaci, however, is a print journalist rather than a television personality, and Jonathan Cott calls her "the greatest political interviewer of modern times." In this article Fallaci has the tables turned on her; she herself is interviewed by Jonathan Cott. Cott, who has also written, among other things, a biography of Bob Dylan, originally published his interview in Rolling Stone.

WHEN Oriana Fallaci went to interview Ethiopia's Haile Selassie, the emperor's two pet Chihuahuas, named Lulu and Papillon — sensitive antennae of the monarch's autonomic nervous system, geiger counters registering the presence of friend or foe — stopped dead in their tracks. And after this interview (in which the emperor sounded "sick or drunk") was published in Italy, the Ethiopian ambassador in Rome was recalled to his homeland, and no word of or from him was ever heard again.

It is not uncommon for political repercussions to result from a Fallaci interview. Her uncomplimentary portrait of Yasir Arafat attracted scores of threatening letters and letter-bomb scares. The original tapes of her conversation with Golda Meir, Fallaci claims, were stolen by agents of Libya's Colonel Qaddafi. Her interview with Pakistan's Ali Bhutto delayed a peace agreement between Pakistan and India. And Henry Kissinger paid Oriana Fallaci one of her greatest compliments, saying that his having consented to an interview with her was the "stupidest" thing he had ever done.

Like the child in "The Emperor's New Clothes," and like the "Plain Dealer" of Restoration comedy, whose unremitting rudeness signified to the audience that this stock character was being true to himself, Oriana Fallaci has, simply with a tape recorder, exposed the inanities and pretensions of those contumelious rascals and fat-hearted popinjays who pose and act as the powerful leaders and manipulators of the world's destiny.

After years of interviewing "vacuous" movie stars, this slight (in stature), passionate, and mettlesome woman — who speaks in a candent, husky tone — has become the greatest political interviewer of modern times. The Oriana Fallaci Tape Collection is now housed in humidified shelves at Boston University. And just this month [June 1976] Liveright is publishing *Interview with History* — a book consisting of fourteen of Fallaci's extraordinary interviews with persons such as Kissinger, President Thieu, General Giap, Golda Meir, the Shah of Iran, Archbishop Makarios, and Indira Gandhi. As an international correspondent for the Italian magazine *L'Europeo*, she has become a star throughout Europe — where her articles, interviews, and books appear regularly in translation — and has attracted a devoted following in this country through the publication of her interviews in magazines and newspapers such as the *New Republic*, the Washington *Post*, the *New York Review of Books*, and the *New York Times Magazine*. Her most recent work — a spare, annealed dramatic monologue entitled *Letter to a Child Never Born* — has sold almost a million copies in Italy and was published by Simon and Schuster in 1977.

Oriana Fallaci claims that she prepares herself for her interviews "as a boxer prepares for the ring," but it is as a "midwife" — as she defines her role in the following interview — that she has drawn from her subjects many astonishing revelations. Through her gentle ministration, Kissinger finally explained the reason for his abiding popularity: "Well, yes, I'll tell you. What do I care? The main point arises from the fact that I've always acted alone. Americans like that immensely. Americans like the cowboy who leads the wagon train by riding ahead alone on his horse, the cowboy who rides all alone into the town, the village, with his horse and nothing else. Maybe even without a pistol, since he doesn't shoot. He acts, that's all, by being in the right place at the right time. In short, a western."

From the Shah of Iran, Fallaci received the following remarks concerning the role of women in his life: "Women, you know. . . . Look, let's put it this way. I don't underrate them; they've profited more than anyone else from my White Revolution. . . . And let's not forget I'm the son of the man who took away women's veils in Iran. But I wouldn't be sincere if I stated I'd been influenced by a single one of them. Nobody can influence me, nobody. Still less a woman. Women are important to a man's life only if they're beautiful and charming and keep their femininity and. . . . This business of feminism, for instance. What do these feminists want? What do you want?

You say equality. Oh! I don't want to seem rude but. . . . You're equal in the eyes of the law, but not, excuse my saying so, in intelligence."

From the tortured leader of the Greek Resistance, Alexandros Panagoulis, Fallaci elicited his haunting description of how it felt to rediscover space after years sequestered in the darkness of prison: "I made a terrible effort to go forward in all that sun, all that space. Then all of a sudden, in all that sun, in all that space, I saw a spot. And the spot was a group of people. And from that group of people a black figure detached itself. And it came toward me, and little by little it became my mother. And behind my mother, another figure detached itself. And this one too came toward me. And little by little it became Mrs. Mandilaras, the widow of Nikoforos Mandilaras, murdered by the colonels. And I embraced my mother, I embraced Mrs. Mandilaras." [Alexandros Panagoulis was killed in Greece on May Day, 1976.]

And at the conclusion of her conversation with the ill-fated President Thieu, Oriana Fallaci presented the following dialogue that extends the interview form into the realm of the greatest comic farce:

> THIEU: *Voyez bien, mademoiselle*, anything I do I like to do well. Whether it's being converted, or playing tennis, or riding a horse, or holding the office of president. I like responsibility more than power. That's why I say that power should never be shared with others. That's why I'm always the one to decide! Always! I may listen to others suggest some decision, and then make the opposite decision. *Oui, c'est moi qui décide*. If one doesn't accept responsibility, one isn't worthy to be the chief and . . . *mademoiselle*, ask me this question, "Who's the chief here?"
>
> FALLACI: Who's the chief here?
>
> THIEU: I am! I'm the chief! *Moi! C'est moi le chef!*
>
> FALLACI: Thank you, Mr. President. Now I think I can go.
>
> THIEU: Are you leaving? Have we finished? Are you satisfied, *mademoiselle*? Because if you're not satisfied, you must tell me. *Mademoiselle*, I hope you're satisfied because I've hidden nothing from you and I've spoken to you with complete frankness. I swear. I didn't want to in the beginning. But then . . . what can I do? That's the way I am. Come on, tell me. Did you ever expect to find such a fellow?
>
> FALLACI: No, Mr. President.
>
> THIEU: *Merci, mademoiselle*. And, if you can, pray for peace in Vietnam. Peace in Vietnam means peace in the world. And sometimes I feel as though there's nothing left to do except pray to God.

At their best, Oriana Fallaci's brilliantly theatrical interviews remind us of the aims of historians and playwrights such as Thucydides and Ben Jonson, in whose works history and human relations are seen as nothing less than moral drama.

Interviewing Oriana Fallaci is an instructive and reassuring experience. She approved of the kind of cassette recorder I use (she has the same model) and, as well, my 90-minute tapes (120-minute tapes jam up, as interviewers learn not soon enough). And throughout the interview, which took place in February 1976, she positioned the machine and checked the battery indicator, turned over the tapes while remembering and repeating the last words of her unfinished sentences on the new side, then numbered the tapes for me. She suggested that I learn how to ask one question at a time instead of rambling and ranging over a series of suggestive ideas, and turned the recorder off when she wanted to say something off the record. "Only Nixon," she once stated, "knows more about tape recorders than I do."

It wasn't so long ago that advice-to-the-lovelorn columnists used to suggest that all a woman had to do to get a man interested in her was to cajole him gently into talking about himself all evening, thereby flattering him and bolstering his sense of self-importance. In your interviews you seem, almost unconsciously, to have taken this piece of folk wisdom and pushed it very far down the line, using it in order to expose your grandiloquent subjects for what they really are.

I've never thought of that. Neither in my private nor my public life have I ever thought in terms of "seducing" somebody, using what are called the "feminine arts" — it makes me vomit just to think of it. Ever since I was a child — and way before the recent feminist resurgence — I've never conceived of . . . I'm very surprised by what you say. There might be some truth here, but you've really caught me by surprise.

What you're talking about implies a kind of psychological violence which I never commit when I interview someone. I never force a person to talk to me. If he doesn't want to talk, or if he talks without pleasure, I just walk out; I've done that many times. There's no courting or seducing involved. The main secret of my interviews lies in the fact that there's no trick whatsoever. None.

You know, there are many students who write about my interviews — in Italy, France, and America, too. And they always ask me how I go about it and if I could teach them to do it. But it's impossible, for these interviews are what they are, good or bad, because they're made by me, with this face, with this voice. They have to do with my personality, and I bring too much of myself into them to teach them.

When I was reading Interview with History, *I began thinking of the great Enlightenment author Diderot, who, it's been said, had an "instinctual" urge to expose what was concealed. And it seems to me that one of the underlying impulses of your work — along with your unmediated hatred for fascism and authoritarianism — is exactly this instinctual urge to expose. Do you feel that this is true?*

All right. You must give me a little time to answer, as I do with the people I interview. It's a difficult question, very difficult. As I told you before, I bring myself into these interviews completely, as a human being, as a personality; I bring what I know, what I don't know, what I am. Oriana is in there, as an actor. And I bring into these encounters all my choices, all my ideas, and my temperament as well. So, being at the same time very antifascist and very passionate, it's very difficult for me to interview the fascist, in the broad sense of the word. And I say it with shame, since I'm perfectly aware of how ridiculous this is. If I am, as I claim to be, a historian as much as a journalist (I claim that a journalist is a historian of his time), how can I reject at least half of humanity? Because at least half of humanity is fascist.

And when I happen to be interviewing a fascist, and if he really "counts" in history and the interview is going well, I get fascinated. I want so much to know *why* he's a fascist. And this "fascination" on my part then leads to what Socrates called *maieutica* — the work of the *midwife*, whose role becomes especially interesting when I have in front of me someone like Thieu. You see, I think that *power* itself is in some sense fascism by definition (I'm not speaking here of the Mussolini-type of fascism but am rather referring to it in the philosophical sense of the word). And I almost always end by being captivated by it.

Do you think that your forceful way of doing interviews was in any way determined by the humiliation and contemptuousness you might have felt being a girl growing up in a world of political men?

Absolutely not. I can't complain too much about men because, number one, I had the luck to be born into a feminist family — they didn't know it, but indeed they were. To begin with: my father. He always believed in women. He had three daughters, and when he adopted the fourth child, he chose a girl — my youngest sister — because . . . he trusts women. And my parents educated me with the attitude of: you *must* do it because you are a woman. It was, for sure, a challenge, which implies the recognition of a certain reality. But they never thought that I couldn't do it.

In the beginning I wanted to become either a surgeon or a journalist. And the only reason why I didn't choose medicine was because we were too poor to afford six years of medical school. So then it seemed obvious for me to get a job as a reporter when I was sixteen. I gave up medicine because I was poor, not because I was a woman. What I never forget is that I was *poor*. And this is probably at the roots of my moralistic attitude that we were speaking about before. Not the fact that I was a woman.

I noticed that you dedicated your book to your mother. Was she a strong influence on you?

She pushed me. She pushed all of us. But my father did, too. I dedicated it to her more than to him because she's dying from cancer, but I should have dedicated it to both of them, because the person who gave me my political ideas was my father. I've changed my mind about many things, but not about my belief in freedom, social justice, and socialism — *that* came from him. And when we get to this point, it doesn't matter whether one is a man or a woman.

We were speaking before of Golda and Indira. The feminists are wrong to say: "Ha, ha! Indira behaves the way she does because she lives in a society of men." No, sir. She does it simply because she's a person of power who wanted more power. She wasn't ready to give it up and she acted as a man would have acted. At that point, it was the moment of truth — *el momento de la verdad*, as the Spanish call it. She could have said goodbye, sir, thank you very much. *That* means democracy to me. But instead she became a dictator, she demonstrated that being a woman makes no difference, she was no better because she was a woman. . . .

You'd be the person I'd choose to interview the first being we met from outer space.

And I would do it like a *child*. That's the secret. . . . I'll tell you something. During the first moonshot, there was a press conference just before the launch. There was a group of Very Important American Journalists there, and, thank God, there was also my dear friend Cronkite among them. And Cronkite sent me a note — we were in the same room because the press was interviewing the astronauts via TV — asking me if I wanted to ask them a question. "Put a question to them? Thank you." And I wrote down my little question — three words — and sent it to Cronkite.

The other questions went on and on . . . about the fuel and not the fuel, about the gas and the starter and the trajectory. . . . I didn't understand anything being said. You know, I wrote a book about the conquest of the moon and I still don't know how and why a rocket goes up. I'm very proud of that. And I didn't understand the questions of the journalists, who were extremely pompous. Everybody was pompous. And then Cronkite said: "I have a question here from Oriana Fallaci." Pause. And he didn't ask the question. (He was marvelous, he was a real actor.) Then, dramatically: "The question is: *Are you scared?*"

Well, after discussing it with Aldrin and Collins, Neil Armstrong was elected to take the walk: "Well," he hesitated, "you know, the adrenalin goes up." "Ah, bullshit. Say you're scared!" I yelled out loud to everybody in the pressroom. "Who cares about the adrenalin! Tell me, tell me, fear, *fear*! Walter, ask them about *fear*!"

And that was the question of the child. If you asked my youngest sister to put a question to the astronauts, she'd say: "Are you afraid going to the moon?" Of course. That's what she'd want to know.

QUESTIONS

1. Does this excerpt of the interview make you want to know more about Fallaci? What facts about her does Cott most want to reveal to his readers? What direction do his questions seem to lead?

2. Not all readers of *Rolling Stone* may be familiar with Fallaci's work. How does Cott remedy this? Does he include enough information?

3. Do you find any evidence that Fallaci, as an accomplished interviewer herself, tries to steer Cott's interview in a particular direction? Does she always answer his questions? Does he ask his questions in the best possible way?

4. It has recently been suggested that interviewers essentially "betray" the people they interview by encouraging a false intimacy and urging the interviewees to speak frankly and freely. Later, the interviewers will use the interviewees' comments as they see fit, forgetting that some remarks may have been made because of this false sense of rapport. We, of course, have no way of knowing whether Fallaci was "betrayed" in this interview, but do you see any evidence in this conversation of a rapport being established between the participants?

5. If your class has done interviews, select one of your classmates and interview him about his role as an interviewer. Ask questions similar to those asked in this essay.

ON A CONSTITUTIONAL CONVENTION

Cokie Roberts

National Public Radio (NPR) provides a service that television and local radio usually cannot, the extended analysis of major news stories as well as features and in-depth interviews. In this report from NPR's "Morning Edition," reporter Cokie Roberts discusses the issue of a Constitutional Convention. In this transcription of the actual broadcast, Roberts is first introduced by commentator Bob Edwards. This report was originally broadcast on September 3, 1987.

BOB EDWARDS: As we celebrate the two hundredth anniversary of the U.S. Constitution, the call for a new Constitutional Convention has been sounded by many states. During his nationally broadcast speech last month, President Reagan seemed ready to join that call. The President said the nation desperately needs the power of a Constitutional amendment to help balance the budget. Forty-four state governments already have such an amendment and are pressuring Congress to approve one on the Federal level. If Congress refuses, a majority of the states can force Congress to convene a Constitutional Convention to debate the matter. It's unclear, however, whether such a convention could be limited to a single issue, and that's what worries some people. In the first of a three-part series on Congress and the Constitution, NPR's Cokie Roberts examines the questions surrounding a second Constitutional Convention.

COKIE ROBERTS: President Reagan has pushed Congress for a Constitutional amendment to balance the budget since he came to Washington, but in his August speech to the nation, the President injected a new threat into his lobbying effort: "If the Congress continues to oppose the wishes of the people by avoiding a vote on our balanced budget amendment, the call for a Constitutional Convention is only two states away from approval, and one way or another the will of the people always prevails."

The idea of a Constitutional Convention is one which strikes fear in the heart of many Americans, conservatives and liberals alike. One of Ronald Reagan's most loyal allies strenuously disagrees with the President on this question; Phyllis Schlafly heads the Eagle Forum: "A new convention could undertake to rewrite the Constitution, which is something we don't need. I think there isn't any evidence that they could do as good a job as the one we already have. It's stood the test of time."

Before the framers of the Constitution left Philadelphia, they provided for future conclaves; Article 5 begins: "The Congress, whenever two-thirds of both houses shall deem it necessary, shall propose amendments to this Constitution, or on the application of the legislatures of two-thirds of the several states shall call a convention for proposed amendments."

"We recognize that it's a legitimate part of the Constitution; however, I think that this country is going through enough tumult at this point that we don't need the addition of a Constitutional Convention." Linda Rodgers Kingsbury heads a coalition of groups lobbying against a Constitutional Convention; it includes elements as diverse as Phyllis Schlafly's Eagle Forum and the American Civil Liberties Union. Heading the lobbying effort for the convention call is the National Tax Limitation Committee helped by the White House. Political Affairs Director John Davis claims the convention call serves more as a threat than a reality: "It's our goal to put enough heat on Congress through the state legislatures to force them to act and give the people what they've been wanting for years, a balanced budget amendment to the Constitution."

Davis declares he has no concerns about a convention, which he believes could be limited to the single question of including a balanced budget amendment in the Constitution, but scholars are not so sure. Walter Burns teaches government at Georgetown University. He asks the question: Can a convention be confined? "My own view is no. This is an assembly of the sovereign people of America, and it would, I think, be inappropriate to try to limit that to that business, and if that is so, then that convention, called ostensibly for the purpose of proposing an amendment to balance the budget, to require it, will be open to proposed amendments to permit school prayer, to abolish abortion, to permit abortion, one thing or the other." The only precedent we have for a Constitutional Convention does not give comfort to those who say a meeting would be limited. Fred Barbash's book *The Founding* explains what those conventioneers did two hundred years ago: "They were instructed by their state, by the then Confederation Congress, to devise a few amendments to the Articles of Confederation, but when they got behind closed doors, and they were closed, they decided to write a whole new Constitution. And I think it was really the first runaway convention in our history, one that has haunted all convention ideas since then."

That runaway convention produced a result this country has revered for two hundred years. The Constitution has only incorporated twenty-six of the more than 10,000 amendments proposed to Congress, and another convention has never been called. Professor Burns doubts that a second Constitutional Convention would end so happily because the cast of characters would not be the same: "That was an extraordinary group of men. You know, they were right when Jefferson called them an assembly of demigods and so forth. The best index I have of that is the judgment of Tallyrand; you know, here is this European, this man who knew everybody in the late eighteenth, early nineteenth century. Someone asked him who are the greatest men you have ever met, and he said the younger Pitt, Napoleon, and Hamilton, and of those three probably Hamilton was the greatest."

If we know there would not be any Hamiltons or Madisons at a second convention, we do not know who would be there or how they would be chosen, a problem that James Madison saw immediately, according to Fred Barbash: "Even in '87 Madison was very concerned about it and complained about it in the convention. What would it do, how would it make its will felt? He thought that it was just too vague to leave it there; he knew the power of a convention because he was wielding it." Madison's argument has been taken up by modern-day opponents of a Constitutional convention. How would votes be determined, they ask, by state or by population? Linda Rodgers Kingsbury poses the question of campaigning for delegate: "One is going to stand up and say 'I am in favor of a balanced budget amendment and I think we ought to do something about this, and this, and this, and this while we're there.' The other will stand up and say, 'I don't think we ought do anything but just look at a balanced budget amendment. Maybe we should take a look at abortion.'"

Two procedure bills to set the rules for conventions have been introduced in Congress, but John Davis argues they have been shelved by anti-convention forces who want to use the uncertainty of process as a tool to defeat a convention. He would welcome such a bill: "That would give us, I am afraid, a good bit of ammunition in putting down those people that would tell us that there is a possibility of a runaway, and I don't think that's a card they want to put in our hand at this point." If a convention should take place, this time it would be almost impossible to do what the founders did — lock the doors and close the curtains, keep the press and public out. And while daily headlines emerge from the convention center, opponents contend the nation's government and economy would stand on shaky ground. Constitutional author Fred Barbash sees that scenario as somewhat over-dramatic along with other dire predictions: "You get this sense now, a lot of hammering about a convention for wiping out the Bill of Rights, and we wake up one morning and the Bill of Rights is gone. Well, it doesn't happen that way. The convention might propose that, but then it's got to make the rounds once more of all the state legislatures, or conventions in the states, and be ratified, which is no easy matter. So there are so many checks on that process that I think you really have to have a real national consensus to change the Constitution."

Rather than take a risk, the Congress is much more likely to respond to calls for a Constitutional Convention the way it has on a couple of occasions in the past, by approving the amendment to balance the budget. The lawmakers of today, like the men who met in Philadelphia two hundred years ago, are not eager to go through the exercise of another convention. The only founding father who argued strongly for frequent conventions was Thomas Jefferson, and he spent the summer of 1787 in Paris, while his colleagues sweated through their ordeal in Philadelphia.

I'm Cokie Roberts, in Washington.

QUESTIONS

1. The Roberts report was of course written to be delivered orally, not read in print. Is there anything about it that suggests to you it is meant to be heard, rather than seen on a page?

2. Roberts' quotations are not completely edited, because these statements are comments actually spoken by the individuals named; she merely introduces their remarks. If you were going to take these taped comments and write a report, would you edit these speeches any differently? How?

3. What purpose does the Edwards introduction serve? Do you find it useful? What assumptions does he make about the audience who is listening to this broadcast?

THE WORLD OF THE FOREST

Colin M. Turnbull

Colin Turnbull has devoted his life to studying native African culture, particularly the culture of the BaMbuti Pygmies in the Ituri forest of Zaire (formerly the Belgian Congo). In this chapter from his book The Forest People *(1961) he introduces his readers to this mysterious world.*

I N the northeast corner of the Belgian Congo, almost exactly in the middle of the map of Africa, . . . lies the Ituri Forest, a vast expanse of dense, damp and inhospitable-looking darkness. Here is the heart of Stanley's Dark Continent, the country he loved and hated, the scene of his ill-fated expedition to relieve Emin Pasha, an expedition costing hundreds of lives and imposing almost unbearable hardships on the survivors, who trekked across the great forest not once, but three times, losing more lives each time through fighting, sickness and desertion.

Anyone who has stood in the silent emptiness of a tropical rain forest must know how Stanley and his followers felt, coming as they all did from an open country of rolling plains, of sunlight and warmth. Many people who have visited the Ituri since, and many who have lived there, feel just the same, overpowered by the heaviness of everything — the damp air, the gigantic water-laden trees that are constantly dripping, never quite drying out between the violent storms that come with monotonous regularity, the very earth itself heavy and cloying after the slightest shower. And, above all, such people feel overpowered by the seeming silence and the age-old remoteness and loneliness of it all.

But these are the feelings of outsiders, of those who do not belong to the forest. If you *are* of the forest it is a very different place. What seems to other people to be eternal and depressing gloom becomes a cool, restful, shady world with light filtering lazily through the tree tops that meet high overhead and shut out the direct sunlight — the sunlight that dries up the non-forest world of the outsiders and makes it hot and dusty and dirty.

Even the silence is a myth. If you have ears for them, the forest is full of sounds — exciting, mysterious, mournful, joyful. The shrill trumpeting of an elephant, the sickening cough of a leopard (or the hundred and one sounds that can be mistaken for it), always makes your heart beat a little unevenly, telling you that you are just the slightest bit scared, or even more. At night, in the honey season, you hear a weird, long-drawn-out, soulful cry high up in the trees. It seems to go on and on, and you wonder what kind of creature can cry for so long without taking breath. The people of the forest say it is the chameleon, telling them that there is honey nearby. Scientists will tell you that chameleons are unable to make any such sound. But the forest people of faraway Ceylon also know the song of the chameleon. Then in the early morning comes the pathetic cry of the pigeon, a plaintive cooing that slides from one note down to the next until it dies away in a soft, sad, little moan.

There are a multitude of sounds, but most of them are as joyful as the brightly colored birds that chase one another through the trees, singing as they go, or the chatter of the handsome black-and-white Colobus monkeys as they leap from branch to branch, watching with curiosity everything that goes on down below. And the most joyful sound of all, to me, is the sound of the voices of the forest people as they sing a lusty chorus of praise to this wonderful world of theirs — a world that gives them everything they want. This cascade of sound echoes among the giant trees until it seems to come at you from all sides in sheer beauty and truth and goodness, full of the joy of living. But if you are an outsider from the non-forest world, I suppose this glorious song would just be another noise to grate on your nerves.

The world of the forest is a closed, possessive world, hostile to all those who do not understand it. At first sight you might think it hostile to all human beings, because in every village you find the same suspicion and fear of the forest, that blank, impenetrable wall. The villagers are friendly and hospitable to strangers, offering them the best of whatever food and drink they have, and always clearing out a house where the traveler can rest in comfort and safety. But these villages are set among plantations in great clearings cut from the forest for many thousands of years. It is their world, and in return for their affection and trust it supplies them with all their needs. They do not have to cut the forest down to build plantations, for they know how to hunt the game of the region and gather the wild fruits that grow in abundance there, though hidden to outsiders. They know how to distinguish the innocent-looking *itaba* vine from the many others it resembles so closely, and they know how to follow it until it leads them to a cache of nutritious, sweet-tasting roots. They know the tiny sounds that tell where the bees have hidden their honey; they recognize the kind of weather that brings a multitude of different kinds of mushrooms springing to the surface; and they know what kinds of wood and leaves often disguise this food. The exact moment when termites swarm, at which they must be caught to provide an important delicacy, is a mystery to any but the people of the forest. They know the secret language that is denied all outsiders and without which life in the forest is an impossibility.

The BaMbuti roam the forest at will, in small isolated bands or hunting groups. They have no fear, because for them there is no danger. For them there is little hardship, so they have no need for belief in evil spirits. For them it is a good world. The fact that they average less than four and a half feet in height is of no concern to them; their taller neighbors, who jeer at them for being so puny, are as clumsy as elephants — another reason why they must always remain outsiders in a world where your life may depend on your ability to run swiftly and silently. And if the Pygmies are small, they are powerful and tough.

Whereas my first visit to the Ituri Forest, in 1951, had been made mainly out of curiosity, I had seen enough to make me want to return to this area for more intensive study. An ideal location was provided by a strange establishment set up on the banks of the Epulu River back in the nineteen-twenties by an American anthropologist, Patrick Putnam.* He had gone there to do his field work but had liked the place and the people

---

*Patrick Putnam first went to the Belgian Congo in 1927 to do field work for Harvard University. Apart from one or two brief return visits to the United States he remained there until his death at the end of 1953. At Camp Putnam he established a dispensary and a leper colony, turning his home into a guest house to help pay the expenses of his hospital work.

so much that he decided to stay. He built himself a huge mud mansion, and gradually a village grew up around him and became known as "Camp Putnam." The Pygmies treated it just as they treated any other Bantu village (the main Negro tribes nearby were the BaBira and BaNdaka, with a few Moslem BaNgwana), and used to visit it to trade their meat for plantation products. This was where I first met them.

But on my second visit, in 1954, I was provided with a real opportunity for studying the relationship between the Pygmies and their village neighbors. The event was the decision of the local Negro chief to hold a tribal nkumbi initiation festival. This is a festival in which all boys between the ages of about nine and twelve are circumcised, then set apart and kept in an initiation camp where they are taught the secrets of tribal lore, to emerge after two or three months with the privileges and responsibilities of adult status.

The nkumbi is a village custom, but in areas where the practice prevails the Pygmies always send their children to be initiated along with the Negro boys. This has been cited as an example of their dependence on the Negroes and of their lack of an indigenous culture. The Negroes take all the leading roles in the festival, and as no Pygmy belongs to the tribe, none can become a ritual specialist, so the Pygmy boys always have to depend on the Negroes for admission to an initiation, and for the subsequent instruction. An uninitiated male, Pygmy or Negro, young or old, is considered as a child — half a man at best.

Only relatives of the boys undergoing initiation are allowed to live in the camp, though any adult initiated male can visit the camp during the daytime.

But it so happened that on this occasion there were no Negro boys of the right age for initiation, so the only men who could live in the camp and stay there all night were Pygmies. To go against the custom of allowing just relatives to live in the camp would have brought death and disaster. Nevertheless the Negroes went ahead with the festival because it has to be held to avoid offending the tribal ancestors. The Negro men would have liked to stay in the camp all night, as normally instruction goes on even then, the boys being allowed to sleep only for short periods. But custom was too strong, and they had to rely on the Pygmy fathers to maintain order in the camp after dark and not allow the children to have too much sleep.

The Pygmies, however, did not feel bound by the custom, as it was not theirs anyway, and they invited me to stay with them, knowing perfectly well that I would bring with me plenty of tobacco, palm wine, and other luxuries. I was, after all, they said, father of all the children, so I was entitled to stay. The Negroes protested, but there was nothing they could do. On the one hand they felt that I would be punished for my offense by their supernatural sanctions; on the other they themselves hoped to profit by my presence. At least I could be expected to share in the expenses, which otherwise they would have to bear, of initiating the eight Pygmy boys.

And so I entered the camp and saw the initiation through from beginning to end. It was not a particularly comfortable time, as we got very little sleep. The Pygmy fathers were not in the least interested in staying awake simply to keep their children awake and teach them nonsensical songs, so the Negroes used to make periodic raids during the night, shouting and yelling and lashing out with whips made of thorny branches, to wake everyone up. Besides that, the camp was not very well built and the heavy rains used to soak the ground we slept on; only the boys, sleeping on their rough bed made of split logs, were dry. In the end we all used to climb up there and sit — there was not room for everyone to lie down — cold and miserable, waiting for the dawn to bring another daily round of exhausting singing and dancing.

But at the end of it all I knew something about the Pygmies, and they knew something about me, and a bond had been made between us by all the discomforts we had shared together as well as by all the fun. And when the initiation was over and we were off in the forest I learned still more. It was then that I knew for sure that much of what had been written about the Pygmies to date gave just about as false a picture as did the thirteenth-century cartographer who painted them as one-legged troglodytes. In the village, or in the presence of even a single Negro or European, the Pygmies behave in one way. They are submissive, almost servile, and appear to have no culture of their own. But at night in the initiation camp when the last Negro had left, or off in the forest, those same Pygmies were different people. They cast off one way of life and took on another, and from the little I saw of their forest life it was as full and satisfactory as village life seemed empty and meaningless.

The Pygmies are no more perfect than any other people, and life, though kind to them, is not without hardships. But there was something about the relationship between these simple, unaffected people and their forest home that was captivating. And when the time came that I had to leave, even though we were camped back near the village, the Pygmies gathered around their fire on the eve of my departure and sang their forest songs for me; and for the first time I heard the voice of the molimo. Then I was sure that I could never rest until I had come out again, free of any obligations to stay in the village, free of any limitations of time, free simply to live and roam the forest with the BaMbuti, its people; and free to let them teach me in their own time what it was that made their life so different from that of other people.

The evening before I left, before the singing started, three of the great hunters took me off into the forest. They said they wanted to be sure that I would come back again, so they thought they would make me "of the forest." There was Njobo, the killer of elephants; his close friend and distant relative, Kolongo; and Moke, an elderly Pygmy who never raised his voice, and to whom everyone listened with respect. Kolongo held my head and Njobo casually took a rusty arrow blade and cut tiny but deep vertical slits in the center of my forehead and above each eye. He then gauged out a little flesh from each slit and asked Kolongo for the medicine to put in. But Kolongo had forgotten to bring it, so while I sat on a log, not feeling very bright, Kolongo ambled off to get the medicine, and Moke wandered around cheerfully humming to himself, looking for something to eat. It began to rain, and Njobo decided that he was not going to stay and get wet, so he left. Moke was on the point of doing the same when Kolongo returned. Obviously anxious to get the whole thing over with as little ceremony as possible and return to his warm dry hut, he rubbed the black ash-paste hard into the cuts until it filled them and congealed the blood that still flowed. And there it is today, ash made from the plants of the forest, a part of the forest that is a part of the flesh, carried by every self-respecting Pygmy male. And as long as it is with me it will always call me back.

The women thought it a great joke when I finally got back to camp, wet and still rather shaky. They crowded around to have a look and burst into shrieks of laughter. They said that now I was a real man with the marks of a hunter, so I would have to get married and then I would never be able to leave. Moke looked slyly at me. He had not explained that the marks had quite that significance.

It was later that evening when the men were singing that I heard the molimo. By then I had learned to speak the language quite well, and I had heard them discussing whether or not to bring the molimo out; there was some opposition on the grounds that it was "a thing of the forest," and not of the village, but old Moke said it was good for me to hear it before I left, as it would surely not let me stay long away but would bring me safely back.

First I heard it call out of the night from the other side of the Nepussi River, where three years earlier I had helped Pat Putnam build a dam. The dam was still there, though breached by continuous flooding. The hospital where Pat had given his life lay just beyond, now an overgrown jungle, only a few crumbling vine-covered walls left standing, the rest lost in a wilderness of undergrowth. Somewhere over there, in the darkness, the molimo now called; it sounded like someone singing but it was not a human voice. It was a deep, gentle, lowing sound, sometimes breaking off into a quiet falsetto, sometimes growling like a leopard. As the men sang their songs of praise to the forest, the molimo answered them, first on this side, then on that, moving around so swiftly and silently that it seemed to be everywhere at once.

Then, still unseen, it was right beside me, not more than two feet away, on the other side of a small but thick wall of leaves. As it replied to the song of the men, who continued to sing as though nothing were happening, the sound was sad and wistful, and immensely beautiful. Several of the older men were sitting near me, and one of them, without even looking up, asked me if I wanted to see the molimo. He then continued singing as though he didn't particularly care what my reply was, but I knew that he did. I was so overcome by curiosity that I almost said "yes"; I had been fighting hard to stop myself from trying to peer through the leaves to where it was now growling away almost angrily. But I knew that Pygmy youths were not allowed to see it until they had proved themselves as hunters, as adults in Pygmy eyes, and although I now carried the marks on my forehead I still felt unqualified. So I simply said, no, I did not think I was ready to see it.

The molimo gave a great burst of song and with a wild rush swept across the camp, surrounded by a dozen youths packed so tightly together that I could see nothing, and disappeared into the forest. Those left in the camp made no comment; they just kept on with their song, and after a while the voice of the molimo, replying to them, became fainter and fainter and was finally lost in the night and in the depths of the forest from where it had come.

This experience convinced me that here was something that I could do that was really worth while, and that I was not doing it justice by coming armed with cameras and recording equipment, as I had on this trip. The Pygmies were more than curiosities to be filmed, and their music was more than a quaint sound to be put on records. They were a people who had found in the forest something that made their life more than just worth living, something that made it, with all its hardships and problems and tragedies, a wonderful thing full of joy and happiness and free of care.

QUESTIONS

1. Turnbull's description doesn't read like the usual anthropological study. How does it differ? Is there anything about it that surprises you?

2. Describe Turnbull's relationship with the BaMbuti Pygmies. How does this relationship affect the persona he presents to the reader? What other attitudes might he have taken toward the BaMbuti? How might these have affected his book?

3. Turnbull reports much of what happened without using quotations or dialogue. How does this relative lack of dialogue affect his description? How would using more dialogue have affected the tone of his piece?

4. Does this chapter have a thesis? What is it?

• • • • •

THE MAN WHO CRIES WOLF

Fred H. Harrington

Fred Harrington is an ethologist, one who scientifically studies animal behavior. This study of the cries and silences of wolves originally appeared in Natural History, *a magazine published by the American Museum of Natural History.*

THE winter night was perfect for howling. The air was cold and motionless. Light, fluffy snow blanketed the ground, cushioning my steps as I edged closer to the wolf pack. Best of all, a full moon hung in the clear black sky, illuminating my way and perhaps stirring a few primordial howls within the wolves. Soon I came across wolf tracks that crossed the road and headed toward a spruce bog. I tried to follow, but at every third step I broke through the crust and was left floundering midthigh in powdery snow. I stopped trying to walk, set my microphone on its tripod, and switched on my tape recorder. Then I howled.

Within seconds, a pack of radio-collared wolves answered. For nearly a minute the spruce woods reverberated with a cacophony of yips, yaps, and yowls, anchored by an occasional low bass note. Finally, the wolves' reply ended with a series of staccato, barklike yaps.

At the time, I was studying timber wolf howling in Superior National Forest in northeastern Minnesota. Working in conjunction with L. David Mech, of the U.S. Fish and Wildlife Service, I was trying to test a theory that howling plays a role in the establishment and maintenance of wolf pack territories. Each night I searched a vast network of logging roads from an antenna-equipped truck, patiently listening for radio signals from wolves Dave had radio-collared.

Populating the forest were about forty packs of wolves, each occupying some twenty-five to one hundred square miles. Under normal conditions, a pack could satisfy all its needs within an area that size — there would be an adequate number of dens, for example, and sufficient prey throughout the year. Virtually every square mile in the forest was claimed by at least one pack, so at the edges of adjacent territories, a one- or two-mile-wide overlapping strip was shared. If at all possible, these overlapping areas were typically avoided by neighboring packs and were thus underused compared with the packs' exclusive territories. Lone wolves accordingly found these areas relatively safe and therefore made frequent use of them. And since the packs tended to stay in their own areas, they rarely met one another or even crossed the path of a lone wolf.

Observing all this led me to wonder if wolves communicate to maintain this quiltlike pattern. So each night I would set out by truck in search of a radio-collared wolf. Once I located one, I would drive as close to the animal as the road allowed. Then I'd howl.

Most animal-vocalization studies use playbacks of recorded calls to provoke live responses. My studies had started that way too. Using several different taped howls, I had attempted playbacks but had been plagued by poor fidelity and equipment failure. My tape recorder, for instance, became very sluggish as the temperature dropped toward freezing. When the speed of the machine slowed, pups' voices deepened and they began to sound like adults. Adult howls took on an unearthly quality that can only be compared to the moaning of lost souls in a horror film. So after three months with no success, I dumped the playback gear and developed my own personal howl.

Getting a howl that fooled the wolves, I soon discovered, was not at all difficult. After learning to maintain enough wind to sustain a loud, six-second howl, I soon developed a standard series of five howls, which I used for the rest of the study. By this time I had been in the field four months and had not heard a single wolf howl. Soon, however, the wolves began to reply to me, and when I left the forest two years later, nearly five hundred of my howls had evoked some sort of vocal reply.

Once I knew my howls were being interpreted as those of an intruding wolf, I was ready to force encounters with packs and then note the conditions under which they replied.

A pack's responses, I learned, could be divided into two major categories based on their howling. If a pack responded by howling, it nearly always stood its ground. (Only 3 percent of the time did the pack reply and then retreat.) If it kept quiet, it either stayed put or it fled. Thus, if there is a message to a pack's reply, it probably reads, "We are a wolf pack, we are here, and we intend to stay here." Implicit in this message is the threat that "if you get closer, we might attack."

Of course, there could be a good deal of bluff involved in a reply. I soon found out that there were times when packs would turn tail and run if an intruder ignored their replies and continued to close in. I also learned that if an encounter does occur, a pack's actual response might depend on a quick appraisal of the odds.

When a pack did not reply, it retreated about a third of the time. These retreats ranged from a fraction of a mile to more than a mile. Dave Mech and I watched one small retreat in progress. I was on the ground, howling to a pack about a mile away, while Dave watched from a circling aircraft as the pack rested on a frozen lake. When I howled, one wolf leaped up and appeared to bark once or twice, perhaps to arouse the rest of the pack. Within minutes the wolves retreated from the open ice and into the woods north of the lake, where they lay down again, less than a mile from shore. Now that the wolves knew my location, and had placed a lake between us, they would have ample warning if I moved closer. In addition, fresh scent from urination, defecation, feet, and bodies would act as an additional olfactory warning.

One probable reason why packs don't forcibly evict intruders is that direct physical encounters carry the risk of severe injury or even death. Dave has now watched several direct encounters between packs, and in each case at least one animal was seriously wounded.

Howling thus serves the pack as a long-distance defense system. Wolves may be able to hear howls from as far away as five miles, making them aware of one another's locations long before an accidental encounter can take place. Once aware of a neighboring pack's position, a pack can avoid traveling into an area where a chance meeting would be likely.

Packs typically tried to avoid other packs that were too far away to be seen. The reason for this seemed clear: encounters between packs could be dangerous if one pack turned out to be larger. Once two packs could see each other, they would quickly discover which had the advantage of size, and usually the larger pack would chase after the smaller. We haven't been able to determine, however, whether the smaller pack flees first, thus drawing the chase, or whether the larger pack attacks the smaller first.

When a pack does reply, it may "hope" the intruder will go away. But that doesn't always happen. On an increasing number of occasions, both Dave Mech in Minnesota and researchers elsewhere have watched packs leave their territories and invade those of their neighbors. In some cases, the intruders seemed content merely to filch a deer or moose, eat it hurriedly, and return to their own territory. But other intrusions were different. The invading packs picked up the residents' trail and excitedly followed it, not repelled by the residents' scent, as might normally be expected. In several cases in Minnesota, the intruders pressed on until they had located the residents and atttacked them. Most of these incursions resulted in at least one mortally wounded resident. What motivated these attacks is unknown.

This introduces the crux of a pack's howling dilemma. If a pack howls and its neighbors answer, and if each pack is content to leave the other alone, then the howling has served its function: a potentially destructive encounter has been averted. But if one pack intent on attack howls and the other answers, then the second pack has given away its location and has facilitated its potential demise. This may explain why packs only answered me on half of the occasions on which I howled.

On each howling occasion, I tried to note various kinds of information, such as where I was in relation to the territory edge or center, whether the pack was traveling or stationary; whether it was at a den, a rendezvous site, or out hunting; whether the pups were present; and which adults were there. Despite my sketchy data, a number of striking patterns emerged, which fleshed out an answer to the "howl or not to howl" question.

If replying to intruders carries the risk of attack, then wolves should expect to reap benefits that make the risk worth taking. One such benefit is the advantage of staying put. For the most part, wolves have no overriding reason to stay put. They can afford to get up, move off, and start hunting again, rather than risk an attack. But if a site contains an important resource, such as their favorite prey or their pups, there is no incentive to move.

Just one of the large ungulates that wolves hunt in Minnesota can keep the average pack well fed for a few days to a week or more. The typical wolf needs about four to eight pounds of meat each day to survive. An adult male moose provides about 725 pounds of edible meat, enough to fuel a pack of six wolves for two to four weeks. Packs are understandably reluctant to leave their kills.

But the kills get old, their meat and marrow are consumed, and soon nothing but hair, bones, and pieces of hide remain. When a pack was ready to move on, howls to them often resulted in a silent retreat. Thus an interesting pattern developed at kills. The freshest of largest kills were associated with the highest reply rates. I located one pack feeding on a six- to seven-month-old fawn that had been killed less than four hours before. It replied to my howls nine times in less than one and a half hours. When I returned the following day, the pack was still there but refused to answer any of my howls. It was gone when I checked again a few hours later, leaving nothing but the fawn's lower jawbone.

Pups also tie a pack to a specific site, but for a much longer period. Once out of the den at three to four weeks of age, the pups spend the next three to four months at rendezvous sites, where they grow and mature as rapidly as the adults can keep them supplied with food. During this period, the pups become increasingly capable of traveling but still cannot match the endurance of an adult. Should danger threaten while the pups are near the den, they can scamper back into it and take refuge. But most rendezvous sites lack such havers and the pups are more exposed to danger, making them more dependent on protection by the adults.

Packs are therefore quite vocal at rendezvous sites. For each pack I studied, the highest reply rates were obtained at rendezvous sites during the summer. One pack replied on all twenty-four nights I howled to it in July and August, while another replied on seventeen of twenty nights in July and on all thirty-two howling sessions in August.

During these pack replies, the pups readily joined in. Pups are accustomed to replying to packmates on their return to the rendezvous site. I found that when pups were left alone, they frequently approached me when I howled near the rendezvous site. On one occasion a pup traveled nearly half a mile toward me. It was panting and whimpering when it crashed through the brush a few feet away. Once it caught my scent it circled around me, still looking for the phantom adult wolf it was so anxious to meet. When I couldn't hear it anymore, I howled, and within seconds the pup came panting and whimpering toward me again. To the pups I must have seemed one of the pack's adults, coming back to the rendezvous site with food and perhaps in the mood to play.

The adults, however, made no such errors in identification. To them, I was an intruder and a real threat to their pups. Therefore, replying to my howls was a serious matter. If I pressed the pack by continuing to howl, the adults led the pups several hundred feet away, giving up some ground rather than endanger the pups in a fight.

As their pups grew and developed, however, packs became less and less responsive. Sometimes in late November or early December, by which time pups had been traveling with the adults for some two months, packs were unlikely to reply unless they were camped at a kill. Because the pups were now very mobile, there was no need to stay on their account. Silence, and perhaps retreat, might be the best response to an intruder's howling. Accordingly, in December and January, replies came sporadically. If a pack had just made a kill, I could expect a day or two of replies before the pack clammed up. But I soon discovered that more than kills or pups influenced a pack's decision about replying.

When the breeding season approached in late February, reply rates went up for all my study packs; kills at that time made no difference in responses. With the increased production of reproductive hormones at the onset of the breeding season, there is a parallel rise in aggressiveness. Within the pack, wolves of the same sex jealously compete for the privilege of mating. This aggression is directed toward strangers as well. Most fatality-producing encounters between packs occur during the mating season, when the dominant wolves seem unwilling to tolerate a threat to their status from any corner. But the breeding season ends even more suddenly than it begins, and as aggressiveness wanes, the number of replies to howling plummets. By April, a month after mating activity had ceased, replies were extremely difficult to elicit.

One last factor seemed to influence the pack's decision whether to reply — its size. One pack of seven to twelve wolves replied twice as frequently as a smaller pack with four to six members. This was true at kill sites, around rendezvous sites, and elsewhere in the packs' territories. Being in a group appears to make wolves more confident in replying to an intruder's threat. As the size of the group increases, individuals become bolder and therefore more likely to reply.

Such group support seems to make larger packs more aggressive than smaller ones. They are accordingly more likely to trespass into neighboring territories, to attack their neighbors, and to chase away any strangers they encounter in their own territories. When deer were in short supply recently in Minnesota's Superior National Forest, packs were occasionally forced to trespass in order to find food. Most were content to make brief forays into alien territory and returned home quickly after finishing their filched kills. One pack of four to six members played this form of Russian roulette once too often; the dominant male was killed when the pack was detected and confronted by the residents. But one of the largest packs, numbering nearly a dozen, trespassed repeatedly during this time and prospered.

In my two years of howling, I had some close encounters with the wolves and experienced moments of fear when the mythology about the animals took over and my imagination got the better of me. But only on seven of more than four hundred occasions did a single wolf leave the pack and approach me. Even these approaches happened only when I continued to howl after the wolves had given me one or more vocal indications of their original position.

Another thing. Even after teasing apart my data in as many ways as I could, I was never able to make any connection between wolf howls and the phases of the moon. I found that especially comforting. Why should wolves pay more attention to the moon than to their families, their food, and their foes?

QUESTIONS

1. In what other publication formats might Harrington have presented his information? How would his report have differed? Why do you think he chose to present the results of his research in *Natural History* rather than in a more technical journal?

2. What effect does his opening paragraph have on this article? Out of a study that lasted for two years, why do you think he chose just this particular incident to begin his essay?

3. At the close of his essay, Harrington mentions that he "had some close encounter with the wolves" during his two-year study. He does not, however, really describe any of these encounters. Why? How do you think he chose the incidents he does include?

4. Is there any data you wish Harrington might have presented in a chart or table? Which information? Why do you suppose he did not do this?

•   •   •   •   •

LIVER

Richard Selzer

Richard Selzer is a surgeon, teacher, and accomplished writer. He has the rare ability to practice medicine and then describe this scientific craft with the eye and the language of a poet. Although he has published several books of nonfiction prose, his first two — Mortal Lessons (1976), from which this essay on the liver was taken and Confessions of a Knife (1979) — remain the most fascinating introduction to his work.

WHAT is the size of a pumpernickel, has the shape of Diana's helmet, and crouches like a thundercloud above its belly-mates, turgid with nourishment? What has the industry of an insect, the regenerative powers of a starfish, yet is turned to a mass of fatty globules by a double martini (two ounces of alcohol)? It is . . . the liver, doted upon by the French, assaulted by the Irish, disdained by the Americans, and chopped up with egg, onion, and chicken fat by the Jews.

Weighing in at three to four pounds, about one fiftieth of the total body heft, the liver is the largest of the glands. It is divided into two great lobes, the right and left, and two small lobes, the caudate and the quadrate, spitefully named to vex medical students. In the strangely beautiful dynamism of embryology, the liver appears as a tree that grows out of the virgin land of the foregut in order to increase its metabolic and digestive function. Its spreading crown of tissue continues to draw nourishment from the blood vessels of the intestine. Legion are the functions of this workhorse, the most obvious of which is the manufacture and secretion of a pint of bile a day, without which golden liquor we could not digest so much as a single raisin; and therefore, contrary to the legend that the liver is an organ given to man for him to be bilious with, in its absence we should become rather more cantankerous and grouchy than we are.

I think it altogether unjust that as yet the liver has failed to catch the imagination of modern poet and painter as has the heart and more recently the brain. The heart is purest theatre, one is quick to concede, throbbing in its cage palpably as any nightingale. It quickens in response to the emotions. Let danger threaten, and the thrilling heart skips a beat or two and tightrope-walks arrhythmically before lurching back into the forceful thump of fight or flight. And all the while we feel it, hear it even — we, its stage and its audience.

One will grant the heart a modicum of history. Ancient man slew his enemy, then fell upon the corpse to cut out his heart, which he ate with gusto, for it was well understood that to devour the slain enemy's heart was to take upon oneself the strength, valor and skill of the vanquished. It was not the livers or brains or entrails of saints that were lifted from the body in sublimest autopsy, it was the heart, thus snipped and cradled into worshipful palms, then soaked in wine and herbs and set into silver reliquaries for the veneration of the faithful. It follows quite naturally that Love should choose such an organ for its bower. In the absence of Love, the canker gnaws it; when Love blooms therein, the heart dances and *tremor cordis* is upon one.

As for the brain, it is all mystery and memory and electricity. It is enough to know of its high-topping presence, a gray cloud, substantial only in the bony box of the skull and otherwise melting into a blob of ghost-colored paste that can be wiped up with a sponge. The very idea of it, teeming with a billion unrealized thoughts, countless circuits breaking and unbreaking, flashing tiny fires of idea on and off, is too much. One bows before the brain, fearing, struck dumb. Or almost dumb, saying pretty things like, "The brain is wider than the sky," or silly things like, "The brain secretes thought as the stomach gastric juice, the kidneys urine." Or this: "Rest, with nothing else, corrodes the brain," which is a damnable lie.

It is time to turn aside from our misplaced meditation on the privileged brain, the aristocratic heart. Let the proletariat arise. I give you . . . the liver! Let us celebrate that great maroon snail, whose smooth back nestles in the dome of the diaphragm, beneath the lattice of the rib cage, like some blind wise slave, crouching above its colleague viscera, secret, resourceful, instinctive. No wave of emotion sweeps it. Neither music nor mathematics gives it pause in its appointed tasks. Consider first its historical role.

Medicine, as is well known, is an offshoot of religion. The predecessor of the physician as healer was the priest as exorciser. It is a quite manageable leap for me from demons to germs as the source of disease. It is equally easy to slide from incantation to prescription. Different incantations for different diseases, I gather, and no less mysterious to the ancient patients than the often mystic formulae of one's family doctor. The mystery was and is part of it. Along with the priest as exorciser was the priest as diviner, who was able to forestall illness by his access to the wishes of the gods, a theory that has since broadened into the field of preventive medicine. The most common method of divination was the inspection of the liver of a sacrificial animal, as is documented in cultures ranging from the Babylonian through the Etruscan to the Greek and Roman. Why the liver as the "organ of revelation par excellence"? Well, here it is:

In the beginning it was the liver that was regarded as the center of vitality, the source of all mental and emotional activity, nay, the seat of the soul itself. Quite naturally, the gods spoke therein. What a gloriously hepatic age! A man could know when and how best to attack his enemy, whether his amorous dallying would bring joy unencumbered with disease, whether the small would be great, the great laid low. All one had to do was to drag a sheep to the temple, flip a drachma to an acolyte, and stand by while the priests slit open the belly and read the markings of the liver, the position of the gallbladder, the arrangement of the ducts and lobes. It was all there, in red and yellow. This sort of thing went on for three thousand years and, one might ask, what other practice has enjoyed such longevity? Even so recent a personality as Julius Caesar learned of the bad vibes of the Ides of March from an old liver lover, although that fellow used a goat instead of a sheep, and a purist might well have been skeptical. Incidentally, the reason the horse was never used for divination is that it is difficult to lift onto altars, and also does not possess a gallbladder, a fact of anatomy that has embarrassed and impoverished veterinarians through the ages.

It was only with the separation of medicine from the apron strings of religion and the rise of anatomy as a study in itself that the liver was toppled from its center role and the heart was elevated to the chair of emotions and intellect. The brain is even more recently in the money, and still has not quite overcome the heart as the seat of the intellect, as witness the quaint reference to learning something "by heart." Soon the heart was added to the organs used for prophecy by the Greeks and Romans, who then threw in the lungs, and finally, with an overdeveloped sense of organic democracy, the intestines. Since the liver was no longer *the* divine organ in the animal, out it transited along with Ozymandias and other sic glorias, which decline so dispirited the hepato-scopists that soon they gave up the whole damned rite and went off to listen sulkily to Hippocrates rhapsodize, tastelessly I think, about the brain and heart. As if that were not bad enough, Plato placed the higher emotions, such as courage, squarely above the diaphragm, and situated the baser appetites below, especially in the liver, where they squat like furry beasts even today, as is indicated in the term "lily-livered," or "choleric," or worse, "bilious." The assassination was complete. Still, there are memories, and the sense of history is a power and glory to all but the most swinish of men.

Today all that is left of the practice of divination is the unofficial cult of phrenology, in which character is interpreted from the bumps of the skull, and the science of palmistry, which is a rather ticklish business to get into, and seems to me merely a vulgar attempt to transfer divination to a more accessible part of the body. Nevertheless, my palmist always places great emphasis on the length and curve of the hand marking known as the "line of the liver."

The closest thing to liver worship still in business is the reverent sorrow with which the French regard their beloved *foie*. It is at once recalcitrant child and stern paterfamilias. This national preoccupation is entirely misunderstood, and thus held in ill-deserve contempt by the rest of the world, which regards such hepatism as a form of mass hypochondria. In fact, it is wholly admirable after the shallow insouciance and hectic swilling of the Americans, for instance. The French understand the absolute fairness of life, that if you want to dance you have to pay the fiddler. Nothing in our country so binds the populace into a single suffering fraternity, any of whose members has but to raise his eyebrows and tap himself below the ribs to elicit a heartfelt moue of commiseration from a passing stranger. In the endless discussions of the relative merits of the various mineral waters, or whether the cure taken at Vichy or Montecatini effects a more enduring remission, class distinctions become as vague as mist. Princes of the Church, Communists of the barricade, légionnaires d'honneur, and chimney sweeps lock hearts and arms in the thrill of fellowship. Napoleon himself, wintering bitterly near Moscow in 1812, yearned not for Paris, or the Seine, or Versailles, or even for Josephine, but for Vichy and *the cure*. Obviously it is in the camaraderie of the liver and not in fragile treaties or grudging coexistence that the hope of the world lies — for ardently though one might wish to wash the brain of one's enemy, to bomb, bug or hijack him, never would one sink to the infliction of harm upon his liver.

That these same French viciously funnel great quantities of grain into the stomachs of their geese in order to fatten the livers for pâté de foie gras, I consider simply a regrettable transference of their own hepatic anxiety onto their poultry. It is as though by bringing on such barnyard *crises de foie* they are in some way exorcised of their own. Ah, the power of insight! To gain it is to forgive and to love.

Deplorable is the constipated English view, delivered with nasal sanctimony, that the Continental liver phobia is an old wives' tale. One has but to glance at any recent map of the British Empire to know the folly of this opinion. Equally regrettable is the *que sera, sera* attitude in the United States, where the last homage to the liver was paid by the faithful users of Carter's Little Liver Pills, until the federal government invaded even that small enclave of devotion by ordering the discontinuance of the word "Liver." Now, oh, God, it's just plain Carter's Little Pills and we are the poorer.

Man's romance with alcohol had its origins in the Neolithic Age or earlier, presumably from the accidental tasting by some curious fellow of, let's say, fermented honey, or mead as it is written in *Beowulf*. The attainment of the resultant euphoria has remained a continuous striving of the human race with the exception of the perverse era of Prohibition, which presumed to tear asunder that which Nature had joined in absolute harmony. Even in the Scriptures it is implied that Noah had a lot to drink, and Lot could not say Noah. From its first appearance on the planet, alcohol has never been absent from the scene. An early hieroglyphic of the Eighteenth Egyptian Dynasty has a woman calling out for eighteen bowls of wine. "Behold," she cries, "I love drunkenness."

The human body is perfectly suited for the ingestion of alcohol, and for its rapid utilization. In that sense we are not unlike alcohol lamps. Endless is our eagerness to devour alcohol. Witness the facts that it is absorbed not only from the intestine, as are all other foods, but directly from the stomach as well. It can be taken in by the lungs as an inhalant, and even by the rectum if given as an enema. Once incorporated into the body, it is to the liver that belongs the task of oxidizing the alcohol. But even the sturdiest liver can handle only a drop or two at a time, and the remainder swirls ceaselesly about the bloodstream, is exhaled by the lungs and thus provides the state police with a crackerjack method of detecting and measuring the presence and amount of alcohol ingested. Along the way it bathes the brain with happiness, lifting the inhibitory cortex off the primal swamp of the id and permitting to surface all sorts of delicious urges such as the one to walk into people's houses wearing your wife's hat. Happily enough, the brain is not organically altered by alcohol unless taken in near-lethal amounts. The brain cells are not destroyed by it in any kind of moderate drinking, and if the alcohol is withdrawn from the diet, the brain rapidly awakens and resumes its function at the usual, if not normal, level. One must reckon, nevertheless, with the hangover, which retributive phenomenon is devised to make the drinker feel guilty. In fact, it is not more than a nightmarish echo of the state of inebriation brought on by excessive fatigue and the toxic effects of congeners, the natural products of the fermentation process that give distinction to the taste of the various forms of alcohol. In *The Adventures of Huckleberry Finn*, we find Huck awakening to "an awful scream. . . . There was pap looking wild, and skipping around every which way, and yelling about snakes. He said they was crawling up his legs; and then he would give a jump and scream, and say one had bit him on the cheek — but I couldn't see no snakes. He started and run round and round the cabin, hollering. 'Take him off. Take him off; he's biting me on the neck!' I never see a man look so wild in the eyes. Pretty soon he was all fagged out, and fell down panting; then he rolled over and over wonderful fast, kicking things every which way, and striking and grabbing at the air with his hands, and screaming, and saying there was devils ahold of him. He wore out by and by, and laid still awhile, moaning. Then he laid stiller, and didn't make a sound."

It was a French physician, quite naturally, who first described the disease known as cirrhosis of the liver, near the turn of the nineteenth century. His name, René Théophile Hyacinthe Laënnec. This fastidious gentleman was the very same whose aversion to applying his naked ear to the perfumed but unbathed bosoms of his patients inspired him to invent the stethoscope, which idea he plagiarized from a group of street urchins playing with rolled-up paper. The entire medical world continues to pay homage to Laënnec for his gift of space interpersonal. As if this were not enough, he permitted himself to be struck by the frequent appearance at autopsy of livers that were yellow, knobby and hard. This marvel he named cirrhosis, from the Greek word for tawny, *kirrhos*. The liver appears yellow because it is fatty, hard because it is scarred, and knobby because the regeneration of liver tissue between the scars produces little mounds or hillocks. It was suspected by Laënnec, and is known by all the rest of us today, that by far the most common cause of cirrhosis is the consumption of alcohol.

It is a matter for future anthropologists to ponder that the two favorite companions of business are Bottle and Board. More than one eminent literary agent, Wall Street broker, and vice-president have died testifying affection for them. Deep drinking and intrigue are part of all the noble professions. These, combined with the studious avoidance of exercise, have conspired to produce a whole race of voluptuaries who, by twos and threes from noon till three, sit at tables in dim restaurants, picking at their sideburns and destroying the furniture with their gigantic buttocks. These same men can be seen after five years of such indiscretion transformed into "lean and slippered pantaloons," with scanty hair that is but the gray garniture of premature senescence.

In the city of New York such is the torrent of spirituous flow as to make the clinking of ice cubes and the popping of corks a major source of noise pollution. It is as though it had been purported by the Surgeon General himself that the best means of maintaining human life from infancy to extreme old age were by the copious use of the Blood of the Grape. It might with equal credibility be put forth that tobacco smoke purifies the air from infectious malignancy by its fragrance, sweetens the breath, strengthens the brain and memory, and restores admiration to the sight.

Counting every man, woman and child in the United States, it is estimated that the average daily intake of calories is thirty-three hundred a person. In this all-inclusive group, one hundred sixty-five calories are ingested as alcohol. Pushing on, if one were to divide these Americans into I Do Drinks and I Don't Drinks, the I Do's take in five hundred calories from this same source. This alcohol is metabolized in the liver by a fiercely efficient enzyme called alcohol dehydrogenase, and transformed directly into energy, which would all be terribly nice were it not for the unjust fact that alcohol is poisonous to the liver, causing it to become loaded with fat. If enough is imbibed, and enough fat is deposited in the liver, this organ takes on the yellowish color noted by Laënnec. Still more booze, and the liver becomes heavy with fat, swelling so that it emerges from beneath the protective rib cage and bulges down into the vulnerable soft white underbelly. There it can be palpated by the examining fingers, and even seen protruding on the right side of the abdomen in some cases.

Even today, the progression from this fatty stage to the frank inflammation and scarring that are the hallmarks of cirrhosis is not well understood. Factors other than continued drinking pertain here. One of these is susceptibility. Jews, for instance, are not susceptible. One sees precious few cirrhotic Jews. It was formerly averred by somewhat chauvinistic Jewish hepatologists that Jews didn't get cirrhosis because they didn't drink much, what with their strong, dependable family ties, and their high motivation, and their absolute need to excel in order to survive. They didn't need to drink. But Jews are now among the most emancipated of drinkers and, with all the fervor of new converts, are causing such virtuosi as the Irish and the French to glance nervously over their shoulders. Still, the Jews do not get cirrhosis. This is not to say that they are not alcoholics. It has been reported by more than one visiting professor of medicine that noticeable segments of the population of Israel get and stay drunk for quite heroic periods of time. It is also reported that their livers remain enviably healthy.

Another measure of susceptibility is, brace yourself, the absence of hair on the chest. In males, of course. Unpelted men of the sort idealized by bathing-suit and underwear manufacturers are sitting ducks for the onset of cirrhosis. All other things being equal, women, the marrying kind, would do well to turn aside from such vast expanses of naked chest skin and to cultivate a taste for the simian. It was formerly thought that cirrhotic men lost their chest hair. Not so. They never had any to begin with.

Lastly, it is said by some that climate is a factor: the closer to the equator, the more vulnerable the liver. Thus, a quantity of alcohol that scarcely ruffles the frozen current of a Norwegian's blood would scatter madness and fever into the brain of a Hindu.

There is a difference, I hasten to add, between imbibers of alcohol and alcoholics. Both develop fatty livers, true, but no one has shown conclusively that a fatty liver is the precursor of cirrhosis. One martini increases the fat content of the liver sufficiently so that it can be seen by the use of special stains under the microscope. In other words, a single martini increases the fat in a liver by one half percent of the weight of the organ, above a normal three percent. In the alcoholic this commonly reaches a death-defying twenty-five percent. But you don't have to be an alcoholic to get cirrhosis. Some quite modest drinkers get it. Nor does it matter the purity of the spirits consumed. Beer, wine, and whiskey equally offend, and he who would take comfort from the idea that he drinks only beer, or only wine, is to be treated with pity and contempt. One correlation that does hold water is the duration of time that one has been drinking. Cirrhosis is primarily a disease of the forties or fifties. Even here we cannot generalize, however, for great numbers of younger people are afflicted, and one patient within my ken was an eighteen-year-old girl whose voluminous liver could be felt abutting on her groin just eight months after she had retired to her room with a continuous supply of Thunderbird wine.

The state of nutrition is also a factor in the development of cirrhosis. It is no secret that boozers, the serious kind, stop eating, especially proteins, either because they can't afford it — what with the cost of a bottle of bourbon these days — or because the sick liver just can't handle the metabolism of protein well, and the appetite is warned off.

The nitrogenous material of protein passes directly through the diseased liver and exerts a toxic effect on the brain. If one restricts protein in the diet of cirrhotics, the brain improves. A case in point is Sir Andrew Aguecheek of *Twelfth Night*, whose fervent wish to cut a dash was aborted by stupidity, cowardice, and social gaucherie. His eccentricity, emotional lability and restricted vocabulary were almost certainly due to the organic brain syndrome of liver disease due to intolerance of nitrogen. Sir Toby Belch assesses Sir Andrew rather highly. Still, Sir Toby cannot resist the clinical judgment that "For Andrew, if he were opened, and you find so much blood in his liver as will clog the foot of a flea, I'll eat the rest of the anatomy." Such as Sir Andrew Aguecheek are thrown into mental confusion, confabulation and even coma by no more than a single ounce of beef. Thus their medical nickname, "one meatballers."

In an analysis of the inhabitants of Chicago's Skid Row, it was observed that a customary diet consisted of alcohol in any form and jelly doughnuts. Yet in the cases of thirty-nine hundred such folk whose death certificates were signed out as cirrhosis, only ten percent were actually found to have the disease at autopsy. Thus it might be stated that alcoholics exceed cirrhotics by nine to one — or that only ten percent of alcoholics get cirrhosis.

What is clearly needed is a test to find out which are the ten percent that are going to get it, so that the rest of us can enjoy ourselves. At the moment I prefer to take comfort from the example of such valiant topers as Winston Churchill, who swallowed a fifth of whiskey a day all the while leading Great Britain in her finest hour, and went on to die in his nineties, still holding his fingers up like that. It is also true that if one, moved by some transcendental vision or goaded by ill-conceived guilt, abstains from further drinking, in short order all the excess fat departs from the liver and it once again regains its pristine color and size. In this way do spree drinkers inadvertently rest their livers and avoid the cirrhosis we slow but steadies risk. Thus something can be said for periodic abstinence, a wisdom one would hesitate to translate into other vices.

Before enumerating the signs and symptoms of cirrhosis, and thus running the risk of offending sensibility, it should be unequivocally affirmed that he is no gentleman, in fact a very milksop, of no bringing up, that will not drink. He is fit for no company, for it is a credit to have a strong brain and carry one's liquor well. Saith Pliny, "'Tis the greatest good of our tradesmen, their felicity, life and soul, their chiefest comfort, to be merry together in a tavern."

Envision, if you will, a house whose stones are living hexagonal tiles not unlike those forming the bathroom floors of first-class hotels. These are the hepatocytes, the cellular units of the liver. Under the microscope they have a singular uniformity, each as like unto its fellow as the antlers of a buck, and all fitted together with a lovely imprecision so as to form a maze of crooked hallways and oblong rooms. Coursing through this muralium of tissue are two arborizations of blood vessels, the one bringing food and toxins from the intestine, the other delivering oxygen from the heart and lungs. Winding in and among these networks is a system of canaliculi that puts to shame all the aqueductal glories of Greece and Rome. Through these sluice the rivers of bile, gathering strength and volume as the little ducts at the periphery meet others, going into ones of larger caliber, which in turn fuse, and so on until there are two large tubes emerging from the undersurface of the liver. Within this magic house are all the functions of the liver carried out. The food we eat is picked over, sorted out, and stored for future use in the cubicles of the granary. Starch is converted to glycogen, which is released in the form of energy as the need arises. Protein is broken down into its building blocks, the amino acids, later to be fashioned into more YOU, as old tissues die off and need to be replaced. Fats are stored until sent forth to provide warmth and comfort. Vitamins and antibodies are released into the bloodstream. Busy is the word for the liver. Deleterious substances ingested, inadvertently like DDT or intentionally like alcohol, are either changed into harmless components and excreted into the intestine, or stored in locked closets to be kept isolated from the rest of the body. Even old blood cells are pulverized and recycled. Such is the ole catfish liver snufflin' along at the bottom of the tank, sweepin', cleanin' up after the gouramis, his whiskey old face stirrin' up a cloud of rejectimenta, and takin' care of everything.

But there are limits. Along comes that thousandth literary lunch and — Pow! the dreaded wrecking ball of cirrhosis is unslung. The roofs and walls of the hallways, complaining under their burden of excess fat, groan and buckle. Inflammation sets in, and whole roomfuls of liver cells implode and die, and in their place comes the scarring that twists and distorts the channels, pulling them into impossible angulation. Avalanches block the flow of bile and heavy tangles of fiber impede the absorption and secretion. This happens not just in one spot but all over, until the gigantic architecture is a mass of sores and wounds, the old ones scarring over as new ones break down.

The obstructed bile, no longer able to flow down to the gut, backs up into the bloodstream to light up the skin and eyes with the sickly lamp of jaundice. The stool turns toothpaste white in commiseration, the urine dark as wine. The belly swells with gallons of fluid that weep from the surface of the liver, no less than the tears of a loyal servant so capriciously victimized. The carnage spreads. The entire body is discommoded. The blood fails to clot, the palms of the hands turn mysteriously red, and spidery blood vessels leap and crawl on the skin of the face and neck. Male breasts enlarge, and even the proud testicles turn soft and atrophy. In a short while impotence develops, an irreversible form of impotence which may well prod the invalid into more and more drinking.

Scared? Better have a drink. You look a little pale. In any case there is no need to be all that glum. Especially if you know something that I know. Remember Prometheus? That poor devil who was chained to a rock, and had his liver pecked out each day by a vulture? Well, he was a classical example of the regeneration of tissue, for every night his liver grew back to be ready for the dreaded diurnal feast. And so will yours grow back, regenerate, reappear, regain all of its old efficiency and know-how. All it requires is quitting the booze, now and then. The ever-grateful, forgiving liver will respond joyously with a multitude of mitoses and cell divisions that will replace the sick tissues with spanking new nodules and lobules of functioning cells. This rejuvenation is carried on with the speed and alacrity of a starfish growing a new ray from the stump of the old. New channels are opened up, old ones dredged out, walls are straightened and roofs shored up. Soon the big house is humming with activity, and all those terrible things I told you happen go away — all except that impotence thing. Well, you didn't expect to get away scot-free, did you?

And here's something to tuck away and think about whenever you want to feel good. Sixty percent of all cirrhotics who stop drinking will be alive and well five years later. How unlike the lofty brain which has no power of regeneration at all. Once a brain cell dies, you are forever one shy.

Good old liver!

QUESTIONS

1. How would you describe Selzer's prose? What have you read that is most like it?
2. Are Selzer's descriptions effective? What do you like or dislike about them?
3. Look up an encyclopedia entry on the liver. How does it differ from Selzer's discussion? Which do you prefer? Why?
4. Selzer relies highly on metaphor to make his point. Notice, for example, the passage that begins "Envision, if you will, a house. . ." (p. 285). Do you find this effective? Why or why not?
5. Selzer is a physician and is used to discussing the body with a physician's vocabulary. Are there any parts of his discussion that need clarification for you?
6. Imitating a craftsman like Selzer is not easy, but give it a try. Select a simple topic (an inanimate object would work best—a vegetable, an article of clothing, a household utensil) and try to describe it using the swooping metaphors Selzer employs.

•   •   •   •   •

TRAVELING WITH TASTE: NASHVILLE

Jefferson Morgan

Bon Appetit *is a magazine for gourmet cooks and those who enjoy food. In this recent column, staff writer Jefferson Morgan takes his readers on a culinary tour of Nashville, Tennessee.*

THE last time I had seen Nashville was just after World War II, from the observation platform of the smoking car on the Dixie Flyer, as she steamed out of Union Station toward the north.

Lest you think I'm more of an antique than I really am, I should point out that I was sitting on my father's knee so I could get a better view.

My family had spent some months in Tennessee. Before that, we lived in Minnesota, and in those days, before true network radio, one of the only "foreign" stations that reached us in Minneapolis was Nashville's WSM, home of Minnie Pearl and Red Foley and a number of other folks who played strange instruments and sang in funny accents. I don't remember much about the food in Nashville then, but I do recall vividly sitting in the old gospel hall built by "Captain Tom" Ryman and watching the people in cowboy hats who had heretofore been only disembodied voices.

Back then, Conway Twitty (a.k.a. Harold Lloyd Jenkins) was 11 years old, and Sarah Ophelia Colley Cannon was a young woman earning pin money by singing a few songs and telling a few jokes about her childhood home of Grinder's Switch.

Today, as you drive into the city from its airport, you see the rising skyline almost blotted out at one point by a hugh billboard proclaiming "Twitty City"; and Henry Cannon's wife (a.k.a. Minnie Pearl) has become something of an international institution celebrated by her own museum.

Union Station is still there, by the way, looming silently over the rusting rails under the Broadway overpass. One of the best examples extant of turn-of-the-century Romanesque excess, it eventually will be preserved as a hotel and new restaurants.

Nashville is a classic example of a city with a split personality.

It is a place in, but not necessarily *of*, the South. Although Tennessee was a member of the "Confredracy," the state capital was a Union base throughout most of the "War of Northern Aggression," as that conflict is still known around here.

To millions of country and western fans around the globe, Nashville is "Music City," home not only of the Grand Ole Opry but also of a rich collection of ribald honky-tonks that were the whelping ground for countless stars, from Eddy Arnold and Hank Williams to Pat Boone (who successfully wooed his Nashville high school sweetheart, Red Foley's daughter, Shirley), Tammy Wynette and Marty Robbins. But in the hushed foyers of the homes surrounding the antebellum mansion Belle Meade, citizens still cling to the city's other sobriquet, "the Athens of the South," an image made tangible during Nashville's first hundredth birthday, in 1897 when a faithful replica of the Parthenon was built in Centennial Park. (Actually, the edifice there now was reconstructed in concrete in 1931, to replace the original wood and plaster building, which had deteriorated.)

With a population of only about half a million, Nashville is the home of 16 colleges and universities, including Vanderbilt and Fisk. Despite their attraction, probably more of the seven million visitors a year are drawn by the music saloons, such as Boots Randolph's in Printer's Alley and the legendary Tootsies Orchid Lounge, where you can sip a beer on the same front stool that Roger Miller occupied when he placed two royalty checks for $250,000 each on the bar and ordered drinks for the house — after "King of the Road" won him his first gold record.

Nashville is a city of museums and graceful public buildings set cheek by jowl with places such as the renovated Second Avenue district of once-decaying warehouses along the Cumberland River. Downtown there is the preserved Ryman Auditorium, where the Opry performed for 31 years from 1943 until it decamped in 1974, to the Opryland theme park, 11 miles upriver; and the Country Music Hall of Fame and Museum, housing mementos of such worthies as Willie Nelson and Johnny Cash. On the other hand, there is the Tennessee Performing Arts Center, where the Nashville Symphony performs in the two-thousand-plus-seat Andrew Jackson Hall and where an audience of over one thousand can enjoy stage productions in the James K. Polk Theater. It is a fairly easy drive from the State Fairgrounds, venue of one of the larger and most eccentric flea markets in America, to the Tennessee Botanical Gardens and Fine Arts Center (Cheekwood), a gallery that attracts major traveling art exhibitions. Or, perhaps after visiting the beautifully restored Hermitage, President Jackson's mansion, you will want to finish the day listening to some of the world's best bluegrass in the dingy atmosphere of the Station Inn.

In no respect do the contrasts of Nashville reveal themselves more than in the areas of food, dining and accommodation. Now there are classical and nouvelle French restaurants, such as Julian's, and hostelries, like the excuisite 77-year-old Hermitage, one of the finest examples of the trend toward small, restored downtown hotels. Then there is the artfully named Loveless Motel just out of town, where the cafe specializes in country ham, fried chicken, grits, collards and biscuits. And perish forfend you should miss the fried catfish at Bud's or fail to make the pilgrimage to Mayo's on Charlotte Road to buy what may arguably be the best hickory-smoked country sausage in the Republic. Formal dining of a decidedly European persuasion is offered at Hugo's in the huge Hyatt Regency, as well as at posh restaurants such as Mario's. For a downhome breakfast or lunch, try Hap Towns's diner near Greer Stadium. Even within the great hotel complex at Opryland there are half a dozen restaurants, with offerings ranging from haute cuisine to barbecued ribs.

And all of this culinary diversity exists in a city where, up until relatively recently, the foremost epicurean shrine was the factory that turns out Goo Goo Clusters, a confection of chocolate, marshmallows, caramel and peanuts that has been rotting the teeth of the Deep South since 1912. After moving away, former senator Howard Baker and Dinah Shore, among other expatriates, had their supplies shipped direct from the Nashville plant.

A lot of people, when they travel to a new or changed city, go to the chamber of commerce or some such place for information. I like to do that last.

Instead, I buy all the local newspapers I can get my hands on and read them cover to cover to learn what the denizens are doing — what they're proud of, afraid of, concerned about, and how they amuse themselves in their spare time. Then I settle down in my hotel room with the Yellow Pages. You would be amazed at what you can glean from that volume. The restaurant section, naturally, is revealing, but so are the other classifications. The South Central Bell book for Greater Nashville, for example, has ten pages devoted to 16 headings under "Music" alone, from "Music Arrangers and Composers" to "Musicians." This will bring me back to Mr. Twitty and Mrs. Cannon later.

When I awoke on the first morning of my triumphal return to Nashville, I was feeling a bit peckish. I hadn't eaten since the night before, when an otherwise blameless cabin attendant on my delayed flight from Atlanta had offered me the now universal airline choice of boiled white paste, or boiled gray gristle masked with axle grease. And I had arrived too late to get any real food. So now I set off straightaway for the Loveless Motel & Cafe on Highway 100, 20 miles west of town.

Pounding down the interstate toward Memphis, through the rolling hills of the Cumberland Valley, listening to Tanya Tucker and Waylon Jennings on the car radio, I debated breakfast choices: hotcakes and fresh smoked sausage; maybe waffles and hickory-smoked bacon. By the time I crossed the Harpeth River, I was pretty near faint with hunger.

The old Loveless — "CAFE — MOTEL — AIR-CONDITIONED" — had the "No" lighted on front of its Vacancy sign. The motel can best be described as Early Auto Court, with a small playground that doubles as a Christmas tree lot every December. But the parking lot was full of vehicles, ranging from pickup trucks to Beemers and Volvos and that crowd.

The cafe itself is an old frame house with an artificial stone facade. The waiting room — and it needs one — is the front porch, screened in summer and storm-windowed in winter.

When I was admitted to the plain, tidy dining room, which is enlivened by the watercolors of local artist Bill Kidwell, I placed my order. I also had the friendly waitress bring me a bowl of grits and butter to go with my tomato juice, just to take the edge off.

Then she came back with a platter covered with scrambled eggs and a slab of fried smoked country ham accompanied by a bowl of redeye gravy. Moments later she returned with a dozen biscuits still hot from the oven, a bowl containing about half a pound more of high-score butter, and homemade blackberry and peach preserves. The sorghum molasses and clover honey were already on the table. And when I asked for a glass of milk, she brought me a pint.

Country ham, smoked or cured, is an acquired taste, one that I fortunately acquired before I earned my first pair of long pants and low-sided shoes. The good burghers of Tennessee, Kentucky and Virginia squabble endlessly about who does it better. It is never, shall we say, fork tender. Its detractors tend to describe it as over-salted shoe leather. I find that these people are either toothless, or sissies raised on those so-called hams that come out of the can jiggling in a mass of some obscene gelatinous substance.

On a scale of 1 to 10, my breakfast at the Loveless came in at about a 14. When I left, after tipping lavishly, I still had change from a $10 bill, not counting what I paid for the half-dozen Goo Goo Clusters I bought for my briefcase, just in case I got trapped on an airplane at mealtime on my way home.

The Loveless also serves excellent lunches and dinners, with a menu including things like fried chicken gizzards served with a bowl of gravy, biscuits, salad and fries. Afraid that I might get arrested for loitering if I hung around until lunchtime, I set off back to the city, this time surrounded by the stereophonic attentions of Johnny Cash and Eddy Arnold.

I had already decided that I had to make at least one sentimental pilgrimage, and when I learned from those good old Yellow Pages that the Elliston Place Soda Shop was not only still in business but was, in fact, only five minutes from where I was staying, the matter was settled.

The soda shop is older than I am, and was one of the last places I recall visiting before that train left so long ago. Located near the Vanderbilt campus, it has been run by the same family since 1939. Because I was still digesting breakfast, I postponed lunch until just before 1:00 P.M. That was my first mistake. Well over a hundred people jammed the booths along the wall, the line of Formica-topped tables down the middle of the room and the stools at the long counter. This does not include the platoon or so who waited patiently for seating or take-out orders. I swear, the only thing that had changed was the pay phone, from which you could no longer make a call for a nickel.

Being by myself, I eventually got the last stool next to the cash register, which was nice, because it provided a good view of the take-out operation. I have no statistical proof of this, but I am convinced the soda shop served as many full-course meals of roast turkey with corn bread dressing, homemade cranberry sauce, whipped potatoes, fresh broccoli and yams that day to the pedestrian trade as it did to those inside. It was a Thursday, and that's always one of the specials on Thursdays.

For old time's sake, I replicated my last meal there, a cheeseburger with fries and a chocolate milk shake. That was my second mistake. In most parts of the South, the traditional fare has long been so good that most cooks haven't wasted a lot of time perfecting carpetbagger intrusions such as burgers and burritos. The shake was great, the fries were superb, the cheeseburger was okay, and I ate it glaring enviously at the couple on adjacent stools who were devouring fried chicken with gravy and a meat loaf that any French chef would happily have served as a hot, coarse pâté of the countryside to a checker from the *Guide Michelin*.

I consoled myself with a hot fudge sundae with all the trimmings.

When I paid my bill, the good old boy behind the cash register asked me how everything had been.

"Fine," I said. "I haven't been in here for 40 years."

"Yeah," he replied. "I noticed. Don't make it so long next time."

As an aside, the Elliston Place Soda Shop is next door to one of the best T-shirt stores in the country, aptly named Bad Influence. The ones that you would be afraid to wear in public are vended from lockers.

Tootsies Orchid Lounge is nestled among a welter of pawnshops and porn studios on the east end of Broadway, between Fourth and Fifth Avenues and just around the corner from Ryman Auditorium. When they tried to close it in 1985, the legions of *Time* and *Newsweek*, among others, descended on the community, and such was the public outcry that it was reopened.

The bartender at Tootsies had the eyes of a man who had seen more iniquity than the Tokyo vice squad.

"What'll it be, sport?"

"What kind of beer do you have?" I asked.

"All kinds. Name it."

"Beck's."

"That's not beer, that's *foreign*." He regarded me with the same look another publican someplace in rural Colorado gave a friend of mine once when he bellied up to the bar and asked for a glass of good white wine.

"Son," the Rocky Mountain boniface said to my friend, "I think you may be in the wrong kinda place."

I quickly ordered a longneck, and some peanuts so I shouldn't go hungry until dinnertime. The barkeep did not offer me a glass. I didn't ask for one.

Tootsies is the sort of place in which you squander your milk money without telling your mother. The walls have yellowing images of the great and forgotten of country and western. There is hardly a surface — including the well-worn bar, floor and ceiling — that has not been covered with graffiti. This afternoon's entertainment was a young picker and grinner who played for tips and who made Willie Nelson look like a Mormon missionary. Tootsies is the sort of place where a poor but honest journalist does not whip out his notebook and start jotting things down, for fear someone will mistake him for a minion of law enforcement and take umbrage. In short, it is an ideal bar, the best sort of place in which to idle away an hour in the afternoon, listening to some fine music while the other patrons are drinkin' mash and talkin' trash.

It is only a short walk up the hill from Tootsies Orchid Lounge to The Hermitage, but the two are worlds apart. The Hermitage is one of those small, city hotels that meets the criteria set down for Mr. Ritz by His Royal Majesty Edward VII: "French food, English service, American plumbing."

Constructed in 1910, the ten-story building is the only commercial beaux arts structure in Tennessee. A decade ago it was completely refurbished, and the number of rooms was reduced from 250 to 112 suites. The entrance is of Siena marble, and the walls, steps and floors combine Tennessee and Greek marble. The huge skylight and glass panels soaring above the lobby were crafted by Hotojy. The main dining room, where bandleader Frances Craig introduced singers such as Dinah Shore and Snooky Lanson and Tennessee's first hit song, "Near You," is paneled with Circassian walnut and has a hand-carved ceiling. It is also — and deservedly — regarded as one of Nashville's world-class restaurants.

One way I measure any eatery is how it takes care of singles. I can't recall how many times on the road I've called to reserve a solitary table at a restaurant (one that has a lot of stars and diamonds and stuff on its Yellow Pages ad) and have been told, "We can take you at 6:00 P.M. or 10:00 P.M." And have you noticed that in many restaurants, single tables all have excellent views of the kitchen or the little foyer outside the restrooms where they keep the cigarette machine?

When I booked into The Hermitage Dining Room, I didn't mention that I was staying in the hotel. As soon as I arrived, prepared for a long wait in the bar, I was shown directly to a leather-upholstered banquette more suitable for four, directly across the small dance floor from the pianist. I learned that the staff was trying mightily to get everybody served, fed and into their overcoats in time for an opening that night at the nearby performing arts center, but still I was treated as if I were the only guest in the room. The menu was extensive and innovative, and the long wine list was split fairly evenly between Europe and the United States, something that is relatively rare in the South even now.

For openers I essayed the duck liver pâté, followed by what The Hermitage laughingly calls a small dinner salad — an enormous plate of crisped greens cooled with the piquant house dressing. I then consumed a sizable portion of fresh Coho salmon stuffed with Maryland shrimp and sautéed with a light wine sauce. Belching prettily, I summoned the pastry trolley and, after laying waste to that, toddled off to my room to watch the San Francisco 49ers humiliate the Los Angeles Rams. In all, it had been a good day.

The next morning I got up with a craving for catfish. Since a full breakfast is included in the price of a suite at The Hermitage (like most hotels in the South, the rates are extremely reasonable by East or West Coast standards), I stopped off for a light repast of freshly squeezed orange juice, honeydew melon and cantaloupe and just-baked Danish pastry, washed down with chicory-laced coffee, before setting off for the suburb of Franklin some miles to the south.

Uncle Bud's Restaurant and Sharecropper Lounge has metamorphosed from the original place on Hillsboro Pike into a cavernous barn set back behind a bowling alley in what has grown into a shopping center alongside a freeway. A whole lot of red and white oilcloth covered enough tables to seat the Sixth Army, and the plywood ceiling is decorated with thousands of those kinds of imprinted baseball hats favored by long-line truckers, advertising things like John Deere, Husky Lumber and Co-op Layer Pellets and Hi-Mag Cattle Mineral. The waitresses wear red long johns under bib overalls. The place was about half full at a weekday lunchtime. Although they serve all kinds of things, I didn't see a single patron order anything but catfish.

The catfish came honest-to-God boned, and delicately fried in cornmeal. It was accompanied by hush puppies and crisp french fries. The only things on the table not fried were the napkins, the sweet and sour slaw and the tartar sauce. The tartar sauce is mixed in washtubs and served on the tables in those plastic squeeze bottles normally employed for catsup and ball-park mustard, but with the tubes cut off so the chunks of pickle and onion don't stop them up.

It is not the purpose of this little memoir simply to regale you with tales of my gluttony, nor to imply that the only reason to go to Nashville is to eat and drink. I can do that at home.

Nashville became Music City and the undisputed center of a multi-billion-dollar entertainment industry almost by accident. In the 1920s, a British folklorist named Cecil Sharp wandered into the hills of northwestern Tennessee seeking the Elizabethan folk ballads that were practically unchanged after centuries. When he published these folk songs, the old Victor recording company placed a few ads for hillbilly musicians to record them. The rustics were enchanted that anyone would pay them to do what they had been doing for fun anyway. From that search came names like Jimmie Rodgers and the Carter family. Today, virtually every recording label (and, not incidentally, outfits like ASCAP and BMI) has major facilities in Nashville, which yearly produces half a billion dollars' worth of records alone.

The focus of it all remains the Grand Ole Opry, which, being broadcast continually since 1925, is the oldest running radio show in the world. The 4,400-seat Grand Ole Opry House in the 120-acre Opryland theme park is also the largest broadcasting studio in the world. In contrast to The Hermitage, the huge Opryland Hotel has over one thousand rooms, the center of which is the Conservatory, an indoor tropical garden of ten thousand plants covering nearly three acres, under a skylight that contains, they say, more than an acre of glass.

There are dozens of other music-related attractions in the area, including Twitty City, a tourist complex surrounding a museum devoted to the musician's career. Opening a museum seems to be a growing industry here: Barbara Mandrell, Hank Williams, Johnny Cash and Marty Robbins are a few — and, of course, Minnie Pearl.

And if you make an appointment, the Standard Candy Company will have someone show you the factory where they make Goo Goo Clusters.

QUESTIONS

1. Morgan is ostensibly writing about food. In the course of his discussion, however, other topics work their way into his tour. Do these details seem to fit, or do they seem out of place? Why or why not?

2. How does Morgan organize his tour? Does his organization seem logical to you? What other formats might he have chosen instead? Would any of these have been better?

3. Does this article appeal only to gourmet cooks? Who else might find it interesting? Is there any audience Morgan specifically *excludes*?

4. Morgan occasionally imitates a country dialect — "drinkin' mash and talkin' trash." Does this add anything to the article? What? Does it detract? In what other way might he have achieved the same effect?

5. Visit a local restaurant and draft an informative analysis of the establishment and your meal.

•   •   •   •   •

AMERICA BETRAYS HERSELF IN VIETNAM: IN EMBRYO, 1945–46

Barbara Tuchman

Barbara Tuchman was a masterful historian who won the Pulitzer prize twice for her books The Guns of August *(1962) and* Stillwell and the American Experience in China, 1911–45 *(1971). This essay on America's involvement in Vietnam was taken from her 1984 study* The March of Folly: From Troy to Vietnam.

IGNORANCE was not a factor in the American endeavor in Vietnam pursued through five successive presidencies, although it was to become an excuse. Ignorance of country and culture there may have been, but not ignorance of the contra-indications, even the barriers, to achieving the objectives of American policy. All the conditions and reasons precluding a successful outcome were recognized or foreseen at one time or another during the thirty years of our involvement. American intervention was not a progress sucked step by step into an unsuspected quagmire. At no time were policy-makers unaware of the hazards, obstacles, and negative developments. American intelligence was adequate, informed observation flowed steadily from the field to the capital, special investigative missions were repeatedly sent out, independent reportage to balance professional optimism — when that prevailed — was never lacking. The folly consisted not in pursuit of a goal in ignorance of the obstacles but in persistence in the pursuit despite accumulating evidence that the goal was unattainable, and the effect disproportionate to the American interest and eventually damaging to American society, reputation and disposable power in the world.

The question raised is why did the policy-makers close their minds to the evidence and its implications? This is the classic symptom of folly: refusal to draw conclusions from the evidence, addiction to the counter-productive. The "why" of this refusal and this addiction may disclose itself in the course of retracing the tale of American policy-making in Vietnam.

The beginning lay in the reversal during the last months of World War II of President Roosevelt's previous determination not to allow, and certainly, not to assist, the restoration of French colonial rule in Indochina. The engine of reversal was the belief, in response to strident French demand and damaged French pride resulting from the German occupation, that it was essential to strengthen France as the linchpin in Western Europe against Soviet expansion, which, as victory approached, had become the dominant concern in Washington. Until this time Roosevelt's disgust with colonialism and his intention to see it eliminated in Asia had been firm (and a cause of basic dispute with Britain). He believed French misrule of Indochina represented colonialism in its worst form. Indochina "should not go back to France," he told Secretary of State Cordell Hull in January 1943; "the case is perfectly clear. France has had the country — thirty million inhabitants — for nearly a hundred years and the people are worse off than they were at the beginning. [They] are entitled to something better than that."

The President "has been more outspoken to me on that subject," Churchill informed Anthony Eden, "than on any other colonial matter, and I imagine that it is one of his principal war aims to liberate Indochina from France." Indeed it was. At the Cairo Conference in 1943, the President's plans for Indochina made emphatic capital letters in General Stilwell's diary: "NOT TO GO BACK TO FRANCE!" Roosevelt proposed trusteeship "for 25 years or so till we put them on their feet, just like the Philippines." The idea thoroughly alarmed the British and evoked no interest from a former ruler of Vietnam, China. "I asked Chiang Kai-shek if he wanted Indochina," Roosevelt told General Stilwell, "and he said point blank 'Under no circumstances!' Just like that — 'Under no circumstances!'"

The possibility of self-rule seems not to have occurred to Roosevelt, although Vietnam — the nation uniting Cochin China, Annam and Tonkin — had before the advent of the French been an independent kingdom with a long devotion to self-government in its many struggles against Chinese rule. This deficiency in Roosevelt's view of the problem was typical of the prevailing attitude toward subject peoples at the time. Regardless of their history, they were not considered "ready" for self-rule until prepared for it under Western tutelage.

The British were adamantly opposed to trusteeship as a "bad precedent" for their own return to India, Burma and Malaya, and Roosevelt did not insist. He was not eager to add another controversy to the problem of India, which made Churchill rave every time the President raised it. Thereafter, with liberated France emerging in 1944 under an implacable Charles de Gaulle and insisting on her "right" of return, and with China as a trustee ruled out by her own now too obvious frailties, the President did not know what to do.

International trusteeship slowly collapsed from unpopularity. Roosevelt's military advisers disliked it because they felt it might jeopardize United States freedom of control over former Japanese islands as naval bases. Europeanists of the State Department, always pro-French, thoroughly adopted the premise of French Foreign Minister Georges Bidault that unless there was "whole-hearted cooperation with France," a Soviet-dominated Europe would threaten "Western civilization." Cooperation, as viewed by the Europeanists, meant meeting French demands. On the other hand, their colleagues of the Far East (later the Southeast Asia) desk were urging that the goal of American policy should be eventual independence after some form of interim government which could "teach" the Vietnamese "to resume the responsibilities of self-government."

In the struggle of policies, the future of Asians could not weigh against the Soviet shadow looming over Europe. In August 1944, at the Dumbarton Oaks Conference on post-war organization, the United States proposal for the colonies made no mention of future independence and offered only a weak-kneed trusteeship to be arranged with the "voluntary" consent of the former colonial power.

Already Indochina was beginning to present the recalcitrance to solution that would only deepen over the next thirty years. During the war, by arrangement with the Japanese conquerors of Indochina and the Vichy government, the French Colonial administration with its armed forces and civilian colonists had remained in the country as surrogate rulers. When, at the eleventh hour, in March 1945, the Japanese ousted them from control, some French groups joined the native resistance under the Viet-Minh, a coalition of nationalist groups including Communists which had been agitating for independence since 1939 and conducting resistance against the Japanese. SEAC (Southeast Asia Command), controlled by the British, made contact with them and invited collaboration. Because any aid to resistance groups would now unavoidably help the French return, Roosevelt shied away from the issue; he did not want to get "mixed up" in liberating Indochina from the Japanese, he irritably told Hull in January 1945. He refused a French request for American ships to transport French troops to Indochina and disallowed aid to the resistance, then reversed himself, insisting that any aid must be limited to action against the Japanese and not construed in the French interest.

Yet who was to take over when the war against Japan was won? Experience with China in the past year had been disillusioning, while the French voice was growing shrill and more imperative. Caught between the pressure of his Allies and his own deep-seated feeling that France should not "go back," Roosevelt, worn out and near his end, tried to avoid the explicit and postpone decisions.

At Yalta in February 1945, when every other Allied problem was developing strain with the approach of victory, the conference skirted the subject, leaving it to the forthcoming organizing conference of the UN at San Francisco. Still worrying the problem, Roosevelt discussed it with a State Department adviser in preparation for the San Francisco meeting. He now retreated to the suggestion that France herself might be the trustee "with the proviso that independence was the ultimate goal." Asked if he would settle for dominion status, he said no, "it must be independence . . . and you can quote me in the State Department." A month later, on 12 April 1945, he died.

With the way now clear, Secretary of State Stettinius told the French at San Francisco twenty-six days after Roosevelt's death that United States did not question French sovereignty over Indochina. He was responding to a tantrum staged by de Gaulle for the benefit of the American Ambassador in Paris in which the General had said that he had an expeditionary force ready to go to Indochina whose departure was prevented by the American refusal of transport, and that "if you are against us in Indochina" this would cause "terrific disappointment" in France, which could drive her into the Soviet orbit. "We do not want to become Communist . . . but I hope you do not push us into it." The blackmail was primitive but tailored to suit what the Europeanists of American diplomacy wished to report. In May at San Francisco, Acting Secretary of State Joseph Grew, the dynamic former Ambassador to Japan and polished veteran of the Foreign Service, assured Bidault with remarkable aplomb that "the record is entirely innocent of any official statement of this government questioning, even by implication, French sovereignty over that area." Recognition is a rather different thing from absence of questioning. In the hands of an expert, that is how policy is made.

Roosevelt had been right about the French record in Indochina; it was the most exploitative in Asia. The French administration concentrated on promoting the production of those goods — rice, coal, rubber, silk and certain spices and minerals — most profitable to export while manipulating the native economy as a market for French products. It provided an easy and comfortable living for some 45,000 French bureaucrats, usually those of mediocre talent, among whom a French survey in 1910 discovered three who could speak a reasonably fluent Vietnamese. It recruited as interpreters and middlemen an assistant bureaucracy of "dependable" Vietnamese from the native upper class, awarding jobs as well as land grants and scholarships for higher education mainly to converts to Catholicism. It eliminated traditional village schools in favor of a French-style education which, for lack of qualified teachers, reached barely a fifth of the school-age population and, according to a French writer, left the Vietnamese "more illiterate than their fathers had been before the French occupation." Its public health and medical services hardly functioned, with one doctor to every 38,000 inhabitants, compared with one for every 3000 in the American-governed Philippines. It substituted an alien French legal code for the traditional judicial system and created a Colonial Council in Cochin China whose minority of Vietnamese members were referred to as "representatives of the conquered race." Above all, through the development of large company-owned plantations and the opportunities for corruption open to the collaborating class, it transformed a land-owning peasantry into landless sharecroppers who numbered over 50 percent of the population on the eve of World War II.

The French called their colonial system *la mission civilisatrice*, which satisfied self-image if not reality. It did not lack outspoken opponents on the left in France or well-intentioned governors and civil servants in the colony who made efforts toward reform from time to time which the vested interests of empire frustrated.

Protests and risings against French rule began with its inception. A people proud of their ancient overthrow of a thousand years of Chinese rule and of later more short-lived Chinese conquests, who had frequently rebelled against and deposed oppressive native dynasties, and who still celebrated the revolutionary heroes and guerrilla tactics of those feats, did not acquiesce passively in a foreign rule far more alien than the Chinese. Twice, in the 1880s and in 1916, Vietnamese emperors themselves had sponsored revolts that failed. While the collaborating class enriched itself from the French table, other men throbbed with the rising blood of the nationalistic impulse in the 20th century. Sects, parties, secret societies — nationalist, constitutionalist, quasi-religious — were formed, agitated, demonstrated and led strikes that ended in French prisons, deportations and firing squads. In 1919, at the Versailles Peace Conference, Ho Chi Minh tried to present an appeal for Vietnamese independence but was turned away without being heard. He subsequently joined the Indochinese Communist Party, organized from Moscow in the 1930s. Thousands were arrested and imprisoned, many executed and some 500 sentenced for life.

Amnestied when the Popular Front government came to power in France, the survivors slowly reconstructed the movement and formed the coalition of the Viet-Minh in 1939. When France capitulated to the Nazis in 1940, the moment seemed at hand for renewed revolt. This too was ferociously suppressed, but the spirit and the aim revived in subsequent resistance to the Japanese, in which the Communists, led by Ho Chi Minh, took the most active part. As in China, the Japanese invasion endowed them with a nationalist cause and when the colonial French let the Japanese enter without a fight, the resistance groups learned contempt and found renewed opportunity.

During the war clandestine American OSS groups operated in Indochina, joining or aiding the resistance. Through airdrops they supplied weapons and on one occasion quinine and sulfa drugs that saved Ho Chi Minh's life from an attack of malaria and dysentery. In talks with OSS officers, Ho said he knew the history of America's own struggle for independence from colonial rule and he was sure "the United States would help in throwing out the French and in establishing an independent country." Impressed by the American pledge to the Philippines, he said he believed that "America was for free popular governments all over the world and that it opposed colonialism in all its forms." This of course was not disinterested conversation. He wanted his message to go further; he wanted arms and aid for a government that he said was "organized and ready to go." The OSS officers were sympathetic but their district chief in China insisted on a policy of "giving no help to individuals such as Ho who were known Communists and therefore sources of trouble."

At Potsdam in July 1945, just before the Japanese defeat, the question of who would take control of Indochina and accept the Japanese surrender was resolved by a secret decision of the Allies that the country below the 16th parallel would be placed under British command and that north of the 16th under Chinese. Since the British were obviously dedicated to colonial restoration, this decision ensured a French return. The United States acquiesced because Roosevelt was dead, because American sentiment is always more concerned with bringing the boys home than with caretaking after a war and because, given Europe's weakened condition, America was reluctant to enter into a quarrel with her Allies. Pressed by the French offer of an army corps of 62,000 for the Pacific front, to be commanded by a hero of the liberation, General Jacques Leclerc, the Combined Chiefs at Potsdam accepted in principle on the understanding that the force would come under American or British command in an area to be determined later, and that transport would not be available until the spring of 1946. It was hardly a secret that the area would be Indochina and the mission its reconquest.

French restoration thus slid into American policy. Although President Truman meant to carry out Roosevelt's intentions, he felt no sense of personal crusade against colonialism and found no written directives left by his predecessor. He was moreover surrounded by military chiefs who, according to Admiral Ernest J. King, the Naval Chief of Staff, "are by no means in favor of keeping the French out of Indochina." Rather, they thought in terms of Western military power replacing the Japanese.

American acceptance was confirmed in August when General de Gaulle descended upon Washington and was told by President Truman, now thoroughly indoctrinated in the threat of Soviet expansion, "My government offers no opposition to the return of the French army and authority in Indochina." De Gaulle promptly announced this statement to a press conference next day, adding that "of course [France] also intends to introduce a new regime," of political reform, "but for us sovereignty is a major question."

He was nothing if not explicit. He had told the Free French at their conference at Brazzaville in January 1944 that they must recognize that political evolution of the colonies had been hastened by the war and that France would meet it "nobly, liberally" but with no intention of yielding sovereignty. The Brazzaville Declaration on colonial policy stated that "the aims of the *mission civilisatrice* . . . exclude any idea of autonomy and any possibility of development outside the French empire bloc. The attainment of 'self-government' in the colonies, even in the distant future, must be excluded."

A week after the Japanese surrender in August 1945, a Viet-Minh congress in Hanoi proclaimed the Democratic Republic of Vietnam and after taking control in Saigon declared its independence, quoting the opening phrases of the American Declaration of Independence of 1776. In a message to the UN transmitted by the OSS, Ho Chi Minh warned that if the UN failed to fulfill the promise of its charter and failed to grant independence to Indochina, "we will keep on fighting until we get it."

A moving message to de Gaulle composed in the name of the last Emperor, the flexible Bao Dai, who had first served the French, then the Japanese, and had now amiably abdicated in favor of the Democratic Republic, was no less prophetic. "You would understand better if you could see what is happening here, if you could feel this desire for independence which is in everyone's heart and which no human force can any longer restrain. Even if you come to re-establish a French administration here, it will no longer be obeyed: each village will be a nest of resistance, each former collaborator an enemy, and your officials and colonists will themselves ask to leave this atmosphere which they will be unable to breathe."

It was one more prophecy to fall on deaf ears. De Gaulle, who received the message while he was in Washington, doubtless did not transmit it to his American hosts, but nothing suggests that it would have had any effect if he had. A few weeks later, Washington informed American agents in Hanoi that steps were being taken to "facilitate the recovery of power by the French."

Self-declared independence lasted less than a month. Ferried from Ceylon by American C-47s, a British general and British troops with a scattering of French units entered Saigon on 12 September, supplemented by 1500 French troops who arrived on French warships two days later. Meanwhile, the bulk of two French divisions had sailed from Marseilles and Madagascar on board two American troopships in the first significant act of American aid. Since the shipping pool was controlled by the Combined Chiefs and the policy decision had already been taken at Potsdam, SEAC could request and be allocated the transports from those available in the pool. Afterward, the State Department, closing the stable door, advised the War Department that it was contrary to United States policy "to employ American flag vessels or aircraft to transport troops of any nationality to or from the Netherlands East Indies or French Indochina, or to permit the use of such craft to carry arms, ammunition or military equipment to those areas."

Until the French arrived, the British command in Saigon used Japanese units, whose disarming was postponed, against the rebel regime.* When a delegation of the Viet-Minh waited on General Douglas Gracey, the British commander, with proposals for maintaining order, "They said, 'welcome' and all that sort of thing," he recalled. "It was an unpleasant situation and I promptly kicked them out." Though characteristically British, the remark was indicative of an attitude that was to infiltrate and deeply affect the future American endeavor as it developed in Vietnam. Finding expression in the terms "slopeys" and "gooks," it reflected not only the view of Asians as

---

*Lord Louis Mountbatten, the Theater Commander, reported on 2 October 1945 to the Combined Chiefs of Staff that the only way he could avoid involving British/Indian forces was "to continue using the Japanese for maintaining law and order and this means I can*not* begin to disarm them for another three months."

inferior to whites but of the people of Indochina, and therefore their pretensions to independence, as of lesser account than, say, the Japanese or Chinese. The Japanese, notwithstanding their unspeakable atrocities, had guns and battleships and modern industry; the Chinese were both admired through the influence of the missionaries and feared as the Yellow Peril and had to be appreciated for sheer land mass and numbers. Without such endowments, the Indochinese commanded less respect. Foreshadowed in General Gracey's words, the result was to be a fatal underestimation of the opponent.

The French divisions from Europe arrived in October and November, some of them wearing uniforms of American issue and carrying American equipment. They plunged into the old business of armed suppression during the first fierce days of arrests and massacre. While they regained control of Saigon, the Viet-Minh faded into the countryside, but this time colonial restoration was incomplete. In the northern zone assigned to the Chinese, the Vietnamese, armed with weapons from the Japanese surrender which the Chinese sold them, retained control under Ho's Provisional Government in Hanoi. The Chinese did not interfere and, loaded with booty from their occupation, eventually withdrew over the border.

In the confusion of peoples and parties, OSS units suffered from a "lack of directives" from Washington which reflected the confusion of policy at home. Traditional anti-colonialism had left a reservoir of ambivalence, but the governing assumption that a "stable, strong and friendly" France was essential to fill the vacuum in Europe tipped the balance of policy. Late in 1945, $160 million of equipment was sold to the French for use in Indochina and remaining OSS units were instructed to serve as "observers to punitive missions against the rebellious Annamites." Eight separate appeals addressed by Ho Chi Minh to President Truman and the Secretary of State over a period of five months asking for support and economic aid went unanswered on the ground that his government was not recognized by the United States.

The snub was not given in ignorance of conditions in Vietnam. A report in October by Arthur Hale, of the United States Information Service in Hanoi, made it apparent that French promises of reform and some vague shape of autonomy, which American policy counted on, were not going to satisfy. The people wanted the French out. Posters crying "Independence or Death!" in all towns and villages of the north "scream at the passerby from every wall and window." Communist influence was not concealed; the flag of the Provisional Government resembled the Soviet flag, Marxist pamphlets lay on official desks, but the same might be said for American influence. The promise to the Philippines was a constant theme, and a vigorous enthusiasm was felt for American prowess in the war and for American productive capacity and technical and social progress. Given, however, the lack of any American response to the Viet-Minh and such incidents "as the recent shipment of French troops to Saigon in American vessels," the goodwill had faded. Hale's report too was prophetic: if the French overcome the Provisional Government, "it can be assumed as a certainty that the movement for independence will not die." The certainty was there at the start.

Other observers concurred. The French might take the cities in the north, wrote a correspondent of the *Christian Science Monitor*, "but it is extremely doubtful if they will ever be able to put down the independence movement as a whole. They have not enough troops to root out every guerrilla band in the north and they have shown little capacity to cope with guerrilla fighting."

Asked by the State Department for an evaluation of American prestige in Asia, which it suspected was "seriously deteriorating," Charles Yost, political officer in Bangkok and a future Ambassador to the UN, confirmed the Department's impression, and he too cited the use of American vessels to transport French troops and "the use of American equipment by these troops." Goodwill toward America as the champion of subject peoples had been very great after the war, but American failure to support the nationalist movement "does not seem likely to contribute to long-term stability in Southeast Asia." The restoration of colonial regimes, Yost warned, was unsuited to existing conditions "and cannot for that reason long be maintained except by force."

That American policy nevertheless supported the French effort was a choice of the more compelling necessity over what seemed a lesser one. George Marshall as Secretary of State acknowledged the existence of "dangerously outmoded colonial outlook and methods in the area," but "on the other hand . . . we are not interested in seeing colonial empire administrations supplanted by philosophy and political organizations emanating from and controlled by Kremlin." This was the crux. The French peppered Washington with "proof" of Ho Chi Minh's contacts with Moscow, and Dean Acheson, Under-Secretary of State, was in no doubt. "Keep in mind," he cabled Abbot Low Moffat, chief for Southeast Asia affairs, who went to Hanoi in December 1946, "Ho's clear record as agent international communism, absence evidence recantation."

Moffat, a warm partisan of the Asian cause, reported that in conversation Ho had disclaimed Communism as his aim, saying that if he could secure independence, that was enough for his lifetime. "Perhaps," he had added wryly, "fifty years from now the United States will be Communist and then Vietnam can be also." Moffat concluded that the group in charge of Vietnam "are at this stage nationalist first" and an effective nationalist state must precede a Communist state, which as an objective "must for the time being be secondary." Whether he was deluded history cannot answer, for who can be certain that, at the time Ho was seeking American support, the development of the Democratic Republic of Vietnam (DRV) was as irrevocably Communist as the course of events was to make it?

The compulsion of the French to regain their empire derived, after the humiliation of World War II, from a sense that their future as a great power was at stake, but they realized the necessity of some adjustment, at least pro forma. During temporary truces with the Viet-Minh in 1946 they tried to negotiate a basis of agreement with promises of some unspecified form of self-government at some unspecified date, so worded as never to ruffle the edges of sovereignty. These were "paper concessions," according to the State Department's Far East desk. When they failed, hostilities resumed and by the end of 1946 the first, or French, Indochina war was fully under way. There was no illusion. If the French resumed the repressive measures and policy of force of the past, reported the American Consul in Saigon, "no settlement of situation can be expected foreseeable future and period guerrilla warfare will follow." The French commander assigned to carry out the reconquest himself saw, or felt, the truth. After his first survey of the situation, General Leclerc said to his political adviser, "It would take 500,000 men to do it and even then it could not be done." In one sentence he laid out the future, and his estimate would still be valid when 500,000 American soldiers were actually in the field two decades later.

Was American policy already folly in 1945–46? Even judged in terms of the thinking of the time, the answer must be affirmative, for most Americans concerned with foreign policy understood that the colonial era had come to an end and that its revival was an exercise in putting Humpty-Dumpty back on the wall. No matter how strong the arguments for bolstering France, folly lay in attaching policy to a cause that prevailing information indicated was hopeless. Policy-makers assured themselves they were not attaching the United States to the cause. They took comfort in French pledges of future autonomy or else in the belief that France lacked the power to regain her empire and would have to come to terms with the Vietnamese eventually. Both Truman and Acheson assured the American public that the U.S. position was "predicated on the assumption that the French claim to have the support of the population of Indochina is borne out by future events." To assist her now for the sake of a strong presence in Europe was therefore no crime — though it was a losing proposition.

The alternative was present and available: to gain for America an enviable primacy among Western nations and confirm the foundation of goodwill in Asia by aligning ourselves with, even supporting, the independence movements. If this seemed indicated to some, particularly at the Far East desk, it was less persuasive to others for whom self-government by Asians was not something to base a policy on and insignificant in comparison to the security of Europe. In Indochina choice of the alternative would have required imagination, which is never a long suit with governments, and willingness to take the risk of supporting a Communist when Communism was still seen as a solid bloc. Tito was then its only splinter, and the possibility of another deviation was not envisaged. Moreover, it would be divisive of the Allies. Support of Humpty-Dumpty was chosen instead, and once a policy has been adopted and implemented, all subsequent activity becomes an effort to justify it.

An uneasy suspicion that we were pursuing folly was to haunt the American engagement in Vietnam from beginning to end, revealing itself in sometimes contorted policy directives. In a summary of the American position for diplomats in Paris, Saigon and Hanoi, the French desk in 1947 drafted for Secretary George Marshall a directive of wishful thinking combined with uncertainty. It saw the independence movements of the new nations of Southeast Asia, representing, so it said, a quarter of the world's inhabitants, as a "momentous factor in world stability"; it believed the best safeguard against this struggle's succumbing to anti-Western tendencies and Communist influence was continued association with former colonial powers; it acknowledged on the one hand that the association "must be voluntary" and on the other hand that the war in Indochina could only destroy voluntary cooperation, and "irrevocably alienate Vietnamese"; it said that the United States wanted to be helpful without wishing to intervene or offer any solution of its own, yet was "inescapably concerned" with the developments in Indochina. Whether foreign service officers were enlightened by this document is questionable.

QUESTIONS

1. Tuchman is attempting to outline the beginnings of a policy that eventually led the U.S. into its involvement in Vietnam twenty years later. Is her explanation satisfactory? Can you follow it? What is not clear to you? Why is it not clear?

2. Tuchman says that government officials refused to draw conclusions from the evidence they had. Why is this clear to her when it was not clear to the officials involved? She says that the U.S. could have chosen to support France and strengthen our European allies, or chosen to end imperialism and strengthen independence in the Far East. Has she overstated the case in her analysis of what was obviously a very complicated situation?

3. Does Tuchman remain objective in her presentation? When, for example, she says that de Gaulle staged a "tantrum," has she slipped into subjectivity, or is she trying to convey the essence of the situation? Where else in her essay does her objectivity seem to waver?

4. How would you characterize the attitude of the British and American diplomats toward the Vietnamese at the end of World War II? How would you characterize the present attitude or "world view" of Tuchman?

5. Does Tuchman's presentation (which in this instance is limited to the years 1945–46) change your understanding of our relationship toward Vietnam? Does it change your attitude about our involvement there twenty years later?

● ● ● ● ●

ETHICS IN EMBRYO

Lewis H. Lapham, Nancy Neveloff Dubler,
Thomas H. Murray, Jeremy Rifkin, Lee Salk

The advance of technology brings with it moral and ethical problems, problems humans have not squarely had to face before the technology that created these problems existed. As we move towards the year 2000, however, some issues that have only recently attracted our attention will surely become more hotly disputed; one of those issues is "human engineering," or what is commonly described as the problem of "test tube babies." Harper's Magazine recently assembled a panel of experts to discuss some of the ethical dilemmas the citizens of the twenty-first century may face if genetic engineering becomes more common.

SOON after the introduction of a controversial technology — nuclear energy, say, or the test-tube baby or the artificial heart — something goes very obviously wrong. A baby dies, a circulatory system fails, a radioactive cloud escapes on an easterly wind.

The event sets in motion an anguished debate between those who believe in what they are pleased to call progress and those who argue unprincipled science will subvert the moral order and diminish the value of human life. The two sets of apologists agree on only one point — that the public debate began only after the damage had been done. In anticipation of this familiar complaint, *Harper's Magazine* assembled a small group of people associated with various aspects of the current discussion about the uses of genetic engineering. No subject excites stronger emotions or opens more doors into a brave new world.

Presented with three proposed techniques — not yet practicable but entirely plausible within the bounds of current laboratory research — the participants were invited to address the embryonic moral questions implicit in the biotechnologies.

The following forum is based on a discussion held at the Cooper Union for the Advancement of Science and Arts in New York City. Lewis H. Lapham served as moderator.

- ▸ LEWIS H. LAPHAM is editor of *Harper's Magazine*.
- ▸ NANCY NEVELOFF DUBLER is the director of the Division of Legal and Ethical Issues in Health Care at the Montefiore Medical Center in New York City. She has written widely about medical dilemmas in contemporary health care.
- ▸ THOMAS H. MURRAY is the director of the Center for Bioethics at the School of Medicine of Case Western Reserve University.
- ▸ JEREMY RIFKIN is president of the Foundation on Economic Trends in Washington, D.C. He is the author of *Entropy, Algeny, Declaration of a Heretic*, and the recently published *Time Wars: The Primary Conflict in Human History*.
- ▸ LEE SALK is clinical professor of psychology in psychiatry and pediatrics at Cornell University Medical Center and professor of child development at Brown University. He is the author of nine books on the parent-child relationship.

Current Technology

In vitro fertilization involves the withdrawal of about six eggs from a woman. All the eggs are fertilized with the father's sperm. Those eggs which show abnormal cell division in the early stages are destroyed. The remaining fertilized eggs are returned to the mother's womb for development.

Proposed Technology

The woman takes fertility drugs, or is "superovulated," to produce around thirty eggs. These are fertilized and genetically profiled to determine whether the embryo has diseases, such as Huntington's chorea; afflictions, such as Down's syndrome, or even simple astigmatism; and finally for characteristics such as eye color, skin color, and physical imperfections.

LAPHAM: I've got thirty fertilized eggs here. Ms. Dubler, am I allowed to throw out the embryos with Down's syndrome or serious disorders?

DUBLER: Yes. We look to find out if there is Down's syndrome or any other affliction that we recognize as exceptionally painful and difficult, those that are not a "good" in human beings.

LAPHAM: How do we know which traits are "not a good in human beings"?

RIFKIN: Exactly. Every year we locate more and more genetic markers for single-gene diseases. When the technology exists to remove them, there will be parental pressure to do so. Soon parents are going to have a genetic read-out of all the traits they can potentially pass on to their children. Parents will become statisticians. They're going to ask, "Do I want to burden my child with a particular trait?"

Where do you draw the line? There are several thousand recessive traits. Leukemia can kill your child at three, heart disease at thirty, and Alzheimer's at fifty. At what point do you say no? Society might even legislate or compel parents not to pass on certain traits because of the health costs likely to be incurred.

We're forcing a profound change in the parent-child relationship. As we introduce predictability, we create more pressure for perfect eggs, perfect sperm, and perfect embryos.

MURRAY: Let's make a distinction. With a disease, a child is sick and in pain. And there are a relative handful of genetic disorders that cause great suffering. But with a recessive trait the gene is not expressed, so the child is not ill. There are thousands of those, so why remove them!

LAPHAM: Let's get back to my petri dish. You've got thirty fertilized eggs. You're going to allow me to take out Down's. What else are you going to let me take out?

DUBLER: Tay-Sachs, Huntington's. If we have the same information about early-onset Alzheimer's as we do about Tay-Sachs I would include early-onset Alzheimer's.

LAPHAM: I'm down to twenty-six. Now let's suppose the twenty-fifth one has got a harelip. Am I allowed to take that one out?

DUBLER: You're not going to test for that, so you're not going to know.

LAPHAM: As soon as I get the technology I'm going to test for that. Mr. Rifkin is right. Once you let me take out Tay-Sachs, there's no stopping.

DUBLER: I don't agree with that at all. There is a fundamental assumption in this discussion with which I disagree profoundly: that we as a society cannot make and enforce decisions. We as a society could have a reproductive policy which stated that we could test for those conditions that burden the life to such a degree that it is permissible to exclude them. The number of conditions would be limited. Aside from those, you would not gather the information. It would be regulated the same way we now regulate research.

RIFKIN: How do you determine "the conditions that burden life"? What about a disease that kills at age five or one that kills at age thirty?

DUBLER: Dying of Huntington's is a terrible death, and I think that society has a shared perception on certain diseases. We can draw lines. We are human beings; we deal with difficult problems all the time.

MURRAY: Jeremy, you lack faith in our ability to make judgments, yet we make judgments all the time. We decide what is a disease and what is not a disease, what's a deformity and what's not a deformity. For example, society says: "If you have a harelip, that's a deformity, and it's enough for one to warrant trying to correct it. We'll even help you pay for it."

That's a social consensus. Whereas if you want a tummy tuck because you don't like your paunch, we say we'll let you do it, but we sure as hell won't pay for it. We draw that line. You may want to argue with me about how to draw it, but we draw it nonetheless.

LAPHAM: But our "society" is defined by the marketplace. And a capitalist ethic does not allow the state to say: Do this, do that.

DUBLER: Sure it does. Let me give you an example. On the black market, you can buy or sell anything. You can torture people. You can pay to have them killed. You can sell human flesh. I don't want to argue that criminals don't exist. On the open market, though, what society professes to believe guides our behavior.

Over the last decade we as a society have said there are certain values in medical research which we will support and ones we will prohibit.

For example, you can't do research on children where there is more than a "minimal risk to the child" unless there is an overwhelming compensating benefit. So we've taken medical research, which is also driven by the marketplace, by gain, by ego, by position, and we've said, *no*, there are certain things that you can't do.

Let me come back to our petri dish. There are certain things you can't do. You can take out Huntington's and you can take out early Alzheimer's and then you are left with a certain number of fertilized eggs. Here's what you do: You will line them up, you will take the first one in line, and you will implant it. I don't think that's any more difficult than regulating research. The black market will exist, but that doesn't invalidate my argument.

RIFKIN: What we're really talking about is eugenics. Professional ethicists keep looking out the front door saying, "I hope this technology isn't abused by a particular government or a particular ideological system. I hope another Adolf Hitler doesn't come along."

Meanwhile a new eugenics has quietly slipped in the back door. You can hear it in our conversation today. We're talking about commercial eugenics. We want perfect babies. We want perfect plants and animals. We want a better economy. There's no evil intent here. The road to the Brave New World is paved with good intentions.

Step-by-step, we are deciding to engineer parts of the genetic code of living things. Two important questions emerge: If we're going to engineer the genetic code, what criteria does this society establish for determining good and bad, useful and dysfunctional genes? And I would like to know whether there is an institution anyone here would trust with the ultimate authority to decide the genetic blueprints for a living thing?

MURRAY: Wait. You asked me to come up with a criterion for a disease everyone thinks should be engineered out. Here it is: a disease that causes a prolonged, painful, and undignified death. How does that sound?

RIFKIN: Would you feel qualified to be on the President's Commission set up to advise on this?

MURRAY: You never answer a question.

RIFKIN: Would you feel qualified to give advice and consent as to what genetic changes in the biological code of human beings are permissible?

MURRAY: Yes. I wouldn't feel qualified to make the ultimate judgment, but I would feel qualified to become part of the discussion. The alternative is to do nothing. Again,

Jeremy, you hold no faith in our ability to make any distinctions, any reasonable judgments.

RIFKIN: I have faith in humanity's ability to make reasonable judgments. The question is who is making the judgments and on behalf of whom? What are the preconceptions and central assumptions that we're using?

SALK: Let's look for a moment at a technology developed two decades ago and see where that's taken us. Neonatology, the medical science devoted to troubled newborns, emerged as a subspecialty around 1965 and created a new breed of physicians. Have we made any reasonable judgments in this field? What I see is a technology driving these doctors to save babies at the lowest birth weight possible. Today I see babies born in our hospital with multiple handicaps. We can save a 600-gram baby, but I don't think the doctors are as concerned with the quality of life as they should be.

DUBLER: I disagree with that entirely. They're very concerned, although puzzled as to how to determine it. They're very aware that it would be unethical to save a 200-gram infant.

SALK: But I'm not sure it's ethical to save a 1,000-gram infant with multiple handicaps.

DUBLER: Many neonatologists would agree.

SALK: But no one is setting up any criteria that they can abide by. Thirty years ago, when a baby was born with respiratory distress, other than giving it oxygen, they would just put it in the corner and let nature take its course. Mothers were told, "This is God's will. You would have had a multiply handicapped child. It's better to let it go." And people accepted that. They had no problems with that at all.

DUBLER: I disagree with almost every one of your statements. There are some babies who are so clearly in intractable pain that they cannot lead any sort of reasonable life. At that point they are let go. Those decisions are made carefully and adequately on moral bases by the medical team and the parents.

Neonatology is a good example where principles — incorporating both science and ethics — have provided real guideposts for caregivers. Similarly, I think a standard for genetic decisions could be developed along the lines of Tom Murray's criterion: when suffering and disease and an undignified death are inevitable.

MURRAY: It's hard to imagine a culture that would not spare people suffering and painful death, as long as it didn't come at a terrible moral price.

LAPHAM: What I hear Nancy and Tom saying is that you are prepared to breed out pain or death in our petri dish but you're not prepared to breed anything in.

DUBLER: Correct.

MURRAY: Right.

LAPHAM: Why not breed in? We could solve the problem of racism, for instance. Let's take out skin color in my petri dish. Why won't you let me do that?

MURRAY: Is that the way to respond to a social problem like discrimination?

LAPHAM: You let me prevent hideous death, but you won't let me put in any "positive" traits.

RIFKIN: When the day comes that we can make these decisions, we will probably be less tolerant of the disabled because we will perceive them as defective *products*.

Also, we're likely to see the beginning of a prejudice based on genetic type, on genetic read-out, which is likely to be just as virulent as prejudice based on race or ethnic background.

Should your employer know that you have a tendency toward Alzheimer's? Should your school system know the genetic read-out of your child? Should a government have these records? I suspect we're going to see the beginning of a biological caste system in the next two to three centuries. We may be seeing the gradual emergence of eugenics in civilization.

MURRAY: You're using the word "eugenics" a little too cavalierly here. Eugenics means the management of the genetic stock of a population.

RIFKIN: To improve it.

MURRAY: To "improve" it, as if we know what that means.

RIFKIN: That's the problem with engineering for improvement. Do you know of any engineer who only wants to make technology *somewhat* efficient but not *perfectly* efficient? Do you know of any engineer who stops midway through the process and decides to accept less than the most efficient solution? I don't. Engineers want to continue the process until they have *perfected* the technology. Why would it be any different in genetic engineering than it is in mechanical or electrical or nuclear engineering?

DUBLER: Because people are not bolts of steel.

RIFKIN: But we are beginning to perceive living things as indistinguishable from bolts of steel.

DUBLER: I don't accept that judgment.

RIFKIN: It depends on what your highest value is. If your highest value is respect for life, then I would agree that we've got a fighting chance here. If, however, the highest value in civilization is efficiency, expediency, and engineering values, then I would say we're in trouble.

MURRAY: If that's the way the values line up, we're in deep trouble. I think fortunately the values don't line up that way.

RIFKIN: The problem with these different values is that they are being developed into a new sociology, one that goes hand-in-hand with genetic engineering. Increasingly we open up the newspaper and find articles saying we have located the newest gene governing personality or social behavior (a good example is the much celebrated but recently discredited "depression" gene).

We're beginning to believe that our social behavior is a direct result of our genetic typing. Social biologists don't come right out and say, "It's all genetics; it's all inheritance." What they do say is more subtle: That genetic inheritance is the *broad determi-*

nant of your personality. Environment, institutions, and values play some role, they say, but it's a smaller role than we had thought.

What happens in a society that has both the technology to manipulate the genetic code and a social biology that suggests that we are no more or less than the genes that make us up? It's a dangerous combination, moving us ever closer to a eugenic civilization.

MURRAY: This is not the first sweeping intellectual change that mankind has experienced. I think Jeremy is right in saying that this challenges the way we think about ourselves. But then again so did Copernicus, so did Darwin, so did Freud. They challenged us to think about ourselves in entirely new ways — in ways at least as profound as those imposed by the genetic-engineering revolution. We still look at ourselves as creatures capable of dignity, capable of meaning, capable of morality.

DUBLER: One example of individual choice — and a simple form of genetic engineering — is choosing your spouse. If you think, for example, that sociological characteristics are linked to behaviors that are determined by genes, then you ought not to choose someone to reproduce with who has a history of assaults or burglaries or murders.

LAPHAM: You're allowing me free choice with my spouse but not my child.

DUBLER: Yes, absolutely. Even though over 50 percent of us in this country make bad decisions in our choice of a spouse, we will not limit that foolishness even when it's repetitive foolishness. That's because there are values inherent in individual choice.

LAPHAM: I don't understand what value system anybody at this table lives by. You'll allow me free choice with a spouse, but not with a child.

SALK: We'll allow you free choice about whether or not to have children.

LAPHAM: And you'll allow me to design my child with enormously expensive neonatal care, private schools, child psychiatrists, Yale University.

DUBLER: That's coping with your decisions.

LAPHAM: No. It's trying to imprint on my descendant a certain set of traits.

DUBLER: You get to rear your child, that's all.

LAPHAM: I get to rear — not design — my child?

DUBLER: Yes.

RIFKIN: But wait a minute. What I gather from you is that some design is permissible and some isn't.

DUBLER: To manipulate for a good — such as ruling out Huntington's — is different than designing.

RIFKIN: To plan in advance the outcome of something: That's what design is. So what you really want is to eliminate the word "design."

DUBLER: Because language helps us distinguish among processes even when they are similar.

RIFKIN: Haven't you introduced design by eliminating one gene? It seems to me you're not taking full responsibility for this. You're saying you are willing to design for some things but not others. It's not semantics. It's a question of whether you're willing to plan any part of the genetic makeup of your offspring in advance.

MURRAY: I'm willing to spare my offspring the horrors of a few terrible diseases.

RIFKIN: It's interesting how we use language. Scientists used the term "genetic engineering" up until the late 1970s. When the controversy over genetics emerged the word was changed from "engineering" to "therapy." Suddenly we're talking about gene therapy. What's the difference between engineering and therapy?

LAPHAM: From this discussion it seems obvious. Therapy connotes taking away the negatives, and engineering connotes putting in the positives. The sentiment here is that it's okay to take away the negatives; that's therapy. It's not okay to put in the positives; that's engineering.

RIFKIN: So when an engineer takes a defect out of a machine, that's not engineering — that's therapy.

MURRAY: We're not talking about engineering; we are talking about eliminating a disease.

RIFKIN: You're talking here about changing the blueprint of life itself.

MURRAY: When a physician cures a disease, is that engineering?

RIFKIN: Yes, if the physician engineers changes into the genetic blueprint. When an engineer eliminates a defect in the design of a tool, that's engineering. Because you're going right to the heart of the actual technology that you've created. Remember, just because something can be done doesn't mean it inevitably should be done. Throughout history many more technologies have been rejected by various cultures than accepted. It's only in the last 200 years of the Western world view that we have come to believe that if it can be done, it's inevitable — a fait accompli. As if new technologies come here in some mysterious way, by the gods, and we just stumble across them and therefore have to live with them as we do the changing seasons. That view allows us not to take responsibility. I don't assume that any of these things are a fait accompli.

DUBLER: It's a wonderful moment: Jeremy and I agree. There is no technological imperative. That's exactly what I've been arguing. Simply because a technology exists is no reason that we must use it or that we can use it.

RIFKIN: But what are you going to do? You have to have a change in world views to deal responsibly with this technology. You can't use this world view to critique this technology because this world view is the architect of this technology.

DUBLER: I believe that scholarly discussion serves as the basis for public discussion and that is how our society should proceed. Ideas are addressed by scholars, which are then discussed by legislators, which then becomes the subject of articles in the public press. Eventually, but not without great difficulty, this debate will produce a consensus on what our overriding values should be.

QUESTIONS

1. A panel discussion such as this one would be easy to follow if it were witnessed by a live audience or broadcast on television. Is it effective to transcribe this conversation and then publish the transcription?

2. What are some alternative ways of presenting the information contained in this debate? Why do you suppose the editors of *Harper's Magazine* did not choose to adopt one of these alternatives?

3. If you were editing this discussion would you have omitted any part of the transcript you have here? (The conversation goes on beyond this excerpt.)

4. What clues do you find in this excerpt about the intended audience? How would you characterize that audience?

5. The moderator of any group discussion cannot always foresee or control the comments of his panel. Since it is not indicated in the text that remarks have been omitted or added, would you say that this moderator was able to keep his panel focused on the relevant issues? What other problems besides the overall focus does a moderator face in a situation such as this?

6. Select a news program such as *Face the Nation* or *Nightline*. Tape the program then write up an abridged transcript of the proceedings. Edit your transcript so that your finished article will capture the essence of the discussion and also be interesting for a reader who did not witness the program firsthand.

SECTION

IV

▼

Crafting
Persuasive
Prose

CONCERNS IN PERSUASIVE PROSE

Persuasive writing emphasizes the reader, rather than the subject or the writer. Generally, persuasion is a "future-oriented" activity. When we attempt to persuade others, we are hoping to affect how they will act, react, or think in the future. We would like to persuade people to buy our product or idea, to vote for our proposal, to think as we do about a project or issue. In short, we wish to affect the behavior of others. These are the basic features of persuasive writing:

1. Reference to the reader, the audience we are attempting to persuade.
2. Emphasis on changing the reader's beliefs or opinions, rather than on expressing the writer's emotions or simply providing objective information.
3. A style that focuses on swaying the reader's opinion; it may use logical appeals, emotional appeals, or both.
4. A degree of reliability that depends on the writer's use of logical, rather than emotional, appeals.

If we think about it for a moment, we can see that we spend a good deal of our lives attempting to persuade others, and, in turn, having others attempt to persuade us. For example, we encounter persuasive prose regularly in advertising, political speeches, business letters, proposals, and editorials, all forms of persuasive prose you may be asked to create. Persuasion is obviously important then, and if we hope to become skilled at persuading people it is worth our time to examine the subject closely.

We might begin by first looking at the ways in which we ourselves are persuaded. Take, for example, the most common form of persuasion we are exposed to — advertising. We are bombarded by advertising appeals daily, in the form of television and radio commercials, as well as the advertisements we see on billboards and in newspapers and magazines. Some of these appeals may be particularly persuasive and may inspire us to take action of some sort. Some we may not find very effective, even annoying. These advertisements may also inspire us to take action; they may inspire us to avoid the products being advertised. Some appeals may stimulate reactions that could best be called neutral. In terms of causing us to take positive action they fail, although presumably they do not alienate us to the products being advertised, and someday we might conceivably try one of these products if another, more effective, appeal does not prevent us from doing so.

Because advertising is the most prominent form of persuasive writing we encounter on a daily basis, it does provide us with many accessible examples of both good and bad persuasive writing, and it also demonstrates some of the central issues persuasive writers regularly encounter. Historically, those who have been able to persuade others effectively have sometimes been distrusted, even feared, because the power of language to sway and convince can be misunderstood. The term "mere rhetoric," for example, is often applied to persuasive arguments that seem to depend more on style than substance, the label itself suggesting that some effort at duplicity or deceit is taking place. In fact, it is frequently asserted that, in attempting to persuade, advertising alters or distorts the truth. Advertising, critics argue, relies on appeals that are largely emotional rather than logical. Advertising may manipulate us, and some ads, the theory goes, may cause us to buy things we do not really need or want.

Advertising, as well as some persuasion, also tends to be self-serving; that is, an advertisement that tries to sell us something will ultimately profit the manufacturer or business that has created the advertisement. This issue of "selfishness" is an important one, and this quality (or the lack of it) is sometimes used to distinguish between ordinary persuasive writing and what is most frequently labeled "propaganda." Here the questions of ethics and morality enter the picture. It is generally considered legitimate and ethical to argue logically for a cause in which you are personally invested. You might also legitimately and ethically use an emotional appeal on behalf of a cause that is in the common interest (presumably, saving whales, baby seals, whooping cranes, and other similar defenseless creatures would be examples of selfless causes, causes that might be defined as for the common good). It is less ethical, however (and strict moralists might even say it is unethical), to use purely emotional appeals to influence others when the issue in question is one by which we might profit financially, socially, or politically. These are the times when the power of language can genuinely be misused, and, some would argue, when the potential for manipulation is at its highest. Although we would like to believe that most of the choices we make in life are arrived at by rational thinking and not irrational reactions, when faced with an argument that is primarily emotional we often need to step back and ask whether we are responding in kind. If you feel that you are being asked to react emotionally to an issue that might otherwise be resolved on purely logical grounds, you may be justified in becoming suspicious and backing away carefully.

13 ▶ Logical Appeals

Persuasive essays are most frequently structured either *inductively* or *deductively*, according to the type of logical arrangement they follow. Although we study *deduction* and *induction* as pure forms of logic, we should remember that these basic patterns of thinking underlie our reasoning when we create all persuasive arguments. If our arguments are to be accepted, if we are to be successful as persuasive writers, we must understand the fundamentals of inductive and deductive logic. As you will see, deductive and inductive arguments, used separately and occasionally combined, are employed throughout the articles in this book, and will also be used by you in your persuasive essays. Because inductive and deductive logic is also used (and perhaps misused) by those whom you are trying to persuade, a clear understanding of these principles will help you understand how your audience is arriving at the conclusions it holds. Once you understand why your audience believes the way it does, you will be more effective in affecting and changing those beliefs. Think of induction and deduction, then, as fundamental patterns of reasoning that apply to all of your persuasive prose, no matter whether you are creating a proposal, a business letter, or an editorial statement.

DEDUCTION

Deduction is a way of reasoning that draws conclusions about specific cases on the basis of statements that are generally valid for classes or groups of examples. It involves making predictions about future cases on the basis of examples that have been validated in the past. These conclusions may be drawn with the use of a structured series of statements (called syllogisms) that may be formally or informally expressed. Syllogisms are usually not directly stipulated in arguments, but rather are implied in the construction of the argument. It is frequently necessary for you to examine an argument carefully, then break it down into the assumptions or premises that comprise it.

In Stephen Jay Gould's article "Evolution as Fact and Theory," for example, Gould points out that modern creationists object to the concept of evolution because these principles are always presented as a "theory" of evolution. A theory, in the minds of many, is speculation only, so evolutionary "theory," the creationists argue, cannot be trusted. If this reasoning were to be expressed as a formal syllogism it would look like this:

Major Premise: Theories are ideas that cannot be proved to be scientific facts.
Minor Premise: Darwin's concept of evolution is only a theory.
Conclusion: Darwin's concept of evolution cannot be proved to be scientific fact.

This example is a *categorical* syllogism, probably the most common type of syllogism you will encounter. A large category is established; in this case the category is ALL THEORIES.

ALL THEORIES

Then a general truth is established about the individual examples within this large category. Here the creationists have declared that *ALL THEORIES* ARE IDEAS THAT CANNOT BE PROVED TO BE FACTS.

ALL THEORIES
(ARE IDEAS THAT CANNOT BE PROVED TO BE FACTS)

The second step in the construction of a categorical syllogism is to declare that a specific example — in this case DARWIN'S EVOLUTIONARY CONCEPT — belongs within the general category we have established.

ALL THEORIES
(ARE IDEAS THAT CANNOT BE PROVED TO BE FACTS)
THEORY: Darwin's
Concept of Evolution

Their conclusion — DARWIN'S CONCEPT OF EVOLUTION CANNOT BE PROVED TO BE A SCIENTIFIC FACT — must be the logical result of their reasoning, because if Darwin's idea belongs within the large category — ALL THEORIES — it must possess the quality we have declared that all samples in that category possess, that is, they cannot be proved and therefore are possibly false. Once Gould understands the principles behind the creationists' argument, that is, once he comprehends the premises they are using, he can then explain what he feels is the fallacy behind their logic. His essay is more effective and clear, because he can expose the assumptions with which he disagrees.

When we make a categorical syllogism, we in effect draw a box around a number of things, people, or ideas, and then declare that certain truths apply to those objects or ideas we have enclosed within our category. Whenever we say things such as "Chevrolets are not reliable," or "Good quarterbacks are quick on their feet," we may be distorting the truth, but we are also creating categorical statements that could be used as Major Premises in categorical syllogisms.

We must follow some simple cautions when we build an essay on a series of categorical syllogisms. We might, for example, have qualified the Major Premise by saying that this truth applied to *most* or *some* of the examples within this category; if we qualify the Major Premise, however, our Conclusion (and the argument we present in our essay) must also be qualified in a similar fashion. So if we state that *MOST* THEORIES ARE IDEAS THAT CANNOT BE PROVED TO BE SCIENTIFIC FACTS, we can conclude only that DARWIN'S CONCEPT OF EVOLUTION *PROBABLY* CANNOT BE PROVED TO BE A SCIENTIFIC FACT; if we state that *SOME* THEORIES ARE IDEAS THAT CANNOT BE PROVED TO BE FACTS, we can say with certainty only that DARWIN'S CONCEPT OF EVOLUTION *MIGHT* NOT PROVED TO BE FACTUAL.

SOME THEORIES
(ARE IDEAS THAT CANNOT BE PROVED TO BE FACTS)

THEORY: Darwin's Concept of Evolution (*May or may not* be proved as fact)

We are not justified in drawing absolutely certain conclusions if our Major Premise is not itself absolutely all-inclusive, that is, if it does not make a statement about all members of a certain category. To overstep the conditions laid down in our premises will create an argument that persuades no one.

We also must insure that our Minor Premise applies to and affirms one of the conditions of the Major Premise. The following, for example, does not allow for a valid conclusion:

Major Premise: Theories are ideas that cannot be proved to be scientific facts.
Minor Premise: The "law of gravity" is not a theory.
Conclusion: The "law of gravity" is a scientific fact. (Invalid)

No valid conclusion can be reached about the law of gravity at this point. We have created a category and placed all theories within this imaginary box. We have then declared that the law of gravity does not belong within this enclosure, and we have no information about the ideas, principles, laws, theories, or concepts that exist outside the box.

> ALL THEORIES
> (ARE IDEAS THAT CANNOT
> BE PROVED TO BE SCIENTIFIC
> FACTS)

> THE LAW OF GRAVITY
> IS *NOT* A THEORY

We cannot say this principle is true, and we cannot say that it is not true. We just cannot (logically) draw any conclusions from the information we have been given. If we do so, we will again create a faulty and unpersuasive argument.

Categorical syllogisms are not the only kind of deductive syllogisms; there are also *conditional* (sometimes called *hypothetical*) syllogisms and (the most difficult to work with) *disjunctive* syllogisms. A *conditional* syllogism is an "*if-then*" syllogism; it asserts that if one condition or situation takes place, then a second condition or situation will result. For example, in Alice Walker's essay "The Civil Rights Movement: What Good Was It?," she asserts that it is not blacks who repeatedly raise questions about the so-called death of the Civil Rights Movement. The chain of reasoning she presents in her explanation could be presented formally as a conditional syllogism. Walker says:

Major Premise: If the white population loses interest in the Civil Rights Movement, the Movement then appears to them to be "dead."

Minor Premise: The white population, because it does not have to live in a world of discrimination on a daily basis, is no longer interested in the Civil Rights Movement.

Conclusion: The Civil Rights Movement appears to be a dead cause to white observers.

A conditional syllogism might be diagrammed like this

> (ANTECEDENT)
> IF CONDITION A
> EXISTS

> (CONSEQUENT)
> THEN SITUATION B
> IS CERTAIN TO FOLLOW

As with the *categorical* syllogism, any qualification of the Major Premise must result in a similarly qualified Conclusion. These premises

Major Premise: If the white population loses interest in the Civil Rights Movement, the cause will *probably* appear to them to be dead.

Minor Premise: The white population, because it does not have to live in a world of discrimination on a daily basis, is no longer interested in the Civil Rights Movement.

cannot validly produce the Conclusion THE CIVIL RIGHTS MOVEMENT APPEARS TO BE A DEAD CAUSE TO WHITE OBSERVERS. The Conclusion will have to be THE CIVIL RIGHTS MOVEMENT *PROBABLY* APPEARS TO BE A DEAD CAUSE TO WHITE OBSERVERS. Also, the Minor Premise must affirm the conditions of the syllogism. In technical terms this means that it must affirm the antecedent, the "if" part of the Major Premise. Denying the antecedent or affirming the consequent, the "then" part of the Major Premise, does not allow a conclusion. So a Minor Premise such as THE WHITE POPULATION REMAINS INTERESTED IN THE CIVIL RIGHTS MOVEMENT denies the antecedent or "if" condition and does not allow the Conclusion THE CIVIL RIGHTS MOVEMENT APPEARS TO BE A VITAL AND VIABLE CAUSE TO WHITE OBSERVERS.

These premises will lead to a valid conclusion:

Major Premise: If the white population loses interest in the Civil Rights Movement then the movement appears to them to be dead.
Minor Premise: The white population has lost interest in the Civil Rights Movement.
Conclusion: The movement appears to them to be dead.

These premises, because the minor premise does not affirm the antecedent, will allow no conclusion:

Major Premise: If the white population loses interest in the Civil Rights Movement then the movement appears to them to be dead.
Minor Premise: The white population remains interested in the Civil Rights Movement.
Conclusion: ?

Conversely, a Minor Premise such as THE CIVIL RIGHTS MOVEMENT APPEARS TO BE A DEAD CAUSE TO WHITE OBSERVERS affirms the consequent, the "then" part of the Major Premise, and does not allow the Conclusion THE WHITE POPULATION HAS LOST INTEREST IN THE CIVIL RIGHTS MOVEMENT. Naturally, it is possible, assuming for the moment that the white population, in fact, believes that the Civil Rights movement is a dead issue, for them to have reached that conclusion for a number of reasons. Our Major Premise does not address *all* the possibilities that are inherent in this complicated situation; it makes a declarative statement about only *one* possibility. If you misunderstand the mechanics of the syllogism's assertions and base an essay on a faulty conclusion or a conclusion improperly drawn, you will only cause your reader to dismiss your attempt at persuasion and your essay will fail.

A *disjunctive* syllogism uses a pattern of either-or reasoning to reach a conclusion. When we create an either-or situation and argue that there are only two possibilities or solutions, we must first be certain that this is precisely the case; that is what makes this form of syllogism particularly tricky. Because life is complicated and at times abounds with seemingly infinite possibilities, we seldom encounter a true either-or situation in which only two solutions exist. In Gould's discussion of evolution, for instance, he points out that creationists regularly take the position that Darwin's concept of evolution is "either a theory or a fact." But, Gould counters, because "facts and theories are different things," it is possible for Darwin's idea to be *both* a fact and a theory. All issues cannot then be resolved by an either-or approach; notice the very big difference between these two Major Premises:

Major Premise 1:   Darwin's concept of evolution is either a fact or a theory.
Major Premise 2:   Darwin's concept of evolution is either a fact or a theory, *but not both*.

They might be diagrammed this way:

Major Premise 1
Darwin's concept of evolution is either a fact or a theory (i.e. it could be either, and some theories might be facts)

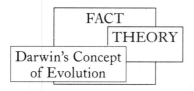

Major Premise 2
Darwin's concept of evolution is either a fact or a theory, *but not both*.

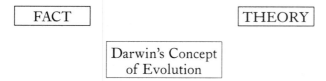

Major Premise 2 establishes a very clear-cut situation, that rare occurrence, a true either-or situation. According to Major Premise 2, Darwin's ideas *must* belong in one category or the other; there is no possibility that the categories overlap. In this case, then, the disjunctive syllogism becomes fairly simple:

Major Premise: Darwin's concept of evolution is either a fact or a theory, *but not both*.
Minor Premise: Darwin's concept of evolution *is* a theory.
Conclusion: Darwin's concept of evolution *is not* a fact.

Without the stipulation that the categories may not overlap, however, the syllogism becomes more complicated. In this situation the Minor Premise must be a negative statement in order for us to reach a valid conclusion.

Major Premise: Darwin's concept of evolution is either a fact or a theory.
Minor Premise: Darwin's concept of evolution is not a theory.
Conclusion: Darwin's concept of evolution is a fact.

An affirmative Minor Premise — DARWIN'S CONCEPT IS A THEORY — does not allow the Conclusion DARWIN'S CONCEPT IS NOT A FACT, because our Major Premise does not state that the categories are mutually exclusive and technically does not rule out the possibility of overlapping conditions.

The creation of mutually exclusive categories is a technique frequently resorted to in faulty arguments, and this strategy is a trap that you as a writer will want to avoid. You want to be certain that you do not create such propositions in your writing, and you particularly want to be wary when such arguments are raised by an opposition you are trying to persuade. To be led into a discussion of an either-or proposition frequently suggests you have been tricked into debating a false dilemma. (For further discussion see Either-Or on p. 326.)

We do not always create formal three-part syllogisms (with a Major Premise, Minor Premise, and Conclusion) when we reason deductively. Frequently our arguments are arranged informally as enthymemes, or compressed syllogisms, where one premise is implicit:

Of course Darwin's concept of evolution is not true; it's just a "theory," isn't it?

Naturally the white population believes the Civil Rights Movement is dead; they lost interest in it years ago.

From both of these examples we can, if we wish, extract a formal three-statement syllogism. And extracting such syllogisms is frequently necessary when we as writers are confronted with an argument that we wish to rebut, for faulty logic can quite readily and easily hide within the compressed structure of an enthymeme. But whether the case is stated with a complete formal syllogism or an implied informal one, the general thinking process — drawing conclusions about specific cases on the basis of statements that are generally valid for classes or groups of examples — is the same.

Finally, it should be pointed out that when one creates a syllogism, that syllogism's conclusion *must* be true *if* the syllogism is validly constructed *and* the syllogism's major and minor premises are true. The following conclusion, for instance, *must* be true:

Major Premise:	All dinosaurs are now extinct.
Minor Premise:	The Stegosaurus was a dinosaur.
Conclusion:	The Stegosaurus is now extinct.

Naturally sometimes problems will occur; as we have seen above, faulty syllogisms can be constructed:

Major Premise:	All dinosaurs are now extinct.
Minor Premise:	The passenger pigeon is extinct.
Conclusion:	The passenger pigeon was a dinosaur.

In this case the error in the syllogism (technically, the lack of a "distributed" middle term) produces a conclusion that is simply false; our common sense tips us off to the problem even if we are not aware of the technical error within the syllogism.

In addition, incorrect premises can be used in validly constructed syllogisms:

> Major Premise: All dinosaurs that ever existed may still be found living in Iowa.
> Minor Premise: The Stegosaurus is a dinosaur that once existed.
> Conclusion: The Stegosaurus may still be found living in Iowa.

Here, the syllogism is correctly constructed and logically valid, but its major premise is not true. The resulting conclusion is complete nonsense; although it is untrue in the real world, however, it is logically sound within the context of the syllogism.

Deduction, because it is an abstract process, is a way of reasoning that may be carried on without empirical validation. We can sit in our favorite chair, with the drapes pulled tightly closed, and reach all manner of conclusions about the world that lies outside our sight. All we need is a supply of premises about that world and we can happily draw our conclusions. Should the premises we are given turn out to be false, our conclusions about life will be incorrect, and perhaps totally bizarre. You will find yourself relying on deductive arguments when you are attempting to draw conclusions about specific cases on the basis of statements that are generally valid for classes or groups of examples. If, for example, you are drafting a proposal that favors the construction of a recycling facility in your community, and you discover that every similar facility in your state has recouped its construction costs within five years, it is legitimate to argue deductively that yours will also. If you are writing a sales letter and you know for a fact that no customer failed to have his auto insurance renewed because of his age, it is reasonable to argue deductively that new customers will not have their policies canceled for this reason either. In all situations like this, of course, the rules governing deductive reasoning must be strictly followed. Here are some questions to keep in mind when using deductive logic:

1. Can your argument be broken down into a formal syllogism? What are your major and minor premises?

2. If you are using a condensed syllogism, or enthymeme, what premises are implied? In condensing your syllogism have you distorted the deductive process in any way?

3. What kind of syllogism are you using in your reasoning? Categorical? Hypothetical? Disjunctive? Is this syllogism correctly presented?

4. Is your syllogism valid? That is, does the conclusion it reaches violate any rules of deductive logic?

5. Is your syllogism true? Is it based on correct information? What are your grounds for knowing this information is true?

6. Has your use of deductive logic strengthened your argument? How has it done so? Would other deductive examples also contribute to the improvement of your argument?

INDUCTION

Induction involves drawing a conclusion after weighing a number of specific cases or considering a body of evidence. This familiar technique is one we frequently use when we create persuasive arguments. When, for example, the National Safety Council concludes that our chances of surviving an automobile accident improve significantly if we fasten our seatbelts, their conclusion is drawn after studying the results of thousands of previous accidents. On the basis of this data — thousands of individual specific cases — a predictive conclusion is drawn. Induction, however, is a less precise way of reaching conclusions than deduction. Why is this so, particularly if, as we have discovered, it is very easy to create valid and therefore apparently true syllogisms that rely on false premises?

Induction, as we have seen, relies on empirical investigation, and the problems inherent in such investigations are easy to demonstrate. In the article "The Feminist Face of Antitechnology," by Samuel Florman, Florman concludes that "most bright young women today do not want to become engineers." Florman, after an hour of sipping sherry with a group of young women at Smith College, first arrived at the idea that young women today view the engineering profession as something that is "beneath them." Naturally, he took these first thoughts and discussed them further with other individuals, modifying his thoughts slightly and adding statistics, facts, and perceptions before presenting his slightly modified thesis. But the critical question we always have to resolve before drawing an inductive conclusion is "How much evidence do we need before we are safe in drawing this conclusion?" Would Florman have been justified in presenting his opinion — that is, in writing his article — after talking to only twenty-five young women at one college? Probably not. But how many students is the proper number? Twenty? Two thousand? Twenty-two thousand? Obviously, the more people Florman speaks with, the more evidence he collects, the more certain he may feel about the validity of his conclusions. But that fact does not tell us when we may safely feel that adequate research has been conducted. How much data will we have to review before we *know* we are safe in drawing a conclusion?

In theory, we can never really *know* for certain; we can only make educated guesses. Philosophers have pointed out that predicting the future on the basis of past experience is always problematic. The "inductive leap," the jump we make from specific evidence to a conclusion always involves a leap of faith, not verifiable truth. Bertrand Russell, for example, has noted that if a turkey could reason inductively, he could conclude, on the basis of his daily experience, that the appearance of the farmer who faithfully feeds him every morning always means a meal. Then the morning before Thanksgiving the farmer shows up with an axe and the turkey is surprised.

A dozen, a hundred, a thousand instances of an event do not necessarily guarantee what will happen on the one thousand and first occurrence of that event. We feel quite certain that when we release a book in mid-air it will fall to the floor with a thud. We even speak authoritatively about the "law" of gravity. Yet, at best, the law of gravity is only a very high degree of probability. We have never seen a book, a pencil, a rock, or an apple fly to the ceiling when released, so we *assume* that such a thing will never happen — surely a reasonable assumption. But few aspects of life have the certainty of gravity, and that is why the debate over many of life's inductive "truths" continues.

The relative "purity" of deductive logic as a manner of reaching conclusions is somewhat misleading, because the premises we rely on in reasoning deductively are generally the result of inductive logic. The assumptions "All dinosaurs are now extinct" and "All pit bulls are dangerous" are conclusions that have been reached after empirical review. The first premise — "All dinosaurs are now extinct" — is somewhat like our conclusions about the "law" of gravity; we have never seen a living dinosaur (aside from the Loch Ness monster, perhaps). The second premise — "All pit bulls are dangerous" — is on much more shaky ground. Is it fair to draw a conclusion about thousands of dogs after reading a few newspaper accounts describing the dogs' alleged ferocity? Pit-bull owners angrily say *no*; many others say *yes*. Unfortunately, no clear guideline will tell us when our inductive leap is justified. If we generalize too quickly, the deductions we may then draw from this generalization will be false, no matter how carefully we construct our syllogisms. So, while deduction and induction are distinct modes of reasoning, we seldom use only one or the other mode to reach conclusions. They work hand in hand and all of us use both methods of reasoning daily.

Many of the conclusions we draw are the result of our applying inductive reasoning. The conclusions you reach in the lab after repeated experimentation, the sales projections you make after considering the records of last year's sales, even your predictions of who will win the next big basketball game — these are all conclusions reached inductively. The accuracy of your own inductive judgments depends on how carefully and thoroughly you have weighed your evidence, and how wisely you make your inductive leap. When you are using inductive logic, consider the following issues:

1. What inductive arguments are you making? How do they contribute to your overall attempt at persuasion?
2. Have you used a sufficient number of examples to make a successful inductive leap? Or, have you generalized too hastily?
3. Is there a high degree of probability in your conclusions? Does the degree of probability you claim reflect the data you have examined? (That is, a claim that applies to thousands of examples should probably not be drawn after examining only a few dozen samples.) Should your claim be qualified slightly or modified on the basis of the data you have examined?

LOGICAL ERRORS

There are several logical errors or fallacies that can entrap an unwary persuasive writer. Here are some common logical fallacies you should watch for and attempt to avoid.

Hasty Generalization

Leaping to an inductive conclusion too quickly. We must always attempt to examine both a sufficient number and a representative sample of cases before we proceed to draw conclusions. The fact that you have had problems with a car stereo you have purchased is important, but it is not conclusive evidence that all the manufacturer's products are flawed. To reach that conclusion you would want to know that many similar car stereos had failed. It would also be helpful if you knew that customers in other parts of the country had been disappointed for some time; then you could assume that a faulty shipment or a temporary manufacturing bug were not to blame. As Lewis Thomas points out in his essay "Humanities and Science," Lord Kelvin, a nineteenth-century British physicist, leapt too quickly when he decided, after reviewing the progress of physics during the nineteenth century, that nearly all the problems of physics had been solved and our knowledge of this discipline was virtually complete. Kelvin thought he had all the facts he needed to make his judgment. But he was wrong.

Ad Hominem

Arguing against the man (or woman). An *ad hominem* argument ignores the case that is being made, and instead focuses on the character of the person who is presenting that case. If, for instance, an angry taxpayer attacks the mayor's annexation plans on the grounds that the mayor owns property whose value could increase if it were annexed, then the taxpayer is arguing *ad hominem* and ignoring the issue of whether the annexation would be beneficial to the community at large.

Bandwagon

An approach based on the assumption that if "everybody else is doing it," you should too. In a democracy we do believe the majority's views should prevail, but the majority's views are not necessarily logically sound. The fact that a particular automobile is "The number one selling import in North America" does not necessarily mean it is the car for you. Numbers are impressive, but popularity and truth are two different things.

Begging the Question

Invoking a circular argument by assuming as true the very premises we hope to prove. The classic example usually cited is the old saw, "Have you stopped beating your wife?" Answering either *yes* or *no* does not deny the fundamental assumption contained in the question. Similarly, the statement "Capital punishment is immoral because executing criminals is wrong!" does not really establish a logical line of reasoning; it simply restates a proposition in slightly different words, something that frequently happens in begging the question.

Equivocation

Misusing language either accidentally or intentionally, usually by confusing the multiple meanings of words. This reasoning, for example, "The best things in life are free, so the United States should abandon all import restrictions and permit free trade," plays on a confusion of meaning. Ignoring for the moment the issue of whether the words of a popular song should be regarded as a serious guide for implementing foreign policy, we can see that the word *free* means "without financial cost" the first time it is used, but it means "unrestrained" in the second part of the sentence. If we are urged to "Obey all laws, particularly the laws of Nature," we should, before we act, remember that *laws* may be both a set of legal rules established by society, and also frequently repeated patterns observed in the natural world. A natural "law" *describes* behavior; a civil "law" attempts to *prescribe* our actions.

Post Hoc, Ergo Propter Hoc

The Latin translates as "after this, therefore because of this." Because one event seems consistently to follow another event, we should not *necessarily* come to believe that the later event is caused by the earlier one. Even if the phone seems to ring every time you get in the bathtub, you cannot necessarily force your friends to call you by taking a bath. The issue here, of course, is consistency as well as the relative connections between the events. If your car's engine seems to sputter and miss on every rainy day, your spark-plug wires or distributor may be cracked and allowing moisture in to cause a misfire. The atmosphere *can* affect your car's performance. On the other hand, if it seems to rain every time you wash your car, it is fairly unlikely you will be able to establish a physical connection that operates in the opposite direction; your car will not affect atmospheric conditions in this way.

Either-Or

An argument that assumes two and only two alternatives are possible. Such arguments, based on disjunctive syllogisms, often mislead by oversimplifying the facts of a situation. For example, an ultimatum — "Either increase the funds for public education or accept the responsibility for an illiterate society" — is frequently presented as an either-or dilemma. The statement "America — love it or leave it!" suggests a clear course of action, but it does not allow Americans the freedom to embrace all possible forms of patriotism.

Non Sequitur

Latin for "it does not follow." There is a sense in which all logical fallacies are *non sequiturs*, because the term applies to arguments with conclusions that do not logically follow. When, for example, we are urged to drink a certain brand of beer "because we only go around once in life," the logic is flawed. We might just as well be told *not* to drink that beer "because we only go around once," or we might decide to use a certain brand of toothpaste, visit the Grand Canyon, or drop out of school for the very same reason; after all, we only go around once.

FACTS AND OPINIONS

When we reason, whether we are doing so inductively or deductively, we build our arguments on evidence. The evidence we use can be either *facts* or *opinions*. The difference between the two is simple but significant. If we say that the Kansas City Royals beat the St. Louis Cardinals, four games to three, in the 1985 World Series, we will have stated a *fact*. If, however, we say that the Royals were the best team in baseball in 1985, or, conversely, that the Cardinals, despite their loss in the Series, were the best team in baseball in 1985, we will be stating an *opinion*. Facts are verifiable, that is, they may be tested or proved. Opinions are not always verifiable; they represent conclusions drawn — sometimes justifiably, sometimes not justifiably — from facts. In this instance it will be easy to look in a record book or almanac and verify that the Royals won the Series in 1985; their victory is a verifiable fact. But how do we go about verifying the "best" overall team? We will not find that statement in our record book. If we decide that the "best" team is always the team that wins the World Series, then we will have to conclude that the Royals were also baseball's best team (although our reasoning here may be circular — see Begging the Question above).

We know, however, that chance or "luck" plays an important part in all sporting events. In Game Six of that World Series, television replays showed that a first base umpire apparently missed a very important call, a call that Cardinal fans, at least, feel robbed them of the game. The Royals won 2–1 and the Series went to a seventh game; a St. Louis victory in this sixth game would have ended the Series and made them the World Champions. Royals fans dispute the importance of this one play and point to the Royals' overwhelming 11–0 victory in the seventh game. So, the issue is not completely clear-cut. Were the Royals the better team, or merely the luckier team? Were both the Cardinals and the Royals the two best teams in their respective leagues, or were they simply the two luckiest teams in their leagues? Or do the best teams, as we sometimes hear, "make their own luck"? Again, the facts here can be verified. The Royals won the Series; the Royals won the seventh game 11–0. The number of hits, the scores, the batting averages, these statistics are facts. The conclusions we draw from these facts, however, are opinions that cannot be verified. Which team was "better," which team was "luckier," which team was "stronger," these issues remain debatable.

FACTS AND STATISTICS

When we deal with statistics and facts, what are sometimes called "hard facts," we want to be certain that we understand what these statistics are measuring, and that they were compiled in a reasonable, objective, and error-free way. A case in point would be the recent questioning of divorce statistics in the United States. For years various researchers have suggested that approximately half of all marriages end in divorce. This conclusion was apparently reached simply by counting the number of marriages each year and comparing it with the number of divorces recorded in the same period. So if in a given community there were 50,000 marriages and 30,000 divorces recorded in a year, the divorce rate for that community was judged to be 60% and it was forecast that 3 out of 5 new marriages would probably fail.

But there is a very real problem with computing these statistics in such a simplistic way, because this system of computing a divorce rate fails to take into account the cumulative nature of the data. Couples who do get divorced do not necessarily get divorced in their first year of marriage, so some of the divorces that are being recorded are stemming from marriages that are five, ten, or even twenty-five years old. Also, couples who do not divorce obviously remain married, but their marriages are not renewed or recorded annually. So if a community continued for a period of time to average 30,000 divorces for every 50,000 weddings, the precise ratio of divorces to married couples would not be 60%, because *each year there are 20,000 couples who remain married* and these couples should be added to the total number of people married at any given time. In the tenth year of this hypothetical survey, for example, there would be 30,000 divorces, 50,000 new marriages, and 180,000 couples (20,000 each year) who had married during the previous nine years *and remained married*. At the end of the tenth year, the 30,000 divorces should be compared to the total number of married couples — 230,000. When this is done the divorce ratio of 60% falls to a ratio of 13%. If the thousands of couples who were married before this hypothetical ten-year survey began are factored in, the divorce rate drops even lower. So how a statistic is arrived at, and precisely what it measures, should be scrutinized carefully. Data and statistics most frequently mislead when they only partly reflect the total issue they purport to measure, as they do in this instance. Most old sayings have more than a grain of truth to them, so when you find yourself attempting to manipulate numbers, remember the ancient saw "Figures don't lie, but any liar can figure." You do not wish to mislead, and, just as important, you don't want others to mislead you. When dealing with statistics and other so-called factual data then, ask the following questions:

1. Is the information you are dealing with factual, or is it based on opinion? Can your data be verified?

2. Have statistics been compiled in an accurate and objective manner? Does anyone stand to gain from a distortion of these statistics?

3. Are the figures being presented oversimplified in any way? Have any of the figures been exaggerated or distorted?

4. Has any of the data been taken out of context? If it has, what are the reasons for this contextual selection?

5. Has there been anything omitted or has any extraneous information been added?

6. Are you satisfied that the data is absolutely complete?

OBSERVATION AND TESTIMONY

Not all factual evidence is statistical; some evidence is gathered by simple observation. If, for example, a courtroom witness states that she saw a suspect leaving the scene of a murder, that testimony must be regarded as factual (assuming that there is absolutely no doubt on the part of the witness and that circumstances were such that she could have seen what she claims to have seen). We must also assume that the witness is sane, that she is telling the truth, and that she has no motives for misreporting what she claims to have seen. Such evidence does not mean that the suspect committed a crime, of course; it is "circumstantial evidence," evidence that pertains to the event being investigated and suggests a possible inference, but evidence that by itself does not establish guilt or innocence. This factual evidence, unlike George Brett's batting average, is not a statistic that we can verify in a record book, but as testimony from a reliable source it can be regarded verifiable.

The incorrect call at first base in Game Six of the 1985 World Series is, to many people, also verifiable. Replays from all angles showed that the batter who was called "safe" by the umpire on the field was apparently "out." But this replay was not necessarily typical, for few television replays are definitive; some sports replays, as the NFL has discovered, may in fact create more controversies than they resolve, leading to the reasonable conclusion that replays cannot always be trusted. And neither can all eyewitnesses. Eyewitness testimony cannot always be proved, but it can be tested. Some dedicated Royals fans will still argue that the replay cameras provided misleading pictures, that their player was safe. If one replay camera shows a player to be out there is always the possibility that the angle of that camera provided a distorted viewpoint. If three cameras show the same results, the likelihood that the player was safe drops dramatically. So personal observation or eyewitness testimony can be regarded as fact, *if* that testimony is carefully tested by attempting to verify the credibility of the witnesses and their ability to attest to what they claim to have observed.

OPINION AND TESTIMONY AS EVIDENCE

Sometimes simply collecting data or recorded observations is not sufficient; sometimes we need to resort to the opinions of experts who can interpret the data for us. When we do turn to such authorities and use their opinions, we need to follow several guidelines.

We always need to be certain that our authority is, in fact, an expert, an expert who does have the experience or training necessary to render a qualified judgment. Here common sense is a fairly reliable guide. Your roommate's notion of whether the ozone layer is in trouble may or may not be relevant. The opinion of a high school chemistry teacher might be more important, but the conclusions of an atmospheric physicist would probably be the strongest evidence you could cite. We also should attempt to find experts who are impartial and objective. Many people, for instance, remain skeptical about the safety of nuclear energy as a power source because most of the authorities who assure us that nuclear reactors are safe are scientists who have committed themselves to careers in nuclear engineering. If the nuclear industry collapses, the argument goes, these scientists will find themselves out of work. So naturally they will tell us reactors are safe. On the other hand, of course, if we do not accept the opinions of those who are admittedly the experts in the field, whose opinions should we accept? Here again, common sense is sometimes our only guide. The opinion of a scientist employed by a power company that is building a reactor *may* be less valid than the opinion of a government scientist employed by the Nuclear Regulatory Commission. For this reason, the hiring of outside consultants, experts who are judged to have nothing to gain or lose by the opinions they render, has become a common practice on most technical projects today.

To be sure, experts, even objective consultants, sometimes disagree, and carefully weighing the credentials of authorities does not always tell us whom we should trust. Sometimes we have to consult other authorities and decide whether sheer numbers will give us any guidance. If the majority of experts in the field are in agreement, we may feel more comfortable accepting the majority's viewpoint. Sometimes we have to become experts ourselves, and see whether we can detect any weaknesses in the arguments or evidence experts provide. It is standard courtroom practice, after all, for attorneys on each side of a case to schedule the appearance of expert witnesses; naturally the witnesses who testify always agree with the attorneys who have arranged their appearances, and the opinions of the experts on one side are usually diametrically opposed to those of the experts on the other side. This does not mean these witnesses are untrustworthy or corrupt; it simply means that they have interpreted data differently. But if we are sitting on the jury of one of these cases, we must decide which expert is "right." Our decision will probably be in favor of the expert who represents the more credible and logical case; frequently that case is the one that most completely accounts for all data, even the data that seems to be at odds with the expert's conclusions.

We need to ascertain that our experts are always experts in the fields in which they are being cited. Albert Einstein, for instance, was universally claimed to be a genius in the field of physics, but it is also common today to hear Einstein's views on world peace quoted. Jonathan Schell, for example, in his article on nuclear disarmament entitled "The Choice," alludes to Einstein's position on this issue. Einstein was certainly entitled to express himself on a topic of global importance, an issue that ultimately may involve all the inhabitants of this planet, but his overwhelming knowledge of physics did not necessarily make him a statesman, philosopher, or political scientist, and the opinions of this Nobel Prize winner on this particular topic are not necessarily more important than those of any other lay person.

Another Nobel Prize winner who has spoken out in recent years is William Shockley, who shared the prize for physics in 1956. Shockley, whose work led to the development of transistors, later went on the college lecture circuit to discuss not physics but genetics. Shockley's views on genetic differences among races were loudly condemned by many scientists, who called them blatantly racist. Shockley clearly had a notion of how researchers collect and analyze data, so his conclusions could not automatically be dismissed as the flawed reasoning of an incompetent thinker. Still, most who heard and read his opinions decided that Shockley had strayed too far out of his field to be taken seriously. He had a Nobel Prize, they concluded, but he was wrong.

Every day, of course, advertising asks us to accept the testimony of other "experts." Actors, actresses, and sports figures regularly endorse products and suggest that we should buy the products they have endorsed. There may be a certain logic in buying a tennis racquet that a famous tennis professional uses, but should we also then buy the same brand of soft drink she claims to be her favorite? Or fly the airline she prefers? Should we also take her advice before buying a computer, an automobile, or fingernail polish? Most of us would probably say *no*, but it is a fact of life that celebrity endorsements do sell products.

It is quite common to cite expert testimony when you are crafting persuasive prose. Whether or not your prose is effective may turn upon your skill in choosing someone whose expertise really is valid. When you rely on testimony and opinion, ask yourself:

1. Whose testimony are you using? What does this witness have to gain or lose by this testimony? What degree of reliability does this testimony have?

2. If the testimony you wish to use is coming from an objective witness, what are the other credentials of this witness? That is, is this witness an authority in the area in which he or she is being cited?

3. Have you misused or misquoted your authority in any way? Is the testimony you are citing in any way distorted by circumstance or external facts? Can you, by adjusting for these circumstances, use this testimony in a meaningful way?

FOCUS . . . .

SUGGESTIONS FOR WRITING

1. Select an editorial from a local newspaper. Examine the argument that underlies it. It is logical? Does it employ inductive or deductive reasoning? What fundamental premises does it reason from? Write a brief analysis describing its persuasive techniques.

2. In 1989 there was a flurry of excitement in the scientific community about a process called "cold fusion," a process that, if it worked, would possibly end the world's energy crisis. After months of testing scientists had not reached a clear consensus on the success of this particular cold fusion technique. Many laboratories had attempted to replicate the original experiments — and failed; some laboratories reported at least partial success. So far at least it would seem that the scientists who did the original experiments may have made their inductive leap — the jump from data to conclusions — too quickly. Look around you at inductive conclusions that have been drawn, from theories about the causes of cancer to theories about the existence of flying saucers and interplanetary life. Draw up two lists, one that contains inductive conclusions you find acceptable, the other containing conclusions you think have been made too quickly. What

similarities do you find among the items that appear in each list? What conclusions can you draw about the nature of the items in each list? Write an essay entitled "They Leapt Too Quickly," about the conclusions that you have placed in your second list.

3. Examine the list of logical errors given in this chapter, then draft an argument that employs as many of these errors as you can include. Feel free to include faulty deductive syllogisms where you can fit them in. Exchange your argument with a classmate and try to identify the logical errors in her essay.

4. Look through the advertisements in several magazines. Collect the ones that (1) use the testimony of "experts," or (2) rely on the use of statistics or other "scientific evidence." Because it is presumably illegal to create an advertisement that is blatantly false or simply lying, determine how much truth is conveyed by these advertisements. What claims does each advertisement actually make? What claims are suggested (but not actually made) by each?

14 ▸ Emotional Appeals

When you wish to appeal to your audience's rational side, when you believe that an argument can be won on the basis of the facts of the case alone, or when you are confronted by those who insist on a careful and sensible presentation of the data involved, then you need to employ a logical appeal. Since Aristotle, however, writers have realized that not all arguments can be won with appeals to logic alone. Appeals that touch our emotions are common and effective, but generally we feel suspicious about adopting strictly emotional appeals because there seems to be something slightly unscrupulous about influencing someone emotionally rather than intellectually. An "emotional reaction" is usually regarded as a sign of weakness in our culture today, and we tend to regard those who attempt to play on our emotions as manipulative and perhaps even dishonest. Certainly we believe that those who attempt to sway our emotions rather than our intellects have their own interests — and not ours — in mind. Advertising, for example, frequently employs emotional appeals, and clearly these advertisers hope to convince us to buy their products; they have designs on our checkbooks.

Perhaps our suspicion of these emotional appeals stems from the fear that advertising may encourage us to act against our better judgment, that we will lose control of our will, that we will be sold something we have no need for and do not want. Such suspicions may be well-founded, for assuredly all of us have been encouraged to buy a product, or attend a movie, or vote for a certain candidate, and later felt that we had been misled into making a hasty decision. Yet it cannot be denied that emotional appeals have their place and such appeals should not be scorned out of hand. All emotional appeals do not attempt to mislead or cheat us, and all who use these appeals are not trying to take advantage of us.

In times of crisis, whether that crisis is an oil shortage, a world war, a great depression, or a period of runaway inflation, governments have attempted to arouse feelings of patriotism, duty, and responsibility among their citizens. They do not always rouse these emotions by appealing to the intellect. For example, the famous World War I recruiting poster showing a determined Uncle Sam pointing his finger and exclaiming "Uncle Sam Wants You!" can be scarcely be regarded as a logical appeal. Charities attempt to touch our emotions to raise money to fight disease or world hunger; environmental groups hope that their appeals will help end pollution or save endangered species. All of these causes attempt to enlist our support by appealing to our sense of what is "right," and our determination of what is right and just is not always arrived at by statistics and facts.

In 1940, for instance, when Great Britain needed to rally her forces after a hurried retreat from Dunkirk, France, Winston Churchill made a memorable speech to Parliament. In his oration he assured England that the fight was far from over:

> We shall go on to the end. We shall fight in France, we shall fight on the seas and the oceans, we shall fight with growing confidence and growing strength in the air, we shall defend our island, whatever the cost may be. We shall fight on the beaches, we shall fight on the landing grounds, we shall fight in the fields and in the streets, we shall fight in the hills; we shall never surrender. . . .

Churchill's ringing statement skillfully included several strategies that appealed to the emotions of those who would hear it and read it:

1. He used a repetitive, parallel structure that suggested order and a systematic response, playing down the heroic but rather chaotic and disorganized incident at Dunkirk.

2. He stressed an absolute commitment of British strength and willpower. Phrases such as "to the end," "whatever the cost," and "never surrender" do not imply a halfhearted effort. Although for many of us the distinction between *shall* and *will* when used with the first or third person has been lost, it was not lost on Churchill's audience. Because the terms connote slightly different meanings in formal usage, we *will* fight did not carry for them the imperative force of we *shall* fight. *Will* would have connoted an *intention* to fight, whereas *shall* suggested an *order* to do so. The difference between the two words is the difference between a hope and a command.

3. Churchill's language sketched a future that had the appearance of fact. He did not say they would *try* to defend the English beaches, or *try* to return to France, he said England *would* do so; *try* sometimes suggests *fail*, so that was a word with negative connotations in this situation, a word to be avoided. After all, his country had already been *trying*, and had not been entirely successful so far. Churchill also stated that England would "fight with growing confidence and strength in the air," a prediction without much substance at the time, but a prediction he hoped would become a self-fulfilling prophecy. The hope that the entire situation described in the speech would come to pass, a situation delineated as though it would become a factual reality, lies at the heart of Churchill's appeal.

When Churchill returned to the House of Commons a few weeks after his famous "We shall never surrender" speech, he hoped once again to rally his countrymen by touching their hearts, not their heads. Churchill succeeded and his plea became an emotional touchstone for millions of dispirited Britons:

> Let us therefore brace ourselves to our duties, and so bear ourselves that, if the British Empire and its Commonwealth last for a thousand years, men will still say: "This was their finest hour."

Churchill's remarks did not focus on the reality of the war, the suffering, the deprivation, the loss of life; they did not give orders or depict the immediate future as did his Dunkirk comments. Instead his words looked far into the oncoming centuries and offered Britons something few people encounter in their lifetimes, an opportunity to experience greatness, an opportunity to be a part of that "finest hour." Such an opportunity is not subject to logical analysis.

In the readings of this section, you will find Edward Kennedy's speech to the Democratic Convention in 1980. Kennedy, although he was not facing a crisis as severe as a world war, was in a situation roughly similar to Churchill's, and he employs several similar strategies in his speech. Kennedy, who had been regarded as a strong potential candidate for the presidency for several years, attempted to wrest the nomination from the incumbent, President Jimmy Carter. He failed, and when he appeared before the convention after this defeat he needed to do several things in his speech. First, he needed to accept his defeat, bring his campaign to a close and thank those who had supported his candidacy. Second and more important, however, he also needed to rally the convention delegates (and the millions of potential voters watching on television) behind the party's nominee, President Carter. Finally, after flirting with presidential politics for several years, Kennedy had apparently decided that this quest was over for him. Although he would continue to have a strong influence on national politics, Kennedy was seemingly bowing out of any future presidential races. In his speech he needed to close the door on that option.

In his attempt to forge unity out of diversity, Kennedy begins with a slight joke and immediately puts his own personal campaign aside until the end of his speech. He begins to speak about a concept that presumably all Democrats in the hall can agree on — their party — and what he calls "its cause" and its "fundamental Democratic principles." Like Churchill, he relies on a parallel structure within his speech, repeatedly returning to certain phrases — "Let us pledge," "We can be proud," "To all those." And Kennedy combines that repetition with particular images to strengthen the message he hopes to communicate. He establishes that they all share a common adversary — the Republicans and their nominee, Ronald Reagan — and then conjures up the image of an elephant turning a handspring and falling flat on its back. Having identified these foes all Democrats have in common, Kennedy hammers away at them on different issues, returning to the same key phrases over and over — "The same Republicans," "that nominee is no friend" — to add force to the negative message he wants associated with the Republicans, while at the same time stating his own positive theme — the Democrats are the party of "new hope" — which he weaves through the second half of his speech.

At the close of his address Kennedy returns to his own supporters. Again he uses parallelism — "I have listened" — to emphasize order and unity as he describes a diverse collection of citizens he has met, supporters whom he describes as his "golden friends." The "golden friends" imagery signals an even more emotional conclusion as Kennedy mixes poetry with politics. He characterizes himself as the representative of these nameless citizens who are battling against "the ravages of inflation," adopting an almost biblical tone ("in their name, I have come here to speak for them") as he asks the delegates in the hall to support them by supporting the ideals he has outlined and allowing "new hope" to flower. Like Churchill in his "finest hour" speech, he closes by looking into the future ("And someday, long after this convention . . . may it be said . . . that we kept the faith . . .that we found our faith again") and giving delegates a chance to participate in a moment of greatness. To complete his exit from the presidential arena, Kennedy chooses some lines from Tennyson's "Ulysses," a poem about a leader and hero who refuses to retire from life's adventures even though he is no longer king. Although the lines ostensibly refer to the Democratic party, which will presumably continue to strive, the connections between Kennedy, the Kennedy legend (notice the almost offhand reference to his brothers), and the retired king were obvious to the convention delegates. Kennedy's address brought forth a response some observers felt was more powerful than the convention's reaction to their actual nominee; it was an eloquent tour de force.

PERSUASIVE PRINCIPLES

If we look at the persuasive addresses of Kennedy and Churchill we can identify within them a common agenda. That agenda consists of (1) *establishing a scapegoat*, (2) *finding a common ground* on which the speaker and his audience can agree, a principle with which they both identify, and (3) *unifying* the speaker and the audience by removing any divisions that might exist between them and stressing their mutual identification with common principles. For Kennedy, establishing a scapegoat means that he must create a "straw man," an adversary he can easily knock down. He does this by citing Republican policies and quoting controversial statements made by Reagan in order to characterize the Republicans and their candidate as insensitive and indifferent to the real problems facing the country. We have only a few paragraphs from Churchill's speeches in this text, but obviously it was not very difficult for him to create an adversary; his foes had already established themselves (by declaring war) and were easily identifiable.

Churchill chooses the concept of the survival of the British Empire as the common principle which presumably all Britons will support (not an economic issue or a political principle which individuals might disagree about); Kennedy selects "old values that will never wear out," values that are difficult for anyone to oppose, such as supporting education, and pits these values against evils that the adversaries allegedly support, such as tax breaks for the wealthy ("instead of shutting down classrooms, let us shut off tax shelters . . . instead of cutting out school lunches, let us cut off tax subsidies . . ."). Both orators rely heavily on the use of personal pronouns to draw their audience into their camp, suggesting an identification with their audience and implying an acknowledged unity — "Let *us* therefore brace *ourselves*. . . ," "Democrats can be proud that *we* chose a different course" (italics added). Kennedy flatters his audience when he addresses his "golden friends" (he does not distinguish these from others who might not have supported his campaign), and when he catalogs the diverse groups "in every state where I have been" who support him, he suggests that he represents the majority of Americans, perhaps in fact "all those who inhabit our land, from California to the New York Island, from the Redwood Forest to the Gulfstream waters." What kind of individual would not want to go along with these speakers, would want to resist identifying herself with these noble goals? Neither writer says so, but presumably those who would not be persuaded must be petty or ignoble individuals, creatures so bound up in their own selfishness that they would flee from what another political leader who was attempting to rally support called "a rendezvous with destiny." The emotional effect of such appeals far outweighs the power of the logical facts and details on which the appeals are based.

You rely on emotional appeals when facts and statistics alone just will not do. When you turn to an emotional appeal, consider the following questions:

1. Is this argument being created for a selfish aim? Or an unselfish cause? Who stands to gain if your argument is successful? Who stands to lose?

2. Can you define your opposition? Can this person, group, or movement be identified and labeled for your audience? Can this group become your "scapegoat"?

3. Do you share a common ground with your audience? With what principles or positions does your reader identify? Can these principles be stressed in your argument?

4. Can you align yourself with your audience by removing any division that may exist between you? On what points can your audience identify with you? What can you do to encourage that process of identification?

PERSUASIVE LANGUAGE

Language and Reality

There is one sense in which language always distorts reality. Language, whether it is sound resonating in the air, ink spots on a page, or dots of phosphorus light on a cathode tube, is always one step removed from the world of "reality," that is, the world whose presence we perceive through our senses, the world of tables, chairs, traffic lights, and thunderstorms. Because language is a symbolic system that has been *created* in order to describe and define reality, it does not always align exactly with the world we are using it to describe. It cannot be as exact as we would like it to be, because language comes in "packets," individual words that are arranged into sentences, and reality often exists as an infinite series of gradations. A variety of phenomena, from faint foggy mist to violent downpours, go under the single label "rain." Additional terms such as "showers" or "light showers" or "sprinkles" create some categories to help us describe and define the weather, but our distinctions and our vocabulary can sometimes break down when we attempt to describe precipitation precisely, as anyone who has spent a summer in London can attest. We have often heard that Eskimos have many more words for snow than we do. This should not be a surprising linguistic difference; establishing more specific categories and distinctions than ours is extremely important if these people are to communicate to each other how to survive in a world dominated by frigid weather, ice, and snow. If our survival depended on staying dry, we would probably need more specific language also. As it is, we can put up our umbrellas and continue to stroll along in a fairly imprecise linguistic fashion.

Weather is not the only place where our language "breaks down" or fails to delineate reality precisely. The spectrum of color extends fluidly without gradations, yet our language comes only in packets. So we sometimes debate whether a flower is red or orange, whether a couch is yellow or green, and all we are doing is arguing about which language packet applies. The flower and the couch are the colors they are, but the language we are trying to align with the reality does not fit neatly. And so it goes with all descriptions of motion and time. (Time, for example, we attempt to describe in terms of packets called "seconds" or "microseconds"; we then lump these packets into categories called "past," "present," and "future" — categories we become quite vague about if we are asked to explain them in any detail.)

When a child runs crying to her mother complaining that her brother has "thrown a rock at her," we would seem to be dealing with a tangible reality (assuming she is telling the truth), until her brother angrily denies the charge, saying he only "tossed a pebble near her." The reality of this situation has suddenly become very slippery. Was the missile in question a "rock" or a "pebble"? How big does a pebble need to be before it becomes a "rock" or a "stone"? The issue here is not which child is telling the truth about the incident, but the relationship between the physical event (which took place without linguistic interpretation) and the interpretation that is placed on this physical event when someone attempts to discuss it. Was the "rock" tossed, thrown, bounced, flipped, heaved, aimed, or hurled? Even if the mother had witnessed the incident she would not *know*; she would only know what she had *seen* (the reality) and then she would have to choose what seemed to be the most appropriate verb to describe the reality. She would, in other words, be trying to align her language and vocabulary with the incident her senses had perceived. The vocabulary she chooses, when she relates the story to her husband, might well determine the unfortunate brother's punishment, because that language will become the father's view of the incident, the father's reality. Ultimately, you see, we never really speak of reality; we simply create a linguistic reality, a web of words that approximately reflects the physical universe. Look around you now. There is reality; it is experienced. Attempt to describe that reality and you begin to weave your linguistic web, a reflective model of the world fabricated from language. Your powers of persuasion are to some degree affected by how well you can manipulate this web.

Concrete and Abstract Language

As a rule, when we use *concrete language* we are using words that have specific referents. When we are trying to encourage a toddler to talk, for example, we can name and then hold up a ball or a stuffed bear. The words directly relate to the specific tangible objects and may in this context be considered fairly concrete. *Abstract language*, on the other hand, names or describes intellectual or spiritual concepts, things we cannot see or touch such as *freedom*, *romanticism*, or *existentialism* (things we have no business discussing with a toddler anyhow).

This simple distinction does not explain all there is to know about abstract and concrete language, however, because the terms are not absolutes; there are degrees of abstraction. When, for example, a surgeon asks for *clamp forceps*, she is asking for a particular two-pronged instrument that will lock together and may be used to compress a blood vessel; if she asks for *obstetric forceps* or *dressing forceps*, she will get something quite different. If she simply asks for *forceps*, a more abstract general term that applies to nearly a dozen various gadgets used to grip or hold, she will probably be handed nothing at all until she chooses language that is more specific. The term *forceps* is more abstract than the term *clamp forceps*, and the term "gripping gadget" is more abstract yet because it includes, presumably, needlenose pliers and monkey wrenches. All of these objects fit into the more abstract category of "tools," and all are part of what may be the highest abstractive category — "things." In the context of teaching a toddler to talk, the word *ball* may be an example of fairly safe concrete language, but the word may also apply to a number of smaller spherical objects (not all of which are perfectly round) that are used in athletics, as well as to any large ball-shaped object (such as a water tower or the sun), whether or not that object actually bounces or rolls.

Metaphor

"In the infancy of society," the poet Shelley wrote, "every author is necessarily a poet, because language itself is poetry." Shelley's comments are true, although we seldom stop to consider the magnitude of their meaning. When language is being shaped, because it is one stage removed from reality, it must rely on comparisons and analogies — metaphors — in order to express what is otherwise inexpressible. When we use a metaphor, after all, we are speaking of one thing in terms of another, attempting to get a handle on a slippery piece of reality. Frequently those slippery pieces are abstractions, concepts that are difficult to visualize without comparing them to something we already can see, experience, and know. These abstractions do not have to be terribly lofty and complicated — like the concept of transcendentalism — for us to need metaphors. For example, mornings can "drag," or they can "fly by." We can be feeling "low," or "high as a kite," or "walking on air." Many metaphors such as these that we use every day are what we call "dead" metaphors; that is, we really do not think of them as metaphors at all. Saying that our morning "limped by" may be more original — and therefore more noticeable — than saying the morning "crawled," but mornings that "crawl," "creep," "drag," and "speed" are also metaphorical in their nature, whether we notice the poetry in our language or not.

Is it possible to remove all metaphors from our language, or even most of the metaphors? Probably not, for the metaphors have become fundamental to our language. Love is something we *fall into*, like we fall into a pit. Sometimes, unfortunately, we *fall out* of it, like we fall out of a tree. Fun is something we can have *loads of*; trouble is something we can *get into* and, fortunately, *get out of*, just like getting in and out of our automobiles. Metaphors are something we *use*, just like we use tools; the number of metaphors *employed* in the *construction* of these paragraphs, and our dependence *on* them *in* our everyday conversation may be *unsettling*, but the fact is we would be *stuck* without them.

What is important for us as persuasive writers is not eliminating metaphors, because that is impossible; we want to learn to use them and not become entrapped by them. Before we acquiesce to the notion that "it's a jungle out there," we should explore the validity of the metaphor. And before we agree that "the country needs an experienced leader at its helm," we should decide whether these rather firmly anchored United States are very much like a ship setting a course across the uncertain surface of the sea. Are we really "working our way up" in "our climb to the top," or do we only speak about it that way? Is "life in the fast lane" getting to us? Do we need to "stop and smell the roses"? Or only "wake up and smell the coffee"? Before we act or react, we need to be positive that we understand the shaping power of the language that is being used to describe and create our concepts, and change that language if it seems appropriate to do so; we want to be certain that we are controlling the metaphors, and they are not controlling us.

Denotation and Connotation

When we speak of the *denotations* of a word, we are talking about what the word specifically means, what the word stands for or is "pointing to" in the real world. The word *aardvark* denotes a furry African anteater largely unfamiliar to most of us unless we are perusing the first page of the dictionary and stumble across a definition and description. Words do not always denote only one thing, however; the word *football*, for instance, refers both to the leather oblate spheroid used to play the game and the game itself.

When we speak of the *connotations* of a word, we are not talking about what the word means or "points to," we are talking about what the word suggests or implies. For most of us, the word *aardvark* probably has few connotations. Perhaps if we had raised aardvarks for a living we would have a soft spot in our hearts for them; or if we had ever been attacked by an aardvark that ran amuck we might now be slightly suspicious or fearful of them. In these cases the word *aardvark* could have strong positive or negative connotations for us, suggesting love and affection or (instead) terror and fear. Chances are, however, the word *aardvark*, if it connotes anything, only suggests something bizarre or unusual, something so odd it may in fact be humorous. We react, if at all, to the strange sound of the word and the laughable look of the creature so designated. Connotatively the word is virtually neutral.

Football, however, is a word with which we are all familiar. For those who love the sport the word may conjure up impressions of autumn, excitement, crowds, bands, color, and parties. For others who are lukewarm about the game the word suggests long weekends when college and professional teams dominate the television schedules, creating a kind of continuous game that begins each Saturday afternoon and only ends late on Monday night. For those who have played the game seriously the word may suggest complicated playbooks, long workouts, numerous injuries, and frequent pain. For others who only bet on the games the word can connote statistics, point spreads, odds, and money (either lost or won). In short, everything we associate with the sport of football can be associated with the word *football*; its connotations are numerous.

Language contains many emotionally charged words, words that suggest the desirable or undesirable. *Clean* has very positive connotations, as does *fresh*. So we are frequently told about detergents that will make our wash smell "fresh" (even the same old socks), a term that may apply to vegetables and other produce but is not particularly appropriate for clothing, or soft drinks that have a "new, clean taste," whatever that is (toothpaste and chewing gum can apparently have it too). Whenever a word's connotations become too unpleasant, it is always possible, in fact desirable, to replace the unpleasant term with one that seems to connote something more lofty, technical, or refined. The company that hauls away our garbage first became an expert in "sanitation," but now is involved only in the rather precise sounding business of "waste management." Hairdressers, who are masters of transformation, first made themselves over into "beauticians," but have since restyled themselves into "cosmetologists," a title suggestive of white lab coats and long hours toiling in research. Everyone knows that "undertakers" had to become "morticians" to sidestep the connotation of being merely "gravediggers." But the more scientific title of "mortician" in turn carried a faint whiff of embalming fluid about it, so the morticians responded by metamorphosing into "funeral directors," a title that suggests something both administrative and vaguely social; it would seem to be a job that has very little to do with embalming and burying dead bodies, and that misperception is exactly what funeral directors intend.

Using Language Persuasively

The ability of language to affect our emotions makes it a powerful persuasive tool, a tool that we can both use and have used against us. When we pick up a newspaper or magazine, when we turn on the television or radio, we find emotional linguistic appeals lying in wait for us. In the presidential campaign of 1988, for example, the Republican candidate, George Bush, repeatedly made the charge that the Democratic candidate was "nothing but a liberal." Clearly the term *liberal* is not being used denotatively here, to define a particular body of beliefs that might be contrasted with another body of beliefs that could be labeled *conservative*. The Republicans hoped that the word *liberal* carried many negative connotations for voters — suggestions of runaway spending, massive welfare programs, and spiraling inflation. To acknowledge he *was* a *liberal* was judged to be a dangerous thing for a Democratic candidate to do. Because of *equivocation* (see Logical Errors) the denotative sense of the word could become overwhelmed by the more powerful pejorative connotations being stressed in the campaign. In the 1964 Republican campaign, for example, Barry Goldwater said in his nomination speech that "Extremism in the defense of liberty is no vice." It was very easy for Democrats to take that word *extremism* and then make much out of what an *extremist* might do in the White House. Whatever Goldwater had hoped to denote by the word, the connotations of it helped cost him the election. And in 1988, a desperate Michael Dukakis, behind in the polls, eventually did declare that he in fact was a liberal — and proud of it — hoping that the label would denote an ideology and rally those who believed in that ideology. Dukakis, however, like Goldwater, did not seem to be able to shed the negative connotations of the label.

Or, to cite an example from another facet of American life, moviemaking, we can look at the firestorm that surrounded the theatrical release of a controversial film, *The Last Temptation of Christ*. The movie, which purported to focus on the humanity of Christ, drew a great deal of criticism from various religious organizations, most of whose members admitted they had never seen the film and did not intend to do so. When one television evangelist was asked how he could be so negative about a movie he had never seen, he replied, "I don't need to open a sewer to know that it stinks." His response employed several persuasive techniques. It begged the question, suggested a metaphorical comparison, and counted on pejorative connotations to evoke a emotional response. His "answer" to the question was really no logical answer at all, but it may have persuaded many listeners to agree with him because it simply "sounded right."

All appeals, both those that are logical and emotional, are constructed from language. Because language is a complicated subject, keep in mind these questions:

1. Does your overall use of language effectively further your appeal? How does it do so?

2. Is your language concrete or abstract? Are there places where your terms might be made more specific or concrete? Are there places where you are too specific?

3. What metaphors do you use? Are any of these "dead" metaphors? What does your choice of metaphors suggest about your subject? Would changing the metaphors create a different atmosphere for your topic? Would changing your metaphors improve your argument?

4. Would changing your metaphors cause you to see or understand your topic differently?

5. How have you used denotative and connotative language? Do key words connote the impressions you want? Would altering some terms create a different impression in your reader's mind? Would altering key terms cause him to change his view of your subject? Would altering these terms cause him to change his attitude towards your argument?

FOCUS · · · · · · · · · · · · ·
SUGGESTIONS FOR WRITING

1. Review your journal for ideas you can return to. Are there issues you examine or comment on repeatedly? What is there about these issues that causes you to return to them more than once?

2. What are some causes you feel strongly about, issues that you eagerly support? What are some causes you do *not* feel strongly about, issues you vehemently oppose? What do these issues, either the ones you support or the ones you oppose, have in common?

3. If you could have a private audience with the president, what would you want to say to him? What changes would you like to see made in government that might affect our society as a whole? What other political figure might you like to speak with? What would you have to say to this person?

4. Turn to a newspaper or newsmagazine and examine political speeches or political statements for the use of connotative language. In general, the more controversial a political policy is, the more likely it is to be surrounded with connotative language intended to slant public opinion. (The United States invasion of Panama in December of 1989 was called "Operation Just Cause," for example.) Write an essay describing how a particular politician uses language to shape opinion about a specific issue or policy.

5. As noted above, certain words — such as "clean" or "fresh" — seem to connote positive qualities no matter whether they are used to describe detergent or tomatoes. Recently another word — "light" (sometimes spelled "lite") became popular in advertising also, and was used to describe beer, TV dinners, and shampoo. The word "system" has also become a popular descriptor; mechanical pencils are described as "writing systems" and there is even one children's cereal on the market that describes itself as a "cereal system" (honest!). Scan advertisements for these words or other popular adjectives and make a list of them. Then write an essay on one of these words that attempts to explain both what the word denotes, and what it seems to connote to advertisers.

15 ▶ Ethical Appeals

PRESENTING THE FACTS

Traditionally, the persuasive writing we do has sometimes been labeled *argumentative writing* rather than *persuasive writing*, because persuasion is a term associated with an appeal to emotion. *Argumentative writing*, on the other hand (according to this definition, at least), avoids emotional appeals and presents the facts — the argument — without (it is hoped) distortion. The label *argumentative writing* can be misleading, however, for it suggests a debate or confrontation — resolving an issue that perhaps has a right and a wrong side. What this term connotes does not always accurately reflect the situation, for an issue can sometimes be resolved in a number of ways, and none of these resolutions will really be "right" or "wrong." Some resolutions will simply be preferable or more reasonable than others, and those are the persuasive appeals that are likely to sway a reader. The distinction between *persuasive* and *argumentative* writing is useful for us, however, because it reflects an ethical dilemma central to much persuasive writing. That dilemma is simply put: How can one write persuasively while remaining strictly truthful? Does a writer who is committed to a strictly factual presentation of material have any options when he is presenting a piece of writing he hopes will affect the behavior or ideas of others?

METHODS OF EMPHASIS: REPETITION, PROPORTION, AND POSITION

The answer is *yes*, a writer who is committed to the facts does have options when he is attempting to create persuasive prose, but it has to be a qualified *yes*. The principal technique to employ involves the *emphasis* of data or information. There are several ways to achieve this emphasis. You can emphasize a point by *repetition* of that point. Naturally, if you repeat something often enough your reader will begin to notice. At the same time, however, if you repeat something too much your reader will stop paying attention and you will lose his interest. *Repetition* can be a technique that backfires and therefore should be used carefully.

A second way to achieve emphasis is through *proportion*. By expanding and elaborating on those points in your argument that are particularly strong, and, conversely, by discussing only briefly those aspects that do not help your case (or that damage your case), you will build a strong persuasive argument. Here also caution must be exercised. Expansion can lead to repetition, and excessive repetition might be counterproductive. You must also remember your commitment to the facts. If your presentation contains negative points, you do not want to emphasize them. At the same time it could be less than honest to ignore these points completely. Depending on the seriousness of this negative information, it might also be misleading to "bury" it in a footnote and then ease your conscience by telling yourself you dealt fairly with the issue.

In general you should not be afraid to include negative information in your persuasive writing. You want to appear to be a writer who is presenting an objective case (even if you yourself are very subjective about the issue you are debating), and by omitting certain obvious information you will not appear to be objective. Including negative information makes your argument seem more impartial and fair. We tend to be suspicious, after all, of people who acknowledge no weaknesses or flaws; we seldom trust the advocate who urges us to "trust him 100%." In addition, and perhaps paradoxically, presenting negative information concisely, but frankly, can make your argument appear even stronger. Your persuasive presentation acknowledges the existence of such negative evidence (which also makes the presentation seem more thorough and complete), yet in the face of such evidence it still vigorously argues for its course of action. If you believe so strongly in spite of this evidence, then this information itself must truly be inconsequential and should surely be dismissed out of hand.

The third way of achieving emphasis is through *position*. The order in which you arrange your pieces of evidence for presentation may be as important as the evidence itself. The exact guidelines on how to arrange information will vary with the format and purpose of your writing. Sometimes as a writer you are asked to place your most important information first; sometimes you are asked to begin with your least important evidence, and place your most important information last. Sometimes you will be urged to put certain kinds of information in the middle — the middle of a letter, the middle of a paragraph, the middle of a sentence. Although all these variations might seem confusing at first, ordering your information in the most effective sequence is mostly a matter of understanding the purpose of your format, and then adapting your evidence to that format. Of the three methods of achieving emphasis, emphasizing through *position* is usually preferable, because it allows the most objectivity. A careful arrangement of information allows you to be persuasive without any alteration of facts, to be convincing without any distortion of the truth.

CREDIBILITY AND AUDIENCE

We have all been in arguments we could never win, arguments when we and our opponents were locked into contradictory positions, angrily debating, perhaps even shouting, neither side giving an inch and both sides rapidly getting nowhere. When this happens no persuasion is taking place, and no persuasion is likely to take place however logical the case may be. If we want to win such an argument we need to understand that we are sometimes persuaded by what is called the tone or "rhetorical stance" of a writer or speaker. As noted above, the advocate who claims to have all the answers and wants all of our trust is someone we tend to suspect. We do not wish to be told that what we believe is foolish or wrongheaded, and someone who begins an argument by telling us that is not likely to win us over; he will simply arouse our antagonism.

Credibility

A skillful writer hopes to present a reasonable and measured argument, free from exaggeration and hyperbole. An important persuasive strategy is to present yourself as a reasonable person with good intentions, a person of common sense, integrity, and logic. You do not wish to appear to be threatening and uncompromising, for such an attitude may produce a similar response on the part of your audience. If you appear to be trustworthy, then your audience may be induced to accept your opinions. If you seem to be narrow-minded and uncompromising, your opponent will either ignore you completely or engage you in a shouting match. In either case your chance of having your views accepted is eliminated. Look at how Martin Luther King, Jr., begins his "Letter from Birmingham Jail." King's essay is a response to a group of clergymen who had publicly criticized his civil rights activities; he presents his position only after he first attempts to establish his credibility and point out that his reaction is a thoughtful and measured response: "If I sought to answer all the criticisms that cross my desk, my secretaries would have little time for anything else. . . . But since I feel that you are men of genuine good will and that your criticisms are sincerely set forth, I want to try to answer your statement in what I hope will be patient and reasonable terms."

Or notice how Ira Glasser begins his essay "Cigarette Ads and the Press," which argues *against* banning cigarette advertising:

> I don't smoke, never have. Neither do any of my children, for which I am grateful. Years before it became fashionable, I protested having other people's tobacco smoke imposed on me in closed places. I know that nicotine is severely addictive, and I believe the evidence that smoking is a serious health hazard. But I am against legislative bans on cigarette advertising.

If we knew that Glasser were a heavy smoker, or someone who were simply indifferent to the public smoking controversy, we might be inclined to dismiss his stand against banning cigarette advertising. But here is a man who doesn't smoke, a man who frankly states that he believes smoking is a health hazard. Yet he does not want cigarette advertising banned. Why? Because his argument does not seem to be motivated by any personal interest (in fact, his argument would seem to run counter to his own interests), we are inclined to listen to, and ponder, the presentation of someone who appears to be selflessly fairminded.

Audience

A certain amount of empathy or identification with your audience is required. Few opinions are so bizarre that they have no merit whatsoever, so you must discover the strengths of your opponent's argument. If you are the chairperson of a committee that advocates the construction of several little league baseball fields on a tract of now empty land in your community, and your opponent is the leader of a citizen's group dedicated to stopping this construction, you must begin by assuming that this citizen's group has valid reasons for arguing as they do. There are any number of possibilities for their opposition. Perhaps they are concerned with the costs of the construction and the potential increase in taxes. Or maybe they are disturbed about the necessary zoning changes, or the lack of parking and the increased traffic in the area, or the environmental impact — the increase in noise and trash, or the supervision and care of these playing fields during the off-season. Perhaps this group had different plans for this tract of land, plans for the development of a facility even more important to the community. Any of these concerns is legitimate, and there are surely many more objections that are equally valid. What is important is that you do not approach the issue by assuming that your opponents are completely irrational and automatically against children, baseball, and outdoor recreation.

Reaching an Agreement

Once you have determined what your opponents' arguments are, you need to examine your own position and establish where the two sides are in agreement. It is possible that you may agree more than you thought you did before you attempted to understand their case. It is also possible that, on examining the issue carefully, you may find your opponents' viewpoints convincing, so convincing in fact that you find your own opinions changing and modifying slightly. That should not be surprising, for if you really are the reasonable and logical person of goodwill you presented yourself as being, it is just conceivable that another well-informed opinion will reshape your thinking. Communication, after all, is a two-way street.

In any case, you need to structure your argument so that the points of agreement are emphasized, and, if you can, you need to show how your differences might be resolved. Unless you intend to go to court, where you might be simply declared a winner or loser, you need to leave your opponent a way out of the debate, a way to resolve the issue without losing face. It is this unwillingness to lose face, this refusal to back down, that creates an unwinnable and interminable debate. If you wanted to build five ball fields, and can get along by building four and leaving a belt of green space to serve as a buffer between the fields and a nearby subdivision, perhaps you can convince this citizens group to put their stamp of approval on your subject. Furthermore, if you can show them that rezoning of some kind is inevitable, and that a likely developer of this vacant land hopes to build a small shopping center on the property if the tract is not turned over to public recreation (a construction project that will likely have a far greater impact on the environment than some grassy baseball fields), you may not only be the winner of the debate, but hailed as a genius of community development as well.

Understanding your opponent's position and compromising some of your own beliefs are not signs of weakness or a lack of principles. Rachel Richardson Smith, in her essay "Abortion, Right and Wrong," wrestles with the opposing pro-choice and pro-life arguments, weighing the strengths and weaknesses of each camp. Although she finds merits in the arguments of both, she concludes not only that neither side is right, but that we are viewing abortion in the wrong terms and ignoring its tragic human context. If she had not attempted to identify with both sides of this controversy, if she had assumed that one side was absolutely right, and the other in turn absolutely wrong, she presumably would not have arrived at the sensitive new perspective she proposes at the close of her remarks.

When you craft persuasive prose, consider these ethical questions:

1. Have you presented your material in an accurate and honest fashion? Have you exaggerated or distorted your case in order simply to win your audience over?

2. Would your argument benefit if you used repetition, proportion, or position to emphasize your point of view? How would your presentation be affected if you rearranged your material? What could you do to the arrangement to make your case stronger than it is? Do any weaknesses seem to stem from the order in which your case is presented?

3. Do you create the impression that you are a reasonable, logical, and objective person? How do you go about doing this? Is there anything else you might say that would help your audience come to trust you even more?

4. What are some of the opinions that your audience might hold? What are the underlying reasons for these opinions? Are these reasons valid? Have you tried to account for and accommodate these opinions in your argument?

5. Are there any aspects of your argument you are willing to modify or compromise on? Would modifying your position on these points affect your overall argument? Are there points where you may be pushing too hard, points where your argument is really not substantial? Should you adjust your argument and allow your opponent some justified concessions on those points?

FOCUS · · · · · · · · · · · · ·

SUGGESTIONS FOR WRITING

1. If you could make one change in your school, community, or state, what would that change be? What problems do you regularly encounter that seem needlessly

frustrating? What solutions do you have for these problems? Why hasn't some-one already solved these problems before now?

2. Look through a newsmagazine or a current newspaper. What stories do you find that seem particularly distressing to you? Why are they distressing? What might be done to correct the problems you find so distressing? Whom could you write to about this problem?

3. We have all been unfairly wronged at some point in our lives. Think of a time when you were wronged. How were you wronged? Who or what was to blame? How might you go about righting this wrong now? What steps should be taken to see that this injustice is never repeated?

4. We all have our enemies, people whom we do not like at all. Sometimes these are people we know personally, sometimes they are public figures whose poli-cies or principles we find intolerable. Identify one of these public figures; it might be a politician, an entertainer, a journalist, a sports figure. In an essay, explain what there is about this person you just cannot tolerate. Then look at the world from this person's viewpoint and apply some of the questions raised in the guidelines above. Is it possible you could modify your opinion of this public figure?

16 ▶ The Goals of Persuasion

Persuasive writing tasks generally fall into one of three categories: (1) advocating a position or belief; (2) proposing an action or solution; or (3) judging and evaluating. Although these tasks share some similarities, they also share some important differences.

ADVOCATING A POSITION

When we wish to take a stand, when we explain why we think the way we do and encourage others to see the justice of our position, we are advocating a position. Everyday we defend our beliefs and opinions informally in our conversations with our friends, and in our disputes with those who are not so friendly toward us. We see examples of this writing in editorials, in position and policy statements, and in political speeches. In your college classes, of course, you are frequently asked to write essays that take stands and defend positions, so this kind of formal writing should not seem strange to you.

The Topic

One of the distinguishing traits of a good position paper is that it covers the topic thoroughly. How well you are able to cover a topic usually depends on the size of the topic you have chosen. Unless you are writing a book, you seldom have the freedom to take on really large topics, so it is best to try to limit the scope of your paper so that it conforms with the restrictions you may face. If you have an hour-exam, for example, or are assigned a 500-word essay, you will not be able to write a very well-developed paper on "Victoria's Reign" or "The Kennedy Years" within these limitations. If you chose instead a topic such as "England's Strategy in the Crimean War," or "John Kennedy's Relationship with Congress," you may still have to scramble to deal adequately with your subject, but the possibilities of your succeeding will improve. A 500-word essay, or even a 1000-word essay, is really not much space in which to develop a sophisticated topic. If you check, you will see that most magazine articles, even short ones, are generally much longer than 500 or 1000 words.

You also need to choose a topic you feel comfortable with, a topic that you either know something about or one in which you have a strong interest. If a topic falls outside your area of expertise, your ability to research this subject — the amount of time you have or the information that is easily available — may influence your decision to choose it. Our instincts and our common sense will usually keep us away from topics we should avoid, but it is not at all uncommon for indecisive students to ask advice of others, then find themselves involved in projects they are ill-prepared to tackle.

The Thesis

A paper must have something to say or there is no reason to write it, no reason for anyone to read it. Saying something that matters is often the criterion that distinguishes the superior paper from the average one, the above average paper from the mediocre one. Many students fail to realize this fact fully, for they keep digging up the same old topics and theses that should have been left buried years ago. If all the student papers ever written on "Capital Punishment" were to be placed end to end, they should then be left lying there (or the paper recycled). This does not mean that it is impossible to write an excellent paper on "Capital Punishment," but a student who decides to attempt this needs to stop first and consider whether his essay will have anything *new* and *different* to offer, or whether the paper will only repeat things that readers have argued about thousands of times before. If you have something genuinely new to say about such a topic you should indeed plunge ahead, but ask yourself these questions before you begin: (1) Will readers learn anything new from this essay? (2) Will it expose them to points of view with which they may not have been familiar?

A thesis is not a topic, nor is it a statement of intention. A thesis is a statement of *opinion*, a statement of *belief*. Although you believe strongly in what you intend to argue, believe so strongly that you feel your belief is not simply an opinion but a plain and obvious *fact*, some things are facts and therefore cannot be used as viable theses. Ask yourself whether someone could argue logically against you by taking the opposite viewpoint. If you cannot imagine a logical contradictory position, perhaps you do not have a good thesis. For example, the statement "Harry Truman was president of the United States" is no thesis at all. It is simply a statement of fact, for unless we are discussing the subject with someone totally ignorant of American history there can be no logical contradictory position. He *was* president and that is that.

But if that statement is changed to "Harry Truman was a good president" or "Harry Truman was a bad president," it would have the beginnings of a thesis, for the hard fact has been changed to a debatable question. The thesis could be improved further by sharpening our stand somewhat. If we substitute *excellent* for *good*, or *terrible* for *bad*, we have taken an even tougher and more controversial stand. If the thesis is taken one step further to "Harry Truman was undoubtedly the best president the United States has ever had," or "Harry Truman was clearly the worst president ever to occupy the White House," then we will really have climbed out on a limb. If we are skillful we will keep our readers interested, for they will want to see whether we will prove our controversial point, or fall off the limb.

Not every statement of opinion makes a good thesis. "Kittens are cute" may express a point of view, but it is not going to become the foundation of a very informative paper. Little controversy is involved (even confirmed cat-haters may be softened by the sight of kittens), and the issue is not one that is likely to produce a very interesting or sophisticated debate. Similarly, the thesis "I like chocolate cake more than any other food" fails completely. Can this opinion be debated? Could anyone logically take the other side? How would they prove their point? How would you prove yours?

Audience

Even though a position paper involves your statement of your opinion, your statement is going to be addressed to someone else and that someone needs to be considered. Your audience may be specific or general, known to you or unknown. Presumably for your student papers your audience is living, but if you create a paper of enduring value that may be published repeatedly, your audience may be living sometime in the future, may not even be born at the time you are writing. In addition, the audience's attitude toward the subject, and general level of knowledge about the subject needs to be taken into consideration. Furthermore, we occasionally need to create our audiences. That is, although sometimes we know our audience so well that we can pinpoint them exactly, other times we are uncertain and must rely upon our suppositions; those times we must write for an audience that we simply imagine exists. This diagram illustrates some of the possible audiences you may be attempting to persuade.

	FRIENDLY (or INTERESTED)	NEUTRAL (or DISINTERESTED)	HOSTILE (or UNINTERESTED)
UNINFORMED			
EDUCATED			
EXPERT			

Each audience has its own particular demands. If you are writing for an *uninformed* audience you will have to define terms, explain issues, summarize histories. An *educated* audience may be generally familiar with these aspects of the subject, but not as familiar as the *expert* audience, whose time you will be wasting if you spend too much time on preliminaries. A *friendly* or *interested* audience is presumably on your side to begin with, so they may be prepared to accept your assertions with little challenge. A *neutral* audience may question your arguments more strongly, and a *hostile* or *uninterested* audience will either approach your presentation with a list of objections already formulated, or need to be convinced of the importance of your cause. If you are writing for this last audience you need to have apprised all sides of the issue, and you need to address their objections squarely.

Arrangement

You can either present your thesis first and use your evidence and proof to support your case, or you can build your argument bit by bit and present your thesis as the conclusion or summary. Although it is not difficult to find examples of either arrangement, the former is probably the more common and accepted pattern used today. Normally, evidence is presented in the order of increasing importance, so that you begin with your least significant point, and build toward your most important one. The counterarguments, if they are fairly simple, can be raised all at once (preferably at an early point in the essay so they do not distract from your own increasingly stronger argument). If the counterarguments are complex, they may be raised, discussed, and dismissed on a point-by-point basis throughout your paper. Remember the guiding thrust of your thesis; return to it frequently and reiterate it by demonstrating how each piece of evidence complements and strengthens your overall proposition.

A successful essay must have a solid conclusion that restates the thesis and summarizes briefly the major points that have been made. Do not be afraid of repeating yourself; most students underwrite their papers by never being explicit enough. Whatever you do, do not attempt to conclude your essay by backing away from your position. The worst student essays end with a timid statement such as this: "Of course there are two sides to every question and someone else might see this differently. Who's to say what the right position is on such an important question?" If your position on the issue you examine is one you are really not certain about, do not waste your readers' time by making them read your essay. Every day, all over the world, people from all walks of life — judges, politicians, ministers, parents — make decisions on legal issues, political issues, religious questions, and moral problems. You also should have the courage of your convictions; do not ever duck an issue by shrugging your shoulders at the end of your paper and inquiring "Who's to say on this issue?" *You* are to say.

Here are some questions to ask when you are advocating a position.

1. Is your topic manageable? That is, can you cover it adequately within the time or space limitations you face?
2. Is the topic something you feel competent to examine? How much do you really know about the topic? How much will you have to learn?

3. Are there adequate materials available if you must do research? What will some of your sources be? Will you be able to find these sources in a library? Will you have to do field work or conduct interviews to obtain the necessary information?

4. Will you have time to conduct research? Could the topic be simplified or altered to make it more manageable? How would you go about doing this?

5. What is the thesis of your paper? Does it take a clear stand? Is it a statement of opinion, not simply a fact?

6. Can this thesis be proved? Is this a thesis others might find controversial? Can it be sharpened or focused?

7. What is your audience's stance? Are they friendly, hostile, or somewhere in between?

8. How much information about the topic does your audience have? What details will you need to provide to make them understand this subject? What aspects of the subject are they likely to understand already?

9. Does your presentation account for opposing viewpoints? What opposing viewpoints are you likely to encounter? How valid are these points of view? Should these viewpoints affect your position in any way?

10. What would be the most effective arrangement for your argument? Could the arrangement of your presentation be improved by altering the order of your major points?

11. Do you take a clear, unambiguous stand in your paper? Do you leave any issues up in the air for your reader to resolve?

PROPOSING AN ACTION OR SOLUTION

When we attempt to influence action or beliefs, when we want to evoke a response beyond simple agreement, we are proposing actions and solutions. This kind of persuasive writing appears in advertising, of course, but it is also found in proposals, business letters, propaganda, solicitations, grant requests, and editorials — whenever we are urging people to agree with us and then take action.

Topic and Thesis

When we propose an action or a solution we are usually responding to a problem that we have recognized. The topic, in a sense, comes to us, then; we do not necessarily go out looking for it. Sometimes others have recognized this problem and have solicited a proposal or solution. Our response is then governed by their definition of the problem, although it is always possible, and sometimes desirable, for us to analyze and redefine the problem. One reason some problems have not been solved, in fact, is that they have been defined in only one way. For some time now, for example, the United States government has been involved in a "war on drugs." Its approach has been to label those who possess drugs as criminals, and to attempt to eliminate physically all drugs, drug dealers, and drug smugglers. In essence we have seen the problem in terms of a military confrontation, as combat between two rival armies. We are all aware of the difficulties of this approach. We have attempted to guard our borders against those who are smuggling drugs in, and have created an elaborate and extremely expensive surveillance system to prevent infiltration. The enemy has in turn developed more sophisticated and powerful equipment to fight back against our anti-drug forces. The "war" has generated many actual battles, some between rival drug dealers, some between drug dealers and the police; many "soldiers" on both sides have been killed, along with many uninvolved civilians.

A different, and admittedly very controversial, solution to this problem has been suggested. If we make some drugs available free to those who are hooked on them, we can then lower the market value of all illegal drugs. (After all, limiting the supply that flows into the country, as we are attempting to do now, only raises the value of the diminished supply that does make it in successfully.) Essentially this approach sees the dilemma as an *economic* problem rather than a *military* one, an economic problem that can be solved with the simple business principle of supply and demand. By making the business of selling drugs less profitable we can sharply curtail the number of drug smugglers; by lowering the cost of drugs on the street we can also curtail the crime that addicts commit to support their habits. By educating young people about the potential hazards of drug use we can then cut down on the number of new addicts. This solution may or may not be a valid one, but it does analyze and then redefine the way the problem is currently seen. If our proposal is to be accepted, we shall first have to convince our audience of the validity of our viewpoint (advocate a position), and then persuade them that our solution is the correct one for the problem as it has been redefined.

If others have not sensed that a problem exists, we may then be providing an unsolicited proposal or solution. Such a situation occurs when our audience is either not aware that a problem exists, or when the audience knows the problem exists, but is not aware that a solution exists. In the former case, your job is first to make your audience aware that there is a problem, then show them how to go about solving it. In the latter, the task is first to convince your audience that the problem *can* be solved, then persuade your audience that your solution is the correct way to resolve the dilemma. In either case you will have to advocate a position first, then make your argument.

Audience

Theoretically, when we are attempting to propose actions or solutions, our potential audience can be as varied as the audience we may be writing for when we advocate a position. The same diagram would apply, in principle (see page 352).

In practice, however, because we are usually trying to provide solutions to people who presumably *need* solutions, we may frequently find our audience to be receptive rather than hostile to our ideas. Our readers are trying to decide which candidate to vote for, which automobile to buy, or how best to resolve a problem in the shipping department. They want answers — even need answers — and are grateful to someone who can fulfill that need. An unsolicited proposal or solution may of course draw more hostility than a solicited one, particularly if we are pointing out a problem to an audience who was not aware of its existence. If we as writers can empathize with the problems our readers may be facing, they in turn may find our solutions more acceptable. It is not wise to belittle the difficulties inherent in a problem, nor is it good to tout too heavily the simplicity of our solution or the cleverness of our proposal. Making the reader feel stupid will scarcely bring the accord we hope our proposal will create.

Arrangement and Structure

Generally a successful appeal or proposal will contain three elements. You must convince your reader that

1. *You understand the problem*. Clearly, misstating or misinterpreting the case means you will lose your reader's empathy — instantly.
2. *Your solution or proposal is feasible and reliable*. Whether or not a similar idea has worked in the past is an important consideration. One would not want to propose the construction of a subway system for Los Angeles, for example, without first looking at the success of the city's present public transportation system.
3. *Your solution or proposal is practical*. The "bottom line" is sometimes a financial sum, sometimes an emotional, technical, or psychological limit. For example, four-wheel drive has proved to be a popular automotive option. Now some manufacturers are beginning to market automobiles with four-wheel steering, that is, cars with rear wheels that can be turned or steered as front wheels always have. For this concept to be successful this innovation will have to be made both economically and technically practical. A system that adds hundreds of pounds to a car, or a system that is infinitely more complex than the problem it proposes to remedy, will ultimately not be acceptable. An atomic-powered can-opener, for instance, is of little use if it occupies all the counterspace in our kitchen.

Solicited and Unsolicited Proposals

The arrangement and emphasis you give to these three basic elements will depend to some degree of what type of proposal you are writing. The proposals we have been examining up to this point have generally been *unsolicited proposals*. That is, the writers who have created them have been not been requested to do so. In this type of proposal, special emphasis must always be given to presenting the problem. Your audience may not be aware that the problem you are attempting to resolve even exists, so you must first convince them that this problem exists and that the consequences of not finding a solution to it are serious. Although your solution, since it has not been solicited, is presumably the only one before your reader at the present time, you must anticipate the possible counterarguments your reader might propose. These might be immediate responses, apparently simple solutions that could instantly solve the problem you have delineated. For example, if you have pointed out that poison ivy is taking over the local school playground, your reader may react by suggesting that you simply spray the lot with herbicides. You will need to anticipate that argument and explain that such chemicals may be more dangerous to the children who play there than the poison ivy you are trying to eradicate. Finally, you may have to outline the steps that must be taken to implement your solution. If your audience has not been aware of the problem you are attempting to resolve, they also may not understand what action should be taken first. It is your job to create an agenda and explain the procedures that should be followed.

In many ways *solicited proposals* are easier for us to write, because solicited proposals are responses to requests for solutions. This means the problem, or at least some facet of the problem, has already been defined. When a company or government agency decides that it needs a product or service, it draws up a set of specifications outlining its requirements, and then solicits proposals from companies or individuals who would like to supply the needed product or service. The competition for such a contract can be very keen, so a good deal of pre-writing analysis must take place before the actual writing begins. Successful solicited proposals are most often the result of successful strategical thinking, for although the "problem" has been generally defined by the company or agency soliciting the proposal, solutions are limited only by the writer's imagination. For example, when a community's waste landfill becomes full, it may need to find a new landfill site. Or it may need to build an waste incinerator. Or it may need to begin a massive recycling program. When a hospital finds its laundry bills are too high, it may need to contract with an outside laundry. Or it may need to increase its rates. Or it may need to buy disposable hospital gowns. Or it may need to eliminate some of its services.

Although analyzing the specific request and tailoring your proposal to it is more important than following a prescribed formula, basically a solicited proposal will do four things:

1. Make an offer to provide the product or services described in the request.
2. Establish that the product or services being offered will meet or exceed the specifications stipulated in the request.
3. Provide a cost figure for the product or services offered.
4. Make some kind of presentation stressing the desirability of contracting for the product or service offered in your proposal.

When preparing commercial proposals keep in mind that a solicited proposal will usually be one that is being read along with a number of other possible solutions, so a good deal of your success will depend on how well you "sell" your solution. The cost of a solution is always important, but, again, costs cannot always be calculated in financial terms. The cheapest solution at the outset may eventually cost the most in terms of problems and unexpected difficulties. As you know from your own everyday experiences, sometimes you want to buy the best product available, regardless of its price, and other times you want to purchase the cheapest product you can find, as long as it will solve your problem and meet your minimum requirements.

Here are some questions to ask when you are proposing an action or solution:

1. Is your proposal solicited or unsolicited? If it is solicited, what does your audience understand about the problem you are attempting to solve? Have they misperceived this problem in any way? Does your solution turn upon a new perception or understanding of this problem?

2. If the proposal is unsolicited, what is your audience's perception of the problem you are attempting to solve? Why have they not recognized that this problem exists? Will a new understanding of their situation allow them to see the problem and solution as you see it? Is there something they might know about this problem that you do not? That is, is there a good reason they might not have resolved this problem before now, or even recognized that it existed before now?

3. What is your audience's actual stance towards this problem? Are they likely to be interested in your solution, hostile towards it, or somewhere in between?

4. What does your audience know about this problem? What details will you have to provide to make them understand the proposal you are presenting? What aspects of the problem do you need to understand better before you can provide a viable solution?

5. If your proposal is one of several that might be considered, what aspects of your solution suggest it might be the most acceptable? Have you explored all the possible ways this problem might be resolved?

6. What are your proposal's strengths? What possible weaknesses does it have?

7. Does your proposal sufficiently demonstrate that you understand the problem in question? Is your solution to the problem likely to be seen as workable? Is it practical?

8. Have you adequately sold your solutions? Will your audience see your solution as desirable?

JUDGING AND EVALUATING

When we evaluate the work, opinions, or beliefs of others, we hope to persuade our readers to agree with us and accept our judgments. These judgments reflect our values, as the word evaluation itself suggests. Values, as you know, can be slippery things, for they tend to reflect relative, rather than absolute, truths. One person, for example, may argue that the movie *Star Wars* marked a significant turning point in American filmmaking. Another may see the film as overblown, overrated, and corny. This does not mean it is impossible to make meaningful evaluations, that we simply say everyone is entitled to his own opinion and we therefore can not make an overall judgment about the film. It does mean, however, that we must first understand what value judgments are, and how we arrive at them before we write evaluative essays. There are good evaluations, and bad evaluations, good film and book reviews, and bad film and book reviews. While we may wish to say in a democracy that everyone is entitled to his own opinions, some people express their opinions in a more intelligent and meaningful way than others. That does not necessarily make their opinions right, but we may be more inclined to be influenced by their judgments.

Basic Assumptions

When we discuss value, our judgments are based on contextual assumptions, underlying criteria we feel are important. For example, the person who sees *Star Wars* as a wonderful movie may point out that its use of elaborate sets and costumes as well as extravagant special effects generated an interest in spectacular visual effects that influenced dozens of other movies — horror and adventure films, as well as science-fiction movies. The fundamental underlying assumption in this case might be "A movie that influences other movies must be a good, as well as a significant, film." Conversely, the person who believes *Star Wars* was a terrible movie might point to its relatively simple plot and the way that the special effects overpower the story and the acting. The underlying assumption that generates this value judgment might be "A good movie is a film that combines a sophisticated, literate plot with superb performances by talented actors and actresses." These are only two positions; obviously there are many others. The person who says "*Star Wars* was great entertainment, but it was not a great movie," is apparently basing that judgment on a perceived distinction between movies that are "good" and movies that "entertain." Do we believe that this distinction can be made? Are the categories "entertaining" and "good" compatible with each other? Or are they mutually exclusive? Whether we accept this judgment, or any of the above judgments and evaluations, depends on how well the writers can establish the apparent validity of these underlying criteria.

Look for a moment at Pauline Kael's review of *E.T.* Clearly she loved the movie, and although she does not say so in just these words, she apparently sees it as an excellent film. Some people argue that all our intellectual value judgments originate in our spontaneous reactions. That is, we come away from a movie, we listen to a new compact disc, or we eat at a new restaurant, and, without thinking about our reasons very much, we immediately form an opinion. It is only later, the theory goes, when we are asked to defend our opinion, that we come up with reasons and justifications for our reactions. Whether this theory is true or not, many writers begin their evaluations with their immediate emotional responses, their spontaneous reactions to the subject that is being evaluated. Pauline Kael begins by simply calling *E.T.* "a bliss-out," a term that certainly connotes an emotional response, but is not very helpful if we are looking for an intellectual explanation of the film.

What fundamental assumptions does Kael seem to have that cause her to reach her judgment about *E.T.*? One key to her criteria can be found in what she praises about the movie. She notes that it "envelops," that it is "a dream of a movie" and (as we have noted) "a bliss-out." Kael points out that the movie presents us with a "dreamscape," that it offers a world "bathed in warmth" with a "mythic" atmosphere. Does this mean she likes the film because of its dreamy, romantic quality, that her underlying assumption is that romantic films are good, while realistic films are bad? Perhaps. But if we pay close attention to what she does not like about the film, what she calls the "intrusive" and "discordant" treatment of the adult scientists who are tracking E.T., we may arrive at a more precise understanding of her fundamental assumptions. The fear these mysterious figures generate in the movie shatters the dreamlike atmosphere, Kael contends. "This movie doesn't need faceless men," she argues, "it has its own terror."

What Pauline Kael values about *E.T.* are both its entrancing quality and (with the one exception noted above) its nearly perfect unity. The unity of the film, in fact, creates its magical atmosphere; it is full of touches (like the scene in which E.T. is attracted to the child in the Yoda Halloween costume) that are "so unaccountably right." Spielberg's camera angles, his editing, his use of light, all fit, all belong, Kael contends. The movie works not because it possesses any one extraordinary quality; it works because all of its parts fit together perfectly. It is a unified whole. If you did not enjoy the movie *E.T.*, you may find it easy to disagree with Kael's conclusions. To create a meaningful rebuttal, however, you would first have to discredit her fundamental assumptions, her underlying criteria, and then find a way to replace them with assumptions of your own.

Audience

Naturally you will need to consider what your audience knows about the subject you are attempting to evaluate. For this reason most evaluations and reviews devote a fair amount of space to a description of the subject they are evaluating. Most reviews of records, movies, and plays, for example, are written when these things are new and have not yet been seen or heard by most readers. Evaluations of products — computers, software, cameras, bicycles, automobiles — also tend to be written when the products are new and just being introduced. In one sense then the audience for a great many evaluations is uninformed on one level, and needs to have the subject described, and perhaps explained, in some detail.

Beyond this first level of knowledge about the subject being evaluated, a writer must of course consider the general level of background information the audience possesses, and return to the diagram we have used before (see page 352). Here you are going to have to compare your expertise in the subject area with that of your intended audience's. If you are going to evaluate your dormitory food, or fast-food restaurants, and you are writing an evaluation for your fellow students, you can expect that most students will have had some experience with these culinary experiences. But if you are something of a gourmet and you intend to review the food in a new Nepalese restaurant in your town, your audience may need certain background information before they will be able to understand your judgments.

The same rule of thumb applies to all judgments and evaluations. Presumably you are making the evaluation because you have (or believe you have) some expertise in this area. The more expertise you have, the more you will have to explain about your underlying criteria. It is easy for your audience to understand if you do not like eating at McDonald's because you do not like plastic forks and styrofoam plates. But if you want to discuss the texture of the guacamole dip you encountered at your favorite Mexican restaurant, or analyze in detail the cinematography of *Citizen Kane*, you will first need to educate your readers to some of the nuances that have had such a powerful effect on your judgment.

Published reviews will give you some guidelines on how to treat your audience, but such reviews do not always help as much as you might think. For example, Pauline Kael's movie reviews appear in *The New Yorker* on a regular basis. She can assume that her readers are fairly sophisticated and literate, and that they probably see a fair number of movies. She probably can also assume that her readers read her reviews fairly regularly. She has an audience that "returns" every week, one that has some familiarity with what she expects and values in films. Her situation is somewhat typical of most evaluators. Unless you are a professional reviewer you probably do not have such an regular audience; it may therefore be necessary for you to be more explicit about your values in a single specific evaluation than Kael is about hers.

Arrangement and Structure

Evaluations tend to have at least four elements:

1. A description
2. A judgment
3. A statement of the underlying assumptions that have produced this judgment
4. The evidence, the specific links between the underlying assumption and the judgment

Generally these elements appear in this order, although the exact arrangement of these details varies from evaluation to evaluation. Some evaluations begin with the judgment, then move to a description; some place the description first and save the overall judgment for last. Some weave the description throughout the evaluation, letting the order of the description determine the order in which evidence is presented.

Pauline Kael's review of *E.T.* demonstrates just how sophisticated an evaluation's structure can be. She begins with a very brief judgment — "a dream of a movie" (although *dream* is surely a pun here) — and then immediately moves into a description of the film. Throughout her description (which makes up nearly all of her review) she presents both judgments and evidence of the film's unity. It is the unity of the film, of course, that, according to her underlying assumption, makes it such an excellent movie. She has so skillfully woven the elements of her presentation together into an integrated review it is virtually impossible to break her review down into separate "blocks." If you have difficulty producing such a smoothly integrated evaluation (and most of us would), it is perfectly acceptable to follow the format outlined above.

Here are some questions to ask when you are evaluating or judging:

1. What values or beliefs are you attempting to evaluate or judge?

2. What fundamental assumptions or underlying criteria are you basing your evaluation on? Would others automatically use these same criteria, or would they base their judgments on other assumptions?

3. What information does your audience have about the subject being evaluated? Will you need to describe this subject in detail for them? What background information might they have that will help them understand the subject better? What comparisons might you draw that will help them to comprehend more fully?

4. Will your audience grasp the criteria you are presenting in your evaluation, or will you have to explain these criteria to them? Are there technical terms you need to explain to them before they can understand your evaluation? Are there technical terms you need to learn yourself?

5. Is your audience likely to accept your judgment automatically, or will you have to establish your authority in this area first? How might you go about establishing this authority?

6. What evidence can you point to that will support your judgmental assumptions? Will this same evidence, or other evidence, support a contradictory viewpoint?

7. Is your case one that is likely to convince your audience? How might you modify it to improve its effectiveness?

FOCUS • • • • • • • • • • • • • •

SUGGESTIONS FOR WRITING

1. Who is your favorite recording artist, athlete, or actor? What makes this person good at what he or she does? How would you go about explaining this person's excellence to someone who was unfamiliar with it?

2. Go to a sporting event — a game, gymnastics tournament, or 5 km run — and instead of reporting on it as a newspaper sports reporter might, that is, simply reporting the facts, write a review of what you saw. What information will you need to acquire before you can write your review?

3. Make a list of your ten favorite books, movies, plays, and television programs. What qualities do the items in each category have in common? Make a list of ten books, movies, plays, or television programs that you absolutely hate. What qualities do the items in each of these categories have in common? Make a list of

these specific qualities. What do your lists say about your own evaluative standards? How would you go about convincing someone else that your standards are valid?

4. Everyone has at least one "bright idea" for an invention or product that the world needs, but for some reason has never developed. What is your "bright idea"? What uses could your invention be put to? Why do you think no one has ever invented this product? Whom should you write to or contact to sell your invention?

PERSUASIVE PROSE

Persuasive prose emphasizes the reader, rather than the subject or the writer. It focuses on affecting the reader, on changing her beliefs or opinions, rather than on expressing the writer's emotions or presenting objective information. Persuasive prose is found in advertising, political speeches, editorials, proposals, argumentative essays, propaganda, and business letters. The following readings represent various forms of persuasive prose.

THE MOST INFLAMMATORY QUESTION OF OUR TIME

R. J. Reynolds Tobacco Company

In the last twenty years smoking has become a very controversial health issue; cigarette advertising has been banned from television and radio, increasingly ominous warnings have been placed on cigarette packages, and smoking has been banned in many public places. The following statement has been placed in magazines and newspapers by R. J. Reynolds Tobacco Company, a company that is obviously concerned about the antismoking trend.

The most inflammatory question of our time.

"Hey, would you put out that cigarette?"

Just seven little words. But in today's over-heated climate of opinion, they can make sparks fly.

For with all the rhetoric about "second-hand smoke," many non-smokers are beginning to feel not just bothered but threatened by cigarettes.

And with all the talk about anti-smoking legislation, many smokers are beginning to feel threatened by non-smokers.

This is not exactly a recipe for social harmony. In fact, it's practically a guarantee of further discord.

Since we have discussed scientific aspects of the "passive smoking" controversy in previous messages, we'd like to focus here on the social questions.

Will more confrontation or more segregation produce less abrasion? Do we solve anything by creating yet another way to divide our society? Shouldn't all of us be wary of inviting government to involve itself further in our private lives?

At R.J. Reynolds, we see an alternative.

We think we should start not by raising barriers, but by lowering our voices. We think smokers and non-smokers can work out their differences together, in a spirit of tolerance and fairness and respect for each other's rights and feelings. We think common courtesy can succeed where coercion is bound to fail.

And maybe, after we have learned peaceful coexistence by talking to each other civilly and sensibly, we can apply the same approach to our many other problems.

Because, after all, this is hardly the most inflammatory question of our time.

Brought to you in the interest of common courtesy by

R.J. Reynolds Tobacco Company

QUESTIONS

1. R. J. Reynolds has published this as a "public issues statement" and does not regard it as an "advertisement." You should notice that it does not carry the standard health warnings that are required to accompany all cigarette advertising. Is there a consumer being appealed to in this statement? What is R. J. Reynolds' goal in publishing this statement?

2. Reread the statement and pay particular attention to the diction. Is it slanted to imply that either smokers or nonsmokers are more or less reasonable than the other group? Cite particular words with strong connotations and explain those connotations.

3. Look for evidence to support both views of the issue. What kind of evidence is included and what kind is excluded? Explain why the tobacco company made the choices it did in terms of including factual evidence.

4. Notice that the statement ends by denying the original assertion. What is R. J. Reynolds' purpose in reversing its original stand? How does this reversal affect a reader or change a reader's view of the tobacco company?

5. Does R. J. Reynolds resolve the controversy of smokers' right to smoke and nonsmokers' right to avoid passive smoking? Explain how the statement defuses the controversy.

•   •   •   •   •

WHAT DOES A CONVENIENCE STORE CLERK THINK JUST BEFORE HE IS ATTACKED?

National Rifle Association of America

One of the primary activities of the National Rifle Association of America (or NRA) is the continued opposition to gun control; the NRA justifies this opposition by citing the Second Amendment to the United States Constitution, the right to keep and bear arms. The NRA advertises widely and, probably more important, maintains a powerful political lobby that opposes all forms of gun control. When this advertisement appeared in newspapers it usually occupied a full page.

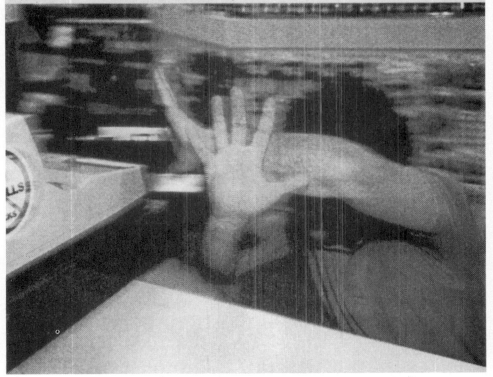

WHAT DOES A CONVENIENCE STORE CLERK THINK JUST BEFORE HE IS ATTACKED?

According to the U.S. Department of Justice, one in three Americans will be a victim of robbery or attempted robbery in their lifetime.

He has no time to think. Instead, his instinct to survive takes over as he attempts to defend himself.

He deserves a fighting chance in the face of vicious criminal assault. That's why our constitution guarantees his right to own a firearm. A right that can be as precious as life itself.

Don't own a firearm if you choose not to. But never let anyone deny or delay your constitutional freedom to make that choice.

DEFEND YOUR RIGHT TO DEFEND YOURSELF.

QUESTIONS

1. What effect is created by the blurry photograph? How does this contribute to the overall message of the advertisement?

2. The statement "Defend Your Right to Defend Yourself" is prominently displayed. What emotional response is this likely to evoke? Would anyone, given the opportunity, *not* want to defend himself in a life-threatening situation?

3. To those who might favor gun control of some kind, there is an implicit irony in this advertisement. These people would argue that if guns were restricted then the convenience store clerk would not have to worry about an attack in the first place. How does the advertisement sidestep that issue?

4. How does this advertisement attempt to appeal to those who may favor gun control? Is that appeal effective? Why or why not?

•   •   •   •   •

WHAT GOOD ARE DESIGNER CLOTHES?

Marcy Fitness Products, Salvati Montgomery Sokoda Advertising

An increasing interest in physical fitness has created a booming market in sporting goods and exercise equipment. Marcy manufactures exercise machines.

WHAT GOOD ARE DESIGNER CLOTHES IF YOU'VE GOT A PLAIN WRAP BODY?

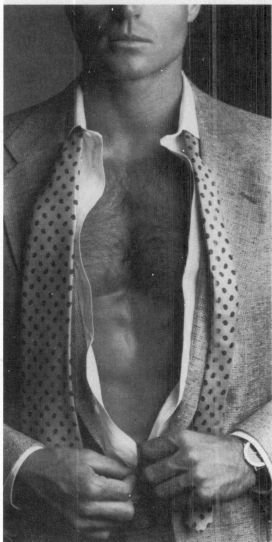

You drive the right car.

You wear the right watch.

You've got the right shoes, shirts and pants.

Don't forget the most important element in any wardrobe.

You.

Put the right shirt on the wrong body and the results can be anything but appealing.

One of the many reasons Marcy builds machines like the EM/1 you see here.

For about the cost of a year's dues at the typical health club, you can own a machine that works virtually every part of your body.

At home. On your own schedule.

Shoulders, thighs, arms, chest, calves.

We'll tighten you up in places you never even knew you had.

Resulting, naturally, in a body that makes anything look great from T-shirts to tuxedos.

Check out the complete Marcy EM/1 series at a Marcy Dealer today.

Do it soon. Not just for the looks, but for the years and vitality you can add to your life.

After all, wardrobes come and go season by season.

But that body you plan to hang them on will be around for a long, long time.

Call 1-800-62MARCY, ext. 12 for your nearest dealer.

MARCY
FITNESS PRODUCTS

WHEN YOU FINALLY GET SERIOUS.

© 1987 MARCY Fitness Products

QUESTIONS

1. Would this advertisement be as effective if it simply reproduced a large photograph of the EM/1 exercise machine? Why or why not?
2. Notice that the word *exercise* does not appear in this advertisement. Why not?
3. Which is emphasized more in this advertisement — appearance or health? Why do you think this is so?
4. Analyze the slogan — "When You Finally Get Serious" — that Marcy puts under its logo. What does this slogan suggest? Is it effective?
5. Count the number of times the word *you* and *your* appear in the advertisement. Rewrite the advertising copy by substituting other pronouns. Does your rewritten advertisement seem more, or less, effective than this one? Why?

● ● ● ● ●

REFLECTIONS ON MELISSA

Hanes Hosiery, Inc.

Hanes Hosiery has created a series of "Reflections" advertisements to promote their Silk Reflections *pantyhose.*

She taught me how to tie
a perfect bow tie.

Says "I love you"
in seventeen languages.

And her legs...
Melissa's incredible legs.

SILK REFLECTIONS
The silkiest Hanes ever

Silk Reflections™
Pantyhose.
In 21 inspiring
colors and designs.

QUESTIONS

1. The advertising copy here consists of only three sentences, one about a bow tie, one about expertise in languages, and one about Melissa's legs. Analyze these sentences. What point is being made in each case?

2. Notice the poses of the models and their clothes. What scene seems to be depicted here? Is there a story the reader should supply? What is that story? What does the advertising copy contribute to that story?

3. To whom is this advertisement addressed? Where do you think it appeared? Is this advertisement sexist? Why or why not?

· · · · ·

"WHOEVER SAID, 'IT'S NOT WHETHER YOU WIN OR LOSE THAT COUNTS,' PROBABLY LOST."

Lufthansa German Airlines, McCann-Erickson Advertising New York

Celebrities, of course, are frequently featured in advertising. This one for Lufthansa German Airlines features tennis star Martina Navratilova.

"Whoever said, 'It's not whether you win or lose that counts', probably lost."

Martina Navratilova, Tennis World champion.

"There are winners, and there are losers. And if you chose to be one of the former, the journey through life can be a little lonely.

When you're a winner, you have to set the standard for excellence wherever you go.

You have to battle against the fatigue, the intimidation, the human tendency to just want to take things a little easier. You have to be able to come up with, time and again, one consistently great performance after another.

It's grueling. And I don't know many people willing to make the effort. But it's those few true professionals you meet along the way that help make the journey just a little easier to manage."

At Lufthansa, we understand the pressures involved in maintaining high standards. But we also know the rewards. For us, they include an outstanding on-time arrival record, a meticulously maintained fleet and friendly, courteous service.

Perhaps that's why in 82 countries Lufthansa is considered by many to be the very best in the world.

People expect the world of us.

 **Lufthansa**
German Airlines

QUESTIONS

1. Assess the impact of the quoted statement from Navratilova. Are we as readers supposed to agree with this sentiment? Disagree? What does the statement suggest about her? About the airlines?

2. Navratilova is Czechoslovakian, not German. Does that fact make any difference? Is her nationality important here, or only the fact that she is an excellent tennis player?

3. Presumably the statement beneath the headline represents Navratilova's views about tennis and athletics. Sports, however, are never mentioned in this statement. Why? What meaning does this statement have for the reader who is simply trying to book a flight, not win at Wimbledon?

4. Why does the airline mention that it flies into 82 countries? Is this important to readers?

5. If Navratilova were advertising tennis racquets, or tennis shoes, her advice and expertise might be significant. Assume for the moment that she was not paid for this statement. Should her opinion about airlines carry any influence? Why or why not?

6. This advertisement has two different parts — the statement by Navratilova and the statement by the airline. Does Navratilova say that she likes Lufthansa Airlines, or that she has ever even flown on Lufthansa Airlines? Is it necessary for her to do so? Would the advertisement be more effective if she did?

•   •   •   •   •

YOU CAN HAVE IT ALL: SEVEN CAMPAIGNS FOR DEADLY SIN

*Fallon McElligott; The Martin Agency; N W Ayer, Inc.; Saatchi &
Saatchi DFS Compton; J. Walter Thompson; Ogilvy & Mather; TBWA
Advertising, Inc.;* **Harper's Magazine**

*We frequently hear the complaint that advertising is capable of selling us inferior products,
or capable of selling us products we do not want or need. When* Harper's Magazine *asked
leading advertising agencies to create advertisements for a set of products we presumably do
not need — the seven deadly sins — the resulting series of tongue-in-cheek ads demonstrated a
good deal about how advertising really does work. Although advertising agencies, of course,
usually want to sell us on the virtue of the products they promote so smoothly that we do not
see the mechanics of the advertising at work, in this case the nature of the "products" allows
the mechanics to show through.*

THE recent public debate on our nation's scandals exposes a fundamental irony.
Amid the moralizing columns of pundits and two-minute homilies by news-
casters warning "Thou Shalt Not" fall the whispers of advertisers: "Who Says You
Can't Have It All?" and "Obsession" and "You Deserve a Break Today" and "The
Pride Is Back!"

With sweet words, Madison Avenue seeks to profit from our longing to lead
ourselves into temptation. The schizophrenia of public puritanism and private liber-
tinism creates a host of charming — and uniquely American — effects. Ivan Boesky
cloisters himself with the Torah. The President publicly offers his urine for official
inspection. Mafia bosses make a public show of attending church. Preachers swear off
adultery.

In the interest of moral instruction and clarification, *Harper's Magazine* asked
leading advertising agencies to develop a campaign *promoting* the seven deadly sins:
Wrath, Lust, Avarice, Gluttony, Sloth, Envy, and Pride. Each agency pitted in-house
teams against one another to perform this public service, to provide grist for tomorrow's sermonizers and to reconcile God and Mammon.

THE GLUTTON SOCIETY
Helping people make the most of themselves for over 100 years.

GLUTTONY

Agency: Fallon McElligott. *Art Director:* Dean Hanson. *Copywriters:* Jarl Olson, Mike Lescarbeau. *Clients:* Federal Express; Wall Street Journal; Lee Jeans.

Do you remember all of the things you told me you wanted as a child?

Well, your list may have changed, but I'll bet it hasn't gotten any shorter.

Perhaps you shouldn't be worried about that.

Greed has always motivated men and women. It has motivated inventors to make better mousetraps, artists to create greater art and scientists to find cures for diseases and pathways to the moon.

Just be sure to use your greed to good ends. Be greedy for knowledge. Be greedy for the kind of success that helps you, your family and your friends. Be greedy for love.

Just don't be greedy in ways that hurt others.

Remember, I'll always be the first one to know if you've been bad or good. So be good for goodness sake.

The world's foremost authority speaks out on the subject of greed.

AVARICE

Agency: The Martin Agency. Art Director: Hal Tench. Copywriter: Mike Hughes. Photographer: Jim Erickson. Production: Chet Booth. Clients: State of Virginia, "Virginia Is for Lovers"; General Motors; Reynolds Aluminum.

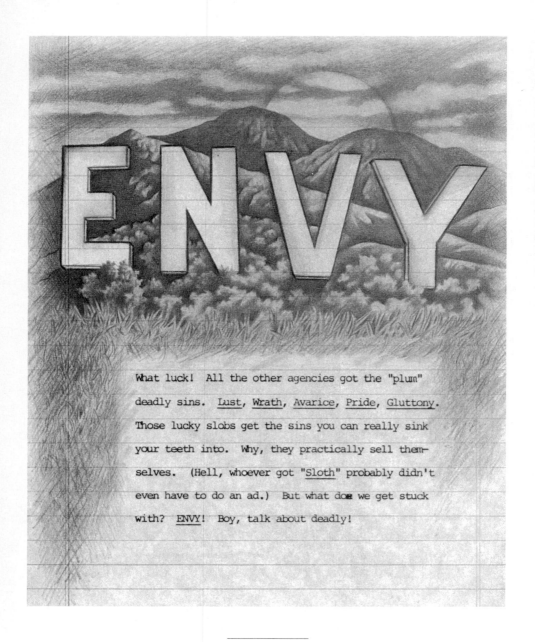

What luck! All the other agencies got the "plum" deadly sins. Lust, Wrath, Avarice, Pride, Gluttony. Those lucky slobs get the sins you can really sink your teeth into. Why, they practically sell themselves. (Hell, whoever got "Sloth" probably didn't even have to do an ad.) But what does we get stuck with? ENVY! Boy, talk about deadly!

ENVY

Agency: NW Ayer, Inc. *Art Director:* Keith Gould. *Copywriter:* Patrick Cunningham. *Clients:* AT&T, "Reach Out and Touch Someone"; DeBeers, "A Diamond Is Forever"; U.S. Army, "Be All That You Can Be."

The only emotion powerful enough both to start a war—

and stop one.

WRATH

Agency: Saatchi & Saatchi DFS Compton. *Creative Director:* Dick Lopez. *Copywriter:* Jeff Frye. *Clients:* Toyota, "Who Could Ask for Anything More? Toyota"; PaineWebber, "Thank You, PaineWebber"; Wendy's, "Where's the Beef?"

SLOTH

Agency: J. Walter Thompson. *Art Director:* Jean Marcellino. *Copywriter:* Chuck Hoffman. *Clients:* Ford, "Have You Driven a Ford Lately?" Pepsi Slice, "We Got the Juice"; U.S. Marine Corps, "We're Looking for a Few Good Men."

It's Time To Start Feeling Good About Yourself–*Really* Good!

"**P**RIDE goeth before a fall"—we've all heard it. But how *TRUE* is it?

It's mostly *BUNK*, agree today's top mental health experts.

Pride: the sin you can feel good about

You've heard all the bad-mouthing.

At home. In Sunday school. In literary magazines. "Pride's a sin!" they proclaim. Well, don't you believe it.

"Pride's gotten a bad rap," says psychiatrist/ornithologist Bernard Warbler.

"It's time this country wakes up and faces facts. Pride, *to whatever extent,* is healthy and natural. The psychiatric community is in complete agreement on this point."

So stick out your chest, for heaven's sake. PRIDE—it's today's "buzz word" for mental health!

Henry VIII

Failure after romantic failure, it was Henry's pride that kept him searching for Mrs. Right. At 52, he finally found her—the lovely Catherine Parr.

William Plover
Dictionary Editor

The most misunderstood word in the English language? "Hubris," or excessive pride, is a word that's quickly leaving our vocabulary. *Good riddance!* The concept of "excessive' pride no longer works—and people are taking notice.

Dictionary editor William Plover: "'Hubris,' of course, comes to us from ancient Greece, and most word-watchers think it's come far enough. It's quite clear, early translators misunderstood the sense of 'wellness' implied by the Greeks. Resulting in centuries of lexicological slander, if you will. To me, hubris is a rather pleasant word."

Next time you run across "hubris' in the dictionary, cross it out—or write a new definition. You'll feel better for doing so!

A poet celebrates pride

And on the pedestal these
words appear.

My name is Ozymandias,
king of kings:

Look on my works, ye Mighty,
and despair!

—*Percy Bysshe Shelley,*
"Ozymandia..."

Shelley was an early advocate of prideful living. His famous king Ozymandias wasn't afraid to put his words—or himself—up on a pedestal.

Shelley's wife, Mary Wollstonecraft Shelley, believed pride enabled men to do the extraordinary. Her novel Frankenstein was a classic celebration of a doctor's pride so great, it was larger than life itself.

Dr. Frankenstein's pride allowed him to create a human being—a task no fictional character had ever before accomplished.

Putting yourself on a pedestal— it's never been more convenient

But how can *you* live more pridefully?

It's easier than you think. We're the Pride Council. A trade association dedicated to bringing fine products—"Prouducts™"—to the American people. At prices that make pride easy to swallow.

ACT NOW! HERE'S HOW!

Just read the coupon below. You'll find carefully screened and selected companies that can help you design the look-down-your-nose lifestyle you've always dreamed of having.

Don't dally—send in your coupon today.

It would be a sin not to.

The Pride Council
Pride. It's not a sin anymore.™

Mail today to:

The Pride Council
666 Broadway
New York, NY 10012

You've got me convinced! Rush me FREE information on the following prideful products and companies, please!

☐ Your Face in Bronze, Inc.
☐ Old World Family Crests
☐ Roots to Royalty Ancestor Investigators
☐ The Freelance Biographers Guild
☐ Acme Pedestal Co.

Name ....

Address ....

City .... State .... Zip ....

© The Pride Council, 1987

PRIDE

Agency: Ogilvy & Mather. *Creative Director:* Jay Jasper. *Art Director:* Carrie Wiesenech. *Copywriter:* Jim Nolan. *Clients:* Hathaway, "The Man in the Hathaway Shirt"; American Express, "Don't Leave Home Without It"; Pepperidge Farm, "Pepperidge Farm Remembers."

Any Sin That's Enabled Us to Survive Centuries of War, Death, Pestilence and Famine Can't Be Called Deadly.

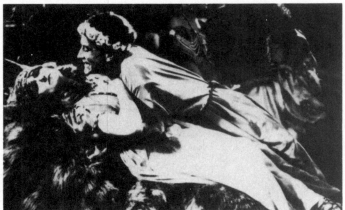

Lust
Where Would We Be Without It?

LUST

Agency: TBWA Advertising, Inc. *Art Director:* Geoff Hayes. *Copywriter:* Evert Cilliers. *Clients:* Absolut Vodka; Bombay Gin; Laughing Cow Cheese.

QUESTIONS

1. These advertisements are obviously not all alike. It seems, in fact, that some of the agencies approached the assignment from a slightly different perspective. How do the advertisements differ in their approaches?

2. How do the advertisements differ in their assessment of audience? Who is the audience for this series?

3. Which advertisements do you find the most effective from a purely persuasive viewpoint? Why? Which advertisements seem to be the least persuasive? Why?

4. Some of these advertisements allude to other famous advertisements. Which ones? What do these allusions suggest about the audience who will read these ads? Allusions like this sometimes appear in regular advertisements also; what do the allusions suggest then?

5. Beneath the captions are listed a few of the advertising campaigns each agency has produced. Do you see any similarities among these campaigns? Can you characterize a "style" for any of these agencies?

6. Try your hand at this campaign by drafting an advertisement for one of the seven cardinal virtues. (If you don't know what these are, look them up.) Don't worry about your artistic skill (or lack of it). Include a rough sketch of the illustration (if any) you would like to appear with your ad copy.

• • • • •

SEX ROLES IN ADVERTISING

Jean Kilbourne

Jean Kilbourne is a media analyst and writer. Her film, Killing Us Softly, *explores the sexual and psychological themes that she finds dominating today's advertising. This essay on sex roles first appeared in an anthology of essays,* TV & Teens *(1982).*

ADVERTISING affects all of us throughout our lives. Adolescents are particularly vulnerable, however, because they are new and inexperienced consumers and are the prime targets of many advertisements. They are in the process of learning their values and roles and developing their self-concepts. Most teenagers are sensitive to peer pressure and find it difficult to resist or even question the dominant cultural messages perpetuated and reinforced by the media. Mass communication has made possible a kind of national peer pressure that erodes private and individual values and standards. Margaret Mead once said that today our children are brought up by the mass media rather than by parents.

Advertisers are aware of their role and do not hesitate to take advantage of the insecurities and anxieties of young people, in the guise of offering solutions. A cigarette provides a symbol of independence. A pair of designer jeans conveys status. The right perfume or beer resolves doubts about femininity or masculinity. Since so many anxieties have to do with sexuality and intimacy and since advertising so often offers products as the answers and uses sex to sell, it is perhaps the concept of sex roles that is most deeply affected.

What do teenagers learn about sex roles from television commercials? On the most obvious level, they learn the stereotypes. These stereotypes have existed for a long time and certainly have not been created or perpetuated solely by advertising. Sexism and sex-role stereotyping exist in every aspect of our society, and we receive these messages from birth. No messenger is more pervasive or persuasive, however, than advertising.

The stereotypes in television commercials have changed very little. Women are shown almost exclusively as sex objects or as demented housewives pathologically obsessed by cleanliness. Men are generally rugged authority figures, dominant and invulnerable. Men who are married or engaged in "women's work" are often betrayed as idiots and buffoons. These stereotypes, and to some extent their effects, have been well documented.

Young people are also affected by advertising in other more subtle ways — ways more indirect but perhaps more powerful than the stereotypes (which increasingly are being recognized and sometimes ridiculed). Advertising could be considered the propaganda of this society. It teaches us to be consumers, to value material things above all else, to feel that happiness can be bought, that there are instant solutions to life's complex problems, and that products can fulfill us and meet our deepest human needs. As a result, objects and things are given great importance and value, and people are often reified and objectified. This is particularly true for women but is increasingly true for men as well. Women, especially young women, are primarily depicted as sex objects and men as success objects. In both cases, the person becomes a thing, and his or her value depends upon the products used.

The sex object is a mannequin, a shell. Conventional beauty is her only attribute. She has no lines or wrinkles (which are, after all, signs of maturity, expression, and experience), no scars or blemishes; indeed, she has no pores. She is thin, generally tall and long legged, and above all young. All "beautiful" women in television commercials, regardless of product or audience, conform to this norm. Women are constantly exhorted to emulate this ideal, to feel ashamed and guilty if they fail, and to feel that their desirability and capacity for being loved are contingent upon physical perfection.

The image is artificial and can only be achieved artificially. Desperate to conform to an ideal and impossible standard, many women go to great lengths to manipulate and change their faces and bodies. More than a million dollars is spent every hour on cosmetics. A woman is conditioned to view her face as a mask and her body as an object, as things separate from and more important than her real self, constantly in need of alteration, improvement, and disguise. She is made to feel dissatisfied with and ashamed of herself, whether she tries to achieve "the look" or not. Objectified constantly by others, she learns to objectify herself.

Women are dismembered in commercials, their bodies separated into parts in need of change or improvement. If a woman has "acceptable" breasts, then she must also be sure that her legs are worth watching, her hips slim, her feet sexy, and that her buttocks look nude under her clothes ("like I'm not wearin' nothin'"). The mannequin has no depth, no totality. She is an aggregate of parts that have been made acceptable.

Girls and young women are primary targets of this message and are socialized to spend enormous amounts of time, energy, and money striving to achieve this ideal. They are made to feel very anxious and insecure about their appearance and their bodies. This preoccupation diverts energy and attention from more important pursuits and the development of their minds and spirits. Ironically, the heavily advertised products, such as cosmetics and soft drinks, are even detrimental to physical attractiveness. There is very little emphasis in the media on good nutrition and exercise and other important aspects of health and vitality.

Most women learn a sense of inferiority and insecurity and of hostile competition with other women. Even the rare teenager who does approximate the ideal suffers. She may experience stunted development in other areas of life and damaged relationships with other women. The constant objectification can lead to callous disregard for others or to a fear that her entire value is contingent upon her appearance. The cultural worship of the adolescent female can lead to unrealistic expectations for the future and can contribute to lifelong rage against women by rejected men. The image harms us all, whether or not we approximate it briefly in our lives.

Young women are also discouraged from growing up and becoming adult. Growing older is the great taboo. Women are encouraged to remain little girls ("because innocence is sexier than you think"), to be passive and dependent, never to mature. The contradictory message, "sensual, but not too far from innocence," places women in a double bind. Somehow women are supposed to be both sexy and virginal, experienced and naive, seductive and chaste. The disparagement of maturity is insulting and frustrating to adult women, and the implication that little girls are seductive is dangerous to real children.

Young people also learn a great deal about sexual attitudes from the media and from advertising in particular. Advertising's approach to sex is pornographic; it reduces people to objects and deemphasizes human contact and individuality. This reduction of sexuality to a dirty joke and of people to objects is the real obscenity of the culture. Although the sexual sell, overt and subliminal, is at a fevered pitch in most commercials, there is at the same time a notable absence of sex as an important and profound human activity. Sex in commercials is narcissistic and autoerotic and exists apart from relationships. Identical models parade alone through the commercials, caressing their own soft skin, stroking and hugging their bodies, shaking their long silky manes, sensually bathing and applying powders and lotions, and then admiring themselves at length in the mirror. Commercials depict a world in which there is pervasive sexual innuendo but no love and in which passion is reserved solely for products.

The curious sterility is due mainly to the stereotypes, which reduce variation and individuality, mock the process of self-realization, and make empathy impossible. When the goal is to embody the stereotype, which is by definition shallow and uniform, depth, passion, and uniqueness are inevitably lost. Men lose, of course, as well as women. Although not as subject to the tyranny of the aesthetic ideal themselves, men are made to feel inadequate if their women — that is, their property — don't measure up ("My wife, I think I'll keep her"). Women are portrayed as sexually desirable only if they are young, thin, carefully polished and groomed, made up, depilated, sprayed, and scented — rendered quite unerotic, in fact — and men are conditioned to seek such partners and to feel disappointed if they fail.

The main goal of sex in advertising, as in pornography, is power over another, either by the physical dominance or preferred status of men or what is seen as the exploitative power of female beauty and female sexuality. Men conquer and women ensnare, always with the essential aid of a product.

Although men are allowed and encouraged to become adults, the acceptable images for males are limited and rigid too. Men are generally conditioned to be obsessed by status and success as measured in material terms and to look upon women as objects, as things to be acquired as further evidence of status. There is a great difference between the portrayal of single men and that of married men. Single men are generally independent and powerful. Married men are often presented as idiots, as if contaminated by their relationship with women. This is particularly true of those few men shown doing domestic chores or relating to children. The stereotypes of men have changed very little.

There have been some changes in the images of women. Indeed a "new woman" has emerged in commercials in recent years. She is generally presented as superwoman, who manages to do all the work at home and on the job (with the help of a product, not of her husband), or as the liberated woman, who owes her independence and self-esteem to the products she uses. These new images do not represent any real progress but rather create a myth of progress, an illusion that reduces complex sociopolitical problems to mundane personal ones, thereby trivializing the issues and diverting energy and attention from a search for genuine solutions.

Superwoman is perhaps the most damaging stereotype of all. Many young women now seem to feel that they can effortlessly combine marriage and a career. The myth of progress obscures the fact that the overwhelming majority of women are in low-status, low-paying jobs and are as far removed from superwoman's elite executive status as the majority of men have always been removed from her male counterpart. The definition of success is still entirely male. The successful woman is presented as climbing up the corporate ladder, seeking money and power. The working woman is expected to get ahead in this man's world, which requires strict adherence to male values, while always giving first priority to her role as wife and mother. In addition, the myth of superwoman places total responsibility for change on the individual woman and exempts men from the responsibilities and rewards of domestic life and child care.

The models for adulthood that commercials offer adolescents are extremely limited and contradictory. Women are supposed to be little girls or superwomen or both. Men are rigidly socialized to repress all feelings of vulnerability, thereby virtually guaranteeing that intimate relationships will be impossible. Motherhood is presented as essential for women and fatherhood as irrelevant for men. Sexuality becomes a commodity.

QUESTIONS

1. Do you agree with Kilbourne's opinions? Have you personally ever attempted to imitate an image you saw portrayed in advertising? Do you think most people do this?
2. Kilbourne argues that advertising shapes our culture. Is it possible that the reverse is actually true, that advertising simply reflects the values already imbedded in the culture? How would we go about determining which is the cause and which the effect?

3. Kilbourne's article was written before the influx of MTV and music videos, which many feel have affected television advertising. Are her assertions about stereotypes still true? If they have changed, how have they changed?

4. Kilbourne's essay appeared in a book called *TV & Teens*. Are teenagers more vulnerable to these sexist images than other segments of the population? Why or why not?

●   ●   ●   ●   ●

BUGS BUNNY SAYS THEY'RE YUMMY

Dawn Ann Kurth

In 1972 a U.S. Senate subcommittee met to consider the effects of television advertising. One of the witnesses before the committee was Dawn Ann Kurth, then a child of eleven. Here is her testimony as it was reported in The New York Times.

Mr. Chairman:

MY name is Dawn Ann Kurth. I am 11 years old and in the fifth grade at Meadowlane Elementary School in Melbourne, Florida. This year I was one of the 36 students chosen by the teachers out of 20,000 5th-through-8th graders to do a project in the Talented Student Program in Brevard County. We were allowed to choose a project in any field we wanted. It was difficult to decide. There seem to be so many problems in the world today. What could I do?

A small family crisis solved my problem. My sister Martha, who is 7, had asked my mother to buy a box of Post Raisin Bran so that she could get the free record that was on the back of the box. It had been advertised several times on Saturday morning cartoon shows. My mother bought the cereal, and we all (there are four children in our family) helped Martha eat it so she could get the record. It was after the cereal was eaten and she had the record that the crisis occurred. There was no way the record would work.

Martha was very upset and began crying and I was angry too. It just didn't seem right to me that something could be shown on TV that worked fine and people were listening and dancing to the record and when you bought the cereal, instead of laughing and dancing, we were crying and angry. Then I realized that perhaps here was a problem I could do something about or, if I couldn't change things, at least I could make others aware of deceptive advertising practices to children.

To begin my project I decided to keep a record of the number of commercials shown in typical Saturday morning TV shows. There were 25 commercial messages during one hour, from 8 to 9 A.M., not counting ads for shows coming up or public service ads. I found there were only 10 to 12 commercials during shows my parents like to watch. For the first time, I really began to think about what the commercials were saying. I had always listened before and many times asked my mother to buy certain products I had seen advertised, but now I was listening and really thinking about what was being said. Millions of kids are being told:

"Make friends with Kool-aid. Kool-aid makes good friends."

"People who love kids have to buy Fritos."

"Hershey chocolate makes milk taste like a chocolate bar." Why should milk taste like a chocolate bar anyway?

"Cheerios makes you feel groovy all day long." I eat them sometimes and I don't feel different.

"Libby frozen dinners have fun in them." Nothing is said about the food in them.

"Cocoa Krispies taste like a chocolate milk shake only they are crunchy."

"Lucky Charms are magically delicious with sweet surprises inside." Those sweet surprises are marshmallow candy.

I think the commercials I just mentioned are examples of deceptive advertising practices.

Another type of commercial advertises a free bonus gift if you buy a certain product. The whole commercial tells about the bonus gift and says nothing about the product they want you to buy. Many times, as in the case of the record, the bonus gift appears to be worthless junk or isn't in the package. I wrote to the TV networks and found it costs about $4,000 for a 30-second commercial. Many of those ads appeared four times in each hour. I wonder why any company would spend $15,000 or $20,000 an hour to advertise worthless junk.

The ads that I have mentioned I consider deceptive. However, I've found others I feel are dangerous.

Bugs Bunny vitamin ads say their vitamins "taste yummy" and taste good.

Chocolate Zestabs says their product is "delicious" and compare taking it with eating a chocolate cookie.

If my mother were to buy those vitamins, and my little sister got to the bottles, I'm sure she would eat them just as if they were candy.

I do not know a lot about nutrition, but I do know that my mother tries to keep our family from eating so many sweets. She says they are bad for our teeth. Our dentist says so too. If they are bad, why are companies allowed to make children want them by advertising on TV? Almost all of the ads I have seen during children's programming are for candy, or sugar-coated cereal, or even suger-coated cereal with candy in it.

I know people who make these commercials are not bad. I know the commercials pay for TV shows and I like to watch TV. I just think that it would be as easy to produce a good commercial as a bad one. If there is nothing good that can be said about a product that is the truth, perhaps the product should not be sold to kids on TV in the first place.

I do not know all the ways to write a good commercial, but I think commercials would be good if they taught kids something that was true. They could teach about good health, and also about where food is grown. If my 3-year-old sister can learn to sing "It takes two hands to handle a whopper cause the burgers are better at Burger King" from a commercial, couldn't a commercial also teach her to recognize the letters of the alphabet, numbers, and colors? I am sure that people who write commercials are much smarter than I and they should be able to think of many ways to write a commercial that tells the truth about a product without telling kids they should eat because it is sweeter or "shaped like fun" (what shape *is* fun, anyway?) or because Tony Tiger says so.

I also think kids should not be bribed to buy a product by commercials telling of the wonderful free bonus gift inside.

I think kids should not be told to eat a certain product because a well-known hero does. If this is a reason to eat something, then, when a well-known person uses drugs, should kids try drugs for the same reason?

Last of all, I think vitamin companies should never, never be allowed to advertise their product as being delicious, yummy, or in any way make children think they are candy. Perhaps these commercials could teach children the dangers of taking drugs or teach children that, if they do find a bottle of pills, or if the medicine closet is open, they should run and tell a grown-up, and never, never eat the medicine.

I want to thank the Committee for letting me appear. When I leave Washington, the thing that I will remember for the rest of my life is that some people *do* care what kids think. I know I could have led a protest about commercials through our shopping center and people would have laughed at me or thought I needed a good spanking or wondered what kind of parents I had that would let me run around the streets protesting. I decided to gather my information and write letters to anyone I thought would listen. Many of them didn't listen, but some did. That is why I am here today. Because some people cared about what I thought. I hope now that I can tell every kid in America that when they see a wrong, they shouldn't just try to forget about it and hope it will go away. They should begin to do what they can to change it.

People will listen. I know, because you're here listening to me.

QUESTIONS

1. What is there about this statement that suggests it was written by a child? Are there any parts of it that do not seem to reflect a child's point of view?

2. What persuasive strategies does Dawn identify in the commercials she names? What seem to be the dominant strategies employed by advertisers who are attempting to appeal to children?

3. Dawn mentions other ways she could have carried her message to the world. Would these ways have been more, or less, effective than the strategy she chose? Why?

4. Does Dawn Kurth's appeal have anything in common with the appeals she in turn criticizes?

5. Is this appeal more effective because it comes from a child? How would you react if the statement were being read by an adult?

6. Write an essay describing another product that is sold primarily to children using advertising that is deceptive or unfair.

•　　•　　•　　•　　•

CIGARETTE ADS AND THE PRESS

Ira Glasser

As the furor over smoking grows, some have urged that all tobacco advertising be banned from newspapers and magazines, just as it has been banned from television. Those who favor the ban see tobacco as a serious health problem for the country and its citizens; those who oppose this advertising ban question whether any single industry should be singled out for such punitive action. In March, 1987, The Nation *magazine published a symposium on this question and asked several writers to contribute their opinions. Here is the statement of Ira Glasser, the executive director of the American Civil Liberties Union.*

I DON'T smoke, never have. Neither do any of my children, for which I am grateful. Years before it became fashionable, I protested having other people's tobacco smoke imposed on me in closed places. I know that nicotine is severely addictive, and I believe the evidence that smoking is a serious health hazard. But I am against legislative bans on cigarette advertising, for two reasons.

First, censorship is a contagious disease. Many people who fervently support the First Amendment believe that it would be possible to ban cigarette ads without endangering other First Amendment rights. I think they are deluding themselves, and us. They offer two arguments in distinguishing between cigarette ads and other forms of protected expression: the First Amendment does not protect commercial speech as fully as it does political or artistic speech; and the particularly dangerous nature of tobacco justifies making an exception to the First Amendment.

If those two distinctions became codified, what might we expect? Laws would be passed prohibiting advertising for abortion clinics, for example, many of which are commercial, profit-making enterprises. Those laws would be justified by their proponents on the ground that abortion is murder, the worst health hazard imaginable. How would we react to that?

Some of us might see distinctions between tobacco ads and abortion clinic ads. But neither I nor the readers of *The Nation* will get to rule on those distinctions. Many people, including many legislators, believe that abortion is murder. They will write the laws, and people named Scalia and Rehnquist will decide whether the laws are constitutional.

Once danger becomes a permissible basis for abridging speech, the only important question is, Who defines what is dangerous? No one who values the First Amendment can be comforted by the expectation that the Rehnquist-Scalia Court will be able to short-circuit it whenever the Court believes something is harmful. Indeed, the purpose of the First Amendment is precisely to remove such discretion from government officials, including judges. We do not want courts deciding what speech is too dangerous for us to hear. We want courts to decide that the First Amendment prohibits using danger as a basis for banning speech.

The terrible erosion of First Amendment rights in the name of national security is a testament to the tendency of courts to allow illegitimate government claims of danger to justify censorship. It is a standard no one should endorse, least of all the left. When they come after abortion clinic ads, using as precedent the liberal arguments in favor of banning cigarette ads, it will be too late to invoke the protection of the First Amendment.

Second, there is little, if any, evidence that bans on cigarette advertising will reduce the percentage of Americans who smoke. In 1965, 43 percent of the adult population smoked; today, it's down to 30 percent. That is the most substantial reported decline for any widely used addictive drug in the United States. Cigarette smoking began to fall off in the early 1970s, when health warnings first appeared on all cigarette ads and packages, and a couple of years after the Federal Communications Commission required broadcasters to air antismoking replies to cigarette ads. Indeed, much of the decline in smoking occurred before cigarette ads were banned on television. In fact, cigarette smoking increased again immediately after the ban, probably because antismoking replies were no longer required. Over the past ten years the percentage of adults who smoke has continued to drop, almost certainly as a result of public education.

In a fair contest between medical facts and the tobacco industry's self-serving propaganda, the facts will win. That is the premise of the First Amendment. And that is what the past twenty years demonstrate. More public education is what we need, not bans on speech. If the government were serious about responding to smoking as a public health hazard, it would do away with the price-supporting programs for tobacco growers and fund a major national public education campaign, particularly aimed at children, on the harmfulness of smoking. That would be really tough.

But most legislators have little interest in being tough. They just want to appear tough. And the way to do that is to introduce legislation to ban cigarette advertising. There's no cost, except to the First Amendment. That's a cost legislators usually don't worry about, but readers of *The Nation* should.

A related, though less consequential, question is whether magazines and newspapers should publish cigarette ads. More generally, should publishers accept only those ads that are in accord with their politics and reject others? My view is that publishers should treat their advertising space differently from their editorial space.

Advertising space could, and perhaps should, be considered a common carrier, a billboard available for sale to anyone, without legal limits. In the past, the New York Civil Liberties Union has tried to persuade *The New Yorker* to take an ad for the play *MacBird!* and the *New York Post* to accept ads for abortion clinics. I think both publications were wrong in refusing those ads, but they have every right to do so. Still, those who invoke the First Amendment to protect their own right to publish have a moral, though not a legal, obligation to provide access to their advertising columns on a nondiscriminatory basis. Then let them attack the ads in their editorial space if they wish. The First Amendment means that this question must be decided by each individual publisher, not by the government.

QUESTIONS

1. Glasser begins by explaining his own personal feelings about smoking. What effect does this opening have on a reader?

2. Glasser argues for preserving First Amendment rights, saying "when they come after abortion clinic ads . . . it will be too late to invoke the protection of the First Amendment." Who is this *they* he is referring to? How would you characterize this persuasive strategy?

3. Glasser refers to the readers of *The Nation* as though they were a special group — "That's a cost legislators usually don't worry about, but readers of *The Nation* should." What assumptions does he seem to make about this audience?

4. One implication of Glasser's argument is that advertising really does not affect people much anyway. He points out that the number of adults who smoke has continued to drop, and argues that in a contest between the facts and "the tobacco industry's self-serving propaganda, the facts will win." How do you feel about the power of advertising? Do the facts always win?

• • • • •

SCIENCE NEWS SALES LETTER

E. G. Sherburne, Jr.

We all receive a good deal of unsolicited mail, mail that offers us prizes, invites us to participate in sweepstakes, and tries to sell us merchandise. Some of these solicitations we toss aside unread as "junk mail." Direct mail advertising is not necessarily inexpensive, however, and many of the appeals we receive are very carefully crafted. And, of course, many of them get results or the advertisers would not continue to spend their money in this way. Here is an example of a good sales letter, one you may have received.

SCIENCE NEWS

The Weekly Newsmagazine of Science
1719 N Street NW, Washington DC 20036

May I send you twelve issues of SCIENCE NEWS, America's only weekly science report, for just $1.00?

They're yours without any further cost or the least commitment.

Dear Reader:

Frankly, twelve weekly issues of SCIENCE NEWS are worth a lot more than $1.

However, I have a very good reason for making you this no-strings-attached introductory offer.

You see, once someone with your demonstrated interest in science has spent three months with SCIENCE NEWS, I'm fairly sure we'll have gained another regular subscriber.

Why? Consider what a few of our current (and better known) readers have written about our unique weekly:

From Wilbur E. Garrett, Editor of the "National Geographic" . . .

"In no other publication can the intelligent layman get so quick and accurate a summary of the latest findings and the latest thinking in all the sciences. Perhaps the greatest tribute to you is the commendations one often hears from the scientists themselves."

From Isaac Asimov, noted science author and futurist . . .

"The existence of SCIENCE NEWS spans sixty years . . . I am pleased that for one-third of this stretch of time, I have been (and still am) a subscriber."

From Walter Sullivan, science writer for the "New York Times" . . .

"I feel compelled to clip something from almost every issue of SCIENCE NEWS for my files. How can one ignore a source that offers us Jonathan Eberhart, Janet Raloff, Dietrick Thomsen and all the others?"

From Stephen Jay Gould, Professor of Geology at Harvard University . . .

"SCIENCE NEWS has long distinguished itself as America's finest journal of general and accessible science. It

(over, please)

continued

continued

should be everybody's starting point to a necessary
understanding."

Finally, I'd like to pass along this comment by the "Columbia Journalism
Review" . . .

". . . by far the best source of science news is a weekly
magazine called SCIENCE NEWS. It offers prompt, witty
reporting to readers who are not put off by a few such
basic scientific terms as ion or hormone. Evidently
writers of other science magazines read SCIENCE NEWS;
uncredited echoes of its stories often appear elsewhere."

As you can see, while many of our readers are indeed practicing scientists,
you don't have to be one of them to enjoy and benefit from SCIENCE NEWS.

But you <u>will</u> have to be a bit above average in both intellect and interest.

Still, the rewards you'll gain from each of our concise weekly issues will
be of far greater value to you than any you may occasionally pick up from the
current plethora of pseudo-science magazines.

You'll get them far sooner, too.

To illustrate, long before any of those other publications got around to
announcing the existence of an artificial heart . . . the threat to our defense
communications of "EMP" generated by nuclear blasts in space . . . or the use of
bone marrow transplants to save children lacking natural immunity to infection,
<u>SCIENCE NEWS readers already knew the essential details</u>.

How is SCIENCE NEWS able to "scoop" other science periodicals and keep
serious readers like you so exceptionally well informed? Because it offers you
a combination of three advantages you simply can't get in any similar-seeming
publication.

<u>SCIENCE NEWS is uniquely authoritative</u>. Published for over 60 years by the
non-profit Science Service, SCIENCE NEWS is the product of a respected editorial
team that constantly monitors more than 200 specialized sources to capture the
essence of scientific progress for you.

<u>SCIENCE NEWS is delivered to you fresh every week</u>. Keeping you fully
current on the fast-breaking advances in fields like biomedicine and the space
sciences means getting this news to you with the least delay possible. As a
weekly publication, SCIENCE NEWS updates you four times faster (and more often)
than any monthly magazine can.

<u>SCIENCE NEWS gives you only the facts you want</u>. With its trim 16-page
format, SCIENCE NEWS doesn't waste your time. Each issue is a brisk, tautly
telegraphic report that brings you the truly important news from science's many
and varied frontiers -- with a maximum of fact and a minimum of words.

Yet, for all its businesslike brevity, this authoritative weekly will
definitely never bore you!

For while each SCIENCE NEWS article and feature is carefully prepared for fast, easy, informative reading, we keep a tight rein on technical jargon and make every illustration count.

Then, too, there's the <u>breadth</u> of our science coverage. To demonstrate, here are just a few examples of what our readers learned recently. (Don't be surprised if some of them still come as "new" news to you.)

ABSORBING NUCLEAR WASTES IN HAWAII. Researchers from the University of Hawaii report that the fungus "Penicilium digitatum" can absorb uranium from solutions of uranyl chloride. If confirmed, this discovery holds great promise for waste-water decontamination.

DECAFFEINATING YOURSELF MAY NOT BE ENOUGH. Scientists have found that long-term coffee consumption causes brain tissue changes that can lead to dependency. And caffeine isn't the only culprit. Another compound discovered in coffee is now reported to have the same effect.

PLANES OF THE FUTURE FACE A HEAVENLY MENACE. Tomorrow's computer-controlled aircraft made of composite materials and plastic present a new problem that threatens to offset their greater efficiency. They will be far more vulnerable to the effects of lightning. The answer? No one's quite sure yet.

FOUND: THE CHEMICAL KEY TO EMPHYSEMA. Thanks to Dr. Ines Mandl of Columbia University, the chemical role of cigarettes and air pollution in the breakdown of lung elastin which produces emphysema has finally been pinpointed. This breakthrough makes possible rational approaches to treating this disease which afflicts some 11 million Americans, and kills about 56,000 of us annually.

NEW BRAIN PARTS FOR OLD? While transplanting most body parts is fraught with the dangers of biological rejection and other, often fatal complications, animal experiments show that the brain seems among the most immunologically safe sites for tissue transplants. The complexity of the human brain will keep it off-limits for a long time though.

GETTING HIGH ON A CARCINOGEN. People who "smort" cocaine are courting a far deadlier danger than addiction: Cancer of the nasal passages! In fact, even inhaling perfume, nasal decongestants, and household solvents (not to mention nicotine and air pollution) can produce the same unpleasant result. For each contains substances that break down into formaldehyde -- a known nasal carcinogen.

"MODERN" MAN IN ANCIENT ISRAEL. Recent findings near the Sea of Galilee indicate that Homo erectus, the first tool-making man, may well have evolved in the Middle East -- not in Africa as previously believed. Stone tools found in the area could pre-date the Leakey's "Olduvai Man" by as much as a million years.

As you can see, SCIENCE NEWS covers all areas of science for you in a way that is not only informative but genuinely interesting as well.

(over, please)

continued

continued

And now you can try it yourself for twelve weeks just by sending us $1.

All you have to do is initial the enclosed Acceptance Form and mail it back to us -- together with your dollar -- in the postage-paid envelope provided.

>   Please notice that there are no strings attached to this
>   offer. When we receive your acceptance, we will send you
>   the following twelve weeks of SCIENCE NEWS. And that, if
>   you wish, will be all you need be concerned about.

While there is a provision in the Acceptance Form's wording for a 52-week SCIENCE NEWS subscription at just $29.87 (a savings of 13% off our regular $34.50 annual rate), <u>this does not obligate you in any way at all!</u>

For if you choose not to take advantage of this special discount opportunity after receiving your twelve trial issues -- <u>you have only to write the word "cancel" across the invoice we'll send you and return it.</u>

In that case, the matter will be immediately and fully closed.

>   Obviously, though, I'm quite confident that after spending
>   twelve weeks at the "cutting edge" of the sciences and
>   technologies with SCIENCE NEWS, you will decide to take us
>   up on that money-saving opportunity.

However, we'll leave that decision up to you.

As you can see, I've tried to make our "twelve trial issue" offer as attractive as possible. So naturally, I hope you won't put off accepting it for even one minute.

Thank you for reading my letter. I look foward to hearing from you soon.

>   Sincerely,
>
>   *E G Sherburne*
>
>   E. G. Sherburne, Jr.
>   Publisher

P.S. SCIENCE NEWS is not sold at newsstands or bookstores. It is available
      only to those who order subscriptions and, for a limited time, through
      this special introductory offer.

QUESTIONS

1. This advertisement is prepared in the literal form of a sales letter, with a printed headline followed by a text that looks as though it has been hand typed. What effect does the appearance of the "letter" have? Do you respond to a letter differently from the way you might respond to a multi-colored advertising brochure?

2. What kind of direct mail advertising do you personally find most effective? What kind do you find least effective? Why?

3. Sherburne begins his letter with some "testimonials" from present readers. Are you impressed by these readers' statements? Do you find their comments relevant?

4. Outline the letter. How is it structured? Does the order of Sherburne's presentation keep you reading? Where does he discuss the cost? Is there a reason for placing this information where he does?

5. What is the effect of including the postscript? Could this information have been included someplace in the text of the letter? Why wasn't it?

6. Examine your own mail for advertising letters similar to this one. Write an essay analyzing the marketing strategies that seem to be at work in the letter you received.

•   •   •   •   •

THE CIVIL RIGHTS MOVEMENT: WHAT GOOD WAS IT?

Alice Walker

Alice Walker writes fiction, essays, poetry, and biography. Currently her most successful work is her best-selling novel The Color Purple *(1982). This article on the civil rights movement is from her book* In Search of Our Mothers' Gardens *(1983), a collection of essays Walker labels "Womanist Prose." It was Walker's first published essay.*

SOMEONE said recently to an old black lady from Mississippi, whose legs had been badly mangled by local police who arrested her for "disturbing the peace," that the Civil Rights Movement was dead, and asked, since it was dead, what she thought about it. The old lady replied, hobbling out of his presence on her cane, that the Civil Rights Movement was like herself, "if it's dead, it shore ain't ready to lay down!"

This old lady is a legendary freedom fighter in her small town in the Delta. She has been severely mistreated for insisting on her rights as an American citizen. She has been beaten for singing Movement songs, placed in solitary confinement in prisons for talking about freedom, and placed on bread and water for praying aloud to God for her jailers' deliverance. For such a woman the Civil Rights Movement will never be over as long as her skin is black. It also will never be over for twenty million others with the same "affliction," for whom the Movement can never "lay down," no matter how it is killed by the press and made dead and buried by the white American public. As long as one black American survives, the struggle for equality with other Americans must also survive. This is a debt we owe to those blameless hostages we leave to the future, our children.

Still, white liberals and deserting Civil Rights sponsors are quick to justify their disaffection from the Movement by claiming that it is all over. "And since it is over," they will ask, "would someone kindly tell me what has been gained by it?" They then list statistics supposedly showing how much more advanced segregation is now than ten years ago—in schools, housing, jobs. They point to a gain in conservative politicians during the last few years. They speak of ghetto riots and of the survey that shows that most policemen are admittedly too anti-Negro to do their jobs in ghetto areas fairly and effectively. They speak of every area that has been touched by the Civil Rights Movement as somehow or other going to pieces.

They rarely talk, however, about human attitudes among Negroes that have undergone terrific changes just during the past seven to ten years (not to mention all those years when there was a Movement and only the Negroes knew about it). They seldom speak of changes in personal lives because of the influence of people in the Movement. They see general failure and few, if any, individual gains.

They do not understand what it is that keeps the Movement from "laying down" and Negroes from reverting to their former *silent* second-class status. They have apparently never stopped to wonder why it is always the white man — on his radio and in his newspaper and on his television — who says that the Movement is dead. If a Negro were audacious enough to make such a claim, his fellows might hanker to see him shot. The Movement is dead to the white man because it no longer interests him. And it no longer interests him because he can afford to be uninterested: he does not have to live by it, with it, or for it, as Negroes must. He can take a rest from the news of beatings, killings, and arrests that reach him from North and South—if his skin is white. Negroes cannot now and will never be able to take a rest from the injustices that plague them, for they—not the white man—are the target.

Perhaps it is naïve to be thankful that the Movement "saved" a large number of individuals and gave them something to live for, even if it did not provide them with everything they wanted. (Materially, it provided them with precious little that they wanted.) When a movement awakens people to the possibilities of life, it seems unfair to frustrate them by then denying what they had thought was offered. But what was offered? What was promised? What was it all about? What good did it do? Would it have been better, as some have suggested, to leave the Negro people as they were, unawakened, unallied with one another, unhopeful about what to expect for their children in some future world?

I do not think so. If knowledge of my condition is all the –freedom I get from a "freedom movement," it is better than unawareness, forgottenness, and hopelessness, the existence that is like the existence of a beast. Man only truly lives by knowing, otherwise he simply performs, copying the daily habits of others, but conceiving nothing of his creative possibilities as a man, and accepting someone else's superiority and his own misery.

When we are children, growing up in our parents' care, we await the spark from the outside world. Sometimes our parents provide it — if we are lucky — sometimes it comes from another source far from home. We sit, paralyzed, surrounded by our anxiety and dread, hoping we will not have to grow up into the narrow world and ways we see about us. We are hungry for a life that turns us on; we yearn for a knowledge of living that will save us from our innocuous lives that resemble death. We look for signs in every strange event; we search for heroes in every unknown face.

It was just six years ago that I began to be alive. I had, of course, been living before — for I am now twenty-three — but I did not really know it. And I did not know it because nobody told me that I — a pensive, yearning, typical high-school senior, but Negro — existed in the minds of others as I existed in my own. Until that time my mind was locked apart from the outer contours and complexion of my body as if it and the body were strangers. The mind possessed both thought and spirit — I wanted to be an author or a scientist — which the color of the body denied. I had never seen myself and existed as a statistic exists, or as a phantom. In the white world I walked, less real to them than a shadow; and being young and well hidden among the slums, among people who also did not exist — either in books or in films or in the government of their own lives — I waited to be called to life. And, by a miracle, I was called.

There was a commotion in our house that night in 1960. We had managed to buy our first television set. It was battered and overpriced but my mother had gotten used to watching the afternoon soap operas at the house where she worked as maid, and nothing could satisfy her on days when she did not work but a continuation of her "stories." So she pinched pennies and bought a set.

I remained listless throughout her "stories," tales of pregnancy, abortion, hypocrisy, infidelity, and alcoholism. All these men and women were white and lived in houses with servants, long staircases that they floated down, patios where liquor was served four times a day to "relax" them. But my mother, with her swollen feet eased out of her shoes, her heavy body relaxed in our only comfortable chair, watched every movement of the smartly coiffed women, heard every word, pounced upon each innuendo and inflection, and for the duration of these "stories" she saw herself as one of them. She placed herself in every scene she saw, with her braided hair turned blond, her two hundred pounds compressed into a sleek size-seven dress, her rough dark skin smooth and *white*. Her husband became "dark and handsome," talented, witty, urbane, charming. And when she turned to look at my father sitting near her in his sweat shirt with his smelly feet raised on the bed to "air," there was always a tragic look of surprise on her face. Then she would sigh and go out to the kitchen looking lost and unsure of herself. My mother, a truly great woman who raised eight children of her own and half a dozen of the neighbors' without a single complaint, was convinced that she did not exist compared to "them." She subordinated her soul to theirs and became a faithful and timid supporter of the "Beautiful White People." Once she asked me, in a moment of vicarious pride and despair, if I didn't think that "they" were "jest naturally smarter, prettier, better." My mother asked this: a woman who never got rid of any of her children, never cheated on my father, was never a hypocrite if she could help it, and never even tasted liquor. She could not even bring herself to blame "them" for making her believe what they wanted her to believe: that if she did not look like them, think like them, be sophisticated and corrupt-for-comfort's sake like them, she was a nobody. Black was not a color on my mother; it was a shield that made her invisible.

Of course, the people who wrote the soap-opera scripts always made the Negro maids in them steadfast, trusty, and wise in a home-remedial sort of way; but my mother, a maid for nearly forty years, never once identified herself with the scarcely glimpsed black servant's face beneath the ruffled cap. Like everyone else, in her day-dreams at least, she thought she was free.

Six years ago, after half-heartedly watching my mother's soap operas and wondering whether there wasn't something more to be asked of life, the Civil Rights Movement came into my life. Like a good omen for the future, the face of Dr. Martin Luther King, Jr., was the first black face I saw on our new television screen. And, as in a fairy tale, my soul was stirred by the meaning for me of his mission — at the time he was being rather ignominiously dumped into a police van for having led a protest march in Alabama — and I fell in love with the sober and determined face of the Movement. The singing of "We Shall Overcome" — that song betrayed by non-believers in it — rang for the first time in my ears. The influence that my mother's soap operas might have had on me became impossible. The life of Dr. King, seeming bigger and more miraculous than the man himself because of all he had done and suffered, offered a pattern of strength and sincerity I felt I could trust. He had suffered much because of his simple belief in nonviolence, love, and brotherhood. Perhaps the majority of men could not be reached through these beliefs, but because Dr. King kept trying to reach them in spite of danger to himself and his family, I saw in him the hero for whom I had waited so long.

What Dr. King promised was not a ranch-style house and an acre of manicured lawn for every black man, but jail and finally freedom. He did not promise two cars for every family, but the courage one day for all families everywhere to walk without shame and unafraid on their own feet. He did not say that one day it will be us chasing prospective buyers out of our prosperous well-kept neighborhoods, or in other ways exhibiting our snobbery and ignorance as all other ethnic groups before us have done; what he said was that we had a right to live anywhere in this country we chose, and a right to a meaningful well-paying job to provide us with the upkeep of our homes. He did not say we had to become carbon copies of the white American middle class; but he did say we had the right to become whatever we wanted to become.

Because of the Movement, because of an awakened faith in the newness and imagination of the human spirit, because of "black and white together" — for the first time in our history in some human relationship on and off TV — because of the beatings, the arrests, the hell of battle during the past years, I have fought harder for my life and for a chance to be myself, to be something more than a shadow or a number, than I had ever done before in my life. Before, there had seemed to be no real reason for struggling beyond the effort of daily bread. Now there was a chance at that other that Jesus meant when He said we could not live by bread alone.

I have fought and kicked and fasted and prayed and cursed and cried myself to the point of existing. It has been like being born again, literally. Just "knowing" has meant everything to me. Knowing has pushed me out into the world, into college, into places, into people.

Part of what existence means to me is knowing the difference between what I am now and what I was then. It is being capable of looking after myself intellectually as well as financially. It is being able to tell when I am being wronged and by whom. It means being awake to protect myself and the ones I love. It means being a part of the world community, and being *alert* to which part it is that I have joined, and knowing how to change to another part if that part does not suit me. To know is to exist: to exist is to be involved, to move about, to see the world with my own eyes. This, at least, the Movement has given me.

The hippies and other nihilists would have me believe that it is all the same whether the people in Mississippi have a movement behind them or not. Once they have their rights, they say, they will run all over themselves trying to be just like everybody else. They will be well fed, complacent about things of the spirit, emotionless, and without that marvelous humanity and "soul" that the Movement has seen them practice time and time again. "What has the Movement done," they ask, "with the few people it has supposedly helped?" "Got them white-collar jobs, moved them into standardized ranch houses in white neighborhoods, given them nondescript gray flannel suits?" "What are these people now?" they ask. And then they answer themselves, "Nothings!"

I would find this reasoning — which I have heard many, many times from hippies and nonhippies alike — amusing if I did not also consider it serious. For I think it is a delusion, a cop-out, an excuse to disassociate themselves from a world in which they feel too little has been changed or gained. The real question, however, it appears to me, is not whether poor people will adopt the middle-class mentality once they are well fed; rather, it is whether they will ever be well fed enough to be able to choose whatever mentality they think will suit them. The lack of a movement did not keep my mother from *wishing* herself bourgeois in her daydream.

There is widespread starvation in Mississippi. In my own state of Georgia there are more hungry families than Lester Maddox would like to admit — or even see fed. I went to school with children who ate red dirt. The Movement has prodded and pushed some liberal senators into pressuring the government for food so that the hungry may eat. Food stamps that were two dollars and out of the reach of many families not long ago have been reduced to fifty cents. The price is still out of the reach of some families, and the government, it seems to a lot of people, could spare enough free food to feed its own people. It angers people in the Movement that it does not; they point to the billions in wheat we send free each year to countries abroad. Their government's slowness while people are hungry, its unwillingness to believe that there are Americans starving, its stingy cutting of the price of food stamps, make many Civil Rights workers throw up their hands in disgust. But they do not give up. They do not withdraw into the world of psychedelia. They apply what pressure they can to make the government give away food to hungry people. They do not plan so far ahead in their disillusionment with society that they can see these starving families buying identical ranch-style houses and sending their snobbish children to Bryn Mawr and Yale. They take first things first and try to get them fed.

They do not consider it their business, in any case, to say what kind of life the people they help must lead. How one lives is, after all, one of the rights left to the individual — when and if he has opportunity to choose. It is not the prerogative of the middle class to determine what is worthy of aspiration. There is also every possibility that the middle-class people of tomorrow will turn out ever so much better than those of today. I even know some middle-class people of today who are not *all* bad.

I think there are so few Negro hippies because middle-class Negroes, although well fed, are not careless. They are required by the treacherous world they live in to be clearly aware of whoever or whatever might be trying to do them in. They are middle class in money and position, but they cannot afford to be middle class in complacency.

They distrust the hippie movement because they know that it can do nothing for Negroes as a group but "love" them, which is what all paternalists claim to do. And since the only way Negroes can survive (which they cannot do, unfortunately, on love alone) is with the support of the group, they are wisely wary and stay away.

A white writer tried recently to explain that the reason for the relatively few Negro hippies is that Negroes have built up a "super-cool" that cracks under LSD and makes them have a "bad trip." What this writer doesn't guess at is that Negroes are needing drugs less than ever these days for any kind of trip. While the hippies are "tripping," Negroes are going after power, which is so much more important to their survival and their children's survival than LSD and pot.

Everyone would be surprised if the Israelis ignored the Arabs and took up "tripping" and pot smoking. In this country we are the Israelis. Everybody who can do so would like to forget this, of course. But for us to forget it for a minute would be fatal. "We Shall Overcome" is just a song to most Americans, *but we must do it*. Or die.

What good was the Civil Rights Movement? If it had just given this country Dr. King, a leader of conscience, for once in our lifetime, it would have been enough. It it had just taken black eyes off white television stories, it would have been enough. If it had fed one starving child, it would have been enough.

If the Civil Rights Movement is "dead," and if it gave us nothing else, it gave us each other forever. It gave some of us bread, some of us shelter, some of us knowledge and pride, all of us comfort. It gave us our children, our husbands, our brothers, our fathers, as men reborn and with a purpose for living. It broke the pattern of black servitude in this country. It shattered the phony "promise" of white soap operas that sucked away so many pitiful lives. It gave us history and men far greater than Presidents. It gave us heroes, selfless men of courage and strength, for our little boys and girls to follow. It gave us hope for tomorrow. It called us to life.

Because we live, it can never die.

QUESTIONS

1. Walker argues that the civil rights movement has not benefitted most black people materially. According to her, how have they benefitted? Do you agree?

2. Walker makes a distinction between the attitudes of some white Americans (who ask questions about the death of the civil rights movement) and most black Americans (who do not see the movement as dead). What audience do you think she had in mind when she wrote this essay? Is it black? White? People from both groups?

3. Walker discusses the impact of television on her life (and on her mother's life) when she was young. What was wrong with the influence of television, according to Walker? Has television changed since the time she describes? Does it still create daydreams for a disadvantaged audience?

4. Walker labels her volume "Womanist Prose." Does this label seem to apply to this essay? Does the article seem to be concerned with issues that are more relevant to women than men? Why or why not?

5. This article was written in the winter of 1966–67. Do you think the issues it raises are still valid? How has the country changed since this essay was written?

•   •   •   •   •

LETTER FROM BIRMINGHAM JAIL

Martin Luther King, Jr.

Martin Luther King was a world-renowned civil rights leader and the winner of the Nobel Peace Prize in 1964. In 1963 he was jailed in Birmingham, Alabama, for leading a protest and his actions were heavily criticized. The following letter was written in response to that public criticism.

April 16, 1963

My Dear Fellow Clergymen:

WHILE confined here in the Birmingham city jail, I came across your recent statement calling my present activities "unwise and untimely." Seldom do I pause to answer criticism of my work and ideas. If I sought to answer all the criticisms that cross my desk, my secretaries would have little time for anything other than such correspondence in the course of the day, and I would have no time for constructive work. But since I feel that you are men of genuine good will and that your criticisms are sincerely set forth, I want to try to answer your statements in what I hope will be patient and reasonable terms.

I think I should indicate why I am here in Birmingham, since you have been influenced by the view which argues against "outsiders coming in." I have the honor of serving as president of the Southern Christian Leadership Conference, an organization operating in every southern state, with headquarters in Atlanta, Georgia. We have some eighty-five affiliated organizations across the South, and one of them is the Alabama Christian Movement for Human Rights. Frequently we share staff, educational and financial resources with our affiliates. Several months ago the affiliate here in Birmingham asked us to be on call to engage in a nonviolent direct-action program if such were deemed necessary. We readily consented, and when the hour came we lived up to our promise. So I, along with several members of my staff, am here because I was invited here. I am here because I have organized ties here.

But more basically, I am in Birmingham because injustice is here. Just as the prophets of the eighth century B.C. left their villages and carried their "thus saith the Lord" far beyond the boundaries of their home towns, and just as the Apostle Paul left his village of Tarsus and carried the gospel of Jesus Christ to the far corners of the Greco-Roman world, so am I compelled to carry the gospel of freedom beyond my own home town. Like Paul, I must constantly respond to the Macedonian call for aid.

AUTHOR'S NOTE: This response to a published statement by eight fellow clergymen from Alabama (Bishop C. C. J. Carpenter, Bishop Joseph A. Durick, Rabbi Hilton L. Grafman, Bishop Paul Hardin, Bishop Holan B. Harmon, the Reverend George M. Murray, the Reverend Edward V. Ramage and the Reverend Earl Stallings) was composed under somewhat constricting circumstances. Begun on the margins of the newspaper in which the statement appeared while I was in jail, the letter was continued on scraps of writing paper supplied by a friendly Negro trusty, and concluded on a pad my attorneys were eventually permitted to leave me. Although the text remains in substance unaltered, I have indulged in the author's prerogative of polishing it for publication.

Moreover, I am cognizant of the interrelatedness of all communities and states. I cannot sit idly by in Atlanta and not be concerned about what happens in Birmingham. Injustice anywhere is a threat to justice everywhere. We are caught in an inescapable network of mutuality, tied in a single garment of destiny. Whatever affects one directly, affects all indirectly. Never again can we afford to live with the narrow, provincial "outside agitator" idea. Anyone who lives inside the United States can never be considered an outsider anywhere within its bounds.

You deplore the demonstrations taking place in Birmingham. But your statement, I am sorry to say, fails to express a similar concern for the conditions that brought about the demonstrations. I am sure that none of you would want to rest content with the superficial kind of social analysis that deals merely with effects and does not grapple with underlying causes. It is unfortunate that demonstrations are taking place in Birmingham, but it is even more unfortunate that the city's white power structure left the Negro community with no alternative.

In any nonviolent campaign there are four basic steps: collection of the facts to determine whether injustices exist; negotiation; self-purification; and direct action. We have gone through all these steps in Birmingham. There can be no gainsaying the fact that racial injustice engulfs this community. Birmingham is probably the most thoroughly segregated city in the United States. Its ugly record of brutality is widely known. Negroes have experienced grossly unjust treatment in the courts. There have been more unsolved bombings of Negro homes and churches in Birmingham than in any other city in the nation. These are the hard, brutal facts of the case. On the basis of these conditions, Negro leaders sought to negotiate with the city fathers. But the latter consistently refused to engage in good-faith negotiation.

Then, last September, came the opportunity to talk with leaders of Birmingham's economic community. In the course of the negotiations, certain promises were made by the merchants — for example, to remove the stores' humiliating racial signs. On the basis of these promises, the Reverend Fred Shuttlesworth and the leaders of the Alabama Christian Movement for Human Rights agreed to a moratorium on all demonstrations. As the weeks and months went by, we realized that we were the victims of a broken promise. A few signs, briefly removed, returned; the others remained.

As in so many past experiences, our hopes had been blasted, and the shadow of deep disappointment settled upon us. We had no alternative except to prepare for direct action, whereby we would present our very bodies as a means of laying our case before the conscience of the local and the national community. Mindful of the difficulties involved, we decided to undertake a process of self-purification. We began a series of workshops on nonviolence, and we repeatedly asked ourselves: "Are you able to accept blows without retaliating?" "Are you able to endure the ordeal of jail?" We decided to schedule our direct-action program for the Easter season, realizing that except for Christmas, this is the main shopping period of the year. Knowing that a strong economic-withdrawal program would be the by-product of direct action, we felt that this would be the best time to bring pressure to bear on the merchants for the needed change.

Then it occurred to us that Birmingham's mayoral election was coming up in March, and we speedily decided to postpone action until after election day. When we discovered that the Commissioner of Public Safety, Eugene "Bull" Connor, had piled up enough votes to be in the run-off, we decided again to postpone action until the day after the run-off so that the demonstrations could not be used to cloud the issues. Like many others, we waited to see Mr. Connor defeated, and to this end we endured postponement after postponement. Having aided in this community need, we felt that our direct-action program could be delayed no longer.

You may well ask: "Why direct action? Why sit-ins, marches and so forth? Isn't negotiation a better path?" You are quite right in calling for negotiation. Indeed, this is the very purpose of direct action. Nonviolent direct action seeks to create such a crisis and foster such a tension that a community which has constantly refused to negotiate is forced to confront the issue. It seeks so to dramatize the issue that it can no longer be ignored. My citing the creation of tension as part of the work of the nonviolent-resister may sound rather shocking. But I must confess that I am not afraid of the word "tension." I have earnestly opposed violent tension, but there is a type of constructive, nonviolent tension which is necessary for growth. Just as Socrates felt that it was necessary to create a tension in the mind so that individuals could rise from the bondage of myths and half-truths to the unfettered realm of creative analysis and objective appraisal, so must we see the need for nonviolent gadflies to create the kind of tension in society that will help men rise from the dark depths of prejudice and racism to the majestic heights of understanding and brotherhood.

The purpose of our direct-action program is to create a situation so crisis-packed that it will inevitably open the door to negotiation. I therefore concur with you in your call for negotiation. Too long has our beloved Southland been bogged down in a tragic effort to live in monologue rather than dialogue.

One of the basic points in your statement is that the action that I and my associates have taken in Birmingham is untimely. Some have asked: "Why didn't you give the new city administration time to act?" The only answer that I can give to this query is that the new Birmingham administration must be prodded about as much as the outgoing one, before it will act. We are sadly mistaken if we feel that the election of Albert Boutwell as mayor will bring the millennium to Birmingham. While Mr. Boutwell is a much more gentle person than Mr. Connor, they are both segregationists, dedicated to maintenance of the status quo. I have hope that Mr. Boutwell will be reasonable enough to see the futility of massive resistance to desegregation. But he will not see this without pressure from devotees of civil rights. My friends, I must say to you that we have not made a single gain in civil rights without determined legal and nonviolent pressure. Lamentably, it is an historical fact that privileged groups seldom give up their privileges voluntarily. Individuals may see the moral light and voluntarily give up their unjust posture; but, as Reinhold Niebuhr has reminded us, groups tend to be more immoral than individuals.

We know through painful experience that freedom is never voluntarily given by the oppressor; it must be demanded by the oppressed. Frankly, I have yet to engage in a direct-action campaign that was "well timed" in the view of those who have not suffered unduly from the disease of segregation. For years now I have heard the word "Wait!" It rings in the ear of every Negro with piercing familiarity. This "Wait" has almost always meant "Never." We must come to see, with one of our distinguished jurists, that "justice too long delayed is justice denied."

We have waited for more than 340 years for our constitutional and God-given rights. The nations of Asia and Africa are moving with jetlike speed toward gaining political independence, but we still creep at horse-and-buggy pace toward gaining a cup of coffee at a lunch counter. Perhaps it is easy for those who have never felt the stinging darts of segregation to say, "Wait." But when you have seen vicious mobs lynch your mothers and fathers at will and drown your sisters and brothers at whim; when you have seen hate-filled policemen curse, kick and even kill your black brothers and sisters; when you see the vast majority of your twenty million Negro brothers smothering in an airtight cage of poverty in the midst of an affluent society; when you suddenly find your tongue twisted and your speech stammering as you seek to explain to your six-year-old daughter why she can't go to the public amusement park that has just been advertised on television, and see tears welling up in her eyes when she is told that Funtown is closed to colored children, and see ominous clouds of inferiority beginning to form in her little mental sky, and see her beginning to distort her personality by developing an unconscious bitterness toward white people; when you have to concoct an answer for a five-year-old son who is asking: "Daddy, why do white people treat colored people so mean?"; when you take a cross-country drive and find it necessary to sleep night after night in the uncomfortable corners of your automobile because no motel will accept you; when you are humiliated day in and day out by nagging signs reading "white" and "colored"; when your first name becomes "nigger," your middle name becomes "boy" (however old you are) and your last name becomes "John," and your wife and mother are never given the respected title "Mrs."; when you are harried by day and haunted by night by the fact that you are a Negro, living constantly at tiptoe stance, never quite knowing what to expect next, and are plagued with inner fears and outer resentments; when you are forever fighting a degenerating sense of "nobodi-ness" — then you will understand why we find it difficult to wait. There comes a time when a cup of endurance runs over, and men are no longer willing to be plunged into the abyss of despair. I hope, sirs, you can understand our legitimate and unavoidable impatience.

You express a great deal of anxiety over our willingness to break laws. This is certainly a legitimate concern. Since we so diligently urge people to obey the Supreme Court's decision of 1954 outlawing segregation in the public schools, at first glance it may seem rather paradoxical for us consciously to break laws. One may well ask: "How can you advocate breaking some laws and obeying others?" The answer lies in the fact that there are two types of laws: just and unjust. I would be the first to advocate obeying just laws. One has not only a legal but a moral responsibility to obey these laws. Conversely, one has a moral responsibility to disobey unjust laws. I would agree with St. Augustine that "an unjust law is no law at all."

Now, what is the difference between the two? How does one determine whether a law is just or unjust? A just law is a man-made code that squares with the moral law or the law of God. An unjust law is a code that is out of harmony with the moral law. To put it in the terms of St. Thomas Aquinas: An unjust law is a human law that is not rooted in eternal law and natural law. Any law that uplifts human personality is just. Any law that degrades human personality is unjust. All segregation statutes are unjust because segregation distorts the soul and damages the personality. It gives the segrega-tor a false sense of superiority and the segregated a false sense of inferiority. Segrega-tion, to use the terminology of the Jewish philosopher Martin Buber, substitutes an "I–it" relationship for an "I–thou" relationship and ends up relegating persons to the status of things. Hence segregation is not only politically, economically and sociologically unsound, it is morally wrong and sinful. Paul Tillich has said that sin is separation. Is not segregation an existential expression of man's tragic separation, his awful estrangement, his terrible sinfulness? Thus it is that I can urge men to obey the 1954 decision of the Supreme Court, for it is morally right; and I can urge them to disobey segregation ordinances, for they are morally wrong.

Let us consider a more concrete example of just and unjust laws. An unjust law is a code that a numerical or power majority group compels a minority group to obey but does not make binding on itself. This is *difference* made legal. By the same token, a just law is a code that a majority compels a minority to follow and that it is willing to follow itself. This is *sameness* made legal.

Let me give another explanation. A law is unjust if it is inflicted on a minority that, as a result of being denied the right to vote, had no part in enacting or devising the law. Who can say that the legislature of Alabama which set up that state's segregation laws was democratically elected? Throughout Alabama all sorts of devious methods are used to prevent Negroes from becoming registered voters, and there are some counties in which, even though Negroes constitute a majority of the population, not a single Negro is registered. Can any law enacted under such circumstances be considered democratically structured?

Sometimes a law is just on its face and unjust in its application. For instance, I have been arrested on a charge of parading without a permit. Now, there is nothing wrong in having an ordinance which requires a permit for a parade. But such an ordinance becomes unjust when it is used to maintain segregation and to deny citizens the First-Amendment privilege of peaceful assembly and protest.

I hope you are able to see the distinction I am trying to point out. In no sense do I advocate evading or defying the law, as would the rabid segregationist. That would lead to anarchy. One who breaks an unjust law must do so openly, lovingly, and with a willingness to accept the penalty. I submit that an individual who breaks a law that conscience tells him is unjust, and who willingly accepts the penalty of imprisonment in order to arouse the conscience of the community over its injustice, is in reality expressing the highest respect for law.

Of course, there is nothing new about this kind of civil disobedience. It was evidenced sublimely in the refusal of Shadrach, Meshach and Abednego to obey the laws of Nebuchadnezzar, on the ground that a higher moral law was at stake. It was practiced superbly by the early Christians, who were willing to face hungry lions and the excruciating pain of chopping blocks rather than submit to certain unjust laws of the Roman Empire. To a degree, academic freedom is a reality today because Socrates practiced civil disobedience. In our own nation, the Boston Tea Party represented a massive act of civil disobedience.

We should never forget that everything Adolf Hitler did in Germany was "legal" and everything the Hungarian freedom fighters did in Hungary was "illegal." It was "illegal" to aid and comfort a Jew in Hitler's Germany. Even so, I am sure that, had I lived in Germany at the time, I would have aided and comforted my Jewish brothers. If today I lived in a Communist country where certain principles dear to the Christian faith are suppressed, I would openly advocate disobeying that country's antireligious laws.

I must make two honest confessions to you, my Christian and Jewish brothers. First, I must confess that over the past few years I have been gravely disappointed with the white moderate. I have almost reached the regrettable conclusion that the Negro's

great stumbling block in his stride toward freedom is not the White Citizen's Coun-
ciler or the Ku Klux Klanner, but the white moderate, who is more devoted to "order"
than to justice; who prefers a negative peace which is the absence of tension to a positive
peace which is the presence of justice; who constantly says: "I agree with you in the goal
you seek, but I cannot agree with your methods of direct action"; who paternalistically
believes he can set the timetable for another man's freedom; who lives by a mythical
concept of time and who constantly advises the Negro to wait for a "more convenient
season." Shallow understanding from people of good will is more frustrating than
absolute misunderstanding from people of ill will. Lukewarm acceptance is much
more bewildering than outright rejection.

I had hoped that the white moderate would understand that law and order exist for
the purpose of establishing justice and that when they fail in this purpose they become
the dangerously structured dams that block the flow of social progress. I had hoped that
the white moderate would understand that the present tension in the South is a necessary phase of the transition from an obnoxious negative peace, in which the Negro
passively accepted his unjust plight, to a substantive and positive peace, in which all
men will respect the dignity and worth of human personality. Actually, we who engage
in nonviolent direct action are not the creators of tension. We merely bring to the
surface the hidden tension that is already alive. We bring it out in the open, where it
can be seen and dealt with. Like a boil that can never be cured so long as it is covered up
but must be opened with all its ugliness to the natural medicines of air and light,
injustice must be exposed, with all the tension its exposure creates, to the light of
human conscience and the air of national opinion before it can be cured.

In your statement you assert that our actions, even though peaceful, must be condemned because they precipitate violence. But is this a logical assertion? Isn't this like
condemning a robbed man because his possession of money precipitated the evil act of
robbery? Isn't this like condemning Socrates because his unswerving commitment to
truth and his philosophical inquiries precipitated the act by the misguided populace in
which they made him drink hemlock? Isn't this like condemning Jesus because his
unique God-consciousness and never-ceasing devotion to God's will precipitated the
evil act of crucifixion? We must come to see that, as the federal courts have consistently
affirmed, it is wrong to urge an individual to cease his efforts to gain his basic constitutional rights because the quest may precipitate violence. Society must protect the
robbed and punish the robber.

I had also hoped that the white moderate would reject the myth concerning time in
relation to the struggle for freedom. I have just received a letter from a white brother
in Texas. He writes: "All Christians know that the colored people will receive equal
rights eventually, but it is possible that you are in too great a religious hurry. It has
taken Christianity almost two thousand years to accomplish what it has. The teachings
of Christ take time to come to earth." Such an attitude stems from a tragic misconception of time, from the strangely irrational notion that there is something in the very
flow of time that will inevitably cure all ills. Actually, time itself is neutral; it can be
used either destructively or constructively. More and more I feel that the people of ill
will have used time much more effectively than have the people of good will. We will
have to repent in this generation not merely for the hateful words and actions of the bad
people but for the appalling silence of the good people. Human progress never rolls in

on wheels of inevitability; it comes through the tireless efforts of men willing to be co-workers with God, and without this hard work, time itself becomes an ally of the forces of social stagnation. We must use time creatively, in the knowledge that the time is always ripe to do right. Now is the time to make real the promise of democracy and transform our pending national elegy into a creative psalm of brotherhood. Now is the time to lift our national policy from the quicksand of racial injustice to the solid rock of human dignity.

You speak of our activity in Birmingham as extreme. At first I was rather disappointed that fellow clergymen would see my nonviolent efforts as those of an extremist. I began thinking about the fact that I stand in the middle of two opposing forces in the Negro community. One is a force of complacency, made up in part of Negroes who, as a result of long years of oppression, are so drained of self-respect and a sense of "somebodiness" that they have adjusted to segregation; and in part of a few middle-class Negroes who, because of a degree of academic and economic security and because in some ways they profit by segregation, have become insensitive to the problems of the masses. The other force is one of bitterness and hatred, and it comes perilously close to advocating violence. It is expressed in the various black nationalist groups that are springing up across the nation, the largest and best-known being Elijah Muhammad's Muslim movement. Nourished by the Negro's frustration over the continued existence of racial discrimination, this movement is made up of people who have lost faith in America, who have absolutely repudiated Christianity, and who have concluded that the white man is an incorrigible "devil."

I have tried to stand between these two forces, saying that we need emulate neither the "do-nothingism" of the complacent nor the hatred and despair of the black nationalist. For there is the more excellent way of love and nonviolent protest. I am grateful to God that, through the influence of the Negro church, the way of nonviolence became an integral part of our struggle.

If this philosophy had not emerged, by now many streets of the South would, I am convinced, be flowing with blood. And I am further convinced that if our white brothers dismiss as "rabble-rousers" and "outside agitators" those of us who employ nonviolent direct action, and if they refuse to support our nonviolent efforts, millions of Negroes will, out of frustration and despair, seek solace and security in black-nationalist ideologies — a development that would inevitably lead to a frightening racial nightmare.

Oppressed people cannot remain oppressed forever. The yearning for freedom eventually manifests itself, and that is what has happened to the American Negro. Something within has reminded him of his birthright of freedom, and something without has reminded him that it can be gained. Consciously or unconsciously, he has been caught up by the *Zeitgeist*, and with his black brothers of Africa and his brown and yellow brothers of Asia, South America and the Caribbean, the United States Negro is moving with a sense of great urgency toward the promised land of racial justice. If one recognizes this vital urge that has engulfed the Negro community, one should readily understand why public demonstrations are taking place. The Negro has many pent-up resentments and latent frustrations, and he must release them. So let him march; let him make prayer pilgrimages to the city hall; let him go on freedom rides — and try to understand why he must do so. If his repressed emotions are not released in nonviolent ways, they will seek expression through violence; this is not a threat but a fact of history. So I have not said to my people: "Get rid of your discontent." Rather, I have tried to say that this normal and healthy discontent can be channeled into the creative outlet of nonviolent direct action. And now this approach is being termed extremist.

But though I was initially disappointed at being categorized as an extremist, as I continued to think about the matter I gradually gained a measure of satisfaction from the label. Was not Jesus an extremist for love: "Love your enemies, bless them that curse you, do good to them that hate you, and pray for them which despitefully use you, and persecute you." Was not Amos an extremist for justice: "Let justice roll down like waters and righteousness like an ever-flowing stream." Was not Paul an extremist for the Christian gospel: "I bear in my body the marks of the Lord Jesus." Was not Martin Luther an extremist: "Here I stand; I cannot do otherwise, so help me God." And John Bunyan: "I will stay in jail to the end of my days before I make a butchery of my conscience." And Abraham Lincoln: "This nation cannot survive half slave and half free." And Thomas Jefferson: "We hold these truths to be self-evident, that all men are created equal . . ." So the question is not whether we will be extremists, but what kind of extremists we will be. Will we be extremists for hate or for love? Will we be extremists for the preservation of injustice or for the extension of justice? In that dramatic scene on Calvary's hill three men were crucified. We must never forget that all three were crucified for the same crime—the crime of extremism. Two were extremists for immorality, and thus fell below their environment. The other, Jesus Christ, was an extremist for love, truth and goodness, and thereby rose above his environment. Perhaps the South, the nation and the world are in dire need of creative extremists.

I had hoped that the white moderate would see this need. Perhaps I was too optimistic; perhaps I expected too much. I suppose I should have realized that few members of the oppressor race can understand the deep groans and passionate yearnings of the oppressed race, and still fewer have the vision to see that injustice must be rooted out by strong, persistent and determined action. I am thankful, however, that some of our white brothers in the South have grasped the meaning of this social revolution and committed themselves to it. They are still all too few in quantity, but they are big in quality. Some—such as Ralph McGill, Lillian Smith, Harry Golden, James McBride Dabbs, Ann Braden and Sarah Patton Boyle—have written about our struggle in eloquent and prophetic terms. Others have marched with us down nameless streets of the South. They have languished in filthy, roach-infested jails, suffering the abuse and brutality of policemen who view them as "dirty nigger-lovers." Unlike so many of their moderate brothers and sisters, they have recognized the urgency of the moment and sensed the need for powerful "action" antidotes to combat the disease of segregation.

Let me take note of my other major disappointment. I have been so greatly disappointed with the white church and its leadership. Of course, there are some notable exceptions. I am not unmindful of the fact that each of you has taken some significant stands on this issue. I commend you, Reverend Stallings, for your Christian stand on this past Sunday, in welcoming Negroes to your worship service on a nonsegregated basis. I commend the Catholic leaders of this state for integrating Spring Hill College several years ago.

But despite these notable exceptions, I must honestly reiterate that I have been disappointed with the church. I do not say this as one of those negative critics who can always find something wrong with the church. I say this as a minister of the gospel, who loves the church; who was nurtured in its bosom; who has been sustained by its spiritual blessings and who will remain true to it as long as the cord of life shall lengthen.

When I was suddenly catapulted into the leadership of the bus protest in Montgomery, Alabama, a few years ago, I felt we would be supported by the white church. I felt that the white ministers, priests and rabbis of the South would be among our strongest allies. Instead, some have been outright opponents, refusing to understand the freedom movement and misrepresenting its leaders; all too many others have been more cautious than courageous and have remained silent behind the anesthetizing security of stained-glass windows.

In spite of my shattered dreams, I came to Birmingham with the hope that the white religious leadership of this community would see the justice of our cause and, with deep moral concern, would serve as the channel through which our just grievances could reach the power structure. I had hoped that each of you would understand. But again I have been disappointed.

I have heard numerous southern religious leaders admonish their worshipers to comply with a desegregation decision because it is the law, but I have longed to hear white ministers declare: "Follow this decree because integration is morally right and because the Negro is your brother." In the midst of blatant injustices inflicted upon the Negro, I have watched white churchmen stand on the sideline and mouth pious irrelevancies and sanctimonious trivialities. In the midst of a mighty struggle to rid our nation of racial and economic injustice, I have heard many ministers say: "Those are social issues, with which the gospel has no real concern." And I have watched many churches commit themselves to a completely otherworldly religion which makes a strange, un-Biblical distinction between body and soul, between the sacred and the secular.

I have traveled the length and breadth of Alabama, Mississippi and all the other southern states. On sweltering summer days and crisp autumn mornings I have looked at the South's beautiful churches with their lofty spires pointing heavenward. I have beheld the impressive outlines of her massive religious-education buildings. Over and over I have found myself asking: "What kind of people worship here? Who is their God? Where were their voices when the lips of Governor Barnett dripped with words of interposition and nullification? Where were they when Governor Wallace gave a clarion call for defiance and hatred? Where were their voices of support when bruised and weary Negro men and women decided to rise from the dark dungeons of complacency to the bright hills of creative protest?"

Yes, these questions are still in my mind. In deep disappointment I have wept over the laxity of the church. But be assured that my tears have been tears of love. There can be no deep disappointment where there is not deep love. Yes, I love the church. How could I do otherwise? I am in the rather unique position of being the son, the grandson and the great-grandson of preachers. Yes, I see the church as the body of Christ. But, oh! How we have blemished and scarred that body through social neglect and through fear of being nonconformists.

There was a time when the church was very powerful — in the time when the early Christians rejoiced at being deemed worthy to suffer for what they believed. In those days the church was not merely a thermometer that recorded the ideas and principles of popular opinion; it was a thermostat that transformed the mores of society. Whenever the early Christians entered a town, the people in power became disturbed and immediately sought to convict the Christians for being "disturbers of the peace" and "outside agitators." But the Christians pressed on, in the conviction that they were "a colony of heaven," called to obey God rather than man. Small in number, they were big in commitment. They were too God-intoxicated to be "astronomically intimidated." By their effort and example they brought an end to such ancient evils as infanticide and gladiatorial contests.

Things are different now. So often the contemporary church is a weak, ineffectual voice with an uncertain sound. So often it is an archdefender of the status quo. Far from being disturbed by the presence of the church, the power structure of the average community is consoled by the church's silent — and often even vocal — sanction of things as they are.

But the judgment of God is upon the church as never before. If today's church does not recapture the sacrificial spirit of the early church, it will lose its authenticity, forfeit the loyalty of millions, and be dismissed as an irrelevant social club with no meaning for the twentieth century. Every day I meet young people whose disappointment with the church has turned into outright disgust.

Perhaps I have once again been too optimistic. Is organized religion too inextricably bound to the status quo to save our nation and the world? Perhaps I must turn my faith to the inner spiritual church, the church within the church, as the true *ekklesia* and the hope of the world. But again I am thankful to God that some noble souls from the ranks of organized religion have broken loose from the paralyzing chains of conformity and joined us as active partners in the struggle for freedom. They have left their secure congregations and walked the streets of Albany, Georgia, with us. They have gone down the highways of the South on tortuous rides for freedom. Yes, they have gone to jail with us. Some have been dismissed from their churches, have lost the support of their bishops and fellow ministers. But they have acted in the faith that right defeated is stronger than evil triumphant. Their witness has been the spiritual salt that has preserved the true meaning of the gospel in these troubled times. They have carved a tunnel of hope through the dark mountain of disappointment.

I hope the church as a whole will meet the challenge of this decisive hour. But even if the church does not come to the aid of justice, I have no despair about the future. I have no fear about the outcome of our struggle in Birmingham, even if our motives are at present misunderstood. We will reach the goal of freedom in Birmingham and all over the nation, because the goal of America is freedom. Abused and scorned though we may be, our destiny is tied up with America's destiny. Before the pilgrims landed at Plymouth, we were here. Before the pen of Jefferson etched the majestic words of the Declaration of Independence across the pages of history, we were here. For more than two centuries our forebears labored in this country without wages; they made cotton king; they built the homes of their masters while suffering gross injustice and shameful humiliation — and yet out of a bottomless vitality they continued to thrive and develop. If the inexpressible cruelties of slavery could not stop us, the opposition we now face will surely fail. We will win our freedom because the sacred heritage of our nation and the eternal will of God are embodied in our echoing demands.

Before closing I feel impelled to mention one other point in your statement that has troubled me profoundly. You warmly commended the Birmingham police force for keeping "order" and "preventing violence." I doubt that you would have so warmly commended the police force if you had seen its dogs sinking their teeth into unarmed, nonviolent Negroes. I doubt that you would so quickly commend the policemen if you were to observe their ugly and inhumane treatment of Negroes here in the city jail; if you were to watch them push and curse old Negro women and young Negro girls; if you were to see them slap and kick old Negro men and young boys; if you were to observe them, as they did on two occasions, refuse to give us food because we wanted to sing our grace together. I cannot join you in your praise of the Birmingham police department.

It is true that the police have exercised a degree of discipline in handling the demonstrators. In this sense they have conducted themselves rather "nonviolently" in public. But for what purpose? To preserve the evil system of segregation. Over the past few years I have consistently preached that nonviolence demands that the means we use must be as pure as the ends we seek. I have tried to make clear that it is wrong to use immoral means to attain moral ends. But now I must affirm that it is just as wrong, or perhaps even more so, to use moral means to preserve immoral ends. Perhaps Mr. Connor and his policemen have been rather nonviolent in public, as was Chief Pritchett in Albany, Georgia, but they have used the moral means of nonviolence to maintain the immoral end of racial injustice. As T. S. Eliot has said: "The last temptation is the greatest treason: To do the right deed for the wrong reason."

I wish you had commended the Negro sit-inners and demonstrators of Birmingham for their sublime courage, their willingness to suffer and their amazing discipline in the midst of great provocation. One day the South will recognize its real heroes. They will be the James Merediths, with the noble sense of purpose that enables them to face jeering and hostile mobs, and with the agonizing loneliness that characterizes the life of the pioneer. They will be old, oppressed, battered Negro women, symbolized in a seventy-two-year-old woman in Montgomery, Alabama, who rose up with a sense of dignity and with her people decided not to ride segregated buses, and who responded with ungrammatical profundity to one who inquired about her weariness: "My feets is tired, but my soul is at rest." They will be the young high school and college students, the young ministers of the gospel and a host of their elders, courageously and nonviolently sitting in at lunch counters and willingly going to jail for conscience' sake. One day the South will know that when these disinherited children of God sat down at lunch counters, they were in reality standing up for what is best in the American dream and for the most sacred values in our Judaeo-Christian heritage, thereby bringing our nation back to those great wells of democracy which were dug deep by the founding fathers in their formulation of the Constitution and the Declaration of Independence.

Never before have I written so long a letter. I'm afraid it is much too long to take your precious time. I can assure you that it would have been much shorter if I had been writing from a comfortable desk, but what else can one do when he is alone in a narrow jail cell, other than write long letters, think long thoughts and pray long prayers?

If I have said anything in this letter that overstates the truth and indicates an unreasonable impatience, I beg you to forgive me. If I have said anything that understates the truth and indicates my having a patience that allows me to settle for anything less than brotherhood, I beg God to forgive me.

I hope this letter finds you strong in the faith. I also hope that circumstances will soon make it possible for me to meet each of you, not as an integrationist or a civil-rights leader but as a fellow clergyman and a Christian brother. Let us all hope that the dark clouds of racial prejudice will soon pass away and the deep fog of misunderstanding will be lifted from our fear-drenched communities, and in some not too distant tomorrow the radiant stars of love and brotherhood will shine over our great nation with all their scintillating beauty.

Yours for the cause of Peace and Brotherhood,
MARTIN LUTHER KING, JR.

QUESTIONS

1. Ostensibly King is addressing his remarks to the eight clergymen who objected to protest. His "letter," however, has been published widely and read by a much larger audience. Was King aware of this potentially larger audience at the time? What evidence do you find of this?

2. King mentions Adolph Hitler in the course of his argument. Is the comparison he draws here valid? The names of other famous historical figures — Thomas Jefferson, Abraham Lincoln, Martin Luther, John Bunyan — are also invoked. Why does King do this? Is his strategy successful?

3. King selects language from the clergymen's letter, words such as *violence* and *order*, and examines what this language really means in this situation. How does he redefine these terms?

4. Find examples of King identifying with his audience. What other postures might he have adopted instead? Would these have been more — or less — effective than the one he has chosen? Why?

5. Historians frequently debate whether "men make the times" or "times make the men." Which point of view does King present in this essay? Which point of view is held by his critics? Which point of view is correct in this case?

6. Notice King's use of allusions, metaphors, rhythm, and repetition. How does he use his training as a minister to influence his audience here?

•　　•　　•　　•　　•

THE CHOICE

Jonathan Schell

We are living in what might be called the second wave of nuclear protests, the first wave having peaked and subsided somewhat in the early sixties. Jonathan Schell has written articles for The New Yorker *and published books on Vietnam, Watergate, and nuclear disarmament. This piece comes from his 1982 book,* The Fate of the Earth.

FOUR and a half billion years ago, the earth was formed. Perhaps a half billion years after that life arose on the planet. For the next four billion years, life became steadily more complex, more varied. and more ingenious, until, around a million years ago, it produced mankind—the most complex and ingenious species of them all. Only six or seven thousand years ago—a period that is to the history of the earth as less than a minute is to a year—civilization emerged, enabling us to build up a human world, and to add to the marvels of evolution marvels of our own: marvels of art, of science, of social organization, of spiritual attainment. But, as we built higher and higher, the evolutionary foundation beneath our feet became more and more shaky, and now, in spite of all we have learned and achieved—or, rather, because of it— we hold this entire terrestrial creation hostage to nuclear destruction, threatening to hurl it back into the inanimate darkness from which it came. And this threat of self-destruction and planetary destruction is not something that we will pose one day in the future, if we fail to take certain precautions; it is here now, hanging over the heads of all of us at every moment. The machinery of destruction is complete, poised on a hair trigger, waiting for the "button" to be "pushed" by some misguided or deranged human being or for some faulty computer chip to send out the instruction to fire. That so much should be balanced on so fine a point—that the fruit of four and a half billion years can be undone in a careless moment—is a fact against which belief rebels. And there is another, even vaster measure of the loss, for stretching ahead from our present are more billions of years of life on earth, all of which can be filled not only with human life but with human civilization. The procession of generations that extends onward from our present leads far, far beyond the line of our sight, and, compared with these stretches of human time, which exceed the whole history of the earth up to now, our brief civilized moment is almost infinitesimal. And yet we threaten, in the name of our transient aims and fallible convictions, to foreclose it all. If our species does destroy itself, it will be a death in the cradle—a case of infant mortality. The disparity between the cause and the effect of our peril is so great that our minds seem all but powerless to encompass it. In addition, we are so fully enveloped by that which is menaced, and so deeply and passionately immersed in its events, which are the events of our lives, that we hardly know how to get far enough away from it to see it in its entirely. It is as though life itself were one huge distraction, diverting our attention from the peril to life. In its apparent durability, a world menaced with imminent doom is in a way deceptive. It is almost an illusion. Now we are sitting at the breakfast table drinking our coffee and reading the newspaper, but in a moment we may be inside a fireball whose temperature is tens of thousands of degrees. Now we are on our way to work, walking through the city streets, but in a moment we may be standing on an empty plain under a darkened sky looking for the charred remnants of our children. Now we are alive, but in a moment we may be dead. Now there is human life on earth, but in a moment it may be gone.

Once, there was time to reflect in a more leisurely way on our predicament. In August, 1945, when the invention of the bomb was made known through its first use on a human population, the people of Hiroshima, there lay ahead an interval of decades which might have been used to fashion a world that would be safe from extinction by nuclear arms, and some voices were in fact heard counseling deep reflection on the looming peril and calling for action to head it off. On November 28, 1945, less than four months after the bombing of Hiroshima, the English philosopher Bertrand Russell rose in the House of Lords and said:

> We do not want to look at this thing simply from the point of view of the next few years; we want to look at it from the point of view of the future of mankind. The question is a simple one: Is it possible for a scientific society to continue to exist, or must such a society inevitably bring itself to destruction? It is a simple question but a very vital one. I do not think it is possible to exaggerate the gravity of the possibilities of evil that lie in the utilization of atomic energy. As I go about the streets and see St. Paul's, the British Museum, the Houses of Parliament, and the other monuments of our civilization, in my mind's eye I see a nightmare vision of those buildings as heaps of rubble with corpses all round them. That is a thing we have got to face, not only in our own country and cities, but throughout the civilized world.

Russell and others, including Albert Einstein, urged full, global disarmament, but the advice was disregarded. Instead, the world set about building the arsenals that we possess today. The period of grace we had in which to ward off the nuclear peril before it became a reality — the time between the moment of the invention of the weapons and the construction of the full-scale machinery for extinction — was squandered, and now the peril that Russell foresaw is upon us. Indeed, if we are honest with ourselves we have to admit that unless we rid ourselves of our nuclear arsenals a holocaust not only *might* occur but *will* occur — if not today, then tomorrow; if not this year, then the next. We have come to live on borrowed time: every year of continued human life on earth is a borrowed year, every day a borrowed day.

In the face of this unprecedented global emergency, we have so far had no better idea than to heap up more and more warheads, apparently in the hope of so thoroughly paralyzing ourselves with terror that we will hold back from taking a final, absurd step. Considering the wealth of our achievement as a species, this response is unworthy of us. Only by a process of gradual debasement of our self-esteem can we have lowered our expectations to this point. For, of all the "modest hopes of human beings," the hope that mankind will survive is the most modest, since it only brings us to the threshold of all the other hopes. In entertaining it, we do not yet ask for justice, or for freedom, or for happiness, or for any of the other things that we may want in life. We do not even necessarily ask for our personal survival; we ask only that we *be survived*. We ask for assurance that when we die as individuals, as we know we must, mankind will live on. Yet once the peril of extinction is present, as it is for us now, the hope for human survival becomes the most tremendous hope, just because it is the foundation for all the other hopes, and in its absence every other hope will gradually wither and die. Life without the hope for human survival is a life of despair.

The death of our species resembles the death of an individual in its boundlessness, its blankness, its removal beyond experience, and its tendency to baffle human thought and feeling, yet as soon as one mentions the hope of survival the similarities are clearly at an end. For while individual death is inevitable, extinction can be avoided; while every person must die, mankind can be saved. Therefore, while reflection on death may lead to resignation and acceptance, reflection on extinction must lead to exactly the opposite response: to arousal, rejection, indignation, and action. Extinction is not something to contemplate, it is something to rebel against. To point this out might seem like stating the obvious if it were not that on the whole the world's reaction to the peril of extinction has been one of numbness and inertia, much as though extinction were as inescapable as death is. Even today, official response to the sickening reality before us is conditioned by a grim fatalism, in which the hope of ridding the world of nuclear weapons, and thus of surviving as a species, is all but ruled out of consideration as "utopian" or "extreme" — as though it were "radical" merely to want to go on living and to want one's descendants to be born. And yet if one gives up these aspirations one has given up on everything. As a species, we have as yet done nothing to save ourselves. The slate of action is blank. We have organizations for the preservation of almost everything in life that we want but no organization for the preservation of mankind. People seem to have decided that our collective will is too weak or flawed to rise to this occasion. They see the violence that has saturated human history, and conclude that to practice violence is innate in our species. They find the perennial hope that peace can be brought to the earth once and for all a delusion of the well-meaning who have refused to face the "harsh realities" of international life — the realities of self-interest, fear, hatred, and aggression. They have concluded that these realities are eternal ones, and this conclusion defeats at the outset any hope of taking the actions necessary for survival. Looking at the historical record, they ask what has changed to give anyone confidence that humanity can break with its violent past and act with greater restraint. The answer, of course, is that everything has changed. To the old "harsh realities" of international life has been added the immeasurably harsher new reality of the peril of extinction. To the old truth that all men are brothers has been added the inescapable new truth that not only on the moral but also on the physical plane the nation that practices aggression will itself die. This is the law of the doctrine of nuclear deterrence — the doctrine of "mutual assured destruction" — which "assures" the destruction of the society of the attacker. And it is also the law of the natural world, which, in its own version of deterrence, supplements the oneness of mankind with a oneness of nature, and guarantees that when the attack rises above a certain level the attacker will be engulfed in the general ruin of the global ecosphere. To the obligation to honor life is now added the sanction that if we fail in our obligation life will actually be taken away from us, individually and collectively. Each of us will die, and as we die we will see the world around us dying. Such imponderables as the sum of human life, the integrity of the terrestrial creation, and the meaning of time, of history, and of the development of life on earth, which were once left to contemplation and spiritual understanding, are now at stake in the political realm and demand a political response from every person. As political actors, we must, like the contemplatives before us, delve to the bottom of the world, and, Atlas-like, we must take the world on our shoulders.

The self-extinction of our species is not an act that anyone describes as sane or sensible; nevertheless, it is an act that, without quite admitting it to ourselves, we plan in certain circumstances to commit. Being impossible as a fully intentional act, unless the perpetrator has lost his mind, it can come about only through a kind of inadvertence — as a "side effect" of some action that we do intend, such as the defense of our nation, or the defense of liberty, or the defense of socialism, or the defense of whatever else we happen to believe in. To that extent, our failure to acknowledge the magnitude and significance of the peril is a necessary condition for doing the deed. We can do it only if we don't quite know what we're doing. If we did acknowledge the full dimensions of the peril, admitting clearly and without reservation that any use of nuclear arms is likely to touch off a holocaust in which the continuance of all human life would be put at risk, extinction would at that moment become not only "unthinkable" but also undoable. What is needed to make extinction possible, therefore, is some way of thinking about it that at least partly deflects our attention from what it is. And this way of thinking is supplied to us, unfortunately, by our political and military traditions, which, with the weight of almost all historical experience behind them, teach us that it is the way of the world for the earth to be divided up into independent, sovereign states, and for these states to employ war as the final arbiter for settling the disputes that arise among them. This arrangement of the political affairs of the world was not intentional. No one wrote a book proposing it; no parliament sat down to debate its merits and then voted it into existence. It was simply there, at the beginning of recorded history; and until the invention of nuclear weapons it remained there, with virtually no fundamental changes. Unplanned though this arrangement was, it had many remarkably durable features, and certain describable advantages and disadvantages; therefore, I shall refer to it as a "system" — the system of sovereignty. Perhaps the leading feature of this system, and certainly the most important one in the context of the nuclear predicament, was the apparently indissoluble connection between sovereignty and war. For without sovereignty, it appeared, peoples were not able to organize and launch wars against other peoples, and without war they were unable to preserve their sovereignty from destruction by armed enemies. (By "war" I here mean only international war, not revolutionary war, which I shall not discuss.) Indeed, the connection between sovereignty and war is almost a definitional one — a sovereign state being a state that enjoys the right and the power to go to war in defense or pursuit of its interests.

It was into the sovereignty system that nuclear bombs were born, as "weapons" for "war." As the years have passed, it has seemed less and less plausible that they have anything to do with war; they seem to break through its bounds. Nevertheless, they have gone on being fitted into military categories of thinking. One might say that they appeared in the world in a military disguise, for it has been traditional military thinking, itself an inseparable part of the traditional political thinking that belonged to the system of sovereignty, that has provided those intentional goals — namely, national interests — in the pursuit of which extinction may now be brought about unintentionally, or semi-intentionally, as a "side effect." The system of sovereignty is now to the earth and mankind what a polluting factory is to its local environment. The machine produces certain things that its users want — in this case, national sovereignty — and as an unhappy side effect extinguishes the species.

In the decades since nuclear arms first appeared in the world, the doctrine of nuclear deterrence has commanded the sincere respect and adherence of many people of good will — especially when they found themselves arguing, as they so often did, with the adherents of traditional military doctrine, who even today, in the face of extinction itself, go on arguing for "military superiority," and the like. And if one once accepts the existence of the doomsday machine, then deterrence theory, however flawed, does offer the hope of certain benefits, the main one being a degree of "stability." Therefore, the perpetual struggle of its adherents against the sheer lunacy of "fighting a nuclear war" is a creditable one. But the fundamental truth about the doctrine and about its role in the wider political — and, it must be added, biological — scheme of things also has to be recognized. For the doctrine's central claim — that it deploys nuclear weapons only in order to prevent their use — is simply not true. Actually, it deploys them to protect national sovereignty, and if this aim were not present they could be quickly dismantled. The doctrine, then, has been the intellectual screen behind which the doomsday machine was built. And its deceptive claim that only by building nuclear weapons can we save ourselves from nuclear weapons lent the doomsday machine a veneer of reason and of respectability — almost of benevolence — that it should never have been given. For to build this machine at all was a mistake of the hugest proportions ever known — without question the greatest ever made by our species. The only conceivable worse mistake would be to put the machine to use. Now deterrence, having rationalized the construction of the machine, weds us to it, and, at best, offers us, if we are lucky, a slightly extended term of residence on earth before the inevitable human or mechanical mistake occurs and we are annihilated.

Yet the deterrence policy in itself is clearly not the deepest source of our difficulty. Rather, as we have seen, it is only a piece of repair work on the immeasurably more deeply entrenched system of national sovereignty. People do not want deterrence for its own sake; indeed, they hardly know what it is, and tend to shun the whole subject. They want the national sovereignty that deterrence promises to preserve. National sovereignty lies at the very core of the political issues that the peril of extinction forces upon us. Sovereignty is the "reality" that the "realists" counsel us to accept as inevitable, referring to any alternative as "unrealistic" or "utopian." If the argument about nuclear weapons is to be conducted in good faith, then just as those who favor the deterrence policy (not to speak of traditional military doctrine) must in all honesty admit that their scheme contemplates the extinction of man in the name of protecting national sovereignty, so must those who favor complete nuclear and conventional disarmament, as I do, admit that their recommendation is inconsistent with national sovereignty; to pretend otherwise would be to evade the political question that is central to the nuclear predicament. The terms of the deal that the world has now struck with itself must be made clear. On the one side stand human life and the terrestrial creation. On the other side stands a particular organization of human life — the system of independent, sovereign nation-states. Our choice so far has been to preserve that political organization of human life at the cost of risking all human life. We are told that "realism" compels us to preserve the system of sovereignty. But that political realism is not biological realism; it is biological nihilism — and for that reason is, of course, political nihilism, too. Indeed, it is nihilism in every conceivable sense of that word. We are told that it is human fate — perhaps even "a law of human nature" — that, in obedience, perhaps, to some "territorial imperative," or to some dark and ineluctable truth in the bottom of our souls, we must preserve sovereignty and always settle our differences with violence. If this is our fate, then it is our fate to die. But must we embrace nihilism? Must we die? Is self-examination a law of our nature? Is there nothing we can do? I do not believe so. Indeed, if we admit the reality of the basic terms of the nuclear predicament — that present levels of global armament are great enough to possibly extinguish the species if a holocaust should occur; that in extinction every human purpose would be lost; that because once the species has been extinguished there will be no second chance, and the game will be over for all time; that therefore this possibility must be dealt with morally and politically as though it were a certainty; and that either by accident or by design a holocaust can occur at any second — then, whatever political views we may hold on other matters, we are driven almost inescapably to take action to rid the world of nuclear arms. Just as we have chosen to make nuclear weapons, we can choose to unmake them. Just as we have chosen to live in the system of sovereign states, we can choose to live in some other system. To do so would, of course, be unprecedented, and in many ways frightening, even truly perilous, but it is by no means impossible. Our present system and the institutions that make it up are the debris of history. They have become inimical to life, and must be swept away. They constitute a noose around the neck of mankind, threatening to choke off the human future, but we can cut the noose and break free. To suppose otherwise would be to set up a false, fictitious fate, molded out of our own weaknesses and our own alterable decisions. We are indeed fated by our acquisition of the basic knowledge of physics to live for the rest of time with the knowledge of how to destroy ourselves. But we are not for that reason fated to destroy ourselves. We can choose to live.

QUESTIONS

1. Schell must make his readers confront and understand the destruction inherent in nuclear war. How does he go about doing this? In your opinion, is he successful?

2. Where does Schell choose emotive language to make his case? What metaphors does he employ? Are these metaphors valid ones?

3. Schell advocates the abandonment of the concept of national sovereignty. Is this abandonment necessary? Is it possible? Is it likely? Is Schell's argument convincing on this point? What are the consequences of refusing to abandon this concept, according to Schell?

4. Schell argues that a nuclear accident and holocaust is inevitable. Outline the syllogism he is using that produces this conclusion. Are his premises valid? Why or why not?

•　　•　　•　　•　　•

THE FEMINIST FACE OF ANTITECHNOLOGY

Samuel C. Florman

Conventional wisdom has frequently separated the arts from the sciences, the humanities from the technical world of engineering. Samuel Florman is an engineer who disagrees with this separation, and he has written numerous articles attempting to bridge the gap between engineering and the humanities. His first two books — Engineering and the Liberal Arts *(1968) and* The Existential Pleasures of Engineering *(1976) — focus on the interaction between the humanities and engineering; his third book, however, takes a slightly different tack. In* Blaming Technology: The Irrational Search for Scapegoats *(1981), Florman takes issue with what he perceives is becoming a social trend, blaming technology — and the engineers that created that technology — for many of the world's ills.*

THE campus of Smith College in Northampton, Massachusetts, is one of the pleasantest places in the world to be on a sunny spring afternoon. The setting is so lovely, the academic atmosphere so tranquil, that when I arrived there on such an afternoon in April, I was totally captivated. The spell of the place, however, made me uneasy about my mission, which was to convince a few of the students at this premier, all-female liberal arts college that they ought to become engineers.

The mission, as it turned out, was destined to fail. Most bright young women today do not want to become engineers. At first hearing this might not seem to be a matter of grave consequence, but since engineering is central to the functioning of our society, its rejection as a career option by female students raises the most profound questions about the relationship of women to technology, and about the objectives of the women's movement.

It is not generally recognized that at the same time that women are making their way into every corner of the work-world, less than 3 percent of the professional engineers in the nation are female. A generation ago this statistic would have raised no eyebrows, but today it is difficult to believe. The engineering schools, reacting to social and governmental pressures, have opened wide their gates and are zealously recruiting women. The major corporations, reacting to even more intense pressures, are offering attractive employment opportunities to nearly all women engineering graduates. According to the College Placement Council, engineering is the only field in which average starting salaries for women are higher than those for men. Tokenism is disappearing, according to the testimony of women engineers themselves. By every reasonable standard one would expect women to be attracted to the profession in large numbers. Yet less than 10 percent of 1980's 58,000 engineering degrees were awarded to women (compared to 30 percent in medicine, 28 percent in law, and 40 percent in the biological sciences). By 1984 the total may reach 15 percent, still a dismal figure when one realizes that more women than men are enrolled in American colleges. Unless this situation changes dramatically, and soon, the proportion of women engineers in practice, among more than 1.25 million males, will remain insignificant for many decades. While women are moving vigorously — assertively, demandingly — toward significant numerical representation in industry, the arts, and the other professions, they are, for reasons that are not at all clear, shying away from engineering.

At Smith I was scheduled to partipate in a seminar entitled "The Role of Technology in Modern Society." The program called for a "sherry hour" before dinner, during which the speakers had an opportunity to talk informally with the students. In a stately paneled room the late-afternoon light sparkled on crystal decanters as we sipped our sherry from tiny glasses. The students with whom I conversed were as elegant as the surroundings, so poised, so *ladylike*. I found myself thinking, "These girls are not going to become engineers. It's simply not their style." The young women were not vapid in the way of country gentry. Far from it. They were alert and sensible, well-trained in mathematics and the sciences. I could imagine them donning white coats and conducting experiments in quiet laboratories. But I could not see them as engineers. It is a hopeless cause, I thought. They will not become engineers because it is "beneath" them to do so. It is a question of social class.

This was an intuitive feeling of the moment, although, when scrutinized, it made sociological sense. Traditionally, most American engineers have come from working-class families. In the words of a post-Sputnik National Science Foundation study, "Engineering has a special appeal for bright boys of lower and lower-middle-class origins." Yet in many of the blue-collar families that have been such a fertile source for male engineers, the idea of a scientific education for women has not taken hold. Therefore, most of the young women who have the educational qualifications to become engineers are likely to come from the middle and upper classes. But the upper classes do not esteem a career in engineering: thus few women engineers.

We have inherited much of our class consciousness from England, and so it is with our attitude toward engineering, which the English have always considered rather a "navvy" occupation. Because engineering did not change from a craft to a profession until the mid-nineteenth century, and never shed completely its craftsman's image, it was fair game for the sneers of pretentious social arbiters. Herbert Hoover, a successful mining engineer before he became President, and something of a scholar who translated Agricola from the Latin, enjoyed telling about an English lady whom he met during the course of an Atlantic crossing. When, near the end of the voyage, Hoover told her that he was an engineer, the lady exclaimed, "Why, I thought you were a gentleman!" The fact that this anecdote is told and retold whenever conversation turns to the role of engineers in American society indicates how basic is the point that it illustrates.

It may not be realistic to expect women to break down class barriers that were created mostly by men. Yet feminists, if they are serious in their avowed purposes, should by now have taken the lead in changing this situation, encouraging the elite among educated young women to reevaluate their social prejudices. For until upper-class aversion to engineering is overcome, or until lower-class women take to studying the sciences in earnest, engineering will remain largely a male profession. And while this condition prevails, the feminist movement will be stalled, probably without even knowing it. For, in a man-made world, how can women achieve the equality they seek?

My view, needless to say, is not shared by the feminists of the United States. Judging by their literature, they seem to attach no particular importance to increasing female enrollment in engineering, perhaps because they are more concerned about battering on closed doors than they are about walking through those that are open. When they do consider the problem, it is not to question or criticize choices being made by women, but only to deplore the effect of external forces.

There is an entire literature devoted to explaining how engineering, and to a lesser degree science and mathematics, has developed a "male image." The terminology of this literature has been ringing in our ears for a long time — "sex role socialization," "undoing sex stereotypes," "self-fulfilling prophecy," and so forth. We know the facts by heart: girls learn early that it is not socially acceptable for them to play with trains and trucks. They learn from teachers that boys perform better than girls in math and science. A condition called "math anxiety" is attributed to these social pressures. As girls mature, they are persuaded by counselors and family that it is not feminine to enter traditionally male professions. They are afraid to compete with men or to let their intelligence show, lest they seem sexually less desirable. Finally, there is a shortage of "role models" with whom a young girl can identify.

Yes, yes, yes, of course, but these facts, which seemed so interesting and important a decade and more ago, are now stale. As the sociologists busy themselves collating their data and getting it published, the times invariably pass them by. After all, *The Feminine Mystique* was published in 1963, and the Equal Pay Act was enacted by Congress that same year. Since then a social revolution has taken place. Educated young women know well enough that they can become engineers. Surely the women who are planning to be biologists and doctors know that they could choose engineering instead, and those who are crowding into the fields of law, business, and journalism know that they could have opted for engineering if they had been willing to take a little calculus and physics. Women's magazines that once specialized in menus and sewing patterns are now overflowing with advice on how to compete in what used to be a man's world — how to dress, sit, talk, intimidate, and in general "make it." Engineering's purported male image is no longer an adequate explanation for female aversion to the profession.

It has been hypothesized that women avoid engineering because it has to do with technology, an aspect of our culture from which they recoil instinctively. Ruth Cowan, a historian at the State University of New York, has done research on the influence of technology on the self-image of the American woman. The development of household appliances, for example, instead of freeing the housewife for a richer life as advertised, has helped to reduce her to the level of a maidservant whose greatest skill is consumerism. Factory jobs have attracted women to the workplace in roles they have come to dislike. Innovations affecting the most intimate aspects of women's lives, such as the baby bottle and birth-control devices, have been developed almost exclusively by men. Dependent upon technology, but removed from its sources and, paradoxically, enslaved by it, women may well have developed deep-seated resentments that persist even in those who consider themselves liberated.

If this situation does exist, we might expect that the feminists would respond to it as a challenge. The brightest and most ambitious women should be eager to bend technology, at long last, to their own will. But this is not happening. The feminists seem content to write articles assuring each other that they have the talent to fix leaky faucets.

Wherever the enemies of technology gather, women are to be found in large numbers. The transcendental movement that arose out of the counterculture of the 1960s — what Marilyn Ferguson has called *The Aquarian Conspiracy* — pits feminine sensitivity against a "macho" materialism. "Wherever the Aquarian Conspiracy is at work," writes Miss Ferguson, "women are represented in far greater numbers than they are in the establishment." This follows from basic physical and social realities:

"Women are neurologically more flexible than men, and they have had cultural permission to be more intuitive, sensitive, feeling."

Such an outlook not only explains why women are likely to be hostile to technology, but also raises the question of whether or not women are equipped biologically to excel in engineering. This is a theory that arouses such rancor that I hesitate to bring it up, and yet it must be confronted. The intellectual factor most closely related to achievement in science is spatial ability, the ability to manipulate objects mentally. Experiments have shown that males are, on average, better at this than females, and that this superiority appears to be related to levels of the male hormone testosterone.

It is a mistake, I think, to argue as some feminists do that there is no discernible difference between the male and female brain. It would be more sensible to say that because of substantial overlap in test scores, the differences that do exist are not practically significant when one considers a large group of potential engineers of both sexes. It would be better yet to point out that such differences as there are would serve to enrich the profession, since good engineering requires intuition and verbal imagination as well as mathematical adeptness and spatial ability. In their so-called weakness may be women's hidden strength.

This is considered to be a reactionary view, I learned to my sorrow when I proposed it to a female executive at RCA whose special interest is the careers of professional women. In response to my remark, she said, "I know that you mean well, but to tell a woman engineer that she has female intuition is like telling a black that he has rhythm."

Inevitably it occurred to me that anyone wondering why women do not become engineers would be well advised to learn something about the few women who *do* become engineers. So one day I took myself to the Engineering Societies Building, a large stone-and-glass structure overlooking the East River near the United Nations in New York City. In this stately edifice are housed most of the major professional societies that represent American engineers. On the third floor, past the imposing offices of the Engineering Foundation and the American Association of Engineering Societies, there is a single room that serves as the home of the Society of Women Engineers. The society, founded in 1959 by 50 women engineers, has grown from a membership of just a few hundred in 1970 to more than 9,000 in 1980. Still, compared to the other engineering societies, it seems pitifully small.

During my visit I browsed through a pile of career guidance pamphlets, newsletters full of recruiting ads from DuPont, Boeing, Ford, and IBM, and also a booklet telling about the society's achievement award, given annually since 1952. The winners of this award are talented women who have made contributions in many fields: solar energy, circuit analysis, metallurgy, missile launchers, rubber reclamation, computers, fluid mechanics, structural design, heat transfer, radio-wave propagation, and so on. Their undeniable ability adds poignancy to the fact that they and their fellow women engineers are so few that their overall contributions to the profession have been, in essence, negligible.

In some of the society's literature I discovered a series of autobiographical essays prepared by society members. In each of these life-stories there was evidence of relatively humble family origins and of success earned through struggle. I also came across photographs of student-chapter members, smiling young women, mostly from the

Midwest, who seemed — was it my imagination? — not at all like the sophisticated young women I had met at Smith.

Of course, the students at Smith do not study engineering. Neither do the students — male or female — at Harvard and Yale, which venerable institutions closed their professional schools of engineering years ago (although they still have some courses in engineering science), and neither of which deigned to respond to a recent statistical questionnaire from the Society of Women Engineers. All the circumstantial evidence I could garner served to reinforce my ideas about the class origins of the problem.

Wanting more information, I visited Carl Frey, executive director of the American Association of Engineering Societies, that organization of organizations to which most of the major professional engineering societies belong. In his position at the top of the organization pyramid, Frey has long lived with the many discontents and disputes endemic to the sprawling, variegated profession: four-year colleges versus five- and six-year programs (what constitutes a professional education?); state licensing (is an engineer a professional without it?); salaries (why do lawyers make so much more than engineers?); prestige (why do scientists get all the credit for engineering achievement?); leadership (why are there so few engineers in elective office?); conservatism of the self-employed versus radicalism of the hired hands; conscience, responsibility, the environmental crisis. Frey could not survive in his position without a genial disposition and a calm sense of history. From his point of view, women in engineering is just one more problem that the profession will cope with in due time.

"I wouldn't get hung up on any fancy theories about class," Frey said, after I outlined my hypothesis. "It's harder and harder to tell who comes from what class, and things are changing so fast that I wouldn't rely on any old statistics you might have seen about the social origins of engineers."

"Well, how do you explain it?" I asked. "Why aren't more bright young women getting into engineering?"

"I think that it has to do with their perception of power. These kids today — the bright girls particularly — they want to be where the action is, where the sources of power are. They don't see engineers as the ones who have the say in our society. And, let's face it, to a great extent they're right. We may have the knowhow, but we don't have the power."

Perception of power. The phrase kept going through my mind. It had a nice ring to it, and it had the ring of truth as well. It did not seem to contradict my ideas about class so much as to encompass them, for what is the origin of class structure if not the desire to perpetuate power?

Every engineer knows that the profession is relatively powerless. Engineers do not make the laws; they do not have the money; they do not set the fashions; they have no voice in the media. It is one of the most irritating ironies of our time that intellectuals constantly complain about being in the grip of a technocratic elite that does not exist.

To the extent that today's young women are not fooled by such nonsense, they are deserving of credit. But if intelligent, energetic women reject engineering because of an all-consuming desire to sit on the thrones of power, then woe to us all in the age of feminism.

When the National Organization for Women was formed in 1966, its Statement of Purpose spoke of bringing women "into full participation in the mainstream of American society *now*, exercising all the privileges and responsibilities thereof in truly equal partnership with men." Yet judging from the way that most advantaged women are selecting their careers, they seem to be a lot more interested in the privileges than in the responsibilities. In this they are following the lead of those males who appear to be in control of our society — the lawyers, writers, politicians, and business managers. This is all very well, but somebody in our society has to design, create, fabricate, build — to *do*. A world full of coordinators, critics, and manipulators would have nothing in it but words. It would be a barren desert, totally devoid of *things*.

Feminist ideology, understandably adopting the values of the extant, i.e., male, establishment, is founded on a misapprehension of what constitutes privilege. The feminist leaders have made the deplorable mistake of assuming that those who work hard without public recognition, and for modest rewards, are necessarily being exploited. "Man's happiness lies not in freedom but in his acceptance of a duty," said André Gide. When the duty turns out to be work that is creative and absorbing, as well as essential, then those who had been patronized for being the worker bees are seen to be more fortunate than the queen.

Studies have shown that young engineers, women as well as men, pursue their career because it promises "interesting work." This is more important to them than money, security, prestige, or any of the other trappings of power. They seem to recognize that a fulfilling career does not have to consist of a continuous ego trip.

Although power, in the popular imagination, is identified with wealth and domination, there is another kind of power that lies beneath the surface of our petty ambitions, and that is the engineer's in full measure. It is the force that Henry Adams had in mind when he wrote of the dynamo and the Virgin. The power of the Virgin raised the medieval cathedrals, although, as Adams noted, the Virgin had been dead for a millennium and had held no real power even when she lived. For better or for worse, technology lies at the heart of our contemporary culture, and the technologist is akin to a priest who knows the secrets of the temple. In this sense, and in this sense only, those who speak of a technocratic elite are touching on a profound truth. Until women share in the understanding and creation of our technology — which is to say, until large numbers of women become engineers — they will suffer from a cultural alienation that ordinary power cannot cure.

The feminist movement means different things to different people. Many of its goals, such as mutual respect and equality before the law, can be achieved even if there are no women engineers. But the ultimate feminist dream will never be realized as long as women would rather supervise the world than help build it.

QUESTIONS

1. Is Florman's assertion true? Is there something "unfeminine" about becoming an engineer? Is there something "unfeminist" about it?

2. Florman points out that Yale and Harvard closed their professional engineering schools years ago. What conclusion does he draw from that fact? Is his conclusion valid?

3. Florman compares engineers with "worker bees," suggesting that they work long hours, go unrecognized, and reap few rewards. Is that your assessment of engineering also?

4. Assuming for the moment that Florman's assertions are true, can you think of other professions that are also snubbed by feminists? What reasons can you give for these professions being ignored or scorned?

5. Write an essay arguing that a certain profession is shunned by women (or men). Include an analysis similar to Florman's explaining why one sex avoids this profession.

•   •   •   •   •

IN DEFENSE OF LITERACY

Wendell Berry

Wendell Berry has published over twenty volumes of poetry, fiction, and essays. Although it is difficult to characterize such a varied body of work, Berry's writing tends to focus on tradition, individualism, and the fundamental values inherent in country life. This article comes from his 1972 book, A Continuous Harmony.

IN a country in which everybody goes to school, it may seem absurd to offer a defense of literacy, and yet I believe that such a defense is in order, and that the absurdity lies not in the defense, but in the necessity for it. The published illiteracies of the certified educated are on the increase. And the universities seem bent upon ratifying this state of things by declaring the acceptability, in their graduates, of adequate — that is to say, of mediocre — writing skills.

The schools, then, are following the general subservience to the "practical," as that term has been defined for us according to the benefit of corporations. By "practicality" most users of the term now mean whatever will most predictably and most quickly make a profit. Teachers of English and literature have either submitted, or are expected to submit, along with teachers of the more "practical" disciplines, to the doctrine that the purpose of education is the mass production of producers and consumers. This has forced our profession into a predicament that we will finally have to recognize as a perversion. As if awed by the ascendency of the "practical" in our society, many of us secretly fear, and some of us are apparently ready to say, that if a student is not going to become a teacher of his language, he has no need to master it.

In other words, to keep pace with the specialization — and the dignity accorded to specialization — in other disciplines, we have begun to look upon and to teach our language and literature as specialties. But whereas specialization is of the nature of the applied sciences, it is a perversion of the disciplines of language and literature. When we understand and teach these as specialties, we submit willy-nilly to the assumption of the "practical men" of business, and also apparently of education, that literacy is no more than an ornament: when one has become an efficient integer of the economy, *then* it is permissible, even desirable, to be able to talk about the latest novels. After all, the disciples of "practicality" may someday find themselves stuck in conversation with an English teacher.

I may have oversimplified that line of thinking, but not much. There are two flaws in it. One is that, among the self-styled "practical men," the practical is synonymous with the immediate. The long-term effects of their values and their acts lie outside the boundaries of their interest. For such people a strip mine ceases to exist as soon as the coal has been extracted. Short-term practicality is long-term idiocy.

The other flaw is that language and literature are always *about* something else, and we have no way to predict or control what they may be about. They are about the world. We will understand the world, and preserve ourselves and our values in it, only insofar as we have a language that is alert and responsive to it, and careful of it. I mean that literally. When we give our plows such brand names as "Sod Blaster," we are imposing on their use conceptual limits which raise the likelihood that they will be used destructively. When we speak of man's "war against nature," or of a "peace offensive," we are accepting the limitations of a metaphor that suggests, and even proposes, violent solutions. When students ask for the right of "participatory input" at the meetings of a faculty organization, they are thinking of democratic process, but they are *speaking* of a convocation of robots, and are thus devaluing the very tradition that they invoke.

Ignorance of books and the lack of a critical consciousness of language were safe enough in primitive societies with coherent oral traditions. In our society, which exists in an atmosphere of prepared, public language — language that is either written or being read — illiteracy is both a personal and a public danger. Think how constantly "the average American" is surrounded by premeditated language, in newspapers and magazines, on signs and billboards, on TV and radio. He is forever being asked to buy or believe somebody else's line of goods. The line of goods is being sold, moreover, by men who are trained to make him buy it or believe it, whether or not he needs it or understands it or knows its value or wants it. This sort of selling is an honored profession among us. Parents who grow hysterical at the thought that their son might not cut his hair are *glad* to have him taught, and later employed, to lie about the quality of an automobile or the ability of a candidate.

What is our defense against this sort of language — this language-as-weapon? There is only one. We must know a better language. We must speak, and teach our children to speak, a language precise and articulate and lively enough to tell the truth about the world as we know it. And to do this we must know something of the roots and resources of our language; we must know its literature. The only defense against the worst is a knowledge of the best. By their ignorance people enfranchise their exploiters.

But to appreciate fully the necessity for the best sort of literacy we must consider not just the environment of prepared language in which most of us now pass most of our lives, but also the utter transience of most of this language, which is meant to be merely glanced at, or heard only once, or read once and thrown away. Such language is by definition, and often by calculation, not memorable; it is language meant to be replaced by what will immediately follow it, like that of shallow conversation between strangers. It cannot be pondered or effectively criticized. For those reasons an unmixed diet of it is destructive of the informed, resilient, critical intelligence that the best of our traditions have sought to create and to maintain — an intelligence that Jefferson held to be indispensable to the health and longevity of freedom. Such intelligence does not grow by bloating upon the ephemeral information and misinformation of the public media. It grows by returning again and again to the landmarks of its cultural birthright, the works that have proved worthy of devoted attention.

"Read not the Times. Read the Eternities," Thoreau said. Ezra Pound wrote that "literature is news that STAYS news." In his lovely poem, "The Island," Edwin Muir spoke of man's inescapable cultural boundaries and of his consequent responsibility for his own sources and renewals:

> Men are made of what is made,
> The meat, the drink, the life, the corn,
> Laid up by them, in them reborn.
> And self-begotten cycles close
> About our way; indigenous art
> And simple spells make unafraid
> The haunted labyrinths of the heart . . .

These men spoke of a truth that no society can afford to shirk for long: we are dependent, for understanding, and for consolation and hope, upon what we learn of ourselves from songs and stories. This has always been so, and it will not change.

I am saying, then, that literacy — the mastery of language and the knowledge of books — is not an ornament, but a necessity. It is impractical only by the standards of quick profit and easy power. Longer perspective will show that it alone can preserve in us the possibility of an accurate judgment of ourselves, and the possibilities of correction and renewal. Without it, we are adrift in the present, in the wreckage of yesterday, in the nightmare of tomorrow.

QUESTIONS

1. Berry suggests that the culture has designated certain skills or disciplines as "practical," and others as "impractical." What would be an example of an "impractical" skill or discipline? What makes that skill seem impractical? Is it really impractical?

2. Berry speaks disparagingly of what he calls "short-term practicality" and cites a strip mine as an example of this thinking. What other examples of short-term practicality can you name?

3. Literacy to Berry seems to mean more than simply the ability to read and write. How would you define what he means by literacy?

4. Compare the views of Berry with those of Florman (p. 421). Are these men discussing the same issues? Where would they agree or disagree?

5. Berry quotes Ezra Pound and says we should "read the Eternities." What specifically does that mean? Can you give an example of how we might go about reading the "Eternities"?

● ● ● ● ●

HUMANITIES AND SCIENCE

Lewis Thomas

Lewis Thomas is a physician whose essays on medicine and life in The New England Journal of Medicine *have been highly praised. His first book, a collection of those essays, became a best-seller* (The Lives of a Cell *[1974]); it has been followed by other popular books that explore medicine, biology, and philosophy —* The Medusa and the Snail *(1979),* The Youngest Science *(1983), and the volume from which this essay was taken,* Late Night Thoughts on Listening to Mahler's Ninth Symphony *(1983).*

LORD Kelvin was one of the great British physicists of the late nineteenth century, an extraordinarily influential figure in his time, and in some ways a paradigm of conventional, established scientific leadership. He did a lot of good and useful things, but once or twice he, like Homer, nodded. The instances are worth recalling today, for we have nodders among our scientific eminences still, from time to time, needing to have their elbows shaken.

On one occasion, Kelvin made a speech on the overarching importance of numbers. He maintained that no observation of nature was worth paying serious attention to unless it could be stated in precisely quantitative terms. The numbers were the final and only test, not only of truth but about meaning as well. He said, "When you can measure what you are speaking about, and express it in numbers, you know something about it. But when you cannot — your knowledge is of a meagre and unsatisfactory kind."

But, as at least one subsequent event showed, Kelvin may have had things exactly the wrong way round. The task of converting observations into numbers is the hardest of all, the last task rather than the first thing to be done, and it can be done only when you have learned, beforehand, a great deal about the observations themselves. You can, to be sure, achieve a very deep understanding of nature by quantitative measurement, but you must know what you are talking about before you can begin applying the numbers for making predictions. In Kelvin's case, the problem at hand was the age of the earth and solar system. Using what was then known about the sources of energy and the loss of energy from the physics of that day, he calculated that neither the earth nor the sun were older than several hundred million years. This caused a considerable stir in biological and geological circles, especially among the evolutionists. Darwin himself was distressed by the numbers; the time was much too short for the theory of evolution. Kelvin's figures were described by Darwin as one of his "sorest troubles."

T. H. Huxley had long been aware of the risks involved in premature extrapolations from mathematical treatment of biological problems. He said, in an 1869 speech to the Geological Society concerning numbers, "This seems to be one of the many cases in which the admitted accuracy of mathematical processes is allowed to throw a wholly inadmissible appearance of authority over the results obtained by them. . . . As the grandest mill in the world will not extract wheat flour from peascods, so pages of formulas will not get a definite result out of loose data."

The trouble was that the world of physics had not moved fast enough to allow for Kelvin's assumptions. Nuclear fusion and fission had not yet been dreamed of, and the true age of the earth could not even be guessed from the data in hand. It was not yet the time for mathematics in this subject.

There have been other examples, since those days, of the folly of using numbers and calculations uncritically. Kelvin's own strong conviction that science could not be genuine science without measuring things was catching. People in other fields of endeavor, hankering to turn their disciplines into exact sciences, beset by what has since been called "physics envy," set about converting whatever they knew into numbers and thence into equations with predictive pretensions. We have it with us still, in economics, sociology, psychology, history, even, I fear, in English-literature criticism and linguistics, and it frequently works, when it works at all, with indifferent success. The risks of untoward social consequences in work of this kind are considerable. It is as important — and as hard — to learn *when* to use mathematics as *how* to use it, and this matter should remain high on the agenda of consideration for education in the social and behavioral sciences.

Of course, Kelvin's difficulty with the age of the earth was an exceptional, almost isolated instance of failure in quantitative measurement in nineteenth-century physics. The instruments devised for approaching nature by way of physics became increasingly precise and powerful, carrying the field through electromagnetic theory, triumph after triumph, and setting the stage for the great revolution of twentieth-century physics. There is no doubt about it: measurement works when the instruments work, and when you have a fairly clear idea of what it is that is being measured, and when you know what to do with the numbers when they tumble out. The system for gaining information and comprehension about nature works so well, indeed, that it carries another hazard: the risk of convincing yourself that you know everything.

Kelvin himself fell into this trap toward the end of the century. (I don't mean to keep picking on Kelvin, who was a very great scientist; it is just that he happened to say a couple of things I find useful for this discussion.) He stated, in a summary of the achievements of nineteenth-century physics, that it was an almost completed science; virtually everything that needed knowing about the material universe had been learned; there were still a few anomalies and inconsistencies in electromagnetic theory, a few loose ends to be tidied up, but this would be done within the next several years. Physics, in these terms, was not a field any longer likely to attract, as it previously had, the brightest and most imaginative young brains. The most interesting part of the work had already been done. Then, within the next decade, came radiation, Planck, the quantum, Einstein, Rutherford, Bohr, and all the rest — quantum mechanics — and the whole field turned over and became a brand-new sort of human endeavor, still now, in the view of many physicists, almost a full century later, a field only at its beginnings.

But even today, despite the amazements that are turning up in physics each year, despite the jumps taken from the smallest parts of nature — particle physics — to the largest of all — the cosmos itself — the impression of science that the public gains is rather like the impression left in the nineteenth-century public mind by Kelvin. Science, in this view, is first of all a matter of simply getting all the numbers together. The numbers are sitting out there in nature, waiting to be found, sorted and totted up. If only they had enough robots and enough computers, the scientist could go off to the beach and wait for their papers to be written for them. Second of all, what we know about nature today is pretty much the whole story: we are very nearly home and dry. From here on, it is largely a problem of tying up loose ends, tidying nature up, getting the files in order. The only real surprises for the future — and it is about those that the public is becoming more concerned and apprehensive — are the technological applications that the scientists may be cooking up from today's knowledge.

I suggest that the scientific community is to blame. If there are disagreements between the world of the humanities and the scientific enterprise as to the place and importance of science in a liberal-arts education, and the role of science in twentieth-century culture, I believe that the scientists are themselves responsible for a general misunderstanding of what they are really up to.

Over the past half century, we have been teaching the sciences as though they were the same academic collection of cut-and-dried subjects as always, and — here is what has really gone wrong — as though they would always be the same. The teaching of today's biology, for example, is pretty much the same kind of exercise as the teaching of Latin was when I was in high school long ago. First of all, the fundamentals, the underlying laws, the essential grammar, and then the reading of texts. Once mastered, that is that: Latin is Latin and forever after will be Latin. And biology is precisely biology, a vast array of hard facts to be learned as fundamentals, followed by a reading of the texts.

Moreover, we have been teaching science as though its facts were somehow superior to the facts in all other scholarly disciplines, more fundamental, more solid, less subject to subjectivism, immutable. English literature is not just one way of thinking, it is all sorts of ways. Poetry is a moving target. The facts that underlie art, architecture, and music are not really hard facts, and you can change them any way you like by arguing about them, but science is treated as an altogether different kind of learning: an unambiguous, unalterable, and endlessly useful display of data needing only to be packaged and installed somewhere in one's temporal lobe in order to achieve a full understanding of the natural world.

And it is, of course, not like this at all. In real life, every field of science that I can think of is incomplete, and most of them — whatever the record of accomplishment over the past two hundred years — are still in the earliest stage of their starting point. In the fields I know best, among the life sciences, it is required that the most expert and sophisticated minds be capable of changing those minds, often with a great lurch, every few years. In some branches of biology the mind-changing is occurring with accelerating velocities. The next week's issue of any scientific journal can turn a whole field upside down, shaking out any number of immutable ideas and installing new bodies of dogma, and this is happening all the time. It is an almost everyday event in physics, in chemistry, in materials research, in neurobiology, in genetics, in immunology. The hard facts tend to soften overnight, melt away, and vanish under the pressure of new hard facts, and the interpretations of what appear to be the most solid aspects of nature are subject to change, now more than at any other time in history. The conclusions reached in science are always, when looked at closely, far more provisional and tentative than are most of the assumptions arrived at by our colleagues in the humanities.

The running battle now in progress between the sociobiologists and the anti-sociobiologists is a marvel for students to behold, close up. To observe, in open-mouthed astonishment, the polarized extremes, one group of highly intelligent, beautifully trained, knowledgeable, and imaginative scientists maintaining that all sorts of behavior, animal and human, are governed exclusively by genes, and another group of equally talented scientists saying precisely the opposite and asserting that all behavior is set and determined by the environment, or by culture, and both sides brawling in the pages of periodicals such as *The New York Review of Books*, is an educational experience that no college student should be allowed to miss. The essential lesson to be learned has nothing to do with the relative validity of the facts underlying the argument, it is the argument itself that is the education: we do not yet know enough to settle such questions.

It is true that at any given moment there is the appearance of satisfaction, even self-satisfaction, within every scientific discipline. On any Tuesday morning, if asked, a good working scientist will gladly tell you that the affairs of the field are nicely in order, that things are finally looking clear and making sense, and all is well. But come back again, on another Tuesday, and he may let you know that the roof has just fallen in on his life's work, that all the old ideas — last week's ideas in some cases — are no longer good ideas, that something strange has happened.

It is the very strangeness of nature that makes science engrossing. That ought to be at the center of science teaching. There are more than seven-times-seven types of ambiguity in science, awaiting analysis. The poetry of Wallace Stevens is crystal-clear alongside the genetic code.

I prefer to turn things around in order to make precisely the opposite case. Science, especially twentieth-century science, has provided us with a glimpse of something we never really knew before, the revelation of human ignorance. We have been used to the belief, down one century after another, that we more or less comprehend everything bar one or two mysteries like the mental processes of our gods. Every age, not just the eighteenth century, regarded itself as the Age of Reason, and we have never lacked for explanations of the world and its ways. Now, we are being brought up short, and this has been the work of science. We have a wilderness of mystery to make our way through in the centuries ahead, and we will need science for this but not science alone. Science will, in its own time, produce the data and some of the meaning in the data, but never the full meaning. For getting a full grasp, for perceiving real significance when significance is at hand, we shall need minds at work from all sorts of brains outside the fields of science, most of all the brains of poets, of course, but also those of artists, musicians, philosophers, historians, writers in general.

It is primarily because of this need that I would press for changes in the way science is taught. There is a need to teach the young people who will be doing the science themselves, but this will always be a small minority among us. There is a deeper need to teach science to those who will be needed for thinking about it, and this means pretty nearly everyone else, in hopes that a few of these people — a much smaller minority than the scientific community and probably a lot harder to find — will, in the thinking, be able to imagine new levels of meaning that are likely to be lost on the rest of us.

In addition, it is time to develop a new group of professional thinkers, perhaps a somewhat larger group than the working scientists, who can create a discipline of scientific criticism. We have had good luck so far in the emergence of a few people ranking as philosophers of science and historians and journalists of science, and I hope more of these will be coming along, but we have not yet seen a Ruskin or a Leavis or an

Edmund Wilson. Science needs critics of this sort, but the public at large needs them more urgently.

I suggest that the introductory courses in science, at all levels from grade school through college, be radically revised. Leave the fundamentals, the so-called basics, aside for a while, and concentrate the attention of all students on the things that are *not* known. You cannot possibly teach quantum mechanics without mathematics, to be sure, but you can describe the strangeness of the world opened up by quantum theory. Let it be known, early on, that there are deep mysteries, and profound paradoxes, revealed in their distant outlines, by the quantum. Let it be known that these can be approached more closely, and puzzled over, once the language of mathematics has been sufficiently mastered.

Teach at the outset, before any of the fundamentals, the still imponderable puzzles of cosmology. Let it be known, as clearly as possible, by the youngest minds, that there are some things going on in the universe that lie beyond comprehension, and make it plain how little is known.

Do not teach that biology is a useful and perhaps profitable science; that can come later. Teach instead that there are structures squirming inside all our cells, providing all the energy for living, that are essentially foreign creatures, brought in for symbiotic living a billion or so years ago, the lineal descendants of bacteria. Teach that we do not have the ghost of an idea how they got there, where they came from, or how they evolved to their present structure and function. The details of oxidative phosphorylation and photosynthesis can came later.

Teach ecology early on. Let it be understood that the earth's life is a system of interliving, interdependent creatures, and that we do not understand at all how it works. The earth's environment, from the range of atmospheric gases to the chemical constituents of the sea, has been held in an almost unbelievably improbable state of regulated balance since life began, and the regulation of stability and balance is accomplished solely by the life itself, like the internal environment of an immense organism, and we do not know how *that* one works, even less what it means. Teach that.

Go easy, I suggest, on the promises sometimes freely offered by science. Technology relies and depends on science these days, more than ever before, but technology is nothing like the first justification for doing research, nor is it necessarily an essential product to be expected from science. Public decisions about what to have in the way of technology are totally different problems from decisions about science, and the two enterprises should not be tangled together. The central task of science is to arrive, stage by stage, at a clearer comprehension of nature, but this does not mean, as it is sometimes claimed to mean, a search for mastery over nature. Science may provide us, one day, with a better understanding of ourselves, but never, I hope, with a set of technologies for doing something or other to improve ourselves. I am made nervous by assertions that human consciousness will someday be unraveled by research, laid out for close scrutiny like the workings of a computer, and then, *and then!* I hope with some fervor that we can learn a lot more than we now know about the human mind, and I see no reason why this strange puzzle should remain forever and entirely beyond us. But I would be deeply disturbed by any prospect that we might use the new knowledge in order to begin doing something about it, to improve it, say. This is a different matter from searching for information to use against schizophrenia or dementia, where we are badly in need of technologies, indeed likely one day to be sunk without them. But the ordinary, everyday, more or less normal human mind is too marvelous an instrument ever to be tampered with by anyone, science or no science.

The education of humanists cannot be regarded as complete, or even adequate, without exposure in some depth to where things stand in the various branches of science, and particularly, as I have said, in the areas of our ignorance. This does not mean that I know how to go about doing it, nor am I unaware of the difficulties involved. Physics professors, most of them, look with revulsion on assignments to teach their subject to poets. Biologists, caught up by the enchantment of their new power, armed with flawless instruments to tell the nucleotide sequences of the entire human genome, nearly matching the physicists in the precision of their measurements of living processes, will resist the prospect of broad survey courses; each biology professor will demand that any student in his path must master every fine detail within that professor's research program. The liberal-arts faculties, for their part, will continue to view the scientists with suspicion and apprehension. "What do the scientists want?" asked a Cambridge professor in Francis Cornford's wonderful *Microcosmographia Academica*. "Everything that's going," was the quick answer. That was back in 1912, and universities haven't much changed.

The worst thing that has happened to science education is that the great fun has gone out of it. A very large number of good students look at it as slogging work to be got through on the way to medical school. Others look closely at the premedical students themselves, embattled and bleeding for grades and class standing, and are turned off. Very few see science as the high adventure it really is, the wildest of all explorations ever undertaken by human beings, the chance to catch close views of things never seen before, the shrewdest maneuver for discovering how the world works. Instead, they become baffled early on, and they are misled into thinking that bafflement is simply the result of not having learned all the facts. They are not told, as they should be told, that everyone else — from the professor in his endowed chair down to the platoons of postdoctoral students in the laboratory all night — is baffled as well. Every important scientific advance that has come in looking like an answer has turned, sooner or later — usually sooner — into a question. And the game is just beginning.

An appreciation of what is happening in science today, and of how great a distance lies ahead for exploring, ought to be one of the rewards of a liberal-arts education. It ought to be a good in itself, not something to be acquired on the way to a professional career but part of the cast of thought needed for getting into the kind of century that is now just down the road. Part of the intellectual equipment of an educated person, however his or her time is to be spent, ought to be a feel for the queernesses of nature, the inexplicable things.

And maybe, just maybe, a new set of courses dealing systematically with ignorance in science might take hold. The scientists might discover in it a new and subversive technique for catching the attention of students driven by curiosity, delighted and surprised to learn that science is exactly as Bush described it: an "endless frontier." The humanists, for their part, might take considerable satisfaction watching their scientific colleagues confess openly to not knowing everything about everything. And the poets, on whose shoulders the future rests, might, late nights, thinking things over, begin to see meanings that elude the rest of us. It is worth a try.

QUESTIONS

1. Thomas makes a clear distinction between *technology* and *science*. Explain how these are different. Which does he believe is more important? Why?

2. Thomas attacks what he believes is a common misconception, that the humanities are "fuzzy" and imprecise, while the sciences are neatly ordered factual disciplines. If the sciences are also imprecise, as Thomas asserts, why are they? Can they simply be made more precise?

3. Why does Thomas say that the poets are the ones "on whose shoulders the future rests"? What do you take this to mean?

4. What does the example of Kelvin teach us about inductive reasoning? What does the current dispute between the geneticists and the behaviorists teach us about inductive reasoning?

5. Thomas himself reasons inductively. Are his conclusions faulty also? How does he know whether they are or not?

• • • • •

THE SCOPES TRIAL IN REVERSE

Duane T. Gish

The Humanist *is a journal published by the American Humanist Association, a group that, according to its literature, sees human beings "as the product of this world, of evolution, and human history." Humanism, to quote from an essay in the first issue of the journal, "symbolizes man's discovery of himself, and therein, of his possibilities. It signifies human endeavor, human achievements, the sweetness and bright promise of life." In the following reading, Duane Gish responds to criticisms of creationism that appeared in a previous* Humanist *article. At the time it was written, Gish was the associate director of the Institute for Creation Research, an organization that opposes the tenets of humanism.*

IN the fifty years or so since the Scopes Trial in 1925, events have taken a 180-degree turn. Then, in violation of constitutional guarantees of academic and religious freedoms, the only theory concerning man's origin permissible under Tennessee law was that of special creation. The teaching of evolutionary theory was proscribed by law. In 1977, many are advocating that the theory of creation be proscribed by administrative or legal fiat and that the theory of evolution be taught exclusively in textbooks and classrooms of public schools and universities. As was the case with the medieval church, ruling circles in our educational and scientific establishments are asserting that they are in sole possession of the truth and believe it is their duty to protect others from error.

Regardless of where they feel the truth lies, members of the American Humanist Association should be foremost in the ranks of those demanding the right to teach both theories of origins in the schools of our democratic, pluralistic society. A threat to the academic and religious freedoms of any segment of our society is a threat to all of us. Those who were pleading so eloquently in 1925 that teachers have a constitutionally guaranteed right to teach both creation and evolution theories are now insisting that only evolution be taught in public schools.

Thus, through its president and the pages of *The Humanist*, the American Humanist Association has launched a determined campaign aimed at elimination of all efforts to present the scientific case for creation in public schools. Humanists have cast themselves in the bigoted, narrow position of denying academic and religious freedoms to those who dissent from their position. Such a course, if successful, will establish their religion of secular humanism as a state-supported religion in violation of constitutional doctrine of separation of church and state.

In "A Statement Affirming Evolution as a Principle of Science" (*The Humanist*, Jan./Feb. 1977) it was stated that creationism is not science but that evolution is scientific and nonreligious. As a matter of fact, evolution theory is no more scientific than creation theory, and it is just as religious. Neither evolution nor creation is a valid scientific theory. Evolutionist Norman Macbeth flatly states that "Darwinism is not science" (*American Biology Teacher*, Nov. 1976). Ehrlich and Birch (evolutionists) state that evolution theory is "outside of empirical science, but not necessarily false. No one can think of ways in which to test it" (*Nature*, Vol. 214, 1967).

In his article "An Axiomatic Interpretation of the Neo-Darwinian Theory of Evolution" (*Perspectives in Biology and Medicine*, Winter 1975) evolutionist C. Leon Harris states that "the axiomatic nature of the neo-Darwinian theory of evolution places the debate between evolutionists and creationists in a new perspective. Evolutionists have often challenged creationists to provide experimental proof that species have been fashioned *de novo*. Creationists have often demanded that evolutionists show how chance mutations can lead to adaptability, or to explain why natural selection has favored some species but not others with special adaptations, or why natural selection allows apparently detrimental organs to persist. We may now recognize that neither challenge is fair. If the neo-Darwinian theory is axiomatic, it is not valid for creationists to demand proof of the axioms, and it is not valid for evolutionists to dismiss creation as unproved so long as it is stated as an axiom."

Evolutionist L. Harrison Matthews states in his Introduction to the 1971 edition of Darwin's *Origin of Species* (J. M. Dent and Sons, London), "Belief in the theory of evolution is thus exactly parallel to belief in special creation — both are concepts which believers know to be true but neither, up to the present, has been capable of proof."

We have thus adequately documented from the scientific literature of evolutionists that evolution is no more scientific than creation. Both can be discussed in scientific terms, of course, and one or the other must be true, but neither is observable, testable, or falsifiable, so neither is a scientific theory.

Furthermore, evolution is intrinsically as religious as creation. Both involve commitments to a particular philosophy or world view. The American Humanist Association has defined humanism as a nontheistic religion. The literature of the association quotes Sir Julian Huxley as saying, "I use the word 'Humanist' to mean someone who believes that man is just as much a natural phenomenon as an animal or plant; that his body, mind and soul were not supernaturally created but are the products of evolution, and that he is not under the control or guidance of any supernatural being or beings, but has to rely on himself and his own powers." The inseparable link between the "nontheistic religion" of humanism and belief in evolution is evident. Faith in evolution theory is a basic dogma of atheistic humanists.

Theistic evolution is not a viable alternative for either creationists or humanists, since it is as evolutionistic and mechanistic as atheistic evolution and, to humanists, it is as theistic as creation. Special creation and evolution are the only valid alternatives as conceptual schemes that have been devised to explain origins.

The "Statement" in *The Humanist* claimed: "There are no alternative theories to the principle of evolution . . . that any competent biologist of today takes seriously." There are actually many competent scientists today who reject evolution as untenable scientifically and are convinced that creation is a far better conceptual model for correlating and explaining the scientific evidence related to origins. Many are biologists, including some who are heads of biology departments at major universities. The Creation Research Society, founded in 1963, now has over five hundred members, all of whom are creationists and hold advanced degrees in sciences.

Much of the available scientific evidence is directly contradictory to evolution theory, but can be admirably correlated and explained by special creation. This is not to say, of course, that there is no evidence that can be adduced in favor of evolution, nor does it mean that all of the evidence is easily and readily explained by creation. Creation scientists insist, however, that the scientific evidence that is available renders creation far more credible than evolution.

Evolution is contradicted and creation is supported by the laws of thermodynamics, the laws of probability, the law of biogenesis (life comes only from preexisting life), the evidence for design and purpose in the natural world, and the fossil record. Concerning the fossil record (paleontology), evolutionist David Kitts, in *Evolution* (Vol. 28, 1974), states: "Despite the bright promise that paleontology provides a mean of 'seeing' evolution, it has presented some nasty difficulties for evolutionists, the most notorious of which is the presence of 'gaps' in the fossil record. Evolution requires intermediate forms between species, and paleontology does not provide them." Evolutionist E. J. H. Corner states, in *Contemporary Botanical Thought*, edited by Macleod and Cobley (1961), "I still think that, to the unprejudiced, the fossil record of plants is in favor of special creation."

Preston Cloud, in "'Scientific Creationism' — A New Inquisition Brewing" (*The Humanist*, Jan./Feb. 1977), denies the statement in my little booklet "Have you Been Brainwashed?" (which he also misquotes) that not a single indisputable multicellular fossil has been found in a Precambrian rock (the Cambrian rocks contain a great variety of fossils of highly complex animals for which no evolutionary ancestors can be found). Yet this is precisely what Cloud states and extensively documents in several articles, the latest appearing in *Geology* (Vol. 1, 1973). In that article, he states: "Cloud (1968), Hofmann (1971), Glaessner (1965, 1969), Sokolov (1971), Sando (1972), and others have established that, in spite of many published records, there are as yet no unequivocal Metazoa in rocks of indisputable Proterozoic or older age." Cloud thus explicitly states that no unequivocal Metazoa (that is, fossils of multicellular animals) have been found in Proterozoic (Precambrian) or older rocks.

In fact, in a debate at the University of California, Santa Barbara, on May 24, 1976, between Cloud and Aharon Gibor, on one hand, and Dr. Henry Morris and me, on the other hand, I explicitly stated that no indisputable multicellular fossils had been found in Precambrian rocks and quoted the article by Cloud (cited above) in support. Cloud offered not a word of rebuttal. What Cloud is willing to publish in *The Humanist* in defense of evolution theory is apparently quite different from what he publishes in the geological literature.

In any case, the fossil record reveals an explosive appearance of a great variety of highly complex animals with absence of ancestors and the systematic absence of transitional forms between higher categories of plants and animals, just as predicted on the basis of creation.

In *Mathematical Challenges to the Neo-Darwinian Interpretation of Evolution* (Philadelphia: Wistar Institute Press, 1967), a group of mathematicians, all evolutionists, have challenged the modern neo-Darwinian theory of evolution, based on random, chance mutations, as totally inadequate. Murray Eden, one of these mathematicians, states that "an adequate scientific theory of evolution must await the discovery of new laws, physical, physico-chemical, and biological." These mathematicians believe that the evolutionists would require millions of times longer than five billion years to produce man from a single-celled organism. Creation scientists maintain that there is no conceivable natural mechanism, including natural selection, for overcoming the impossible odds against getting man from a single-celled organism by pure chance. Intelligent, purposeful activity by a supernatural creator must have been required.

The second law of thermodynamics, regardless of denials by evolutionists, including Cloud, is fatal to evolution theory. Evolution theory postulates an enormous spontaneous increase in order during the evolution of the universe, the origin of life, and the evolution of living things. The second law of thermodynamics tells us that there could have been no such *spontaneous* increase in order. All natural systems tend to proceed toward greater disorder.

In an article in the *Smithsonian Institution Journal* (June 1970), Isaac Asimov put it this way: "Another way of stating the second law then is: 'The Universe is constantly getting more disorderly!' Viewed that way, we can see the second law all about us. We have to work hard to straighten a room, but left to itself it becomes a mess again very quickly and very easily. Even if we never enter it, it becomes dusty and musty. How difficult to maintain houses and machinery, and our own bodies, in perfect working order; how easy to let them deteriorate. In fact, all we have to do is nothing, and everything deteriorates, collapses, breaks down, wears out, all by itself — and that is what the Second Law is all about."

This universal tendency toward disorder applies to all systems, open or closed. Certain open systems, due to very special conditions, can exist and increase in complexity temporarily, but eventually all systems succumb. Such special conditions are possessed by green plants and automobile factories due to the preexisting energy conversion systems (photosynthesis and machines) and the control and maintenance systems (the incredibly complex genetic system of the plant and the assembly line and humans of the factory) possessed by green plants and automobile factories.

That it takes more than just energy to generate order in natural systems is evident, when, forgetting evolutionary theory and speaking as scientists, evolutionists George Simpson and William Beck state, in *Life: An Introduction to Biology*: "The simple expenditure of energy is not sufficient to develop and maintain order. A bull in a china shop performs work, but he neither creates nor maintains organization. The work needed is *particular* work; it must follow specifications; it requires information on how to proceed."

Could an explosion of some primeval cosmic egg (whose origin has no explanation) produce the highly ordered universe? Could a living thing, necessarily incredibly complex, arise spontaneously from simple gases? There could have been energy aplenty, but where was the information on how to proceed to assemble large and complex protein, DNA and RNA molecules? Where were the energy conversion machines? Machines and control systems, in perfect obedience to the second law, do not arise spontaneously; they spontaneously deteriorate. The hypothetical primitive earth would have been bathed in the deadly destructive ultraviolet light of the sun, but there were no machines to convert this energy into constructive energy and nothing to operate, control, and maintain the machinery, even if it did exist.

Certainly no rational scientist could suggest that an isolated natural system could spontaneously transform itself from a disordered state to an ordered state. Atheistic evolutionists believe, however, that the universe is an isolated natural system that transformed itself from a disordered to an ordered state. This is unscientific and irrational. Creationists maintain that the only rational answer is the existence of a self-maintaining, eternally existent, supernatural creator.

Ultimately, acceptance of either creation or evolution involves a faith commitment, but creationists maintain that the scientific evidence that is available provides a much more rational basis for belief in creation than for belief in evolution. At the very least, the scientific case for creation, devoid of all references to the Bible or Genesis, should be fully available to students in public schools and universities. A logical, rational study of all the data and a consideration of all alternatives, so important to good education, as well as to academic and religious freedoms, require it.

QUESTIONS

1. What makes the present situation the "Scopes trial in reverse," according to Gish? Is this summary of the situation accurate?

2. After quoting several authorities he labels as evolutionists, Gish states "We have thus adequately documented from the scientific literature of evolutionists that evolution is no more scientific than creation." Has he adequately documented this fact? Are you convinced that he has treated the evolution argument fairly and objectively?

3. Gish accuses Preston Cloud of misquoting him (p. 438), but he does not say how he was misquoted. What is the effect of including this remark? What logical fallacy is involved here?

4. Outline Gish's argument. What seem to be his major points? Does he prove to you that creationism explains the universe? Why or why not?

5. Gish spends some time discussing and attacking "humanism." What do you take this term to mean? What does "humanism" seem to mean to Gish? What is the denotation of this term? What are the connotations?

•   •   •   •   •

EVOLUTION THEORY AND CREATION MYTHOLOGY

Preston Cloud

Preston Cloud is a professor emeritus of biogeology at the University of California at Santa Barbara. It was his article "'Scientific Creationism'—A New Inquisition Brewing" (The Humanist, *January/February 1977) that partly drew the wrath of Duane Gish in the previous reading. Here is Cloud's response to Gish.*

Central Issues

D R. Duane Gish concludes that objection to the compulsory inclusion of Hebraic creation mythology as an alternative to biological evolution in natural-science textbooks somehow threatens academic and religious freedoms. He also professes to believe that evolutionists seek "by administrative or legal fiat" to exclude creation legends from "textbooks and classrooms."

The logic by which he arrives at these and other conclusions presented defies rational comprehension. In fact, people other than fundamentalist religious activists generally regard as entirely sensible, fair, and wholesome the prevailing legal climate that allows the qualified author of a textbook and the qualified teacher of a class to write or say what she or he wishes as long as it does not advocate violent overthrow of the state or misrepresent or abridge standards of public decency. The statements on evolution and creation in the January/February 1977 issue of *The Humanist* do not take exception to the creation dogma itself, the acceptance or rejection of which is and should be a matter of personal taste; rather, they oppose the creationist campaign to *require* the presentation of a thinly disguised version of Old Testament Judeo-Babylonian-Sumerian creation mythology as a serious scientific alternative to evolution in natural-science textbooks and classrooms.

The director of the Institute for Creation Research makes a great pretense of stressing "that creationists are not proposing to teach the 'creation story of Genesis' in the schools, but only to show that the facts of science can be explained in terms of the scientific model of creation (without reference to Genesis)" (H. M. Morris, *Acts & Facts*, April 1977). However, there is nothing scientific about any effort to explain natural phenomena by supernatural causes. It is also clear from other pronouncements by Drs. Morris and Gish that the ideas they seek to impose on science are vintage Old Testament. Their position is unequivocally and repeatedly stated in a number of recent creationist publications: for instance, Morris (*The Remarkable Birth of Planet Earth*, 1972) asserts that "for whom Biblical and theological considerations are of first importance, there can be no compromise with the evolutionary system," and "the problem is completely settled, of course, by the scriptures." In the words of Gish: "By creation we mean the bringing into being of the basic kinds of plants and animals by the process of sudden or fiat creation described in the first two chapters of Genesis" (*Evolution—the Fossils Say No*, 1973).

Evolutionists do not propose the inclusion of a section on evolution parallel to the Book of Genesis in Bibles for public or church-school use. Nor do they propose the exclusion of biblical or other forms of creationism from textbooks of religion, mythology, history, or even sociology (as a social, not a biological, phenomenon). Freedom is not impaired where the content of textbooks is a matter of relevance to the subject based on qualified professional judgment. It is impaired where textbook or course content is prescribed by law or regulation beyond the requirements of relevance, good taste, and truth in advertising. It is just such meddlesome regulation that Dr. Gish's Creation Research Society and their political allies seek. *It is not freedom for which they carry the torch, but the suppression of freedom.*

Since Dr. Gish himself admits in the middle of his fourth paragraph that creation is not "a valid scientific theory," one might think that this should settle the issue. However, he claims that "evolution theory" is also unscientific, based on his assertion that neither creation nor evolution is testable. True though that is of creation, it is not true of evolution, which does have testable consequences, as inadvertently conceded by Gish in a different context. There he states (*op. cit.*, 1973) that "whether evolution actually did happen or not can only be decided, scientifically, by an examination of the historical record, that is, the fossil record."

Consider that fossil record, to which I have devoted a lifetime of research. It contains unequivocal indigenous microbial *fossils in rocks two billion years or more old.* These are all of very simple cellular types. At successive intervals over the two billion years since then, advances in biological complexity of interest from the viewpoint of creationist concerns about human origins are documented by fossils in the following table.

Approximate Age of Oldest Fossils Known, in Years Before Present

Level of Biological Complexity

1. Advanced cellular types	1,300 million
2. Soft-bodied multicellular animal life (Metazoa)	680 million
3. Shelly Metazoa	600 million
4. Vertebrate animals (simple fishes)	490 million
5. Land Plants	400 million
6. First land animals	390 million
7. Amphibians	350 million
8. Reptiles	310 million
9. Mammals	200 million
10. Birds (arose independently of and later than mammals)	150 million
11. Primates	60 million
12. Anthropoids	35 million
13. Hominid family	15 million
14. Genus *Homo*	1.2 million
15. Species *Homo sapiens*	250 thousand
16. Subspecies *H. sapiens sapiens* ("modern man")	50 thousand

This succession of radiometrically dated biological events, actually much more complete in detail, established that life has changed progressively through time. That is to say, it has *evolved* in an orderly, albeit not in a uniform, progresssion from simpler to more complex organisms. *The question, therefore, is not whether biological revolution*

appened. Of the various testable, and thus scientific, mechanisms
happened, but bsed, only that of evolutionary progression by means of natural
that have ed by Darwin and modified by the findings of modern genetics,
selection and paleontology, has so far withstood all opportunities for dis-
molecu alifies to be considered as a theory. That, of course, does not mean
proof y not be further modified by future scientific discoveries or new ways
tha discoveries. That is the nature of science.

ssible creation model that is consistent with the facts known is either
s the creator with natural laws or one that calls on a multitudinous
increasingly complex and frequently intergrading creation events—a
s in no way testable and thus cannot be considered as part of science.
ese versions, however, is acceptable to the Creation Research Society.

ists in the mold of Gish, Morris, and their associates are not actually
the fossil record. They simply choose to deny that evolution has occurred,
modern versions of the theory of biological evolution, by means of natural
They must, therefore, also deny, and they do deny, the well-established and
ly validated primary facts on which the record of evolution is based—the
gressive succession of biological types and the repeatable, self-checking, geo-
nronological measurements that place them in scale of time billions of years long.
They further consider as irrelevant or insignificant the findings of modern genetics and
molecular biology with respect to evolutionary processes. As Gish puts it (*op. cit.*,
1973), "We are not referring to the limited variations that can be seen to occur, or
which can be inferred to have occurred in the past but which do not give rise to a new
basic kind," the creationese expression *basic kind* increasing generally in inclusiveness
with biological distance from Homo sapiens.

What is the "scientific case for creation, devoid of all references to the Bible or
Genesis" that Dr. Gish argues "should be fully available to students in public schools
and universities"? Since Dr. Gish admits that creation is not a valid scientific theory,
how can there be a *scientific* case for it? Since creationists assert that all we need to know
about origins is contained in the first two chapters of Genesis, why would they wish to
exclude reference to their primary "evidence" unless they fear to have it exposed to
objective scientific scrutiny?

Indeed this "evidence" is fully available now to anyone wishing to read it—not
only in schools and churches but in a great many or most hotel rooms and homes in the
United States. And it is exactly because the well and repeatedly documented findings of
geology and paleontology contradict the accounts of Genesis in all respects that creationists deny those facts and insist that all levels of biological complexity cited above,
and many more, appeared during six literal twenty-four-hour days of creation and in a
grossly different order from that found in the geological record.

In bald fact, Gish, Morris, and other creationists claim that geologists the world
over are mistaken, or even lying, about the great age of the earth and its geologic
record and that geneticists and molecular biologists have misinterpreted their data.
They see no progress in the understanding of origins, no improvement since early
biblical times in the capability of the human mind to grasp sophisticated concepts.

What are the constructive aspects of such a position? I can only think of one. It
informs us that biologists and biogeologists must do a better job of presenting the

evidence for evolution in the schools. For when the facts are fairly a
and their implications understood, no reasonable person can fail to a
that life has changed and increased in variety and complexity over bil-
geologic time or that the advances of modern biology (including medicin
keyed to viewing that progression as a naturalistic and thus comprehens.

Other Considerations

So much for the main points at issue. It remains to deal more explicitly wi
of the arguments advanced by Dr. Gish, for the sake of readers who may find
selves honestly confused by his remarks.

1. *The "explosive appearance" of early multicellular animal diversity related by G
actually occupied an interval of some 80 to 100 million years* between about 680 and 5
million years ago. My 1973 remark as given by Gish in the preceding article is correctly quoted in this instance and I stand by it. As he apparently does not understand
the geological terminology, however, and makes unwarranted extensions of the data,
he reaches false conclusions. I have therefore repeated my conclusions in the preceding
statement and tabulation using numbers of radiometric years instead of geologic terms.
It is unfortunately true that geologists have used the term *explosive* to dramatize events
that appear to take place relatively abruptly in a geological sense, but which actually
require million or tens of millions of years. Focus on geologically ancient intervals of
seemingly rapid evolutionary diversification on the part of creationists, however, is
pure obfuscation, for they insist that everything from the simplest microbes to man was
created in six days only seven to ten thousand years ago.

2. *A "systematic absence of transitional forms between higher categories of plants and
animals" as claimed by Gish is not borne out by the geologic record.* There are, of course,
many puzzling gaps in the sequence of evolution among the main groups of *invertebrate* animals, probably due to rapid evolution in small peripheral populations at times
of ecologic change or pressure combined with a geological succession that tends to be
more incomplete in detail the further back in time. The record of more recent transitions, as between the major classes of the vertebrates, however, is surprisingly good,
including that of fossil hominids of the line of evolution toward Homo sapiens. Indeed
the emergence of modern man from his hominid ancestors is within the range of
evolutionary variation conceded by Gish (*op. cit.*, 1973) for the Galapagos finches,
which have been evolved from a parent finch stock of mainland affinities into thirteen
species, three genera, and one subfamily over the past couple of million years or so.

3. *Gish's insistence on the old and untenable argument that the second law of thermodynamics prohibits evolution by naturalistic processes is discredited* by his own concession
that the capture of solar energy by green-plant photosynthesis temporarily defers the
onset of entropic disorder. *Temporarily*, in this sense, can be as short as the lifetime of
a given plant or as long as the lifetime of the sun within a life-supporting temperature range.

4. *Finally, Gish argues (correctly) that no "isolated natural system could spontaneously transform itself from a disordered state to an ordered state." The critical points he
omits are that we know of no isolated natural systems and that the theory of evolution by
natural selection provides the necessary guiding forces.* All systems interact with factors
seemingly outside them. Even the mysterious astronomical black holes engulf new

matter and affect the gravitational characteristics of their surroundings. The now numerous complex polyatomic organic molecules observed in interstellar space by means of radio telescopes record stages of organic chemical evolution, presumably driven, against great odds, by high-energy ultraviolet or other radiation. If we use *creative* in the broad sense, no creative process is completely random. It is, of course, not random mutation of itself that leads to evolution. Rather, selective pressures among mutants and their descendants determine which shall survive and reproduce, complemented importantly by genetic exchange and the improved chances for survival and reproduction of favored genetic variants. In this way the mean characteristics of surviving populations are moved away from ancestral means, as is done regularly in selective plant and animal breeding. The mechanisms are well explained by Dr. W. V. Mayer in his article in the January/February 1977 issue of *The Humanist*, which should be studied carefully by all who are really interested in understanding evolutionary processes.

A crude analogy is familiar to skiers in the form of the development of the bumps on a ski slope called "moguls." The seemingly random movements of a number of skiers down a previously unskied or smoothed-over snowy slope quickly generates a regular pattern of these bumps, or moguls. The only concern of the skier is to get down the hill in the preferred way. He is not trying to make a bumpy slope, nor has he any real control over or design for the movements of other skiers. Gravity and whatever other physical constraints there may be provide the creative or selective forces that constrain the movements of skiers in such a way as to quickly and invariably transform initially smooth slopes into bumpy patterns of great regularity.

No creationist attack on evolution seems to be complete without emotion-generating attention to the supposedly anti-Christian views of the opposition. Inasmuch as the creationist position on origins is straight Old Testament legend, however, it is hard to see where Christianity is involved in a discussion or refutation of it. Having been raised in a family that read the Bible regularly and gave two sons to the Christian ministry, I harbor the impression that the Christian preachment of love and tolerance amounts to a rejection of Old Testament severity, bloodshed, mass homicide, and crimes of passion. If stories such as those of mass drowning in the Noachian flood (Genesis 6–9), the brutal revenge of the Passover and other plagues on Egypt (Exodus 2:7–14), and the bloody conquest of small states on the way to Palestine (Deuteronomy 20) are indeed the authentic written record of actions by, or instigated by, the creator and not the legends and secular history of primitive tribal peoples, then it is easy to see why modern advocates of a literal interpretation of the Bible wish analysis of it to be omitted from public discussion. If they and their followers actually regard the matter referred to as an accurate description of divine or divinely ordered events, I would like to know how they reconcile such events either with the teachings of Christianity or with civilized concepts of morality. If, contrariwise, they believe the parts noted to be allegorical or secular history, I would like to know why, in contrast, the Book of Genesis is to be taken as an accurate transcript of the work and actions of a merciful god.

Considering that anyone who wishes to read and believe these things is free to do so, in what way is it crucial to academic or religious freedom that they become a legally or administratively required part of the natural-science curriculum, as creationists are demanding all over the nation? At what point does tolerance and open-mindedness succumb to the substitution of assertion for evidence, surrender judgment to dogma, abdicate reason to sophistry?

We have fought too hard for our intellectual freedoms to see them compromised by false demands for objectivity and fair play from those who understand neither the nature of objectivity nor the rules of fair play.

QUESTIONS

1. Whose argument do you find easier to follow — Cloud's or Gish's? Why? Is the chart Cloud includes helpful?

2. These writers present the issue of teaching creationism and evolutionism in schools in slightly different ways. What does Gish say the evolutionists want to do in the schools? What does Cloud say the creationists want to do? Do they agree?

3. Cloud points out that Darwin's theory may in time be replaced by a more thorough and comprehensive theory. How did Darwin arrive at his theory? Exactly what is a scientific theory in this context? Was Darwin in any sense a "poet" (see Lewis Thomas, p. 430)? Was he a storyteller?

4. Gish spends several paragraphs explaining and discussing the second law of thermodynamics, a principle that he feels supports his argument. Cloud dismisses this point in two sentences. Is Cloud's treatment of this issue clear to you? Is it satisfactory?

5. Gish uses the analogy of cleaning up a room to demonstrate the universe's tendency toward disorder; Cloud discusses skiers to point out how apparently random behavior can be selectively shaped to produce regular patterns. Why do these men rely on metaphors to explain their positions?

6. Cloud denies that evolution is anti-Christian. Just as there is some disagreement between these men about the term "humanism," there seems to be some disagreement about what the term "Christian" suggests. What does the term seem to mean to Cloud? What does it seem to mean to Gish? Are their mutual definitions incompatible?

•   •   •   •   •

EVOLUTION AS FACT AND THEORY

Stephen Jay Gould

Stephen Jay Gould is an evolutionary biologist and paleontologist. A professor at Harvard University, his books also have a popular appeal to the mass audience, for he can write entertainingly about subjects as diverse as the flamingo's smile or the evolution of Mickey Mouse. The Panda's Thumb *(1980) won the American Book Award for Science;* The Mismeasure of Man *(1981) won the National Book Critic's Circle Award. This discussion of evolution comes from* Hen's Teeth and Horse's Toes *(1983); it was first published in* Discover Magazine *in 1981.*

KIRTLEY Mather, who died last year at age ninety, was a pillar of both science and Christian religion in America and one of my dearest friends. The difference of a half-century in our ages evaporated before our common interests. The most curious thing we shared was a battle we each fought at the same age. For Kirtley had gone to Tennessee with Clarence Darrow to testify for evolution at the Scopes trial of 1925. When I think that we are enmeshed again in the same struggle for one of the best documented, most compelling and exciting concepts in all of science, I don't know whether to laugh or cry.

According to idealized principles of scientific discourse, the arousal of dormant issues should reflect fresh data that give renewed life to abandoned notions. Those outside the current debate may therefore be excused for suspecting that creationists have come up with something new, or that evolutionists have generated some serious internal trouble. But nothing has changed; the creationists have presented not a single new fact or argument. Darrow and Bryan were at least more entertaining than we lesser antagonists today. The rise of creationism is politics, pure and simple; it represents one issue (and by no means the major concern) of the resurgent evangelical right. Arguments that seemed kooky just a decade ago have reentered the mainstream.

The basic attack of modern creationists falls apart on two general counts before we even reach the supposed factual details of their assault against evolution. First, they play upon a vernacular misunderstanding of the word "theory" to convey the false impression that we evolutionists are covering up the rotten core of our edifice. Second, they misuse a popular philosophy of science to argue that they are behaving scientifically in attacking evolution. Yet the same philosophy demonstrates that their own belief is not science, and that "scientific creationism" is a meaningless and self-contradictory phrase, an example of what Orwell called "newspeak."

In the American vernacular, "theory" often means "imperfect fact" — part of a hierarchy of confidence running downhill from fact to theory to hypothesis to guess. Thus, creationists can (and do) argue: evolution is "only" a theory, and intense debate now rages about many aspects of the theory. If evolution is less than a fact, and scientists can't even make up their minds about the theory, then what confidence can we have in it? Indeed, President Reagan echoed this argument before an evangelical group in Dallas when he said (in what I devoutly hope was campaign rhetoric): "Well, it is a theory. It is a scientific theory only, and it has in recent years been challenged in the world of science — that is, not believed in the scientific community to be as infallible as it once was."

Well, evolution *is* a theory. It is also a fact. And facts and theories are different things, not rungs in a hierarchy of increasing certainty. Facts are the world's data. Theories are structures of ideas that explain and interpret facts. Facts do not go away while scientists debate rival theories for explaining them. Einstein's theory of gravitation replaced Newton's, but apples did not suspend themselves in mid-air pending the outcome. And human beings evolved from apelike ancestors whether they did so by Darwin's proposed mechanism or by some other, yet to be discovered.

Moreover, "fact" does not mean "absolute certainty." The final proofs of logic and mathematics flow deductively from stated premises and achieve certainty only because they are *not* about the empirical world. Evolutionists make no claim for perpetual truth, though creationists often do (and then attack us for a style of argument that they themselves favor). In science, "fact" can only mean "confirmed to such a degree that it would be perverse to withhold provisional assent." I suppose that apples might start to rise tomorrow, but the possibility does not merit equal time in physics classrooms.

Evolutionists have been clear about this distinction between fact and theory from the very beginning, if only because we have always acknowledged how far we are from completely understanding the mechanisms (theory) by which evolution (fact) occured. Darwin continually emphasized the difference between his two great and separate accomplishments: establishing the fact of evolution, and proposing a theory — natural selection — to explain the mechanism of evolution. He wrote in *The Descent of Man:* "I had two distinct objects in view; firstly, to show that species had not been separately created, and secondly, that natural selection had been the chief agent of change . . . Hence if I have erred in . . . having exaggerated its [natural selection's] power . . . I have at least, as I hope, done good service in aiding to overthrow the dogma of separate creations."

Thus Darwin acknowledged the provisional nature of natural selection while affirming the fact of evolution. The fruitful theoretical debate that Darwin initiated has never ceased. From the 1940s through the 1960s, Darwin's own theory of natural selection did achieve a temporary hegemony that it never enjoyed in his lifetime. But renewed debate characterizes our decade, and, while no biologist questions the importance of natural selection, many now doubt its ubiquity. In particular, many evolutionists argue that substantial amounts of genetic change may not be subject to natural selection and may spread through populations at random. Others are challenging Darwin's linking of natural selection with gradual, imperceptible change through all intermediary degrees; they are arguing that most evolutionary events may occur far more rapidly than Darwin envisioned.

Scientists regard debates on fundamental issues of theory as a sign of intellectual health and a source of excitement. Science is — and how else can I say it? — most fun when it plays with interesting ideas, examines their implications, and recognizes that old information may be explained in surprisingly new ways. Evolutionary theory is now enjoying this uncommon vigor. Yet amidst all this turmoil no biologist has been led to doubt the fact that evolution occurred; we are debating *how* it happened. We are all trying to explain the same thing: the tree of evolutionary descent linking all organisms by ties of genealogy. Creationists pervert and caricature this debate by conveniently neglecting the common conviction that underlies it, and by falsely suggesting that we now doubt the very phenomenon we are struggling to understand.

Secondly, creationists claim that "the dogma of separate creations," as Darwin characterized it a century ago, is a scientific theory meriting equal time with evolution in high school biology curricula. But a popular viewpoint among philosophers of science belies this creationist argument. Philosopher Karl Popper has argued for decades that the primary criterion of science is the falsifiability of its theories. We can never prove absolutely, but we can falsify. A set of ideas that cannot, in principle, be falsified is not science.

The entire creationist program includes little more than a rhetorical attempt to falsify evolution by presenting supposed contradictions among its supporters. Their brand of creationism, they claim, is "scientific" because it follows the Popperian model in trying to demolish evolution. Yet Popper's argument must apply in both directions. One does not become a scientist by the simple act of trying to falsify a rival and truly scientific system; one has to present an alternative system that also meets Popper's criterion — it too must be falsifiable in principle.

"Scientific creationism" is a self-contradictory, nonsense phrase precisely because it cannot be falsified. I can envision observations and experiments that would disprove any evolutionary theory I know, but I cannot imagine what potential data could lead creationists to abandon their beliefs. Unbeatable systems are dogma, not science. Lest I seem harsh or rhetorical, I quote creationism's leading intellectual, Duane Gish, Ph.D., from his recent (1978) book, *Evolution? The Fossils Say No!* "By creation we mean the bringing into being by a supernatural Creator of the basic kinds of plants and animals by the process of sudden, or fiat, creation. We do not know how the Creator created, what processes He used, *for He used processes which are not now operating anywhere in the natural universe* [Gish's italics]. This is why we refer to creation as special creation. We cannot discover by scientific investigations anything about the creative processes used by the Creator." Pray tell, Dr. Gish, in the light of your last sentence, what then is "scientific" creationism?

Our confidence that evolution occurred centers upon three general arguments. First, we have abundant, direct, observational evidence of evolution in action, from both field and laboratory. This evidence ranges from countless experiments on change in nearly everything about fruit flies subjected to artificial selection in the laboratory to the famous populations of British moths that become black when industrial soot darkened the trees upon which the moths rest. (Moths gain protection from sharp-sighted bird predators by blending into the background.) Creationists do not deny these observations; how could they? Creationists have tightened their act. They now argue that God only created "basic kinds," and allowed for limited evolutionary meandering within them. Thus toy poodles and Great Danes come from the dog kind and moths can change color, but nature cannot convert a dog to a cat or a monkey to a man.

The second and third arguments for evolution — the case for major changes — do not involve direct observation of evolution in action. They rest upon inference, but are no less secure for that reason. Major evolutionary change requires too much time for direct observation on the scale of recorded human history. All historical sciences rest upon inference, and evolution is no different from geology, cosmology, or human history in this respect. In principle, we cannot observe processes that operated in the past. We must infer them from results that still surround us: living and fossil organisms for evolution, documents and artifacts for human history, strata and topography for geology.

The second argument — that the imperfection of nature reveals evolution — strikes many people as ironic, for they feel that evolution should be most elegantly displayed in the nearly perfect adaptation expressed by some organisms — the camber of a gull's wing, or butterflies that cannot be seen in ground litter because they mimic leaves so precisely. But perfection could be imposed by a wise creator or evolved by natural selection. Perfection covers the tracks of past history. And past history — the evidence of descent — is the mark of evolution.

Evolution lies exposed in the *imperfections* that record a history of descent. Why should a rat run, a bat fly, a porpoise swim, and I type this essay with structures built of the same bones unless we all inherited them from a common ancestor? An engineer, starting from scratch, could design better limbs in each case. Why should all the large native mammals of Australia be marsupials, unless they descended from a common ancestor isolated on this island continent? Marsupials are not "better," or ideally suited for Australia; many have been wiped out by placental mammals imported by man from other continents. This principle of imperfection extends to all historical sciences. When we recognize the etymology of September, October, November, and December (seventh, eighth, ninth, and tenth), we know that the year once started in March, or that two additional months must have been added to an original calendar of ten months.

The third argument is more direct: transitions are often found in the fossil record. Preserved transitions are not common — and should not be, according to our understanding of evolution (see next section) — but they are not entirely wanting, as creationists often claim. The lower jaw of reptiles contains several bones, that of mammals only one. The non-mammalian jawbones are reduced, step by step, in mammalian ancestors until they become tiny nubbins located at the back of the jaw. The "hammer" and "anvil" bones of the mammalian ear are descendants of these nubbins. How could such a transition be accomplished? the creationists ask. Surely a bone is either entirely in the jaw or in the ear. Yet paleontologists have discovered two transitional lineages of therapsids (the so-called mammal-like reptiles) with a double jaw joint — one composed of the old quadrate and articular bones (soon to become the hammer and anvil), the other of the squamosal and dentary bones (as in modern mammals). For that matter, what better transitional form could we expect to find than the oldest human, *Australopithecus afarensis*, with its apelike palate, its human upright stance, and a cranial capacity larger than any ape's of the same body size but a full 1,000 cubic centimeters below ours? If God made each of the half-dozen human species discovered in ancient rocks, why did he create in an unbroken temporal sequence of progressively more modern features — increasing cranial capacity, reduced face and teeth, larger body size? Did he create to mimic evolution and test our faith thereby?

Faced with these facts of evolution and the philosophical bankruptcy of their own position, creationists rely upon distortion and innuendo to buttress their rhetorical claim. If I sound sharp or bitter, indeed I am — for I have become a major target of these practices.

I count myself among the evolutionists who argue for a jerky, or episodic, rather than a smoothly gradual, pace of change. In 1972 my colleague Niles Eldredge and I developed the theory of punctuated equilibrium. We argued that two outstanding facts of the fossil record — geologically "sudden" origin of new species and failure to change thereafter (stasis) — reflect the predictions of evolutionary theory, not the imperfections of the fossil record. In most theories, small isolated populations are the source of new species, and the process of speciation takes thousands or tens of thousands of years. This amount of time, so long when measured against our lives, is a geological microsecond. It represents much less than 1 per cent of the average life span for a fossil invertebrate species — more than ten million years. Large, widespread, and well established species, on the other hand, are not expected to change very much. We believe that the inertia of large populations explains the stasis of most fossil species over millions of years.

We proposed the theory of punctuated equilibrium largely to provide a different explanation for pervasive trends in the fossil record. Trends, we argued, cannot be attributed to gradual transformation within lineages, but must arise from the differential success of certain kinds of species. A trend, we argued, is more like climbing a flight of stairs (punctuations and stasis) than rolling up an inclined plane.

Since we proposed punctuated equilibria to explain trends, it is infuriating to be quoted again and again by creationists — whether through design or stupidity, I do not know — as admitting that the fossil record includes no transitional forms. Transitional forms are generally lacking at the species level, but they are abundant between larger groups. Yet a pamphlet entitled "Harvard Scientists Agree Evolution Is a Hoax" states: "The facts of punctuated equilibrium which Gould and Eldredge . . . are forcing Darwinists to swallow fit the picture that Bryan insisted on, and which God has revealed to us in the Bible."

Continuing the distortion, several creationists have equated the theory of punctuated equilibrium with a caricature of the beliefs of Richard Goldschmidt, a great early geneticist. Goldschmidt argued, in a famous book published in 1940, that new groups can arise all at once through major mutations. He referred to these suddenly transformed creatures as "hopeful monsters." (I am attracted to some aspects of the non-caricatured version, but Goldschmidt's theory still has nothing to do with punctuated equilibrium — see essays in section 3 and my explicit essay on Goldschmidt in *The Panda's Thumb*.) Creationist Luther Sunderland talks of the "punctuated equilibrium hopeful monster theory" and tells his hopeful readers that "it amounts to tacit admission that anti-evolutionists are correct in asserting there is no fossil evidence supporting the theory that all life is connected to a common ancestor." Duane Gish writes, "According to Goldschmidt, and now apparently according to Gould, a reptile laid an egg from which the first bird, feathers and all, was produced." Any evolutionist who believed such nonsense would rightly be laughed off the intellectual stage; yet the only theory that could ever envision such a scenario for the origin of birds is creationism — with God acting in the egg.

I am both angry at and amused by the creationists; but mostly I am deeply sad. Sad for many reasons. Sad because so many people who respond to creationist appeals are troubled for the right reason, but venting their anger at the wrong target. It is true that scientists have often been dogmatic and elitist. It is true that we have often allowed the white-coated, advertising image to represent us — "Scientists say that Brand X cures bunions ten times faster than . . ." We have not fought it adequately because we derive benefits from appearing as a new priesthood. It is also true that faceless and bureaucratic state power intrudes more and more into our lives and removes choices that should belong to individuals and communities. I can understand that school curricula, imposed from above and without local input, might be seen as one more insult on all these grounds. But the culprit is not, and cannot be, evolution or any other fact of the natural world. Identify and fight your legitimate enemies by all means, but we are not among them.

I am sad because the practical result of this brouhaha will not be expanded coverage to include creationism (that would also make me sad), but the reduction or excision of evolution from high school curricula. Evolution is one of the half dozen "great ideas" developed by science. It speaks to the profound issues of genealogy that fascinate all of us — the "roots" phenomenon writ large. Where did we come from? Where did life arise? How did it develop? How are organisms related? It forces us to think, ponder, and wonder. Shall we deprive millions of this knowledge and once again teach biology as a set of dull and unconnected facts, without the thread that weaves diverse material into a supple unity?

But most of all I am saddened by a trend I am just beginning to discern among my colleagues. I sense that some now wish to mute the healthy debate about theory that has brought new life to evolutionary biology. It provides grist for creationist mills, they say, even if only by distortion. Perhaps we should lie low and rally around the flag of strict Darwinism, at least for the moment — a kind of old-time religion on our part.

But we should borrow another metaphor and recognize that we too have to tread a straight and narrow path, surrounded by roads to perdition. For if we ever begin to suppress our search to understand nature, to quench our own intellectual excitement in a misguided effort to present a united front where it does not and should not exist, then we are truly lost.

QUESTIONS

1. Gould defines *fact* as meaning "confirmed to such a degree that it would be perverse to withhold provisional assent." Is this the way you would define *fact*? Why is Gould's definition different? How would he define *truth*?

2. Gould makes the point that evolutionists frequently debate Darwin's theory, but the fact that evolution took place is undeniable. Return to the Gish article (p. 436). Is it possible that some of the evolutionists he quotes are simply participating in this evolutionary debate — that is, the debate over *how* evolution took place not *whether* it took place?

3. Gould repeatedly labels "scientific creationism" a contradiction in terms. What are his reasons for doing so? Does his argument make sense?

4. Gould closes by lamenting that some of his colleagues wish to end their investigations of Darwin's theory and unify behind it. What would be the result if this occurred? Have similar things occurred in science in the past? Have similar things occurred in other disciplines? Are there any researchers you can think of today who may have their work inhibited by social pressures? Are there any researchers who may receive the positive benefits of social pressures?

•   •   •   •   •

TENTATIVE REPORT ON THE HUDSON RIVER BRIDGE

O. H. Ammann

In 1926, O. H. Ammann, the chief engineer of the project, submitted to the New York Port Authority a proposal to build a bridge across the Hudson River from New Jersey to Manhattan. The estimated cost for the project at that time was $50,000,000, a sum that would be even larger in today's dollars. To sell a project of such magnitude requires research, careful preparation, and persuasive skill; here is the actual proposal Ammann used to sell the bridge to the states of New Jersey and New York.

THE PORT OF NEW YORK AUTHORITY

March 11, 1926

To the Governor of the State of New York:

To the Governor of the State of New Jersey:

Sirs: — We herewith transmit to you the Tentative Report of our Bridge Engineer dealing with a bridge across the Hudson River between Fort Washington and Fort Lee, which gives the engineers' tentative conclusions.

We send this report at this time in order that you may have the latest available engineering information on this matter. The Commission has not yet determined the design or location of the bridge.

We have the honor to remain,

Respectfully,

The Port of
New York Authority
{

JULIAN A. GREGORY, Chairman,
JOHN F. GALVIN, Vice-Chairman,
FRANK C. FERGUSON,
OTTO B. SHULHOF,
SCHUYLER N. RICE
HERBERT K. TWITCHELL,

Commissioners

THE PORT OF NEW YORK AUTHORITY

February 25, 1926

To the Commissioners of the Port of New York Authority:

DEAR SIRS — The preliminary work necessary for the planning and construction of the Hudson River Bridge between Fort Washington and Fort Lee, with which The Port of New York Authority has been charged by the Legislatures of New York and New Jersey, has now advanced to a point where conclusions can be drawn regarding the physical and financial feasibility of this bridge, its necessity as a link in the local and interstate transportation systems, its location, size, type, method of construction, approximate cost and aesthetic merits.

Briefly the work so far accomplished embraces comprehensive traffic studies to determine the probable volume of traffic over the bridge and the revenues to be derived therefrom, topographical surveys, river borings and engineering design studies to determine the suitable site, size and type of crossing and its cost, and finally, architectural studies to determine the feasibility of rendering the bridge a befitting object in a charming landscape.

The project being of exceptional magnitude, and complex aspect, it was necessary that the preliminary studies be undertaken with great care and thoroughness. The appropriations by the two States for these preliminary studies, amounting to $200,000, became available only on July 1, 1925, and the time has not been sufficient to permit either the completion of the studies or the rendering of a comprehensive report on the project. However, it is believed that from the studies so far completed the following conservative conclusions may be drawn:

Conclusions

(1) The traffic studies reveal an urgent demand for a crossing for vehicular traffic in the vicinity of the proposed bridge to relieve the present intolerable traffic situation. The traffic volume is of more than sufficient magnitude to make it financially feasible to construct, operate and maintain, from tolls, such a crossing, not considering the broader benefits to the people of both States as well as to the local community.

(2) The general location of the bridge is well chosen with regard to topography in its vicinity and the feasibility of convenient connections to the important local and arterial highway routes on both sides of the river. A crossing at this point also appears to be the next logical step after construction of the vehicular tunnel at Canal Street, since the two crossings are far enough apart not to influence materially each other's traffic quota.

(3) From the engineering point of view the construction of the bridge is in every respect feasible and, while of unusual magnitude, will involve no extraordinary difficulties, nor hazardous or untried operations. The bridge will have a single river span of at least 3500 feet and a clear height above water of about 200 feet. The piers will be located within pier-head lines, as established by the War Department, and will therefore be no obstruction to navigation.

(4) The bridge is to be the suspension type, the most economical and aesthetically superior type available. It will be of extremely simple construction, and its design is conceived so that it will be feasible to build the bridge at a minimum initial expenditure to serve present traffic needs, and to enlarge its capacity as the traffic volume increases.

(5) If funds for construction of the bridge shall become available in 1927, it is expected that not later than 1933 the bridge will be open for four-lane vehicular and bus passenger traffic and for pedestrians. It is estimated that this capacity will suffice to take care of the initial traffic and the expected increase until about 1943, and then it will probably become necessary to enlarge to an eight-lane vehicular capacity.

(6) While it is not possible, at the present time, to report definite cost figures, it is estimated, upon information so far available and upon such forecast of real estate values as may now reasonably be made, that the bridge can be opened for highway traffic at a cost of less than $50,000,000, inclusive of interest during construction.

(7) Depending upon traffic capacity finally to be decided upon, it is estimated that the bridge can later be enlarged at an additional cost of between $15,000,000 and $25,000,000, if, and when, the vehicular and passenger traffic will have grown in volume to pay for this additional cost.

(8) On the basis of conservative traffic analysis, and without counting upon the vehicular traffic which will be generated by the construction of the bridge, nor upon possible income from other than vehicular traffic, it is estimated that during the first year after completion the revenue will more than cover the annual interest charge, administration, maintenance, and amortization. The bridge will thus be self-sustaining in every respect from the first year without imposing unreasonable toll charges upon the traffic.

(9) On the basis of conservative assumptions for future growth of traffic, and counting upon revenue from vehicular traffic alone, it is estimated that within ten years after opening to traffic the bridge may be enlarged to eight-lane capacity, and that within twenty years thereafter the entire bond issue raised to cover construction cost can be amortized.

(10) The architectural studies so far made, while yet tentative, indicate clearly that the bridge may be so designed as to form an object of grace and beauty as well as utility, and to blend harmoniously with the grandeur of its natural setting.

(11) In view of this favorable aspect of the bridge, its urgent necessity to relieve traffic conditions and in order to derive the benefit of a complete investigation, it is recommended that the preliminary work be carried to completion, and that the States be asked to appropriate an additional sum of $100,000 to make that completion possible.

Following is a more complete and detailed account of the work so far accomplished:

Traffic Studies

Since the Legislative Acts provide that the Port Authority may levy charges for the use of the bridge and that the bridge shall be built and paid for in whole or in part by bonds of the Port Authority, or other securities, it has been necessary to ascertain whether or not the revenues from tolls for vehicles and pedestrians, and possibly franchise rights for rail passenger facilities, will be adequate to meet the cost of construction. This involves the study of a number of traffic factors, viz.:

First: The present volume of vehicular and pedestrian traffic over each of the seventeen ferries across the Hudson River.

Second: The volume of traffic the bridge will be expected to attract when it is opened to traffic. This requires an estimate of the effect on the bridge traffic of the opening of the vehicular tunnel in 1926.

Third: The volume of traffic that can reasonably be expected to be diverted to the bridge from each of the other crossings in that year.

Fourth: The volume of traffic over the bridge for each year, for twenty years subsequent to the opening of the bridge, proper allowance being made for the effect upon the bridge traffic of the possible construction of other crossings below 179th Street, Manhattan.

This necessitates the determination of the origin and destination of vehicles by types for the existing ferries and apportioning the divertible traffic to each of the proposed crossings in such a way as to take into account relative distances and ferry, tunnel, and bridge charges and the elimination of undue congestion on the approach streets to each of the proposed facilities.

Fifth: An estimate of the revenues for each year subsequent to the opening of the bridge, based upon an average toll per vehicle and per pedestrian.

In order to estimate the vehicular traffic, it was necessary to obtain the trend or rate of growth of the present-day traffic over seventeen ferries between the Battery and Tarrytown (for the most recent normal year). This required the records, by classes of vehicles, kept by each of the ferry companies from 1914 to date. Where revenues only are available for this traffic, average tolls for each class of vehicle must be applied to the revenues to estimate the number of vehicles. From these records the volume of traffic over each of the ferries can be forecast for each of the years subsequent to 1932.

Instead of forecasting the traffic for each of the ferries it is better to forecast the volume of traffic that will be diverted from the existing ferries to the bridge. To obtain this divertible bridge traffic it is necessary first to ascertain the distribution of the present-day traffic over each of the ferries for the most recent normal year. To do this the origin and destination of each vehicle is necessary for a sample period of time, so selected that the peak and the average traffic condition in the year will be reflected. These occur in the months of July and October. The variations of traffic between week-days and Sundays from hour to hour, or both, are necessary to estimate the peak traffic conditions to test out the roadway capacities on the bridge. Field clockings, therefore, were taken by placing inspectors on each of the ferry boats of every route to ride the boats throughout the day. The inspectors ascertained and recorded the following information respecting each vehicle crossing the river by ferry:

(a) Type of vehicle, that is, whether horse drawn or motor propelled. A division of motor vehicles was made as between commercial and pleasure, and again sub-divided to indicate the carrying capacity of the commercial vehicles and the seating capacity of the pleasure vehicles:

(b) Number of persons carried in each vehicle;

(c) State License;

(d) Origin and destination of each vehicle;

(e) Frequency of use of ferry route by each vehicle.

These clockings were made throughout the months of July, August, September and October, 1925. In carrying forward the clockings a field force of fifty-six men was employed on the seventeen ferry routes. The detailed information noted above was ascertained and recorded for a total of 242,000 vehicles.

Clockings were made of the vehicular traffic now passing over the streets and street intersections in the vicinity of the proposed location of the bridge, to determine the degree to which capacity of these streets is now used. Also a study was made to determine the volume of traffic carried at present by the East River bridges, particularly during the peak of travel; and the extent of saturation.

Examination of the records of the various ferry companies operating the seventeen ferry routes, for the purpose of ascertaining the volume of traffic and its classification handled by the ferries of each route for the past ten years, has required a force of three to four men constantly from July to the present date.

After having completed the field clockings, the next step was the tabulation and summarization of the data. The work of tabulating was carried on in part during the period of clocking and has proceeded since the clockings were completed in October, to bring it to a point to permit of detailed analysis.

These analyses are for the purpose of determining future distribution of vehicular traffic among the present crossings, the proposed 178th Street bridge, and any other crossings that might later be constructed and which might affect the future revenues of the 178th Street bridge.

One of the first determinations to be arrived at by analysis is the probable volume of traffic that may be expected to use the 178th Street bridge when it is opened, assuming that were the only highway across the Hudson River between Manhattan and New Jersey.

The second determinations to be made is the volume of traffic which will be attracted to the vehicular tunnel, when it is opened, which otherwise might, in part at least, have used the 178th Street Bridge.

The third determination is the probable effect on the 178th Street bridge traffic by the opening of any additional highway crossing over the Hudson in the future.

Each of these steps involves a large number of intermediate steps. For example: highway access to the bridge; determination of a toll which will secure maximum traffic and maximum revenue; future crossings to be constructed by the City of New York across the East and Harlem Rivers; and traffic that will be generated by the stimulation of industrial and residential development, particularly on the Jersey side.

The results of all of these traffic studies are now being carefully recorded and will be included in a later report on the project.

Exhibit (A) illustrates the growth of the total trans-Hudson vehicular traffic as tentatively estimated from 1924 to 1960, inclusive, and the number of vehicles of this total traffic which would have been, or will be, diverted to the 178th Street bridge.

Below is recorded the first tentative estimate of total trans-Hudson vehicular traffic for all ferries from the Battery to and including Tarrytown, and the traffic that the bridge will divert from these ferries and the tunnel.

Year	Hudson River Traffic	Bridge Traffic	Year	Hudson River Traffic	Bridge Traffic
1924	11,706,000	3,208,000	1944	36,055,000	11,476,000
1925	12,912,000	3,596,000	1945	36,767,000	11,723,000
1926	14,185,000	4,017,000	1946	37,408,000	11,944,000
. . . .			. . . .		
1934	25,607,000	7,889,000	1953	40,841,000	13,144,000
1935	26,984,000	8,364,000	1954	41,172,000	13,263,000
1936	28,280,000	8,807,000	1955	41,478,000	13,369,000
			1956	41,765,000	13,471,000

These figures must be revised as the analysis proceeds to take into account the effect of the opening of additional crossings. The above figures do not include traffic which will be generated from the adjacent territories, whose growth the bridge will stimulate. While this cannot be measured accurately, an analysis of the growth of population, intensity of realty development, and motor vehicle registration is in process to determine the effect of the East River bridges upon Brooklyn and Queens, in order to gauge roughly the effect that the Hudson River bridge will have upon Fort Lee and its contiguous communities. The amount of this traffic will be considerable and eventually will be added to the above estimates.

While the above traffic is the principal source of revenue, there are four other sources which will contribute to the income of the bridge. This revenue will come from passengers in vehicles, pedestrians, bus lines and rapid transit facilities. Studies are under way to ascertain the potential traffic which will give rise to this income and will be represented in a later report.

Tables (I-a), and (I-c), appended to this report, give the gross revenues estimated to date for a 50¢ rate, a 60¢ rate, a 70¢ rate, respectively, from vehicles only. It will be seen that for 1933, or the first year of operation, the income from vehicles alone is forecast as at least $3,700,000. Subtracting the charges for administration, maintenance and operation, the net operating income is close to 6½% on the $50,000,000, the probable maximum initial cost of the bridge. In addition, there will be revenue from passengers in vehicles, pedestrians, and bus lines, and from vehicular traffic which will be generated by the bridge. Consequently, it is safe to conclude at this time that the charges on the initial and ultimate cost of construction can be met out of the potential revenue from traffic, and that therefore the project is economically sound.

Location Studies

The Legislative Acts of New York and New Jersey provide that the bridge shall be located at a point between 170th and 185th Streets in Manhattan, New York City, and a point approximately opposite thereto in the borough of Fort Lee, New Jersey.

After a general examination of the territory on both sides of the river, within these limits, three specific sites which appeared to offer possibilities were tentatively selected for more careful study. (See location map, Exhibit B.) The three sites chosen are those in close vicinity of 181st Street, 179th Street, and 175th Street, Manhattan, respectively. River borings, studies of approaches, grades, street connections, tentative designs and comparative cost estimates were made for these locations. These studies revealed the central location near 179th Street as being not only the most economical, but also the most desirable with respect to approach grades and street connections and natural setting, and it was therefore decided to confine the elaboration of more complete plans and estimates to this location.

In the selection of the locations, careful consideration was also given to the scenic effect of the bridge, more particularly with regard to the effect upon Fort Washington Park. While, by locating the bridge at 181st Street or 175th Street, encroachment upon this park by bridge piers might be avoided, the much longer river span required at these locations, and the consequent greater proportions of the bridge, would not be as favorable, aesthetically, as a bridge at 179th Street. Moreover, the location of a pier in the Park is not believed to curtail in any way the usefulness of the Park or to mar its beauty.

Topographical Surveys, Mapping and Triangulation

Owing to lack of maps, sufficiently accurate and complete for preliminary planning and reliable estimates of cost, it has been necessary to undertake extensive and accurate topographical surveys extending over the territories on which the bridge approaches and street connections may be located. These surveys are now nearing completion and will form a valuable basis for the final planning and construction of the bridge. The results of these surveys have been embodied in a large map to the scale of $1'' = 100'$.

Owing to the lateness of the season it has been found impracticable to undertake an accurate triangulation across the river, but the necessary base lines have been established, and all other preparations for these measurements have been made, and it is expected that they can be accomplished in the Spring as soon as weather conditions permit. For the tentative studies, the triangulation made by the U.S. Coast and Geodetic Survey was considered to be sufficiently reliable.

River Borings

In order to obtain reliable information on the character of the river bottom and to establish beyond question the surface of the solid bedrock upon which the bridge piers have to rest, it was necessary to undertake borings carried well into the solid rock.

In all, sixteen borings, at the three locations tentatively selected, have been sunk, the results carefully recorded and the rock cores preserved. These borings have established the fact that, outside of the pierhead lines established by the War Department, that is, within the width of river reserved for navigation, bedrock is too deep to permit of economical construction of bridge piers and that such piers must, and can, be placed between the pierhead lines and the shore, or on shore. Moreover, thus located, the piers will form no obstructions to navigation. . . .

Additional borings will have to be made when the location of the bridge is definitely established.

The character of rock revealed by these borings corresponds to that prognosticated by the U.S. Geological Survey. On the New Jersey side bedrock was found to consist partly of solid red sandstone and shale, known as the "Newark Formation," partly of the so-called "Stockbridge Dolomite" which forms the major portion of the rockbed under the Hudson River. The borings on the New York side revealed a solid bed of "Hudson Shist" (mica shist), which is the prevailing rock of Manhattan Island. All of these rock formations are sufficiently hard to constitute a solid and permanent foundation for the bridge piers and to safely sustain the great pressure from them.

The material overlying the rock is almost entirely river silt, unsuitable for foundation purposes.

Engineering Design Studies

In order to determine the most economical and suitable type and general proportions of the structure, for various possible locations, it was essential to undertake extended comparative design studies and cost estimates, before any final planning could be undertaken. Complete tentative designs were made for a 3500 foot river span and a 3900 foot span, as required for the 179th and 181st Street locations, respectively. Comparative estimates of cost have also been prepared for various capacities for highway traffic and for combined highway and rail passenger traffic.

Various possible forms and materials for the individual parts of this structure were given most careful consideration, and all essential features of the structure have been studied in detail with a view to assure not only economy, but conformity to the most advanced standards of design and methods of fabrication and construction.

Tentative schemes of erection have been evolved, inasmuch as the method of erection of a large bridge not only has an important bearing upon its design and economy, but because in this case it involves operations of unprecedented proportions.

As a result of these studies a tentative design has been developed which, for the 179th Street location, may be briefly described as follows:

Type and General Proportions of Bridge

Little study was necessary to determine the suspension bridge as the most suitable type, because its superior economy for such great spans and capacities is now generally recognized by engineers. Its superior aesthetic merits, when properly designed, further single it out as the best adapted type in this case.

A cantilever bridge, the nearest other possibility, would, with its dense and massive network of steel members, form a monstrous structure and truly mar forever the beauty of the natural scenery.

The general proportions of the bridge, as to length of spans and height above water, were sharply defined by the topographical and geological conditions of the site. As a result of the borings, heretofore described, the main pier on the New Jersey side was located well within the pierhead line at a point where rock can be reached at a depth of about 100 feet, which is the approximate limit for the pneumatic process, the safest and most reliable foundation method. On the New York side the logical and natural place for the pier is the rocky point of Fort Washington Park close to the pierhead line. This results in a central span of 3500 feet between centers of piers, or twice the span of the Philadelphia-Camden bridge, the longest suspension bridge so far built.

The rock cliffs of the Palisades form the natural abutment and anchorage on the New Jersey side and, for the sake of symmetry, which is an essential aesthetic requirement, the side span on the New York side is made the same, or approximately 700 feet.

The clear height of the bridge floor above water is approximately 200 feet, this height resulting from the elevations of the connecting streets on both sides of the river and the limiting grades of the approaches. Incidentally, this height is ample to permit passage of the largest vessels which are likely to go up the river beyond this point.

The general form and arrangement of the structure are of extreme simplicity. Essentially the floor deck is suspended throughout its length from simple cables or chains. The latter will pass over the two towers and are to be firmly anchored in rock or massive concrete blocks at their ends.

To enhance the gracefulness of the bridge, the cables are to have a comparatively small sag or flat catenary. Structurally, the cables are to be built either of steel wires or of high grade steel eyebars, both types of construction having reached a high degree of perfection in American bridge practice and a degree of safety superior to that of any other type of structural members.

Detailed studies have been made of two essentially different types of towers, a slender steel tower, as exemplified in the Manhattan bridge, and a combined steel and masonry tower of massive appearance. While the economic merits of the slender steel tower, and its justification in some localities, are recognized, it is felt that the conspicuous location of the proposed bridge in the midst of a bold and impressive landscape makes the selection of the aesthetically superior massive tower imperative.

Traffic Capacity of Bridge

One of the most important and complex questions which had to be solved, and will involve further careful study in connection with the planning of this bridge, is the determination of its traffic capacity, as regards both kinds and volume of traffic.

The question is necessarily closed related to the study of the traffic situation and definite solution has to await the results of these studies. While the Legislative Acts do not specify the kind of traffic to be accommodated, existing conditions point clearly to the need of a crossing primarily for vehicular traffic. Furthermore, while the development of the territories contiguous to the bridge will, sooner or later, call for the accommodation of a considerable volume of passenger traffic, it is not likely that rapid transit or other rail passenger traffic facilities will be needed for many years to come.

It is also realized that the demand for passenger traffic in the immediate future, and possibly for many years to come, may be filled by passenger buses running over the bridge roadway. Any provisions for the accommodation of rail traffic, which would involve a comparatively large outlay at present, would therefore not be warranted.

As a result of our studies it now appears quite feasible, however, to build the bridge initially for highway traffic only, but with provision, at a small extra expenditure, for the future accommodation of rail passenger, or additional bus passenger traffic.

In fact the design, as now developed (see Exhibit C), is exceptionally far-reaching in its provision for a gradual increase in traffic capacity with a minimum possible initial expenditure, and with the least possible time of construction before the bridge can be opened to traffic.

The plan provides for an initial capacity of two 24-foot roadways which will conveniently accommodate four lanes of vehicular traffic, two in each direction. Two footwalks for pedestrians are also provided for. It is estimated that these two roadways will be sufficient to fill the demand for highway traffic for about ten years after the opening of the bridge.

If and when justified by increased volume of vehicular traffic, another four-lane roadway can be added, and used for truck traffic, while the two initial roadways may be reserved for the faster passenger automobiles. It is estimated that the eight lanes will be ample to take care of all vehicular traffic which may be concentrated at this crossing. All of this highway traffic is to be accommodated on an upper deck of the structure.

If and when accommodation for rail passenger traffic, or for additional bus passenger traffic, across the bridge becomes necessary, two or four lanes, or tracks, of either form of such traffic can be added on a lower deck.

The question as to whether, and to what extent, rail passenger traffic should be provided for on the bridge is still under consideration, and the cooperation and advice of the transit authorities in the two States have been sought in order to arrive at a satisfactory solution.

Approaches and Highway Connections

Tentative studies for the approaches and highway connections on both sides of the river have been made, but further studies in cooperation with the proper municipal and State highway authorities are necessary. The studies so far completed indicate conclusively that direct connections of the bridge approaches with important highway arteries, such as Broadway and Riverside Drive in Manhattan, and Lemoine Avenue in New Jersey, are entirely feasible and involve no extensive changes in the street system, at least for many years after completion of the bridge.

It would be lacking in foresight, however, not to recognize the fact that when the bridge is to be completed to capacity the vehicular traffic will have grown to such an extent that new arteries will become necessary on both sides of the river, more particularly for that traffic which will flow to and from the bridge in an easterly and westerly direction. While such new arteries will not form part of the bridge project proper, studies are being made with respect to them and with a view to give the bridge a proper setting in the future net of highway arteries.

Regarding the structural arrangement of the approaches, more particularly that on the New York side, it should be mentioned that aesthetic considerations have been paramount in developing their design.

The New York approach is designed as a short viaduct of monumental appearance which will enhance rather than destroy the good character of the neighborhood (see Exhibit D). The New Jersey approach is designed as a cut through the top of the Palisades so marked at the face of the cliffs as not to destroy the appearance of the latter or to break their natural silhouette.

Tracks, if any are provided, will be hidden from view on the approaches.

Architectural Studies

The commanding location of the bridge in a charming landscape made it imperative to give prominent consideration to the aesthetic side of the bridge design; in other words, to combine beauty with utility and strength. For this purpose the Port Authority has engaged an eminent architect, Mr. Cass Gilbert, to assist the engineering staff in the preparation of the plans. A statement by the architect on the architectural aspect of the project is appended.

Estimates of Cost

In view of the incompleted state of the preliminary work and certain as yet unsettled questions, such as provision for passenger traffic, extent of architectural treatment of the bridge and approaches, more accurate appraisal of property and damages, etc., it is impossible to give at the present time reliable cost estimates. Making reasonable allowance for the uncertain features, it is estimated that the bridge can be constructed, ready for the initial highway capacity, at a cost of less than $50,000,000 inclusive of interest during construction, and that it can later be strengthened for the eight-lane highway capacity, and provision for from two to four electric railway tracks, at an additional cost of between $15,000,000 and $20,000,000.

Financial Statement

The financial statement following gives, for the years 1933, 1943, 1953 and 1960, the gross revenue and net operating income from vehicles only, based upon average toll rates of 50¢, 60¢, and 70¢, respectively, an initial cost of $50,000,000 and an additional expenditure, ten years later, of $15,000,000, as required for the increased vehicular capacity.

Year	Gross Revenue from Vehicles Only	Administration Operation Maintenance	Net Operating Income Available for Interest and Amortization	Per Cent of Net Operating Income to Estimated Cost
A. Average Toll Charge 50¢				
1933	$3,700,000	$ 500,000	$3,200,000	6.40%
1943	5,608,000	750,000	4,858,000	9.72
1953	6,572,000	1,000,000	5,572,000	8.57
1960	6,910,000	1,000,000	5,910,000	9.09
B. Average Toll Charge 60¢				
1933	4,441,000	500,000	3,941,000	8.76
1943	6,730,000	750,000	5,980,000	13.29
1953	7,886,000	1,000,000	6,886,000	10.59
1960	8,293,000	1,000,000	7,293,000	11.22
C. Average Toll Charge 70¢				
1933	5,181,000	500,000	4,681,000	10.40
1943	7,851,000	750,000	7,101,000	15.78
1953	9,201,000	1,000,000	8,201,000	12.62
1960	9,675,000	1,000,000	8,675,000	13.35

Note: — Additional revenue from generated vehicular traffic and from bus and rail passenger traffic is expected to increase materially the potential net operating income.

Acknowledgement

The Engineering Staff has been aided in its studies so far made by valuable advice and information from various individuals and organizations to whom due credit will be given at the proper time.

The undersigned also takes this occasion to express their acknowledgement for the valuable services so far rendered by other members of the engineering staff, more particularly, R. A. Lesher, Traffic Engineer, in charge of traffic studies; W. J. Boucher, Engineer of Construction, and R. Hoppen, Jr., Resident Engineer, in charge of surveys and borings; W. A. Cuenot and A. Andersen, Assistant Engineers, in charge of design studies.

Respectfully submitted
(Signed) O. H. AMMANN,
Bridge Engineer

QUESTIONS

1. A project this size would require several years to complete, and, obviously, would be used for years to come. A certain amount of prediction and forecasting is necessary. Do Ammann's projections seem reasonable? Were they accurate? What things did he not foresee?

2. Where could Ammann's report have been more technical than it is? Why isn't it more technical?

3. Refer to the audience chart on p. 352. How would you characterize the audience for this report?

4. What features of the proposed bridge does Ammann stress the most? Why? What features does he stress least? Why? What does this tell you about his intended audience?

5. If a similar bridge were being proposed today, what features or aspects would a proposal be likely to emphasize?

• • • • •

ADDRESS TO THE DEMOCRATIC CONVENTION

Edward M. Kennedy

Revered and respected by some, disliked by others, Senator Edward Kennedy has been one of the most prominent American politicians, and probably the most prominent Democrat, of the last twenty-five years. In 1980, after having been the center of speculation in several presidential elections, Kennedy attempted to wrest the Democratic nomination from the incumbent Jimmy Carter. Kennedy won several important primaries, but appeared to have entered the campaign too late to prevent the renomination of Carter. At the 1980 Democratic Convention it was necessary for Kennedy to appear (after Carter had the nomination in hand) to help reunite the party that was more than a little apprehensive about Carter's chances against the popular Ronald Reagan. Here is Kennedy's speech.

WELL, things worked out a little differently from the way I had planned, but I still love New York.

My fellow Democrats and my fellow Americans: I have come here tonight not to argue for a candidacy, but to affirm a cause.

I am asking you . . . I am asking you to renew the commitment of the Democratic Party to economic justice. I am asking you to renew our commitment to a fair and lasting prosperity that can put America back to work.

This is the cause that brought me into the campaign and that sustained me for nine months, across a hundred thousand miles, in 40 different states. We had our losses; but the pain of our defeats is far, far less than the pain of the people that I have met. We have learned that it is important to take issues seriously, but never to take ourselves too seriously.

The serious issue before us tonight is the cause for which the Democratic Party has stood in its finest hours — the cause that keeps our party young — and makes it, in the second century of its age, the largest political party in this Republic and the longest lasting political party on this planet.

Our cause has been, since the days of Thomas Jefferson, the cause of the common man and the common woman. Our commitment has been, since the days of Andrew Jackson, to all those he called "the humble members of society — the farmers, mechanics, and laborers." On this foundation, we have defined our values, refined our policies, and refreshed our faith.

Now I take the unusual step of carrying the cause and the commitment of my campaign personally to our national convention. I speak out of a deep sense of urgency about the anguish and anxiety I have seen across America. I speak out of a deep belief in the ideals of the Democratic Party, and in the potential of that party and of a president to make a difference. And I speak out of a deep trust in our capacity to proceed with boldness and a common vision that will feel and heal the suffering of our time — and the division of our party.

Economic Plank

The economic plank of this platform on its face concerns only material things; but is also a moral issue that I raise tonight. It has taken many forms over many years. In this campaign, and in this country that we seek to lead, the challenge in 1980 is to give our voice and our vote for these fundamental Democratic principles:

Let us pledge that we will never misuse unemployment, high interest rates, and human misery as false weapons against inflation.

Let us pledge that employment will be the first priority of our economic policy.

Let us pledge that there will be security for all those who are now at work. And let us pledge that there will be jobs for all who are out of work. And we will not compromise on the issue of jobs.

These are not simplistic pledges. Simply put, they are the heart of our tradition, and they have been the soul of our party across the generations. It is the glory and the greatness of our tradition to speak for those who have no voice, to remember those who are forgotten, to respond to the frustrations and fulfill the aspiration of all Americans seeking a better life in a better land.

We dare not forsake that tradition. We cannot let the great purpose of the Democratic Party become the bygone passages of history. We must not permit the Republicans to seize and run on the slogans of prosperity.

Reagan's Stand on Issues

We heard the orators at their convention all trying to talk like Democrats. They proved that even Republican nominees can quote Franklin Roosevelt to their own purpose. The Grand Old Party thinks it has found a great new trick. But 40 years ago, an earlier generation of Republicans attempted the same trick. And Franklin Roosevelt himself replied "Most Republican leaders . . . have bitterly fought and blocked the forward surge of average men and women in their pursuit of happiness. Let us not be deluded that overnight those leaders have suddenly become the friends of average men and women. . . . You know," he continued, "very few of us are that gullible."

And four years later, when the Republicans tried that trick again, Franklin Roosevelt asked: "Can the Old Guard pass itself off as the New Deal? I think not. We have all seen many marvelous stunts in the circus — but no performing elephant could turn a handspring without falling flat on its back."

The 1980 Republican convention was awash with crocodile tears for our economic distress but it is by their long record and not their recent words that you shall know them.

The same Republicans who are talking about the crisis of unemployment have nominated a man who once said — and I quote: "Unemployment insurance is a prepaid vacation plan for freeloaders." And that nominee is no friend of labor.

The same Republicans who are talking about the problems of the inner cities have nominated a man who said — and I quote: "I have included in my morning and evening prayers every day the prayer that the federal government not bail out New York." And that nominee is no friend of this city and our great urban centers across this nation.

The same Republicans who are talking about security for the elderly have nominated a man who said just four years ago that participation in Social Security "should be made voluntary." And that nominee is no friend of the senior citizens of this nation.

The same Republicans who are talking about preserving the environment have nominated a man who last year made the preposterous statement, and I quote: "Eighty percent of our air pollution comes from plants and trees." And that nominee is no friend of the environment.

And the same Republicans who are invoking Frankin Roosevelt have nominated a man who said in 1976 — and these are his exact words: "Fascism was really the basis of the New Deal." And that nominee, whose name is Ronald Reagan, has no right to quote Franklin Delano Roosevelt.

Democratic Values

The great adventure which our opponents offer is a voyage into the past. Progress is our heritage, not theirs. What is right for us as Democrats is also the right way for Democrats to win.

The commitment I seek is not to outworn views, but to old values that will never wear out. Programs may sometimes become obsolete, but the ideal of fairness always endures. Circumstances may change, but the work of compassion must continue. It is surely correct that we cannot solve problems by throwing money at them; but it is also correct that we dare not throw out our national problems onto a scrap heap of inattention and indifference. The poor may be out of political fashion, but they are not without human needs. The middle-class may be angry, but they have not lost the dream that all Americans can advance together.

The demand of our people in 1980 is not for smaller government or bigger government, but for better government. Some say that government is always bad, and that spending for basic social programs is the root of our economic evils. But we reply: The present inflation and recession cost our economy $200 billion a year. We reply: Inflation and unemployment are the biggest spenders of all.

The task of leadership in 1980 is not to parade scapegoats or to seek refuge in reaction but to match our power to the possibilities of progress.

While others talked of free enterprise, it was the Democratic Party that acted — and we ended excessive regulation in the airline and trucking industries. And we restored competition to the marketplace. And I take some satisfaction that this deregulation was legislation that I sponsored and passed in the Congress of the United States.

Fellow Democrats, we realize that each generation of Americans has a rendevous with a different reality. The answers of one generation become the questions of the next generation. But there is a guiding star in the American firmament. It is as old as the revolutionary belief that all people are created equal — and as clear as the contemporary condition of Liberty City and the South Bronx. Again and again, Democratic leaders have followed that star — and they have given new meaning to the old values of liberty and justice for all.

Party of New Hope

We are the party of the New Freedom, the New Deal, and the New Frontier. We have always been the party of hope. So this year, let us offer new hope — new hope to an America uncertain about the present, but unsurpassed in its potential for the future.

To all those who are idle in the cities and industries of America, let us provide new hope for the dignity of useful work. Democrats have always believed that a basic civil right of all Americans is the right to earn their own way. The party of the people must always be the party of full employment.

To all those who doubt the future of our economy, let us provide new hope for the reindustrialization of America. And let our vision reach beyond the next election or the next year to a new generation of prosperity. If we could rebuild Germany and Japan after World War II, then surely we can reindustrialize our own nation and revive our inner cities in the 1980s.

To all those who work hard for a living wage, let us provide new hope that the price of their employment shall not be an unsafe workplace and death at an earlier age.

To all those who inhabit our land, from California to the New York Island, from the Redwood Forest to the Gulfstream waters, let us provide new hope that prosperity shall not be purchased by poisoning the air, the rivers and the natural resources that are the greatest gift of this continent. We must insist that our children and grandchildren shall inherit a land which they can truly call America the beautiful.

To all those who see the worth of their work and their savings taken by inflation, let us offer new hope for a stable economy. We must meet the pressures of the present by invoking the full power of government to master increasing prices. In candor, we must say that the federal budget can be balanced only by policies that bring us to a balanced prosperity of full employment and price restraint.

Democratic Tax Reform

And to all those overburdened by an unfair tax structure, let us provide new hope for real tax reform. Instead of shutting down classrooms, let us shut off tax shelters.

Instead of cutting out school lunches, let us cut off subsidies for expensive business lunches that are nothing more than food stamps for the rich.

The tax cut of our Republican opponents takes the name of tax reform in vain. It is a wonderfully Republican idea that would redistribute income in the wrong direction. It is good news for any of you with incomes over $200,000 a year. For the few of you, it offers a pot of gold worth $14,000. But the Republican tax cut is bad news for the middle income families. For the many of you, they plan a pittance of $200 a year. And that is not what the Democratic Party means when we say tax reform.

The vast majority of Americans cannot afford this panacea from a Republican nominee who has denounced the progressive income tax as the invention of Karl Marx. I am afraid he has confused Karl Marx with Theodore Roosevelt, that obscure Republican president who sought and fought for a tax system based on ability to pay. Theodore Roosevelt is not Karl Marx — and the Republican tax scheme is not tax reform.

National Health Insurance

Finally, we cannot have a fair prosperity in isolation from a fair society.

So I will continue to stand for a national health insurance. We must not surrender to the relentless medical inflation that can bankrupt almost anyone — and that may soon break the budgets of government at every level.

Let us insist on real controls over what doctors and hospitals can charge. And let us resolve that the state of a family's health shall never depend on the size of a family's wealth.

The president, the vice president, and the members of Congress have a medical plan that meets their needs in full. And whenever senators and representatives catch a little cold, the Capitol physician will see them immediately, treat them promptly, and fill a prescription on the spot. We do not get a bill even if we ask for it. And when do you think was the last time a member of Congress asked for a bill from the federal government?

And I say again, as I have said before: If health insurance is good enough for the president, the vice president and the Congress of the United States, then it is good enough for all of you and for every family in America.

Democatic-GOP Differences

There are some who said we should be silent about our differences on issues during this convention. But the heritage of the Democratic Party has been a history of democracy. We fight hard because we care deeply about our principles and purposes. We did not flee this struggle. We welcome this contrast with the empty and expedient spectacle last month in Detroit where no nomination was contested, no question was debated and no one dared to raise any doubt or dissent.

Democrats can be proud that we chose a different course — and a different platform.

We can be proud that our party stands for investment in safe energy instead of a nuclear future that may threaten the future itself. We must not permit the neighborhoods of America to be permanently shadowed by the fear of another Three Mile Island.

We can be proud that our party stands for a fair housing law to unlock the doors of discrimination once and for all. The American house will be divided against itself so long as there is prejudice against any American buying or renting a home.

And we can be proud that our party stands plainly and publicly, and persistently for the ratification of the Equal Rights Amendment. Women hold their rightful place at our convention; and women must have their rightful place in the Constitution of the United States. On this issue, we will not yield, we will not equivocate, we will not rationalize, explain, or excuse. We will stand for E.R.A. and for the recognition at long last that our nation is made up of founding mothers as well as founding fathers.

A fair prosperity and a just society are within our vision and our grasp. And we do not have every answer. There are questions not yet asked, waiting for us in the recesses of the future.

But of this much we can be certain, because it is the lesson of all our history.

Together a president and the people can make a difference. I have found that faith still alive wherever I have traveled across the land. So let us reject the counsel of retreat and the call to reaction. Let us go forward in the knowledge that history only helps those who help themselves.

There will be setbacks and sacrifices in the years ahead. But I am convinced that we as a people are ready to give something back to our country in return for all it has given to us. Let this be our commitment: Whatever sacrifices must be made will be shared — and shared fairly. And let this be our confidence: At the end of our journey and always before us shines that ideal of liberty and justice for all.

To Those Who 'Stayed the Course'

In closing, let me say a few words to all those I have met and all those who have supported me at this convention and across the land.

There were hard hours on our journey. And often we sailed against the wind, but always we kept our rudder true. And there were so many of you who stayed the course and shared our hope. You gave your help; but even more, you gave your hearts. And because of you, this has been a happy campaign. You welcomed Joan and me and our family into your homes and neighborhoods, your churches, your campuses, your union halls. When I think back on all the miles and all the months and all the memories, I think of you. And I recall the poet's words, and I say: "What golden friends I had."

Among you, my golden friends across this land, I have listened and learned.

I have listened to Kenny Dubois, a glass blower in Charleston, W. Va., who has 10 children to support, but has lost his job after 35 years, just three years short of qualifying for his pension.

I have listened to the Trachia family, who farm in Iowa and who wonder whether they can pass the good life and the good earth on to their children.

I have listened to a grandmother in East Oakland, who no longer has a phone to call her grandchildren, because she gave it up to pay the rent on her small apartment.

I have listened to young workers out of work to students without the tuition for college, and to families without the chance to own a home. I have seen the closed factories and the stalled assembly lines of Anderson, Ind., and South Gate, Calif. I have seen too many — far too many — idle men and women desperate to work. I have seen too many — far too many — working families desperate to protect the value of their wages from the ravages of inflation.

Yet I have also sensed a yearning for new hope among the people in every state where I have been. And I have felt it in their handshakes; I saw it in their faces. And I shall never forget the mothers who carried children to our rallies. I shall always remember the elderly who have lived in an America of high purpose and who believe that it can all happen again.

Tonight, in their name, I have come here to speak for them. And for their sake, I ask you to stand with them. On their behalf, I ask you to restate and reaffirm the timeless truth of our party.

I congratulate President Carter on his victory here. I am confident that the Democratic Party will reunite on the basis of Democractic principles — and that together we will march toward a Democratic victory in 1980.

And someday, long after the convention, long after the signs come down, and the crowds stop cheering, and the bands stop playing, may it be said of our campaign that we kept the faith. May it be said of our party in 1980 that we found our faith again.

And may it be said of us, both in dark passages and in bright days, in the words of Tennyson that my brothers quoted and loved — and that have special meaning for me now:

> I am a part of all that I have met . . .
> Tho much is taken, much abides . . .
> That which we are, we are . . .
> One equal temper of heroic hearts . . .
> . . . strong in will
> To strive, to seek, to find, and not to yield.

For me, a few hours ago, this campaign came to an end. For all those whose cares have been our concern, the work goes on, the cause endures, the hope still lives, and the dream shall never die.

QUESTIONS

1. Kennedy is speaking to several different groups of people in this speech. Identify his audience as best you can. How does he attempt to bring these diverse groups together?

2. In 1980 the Republican Convention took place before the Democratic Convention. How does Kennedy use this fact to his advantage?

3. If Kennedy had received the nomination, parts of this speech might have worked their way into his acceptance speech. Do you find any passages within this address that suggest they might have originally been intended to serve that function?

4. The discussion on p. 335 points out that Kennedy uses repetition to reinforce his points. What about his use of metaphor? Where does Kennedy tend to employ his metaphors? Where does he seem to avoid them?

5. Kennedy also frequently uses alliteration. Find some of his alliterative passages; what effect does the alliteration have?

• • • • •

WHAT SHOULD BE DONE ABOUT ROCK LYRICS?

Caryl Rivers

Caryl Rivers is a professor in the College of Communication at Boston University. Besides teaching journalism she also practices it; this commentary originally appeared in the Boston Globe.

AFTER a grisly series of murders in California, possibly inspired by the lyrics of a rock song, we are hearing a familiar chorus: Don't blame rock and roll. Kids will be kids. They love to rebel, and the more shocking the stuff, the better they like it.

There's some truth in this, of course. I loved to watch Elvis shake his torso when I was a teen-ager, and it was even more fun when Ed Sullivan wouldn't let the cameras show him below the waist. I snickered at the forbidden "Rock with Me, Annie" lyrics by a black Rhythm and Blues group which were deliciously naughty. But I am sorry, rock fans, that is not the same thing as hearing lyrics about how a man is going to force a woman to perform oral sex on him at gunpoint in a little number called "Eat Me Alive." It is not in the same league with a song about the delights of slipping into a woman's room while she is sleeping and murdering her, the theme of an AC DC ballad that allegedly inspired the California slayer.

Make no mistake, it is not sex we are talking about here, but violence. Violence against women. Most rock songs are not violent — they are funky, sexy, rebellious, and sometimes witty. Please do not mistake me for a Mrs. Grundy. If Prince wants to leap about wearing only a purple jock strap, fine. Let Mick Jagger unzip his fly as he gyrates, if he wants to. But when either one of them starts garroting, beating, or sodomizing a woman in their number, that is another story.

I always find myself annoyed when "intellectual" men dismiss violence against women with a yawn, as if it were beneath their dignity to notice. I wonder if the reaction would be the same if the violence were directed against someone other than women. How many people would yawn and say, "Oh, kids will be kids," if a rock group did a nifty little number called "Lynchin," in which stringing up and stomping on black people were set to music? Who would chuckle and say, "Oh, just a little adolescent rebellion" if a group of rockers went on MTV dressed as Nazis, desecrating synagogues and beating up Jews to the beat of twanging guitars?

I'll tell you what would happen. Prestigious dailies would thunder on editorial pages; senators would fall over each other to get denunciations into the Congressional Record. The president would appoint a commission to clean up the music business.

But violence against women is greeted by silence. It shouldn't be.

This does not mean censorship, or book (or record) burning. In a society that protects free expression, we understand a lot of stuff will float up out of the sewer. Usually, we recognize the ugly stuff that advocates violence against any group as the garbage it is, and we consider its purveyors as moral lepers. We hold our nose and tolerate it, but we speak out against the values it proffers.

But images of violence against women are not staying on the fringes of society. No longer are they found only in tattered paper-covered books or in movie houses where winos snooze and the scent of urine fills the air. They are entering the mainstream at a rapid rate. This is happening at a time when the media, more and more, set the agenda for the public debate. It is a powerful legitimizing force — especially television. Many people regard what they see on TV as the truth: Walter Cronkite once topped a poll as the most trusted man in America.

Now, with the advent of rock videos and all-music channels, rock music has grabbed a big chunk of legitimacy. American teen-agers have instant access, in their living rooms, to the messages of rock, on the same vehicle that brought them Sesame Street. Who can blame them if they believe that the images they see are accurate reflections of adult reality, approved by adults? After all, Big Bird used to give them lessons on the same little box. Adults, by their silence, sanction the images. Do we really want our kids to think that rape and violence are what sexuality is all about?

This is not a trivial issue. Violence against women is a major social problem, one that's more than a cerebral issue to me. I teach at Boston University, and one of my most promising young journalism students was raped and murdered. Two others told me of being raped. Recently, one female student was assaulted and beaten so badly she had $5,000 worth of medical bills and permanent damage to her back and eyes.

It's nearly impossible, of course, to make a cause-and-effect link between lyrics and images and acts of violence. But images have a tremendous power to create an atmosphere in which violence against certain people is sanctioned. Nazi propagandists knew that full well when they portrayed Jews as ugly, greedy, and powerful.

The outcry over violence against women, particularly in a sexual context, is being legitimized in two ways: by the increasing movement of these images into the mainstream of the media in TV, films, magazines, albums, videos, and by the silence about it.

Violence, of course, is rampant in the media. But it is usually set in some kind of moral context. It's usually only the bad guys who commit violent acts against the innocent. When the good guys get violent, it's against those who deserve it. Dirty Harry blows away the scum, he doesn't walk up to a toddler and say, "Make my day." The A Team does not shoot up suburban shopping malls.

But in some rock songs, it's the "heroes" who commit the acts. The people we are programmed to identify with are the ones being violent, with women on the receiving end. In a society where rape and assaults on women are endemic, this is no small problem, with millions of young boys watching on their TV screens and listening to their Walkmans.

I think something needs to be done. I'd like to see people in the industry respond to the problem. I'd love to see some women rock stars speak out against violence against women. I would like to see disc jockeys refuse air play to records and videos that contain such violence. At the very least, I want to see the end of the silence. I want journalists and parents and critics and performing artists to keep this issue alive in the public forum. I don't want people who are concerned about the issue labeled as blue-noses and bookburners and ignored.

And I wish it wasn't always just women who were speaking out. Men have as large a stake in the quality of our civilization as women do in the long run. Violence is a contagion that infects at random. Let's hear something, please, from the men.

QUESTIONS

1. Rivers says she does not want to be mistaken for 'a Mrs. Grundy." What does this mean? Who was Mrs. Grundy?
2. Rivers does not advocate censorship. What does she advocate?
3. In her argument, Caryl Rivers states that if rock music promoted racism there would be an immediate reaction. What other taboos would bring similar condemnation? Why?
4. By silently ignoring the violence against women, Rivers argues, our culture tacitly promotes that violence. What other injustices like this does our culture permit and thereby silently endorse?
5. Rivers' editorial appeared several years ago. Do you think rock lyrics have improved any in the last five years? Are protests like hers having an effect? Why or why not?
6. Write an essay that either agrees with Rivers, arguing that rock lyrics are in fact harmful, or disagrees with her, arguing that rock music and lyrics are basically harmless.

• • • • •

ABORTION, RIGHT AND WRONG

Rachel Richardson Smith

Abortion has been a political and moral battleground that threatens to become even bigger. Recent court decisions have caused some observers to contend that abortion will be the political issue of the 1990s. This essay by Rachel Richardson Smith, a mother and theology student, originally appeared in the "My Turn" column of Newsweek, a forum where readers are invited to publish their opinions.

I CANNOT bring myself to say I am in favor of abortion. I don't want anyone to have one. I want people to use contraceptives and for those contraceptives to be foolproof. I want people to be responsible for their actions; mature in their decisions. I want children to be loved, wanted, well cared for.

I cannot bring myself to say I am against choice. I want women who are young, poor, single or all three to be able to direct the course of their lives. I want women who have had all the children they want or can afford or their bodies can withstand to be able to decide their future. I want women who are in bad marriages or destructive relationships to avoid being trapped by pregnancy.

So in these days when thousands rally in opposition to legalized abortion, when facilities providing abortions are bombed, when the president speaks glowingly of the growing momentum behind the anti-abortion movement, I find myself increasingly alienated from the pro-life groups.

At the same time, I am overwhelmed with mail from pro-choice groups. They, too, are mobilizing their forces, growing articulate in support of their cause, and they want my support. I am not sure I can give it.

I find myself in the awkward position of being both anti-abortion and pro-choice. Neither group seems to be completely right — or wrong. It is not that I think abortion is wrong for me but acceptable for someone else. The question is far more complex than that.

Part of my problem is that what I think and how I feel about this issue are two entirely different matters. I know that unwanted children are often neglected, even abandoned. I know that many of those seeking abortions are children themselves. I know that making abortion illegal will not stop all women from having them.

Absolutes: I also know from experience the crisis an unplanned pregnancy can cause. Yet I have felt the joy of giving birth, the delight that comes from feeling the baby's skin against my own. I know how hard it is to parent a child and how deeply satisfying it can be. My children sometimes provoke me and cause endless frustration, but I can still look at them with tenderness and wonder at the miracle of it all. The lessons of my own experience produce conflicting emotions. Theory collides with reality.

It concerns me that both groups present themselves in absolutes. They are committed and they want me to commit. They do not recognize the gray area where I seem to be languishing. Each group has the right answer — the only answer.

Yet I am uncomfortable in either camp. I have nothing in common with the pro-lifers. I am horrified by their scare tactics, their pictures of well-formed fetuses tossed in a metal pan, their cruel slogans. I cannot condone their flagrant misuse of Scripture and unforgiving spirit. There is a meanness about their position that causes them to pass judgment on the lives of women in a way I could never do.

The pro-life groups, with their fundamentalist religious attitudes, have a fear and an abhorrence of sex, especially premarital sex. In their view abortion only compounds the sexual sin. What I find incomprehensible is that even as they are opposed to abortion they are also opposed to alternative solutions. They are squeamish about sex education in the schools. They don't want teens to have contraceptives without parental consent. They offer little aid or sympathy to unwed mothers. They are the vigilant guardians of a narrow morality.

I wonder how abortion got to be the greatest of all sins? What about poverty, ignorance, hunger, weaponry?

The only thing the anti-abortion groups seem to have right is that abortion is indeed the taking of human life. I simply cannot escape this one glaring fact. Call it what you will — fertilized egg, embryo, fetus. What we have here is human life. If it were just a mass of tissue there would be no debate. So I agree that abortion ends a life. But the anti-abortionists are wrong to call it murder.

The sad truth is that homicide is not always against the law. Our society does not categorically recognize the sanctity of human life. There are a number of legal and apparently socially acceptable ways to take human life. "Justifiable" homicide includes the death penalty, war, killing in self-defense. It seems to me that as a society we need to come to grips with our own ambiguity concerning the value of human life. If we are to value and protect unborn life so stringently, why do we not also value and protect life already born?

Mistakes: Why can't we see abortion for the human tragedy it is? No woman plans for her life to turn out that way. Even the most effective contraceptives are no guarantee against pregnancy. Loneliness, ignorance, immaturity can lead to decisions (or lack of decisions) that may result in untimely pregnancy. People make mistakes.

What many people seem to misunderstand is that no woman wants to have an abortion. Circumstances demand it; women do it. No woman reacts to abortion with joy. Relief, yes. But also ambivalence, grief, despair, guilt.

The pro-choice groups do not seem to acknowledge that abortion is not a perfect answer. What goes unsaid is that when a woman has an abortion she loses more than an unwanted pregnancy. Often she loses her self-respect. No woman can forget a pregnancy no matter how it ends.

Why can we not view abortion as one of those anguished decisions in which human beings struggle to do the best they can in trying circumstances? Why is abortion viewed so coldly and factually on the one hand and so judgmentally on the other? Why is it not akin to the same painful experience families must sometimes make to allow a loved one to die?

I wonder how we can begin to change the context in which we think about abortion. How can we begin to think about it redemptively? What is it in the trauma of loss of life — be it loved or unloved, born or unborn — from which we can learn? There is much I have yet to resolve. Even as I refuse to pass judgments on other women's lives, I weep for the children who might have been. I suspect I am not alone.

QUESTIONS

1. Outline Smith's essay. How does she structure it?
2. What audience is likely to read Smith's opinions in *Newsweek*? Does her presentation seem appropriate? Has she in any way shaped her essay for this audience?
3. How does Smith propose resolving the abortion dilemma? Does she present any viewpoints that are different from those you have heard before?
4. What are the real causes of unwanted pregnancies according to Smith? How might these causes be avoided or eliminated altogether?
5. Smith does not say that abortion is not wrong, but she mentions other wrongs that seem to be more important. What are they? Do you agree?

● ● ● ● ●

JAPAN: PLAYING BY DIFFERENT RULES

James Fallows

James Fallows is a free-lance writer, who has become an expert on Asian culture and how it intermeshes with American political and economic policies. His latest book, More Like Us: Making America Great Again *(1989), focuses on these issues, as does this article that appeared recently in* The Atlantic.

SOMETHING is peculiar about the way we discuss "trade wars." When America and Japan really were at war, each country was trying to blow the other up. Now the threat from Japan is — what? That its companies will devise more appealing products than our companies can, and will then offer them to us at a lower price. Where's the aggression or hostile intent? What makes this anything like Pearl Harbor?

Economists, of course, have comebacks to such questions. Maybe the Japanese are offering cut-rate goods today purely in hopes of squeezing out the competition and collecting big monopoly profits later on. Maybe we'll be forced into a kind of peonage if Japan comes to control all the high-grade, sophisticated manufacturing and we're left to sell soybeans and rent out our big-league ballplayers for service with the Hiroshima Carp.

Still, according to all the basic logic of our economic system, we shouldn't worry about trade wars, any more than we worry about being offered a gift. If another country will sell us goods for less than it costs us to make them, why should we complain? It doesn't really matter whether the supplying country is more efficient or is merely willing to "dump," selling the goods at a loss. In either case, foreign trade leaves us with the steel girders or the color TVs we might have made ourselves, *plus* the cash we've saved by buying for less. If the Japanese want to exploit themselves and sell below their true cost, that's their problem — all they're doing is raising our standard of living at the expense of theirs. If the Koreans are willing to work for low wages, we should be happy to buy their shoes for $8 instead of $48 and use the $40 for something else. The extra wealth for America — the $40 we get besides the pair of shoes — will presumably give us leeway to invest in newer, more productive industries, or simply to make up the lost incomes of people who used to produce shoes.

So goes the theory of free trade, as I learned it in my economics courses and as it's explained in America whenever someone wants to prove that protectionism is bad. I was steeped in the theory when I arrived in Japan, early last year. I still think it's the right answer to most of what's wrong with the world's economy. But I no longer think that it tells us much about dealing with Japan.

It's hard to make the objections to free trade with Japan sound as neat and elegant as the original theory itself. The objections centers on this point: free trade assumes certain things about human behavior that may not be correct when applied to the Japanese. This is not because the Japanese are a separate species, as they sometimes contend, but because their society's definition of the good life is different from Adam Smith's.

The Adam Smith, free-trade view of life rests on three pillars:

1. Economic problems are always solved by *more* trade, not less. When goods flow from low-cost production sites to markets in higher-cost areas, everyone is better off. The more smoothly they flow, the greater the all-around benefit, since each part of the world is doing what it can do best.

2. The desirability of more trade rests, in turn, on the assumption that the world is full of "economic men," who go through life making rational cost-benefit decisions. Their appetites and preferences may differ — if wages go up, some people will work more, because the payoff is greater, and others will work less, because they can earn what they need in a shorter time. But everyone will respond to market signals to get the best deal for himself. As a result, everyone will *naturally* act in a way that promotes international trade. Everyone wants a bargain; the best bargains are by definition available from the world's lowest-cost producers; freer trade will select the most efficient producers and make more goods available at a lower overall cost.

3. This picture of economic man, in its turn, rests on an even deeper assumption about what life, or at least the commerical part of it, is for. Efficient production is good because it leads to lower prices, and lower prices are good because they let people have "more": more food, more clothes, more leisure, more variety, more of everything money can buy. And in providing more, the capitalist free-trade system offers its only justification for itself. Competitive capitalism is crueler than other economic systems — the bankruptcies, the unemployment. But in return it offers people more material wealth and a higher standard of living than any other system has done. For at least the past century America and most other developed nations have willingly accepted this bargain. No pain, no gain. By the logic of the market, competition is always good, because it offers people more, and a free world trading system is best, because it offers people most.

As long as all the participants are after the same thing — "more" — then the world trading system should work fine. Markets will clear. Like magnetism, sexual attraction, and other powerful interactions, free trade starts with two parties that have symmetrical goals and motivations, and it takes them toward a predictable result.

But suppose one participant doesn't have the same goals as the others. Then the result won't be what was expected — in an electromagnet, at a freshman mixer, or in the world trading system. Suppose, to stick to economics, that one country isn't really interested in buying products from anywhere else, because it is not powerfully motivated by lower prices, *because having more is not its principal goal*. Then free trade's solution to all problems — everyone should buy more from everyone else — won't necessarily make sense.

This, I've come to think, is the basic story of Japan and the United States — really, of Japan and the rest of the world. Japan is not mainly interested in a higher standard of living for its people; America is. Given those different starting points, free trade will almost inevitably lead to chronic trade surpluses for Japan, chronic deficits for the United States. That outcome is not necessarily bad in itself, but it forces us to make a choice that few politicians have yet offered to us. Which really bothers us more: the chronic "failures" in trade with Japan, or the violence we'd have to do to free trade to correct them?

Let me clarify what I'm *not* trying to say. To argue that Japan tends toward surplus does not mean that its industries, managers, and workers are the "best" in the world. Some of them may be; even so, free-trade theory assumes that trade accounts would still balance out. If Japan really were better at manufacturing than any other country, its exports would keep rising and so (because of supply-demand forces on the currency exchange) would the value of the yen. Goods from the rest of the world would become cheaper; its people, wanting "more," would recognize and seize these bargains. Equilibrium would be restored. This is essentially what happened to America in the generation after the Second World War. Our industries were world-beaters; our dollars grew strong, and we spent those dollars — and spent and spent. But the chronic trade imbalance reflects something more than Japanese manufacturing skill.

I also don't mean to say that the United States bears no responsibility for its trade and budget deficits. We're more responsible for the size of the deficits than anyone else is. The U.S. trade deficit was about $150 billion last year, or more than five times larger than the normal rate in the late 1970s. It could never have gotten so large so fast if the federal budget deficit had not been booming at the same time. (To summarize a long but now standard explanation: Japan and Germany *had* to run big trade surpluses with the United States in the 1980s, to earn the dollars they then lent us to cover our budget deficit.) Moreover, eliminating all identifiable trade barriers in Japan would, in the short run, eliminate only part of the U.S.-Japan trade deficit, since so many "imports" are really Japanese-made components for American products and subcontracts for American firms.

Finally, I would never deny that American business, American culture, American habits — let's face it, Americans — are to blame for many of our export failings. Our children don't learn enough about math or science, our smartest people end up planning hostile corporate takeovers or designing attack submarines, we don't naturally think of export markets, but our managers and unions do naturally think of getting all they can out of a company in the shortest possible time. Lee Iacocca tried to make himself the symbol of America's industrial rebirth, but by paying himself $20 million in a year when Chrysler's earnings declined, he has become as grim a symbol as Ivan Boesky of what the Japanese think is killing us.

This cultural-doom analysis is very familiar, and it can be overdone. Do U.S. companies think of the U.S. market first? That may say less about our parochialism than about the size of our market — a lot of Taiwanese companies think of America first too. Still, the charge that we've become culturally unfit is true enough to make us re-examine our schools, our management ethics, and ultimately our values. Unless we start correcting our own failings, we're in no position to hector the Japanese.

But even if America solved its cultural problems, even if our students joyfully tackled extra homework and employees strove always to enhance the honor of the firm, I suspect that Japan would still be involved in trade wars against us and others. The deficits would be smaller, but the tensions would still be there. The reason is that the free-trade solution — everyone buying more from everyone else — runs counter to a deeper value in Japanese life: the non-capitalist desire to preserve every Japanese person's place in the Japanese productive system. In the United States and in most of the world that Adam Smith described, people suffer indignities as *producers* — through layoffs, job changes, shifts into new businesses — in order to improve the welfare of the

society's *consumers*. In Japan it's the other way around. The Japanese consumer's interests comes last — and therefore so does the motivation for buying from overseas.

Of course, the Japanese market is not as self-contained as Albania's, or as obviously tariff-bound as Taiwan's or South Korea's. One of the first things American visitors to Japan see, as they stumble bleary-eyed through Narita Airport, is the sign on every luggage cart reading IMPORT NOW!, conveniently in English. American brand names — McDonald's, Kentucky Fried Chicken, (Tokyo) Disneyland — are ubiquitous in Japan. Kenichi Ohmae, the author of *Beyond National Borders*, and the managing director of McKinsey & Company in Japan, has pointed out time and again that American-*owned* companies sell about as much to Japan as Japanese-owned companies do to the United States. (The difference, of course, is that most of the "American" products are made in Japan, in Japanese-American joint ventures, thereby protecting the Japanese producer's interests.) Japanese trade officials have a standard anyone-can-succeed-in-Japan presentation for foreign visitors, usually starring Mister Donut, Schick razors, and BMW cars. Its moral is, you can sell as long as you make a truly high-quality product (strike one against America) and strive earnestly to meet local tastes (strikes two and three, we're out).

Technically, the trade officials are right. With enough work, almost anything could be sold in Japan, even American rice or Korean cars. The difference is the natural tendency of the system. The United States, putting the consumer's interest first, naturally buys up whatever offers the best value, unless some lobby or cartel stands in the way. Japan, putting the (Japanese) producer's interest first, naturally resists importing anything but raw materials. Selling to America is like rolling a ball downhill. Selling to Japan is like fighting against guerrillas, or bailing against a siphon, or betting against the house. You can win, but the odds are not on your side.

None of the illustrations of this point is conclusive in itself, but together they suggest a deviation from the logic of capitalism and free trade. Capitalist societies are supposed to respond to price, so as to get "more." Japan does not.

Food is the classic illustration. Japan imports about half its calories, but if it cared mainly about price, it would import much more food. By refusing to import rice and blocking many other imports, Japan protects its farmers (and avoids antagonizing the gangsters in the beef industry) but penalizes every consumer in the country, through grotesquely inflated prices for food and land. Food may seem an exceptional case: it's an emotional issue; every major country protects its farmers to some degree; most Japanese still have a sentimental tie to the soil. What makes it so intriguing is that there's almost no complaint from the victims of the policy. Last spring a coalition of Japanese consumer groups protested food policy — but what concerned them was the suggestion that Japan should import more cheap food. They recommended that Japan's superexpensive rice should "never" be exposed to foreign competition.

The retail network is another famous example. A hundred years ago the United States had a retail system much like Japan's today: fragmented, diverse, family-owned, and inefficient. America doesn't have many Mom-and-Pop stores anymore (except for immigrant-run groceries), because they've been bulldozed under by Sears, Safeway, K-mart, and other large-scale, low-cost operations. The Mom-and-Pops put up a political fight in the 1920s and 1930s and tried to outlaw the chain stores. But, as Thomas McCraw and Patricia O'Brien wrote recently in *America versus Japan*, they were

snubbed by courts, legislatures, and even voters in referenda. Chain stores offered lower prices; therefore they were good. Japan has followed just the opposite course. In the past fifteen years government directives have made it harder to open discount stores, supermarkets, or other low-cost outlets that would improve the consumer's standard of living but would threaten the tiny greengrocer down the block.

Right-thinking Americans know that monopolies and cartels are bad, because they hurt the consumer. Japan *likes* cartels and some monopolies, because they strengthen Japanese producers against foreign competition. Japanese steelmakers, in the 1960s and 1970s, and semiconductor makers, in the 1970s and 1980s, have invested more heavily in advanced production equipment than any of them would have dared to on its own. It would be cheaper, in the short term, to keep using the old machines, which is what many American companies have done. The Japanese companies could take this "risk" because of their cartel-based faith that the famous Ministry of International Trade and Industry, MITI, would divide up the work fairly whenever the market went slack.

Japanese taxpayers would save money if they bought military aircraft direct from American producers. Although our own military budget may make this hard to believe, it is cheaper to buy the next F-15 off the production line than to set up a production line of your own. Nonetheless, the F-15s that the Air Self-Defense Force flies are made in Japan, under American license. Japan is scheduled to introduce a new fighter plane late in this decade. Buying an existing American model would be cheaper — that is, would hold down Japanese taxes, would give Japanese consumers "more." But unless the trade-war pressure from America becomes too intense, Japan seems almost sure to build its own fighter, at up to twice the cost of an imported plane.

One last, humble illustration is soda ash. This is an important chemical used for making glass, other chemicals, and detergents. Japanese soda-ash producers use petroleum-fired boilers that even in the cheap-oil days seemed to be burning money. American-made soda ash is cheaper. The American trade association that has been trying to sell it in Japan claims that it could be offered for significantly less than the made-in-Japan price. For years the association made no headway whatsoever. Then, in 1983, Japan's Fair Trade Commission found that Japanese companies were colluding to keep the Americans out. American suppliers quickly expanded their share of the market from three to 15 percent, but then got very little more. The yen has gone up, dollar prices have plummeted, but the market share has barely budged. An executive of Asahi Glass, a major purchaser, recently announced that he'd never leave his high-cost Japanese supplier — they'd been friends in school. "This isn't exactly collusion," an American diplomat told me. "It's simply a refusal to act on price."

Early this year the Organization for Economic Cooperation and Development, in Paris, offered an intriguing analysis of what the cumulative refusals to act on price meant for Japan. For 1986 as a whole, the average yen-dollar exchange rate was 169 to 1. At that rate Japan's per capita income was just below America's, and at the rates prevailing early this year, when the dollar plunged into the 140s, Japan was clearly the "richest" major country in the world. But the OECD went on to adjust incomes in each country for purchasing power and then recalculated the rate. In terms that matter to consumers, the "real" exchange rate was 223 to 1.

This is the single most illuminating statistic to come out of Japan. (Or maybe one of the two most illuminating. The other, which needs to be repeated as often as possible, is that at current market rates Japan's land all together is "worth" more than America's, even though the United States is twenty-five times as large.) It is important because of what it says about the repression of consumer interests in Japan. The gap between the official and "real" exchange rates — between something in the 140s to the 160s and 223 — is the wealth that Japan has denied its own consumers in order to preserve its market share. To put it another way, the gap means that products from the rest of the world are available to the Japanese at astonishing bargain rates. For 140 yen a Japanese consumer can buy a dollar and use it to buy clothes, food, or machinery that would cost him more than 200 yen to buy at home. If Japan wanted to, it could even buy its way out of its domestic-housing problem. It can't import land, but by importing more food it could free up precious flatland now used for farming and let the Japanese move out of their "rabbit hutches."

The world would seem to be Japan's bargain basement, but Japan is not interested. What makes Japan unusual is not that it sells so much to other countries — West Germany's exports make up 34 percent of its gross national product, while Japan's make up 13 percent — but that it buys so little. West Germany imports the equivalent of 30 percent of its GNP, Japan about 10 percent — mainly raw materials it can't produce for itself. If the yen rises high enough, Japan will finally be priced out of its export surplus. But if it were a society of economic men, it would have begun buying its way out of the surplus long before now.

Understanding why Japan behaves this way would be a life's work. One theory, popular among the Japanese, holds that the trade surplus reflects the people's inborn frugality, moderation, and unsurpassed productive skill. Perhaps it reflects the bias of the political system toward paternalistic decisions, made by small elites sheltered from life as the ordinary consumer knows it. Japan is an impeccably free society but in practice not a very democratic one. The most important political decisions are always made by committees, oligarchies, bureaucracies, party-leadership councils. In an article called "The Japan Problem," published in *Foreign Affairs* late last year, the Dutch journalist Karel van Wolferen, who has lived in Japan for twenty-five years, argued that power in Japan was dispersed among a number of semi-autonomous baronies, each of which promoted its own interests and laughed off any attempt to change course. Prime Minister Nakasone, viewing the nation's predicament as a whole, might understand that Japan needed to start spending more on itself. But, van Wolferen said, all the component parts of the system — the huge industrial companies, the labor unions, MITI, the farmers — were programmed to build market share, cut profit when necessary, resist foreign penetration, and export, export, export. Early last year the Japanese government rolled the drums for the Maekawa report, an ambitious proposal to increase imports, improve living standards, shorten the work week to five days, and generally make Japan a nation of economic men. By the end of the year, according to a survey conducted by the Ministry of Labor, the number of firms with a five-day week appeared to have gone *down*. (On the other hand, in the wake of the Maekawa report the average Japanese worker was skipping out of the office at day's end a minute and fifteen

seconds earlier.) The rest of the world may think Japan is rich, but its people seem to regard the *endaka* — "strong-yen" — crisis as the occasion for yet another round of belt-tightening. From September of 1985 to December of 1986 the yen's value against the dollar rose by almost 52 percent. But Toyota, Nissan, and Honda were so determined to hold on to market share that they swallowed most of the currency change and raised their dollar prices by only 15 percent.

There are other theories. For example, maybe the Japanese, with their rapidly aging population, are trying to sock their profits away in American investments even though it means short-term sacrifice. Someday they'll have to start importing, but before then they can build a big endowment of overseas investments that will help pay their big, looming pension bill. Or maybe the Japanese truly reject the "creative destruction" theory of capitalism, since they mourn the destructive part (lost jobs and markets) much more than they welcome the creativity (higher standard of living). In the two years of *endaka* the Japanese press has harped endlessly on the misery of "small and medium size enterprises," which are being squeezed out of their traditional export markets. Last summer I visited a few of these companies, including a knife factory in Seki. In a tin-roofed, junk-filled shed in the mountains I saw Japanese retirees grinding butcher knives by hand on antique grind wheels. An old man and an old woman were hand-gluing the red plastic sides onto "Swiss" army knives. The plant manager, his eyes practically brimming with tears, was sure I'd share his sorrow about his tragic loss of market share. And yes, it was too bad for him. But by any normal standard this factory should have moved out of Japan fifteen years ago, to Taiwan or India. Much more impressive installations in the United States have been destroyed by Japanese competition. The parallel does not seem to have occurred to anyone in Japan.

Preserving the existing order — continuing to buy soda ash from your school chum — seems more important to Japan than anything else. The two kinds of foreign purchases that have boomed in Japan — tourism, and investment in foreign real estate — are different from other imports in that they pose no competition to anyone in Japan. The *Nihon Keizai Shimbun*, a distinguished paper comparable to *The Wall Street Journal*, ran an editorial last spring about low consumption levels, and pointed out that letting in more foreign labor would lower the cost of many services. But such a change would be too disruptive, the paper concluded. "Perhaps the high cost of living is the price we pay for social peace and harmony." When they tire of lending money to Americans, or buying real estate, or going on tours, the Japanese have very little to do with their money since they're so reluctant to import. Shares of stock are one thing they can buy, and prices on the Japanese stock market have been speculated up to stupendous levels. Nippon Telephone traded early this year with a price-to-earnings ratio of 250, and the Tokyo Stock Exchange as a whole had a P/E ratio of 56, about three times higher than that of the New York Stock Exchange. Memberships in Japanese golf clubs are traded on an official exchange; a place in the most prestigious club recently went for 400 million yen, or about $2.7 million. A headline in *The Wall Street Journal* early this year said, "JAPAN: SO MUCH YEN, SO LITTLE ELSE."

No one can say that it's "wrong" for Japan to be a mercantilist society, piling up its trade profits rather than spending them. No one can say whether Japan will always behave the way it does now. Its biggest companies are rushing to set up factories

overseas; unemployment is rising; profits are plunging; the strong yen is having its effect. (If Japan had been more consumer-oriented and willing to "act on price," a gentler shift in exchange rates might have increased domestic spending.) Just before the economic summit in Venice, Japan announced a $40 billion public-works program to boost consumption. It's conceivable that ten years from now warnings about Japan's chronic surplus will look as premature as warnings about the "petrodollar" glut do now. But unless *endaka* or *kokusaika* ("internationalization") changes Japan's basic nature, "free trade" will almost certainly mean something like what it's meant for the past few years: big surpluses for Japan, big deficits everywhere else, a big flow of profits out from Japan to buy companies, buildings, Treasury bonds (but not manufactured products), overseas. That near certainty gives us our choice: do we want to end the deficits or do we want to honor free trade? We can't do both.

Life as chronic debtors (which is to say, as free-traders) might not be so bad. It would accomplish de facto what we could never manage officially: the merger of Japan and the United States. Our two economies are complementary (they make and save, we borrow and buy) and so are our natural resources, human talents, and even our foreign policies. The more deeply the Japanese become enmeshed in our society — owning much of the debt, the real estate, the market share — the more of a stake they will have in its well-being. Everyone in the United States feels bad about foreigners "taking over" American buildings and companies, but is anyone really hurt? When Japanese investors re-open old American factories, they bring new technology and create new jobs. When they buy real estate, they pay money to the (usually American) owners. Japanese investment has helped push the American stock market to its speculative highs, and has buoyed the real-estate market in New York, Honolulu, Washington, and Los Angeles. Some Americans resent the rising prices, but others enjoy the profits.

Permanent debtor status could also have its drawbacks. America would have less independence of action, since it would have to keep foreign investors calm and confident. Putting the United States on a leash might be better for the world, but we would never choose this course ourselves. As our interest burden mounts, we'll have to slide down to a lower standard of living, consuming less and repaying more. (The Japanese are already underconsuming, of course, but they have never done otherwise.) And sometimes debt gets out of control, leading to inflation, panic, collapse.

If consumer welfare remains our goal, the United States would do best to stick to the free-trade route, despite the "deindustrialization" and debt. Restricting trade always means higher prices. We can resolve to work harder, teach our children more math, become more "competitive," all the while recognizing that Japan will never love our exports as much as we do theirs. But if we decide that continued debt is too dangerous, we'll have to go beyond "competitiveness." We'll need to change the rules.

This does not mean making Lee Iacocca speeches about the perfidious Japanese. They're simply doing what comes naturally to them. American politicians have been quoted in Japan as warning that trade sanctions would be the "equivalent of the A-bomb" or "really winning the war." The Japanese are too smart to let themselves be caught saying that a new car or computer chip of theirs will be the "equivalent of the Bataan Death March." In an editorial last spring *The New York Times* urged America to "badger them relentlessly for more access to their markets. . . ." What's the point of badgering them at all? Threats not backed up by action annoy the Japanese, make America look weak and nervous, and leave the bothersome trade patterns unchanged.

Instead of yelling and badgering, we should decide precisely what bothers us about the trade balance and then act calmly, without noise or threats, to change the rules where we think we must. Are we mainly worried about the overall trade balance? The Gephardt amendment, which would require sanctions against nations with chronic export surpluses, enjoys almost no respectable support, but it would force Japan to moderate its mercantilist behavior. Do we think there's too much foreign investment? We can limit it, as Japan has. Japan makes it hard for foreign companies to move in and set up wholly owned subsidiaries. Foreign investment in the United States would seem to help us, by bringing new technology and jobs. But if we feel that it's a threat, let's not yell at the Japanese; let's imitate them, with a change of investment rules.

Do we worry that Matsushita and Nissan will keep all the high-grade manufacturing work back in Osaka and Zama, leaving American workers to bolt parts together from a kit? The rising yen will put pressure on the Japanese to shift whole operations overseas; but if we're concerned, let's pass local-content laws.

Do we seethe about all the areas where American firms are competitive but are being frozen out of Japan? Let's not give speeches urging a more open attitude: when Japanese society does open up, it will be for its own reasons. Let's simply deny it markets reciprocally. For years American shipping firms complained about Japanese rules on "high cube containers"—the large metal boxes that are hauled across the country as truck trailers, loaded on ships, and unloaded in another port. Japan claimed that American containers were too big and dangerous; they had to be unloaded and their contents repacked in Japanese containers on arrival. The speeches and complaints went on; the Japanese stuck to their guns. But last year the U.S. Federal Maritime Commission started investigating the effect of Japanese restrictions, with a thinly veiled threat to restrict Japanese shipments to the United States in retaliation. Japan modified its rules, but after American shippers said the changes made no practical difference, the commission pursued its investigation. Recently the Japanese issued further-relaxed guidelines.

Stated that way, the story may seem to have a bully-boy moral, which is not my point. It's juvenile and dangerous to think that if we just get tough with the Japanese (or Russians), we can make them back down. The point is that in this case, without speeches, our government changed the rules; without rancor, the Japanese adapted. The more typical pattern is for our politicians to yell at the Japanese, without changing the rules. We've yelled because we're uneasy about the deficits, but we haven't done anything, because it would hurt us as consumers and impinge on free trade.

Let's be clear about it: changing the trade imbalance *will* hurt us as consumers, because consumers' interests always suffer from any restriction on trade. Nonetheless, even the United States, consumer heaven, has restricted trade when free trade threatened other values. Child labor would make household help affordable again; totally unlimited immigration would probably take three dollars off the bill for a standard restaurant meal. Product-safety laws make everything cost more. Yet in all these cases our laws recognize that not even Americans live by the "standard of living" alone.

We may feel the same way about trade: that stable communities, predictable jobs, freedom from foreign interference, matter more than the best value for our money. If so, we can change the laws, mandating a different trade balance — and a lower standard of living. The Japanese have made a choice for their society, and we should make one for ours. That's better than thinking that we can talk the Japanese into behaving more like us, or relying on "free trade" to reach equilibrium again.

QUESTIONS

1. Fallows begins by outlining fundamental premises of economics as Americans understand them. Would you agree that these are the premises of the American marketplace? What conclusions logically flow from these premises? What assumptions lead to these premises.?

2. What is "wrong" with Japan, according to Fallows? Why do they not accept our economic premises?

3. Fallows points out that some Japanese manufacturers will simply not purchase supplies for manufacturing that are cheaper than the ones they are using, even though these supplies may be readily available. He quotes an American diplomat who says, "It's simply a refusal to act on price." Are there times in our culture when we refuse to act on price and buy cheaper goods, even when those goods are readily available? When? Why do we do this?

4. Fallows believes that we should change some of our laws — and perhaps our attitudes — in order to change the trade balance. In your opinion, will most Americans be able to accept a change in their standard of living? Why or why not? Fallows gives a few examples of situations where this has occurred. Are they convincing?

5. Japan, according to Fallows, is a producer-oriented culture, while the United States is a consumer-oriented culture. Are these cultures mutually exclusive?

6. Henry Ford agreed to pay his workers the then outrageous sum of five dollars a day because allegedly he believed that many of those workers could then afford to buy the new cars they were building. Was this strategy producer-oriented or consumer-oriented? Can you think of any other situations that might parallel this one?

●   ●   ●   ●   ●

VIEWPOINTS: COMMENCEMENT ADDRESS
AT DUKE UNIVERSITY

Ted Koppel

Ted Koppel has become well known to most Americans as the host of the popular ABC news program Nightline, *where he has developed a reputation for being a tenacious interviewer. On May 15, 1987, however, Ted Koppel exchanged his interviewer's chair for a mortarboard, and addressed the graduating class of Duke University in Durham, North Carolina; here is the text of his speech.*

I'M going to talk to you about a phenomenon that I think is taking place in this country today. America has been Vannatized. That's Vannatized as in Vanna White, "Wheel of Fortune"'s vestal virgin. The young lady may or may not already have appeared on one of those ubiquitous lists of most-admired Americans, but if she has not, it's only a matter of time. Through the mysterious alchemy of popular television, Miss White is roundly, indeed all but universally, adored.

It seems unlikely, but lest there be among you someone who has not thrilled to the graceful ease with which Miss White glides across our television screens, permit me to tell you what she does.

She turns blocks on which blank sides are displayed to another side of the block on which a letter is displayed.

She does this very well, very fluidly, with what appears to be genuine enjoyment. She also does it mutely. Vanna says nothing. She is often seen smiling at, and talking with, winners at the end of the program, but we can only imagine what they are saying to each other.

We don't hear Vanna. She speaks only body language, and she seems to like everything she sees. No, "like" is too tepid. Vanna thrills, rejoices, adores everything she sees. Therein lies her particular magic. We have no idea what, or even if, Vanna thinks. Is she a feminist or every male chauvinist's dream? She is whatever you want her to be. Sister, lover, daughter, friend, never cross, non-threatening and non-judgmental to a fault.

The viewer can, and apparently does, project a thousand different personalities onto that charmingly neutral television image, and she accommodates them all. Even Vanna White's autobiography, an oxymoron if ever there was one, reveals only that her greatest nightmare is running out of cat food and that one of the complexities of her job entails making proper allowance for the greater weight of the letters "M" and "W" over the letter "I", for example. Once, we learn, during her earlier, less-experienced days, she failed to take that heavy-letter factor into proper account and broke a fingernail.

I tremble to think what judgment a future anthropologist finding that book will render on our society. I tremble not out of fear that they will misjudge us, but rather that they will judge us only too accurately. For the Vanna Factor has wormed its way into all too many aspects of our lives. All of us whose success is directly or indirectly a function of television are the beneficiaries of the Vanna Factor. I am, for example. My mail proves it to me on a daily basis.

I am increasingly driven to the conclusion that on television, neutrality or objectivity are simply perceived, or at least treated, as a form of intellectual vaccum, into which the viewer's own opinion is drawn. I find myself being regarded not so much as an objective journalist, but as someone who shares most views, even those that are incompatible with one another. As in the case of Vanna White, although mercifully to a lesser degree, many of "Nightline"'s viewers project onto me those opinions they would like me to hold, and then find me compatible.

In Vanna White's case, in my own, the fostering of such illusions may be not only permissible, but even necessary. We have been hired, Vanna and I, to project neutrality. The problem is that what I am calling the Vanna Factor has evolved more and more into a political, an economic, even a religious necessity.

On television, ambiguity is a virtue, and television these days is our most active marketplace of ideas. Let's take inventory for a moment. Sixty percent or more of the American public, roughly 140 million people, get most or all of their news from television. Presumably some of those people can read, but approximately 60 million of our fellow citizens cannot. They are functional illiterates. For them television is not merely the medium of choice, but of necessity.

What then should we or must we conclude? Whatever your merchandise, if you want to move it in bulk, you flaunt it on television. Merchants trying to sell their goods, politicians trying to sell their ideas, preachers trying to sell their gospel or their morality, all of these items are most efficiently sold on TV. If that doesn't scare the living daylights out of you, you're not paying attention.

Never mind the dry goods; television and toilet paper were made for one another. But let's focus on our national policies. Let's look at our principles. Our ethical and moral standards — how do they fare on television?

You won't be surprised to learn that there is not a great deal of room on television for complexity. We are nothing as an industry if not attuned to the appetites and limitations of our audience. We have learned, for example, that your attention span is brief. We should know. We helped make it that way.

Watch "Miami Vice" some Friday night. You will find not only a pastel-colored world, which neatly symbolizes the moral ambiguity of that program, you will discover that no scene lasts longer than 10 or 15 seconds. It is a direct reflection of the television industry's confidence in your ability to concentrate.

Analyze what our most popular youth-oriented radio stations are doing: seven songs in a row, 10 songs in a row, 16 songs in a row. As Andy Rooney likes to say, "Didn't you ever wonder why?" Many of you, I am told, lack the patience to sit through commercials. As soon as the music stopped, you began scanning the dial looking for more music. And so the media consultants, those lineal descendants of the oracle at Delphi, reprogrammed your itchy dial fingers, fed you multiple morsels of music, one after another, until you learned to sit through the commercials.

Look at MTV or "Good Morning, America," and watch the images and ideas flash past in a blur of impressionistic appetizers. No, there is not much room on television for complexity. You can partake of our daily banquet without drawing on any intellectual resources, without either physical or moral discipline. We require nothing of you. Only that you watch or say that you are watching if Mr. Nielsen's representatives happen to call.

And gradually, it must be said, we are beginning to make our mark on the American people. We have actually convinced ourselves that slogans will save us. Shoot up, if you must, but use a clean needle. Enjoy sex whenever and with whomever you wish, but wear a condom. "No." The answer is "No." Not because it isn't cool or smart or because you might end up in jail or dying in an AIDS ward, but "no" because it's wrong, because we have spent 5,000 years as a race of rational human beings, trying to drag ourselves out of the primeval slime by searching for truth and moral absolutes.

In the place of truth, we have discovered facts. For moral absolutes, we have substituted moral ambiguity. We now communicate with everyone and say absolutely nothing. We have reconstructed the Tower of Babel, and it is a television antenna: a thousand voices producing a daily parody of democracy, in which everyone's opinion is afforded equal weight, regardless of substance or merit. Indeed, it can even be argued that opinions of real weight tend to sink with barely a trace in television's ocean of banalities.

Our society finds truth too strong a medicine to digest undiluted. In its purest form, truth is not a polite tap on the shoulder. It is a howling reproach. What Moses brought down from Mt. Sinai were not the Ten Suggestions. They are commandments. Are, not were. The sheer brilliance of the Ten Commandments is that they codify in a handful of words acceptable human behavior, not just for then or now, but for all time.

Language evolves. Power shifts from one nation to another. Messages are transmitted with the speed of light. Man erases one frontier after another. And yet we and our behavior and the commandments which govern that behavior remain the same. The tension between those commandments and our baser instincts provide the grist for journalism's daily mill. What a huge, gaping void there would be in our informational flow and in our entertainment without the routine violation of the sixth commandment, "Thou shalt not murder." The Gary Hart campaign floundered just this week on violations of the seventh commandment, "Thou shalt not commit adultery."

Relevant? Of course the commandments are relevant. Simply because we use different terms and tools, the eighth commandment is still relevant to the insider trading scandal. The commandments don't get bogged down in methodology. Simple, to the point: "Thou shalt not steal." Watch the Iran-Contra hearings and keep the ninth commandment in mind, "Thou shalt not bear false witness." And the tenth commandment, which seems to have been crafted for the 80s and the Me Generation, the commandment against covetous desires, against longing for anything we cannot get in a honest or legal fashion.

When you think about it, it's curious, isn't it? We've changed in almost all things — where we live, how we eat, communicate, travel — and yet in our moral and immoral behavior, we are fundamentally unchanged. Maimonides and Jesus summed it up in almost identical words. "Thou shalt love thy neighbor as thyself." "Do unto others as you would have them do unto you." So much for our obligations toward our fellow man. That's what the last five commandments are about.

The first five are more complex in that they deal with figures of moral authority. The fifth commandment requires us to honor our father and mother. Religious scholars through the years have concluded that it was inscribed on the first tablet among the laws of piety toward God because as far as children are concerned, parents stand in the place of God. What a strange conclusion — us, in the place of God. We, who set such flawed examples for you.

And yet, in our efforts to love you, to provide for you and in our efforts to forgive you when you make mistakes, we do our feeble best to personify that perfect image of love and forgiveness and providence which some of us find in God.

Which brings me to the first, and in this day and age probably the most controversial of the commandments, since it requires that we believe in the existence of a single, supreme God and then in the second, third, and fourth commandments prohibits the worship of any other God, forbids that that His name be taken in vain, requires that we set aside one day in seven to rest and worship Him.

What a bizarre journey. From sweet, undemanding Vanna White to that all-demanding, jealous Old Testament God.

There have always been imperfect role models, false gods of material success and shallow fame. But now their influence is magnified by television. I caution you, as one who performs daily on that flickering altar, to set your sights beyond what you can see. There is true majesty in the concept of an unseen power which can neither be measured nor weighed. There is harmony and inner peace to be found in following a moral compass that points in the same direction regardless of fashion or trend. There is hope that if we can only set our course according to man's finest aspirations, we can achieve what we all want, and that we can have it without diminishing our neighbor's share.

Peace. May it come to your generation.

QUESTIONS

1. What aspects of this address suggest it was intended to be to be heard rather than seen on a page?

2. If Vanna White is a symbol, what is she a symbol of? What other symbols similar to Vanna does Koppel identify?

3. Is it inconsistent for Koppel to attack television as he does? Why does he do so?

4. Where does Koppel identify with his audience? Where does he establish a distance between himself and his audience? How does the context of this address shape the persona he assumes?

5. What is the central point Koppel is trying to make here? Is his message surprising to you? Why or why not?

6. Koppel criticizes those who accept the values found in television, arguing that we should not reach for easy and simple solutions to life's problems. Then he advocates relying on the values found in the Ten Commandments. Is this also a simple solution? Is he being inconsistent?

7. Every few years a celebrity such as Vanna White catches the public's attention briefly and usually fades just as quickly. What celebrity seems to be in the news now? Write an essay explaining this celebrity's appeal.

•   •   •   •   •

THE PURE AND THE IMPURE

Pauline Kael

Pauline Kael regularly reviews movies for The New Yorker, *where she has gained the reputation of being one of the more perceptive motion picture critics writing today. Her reviews are so good, in fact, that they are regularly collected and republished. This review of Steven Spielberg's film* E.T. *comes from her 1984 collection* Taking It All In.

STEVEN Spielberg's *E.T. The Extra-Terrestrial* envelops you in the way that his *Close Encounters of the Third Kind* did. It's a dream of a movie — a bliss-out. This sci-fi fantasy has a healthy share of slapstick comedy, yet it's as pure as Carroll Ballard's *The Black Stallion*. Like Ballard, Spielberg respects the conventions of children's stories, and because he does he's able to create the atmosphere for a mythic experience. Essentially, *E.T.* is the story of a ten-year-old boy, Elliott, who feels fatherless and lost because his parents have separated, and who finds a miraculous friend — an alien, inadvertently left on Earth by a visiting spaceship.

If the film seems a continuation of *Close Encounters*, that's partly because it has the sensibility we came to know in that picture, and partly because E.T. himself is like a more corporeal version of the celestial visitors at the end of it. Like *Close Encounters*, *E.T.* is bathed in warmth, and it seems to clear all the bad thoughts out of your head. It reminds you of the goofiest dreams you had as a kid, and rehabilitates them. Spielberg is right there in his films; you can feel his presence and his love of surprises. This phenomenal master craftsman plays high-tech games, but his presence is youthful — it has a just-emerged quality. The Spielberg of *Close Encounters* was a singer with a supple, sweet voice. It couldn't be heard in his last film, the impersonal *Raiders of the Lost Ark*, and we may have been afraid that he'd lost it, but now he has it back, and he's singing more melodiously than we could have hoped for. He's like a boy soprano lilting with joy all through *E.T.*, and we're borne along by his voice.

In Spielberg's movies, parents love their children, and children love their siblings. And suburban living, with its comfortable, uniform houses, is seen as a child's paradise — an environment in which children are protected and their imaginations can flourish. There's a luminous, magical view of Elliott's hilly neighborhood in the early-evening light on Halloween, with the kids in their costumes fanning out over the neatly groomed winding streets as each little group moves from one house to another for trick-or-treat, and E.T. swathed in a sheet and wearing red slippers over his webbed feet, waddles along between Elliott and his teen-age brother, Michael — each of them keeping a firm, protective grip on a gray-green four-digit hand. E.T. isn't just Elliott's friend; he's also Elliott's pet — the film catches the essence of the bond between lonely children and their pets. The sequence may call up memories of the trick-or-treat night in Vincente Minnelli's *Meet Me in St. Louis*, but it's more central here. All the imagery in the film is linked to Halloween, with the spaceship itself as a jack-o-lantern in the sky, and the child-size space visitors, who have come to gather specimens of Earth's flora, wrapped in cloaks with hoods and looking much like the trick-or-treaters. (The pumpkin spaceship is silent, though when you see it you may hear in your head the five-

note theme of the mother ship in *Close Encounters*, and the music that John Williams
has written for *E.T.* is dulcet and hushed — it allows for the full score that the movie
gets going in your imagination.)

E.T. probably has the best-worked-out script that Spielberg has yet shot, and since
it seems an emanation of his childlike, playful side and his love of toys, it would be
natural to assume that he wrote it. But maybe it seems such a clear expression of his
spirit because its actual writer, Melissa Mathison, could see what he needed more
deeply than he could himself, and could devise a complete structure that would hold his
feelings in balance. Mathison was one of the scenarists for *The Black Stallion* and is a
co-writer of *The Escape Artist*; it probably isn't a coincidence that all three of these films
have young-boy heroes who miss their fathers. Writers may be typecast, like actors;
having written one movie about a boy, Mathison may have been thought of for another, and yet another. In *E.T.*, she has made Elliott dreamy and a little withdrawn but
practical and intelligent. And very probably she intuited the necessity for Elliott, too,
to be bereft — especially since Spielberg himself had experienced the separation of his
parents. Mathison has a feeling for the emotional sources of fantasy, and although her
dialogue isn't always inspired, sometimes it is, and she has an ear for how kids talk.
Henry Thomas, who plays Elliott, and Kelly Reno in *The Black Stallion* and Griffin
O'Neal as the boy magician in *The Escape Artist* are not Hollywood-movie kids; they
all have an unusual — a magical — reserve. They're all in thrall to their fantasies, and
the movies take us inside those fantasies while showing us how they help the boys grow
up. Elliott (his name begins with an "E" and ends with a "T") is a dutiful, too sober
boy who never takes off his invisible thinking cap; the telepathic communication he
develops with E.T. eases his cautious, locked-up worries, and he begins to act on his
impulses. When E.T. has his first beer and loses his inhibitions, Elliott, at school, gets
tipsy, and in biology class when each student is required to chloroform a frog and then
dissect it he perceives his frog's resemblance to E.T. and sets it free. (His classmates
follow suit.) The means by which Elliott manages to kiss a pretty girl who towers over
him by at least a head is a perfectly executed piece of slapstick.

It's no small feat to fuse science fiction and mythology. *E.T.* holds together the way
some of George MacDonald's fairy tales (*At the Back of the North Wind*, *The Princess
and the Goblin*, *The Princess and Curdie*) do. It's emotionally rounded and complete.
The neighborhood kids whose help Elliott needs all come through for him. Even his
little sister, Gertie (Drew Barrymore), is determined to keep the secret that E.T. is
hidden in Elliott's room. And when Elliott's harried mother (Dee Wallace) rushes
around in her kitchen and fails to see E.T. — fails to see him even when she knocks him
over — the slapstick helps to domesticate the feeling of enchantment and, at the same
time, strengthens it. Adults — as we all know from the children's stories of our own
childhoods, or from the books we've read to our children — are too busy and too preoccupied to see the magic that's right there in front of them. Spielberg's mellow, silly
jokes reinforce the fantasy structure. One of them — Elliott on his bicycle dropping
what look like M&M's to make a trail — seems to come right out of a child's mind.
(Viewers with keen eyes may perceive that the candies are actually Reese's Pieces.)
Among the costumed children radiating out on Halloween is a tiny Yoda, and the
audience laughs in recognition that, yes, this film is part of the fantasy world to which
Yoda (the wise gnome of *The Empire Strikes Back*) belongs. And when E.T. — a goblin

costumed as a ghost — sees the child dressed as Yoda and turns as if to join him it's funny because it's so unaccountably right.

Henry Thomas (who was the older of Sissy Spacek's two small sons in *Raggedy Man*) has a beautiful brainy head with a thick crop of hair; his touching serio-comic solemnity draws us into the mood of the picture. When one of the neighborhood kids makes a fanciful remark about E.T., Elliott reprimands him, rapping out, "This is reality." Dee Wallace as the mother, Peter Coyote as a scientist who from childhood has dreamed the dream that Elliott has realized, and the other adult actors are the supporting cast. Henry Thomas and E.T. (who was designed by one of the authentic wizards of Hollywood, Carlo Rambaldi) are the stars, and Drew Barrymore and Robert Macnaughton, as the teen-ager Michael, are the featured players. Elliott and his brother and sister are all low-key humorists. When Michael first sees E.T., he does a double take that's like a momentary paralysis. Elliott has an honestly puzzled tone when he asks Michael, "How do you explain school to a higher intelligence?" Little Gertie adapts to E.T. very quickly — he may have the skin of a dried fig and a potbelly that just misses the floor, but she talks to him as if he were one of her dolls.

Spielberg changed his usual way of working when he made *E.T.*, and you can feel the difference. The visual energy and graphic strength in his work have always been based on his storyboarding the material — that is, sketching the camera angles in advance, so that the graphic plan was laid out. That way, he knew basically what he was after in each shot and how the shots would fit together; his characteristic brilliantly jagged cutting was largely thought out from the start. On *E.T.* — perhaps because the story is more delicate and he'd be working with child actors for much of the time — he decided to trust his intuition, and the film has a few fuzzy spots but a gentler, more fluid texture. It's less emphatic than his other films; he doesn't use his usual wide-screen format — he isn't out to overpower you. The more reticent shape makes the story seem simpler — plausible. The light always has an apparent source, even when it gives the scenes an other-worldly glow. And from the opening in the dense, vernal woodland that adjoins Elliott's suburb (it's where we first hear E.T.'s frightened sounds), the film has the soft, mysterious inexorability of a classic tale of enchantment. The little shed in back of the house where Elliott tosses in a ball and E.T. sends it back is part of a dreamscape.

The only discordant note is the periodic switch to overdynamic camera angles to show the NASA men and other members of the search party whose arrival frightened off the space visitors and who keep looking for the extraterrestrial left behind. These men are lined up in military-looking groups, and the camera shows us only their stalking or marching bodies — they're faceless, silent, and extremely threatening. Their flashlights in the dark woods could be lethal ray guns, and one of them has a bunch of keys hanging from his belt that keep jangling ominously. The rationale is probably that we're meant to view the men as little E.T. would, or as Elliott would, but most of the time neither E.T. nor Elliott is around when they are. Later in the movie, in the sequences in a room that is used as a hospital, it's clear that when adults are being benevolent in adult terms they may still be experienced by children as enemies. But the frequent intrusive cuts to the uniformed men — in some shots they wear moon-travel gear and head masks — are meant to give us terror vibes. They're abstract figures of evil; even the American-flag insignia on their uniforms is sinister — in modern movie iconology that flag means "bad guys." And this movie doesn't need faceless men; it has its own terror. Maybe Spielberg didn't have enough faith in the fear that is integral to any magical idyll: that it can't last.

When the children get to know E.T., his sounds are almost the best part of the picture. His voice is ancient and otherwordly but friendly, humorous. And this scaly, wrinkled little man with huge, wide-apart, soulful eyes and a jack-in-the-box neck has been so fully created that he's a friend to us, too; when he speaks of his longing to go home the audience becomes as mournful as Elliott. Spielberg has earned the tears that some people in the audience — and not just children — shed. The tears are tokens of gratitude for the spell the picture has put on the audience. Genuinely entrancing movies are almost as rare as extraterrestrial visitors.

QUESTIONS

1. Who is Kael's audience here? Is this audience likely to be interested in a movie such as *E.T.*, which has such a strong appeal for children? How does Kael arouse her audience's interest in this film?

2. Kael employs a number of parenthetical asides. Why? What kind of things does she say in these parenthetical comments? What effect do these remarks have on the overall tone of her review?

3. What kinds of information does Kael assume her audience already possesses? Is it fair for her to make these assumptions?

4. At its release *E.T.* was criticized by some reviewers for being too sentimental and emotional. How would Kael react to that charge? How do *you* react to that charge?

5. You now have much information that readers of *The New Yorker* did not have at the time of this review. You have probably seen the movie, perhaps more than once, and know of its great commercial success. Is there anything missing from this review that you, with the wisdom of your hindsight, think should be mentioned?

6. What standards does Kael use to evaluate *E.T.*? Do these standards seem appropriate and convincing?

7. Write your own review of *E.T.*

•   •   •   •   •

MOZART'S GREATEST HIT

Richard Corliss

A reviewer does not know whether his judgment will be accepted by others, whether his views will coincide with those of other critics. When Richard Corliss, a reviewer for Times *magazine, published this review of the motion picture* Amadeus *he did not know the film would go on to win Academy Awards for Best Picture, Best Director, and Best Actor; it did, however, and his opinions were justified.*

IF mediocrity is the natural condition of humankind, then genius is the purest and rarest of diseases. Tortured writers, earless painters, mad scientists all live inside the quarantine of their own superiority, distanced by their difference from the world they illuminate and help re-create. To 19th century romantics the genius was a superman; to most of us today he may seem both more and less than human, an idiot savant, a freak of nature.

To Antonio Salieri, the 18th century Italian composer whom Peter Shaffer resurrected in fictional form for his 1979 play *Amadeus*, one peculiar genius was even more frightening: a precious gift and a malicious joke from God. The creature's name was Wolfgang Amadeus Mozart — "Spiteful, sniggering, conceited, infantine Mozart!" as the play's Salieri, his contemporary and rival, calls him. "I had heard a voice of God," the Italian mutters after listening to a Mozart adagio, "and it was the voice of an obscene child!" Salieri carried a double curse: to appreciate beyond pain or pleasure Mozart's genius and to realize that his disease was incommunicable.

As staged by Peter Hall, first at Britain's National Theater and then for long runs in London and on Broadway, Shaffer's play was an eloquent tragicomedy swathed in theatrical sorcery. Events in the crisscrossing lives of the two composers were summoned up as spirits — real, distorted or imagined — out of the crumbling mind of Salieri, a man convinced that he had murdered Mozart. Weaving Mozartian facts into the Salieri fantasy, Shaffer conceived his play uniquely for the stage. Surely there was no reason, no excuse for turning it into a film.

Milos Forman found a reason. The director of *One Flew Over the Cuckoo's Nest* saw a way to retain the play's intellectual breadth and formal audacity without betraying the movie medium's demand for matter of fact naturalism. And he persuaded Shaffer, who had been disappointed by film adaptations of his plays, including *The Royal Hunt of the Sun* and *Equus*, to write the *Amadeus* screenplay, reshaping *Amadeus* from a madman's memory play to a more realistic musical biography. Recalls Shaffer: "It was like having the same child twice."

Amadeus the film dramatizes nearly all the major events in the last decade of Mozart's 35 years. His music, which in the play served only as an allusive *ostinato*, seizes center screen with significant excerpts from four Mozart operas, several concerti and the *Requiem*. As seen through the dealer's eye of the movie camera, Salieri looks like a sullen midget next to a Mozart monument; he is Judas to Mozart's Jesus, James Earl Ray to his Martin Luther King, Jr., Bob Uecker to his Babe Ruth. Explains

Shaffer: "Salieri had to give way just a bit to make room for the glory and wonder of his victim's achievement."

The result is a grand, sprawling entertainment that incites enthrallment for much of its 2 hr. 38 min. Shaffer's screenplay retains many of the play's epigrammatic fulminations, deftly synopsizes whole sections, transforms Mozart's father from a hectoring apparition to an onscreen tyrant, and provides a thrilling new climax in which the dying Mozart dictates his *Requiem* to a Salieri racked with guilt, jealousy and awe. If the operatic excerpts occasionally impede dramatic flow, they capture the Mozartian spirit as well as comment, with typical Forman bravura, on the theme of an oaf who makes miracles with music: in the *Don Giovanni* parody, a dove flies out of a horse's ass.

For Forman, returning to his native Czechoslovakia for his first film there since 1968, *Amadeus* marks a sure step forward in dramatic and visual storytelling. Defeated by his two previous challenges — turning the Love Generation *Hair* into a Viet Nam elegy and compressing the epic misanthropy of E. L. Doctorow's novel *Ragtime* — the director has come to some sensitive compromises with narrative reality. Mozart sings the music of God, Salieri schemes and screams in tragic register, and the film keeps humming merrily along with them both.

This *Amadeus* dares to pose the riddle of genius in the form of a traditional celebrity bio pic. In 1781 Mozart (Tom Hulce), once the put-upon prodigy of musical Europe, comes at the age of 26 to the Viennese court of Hapsburg Emperor Joseph II (played with a sly, thin smile and a delicious air of cagey indecisiveness by Jeffrey Jones). There the man of the moment is Antonio Salieri (F. Murray Abraham): court composer, consummate technician and politician, Emperor's favorite, a musical lion of Vienna. Most important, he knows his place, as an educated servant among masters of the blood and the bureaucracy. Mozart, fatally, does not.

So begins the artistic trajectory of surge, transcendence, decline and early death. Mozart takes a lower-class wife (Elizabeth Berridge, with the puffy, smooth face and black button eyes of a rag doll left in grandma's attic), but befuddles her with his excesses at work and play. He fights with his possessive father (Roy Dotrice) and with the arbiters of art in Joseph's court. He is a slave to fashion and passion. His genius continues to consume him, like a virus he is unable or unwilling to shake; at the first performance of *The Magic Flute* he faints dead away at the piano. Portrait of the artist as a great man: while his wife and father bicker over money in the next room, Mozart slumps over a billiard table, takes a swig of wine and fleshes out *Ah tutti contenti* from *The Marriage of Figaro*, creating music of domestic ecstasy out of the discord of his family life.

Salieri stands to the side during all this, stage-managing Mozart's downfall, then appearing to the fevered young man in his dead father's disguise and commissioning the *Requiem*. Similarly, the two main actors, chosen from a thousand who auditioned for the roles, must follow different circuits to their roles. Hulce, who may be remembered by movie fans as the prime nerd in National Lampoon's *Animal House*, must stride on-screen as a fop *manqué*, pinwheeling his arrogance, before the audience can find the obsession at the core of his genius. Hulce prepared for the role by practicing piano four hours a day. "After that," he says, "all I felt like doing was dancing and drinking all night — just like Mozart." In a daring, powerful performance, this boy with the map of White Water, Wis., stamped on his face soon convinces the viewer that he is the pagan saint of classical music.

Hulce's Mozart bears the familiar Forman trademark. The director always seems to be telling his actors: Go bigger, dare more, fill the biggest moviehouse with your passion and technique. Abraham's challenge as Salieri was more daunting. He must be all smoldering menace, a dandy in smirking repose — until, one day, he scans some scribbled Mozart sheet music, and tears of astonishment and fury course down his cheeks. Says Abraham, who has played in everything from Shakespeare to *Scarface* to a leotarded leaf in the Fruit of the Loom TV spots: "Salieri is a figure tragic in Greek proportions because he enters into a competition with God." Forman says he chose these two off-Broadway journeymen over stars, or over actors who had performed in the play, because "I wanted to believe that this person *is* Mozart, *is* Salieri, not just an actor playing a part." Believe who will. The fact remains that Hulce and Abraham move assuredly to the center of this glittery production, finding the souls of their characters and then, at the film's climax, exchanging them.

One wonders: Can this galloping metaphysical thriller find an audience? For the vast majority of today's moviegoers, the 18th century is far more remote than the sci-fi 25th; Salieri is a loser from Loserville; and Mozart, he's the guy who wrote *Elvira Madigan*, and his first name is Mostly, isn't it? The film's $18 million budget may be less than is spent on many a teen-pic flop, but it still makes *Amadeus* a ricochet roll of the dice; the film will have to bring in more than $40 million at the box office just to break even.

To mention these commercial risks, though, is to take a Hapsburg Emperor's narrow view of art's bottom line. *Amadeus* may be a popular film for the same reason it is a good one: it paints, in vibrant strokes, an image of the artist as romantic hero. The textbook Mozart, embalmed in immortality, comes raucously alive as a punk rebel, grossing out the Establishment, confuting his chief rival, working himself to death in an effort to put on paper songs no one else can hear. Who among us cannot sympathize, even identify, with such an icon of iconoclasm? In real life we may all be Salieris, but we can respond to a movie that tells us we are really Mozarts.

QUESTIONS

1. *Time* magazine has frequently been criticized for adopting a style that employs breezy language and sometimes coins new terms. Do you find any evidence of this language in this review?

2. Compare this review with the review of *E.T.* (p. 490). Which review tells you more about the movie? Which review seems to be more judgmental? Which review seems more objective?

3. What fundamental assumptions does Corliss seem to have about what makes a good movie? Does he convince you that *Amadeus* has these qualities?

4. A reviewer can be off-putting if he seems too subjective — too positive or too negative. Does Corliss seem too enthusiastic about this movie? What does he do to maintain an objective appearance?

•   •   •   •   •

MICHAEL JACKSON AT MADISON SQUARE GARDEN

Stephen Holden

As rock concerts become more expensive and elaborate, reviewing the performance also becomes more complicated. Here is the review entertainment critic Stephen Holden wrote for The New York Times *after Michael Jackson's March 3, 1988, concert.*

FOR years, the title of "the hardest working man in show business" has been claimed by the great soul singer James Brown. But after watching Michael Jackson's bravura two-hour show on Thursday at Madison Square Garden, where he performed a benefit for the United Negro College Fund, one wondered if perhaps that sobriquet didn't belong to pop music's lanky 29-year-old Peter Pan, a man who has the gift of appearing to be earthbound only at his own whim.

The elaborate show that Mr. Jackson is touring around the world might be described as a mammoth pop-soul Halloween party staged in an amusement park in which the star plays a host of roles, from wide-eyed kid to werewolf, from romantic supplicant to stealthy criminal, all the time barely touching the floor. While many other performers could play all the roles Mr. Jackson assumes, the notion that another pop singer and dancer could invest anything like the passion he stamps into every detail of the performance is practically inconceivable.

Mr. Jackson is reputed to be an eccentric personality off the stage, but in performance he brings an almost grim intensity and perfectionism to every note, gesture and rhythmic nuance. Translated into a pop stage extravaganza, the star's offstage mystique of a shy misunderstood manchild with a martyr complex becomes sharply focused pop theater of indelibly expressive poses and quick changes, many of them conceived around brilliant stage lighting. The laser beams that periodically zoom from the stage are smoothly synchronized with the star's rippling rag-doll body language. For "Thriller," he and several dancing "zombies" are bedecked with colored lights that at the song's end appear to turn into flames. During "Human Nature," rotating beams of artificial sunlight on both sides of the singer rake the arena.

Musically and gesturally, Mr. Jackson's show is constructed around a basic emotional cycle as the star transforms himself from a sulking downcast victim who seems the quintessence of wounded innocence into a brave spiritual warrior bearing the torch of sweetness and joy in the face of ridicule, shame and rejection. Throughout Thursday's show, the scenario was played out again and again with the inflections varying according to the material. The evening reached a pinnacle of tearful pathos in a medley of "I Just Can't Stop Loving You" and "She's Out of My Life," and of anger in "Dirty Diana," which Steve Stevens capped with a crunching hard-rock guitar solo. And for the climactic "Man In the Mirror," Mr. Jackson mimed a veritable alphabet of expressions, from aggrieved sacrificial sufferer to inspirational messenger of hope.

But the show's most thrilling moment was Mr. Jackson's "Billie Jean," the song that still sums up better than any other the many sides of his performing personality. With its sophisticated melodic syncopation built around assertive phrases that the singer almost spits out, the song triumphantly fuses funkified post-Motown soul grooves with a modern theatrical tradition exemplified by the jazzier songs from "West Side Story." And its lyrics, evoking a treacherous emotional limbo where urban realism meets nightmarish paranoia, carry a powerful but mysterious resonance. Most important, the song is the springboard for Mr. Jackson's famous moonwalk routine in which he seems to loose gravity and skid backward as though suspended from the ceiling by an invisible string. Mr. Jackson executed the maneuver even better, faster and more daringly on Thursday than when he first introduced it on television in Motown's 25th-anniversary celebration. It is now the signature of a great song-and-dance performer who brings the pace of Fred Astaire and the funky acrobatics of James Brown and a long line of vaudevillian soul men into a perfect alignment.

QUESTIONS

1. What does Holden focus on more, Jackson's music or his dancing? Why?
2. Holden calls Jackson's performance "pop theater." How is this label reflected by the emphasis of his review?
3. Holden describes "Billie Jean" as a song "evoking a treacherous emotional limbo where urban realism meets nightmarish paranoia." Is this a phraseology Jackson's fans are likely to understand? Why does Holden use such a description?
4. What details about the concert does Holden omit? Is there a reason he omitted them? What standards does he use as the basis of his review?
5. Write a review of the last concert you attended. Newspapers do not allow unlimited space for such essays, so to make your task realistic place a strict limit on the length of your article — 500 words.

•   •   •   •   •

MICHAEL JACKSON'S *BAD*

Phyl Garland

Phyl Garland teaches in the Graduate School of Journalism at Columbia University, and also regularly reviews recordings for Stereo Review, *a magazine for readers who are interested in stereo equipment, recordings, and the latest trends in the recording industry. Because Michael Jackson's album* Thriller *was the best-selling album of all time, there was a good deal of curiosity and speculation when his next album* Bad *was released. Here is Phyl Garland's review of it.*

No doubt Michael Jackson has found himself his own toughest act to follow. Given the record-shattering success of his "Thriller," which went on to become the bestselling album of all time after its release five years ago, the big question is whether his new album, "Bad," is a worthy successor. Its gestation period has been elephantine, the longest in his fruitful career — although he was busy in the interim doing other things, including co-writing *We Are the World* and starring in a film fantasy for the Disney outfit. But all such considerations aside, the answer must be a resounding "Yes," for "Bad" represents a new level of musical assertiveness for Jackson, who wrote eight of the ten songs (nine of the eleven on the compact disc) compared with three and a half for "Thriller." They were chosen from a total of sixty-two he wrote before the album went into production. At a boyish twenty-nine, Jackson is obviously quite serious about the state of his art, regardless of all the hype about his eccentricities. Now his compositional voice is being projected as prominently as his performance presence, which has been formidable ever since he dazzled the public as the prodigious eleven-year-old lead singer-dancer for the Jackson Five.

Many of the same ingredients that made "Thriller" live up to its name are apparent in this set: state-of-the-art technology in mingling human and electronic sounds, an all-but-uncontainable energy that bubbles upward to captivate the listener, and a careful straddling of musical genres. Sassy rock textures are interspersed with mellow rhythm-and-blues cadences, and sheets of synthesized sound give way to a jazz lick or two.

Like "Thriller," "Bad" is designed to appeal to a vast cross section of tastes, leaving followers of various musical camps with the impression that Jackson has spoken directly to them. He is continually engaging, whether cooing the ingenuous ballad *I Just Can't Stop Loving You* or shouting about being *Bad*. The buckles and black leather cannot really harden him — even in the title song he's more like an irritated kitten than a hood. He is all raw, nervous energy on propulsive numbers like *Speed Demon* and *Smooth Criminal*, all lyrical beauty in *Liberian Girl*. Stevie Wonder joins him in a roof-raiser called *Just Good Friends*, and what sounds like a cast of thousands, including the Andraé Crouch Choir and the Winans, helps made *Man in the Mirror* a riveting experience.

What you like best here will depend on your tastes, but it would take a tin-eared soul to remain totally unresponsive. Perhaps "Bad" won't break the records set by

"Thriller," whose sales were boosted by Jackson's lavish, pioneering video productions. But "Bad" is good enough to keep him well ahead of his imitators.

QUESTIONS

1. Approximately half of Garland's review is devoted to what might be called background remarks. Why?
2. What question does Garland formulate as the central issue of her review? What other questions might she have posed instead of this one?
3. Stephen Holden (p. 497) tended to review Jackson as an entertainer and performer rather than as a singer. Obviously Garland cannot review Jackson's dancing, but she does speak of his energy and presence. Is this also a review of Jackson's "performance"?
4. Every review should present the evidence the reviewer has based her judgment on. Garland does an amazing job of this considering the extremely limited space she is allotted. Make a list of the points she mentions. How is she able to squeeze so much information into a few paragraphs?
5. Write a review of your favorite album. Restrict this review to 500 words or less.

• • • • •

Copyrights and Acknowledgments

Section IV

From *The Fate of the Earth* by Jonathan Schell, pp. 181–187. 217–219. Copyright © 1982 by Jonathan Schell. Reprinted by permission of Alfred A. Knopf, Inc. Originally appeared in *The New Yorker*. **Samuel C. Florman**, "The Feminist Face of Antitechnology." From *Blaming Technology* by Samuel C. Florman, pp. 120–130. Copyright 1981. Reprinted by permission of St. Martin's Press, Inc., New York. **Wendell Berry**, "In Defense of Literacy." From *A Continuous Harmony* by Wendell Berry, pp. 169–173. Copyright © 1972 by Wendell Berry. Reprinted by permission of Harcourt Brace Jovanovich, Inc. **Lewis Thomas**, "Humanities and Science." From *Late Night Thoughts on Listening to Mahler's Ninth Symphony* by Lewis Thomas, pp. 143–155. Copyright © 1980, 1981, 1982, 1983 by Lewis Thomas. All rights reserved. Reprinted by permission of Viking Penguin Inc. **Duane T. Gish**, "The Scopes Trial in Reverse." This article first appeared in the November/December 1977 issue of *The Humanist* and is reprinted by permission. **Preston Cloud**, "Evolution Theory and Creation Mythology." This article first appeared in the November/December 1977 issue of *The Humanist* and is reprinted by permission. **Stephen Jay Gould**, "Evolution as Fact and Theory." "Evolution as Fact and Theory" is reprinted from *Hen's Teeth and Horse's Toes, Further Reflections in Natural History* by Stephen Jay Gould, by permission of W. W. Norton & Company. Copyright © 1983 by Stephen Jay Gould. **Edward M. Kennedy** "Address to the Democratic Convention." From Senator Kennedy's Address to the Democratic Convention, 1980. Reprinted by permission of Senator Edward M. Kennedy. **Caryl Rivers**, "What Should Be Done about Rock Lyrics." This article first appeared in the *Boston Globe* and is reprinted with permission of the author. **Rachel Richardson Smith**, "Abortion: Right and Wrong." This article first appeared in *Newsweek*, March 25, 1985. Reprinted by permission of Rachel Richardson Smith. **James Fallows**, "Japan: Playing by Different Rules." This article appeared in *The Atlantic Monthly*, September 1987, pp. 22–32. Reprinted by permission of James Fallows. **Ted Koppel**, "Viewpoints: Commencement Address at Duke University." From *Duke Dialogue*, May 15, 1987. Reprinted by permission of Duke Dialogue, Duke University, and Ted Koppel **Pauline Kael**, "The Pure and the Impure." From *Taking It All In* by Pauline Kael. Copyright © 1984 by Pauline Kael. Reprinted by permission. **Richard Corliss**, "Mozart's Greatest Hits." From *Time*, September 10, 1984, pp. 74–75. Copyright © 1984 by Time, Inc. All rights reserved. Reprinted by permission. **Stephen Holden**, "Michael Jackson At Madison Square Garden." From *The New York Times*, March 5, 1988. Copyright © 1988 by The New York Times Company. Reprinted by permission. **Phyl Garland**, "Michael Jackson's *Bad*." From *Stereo Review*, December 1987. Reprinted by permission of Phyl Garland.

INDEX

A 0
B 1
C 2
D 3
E 4
F 5
G 6
H 7
I 8
J 9